A history of the french novel

(To the close of the 19th century)
(Volume I)
From the Beginning to 1800

George Saintsbury

Alpha Editions

This edition published in 2019

ISBN : 9789353706999

Design and Setting By
Alpha Editions
email - alphaedis@gmail.com

A HISTORY

OF THE

FRENCH NOVEL

(TO THE CLOSE OF THE 19TH CENTURY)

BY

GEORGE SAINTSBURY

M.A. AND HON. D.LITT. OXON.; HON. LL.D. ABERD.; HON. D.LITT. DURH.;
FELLOW OF THE BRITISH ACADEMY ; HON. FELLOW OF MERTON COLLEGE, OXFORD ;
LATE PROFESSOR OF RHETORIC AND ENGLISH LITERATURE IN THE UNIVERSITY OF EDINBURGH

VOL. I

FROM THE BEGINNING TO 1800

MACMILLAN AND CO., LIMITED
ST. MARTIN'S STREET, LONDON
1917

PREFACE

In beginning what, if it ever gets finished, must in all probability be the last of some already perhaps too numerous studies of literary history, I should like to point out that the plan of it is somewhat different from that of most, if not all, of its predecessors. I have usually gone on the principle (which I still think a sound one) that, in studying the literature of a country, or in dealing with such general characteristics of parts of literature as prosody, or such coefficients of all literature as criticism, minorities are, sometimes at least, of as much importance as majorities, and that to omit them altogether is to risk, or rather to assure, an imperfect—and dangerously im perfect—product.

In the present instance, however, I am attempting something that I have never, at such length, attempted before—the history of a Kind, and a Kind which has distinguished itself, as few others have done, by communicating to readers the *pleasure* of literature. I might almost say that it is the history of that pleasure, quite as much as the history of the kind itself, that I wish to trace. In doing so it is obviously superfluous to include inferiorities and failures, unless they have some very special lesson or interest, or have been (as in the case of the minorities on the bridge of the sixteenth and seventeenth centuries) for the most part, and unduly,

v

neglected, though they are important as experiments and links.[1]   We really do want here—what the reprehensible hedonism of Mr. Matthew Arnold, and his submission to what some one has called " the eternal enemy, Caprice," wanted in all cases—"only the chief and principal things." I wish to give a full history of how what is commonly called the French Novel came into being and kept itself in being ; but I do not wish to give an exhaustive, though I hope to give a pretty full, account of its practitioners.

In another point, however, I have kept to my old ways, and that is the way of beginning at the beginning. I disagree utterly with any Balbus who would build an absolute wall between romance and novel, or a wall hardly less absolute between verse- and prose-fiction. I think the French have (what is not common in their language) an advantage over us in possessing the general term *Roman*, and I have perhaps taken a certain liberty with my own title in order to keep the noun-part of it to a single word.   I shall extend the meaning of " novel " —that of *roman* would need no extension—to include, not only the prose books, old and new, which are more generally called " romance," but the verse romances of the earlier period.

The subject is one with which I can at least plead almost lifelong familiarity.   I became a subscriber to " Rolandi's," I think, during my holidays as a senior schoolboy, and continued the subscriptions during my vacations when I was at Oxford.   In the very considerable leisure which I enjoyed during the six years when I was Classical Master at Elizabeth College, Guernsey,

---

[1] For the opposite or corresponding reasons, it has seemed unnecessary to dwell on such persons, a hundred and more years later, as Voisenon and La Morlière, who are merely "corrupt followers" of Crébillon *fils* ; or, between the two groups, on the numerous failures of the quasi-historical kind which derived partly from Mlle. de Scudéry and partly from Mme. de la Fayette.

I read more French than any other literature, and more novels than anything else in French. In the late 'seventies and early 'eighties, as well as more recently, I had to round off and fill in my knowledge of the older matter, for an elaborate account of French literature in the *Encyclopædia Britannica*, for a long series of articles on French novelists in the *Fortnightly Review*, and for the *Primer* and *Short History* of the subject which I wrote for the Clarendon Press; while from 1880 to 1894, as a *Saturday Reviewer*, I received, every month, almost everything notable (and a great deal hardly worth noting) that had appeared in France.

Since then, the cutting off of this supply, and the extreme and constant urgency of quite different demands on my time, have made my cultivation of the once familiar field "*parc* and infrequent." But I doubt whether any really good judge would say that this was a serious drawback in itself; and it ceases to be one, even relatively, by the restriction of the subject to the close of the last century. It will be time to write of the twentieth-century novel when the twentieth century itself has gone more than a little farther.

For the abundance of translation, in the earlier part especially, I need, I think, make no apology. I shall hardly, by any one worth hearing, be accused of laziness or scamping in consequence of it, for translation is much more troublesome, and takes a great deal more time, than comment or history. The advantage, from all other points of view, should need no exposition: nor, I think, should that of pretty full story-abstract now and then.

There is one point on which, at the risk of being thought to "talk too much of my matters," I should like to say a further word. All my books, before the present volume, have been composed with the aid of a

b

library, not very large, but constantly growing, and always reinforced with special reference to the work in hand; while I was able also, on all necessary occasions, to visit Oxford or London (after I left the latter as a residence), and for twenty years the numerous public or semi-public libraries of Edinburgh were also open to me. This present *History* has been outlined in expectation for a very long time; and has been actually laid down for two or three years. But I had not been able to put much of it on paper when circumstances, while they gave me greater, indeed almost entire, leisure for writing, obliged me to part with my own library (save a few books with a reserve *pretium affectionis* on them), and, though they brought me nearer both to Oxford and to London, made it less easy for me to visit either. The London Library, that Providence of unbooked authors, came indeed to my aid, for without it I should have had to leave the book alone altogether; and I have been " munitioned " sometimes, by kindness or good luck, in other ways. But I have had to rely much more on memory, and of course in some cases on previous writing of my own, than ever before, though, except in one special case,[1] there will be found, I think, not a single page of mere " rehashing." I mention this without the slightest desire to beg off, in one sense, from any omissions or mistakes which may be found here, but merely to assure my readers that such mistakes and omissions are not due to idle and careless bookmaking. That " books have fates " is an accepted proposition. In respect to one of these—possession of materials and authorities—mine have been exceptionally fortunate hitherto, and if they had any merit it was no doubt largely due to this. I have, in the present, endeavoured to make the best of what was not quite such good fortune.

[1] That of the minor " Sensibility " novelists in the last chapter.

And if anybody still says, " Why did you not wait till you could supply deficiencies ? " I can only reply that, after seventy, *νὺξ γὰρ ἔρχεται* is a more insistent warrant, and warning, than ever.[1]

GEORGE SAINTSBURY.

[*EDINBURGH, 1914-15; SOUTHAMPTON, 1915-16*]
1 Royal Crescent, Bath, *May* 31, 1917.

[1] I have once more to thank Professors Ker, Elton, and Gregory Smith for their kindness in reading my proofs and making most valuable suggestions ; as well as Professor Fitzmaurice-Kelly and the Rev. William Hunt for information on particular points.

ADDENDA AND CORRIGENDA

P. 3, *note.*—This note was originally left vague, because, in the first place, to perform public and personal fantasias with one's spear on the shield of a champion, with whom one does not intend to fight out the quarrel, seems to me bad chivalry, and secondly, because those readers who were likely to be interested could hardly mistake the reference. The regretted death, a short time after the page was sent to press, of Mr. W. J. Courthope may give occasion to an acknowledgment, coupled with a sincere *ave atque vale.* Mr. Courthope was never an intimate friend of mine, and our agreement was greater in political than in literary matters : but for more than thirty years we were on the best terms of acquaintance, and I had a thorough respect for his accomplishments.

P. 20, l. 5.—*Fuerres de Gadres.* I wonder how many people thought of this when Englishmen "forayed Gaza" just before Easter, 1917 ?

P. 46, mid-page.—It so happened that, some time after having passed this sheet for press, I was re-reading Dante (as is my custom every year or two), and came upon that other passage (in the *Paradiso*, and therefore not known to more than a few of the thousands who know the Francesca one) in which the poet refers to the explanation between Lancelot and the Queen. It had escaped my memory (though I think I may say honestly that I knew it well enough) when I passed the sheet : but it seemed to me that perhaps some readers, who do not care much for "parallel passages" in the pedantic sense, might, like myself, feel pleasure in having the great things of literature, in different places, brought together. Moreover, the *Paradiso* allusion seems to have puzzled or misled most of the commentators, including the late Mr. A. J. Butler, who, by his translation and edition of the *Purgatorio* in 1880, was my Virgil to lead me through the *Commedia*, after I had sinfully neglected it for exactly half a life-time. He did not know, and might easily not have known, the Vulgate *Lancelot* : but some of those whom he cites, and who evidently *did* know it, do not seem to have recognised the full significance of the passage in Dante. The text will give the original : the *Paradiso* (xvi. 13-15) reference tells how Beatrice (after Cacciaguida's biographical and historical recital, and when Dante, in a confessed outburst of family pride, addresses his ancestor with the stately *Voi*), "smiling, appeared like her who coughed at the first fault which is written of Guinevere." This, of course (see text once more), is the Lady of Malahault, though Dante does not name her as he does Prince Galahault in the other *locus*. The older commentators (who, as has been said, *did* know the original) do not seem to have seen in the reference much more than that both ladies noticed, and perhaps approved, what was happening. But I think there is more in it. The Lady of Malahault (see note in text) had previously been aware that Lancelot was deeply in love, though he would not tell her with whom. Her cough therefore meant : "Ah ! I have found you out." Now Beatrice, well as she knew Dante's propensity to love, knew as well that *pride* was even more of a besetting weakness of his. This was quite a harmless instance of it : but still it *was* an instance—and the "smile" which is *not* recorded of the Arthurian lady meant : "Ah ! I have *caught* you out." Even if this be excessive "reading into" the texts, the juxtaposition of them may not be unsatisfactory to some who are not least worth satisfying. (Since writing this, I have been reminded that Mr. Paget Toynbee did make the "juxtaposition" in his Clarendon Press *Specimens of Old French* (October, 1892), printing there the "Lady of Malahault" passage from MSS. copied by Professor Ker. But there can be no harm in duplicating it.)

P. 121, ll. 8-10. Perhaps instead of, or at least beside, Archdeacon Grantly I should have mentioned a more real dignitary (as some count reality) of the Church, Charles Kingsley. The Archdeacon and the Canon would have fought on many ecclesiastical and some political grounds, but they might have got on as being, in Dr. Grantly's own words at a memorable moment "both gentlemen." At any rate, Kingsley was soaked in Rabelais, and one of the real curiosities of literature is the way in which the strength of *Gargantua* and *Pantagruel* helped to beget the sweetness of *The Water Babies*.

Chap. viii. pp. 163-175.—After I had "made my" own "siege" of the *Astrée* on the basis of notes recording a study of it at the B.M., Dr. Hagbert Wright of the London Library was good enough to let me know that his many years' quest of the book had been at last successful, and to give me the first reading of it. (It was Southey's copy, with his own unmistakable autograph and an inserted note, while it also contained a cover of a letter addressed to him, which had evidently been used as a book-mark.) Although not more than four months had passed since the previous reading, I found it quite as appetising as (in the text itself) I had expressed my conviction that it would be : and things not noticed before cropped up most agreeably. There is no space to notice all or many of them here. But one of the earliest, due to Hylas, cannot be omitted, for it is the completest and most sententious vindication of polyerotism ever phrased : "Ce n'était pas que je n'aimasse les autres : mais j'avais encore, outre leur place, celle-ci vide dans mon âme." And the soul of Hylas, like Nature herself, abhorred a vacuum ! (This approximation is not intended as "new and original" : but it was some time after making it that I recovered, in *Notre Dame de Paris*, a forgotten anticipation of it by Victor Hugo.)

Another early point of interest was that the frontispiece portrait of Astrée (the edition, see *Bibliography*, appears to be the latest of the original and ungarbled ones, *imprimée à Rouen, et se vend à Paris* (1647, 10 vols.)) is evidently a portrait, though not an identical one, of the same face given in the Abbé Reure's engraving of Diane de Chateaumorand herself. The nose, especially, is hardly mistakable, but the eyes have rather less expression, and the mouth less character, though the whole face (naturally) looks younger.

On the other hand, the portrait here—not of Céladon, but admittedly of Honoré d'Urfé himself—is much less flattering than that in the Abbé's book.

Things specially noted in the second reading would (it has been said) overflow all bounds here possible : but we may perhaps find room for three lines from about the best of the very numerous but not very poetical verses, at the beginning of the sixth (*i.e.* the middle of the original *third*) volume :

> Le prix d'Amour c'est l'Amour même.
> Change d'humeur qui s'y plaira,
> Jamais Hylas ne changera,

the two last being the continuous refrain of a "villanelle" in which this bad man boasts his constancy in inconstancy.

P. 265, *note* 1.—It ought perhaps to be mentioned that Mlle. de Lussan's paternity is also, and somewhat more probably, attributed to Eugene's elder brother, Thomas of Savoy, Comte de Soissons. The lady is said to have been born in 1682, when Eugene (b. 1663) was barely nineteen ; but of course this is not decisive. His brother Thomas *Amédée* (b. 1656) was twenty-six at the time. The attribution above mentioned gave no second name, and did not specify the relationship to Eugene : so I had some difficulty in identifying the person, as there were, in the century, three Princes Thomas of Savoy, and I had few books of reference. But my old friend and constant helper in matters historical, the Rev. William Hunt, D.Litt., cleared the point up for me. Of the other two—Thomas *François*, who was by marriage Comte de Soissons and was grandfather of Eugene and Thomas Amédée, died in the same year in which Thomas Amédée was born, therefore twenty-six before Mlle. de Lussan's birth : while the third, Thomas *Joseph*, Eugene's cousin, was not born till 1796, fourteen years after the lady. The matter is, of course, of no literary importance : but as I had passed the sheet for press before noticing the diversity of statements, I thought it better to settle it.

P. 267. Pajon. I ought not to have forgotten to mention that he bears the medal of Sir Walter Scott (Introduction to *The Abbot*) as "a pleasing writer of French Fairy Tales."

Page 453.—Choderlos de Laclos. Some surprise has been expressed by a friend of great competence at my leaving out *Les Liaisons Dangereuses*. I am, of course, aware that "persons of distinction" have taken an interest in it ; and I understand that, not many years ago, the unfortunate author of the beautiful lines *To Cynara* wasted his time and talent on translating the thing. To make sure that my former rejection was not unjustified, I have accordingly read it with care since the greater part of this book was passed for press ; and it shall have a judgment here, if not in the text. I am unable to find any redeeming point in it, except that some ingenuity is shown in bringing about the *dénouement* by a rupture between the villain-hero and the villainess-heroine, M. le Vicomte de Valmont and Mme. la Marquise de Merteuil. Even this, though fairly craftsmanlike in treatment, is banal enough in idea—that idea being merely that jealousy, in both sexes, survives love, shame, and everything else, even community in scoundrelism—in other words, that the green-eyed monster (like "Vernon" and unlike "Ver") *semper viret*. But it is scarcely worth one's while to read six hundred pages of very small print in order to learn this. Of amusement, as apart from this very elementary instruction, I at least can find nothing. The pair above mentioned, on whom practically hangs the whole appeal, are merely disgusting. Their very voluptuousness is accidental : the sum and substance, the property and business of their lives and natures, are compact of mischief, malice, treachery, and the desire of "getting the better of somebody." Nor has this diabolism anything grand or impressive about it—anything that "intends greatly" and glows, as has been said, with a black splendour, in Marlowesque or Websterian fashion. Nor, again, is it a "Fleur du Mal" of the Baudelairian kind, but only an ugly as well as noxious weed. It is prosaic and suburban. There is neither tragedy nor comedy, neither passion nor humour, nor even wit, except a little horseplay. Congreve and Crébillon are as far off as Marlowe and Webster ; in fact, the descent from Crébillon's M. de Clérval to Laclos' M. de Valmont is almost inexpressible. And, once more, there is nothing to console one but the dull and obvious moral that to adopt love-making as an "occupation" (*vide* text, p. 367) is only too likely to result in the τέχνη becoming, in vulgar hands, very βάναυσος indeed.

The victims and *comparses* of the story do nothing to atone for the principals. The lacrimose stoop-to-folly-and-wring-his-bosom Mme. de Tourvel is merely a bore ; the *ingénue* Cécile de Volanges is, as Mme. de Merteuil says, a *petite imbécile* throughout, and becomes no better than she should be with the facility of a predestined strumpet ; her lover, Valmont's rival, and Mme. de Merteuil's plaything, M. le Chevalier Danceny, is not so very much better than *he* should be, and nearly as much an imbecile in the masculine way as Cécile in the feminine ; her respectable mother and Valmont's respectable aunt are not merely as blind as owls are, but as stupid as owls are not. Finally, the book, which in many particular points, as well as in the general letter-scheme, follows Richardson closely (adding clumsy notes to explain the letters, apologise for their style, etc.), exhibits most of the faults of its original with hardly any of that original's merits. Valmont, for instance, is that intolerable creature, a pattern Bad Man—a Grandison-Lovelace—a prig of vice. Indeed, I cannot see how any interest can be taken in the book, except that derived from its background of *tacenda* ; and though no one, I think, who has read the present volume will accuse me of squeamishness, *I* can find in it no interest at all. The final situations referred to above, if artistically led up to and crisply told in a story of twenty to fifty pages, might have some ; but ditchwatered out as they are, I have no use for them. The letter-form is particularly unfortunate, because, at least as used, it excludes the ironic presentation which permits one almost to fall in love with Becky Sharp, and quite to enjoy *Jonathan Wild*. Of course, if anybody says (and apologists *do* say that Laclos was, as a man, proper in morals and mild in manners) that to hold up the wicked to mere detestation is a worthy work, I am not disposed to argue the point. Only, for myself, I prefer to take moral diatribes from the clergy and aesthetic delectation from the artist. The avenging duel between Lovelace and Colonel Morden is finely done ; that between Valmont and Danceny is an obvious copy of it, and not finely done at all. Some, again, of the riskiest passages in subject are made simply dull by a Richardsonian particularity which has no seasoning either of humour or of excitement. Now, a Richardson *de mauvais lieu* is more than a bore — it is a nuisance, not pure and simple, but impure and complex.

I have in old days given to a few novels (though, of course, only when they richly deserved it) what is called a "slating"—an *éreinte-ment*—as I once had the honour of translating that word in conversation, at the request of a distinguished English novelist, for the benefit of a distinguished French one. Perhaps an example of the process is not utterly out of place in a *History* of the novel itself. But I have long given up reviewing fiction, and I do not remember any book of which I shall have to speak as I have just spoken. So *hic caestus*, etc.—though I am not such a coxcomb as to include *victor* in the quotation.

CONTENTS

CHAPTER I

CHAPTER II

CHAPTER III

xvii

CHAPTER VII

CHAPTER VIII

CHAPTER IX

CHAPTER X

CHAPTER XI

CHAPTER XII

CHAPTER I

INTRODUCTORY

ALTHOUGH I have already, in two places,[1] given a somewhat precise account of the manner in which fiction in
The early the modern sense of the term, and especially
history of prose fiction, came to occupy a province in
prose fiction. modern literature which had been so scantily
and infrequently cultivated in ancient, it would
hardly be proper to enter upon the present subject
with a mere reference to these other treatments. It is
matter of practically no controversy (or at least of none
in which it is worth while to take a part) that the history
of prose fiction, before the Christian era, is very nearly
a blank, and that, in the fortunately still fairly abundant
remains of poetic fiction, " the story is the least part "
(as Dryden says in another sense), or at least the *telling*
of the story, in our modern sense, is so. Homer (in
the *Odyssey* at any rate), Herodotus (in what was certainly
not intentional fiction at all), and Xenophon [2] are
about the only Greek writers who can tell a story, for
the magnificent narrative of Thucydides in such cases
as those of the Plague and the Syracusan cataclysm
shows all the " headstrong " *ethos* of the author in its
positive refusal to assume a " story " character. In

---

[1] The article " Romance " in the *Encyclopaedia Britannica*, 11th ed. ; and the volume
on *The English Novel* in Messrs. Dent's series " Channels of English Literature."
London, 1913.

[2] Plato (or Socrates ?) does it only on a small scale and partially, though there are
the makings of a great novelist in the *Dialogues*. Apollonius Rhodius is the next verse-
tale teller to Homer among the prae-Christian Greeks.

Latin there is nothing before Livy and Ovid;[1] of whom the one falls into the same category with Herodotus and Xenophon, and the other, admirable *raconteur* as he is, thinks first of his poetry. Scattered tales we have : " mimes " and other things there are some, and may have been more. But on the whole the schedule is not filled : there are no entries for the competition.

In later classical literature, both Greek and Latin, the state of things alters considerably, though even then
The late it cannot be said that fiction proper—that is classical to say, either prose or verse in which the stage. accomplishment of the form is distinctly subordinate to the interesting treatment of the subject —constitutes a very large department, or even any regular department at all. If Lucius of Patrae was a real person, and much before Lucian, he may dispute with Petronius—that first-century Maupassant or Meredith, or both combined—the actual foundation of the novel as we have it ; but Lucian himself and Apuleius (strangely enough handling the same subject in the two languages) give securer and more solid starting-places. Yet nothing follows Apuleius ; though some time after Lucian the Greek romance, of which we have still a fair number of examples (spread, however, over a still larger number of centuries), establishes itself in a fashion. It does one thing, indeed, which in a way refounds or even founds the whole conception—it establishes the heroine. There are certainly feminine persons, sometimes not disagreeable, who play conspicuous and by no means mute or unpractical parts in both Greek and Latin versions of the Ass-Legend ; but one can hardly call them heroines. There need be no chicane about the application of that title to Chloe or to Chariclea, to Leucippe or to her very remarkable rival, to Anthia or to Hysmine. Without the heroine you can hardly have romance : the novel without her (though her individuality may be put in commission) is an absolute impossibility.

---

[1] Virgil, in the only parts of the *Aeneid* that make a good story, is following either Homer or Apollonius.

The connection between these curious performances (with the much larger number of things like them which *A nexus of* we know to have existed) on the one side, and *Greek and* the Western mediaeval romance on the other, *French romance ?* has been at various times matter of consider- *The facts* able controversy ; but it need not trouble us *about the matter.* much here. The Greek romance was to have very great influence on the French novel later : on the earlier composition, generally called by the same name as itself, it would seem [1] to have had next to none. Until we come to *Floire et Blanchefleur* and perhaps *Parthenopex*, things of a comparatively late stage, obviously post-Crusade, and so necessarily ex- posed to, and pretty clearly patient of, Greek-Eastern in- fluence, there is nothing in Old French which shows even the same kinship to the Greek stories as the Old English *Apollonius of Tyre*, which was probably or rather certainly in the original Greek itself. The sources of French " romance "—I must take leave to request a " truce of God " as to the application of that term and of " epic " for present purposes—appear to have been two—the Saint's Life and the patriotic or family *saga*, the latter in the first place indelibly affected by the Mahometan incursions of the eighth, ninth, and tenth centuries. The story-telling instinct—kindled by, or at first devoted to, these subjects—subsequently fastened on numerous others. In fact almost all was fish that came to the magic net of Romance ; and though two great subjects of ours, the " Matter of Britain " (the Arthurian Legend) and the " Matter of Rome " (classical story generally, including the Tale of Troy), came traditionally to rank themselves with the " Matter of France " and with the great range of hagiology which it might have been dangerous to proclaim a fourth " matter " (even if anybody had been likely to take the view that it was so), these classifications are, like most of their kind, more specious than satisfactory.

---

[1] To me at least the seeming seems to approach demonstration ; and I can only speak as I find, with all due apologies to those who find differently.

Any person—though indeed it is to be feared that
the number of such persons is not very large—who has
The power some knowledge of hagiology *and* some of
and influence literature will admit at once that the popular
of the "Saint's notion of a Saint's Life being necessarily a dull
Life." and " goody " thing is one of the foolishest
pieces of presumptuous ignorance, and one of the
most ignorant pieces of foolish presumption. Not
only have modern novelists sometimes been better informed and better inspired—as in the case of more than
one version of the Legends of St. Mary of Egypt, of St.
Julian, of Saint Christopher, and others—but there
remain scores if not hundreds of beautiful things that
have been wholly or all but wholly neglected. It is
impossible to imagine a better romance, either in verse
or in prose, than might have been made by William Morris
if he had kept his earliest loves and faiths and had taken
the *variorum* Legend of St. Mary Magdalene, as we have
it in divers forms from quite early French and English
to the fifteenth-century English Miracle Play on the
subject. That of St. Eustace (" Sir Isumbras "), though
old letters and modern art have made something of it,
has also never been fully developed in the directions
which it opens up ; and one could name many others.
But it has to be admitted that the French (whether, as
some would say, naturally enough or not) never gave
the Saint's Life pure and simple the development which
it received in English. It started them—I at least
believe this—in the story-telling way ; but cross-roads,
to them more attractive, soon presented themselves.

Still, it started them. I hope it is neither intolerably
fanciful nor the mere device of a compiler anxious to
The Legend make his arrows of all wood, to suggest that
of St. there is something noteworthy in the nature of
Eulalia. the very first piece of actual French which we
possess. The Legend of St. Eulalia can be tried pretty
high ; for we have [1] the third hymn of the *Peristephanon*

---

[1] There is, of course, a Latin " sequence " on the Saint which is nearer to the French
poem ; but that does not affect our present point.

of Prudentius to compare it with. The metre of this
Germine nobilis Eulalia
is not one of the best, and contrasts ill with the stately
decasyllables—perhaps the very earliest examples of that
mighty metre that we have—which the infant daughter-
tongue somehow devised for itself some centuries later.
But Prudentius is almost always a poet, if a poet of the
decadence, and he had as instruments a language and a
prosody which were like a match rifle to a bow and
arrows—*not* of yew and *not* cloth-yard shafts—when contrasted with the dialect and speech-craft of the unknown
tenth-century Frenchman. Yet from some points of
view, and especially from ours, the Anonymus of the
Dark Ages wins. Prudentius spins out the story into
two hundred and fifteen lines, with endless rhetorical
and poetical amplification. He wants to say that
Eulalia was twelve years old; but he actually informs
us that
Curriculis tribus atque novem,
Tres hyemes quater attigerat,

and the whole history of the martyrdom is attitudinised
and bedizened in the same fashion.

Now listen to the noble simplicity of the first French
poet and tale-teller :

A good maiden was Eulalia : fair had she the body, but the
soul fairer. The enemies of God would fain conquer her—would
fain make her serve the fiend. She listened not to the evil counsellors, that she should deny God, who abideth in Heaven aloft—
neither for gold, nor for silver, nor for garments; for the royal
threatenings, nor for entreaties. Nothing could ever bend the
damsel so that she should not love the service of God. And for
that reason she was brought before Maximian, who was the King
in those days over the pagans. And he exhorted her—whereof
she took no care—that she should flee from the name of Christian.
But she assembled all her strength that she might rather sustain
the torments than lose her virginity: for which reason she died
in great honour. They cast her in the fire when it burnt fiercely :
but she had no fault in her, and so it pained her [*or* she burnt [1]] not.

---

[1] The literal "cooked," with no burlesque intention, was used of punitory burning
quite early ; but it is not certain that the transferred sense of *cuire*, " to *pain*," is not
nearly or quite as old.

To this would not trust the pagan king: but with a sword he bade them take off her head. The damsel did not gainsay this thing: she would fain let go this worldly life if Christ gave command. And in shape of a dove she flew to heaven. Let us all pray that she may deign to intercede for us; that Christ may upon us have mercy after death, and of His clemency may allow us to come to Him.

Of course this is story-telling in its simplest form and on its smallest scale: but the essentials are there, The *St.* and the non-essentials can be easily supplied *Alexis.* —as indeed they are to some extent in the *Life of St. Leger* and to a greater in the *Life of St. Alexis*, which almost follow the *Sainte-Eulalie* in the making of French literature. The *St. Alexis* indeed provides something like a complete scheme of romance interest, and should be, though not translated (for it runs to between 600 and 700 lines), in some degree analysed and discussed. It had, of course, a Latin original, and was rehandled more than once or twice. But we have the (apparently) first French form, probably of the eleventh century. The theme is one of the commonest and one of the least sympathetic in hagiology. Alexis is forced by his father, a rich Roman "count," to marry; and after (not before) the marriage, though of course before its consummation, he deserts his wife, flies to Syria, and becomes a beggar at Edessa. After a time, long enough to prevent recognition, he goes back to Rome, and obtains from his own family alms enough to live on, though these alms are dispensed to him by the servants with every mark of contempt. At last he dies, and is recognised forthwith as a saint. This hackneyed and somewhat repulsive *donnée* (there is nothing repulsive to the present writer, let it be observed, either in Stylites or in Galahad) the French poet takes and makes a rather surprising best of it. He is not despicable even as a poet, all things considered; but he is something very different indeed from despicable as a tale-teller. To begin, or, strictly speaking, to end with (R. L. Stevenson never said a wiser thing than that the end must be the necessary result of, and as it were foretold in, the beginning), he has lessened if not wholly destroyed the jar of the situation by (most unusually and considering the mad chastity-worship of the time rather audaciously) associating the deserted wife directly with the Saint's " gustation of God " above :

> Without doubt is St. Alexis in Heaven,
> With him has he God in the company of the Angels,
> *With him the maiden to whom he made himself strange,*
> *Now he has her close to him—together are their souls,*
> *I know not how to tell you how great their joy is.*[1]

But there are earlier touches of that life which makes all literature, and tale-telling most of all. An opening on Degeneracy is scarcely one of these, for this was, of course, a commonplace millenniums earlier, and it had the recent belief about the approaching end of the world at the actual A.D. 1000 to prompt it. The maiden is " bought " for Alexis from her father or mother. Instead of the not unusual and rather distasteful sermons on virginity which later versions have, the future saint has at least the grace to accompany the return of the ring [2] with only a few words of renunciation of his spouse to Christ, and of declaration that in this world " love is imperfect, life frail, and joy mutable." A far more vivid touch is given by the mother who, when search for the fugitive has proved futile, ruins the nuptial chamber, destroys its decorations, and hangs it with rags and sackcloth,[3] and who, when the final discovery is made, reproaches the dead saint in a fashion which is not easy to reply to : " My son, why hadst thou no pity of *us* ? Why hast thou not spoken to me *once* ? " The bride has neither forgotten nor resented : she only weeps her deserter's former beauty, and swears to have no other spouse but God. The poem ends—or all but

[1] Not the least interesting part of this is that it is almost sufficient by itself to establish the connection between Saint's Life and Romance.

[2] By a very curious touch he gives her also " les renges de s'espide," *i.e.* either the other ring by which the sword is attached to the sword-belt, or the belt itself. The meaning is, of course, that with her he renounces knighthood and all worldly rank.

[3] She addresses the room itself, dramatically enough : " Chamber ! never more shalt thou bear ornament : never shall any joy in thee be enjoyed."

ends—in a hurly-burly of popular enthusiasm, which will hardly resign its new saint to Pope or Emperor, till at last, after the usual miracles of healing, the body is allowed to rest, splendidly entombed, in the Church of St. Boniface.

Now the man who could thus, and by many other touches not mentioned, run blood into the veins of mummies,[1] could, with larger range of subject and wider choice of treatment, have done no small things in fiction.

But enough talk of might-have-beens : let us come to the things that were done.

---

[1] Let me repeat that I mean no despite to the "Communion of Saints" or to their records—much the reverse. But the hand of any *purpose*, Religious, Scientific, Political, what not, is apt to mummify story.

CHAPTER II

It has been said already that the Saint's Life, as it seems most probable to the present writer, started the romance in France; but of course we must allow considerable reinforcement of one kind or another from local, traditional, and literary sources. The time-honoured distribution, also given already, of the "matter" of this romance does not concern us so much here as it would in a history of French literature, but it concerns us. We shall indeed probably find that the home-grown or home-fed *Chanson de Geste* did least for the novel in the wide sense—that the "Matter of Rome" chiefly gave it variety, change of atmosphere to some extent, and an invaluable connection with older literatures, but that the central division or "Matter of Britain," with the immense fringes of miscellaneous *romans d'aventures*—which are sometimes more or less directly connected with it, and are always moulded more or less on its patterns—gave most of all.

Of these, however, what has been called the family or patriotic part was undoubtedly the earliest and for The *Chanson* a long time the most influential. There is, *de Geste.* fortunately, not the least need here to fight out the old battle of the *cantilenae* or supposed *ballad*-originals. I see no reason to alter the doubt with which I have always regarded their existence; but it really does not matter, *to us*, whether they existed or not, especially since we have not got them now. What we have got is a vast mass of narrative poetry, which latterly

9

took actual prose form, and which—as early certainly as the eleventh century and perhaps earlier—turns the French faculty for narrative (whether it was actually or entirely fictitious narrative or not does not again matter) into channels of a very promising kind.

The novel-reader who has his wits and his memory about him may perhaps say, "Promising perhaps ; but paying ? " The answer must be that the promise may have taken some time to be fully liquidated, but that the immediate or short-dated payment was great. The fault of the *Chansons de Geste*—a fault which in some degree is to be found in French literature as a whole, and to a greater extent in all mediaeval literature—is that the class and the type are rather too prominent. The central conception of Charlemagne as a generally dignified but too frequently irascible and rather petulant monarch, surrounded by valiant and in a way faithful but exceedingly touchy or ticklish paladins, is no doubt true enough to the early stages of feudalism—in fact, to adapt the tag, there is too much human nature in it for it to be false. But it communicates a certain sameness to the *chansons* which stick closest to the model.

The exact relation of the *Chansons de Geste* to the subsequent history of French fiction is thus an extremely important one, and one that requires, not only a good deal of reading on which to base any opinion that shall not be worthless, but a considerable exercise of critical discretion in order to form that opinion competently. The present writer can at least plead no small acquaintance with the subject, and a full if possibly over-generous acknowledgment of his dealings with it on the part of some French authorities, living and dead, of the highest competence. But the attractions of the vast and strangely long ignored body of *chanson* literature are curiously various in kind, and they cannot be indiscriminately drawn upon as evidence of an early mastery of tale-telling proper on the part of the French as a nation. There is indeed one solid fact, the importance of which

The proportions of history and fiction in them.

can hardly be exaggerated in some ways, though it may be wrongly estimated in others. Here is not merely the largest part proportionately, but a very large bulk positively, of the very earliest part of a literature, devoted to a kind of narrative which, though some of it may be historic originally, is pretty certainly worked up into its concrete and extant state by fiction. The comparison with the two literatures which on the whole bear such comparison with French best—English and Greek— is here very striking. People say that there "must have been" many *Beowulfs* : it can hardly be said that we have so much as a positive assertion of the existence of even one other, though we have allusions and glances which have been amplified in the usual fashion. We have positive and not reasonably doubtful assertion of the existence of a very large body of more or less early Greek epic ; but we have nothing existing except the *Iliad* and the *Odyssey*.

On this fact, be it repeated, if we observe the canons of sound criticism in the process, too much stress in The part played by language, prosody, and manners. general cannot be laid. There must have been some more than ordinary *nisus* towards story-telling in a people and a language which produced, and for three or four centuries cherished, something like a hundred legends, sometimes of great length, on the single general [1] subject of the exploits, sufferings, and what not of the great half-historical, half-legendary emperor *à la barbe florie*, of his son, and of the more legendary than historical peers, rebels, subjects, descendants, and "those about both" generally. And though the assertion requires a little more justification and allowance, there must have been some extraordinary gifts for more or less fictitious composition when such a vast body of spirited fictitious, or even half-fictitious, narrative is turned out.

But in this justification as to the last part of the con-

[1] The subdivision of the *gestes* does not matter : they were all connected closely or loosely—except the Crusading section, and even that falls under the Christian *v.* Saracen grouping if not under the Carlovingian. The real "outside" members are few, late, and in almost every case unimportant.

tention a good deal of care has to be observed.   It will not
necessarily follow, because the metal is attractive, that its
attractiveness is always of the kind purely belonging to
fiction ; and, as a matter of fact, a large part of it is not.
Much is due to the singular sonority and splendour of
the language, which is much more like Spanish than
modern French, and which only a few poets of exceptional power have been able to reproduce in modern
French itself.   Much more is imparted by the equally
peculiar character of the metre—the long *tirades* or
laisses, assonanced or mono-rhymed paragraphs in decasyllables or alexandrines, which, to those who have
once caught their harmony, have an indescribable and
unparalleled charm.   Yet further, these attractions come
from the strange unfamiliar world of life and character
described and displayed ; from the brilliant stock epithets
and phrases that stud the style as if with a stiff but
glittering embroidery ; and from other sources too many
to mention here.

Yet one must draw attention to the fact that all the
named sources of the attraction, and may perhaps ask
Some   the reader to take it on trust that most of the
drawbacks. unnamed, are not essentially or exclusively
attractions of fiction—that they are attractions of
poetry.   And, on the other hand, while the weaving of
so vast a web of actual fiction remains " to credit,"
there are not a few things to be set on the other side of
the account.   The sameness of the *chanson* story, the
almost invariable recurrence of the stock motives and
frameworks—of rebellion, treason, paynim invasion,
petulance of a King's son, somewhat too " coming "
affection of a King's daughter, tyrannical and Lear-like
impotentia of the King himself, etc.—may be exaggerated,
but cannot be denied.   In the greatest of all by general
acknowledgment, the far-famed *Roland*, the economy
of pure story interest is pushed to a point which in a less
unsophisticated age—say the twentieth instead of the
twelfth or eleventh century—might be put down to
deliberate theory or crotchet.   The very incidents,

stirring as they are, are put as it were in skeleton argument
or summary rather than amplified into full story-flesh
and blood ; we see such heroine as there is only to see
her die ; even the great moment of the horn is given
as if it had been " censored " by somebody. People,
I believe, have called this brevity Homeric ; but that
is not how I read Homer.

In fact, so jealous are some of those who well and
wisely love the *chansons*, that I have known objections
taken to ranking as pure examples, despite their undoubted age and merit, such pieces as *Amis et Amiles*
(for passion and pathos and that just averted tragedy
which is so difficult to manage, one of the finest of all)
and the *Voyage à Constantinoble*, the single early specimen
of mainly or purely comic *donnée*.[1] This seems to me,
I confess, mere prudery or else mistaken logic, starting
from the quite unjustifiable proposition that nothing
that is not found in the *Chanson de Roland* ought to be
found in any *chanson*. But we may admit that the
" bones "—the simplest terms of the *chanson*-formula—
hardly include varied interests, though they allow such
interests to be clothed upon and added to them.

Despite this admission, however, and despite the
further one that it is to the " romances " proper—

But a fair
balance of
actual story
merit.

Arthurian, classical, and adventurous—rather
than to the *chansons* that one must look for the
first satisfactory examples of such clothing
and addition, it is not to be denied that the
chansons themselves provide a great deal of it—whether
because of adulteration with strictly " romance " matter
is a question for debate in another place and not here.
But it would be a singularly ungrateful memory which

---

[1] There are comic *episodes* elsewhere ; but almost the whole of this poem turns on
the *gabs* or burlesque boasts of the paladins.—It may be wise here to anticipate an
objection which may be taken to these remarks on the *chansons*. I have been asked
whether I know M. Bédier's handling of them ; and, by an odd coincidence, within a
few hours of the question I saw an American statement that this excellent scholar's
researches " have revised our conceptions " of the matter. No one can exceed me in
respect for perhaps the foremost of recent scholars in Old French. But my "conception" of the *chansons* was formed long before he wrote, not from that of any of his
predecessors, but from the *chansons* themselves. It is therefore not subject to "revisal"
except from my own re-reading, and such re-reading has only confirmed it.

should, in this place, leave the reader with the idea that the *Chanson de Geste* as such is merely monotonous and dull. The intensity of the appeal of *Roland* is no doubt helped by that approach to bareness—even by a certain tautology—which has been mentioned. *Aliscans*, which few could reject as faithless to the type, contains, even without the family of dependent poems which cluster round it, a vivid picture of the valiant insubordinate warrior in William of Orange, with touches of comedy or at least horse-play.

The striking, and to all but unusually dull or hope-lessly "modern" imaginations as unusually beautiful, Some centre-point of *Amis et Amiles*,—where one of instances the heroes, who has sworn a "white" perjury of this. to save his friend and is punished for it by the terror, "white" in the other sense, of leprosy, is abandoned by his wife, and only healed by the blood of the friend's children, is the crowning instance of another set of appeals. The catholicity of a man's literary taste, and his more special capacity of appreciating things mediaeval, may perhaps be better estimated by his opinion of *Amis et Amiles* than by any other touchstone; for it has more appeals than this almost tragic one—a much greater development of the love-motive than either *Roland* or *Aliscans*, and a more varied interest generally. Its continuation, *Jourdains de Blaivies*, takes the hero abroad, as do many other *chansons*, especially two of the most famous, *Huon de Bordeaux* and *Ogier de Danemarche*. These two are also good—perhaps the best—examples of a process very much practised in the Middle Ages and leaving its mark on future fiction—that of expansion and continuation. In the case of Ogier, indeed, this process was carried so far that enquiring students have been known to be sadly disappointed in the almost total disconnection between William Morris's beautiful section of *The Earthly Paradise* and the original French, as edited by Barrois in the first attempt to collect the *chansons* seventy or eighty years ago. The great "Orange" subcycle, of which *Aliscans*

is the most famous, extends in many directions, but is
apt in all its branches to cling more to " war and politics."
William of Orange is in this respect partly matched by
Garin of Lorraine.   No *chanson* retained its popularity,
in every sense of that word, better than the *Quatre Fils
d'Aymon*—the history of Renaut de Montauban and his
brothers and cousin, the famous enchanter-knight
Maugis.   As a " boy's book " there is perhaps none
better, and the present writer remembers an extensive
and apparently modern English translation which was
a favourite " sixty years since."   *Berte aux grands Piés*,
the earliest form of a well-known legend, has the extrinsic
charm of being mentioned by Villon ; while there is no
more agreeable love-story, on a small scale and in a
simple tone, than that of Doon and Nicolette [1] in *Doon
de Mayence*.   And not to make a mere catalogue which,
if supported by full abstracts of all the pieces, would
be inordinately bulky and would otherwise convey little
idea to readers, it may be said that the general *chanson*
practice of grouping together or branching out the poems
(whichever metaphor be preferred) after the fashion of a
family-tree involves of itself no inconsiderable call on the
tale-telling faculties.   That the writers pay little or no
attention to chronological and other possibilities is hardly
much to say against them ; if this be an unforgivable sin
it is not clear how either Dickens or Thackeray is to
escape damnation, with Sir Walter to greet them in
their uncomfortable sojourn.

But it is undoubtedly true that the almost exclusive
concentration of the attention on war prevents the
attainment of much detailed novel-interest.   Love affairs
—some glanced at above—do indeed make, in some of
the *chansons*, a fuller appearance than the flash-light
view of lost tragedy which we have in *Roland*.   But until
the reflex influence of the Arthurian romance begins to
work, they are, though not always disagreeable or

---

[1] It is not of course intended to be preferred to the far more widely known tale
in which the heroine bears the same name, and which will be mentioned below.   But
if it is less beautiful such beauty as it has is free from the slightest *morbidezza*.

ungraceful, of a very simple and primitive kind, as indeed are the delineations of manners generally.

The " matter of Rome the Great," as the original text has it (though, in fact, Rome proper has little to do with the most important examples of the class), adds very importantly to the develop-ment of romance, and through that, of novel. Its bulk is considerable, and its examples have interest of various kinds. But for us this interest is concentrated upon, if not exclusively confined to, the two great groups (undertaken by, and illustrated in, the three great literary languages of the earlier Middle Ages, and, as usual, most remarkably and originally in French) of the Siege of Troy and the life of Alexander. It should be almost enough to say of the former that it introduced,[1] with practically nothing but the faintest suggestion from really classical sources, the great romance-novel of the loves of Troilus and Cressida to the world's literature ; and of the second, that it gives us the first instance of the infusion of Oriental mystery and marvel that we can discern in the literature of the West. For details about the books which contain these things, their authors and their probable sources and development, the reader must, as in other cases, look elsewhere.[2] It is only our business here to say something about the general nature of the things themselves and about the additions that they made to the capital, and in some cases almost to the " plant," of fiction.

The classical borrowings —Troy and Alexander.

That the Troilus and Cressida romance, with its large provision and its more large suggestion of the accomplished love-story, evolved from older tale - tellers by Boccaccio and Chaucer and

Troilus.

[1] And to this introduction our dealings with it here may be confined. The accounts of the siege itself are of much less interest, especially in connection with our special subject.

[2] A sort of companion handbook to the first part of this volume will be found in the present writer's sketch of twelfth and thirteenth century European literature, under the title of *The Flourishing of Romance and the Rise of Allegory*, in Messrs. Blackwood's *Periods of European Literature* (Edinburgh and London, 1897), and another in his *Short History of French Literature* (Oxford, 7th ed. at press).

Henryson and Shakespeare, is not a pure creation of
the earlier Middle Ages, few people who patiently attend
to evidence can now believe. Even in the wretched
summaries of the Tale of Troy by Dictys and Dares
(which again no such person as the one just described
can put very early), the real novel-interest—even the
most slender romance-interest—is hardly present at all.
Benoît de Sainte-More in the twelfth century may not
have actually invented this; it is one of the principles
of this book, as of all that its writer has written, that the
quest of the inventor of a story is itself the vainest of
inventions. But it is certain that nobody hitherto has
been able to " get behind him," and it is still more
certain that he has given enough base for the greater men
who followed to build upon. If he cannot be credited
with the position of the pseudo-Callisthenes (see below)
in reference to the Alexander story, he may fairly share
that of his contemporary Geoffrey of Monmouth, if not
even of Nennius, as regards that of Arthur. The
situation, or rather the group of situations, is of the most
promising and suggestive kind, negatively and positively.
In the first place the hero and heroine are persons about
whom the great old poets of the subject have said little
or nothing; and what an immense advantage this is all
students of the historical novel of the last hundred years
know. In the second, the way in which they are put in
action (or ready for action) is equally satisfactory, or let
us say stimulating. In a great war a prince loves a
noble lady, who by birth and connections belongs to the
enemy, and after vicissitudes, which can be elaborated
according to the taste and powers of the romancer, gains
her love. But the course of this love is interrupted by
her surrender or exchange to the enemy themselves;
her beauty attracts, nay has already attracted, the fancy
of one of the enemy's leaders, and being not merely a
coquette but a light-o'-love [1] she admits his addresses.

---

[1] It is scarcely rash to say that Cressid is the first representative of this dread and
delightful entity, and the ancestress of all its embodiments since in fiction, as Cleopatra
seems to have been in history. No doubt "it" was of the beginning, but it lacked its
vates. Helen was different.

C

Her punishment follows or does not follow, is accomplished during the life of her true lover or not, according again to the taste and fancy of the person who handles the story. But the scheme, even at its simplest, is novel-soil : marked out, matured, manured, and ready for cultivation, and the crops which can be grown on it depend entirely upon the skill of the cultivator.

For all this some would, as has been said above, see sufficient suggestion in the Greek Romance. I have myself known the examples of that Romance for a very long time and have always had a high opinion of it ; but except what has been already noticed—the prominence of the heroine—I can see little or nothing that the Mediaeval romance could possibly owe to it, and as a matter of fact hardly anything else in common between the two. In the last, and to some extent the most remarkable (though very far from the best if not nearly the worst), of the Greek Romances, the *Hysminias and Hysmine* of Eustathius, we have indeed got to a point in advance, taking that word in a peculiar sense, even of *Troilus* at its most accomplished, that is to say, the Marinism or Marivaudage, if not even the Meredithese, of language and sentiment. But *Hysminias and Hysmine* is probably not older than Benoît de Sainte-More's story, and as has just been said, Renaissance, nay post-Renaissance, not Mediaeval in character. We must, of course, abstain from " reading back " Chaucer or even Boccaccio into Benoît or into his probable plagiarist Guido de Columnis ; but there is nothing uncritical or wrong in " reading forward " from these to the later writers. The hedge-rose is there, which will develop into, and serve as a support for, the hybrid perpetual—a term which could itself be developed in application, after the fashion of a mediaeval *moralitas*. And when we have actually come to Pandaro and Deiphobus, to the " verse of society," as it may be called in a new sense, of the happier part of Chaucer and to the intense tragedy of the later part of Henryson, then we are in the workshop, if not in the actual show-room, of the completed novel. It would

be easy, as it was not in the case of the *chansons*, to
illustrate directly by a translation, either here from
Benoît or later from the shortened prose version of the
fourteenth century, which we also possess ; but it is not
perhaps necessary, and would require much space.

The influence of the Alexander story, though scarcely
less, is of a widely different kind.   In *Troilus*, as has been
Alexander. said, the Middle Age is working on scarcely
more than the barest hints of antiquity, which
it amplifies and supplements out of its own head and its
own heart—a head which can dream dream-webs of
subtlest texture unknown to the ancients, and a heart
which can throb and bleed in a fashion hardly shown by
any ancient except Sappho.   With the Alexander group
we find it much more passively recipient, though here
also exercising its talent for varying and amplification.
The controversies over the pseudo-Callisthenes, " Julius
Valerius," the *Historia de Praeliis*, etc., are once more not
for us ; but results of them, which have almost or quite
emerged from the state of controversy, are.   It is certain
that the appearance, in the classical languages, of the
wilder legends about Alexander was as early at least as
the third century after Christ—that is to say, long before
even " Dark " let alone " Middle " Ages were thought
of—and perhaps earlier.   There seems to be very little
doubt that these legends were of Egyptian or Asiatic
origin, and so what we vaguely call " Oriental."   They
long anticipated the importing afresh of such influences
by the Crusades, and they must, with all except Christians
and Jews (that is to say, with the majority), have actually
forestalled the Oriental influence of the Scriptures.
Furthermore, when Mediaeval France began to create
a new body of European literature, the Crusades had
taken place ; the appetite for things Oriental and perhaps
we should say the half-imaginative power of appreciating
them, had become active ; and a considerable amount of
literature in the vernacular had already been composed.
It was not wonderful, therefore, that the *trouvères* should
fly upon this spoil.   By not the least notable of the

curiosities of literature in its own class, they picked out
a historical but not very important episode—the siege
of Gaza and Alexander's disgraceful cruelty to its brave
defender—and made of this a regular *Chanson de Geste*
(in all but " Family " connection), the *Fuerres de Gadres*,
a poem of several thousand lines.   But the most generally
popular (though sometimes squabbled over) parts of the
story, were the supposed perversion of Olympias, not by
the God Ammon but by the magician-king Nectanabus
personating the God and becoming thereby father of the
Hero; the Indian and some other real campaigns (the
actual conquest of Persia was very slightly treated), and,
far above all, the pure Oriental wonder-tales of the descent
into the sea, the march to the Fountain of Youth, and
other myths of the kind.

Few things can be more different than the story-means
used in these two legends ; yet it must be personal taste
rather than strict critical evaluation which pronounces
one more important to the development of the novel
than the other.   There is a little love interest in the
Alexander poems—the heroine of this part being Queen
Candace—but it is slight, episodic, and rudimentary
beside the complex and all-absorbing passions which,
when genius took the matter in hand, were wrought out
of the truth of Troilus and the faithlessness of Cressid.
The joys of fighting or roaming, of adventure and quest,
and above all those of marvel, are the attractions which
the Alexander legend offers, and who shall say that they
are insufficient ?   At any rate no one can deny that
they have been made the seasoning, if not the stuff and
substance, of an enormous slice of the romance interest,
and of a very large part of that of the novel.

It is scarcely necessary to speak of other classical
romances, and it is of course very desirable to keep in
The mind that the Alexander story, in no form in
Arthurian which we have it, attempts any *strictly* novel
Legend. interest ; while though that interest is rife
in some forms of " Troilus," those forms are not exactly
of the period, and are in no case of the language, with

which we are dealing. It was an Italian, an Englishman, and a Scot who each in his own speech—one in the admirable vulgar tongue, of which at that time and as a finished thing, Italian was alone in Europe as possessor ; the others in the very best of Middle English, and, as some think, almost the best of Middle Scots verse—displayed the full possibilities of Benoît's story. But the third " matter," the matter of Britain or (in words better understanded of most people) the Arthurian Legend, after starting in Latin, was, as far as language went, for some time almost wholly French, though it is exceedingly possible that at least one, if not more, of its main authors was no Frenchman. And in this " matter " the exhibition of the powers of fiction—prose as well as verse— was carried to a point almost out of sight of that reached by the *Chansons*, and very far ahead of any contemporary treatment even of the Troilus story.

Before, however, dealing with this great Arthurian story as a stage in the history of the Novel-Romance in and by itself, we must come to a figure which, Chrestien de though we have very little substantial know-Troyes and ledge of it, there is some reason for admitting the theories about him. as one of the first named and " coted " figures in French literature, at least as regards fiction in verse. It is well known that the action of modern criticism is in some respects strikingly like that of the sea in one of the most famous and vivid passages [1] of Spenser's unequalled scene-painting in words with musical accompaniment of them. It delights in nothing so much as in stripping one part of the shore of its belongings, and hurrying them off to heap upon another part. Chrestien de Troyes is one of the lucky personages who have benefited, not least and most recently, by this fancy. It is true that the actual works attributed to him have remained the same—his part of the shore has not been actually extended like part of that of the Humber. But it has had new riches, honours, and decorations heaped upon it till it has become, in the actual Spenserian language

[1] *Faerie Queene*, v. iv. 1-20.

of another but somewhat similar passage (iii. iv. 20), a
" rich strond" indeed. Until a comparatively recent
period, the opinion entertained of Chrestien, by most if
not all competent students of him, was pretty uniform,
and, though quite favourable, not extraordinarily high.
He was recognised as a past-master of the verse *roman
d'aventures* in octosyllabic couplet, who probably took his
heterogeneous materials wherever he found them ; " did
not invent much " (as Thackeray says of Smollett), but
treated whatever he did treat in a singularly light and
pleasant manner, not indeed free from the somewhat
undistinguished fluency to which this " light and lewed "
couplet, as Chaucer calls it, is liable, and showing no
strong grasp either of character or of plot, but on the
whole a very agreeable writer, and a quite capital example
of the better class of *trouvère*, far above the *improvisatore*
on the one hand and the dull compiler on the other ; but
below, if not quite so far below, the definitely poetic poet.

To an opinion something like this the present writer,
who formed it long ago, not at second hand but from
independent study of originals, and who has kept up
and extended his acquaintance with Chrestien, still
adheres.

Of late, however, as above suggested, " Chrestiens "
have gone up in the market to a surprising extent.
Some twenty years ago the late M. Gaston Paris [1] an-
nounced and, with all his distinguished ability and his
great knowledge elaborately supported, his conclusions,
that the great French prose Arthurian romances (which
had hitherto been considered by the best authorities,
including his own no less admirable father, M. Paulin
Paris, slightly anterior to the poet of Troyes, and in
all probability the source of part at least of his work)
were posterior and probably derivative. Now this,
of itself, would of course to some extent put up

---

[1] I hope I may be allowed to emphasise the disclaimer, which I have already made
more than once elsewhere, of the very slightest disrespect to this admirable scholar.
The presumption and folly of such disrespect would be only inferior to its ingratitude,
for the indulgence with which M. Paris consistently treated my own somewhat rash
adventures in Old French was extraordinary. But as one's word is one's word so one's
opinion is one's opinion.

Chrestien's value. But it, and the necessary corollaries from it, as originality and so forth, by no means exhaust the additional honours and achievements which have been heaped upon Chrestien by M. Paris and by others who have followed, more or less accepted, and in some cases bettered his ascriptions. In the first and principal place, there has been a tendency, almost general, to dethrone Walter Map from his old position as the real begetter of the completed Arthurian romance, and to substitute the Troyan. Then, partly in support, but also to some extent, I think, independently of this immense ennoblement, discoveries have been made of gifts and graces in Chrestien himself, which had entirely escaped the eyes of so excellent a critic, so erudite a scholar, and so passionate a lover of Old French literature as the elder M. Paris, and which continue to be invisible to the far inferior gifts and knowledge, but if I may dare to say so, the equal good will and the not inconsiderable critical experience, of the present historian.

Now with large parts of this matter we have, fortunately enough, nothing to do, and the actual authorship of the great Arthurian conception, namely, the interweaving of the Graal story on the one hand and the loves of Lancelot and Guinevere on the other, with the Geoffrey of Monmouth matter, concerns us hardly at all. But some have gone even further than has been yet hinted in the exaltation of Chrestien. They have discovered in him—" him-by-himself-him "—as the author of his actual extant works and not as putative author of the real Arthuriad, not merely a pattern example of the court *trouvère*—as much as this, or nearly as much, has been admitted here—but almost the inventor of romance and even of something very like novel, a kind of mediaeval Scott-Bulwer-Meredith, equally great at adventure, fashion, and character-analysis ; subject only, and that not much, to the limitations of the time. In fact, if I do not do some of these panegyrists injustice, we ought to have a fancy bust of Chrestien, with the titles of his works gracefully inscribed on the pedestal, as a

frontispiece to this book, if not even a full-length statue,
robed like a small St. Ursula, and like her in Memling's
presentation at Bruges, sheltering in its ample folds
the child-like figures of future French novelists and
romancers, from the author of *Aucassin et Nicolette* to
M. Anatole France.

Again, some fifty years of more or less critical reading
of novels of all ages and more than one or two languages,
combined with nearly forty years reading of Chrestien
himself and a passion for Old French, leave the present
writer quite unable to rise to this beatific vision.   But let
us, before saying any more what Chrestien could or could
not do, see, in the usual cold-blooded way, what he *did*.

The works attributed to this very differently, though
never unfavourably, estimated tale-teller—at·least those
which concern us—are *Percevale le Gallois, Le
Chevalier à¹ la Charette, Le Chevalier au Lyon,
Erec et Enide, Cligès,* and a much shorter
Guillaume d'Angleterre.   This last has nothing to do with
the Conqueror (though the title has naturally deceived
some), and is a semi-mystical romance of the group derived
from the above-mentioned legend of St. Eustace, and
represented in English by the beautiful story· of *Sir
Isumbras.*   It is very doubtfully Chrestien's, and in any
case very unlike his other work ; but those who think
him the Arthurian magician might make something of
it, as being nearer the tone of the older Graal stories than
the rest of his compositions, even *Percevale* itself.   Of
these, all, except the *Charette,* deal with what may be
called outliers of the Arthurian story.   ·*Percevale* is the
longest, but its immense length required, by common
confession, several continuators ;² the others have a
rather uniform allowance of some six or seven thousand
lines.   *Cligès* is one of the most "outside" of all, for the
hero, though knighted by Arthur, is the disinherited
heir of Constantinople, and the story is that of the

*His un-
questioned
work.*

---

¹ Sometimes *de*, but *à* seems more analogical.
² Chrestien was rather like Chaucer in being apt not to finish.   Even the *Charette*
owes its completion (in an extent not exactly determinable) to a certain Godfrey de
Lagny (Laigny, etc.).

recovery of his kingdom. *Erec*, as the second part of the title will truly suggest, though the first may disguise it, gives us the story of the first of Tennyson's original *Idylls*. The *Chevalier au Lyon* is a delightful romance of the Gawain group, better represented by its English adaptation, *Ywain*, than any other French example. *Percevale* and the *Charette* touch closest on the central Arthurian story, and the latter has been the chief battle-field as to Chrestien's connection therewith, some even begging the question to the extent of adopting for it the title *Lancelot*.

The subject is the episode, well known to English readers from Malory, of the abduction of Guinevere by
Comparison
of the
Chevalier à
la Charette
and the
prose
Lancelot.
Meleagraunce, the son of King Bagdemagus ; of the inability of all knights but Lancelot (who has been absent from Court in one of the lovers' quarrels) to rescue her ; and of his undertaking the task, though hampered in various ways, one of the earliest of which compelled him to ride in a cart—a thing regarded, by one of the odd [1] conventions of chivalry, as disgraceful to a knight. Meleagraunce, though no coward, is treacherous and " felon," and all sorts of mishaps befall Lancelot before he is able for the second time to conquer his antagonist, and finally to take his over and over again forfeited life. But long before this he has arrived at the castle where Guinevere is imprisoned ; and has been enabled to arrange a meeting with her at night, which is accomplished by wrenching out the bars of her window. The ill chances and *qui-proquos* which result from his having cut his hands in the proceeding (though the actual visit is not discovered), and the arts by which Meleagraunce ensnares the destined avenger for a time, lengthen out the story till, by the final contest, Meleagraunce goes to his own place and the Queen is restored to hers.

---

[1] Of course it is easy enough to assign explanations of it, from the vehicle of criminals to the scaffold downwards ; but it remains a convention—very much of the same kind as that which ordains (or used to ordain) that a gentleman may not carry a parcel done up in newspaper, though no other form of wrapping really stains his honour.

Unfortunately the blots of constant tautology and verbiage, with not infrequent flatness, are on all this gracious story as told by Chrestien.[1]   Among the traps and temptations which are thrown in Lancelot's way to the Queen is one of a highly " sensational " nature.   In the night Lancelot hears a damsel, who is his hostess, though he has refused her most thorough hospitality, shrieking for assistance ; and on coming to the spot finds her in a situation demanding instant help, which she begs, if the irreparable is not to happen.   But the poet not only gives us a heavily figured description of the men-at-arms who bar the way to rescue, but puts into the mouth of the intending rescuer a speech (let us be exact) of twenty-eight lines and a quarter, during which the just mentioned irreparable, if it had been seriously meant, might have happened with plenty of time to spare.   So, in the crowning scene (excellently told in Malory), where the lover forces his way through iron bars to his love, reckless of the tell-tale witness of his bleeding hands, the circumlocutions are *plusquam* Richardsonian—and do not fall far short of a serious anticipation of Shakespeare's burlesque in *A Midsummer Night's Dream*.   The mainly gracious description is spoilt by terrible bathetics from time to time.   Guinevere in her white nightdress and mantle of scarlet and *camus* [2] on one side of the bars, Lancelot outside, exchanging sweet salutes, " for much was he fain of her and she of him," are excellent.   The next couplet, or quatrain, almost approaches the best poetry.   " Of villainy or annoy make they no parley or complaint ; but draw near each other so much at least that they hold each other hand by hand."   But what follows ?   That they cannot come together vexes them so immeasurably that—what ?   They blame the iron work for it.   This certainly shows an acute understanding [3] and a very creditable sense of

---

[1] Neither he nor Malory gives one of the most gracious parts of it—the interview between Lancelot and King Bagdemagus, *v. inf.* p. 54.

[2] Material (chamois skin)? or garment?   Not common in O.F., I think, for *camisia* ; but Spenser (*Faerie Queene*, II. iii. xxvi.) has (as Prof. Gregory Smith reminds me) "a silken *camus* lilly whight."

[3] As does Pyramus's—or Bottom's—objection to the wall.

the facts of the situation on the part of both lovers ; but
it might surely have been taken for granted. Also, it
takes Lancelot forty lines to convince his lady that when
bars are in your way there is nothing like pulling them
out of it. So in the actual pulling-out there is the idlest
exaggeration and surplusage ; the first bar splits one of
Lancelot's fingers to the sinews and cuts off the top joint
of the next. The actual embraces are prettily and gracefully told (though again with otiose observations about
silence), and the whole, from the knight's coming to the
window to his leaving it, takes 150 lines. Now hear
the prose of the so-called " Vulgate *Lancelot*."

And he came to the window : and the Queen, who waited for
him, slept not, but came thither.   And the one threw to the other
their arms, and they felt each other as much as they could reach.
" Lady," said Lancelot, " if I could enter yonder, would it please
you ? "   " Enter," said she, " fair sweet friend ?   How could
this happen ? "   " Lady," said he, " if it please you, it could
happen lightly."   " Certainly," said she, " I should wish it
willingly above everything."   " Then, in God's name," said he,
" that shall well happen.   For the iron will never hold."   " Wait,
then," said she, " till I have gone to bed."   Then he drew the
irons from their sockets so softly that no noise was made and no
bar broke."

In this simple prose, sensuous and passionate for all
its simplicity, is told the rest of the story. There are
eighteen lines of it altogether in Dr. Sommer's reprint,
but as these are long quarto lines, let us multiply them by
some three to get the equivalent of the " skipping octosyllables." There will remain fifty to a hundred and
fifty, with, in the prose, some extra matter not in the
verse. But the acme of the contrast is reached in these
words of the prose, which answer to some forty lines of
the poet's watering-out. " Great was the joy that they
made each other that night, for long had each suffered
for the other. And when the day came, they parted."
Beat that who can !
Many years ago, and not a few before M. Gaston
Paris had published his views, I read these two forms of

the story in the valuable joint edition, verse and prose, of M. Jonckbloet, which some ruffian (may Heaven *not* assoil him!) has since stolen or hidden from me. And I said then to myself, " There is no doubt which of these is the original." Thirty years later, with an unbroken critical experience of imaginative work in prose and verse during the interval, I read them again in Dr. Forster's edition of the verse and Dr. Sommer's of the prose, and said, " There is less doubt than ever." That the prose should have been prettified and platitudinised, decorated and diluted into the verse is a possibility which we know to be not only possible but likely, from a thousand more unfortunate examples. That the contrary process should have taken place is practically unexampled and, especially at that time, largely unthinkable. At any rate, whosoever did it had a much greater genius than Chrestien's.

This is no place to argue out the whole question, but a single particular may be dealt with. The curiously silly passage about the bars above given is a characteristic example of unlucky and superfluous amplification of the perfectly natural question and answer of the prose, " May I come to you ? " " Yes, but how ? " an example to be paralleled by thousands of others at the time and by many more later. Taken the other way it would be a miracle. Prose abridgers of poetry did not go to work like that in the twelfth-thirteenth century—nor, even in the case of Charles Lamb, have they often done so since.

It is, however, very disagreeable to have to speak disrespectfully of a writer so agreeable in himself and so really important in our story as Chrestien. His own gifts and performances are, as it seems to me, clear enough. He took from this or that source—his selection of the *Erec* and *Percivale* matters, if not also that of *Yvain*, suggests others besides the, by that time as I think, concentrated Arthurian story—and from the Arthuriad itself the substance of the *Chevalier à la Charette*. He varied and dressed them up with pleasant

etceteras, and in especial, sometimes, though not always,
embroidered the already introduced love-motive with
courtly fantasies and with a great deal of detail. I
should not be at all disposed to object if somebody says
that he, before any one else, set the type of the regular
verse *Roman d'aventures*. It seems likely, again, from
the pieces referred to above, that he may have had
originals more definitely connected with Celtic sources,
if not actually Celtic themselves, than those which have
given us the mighty architectonic of the "Vulgate"
Arthur. In his own way and place he is a great and an
attractive figure—not least in the history of the novel.
But I can see nothing in him that makes me think him
likely, and much that makes me think him utterly unlikely, to be the author of what I conceive to be the
greatest, the most epoch-making, and almost the origin-
ating conception of the novel-romance itself. Who it
was that did conceive this great thing I do not positively
know. All external evidence points to Walter Map;
no internal evidence, that I have seen, seems to me really
to point away from him. But if any one likes let us leave
him a mere Eidolon, an earlier "Great Unknown."
Our business is, once more, with what he, whoever he
was, did.

The multiplicity of things done, whether by "him"
or "them," is astonishing; and it is quite possible,
indeed likely, that they were not all done by
the same person. Mediaeval continuators (as
has been seen in the case of Chrestien) worked
after and into the work of each other in a rather
uncanny fashion; and the present writer frankly confesses that he no more knows where Godfrey de Lagny
took up the *Charette*, or the various other sequelists the
Percevale, from Chrestien than he would have known,
without confession, the books of the *Odyssey* done by
Mr. Broome and Mr. Fenton from those done by Mr.
Pope. The *grand-œuvre* is the combination of Lancelot
as (1) lover of the Queen; (2) descendant of the Graal-
wards; (3) author, in consequence of his sin, of the

*The con-
stitution
of the
Arthuriad.*

general failure of the Round Table Graal-Quest ; (4)
father of its one successful but half-unearthly Seeker ;
(5) bringer-about (in more ways than one [1]) of the intestine
dissension which facilitates the invasion of Mordred and
the foreigners and so the Passing of Arthur, of his own
rejection by the repentant Queen, and of his death.   As
regards minor details of plot and incident there have to
be added the bringing in of the pre-Round Table part of
the story by Lancelot's descent from King Ban and his
connections with King Bors, both Arthur's old allies,
and both, as we may call them, " Graal-heirs " ; the
further connection with the Merlin legend by Lancelot's
fostering under the Lady of the Lake ; [2] the exaltation,

[1] This part of the matter has received too little attention in modern studies of the
subject : partly because it was clumsily handled by some of the probably innumerable
and certainly undiscoverable meddlers with the Vulgate.   The unpopularity of Lancelot
and his kin is not due merely to his invincibility and their not always discreet partisanship.   The older "Queen's knights" must have naturally felt her devotion to him ; his
"undependableness"—in consequence not merely of his fits of madness but of
his chivalrously permissible but very inconvenient habit of disguising himself and
taking the other side—must have annoyed the whole Table.   Yet these very things,
properly managed, help to create and complicate the "novel" character.   For
one of the most commonly and not the least justly charged faults of the average
romance is its deficiency in combined plot and character-interest—the presence in it,
at most, of a not too well-jointed series of episodes, possibly leading to a death or
a marriage, but of little more than chronicle type.   This fault has been exaggerated,
but it exists.   Now it will be one main purpose of the pages which follow to show that
there is, in the completed Arthuriad, something quite different from and far beyond this
—something perhaps imperfectly realised by any one writer, and overlaid and disarranged
by the interpolations or misinterpretations of others, but still a "mind" at work that
keeps the "mass" alive, and may, or rather surely will, quicken it yet further and into
higher forms hereafter.   (Those who know will not, I hope, be insulted if I mention
for the benefit of those who do not, that the term "Vulgate" is applied to those forms
of the parts of the story which, with slighter or more important variations, are common
to many MSS.   The term itself is most specially applied to the *Lancelot* which, in
consequence of this popularity throughout the later Middle Ages, actually got itself
printed early in the French Renaissance.   The whole has been (or is being) at last most
fortunately reprinted by Dr. Sommer.   See Bibliography.)

[2] This is another point which, not, I suppose, having been clearly and completely
evolved by the first handler, got messed and muddled by successive copyists and continuators.   In what seems to be the oldest, and is certainly the most consistent and
satisfactory, story there is practically nothing evil about Viviane—Nimiane—Nimue,
who is also indisputably identical with the foster-mother of Lancelot, the occasional
Egeria (always for good) of Arthur himself, and the benefactress (this is probably a later
addition though in the right key) of Sir Pelleas.   For anybody who possesses the Power
of the Sieve she remains as Milton saw her, and not as Tennyson mis-saw part of her.
The bewitching of Merlin (who, let it be remembered, was an ambiguous person in several
ways, and whose magic, if never exactly black, was sometimes a rather greyish or
magpied white) was not an unmixed loss to the world ; she seems to have really loved
him, and to have faithfully kept her word by being with him often.   He "could not get
out" certainly, but are there many more desirable things in the outside world than
lying with your head in the lap of the Lady of the Lake while she caresses and talks to

inspiring, and, as it were, unification of the scattered
knight-adventures through Lancelot's constant presence
as partaker, rescuer, and avenger ; [1] the human interest
given to the Graal-Quest (the earlier histories being
strikingly lacking in this) by his failure, and a good many
more.   But above all there are the general characters of
the knight and the Queen to make flesh and blood of
the whole.

Not merely the exact author or authors, but even the
exact source or sources of this complicated, fateful, and
exquisite imagination are, once more, not known.   Years
ago it was laid down finally by the most competent of
possible authorities (the late Sir John Rhys) that " the
love of Lancelot and Guinevere is unknown to Welsh
literature."   Originals for the " greatest knight " have
been sought by guesswork, by idle play on words and
names, if not also by positive forgery, in that Breton
literature which does not exist.   There do exist versions
of the story in which Lancelot plays no very prominent
part, and there is even one singular version—certainly
late and probably devised by a proper moral man afraid
of scandal—which makes Lancelot outlive the Queen,
quite comfortably continuing his adventurous career
(this is perhaps the " furthest " of the Unthinkable in
literature), and (not, it may be owned, quite inconsistently)
hints that the connection was merely Platonic throughout.
These things are explicable, but better negligible.   For
my own part I have always thought that the loves of

---

you? " J'en connais des plus malheureux " as the French poet observed of some one in less
delectable case.   The author of the *Suite de Merlin* seems to have been her first maligner.
Tennyson, seduced by contrast, followed and exaggerated the worst view.   But I am
not sure that the most " irreligious " thing (as Coleridge would have said) was not the
transformation of her into a mere married lady (with a château in Brittany, and an
ordinary knight for her husband) which astounds us in one of the dullest parts of the
Vulgate about Lancelot—the wars with Claudas.

[1] I have always thought that Spenser (whose dealings with Arthuriana are very
curious, and have never, I think, been fully studied) took this function of Lancelot to
suggest the presentation of his Arthur.   But Lancelot has no—at least no continuous—
fairy aid ; he is not invariably victorious, and he is thoroughly human.   Spenser's Prince
began the " blamelessness " which grew more trying still in Tennyson's King.   (In the
few remarks of this kind made here I am not, I need hardly say, " going back upon "
my lifelong estimate of Tennyson as an almost impeccable poet.   But an impeccable
poet is not necessarily an impeccable plot- and character-monger either in tale-telling or
in drama.)

Tristram and Iseult (which, as has been said, were
originally un-Arthurian) suggested the main idea to the
author of it, being taken together with Guinevere's false-
ness with Mordred in the old quasi-chronicle, and
perhaps the story of the abduction by Melvas (Meleagraunce), which seems to be possibly a genuine Welsh
legend.   There are in the Tristram-Iseult-Mark trio quite
sufficient suggestions of Lancelot-Guinevere-Arthur ;
while the far higher plane on which the novice-novelist
sets his lovers, and even the very interesting subsequent
exaltation of Tristram and Iseult themselves to
familiarity and to some extent equality with the other
pair, has nothing critically difficult in it.

But this idea, great and promising as it was, required
further fertilisation, and got it from another.   The
Graal story is (once more, according to authority of the
greatest competence, and likely if anything to be biassed
the other way) pretty certainly not Welsh in origin, and
there is no reason to think that it originally had anything
to do with Arthur.   Even after it obeyed the strange
" suck " of legends towards this centre whirlpool, or
Loadstone Rock, of romance, it yielded nothing intimately
connected with the Arthurian Legend itself at first, and
such connection as succeeded seems pretty certainly [1] to
be that of which Percevale is the hero, and an outlier,
not an integral part.   But either the same genius (as one
would fain hope) as that which devised the profane
romance of Lancelot and Guinevere, or another, further
grafted or inarched the sacred romance of the Graal and
its Quest with the already combined love-and-chivalry
story.   Lancelot, the greatest of knights, and of the true
blood of the Graal-guardians, ought to accomplish the
mysteries ; but he cannot through sin, and that sin is
this very love for Guinevere.   The Quest, in which
(despite warning and indeed previous experience) he
takes part, not merely gives occasion for adventures,
half-mystical, half-chivalrous, which far exceed in interest

[1] Of this we have unusually strong evidence in the shape of MS. interlineations,
where the name "Percevale" is actually struck out and that of "Gala[h]ad" substituted above it.

the earlier ones, but directly leads to the dispersion and
weakening of the Round Table. And so the whole
draws together to an end identical in part with that of
the Chronicle story, but quite infinitely improved upon it.

Now not only is there in this the creation of the novel
in posse, of the romance *in esse*, but it is brought about
Its approxi- in a curiously noteworthy fashion. A hundred
mation to years and more later the greatest known writer
the novel of the Middle Ages, and one of the three
proper. or four greatest of the world, defined the
subjects of poetry as Love, War, and Religion, or in
words which we may not unfairly translate by these.
The earlier master recognised (practically for the first
time) that the romance—that allotropic form (as the
chemists might say) of poetry—must deal with the same.
Now in these forms of the Arthurian legend, which are
certainly anterior to the latter part of the twelfth century,
there is a great deal of war and a good deal of religion,
but these motives are mostly separated from each other,
the earlier forms of the Arthur story having nothing to
do with the Graal, and the earlier forms of the Graal
story—so far as we can see—nothing, or extremely little,
to do with Arthur. Nor had Love, in any proper and
passionate sense of the word, anything to do with either.
Women and marriage and breaches of marriage appear
indeed; but the earlier Graal stories are dominated by
the most ascetic virginity-worship, and the earlier Arthur-
stories show absolutely nothing of the passion which is
the subject of the magnificent overture of Mr. Swinburne's *Tristram*. Even this story of Tristram himself,
afterwards fired and coloured by passion, seems at first
to have shown nothing but the mixture of animalism,
cruelty, and magic which is characteristic of the Celts.[1]
Our magician of a very different gramarye, were he
Walter or Chrestien or some third—Norman, Champenois,
Breton,[2] or Englishman (Welshman or Irishman he
pretty certainly was *not*)—had therefore before him, if

[1] I do not say that this is their *only* character.
[2] Brittany had much earlier and much more tradition of chivalry than Wales.

not exactly dry bones, yet the half-vivified material of
a chronicle of events on the one hand and a mystical
dream-sermon on the other.   He, or a French or English
Pallas for him, had to " think of another thing."

And so he called in Love to reinforce War and Religion
and to do its proper office of uniting, inspiring, and
producing Humanity.   He effected, by the union of the
three motives, the transformation of a mere dull record
of confused fighting into a brilliant pageant of knightly
adventure.   He made the long-winded homilies and
genealogies of the earlier Graal-legend at once take
colour from the amorous and war-like adventures, raise
these to a higher and more spiritual plane, and provide
the due punishment for the sins of his erring characters.
The whole story—at least all of it that he chose to touch
and all that he chose to add—became alive.   The bones
were clothed with flesh and blood, the " wastable country
verament " (as the dullest of the Graal chroniclers says
in a phrase that applies capitally to his own work)
blossomed with flower and fruit.   Wars of Arthur with
unwilling subjects or Saxons and Romans ; treachery of
his wife and nephew and his own death ; miracle-history
of the Holy Vessel and pedigree of its custodians ; Round
Table ; these and many other things had lain as mere
scraps and orts, united by no real plot, yielding no real
characters, satisfying no real interest that could not
have been equally satisfied by an actual chronicle or an
actual religious-mystical discourse.   And then the whole
was suddenly knit into a seamless and shimmering web
of romance, from the fancy of Uther for Igerne to the
" departing of them all " in Lyonnesse and at Amesbury
and at Joyous Gard.   A romance undoubtedly, but also
incidentally providing the first real novel-hero and the
first real novel-heroine in the persons of the lovers who,
as in the passage above translated, sometimes " made
great joy of each other for that they had long caused each
other much sorrow," and finally expiated in sorrow what
was unlawful in their joy.

Let us pass to these persons themselves.

The first point to note about Lancelot is the singular fashion in which he escapes one of the dangers of the hero.   Aristotle had never said that a hero must be faultless; indeed, he had definitely said exactly the contrary, of at least the tragic hero.   But one of the worst of the many misunderstandings of his dicta brought the wrong notion about, and Virgil — that exquisite craftsman in verse and phrase, but otherwise, perhaps, not great poet and very dangerous pattern— had confirmed this notion by his deplorable figurehead. It is also fair to confess that all except morbid tastes do like to see the hero win.   But if he is to be a hero of Rymer, not merely

Especially in the characters and relations of Lancelot and Guinevere.

> Like Paris handsome [1] and like Hector brave,

but as pious as Aeneas ; " a rich fellow enough," with blood hopelessly blue and morals spotlessly copy-bookish —in other words, a Sir Charles Grandison—he will duly meet with the detestation and " conspuing " of the elect.   Almost the only just one of the numerous and generally silly charges latterly brought against Tennyson's Arthurian handling is that his conception of the blameless king does a little smack of this false idea, does something grow to it.   It is one of the chief points in which he departed, not merely from the older stories (which he probably did not know), but from Malory's astonishing redaction of them (which he certainly did).

But Lancelot escapes this worst of fates in the *Idylls* themselves, and much more does he escape it in the originals.   In the first place, though he invariably (or always till the Graal Quest) " wins through," he constantly does not do so without intermediate hairbreadth escapes, and even not a few adventures which are at first not escapes at all.   And

Lancelot.

---

[1] The only fault alleged against Lancelot's person by carpers was that he was something " pigeon "—or " guardsman "—chested.   But Guinevere showed her love and her wit, and her " valiancy " (for so at least on this occasion we may translate *vaillant*) by retorting that such a chest was only big enough—and hardly big enough—for such a heart.

just as his perpetual bafflement in the Quest salts and
seasons his triumphs in the saddle, so does the ruling
passion of his sin save, from anything approaching
mawkishness,[1] his innumerable and yet inoffensive
virtues ; his chastity, save in this instance, which
chastity itself, by a further stroke of art, is saved from
niaiserie by the plotted adventures with Elaine ; his
courtesy, his mercifulness, his wonderfully early notion
of a gentleman (*v. inf.*), his invariable disregard of
self, and yet his equally invariable naturalness. Pious
Aeneas had not the least objection to bringing about the
death of Dido, as he might have known he was doing
(unless he was as great a fool as he is a prig) ; and he is
probably never more disgusting or Pecksniffian than
when he looks back on the flames of Dido's pyre and
is really afraid that something unpleasant must have
happened, though he can't think what the matter can be.
But *he*, one feels sure, would never have lifted up his
hand against a woman, unless she had richly deserved it
on the strictest patriotic scores, as in the case of Helen,
when his mamma fortunately interfered.   On the other
hand, Lancelot was " of the Asra who die when they
love " and love till they die—nay, who would die if they
did not love.   But it is certain (for there is a very nice
miniature of it reproduced from the MS. in M. Paulin
Paris's abstract) that, for a moment, he drew his sword
on Elaine to punish the deceit which made him un-
wittingly false to Guinevere.   It is very shocking, no
doubt, but exceedingly natural ; and of course he did not
kill or even (like Philaster) wound her, though nobody
interfered to prevent him.   Many of the incidents which
bring out his character are well known to moderns by
poem and picture, though others, as well worth knowing,
are not.   But the human contrasts of success and
failure, of merit and sin, have never, I think, been quite

---

[1] Some of the later " redactors " of the Vulgate may perhaps have unduly multiplied
his madnesses, and have exaggerated his early shyness a little. But I am not sure of
the latter point. It is not only " beasts " that, as in the great Theocritean place, " go
timidly because they fear Cythera " ; and a love charged with such dread consequences
was not to be lightly embarked upon.

brought out, and to bring them out completely here would take too much room. We may perhaps leave this other —quite other — " *First* Gentleman in Europe " with the remark that Chrestien de Troyes gives only one side of him, and therefore does not give him at all. The Lancelot of board and bower, of travel and tournament, he does very fairly. But of the Lancelot of the woods and the hermitage, of the dream at the foot of the cross, of the mystic voyage and the just failing (if failing) effort of Carbonek, he gives, because he knows, nothing.

Completed as he was, no matter for the moment by whom, he is thus the first hero of romance and nearly the greatest ; but his lady is worthy of him, and she is almost more original as an individual. Guinevere. It is true that she is not the first heroine, as he is, if not altogether, almost the first hero. Helen was that, though very imperfectly revealed and gingerly handled. Calypso (hardly Circe) *might* have been. Medea is perhaps nearer still, especially in Apollonius. But the Greek romancers were the first who had really busied themselves with the heroine : they took her up seriously and gave her a considerable position. But they did not succeed in giving her much character. The naughty *not*-heroine of Achilles Tatius, though she has less than none in Mr. Pope's supposed innuendo sense, alone has an approach to some in the other. As for the accomplished Guinevere's probable contemporary, the Ismene or Hysmine of Eustathius Macrembolites (*v. sup.* p. 18), she is a sort of Greek-mediaeval Henrietta Temple, with Mr. Meredith and Mr. Disraeli by turns holding the pen, though with neither of them supplying the brains. But Guinevere is a very different person ; or rather, she *is* a person, and the first. To appreciate her she must be compared with herself in earlier presentations, and then considered fully as she appears in the Vulgate—for Malory, though he has given much, has not given the whole of her, and Tennyson has painted only the last panel of the polyptych wholly, and has rather over-coloured that.[1]

---

[1] The early *Sir Lancelot and Queen Guinevere*, though only external, is perfect.

In what we may call the earliest representations of
her, she has hardly any colour at all. She is a noble
Roman lady, and very beautiful. For a time she is apparently very happy with her husband, and he with her ;
and if she seems to make not the slightest scruple about
" taking up with " her nephew, co-regent and fellow
rebel, why, noble Roman ladies thought nothing of
divorce and not much of adultery. The only old Welsh
story (the famous Melvas one so often referred to) that
we have about her in much detail merely establishes the
fact, pleasantly formulated by M. Paulin Paris, that she
was " très sujette à être enlevée," but in itself (unless
we admit the Peacockian triad of the " Three Fatal Slaps
of the Isle of Britain " as evidence) again says nothing
about her character. If, as seems probable if not certain,
the *Launfal* legend, with its libel on her, is of Breton
origin, it makes her an ordinary Celtic princess, a spiritual
sister of Iseult when she tried to kill Brengwain, and
a cross between Potiphar's wife and Catherine of Russia,
without any of the good nature and " gentlemanliness "
of the last named. The real Guinevere, the Guinevere
of the Vulgate and partly of Malory, is freed from the
colourlessness and the discreditable end of Geoffrey's
queen, transforms the promiscuous and rather *louche*
Melvas incident into an important episode of her epic
or romantic existence, and gives the lie, even in her least
creditable or least charming moments, to the *Launfal* libel.
As before in Lancelot's case, details of her presentation had
in some cases best be either translated in full or omitted,
but I cannot refuse myself the pleasure of attempting, with
however clumsy a hand, a portrait of our, as I believe,
English Helen, who gave in French language to French,
and not only French literature, the pattern of a heroine.

There is not, I think, any ancient authority for the
rather commonplace suggestion, unwisely adopted by

Many touches in the *Idylls* other than the title-one are suitable and even subtle ; but the
convertite in that one is (as they say now) "unconvincing." The simpler attitude of
the rejection of Lancelot in the verse *Morte* and in Malory is infinitely better. As for
Morris's two pieces, they could hardly be better in themselves as poems—but they are
scarcely great on the novel side.

Tennyson, that Guinevere fell in love with Lancelot when he was sent as an ambassador to fetch her; thus merely repeating Iseult and Tristram, and anticipating Suffolk and Margaret. In fact, according to the best evidence, Lancelot could not have been old enough, if he was even born. On the contrary, nothing could be better than the presentation of her introduction to Arthur and the course of the wooing in the Vulgate— the other " blessed original." She first sees Arthur as a foe from the walls of besieged Carmelide, and admires his valour; she has further occasion to admire it when, as a friend, he rescues her father, showing himself, as what he really was in his youth, his own best knight. The pair are genuinely in love with each other, and the betrothal and parting for fresh fight are the most gracious passages of the *Merlin* book, except the better version (*v. sup.*) of the love of Merlin himself and the afterwards libelled Viviane. Anyhow, she was married because she fell in love with him, and there is no evidence to show that she and Arthur lived otherwise than happily together. But, if all tales were true, she had no reason to regard him as a very faithful husband or a blameless man. She may not have known (for nobody but Merlin apparently did know) the early and unwitting incest of the King and his half-sister Margause; but the extreme ease with which he adopted her own treacherous foster-sister, the " false Guinevere," and his proceedings with the Saxon enchantress Camilla, were very strong " sets off " to her own conduct. Also she had a most dis-agreeable [1] sister-in-law in Morgane-la-Fée. These are not in the least offered as excuses, but merely as "lights." Indeed Guinevere never seems to have hated or disliked her husband, though he often gave her cause; and if, until the great repentance, she thought more lightly of " spouse-breach " than Lancelot did, that is not un-characteristic of women. [2] In fact, she is a very perfect

[1] Disagreeable, that is to say, as a sister and sister-in-law. There must have been something attractive about her in other relations.

[2] Compare one of the not so very many real examples of Ibsen's vaunted psychology, the placid indifference to her own past of Gina in the *Wild Duck*.

(not of course in the moral sense) gentlewoman. She
is at once popular with the knights, and loses that popularity rather by Lancelot's fault than by her own, while
Gawain, who remains faithful to her to the bitter end,
or at least till the luckless slaughter of his brethren,
declares at the beginning that she is the fairest and most
gracious, and will be the wisest and best of queens. She
shows something very like humour in the famous and fateful remark (uttered, it would seem, without the slightest
ill or double meaning at the time) as to Gawain's estimate
of Lancelot.[1] She seems to have had an agreeable
petulance (notice, for instance, the rebuke of Kay at the
opening of the *Ywain* story and elsewhere), which sometimes, as it naturally would, rises to passionate injustice,
as Lancelot frequently discovered. She is, in fact,
always passionate in one or other sense of that great and
terrible and infinite [2] word, but never tragedy-queenish
or vixenish. She falls in love with Lancelot because he
falls in love with her, and because she cannot help it.
False as she is to husband and to lover, to her court and
her country,[3] it can hardly be said that any act of hers,
except the love itself and its irresistible consequences, is
faulty. She is not capricious, extravagant, or tyrannical ;
in her very jealousy she is not cruel or revengeful (the
original Iseult would certainly have had Elaine poisoned
or poniarded, for which there was ample opportunity).
If she torments her lover, that is because she loves him.
If she is unjust to him, that is because she is a woman. Her
last speech to Lancelot after the catastrophe—Tennyson
should have, as has been said, paraphrased this as he
paraphrased the passing of her husband, and from the
same texts, and we should then have had another of
the greatest things of English poetry—shows a noble
nature with the ἁμαρτία present, but repented in a
strange and great mixture of classical and Christian
tragedy. There is little told in a trustworthy fashion

---

[1] He had said that if he were a woman he would give Lancelot anything he asked ;
and the Queen, following, observes that Gawain had left nothing for a woman to say.
[2] *Nos passions ont quelque chose d'infini*, says Bossuet.
[3] ἔλανδρος, ἑλέπτολις. She had no opportunity of being ἑλέναυς.

about her personal appearance. But if Glastonbury
traditions about her bones be true, she was certainly
(again like Helen) " divinely tall." And if the suggestions of Hawker's " Queen Gwennyvar's Round " [1] in
the sea round Tintagel be worked out a little, it will
follow that her eyes were divinely blue.

When such very high praise is given to the position
of the (further) accomplished Arthur-story, it is of course
Some minor not intended to bestow that praise on any
points.   particular MS. or printed version that exists.
It is in the highest degree improbable that, whether
the original magician was Map, or Chrestien, or
anybody else (to repeat a useful formula), we possess
an exact and exclusive copy of the form into which he
himself threw the story. Independently of the fact that
no MS., verse or prose, of anything like the complete
story seems old enough, independently of the enormous
and almost innumerable separable accretions, the so-
called Vulgate cycle of " *Graal-Merlin-Arthur-Lancelot-
Graal-Quest-Arthur's-Death* " has considerable variants
—the most important and remarkable of which by far
is the large alteration or sequel of the " Vulgate " *Merlin*
which Malory preferred. In the " Vulgate " itself, too,
there are things which were certainly written either by
the great contriver in nodding moods, or by somebody
else,—in fact no one can hope to understand mediaeval
literature who forgets that no mediaeval writer could
ever " let a thing alone ": he simply *must* add or shorten,
paraphrase or alter. I rather doubt whether the Great
Unknown himself meant *both* the amours of Arthur with
Camilla and the complete episode of the false Guinevere
to stand side by side. The first is (as such justifications
go) a sufficient justification of Guinevere by itself; and
the conduct of Arthur in the second is such a combination
of folly, cruelty, and all sorts of despicable behaviour

---

[1] Hawker's security as to Cornish men and things is, I admit, a little Bardolphian.
But did he not write about the Quest? (This sort of argument simply swarms in
Arthurian controversy; so I may surely use it once.) Besides there is no doubt about
the blueness of the sea in question; though Anthony Trollope, in *Malachi's Cove*, has
most falsely and incomprehensibly denied it.

that it overdoes the thing.   So, too, Lancelot's " abscond-
ences," with or without madness, are too many and too
prolonged.[1]   The long and totally uninteresting campaign against Claudas, during the greater part of which
Lancelot (who is most of all concerned) is absent, and
in which he takes no part or interest when present, is
another great blot.   Some of these things, but not all,
Malory remedied by omission.

To sum up, and even repeat a little, in speaking so
highly of this development—French beyond all doubt
as a part of literature, whatever the nationality, domicile,
and temper of the person or persons who brought it
about—I do not desire more to emphasise what I believe
to be a great and not too well appreciated truth than
to guard against that exaggeration which dogs and
discredits literary criticism.   Of course no single redaction
of the legend in the late twelfth or earliest thirteenth
century contains the story, the whole story, and nothing
but the story as I have just outlined it.   Of course the
words used do not apply fully to Malory's English
redaction of three centuries later—work of genius as
this appears to me to be.   Yet further, I should be fully
disposed to allow that it is only by reading the *posse* into
the *esse*, under the guidance of later developments of the
novel itself, that the estimate which I have given can be
entirely justified.   But this process seems to me to be
perfectly legitimate, and to be, in fact, the only process
capable of giving us literary-historical criticism that is
worth having.   The writer or writers, known or unknown, whose work we have been discussing, have got
the plot, have got the characters, have got the narrative
faculty required for a complete novel-romance.   If they
do not quite know what to do with these things it is only
because the time is not yet.   But how much they did,
and of how much more they foreshadowed the doing,
the extracts following should show better than any
" talk about it."

---

[1] That this is a real sign of decadence and unoriginality, the further exaggeration of
it in the case of the knights of the *Amadis* cycle proves almost to demonstration.

[Lancelot, still under the tutelage of the Lady of the Lake and ignorant of his own parentage, has met his cousins, Lionel and Bors, and has been greatly drawn to them.]

Now turns herself the Lady back to the Lake, and takes the children with her.   And when she had gone [1] a good way, she called Lancelot a little way off the road and said to him very kindly, " King's son,[2] how wast thou so bold as to call Lionel thy cousin ? for he *is* a king's son, and of not a little more worth and gentry than men think.' " Lady," said he, who was right ashamed, " so came the word into my mouth by adventure that I never took any heed of it."   " Now tell me," said she, " by the faith thou owest me, which thinkest thou to be the greater gentleman, thyself or him ? "   " Lady," said he, " you have adjured me strongly, for I owe no one such faith as I owe you, my lady and my mother :   nor know I how much of a gentleman I am by lineage.   But, by the faith I owe you, I would not myself deign to be abashed at that for which I saw him weep.[3]   And they have told me that all men have sprung from one man and one woman : nor know I for what reason one has more gentry than another, unless he win it by prowess, even as lands and other honours. But know you for very truth that if greatness of heart made a gentleman I would think yet to be one of the greatest."   " Verily, fair son," said the Lady, " it shall appear.   And I say to you that you lose nothing of being one of the best gentlemen in the world, if your heart fail you not."   " How, Lady ! " said he, " say you this truly, *as* my lady ? "   And she said, " Yes, without fail." " Lady," said he, " blessed be you of God, that you said it to me so soon [*or* as soon as you have said it].   For to that will you make me come which I never thought to attain.   Nor had I so much desire of anything as of possessing gentry."

Illustrative extracts translated from the "Vulgate." The youth of Lancelot.

[The first meeting of Lancelot and Guinevere.   The Lady of the Lake has prevailed upon the King to dub Lancelot on St. John's Day (Midsummer, not Christmas).   His protectress departing, he is committed to the care of Ywain, and a conversation arises about him.   The Queen asks to see him.]

Then bid he [the King] Monseigneur [4] Ywain that he should

---

[1] After the opening sentence I have dropped the historic present, which, for a continuance, is very irritating in English.

[2] Lancelot himself has told us earlier (*op. cit.* i. 38) that, though he neither knew nor thought himself to be a king's son, he was commonly addressed as such.

[3] Lionel (very young at the time) had wept because some one mentioned the loss of his inheritance, and Lancelot (young as he too was) had bidden him not cry for fear of landlessness.   "There would be plenty for him, if he had heart to gain it."

[4] This technical title is usually if not invariably given to Ywain and Gawain as

go and look for Lancelot. "And let him be equipped as handsomely as you know is proper : for well know I that
he has plenty." Then the King himself told the
Queen how the Lady of the Lake had requested that he
would not make Lancelot knight save in his own arms
and dress. And the Queen marvelled much at this, and thought
long till she saw him. So Messire Ywain went to the Childe
[*vallet*] and had him clothed and equipped in the best way he
could : and when he saw that nothing could be bettered, he led
him to Court on his own horse, which was right fair. But he
brought him not quietly. For there was so much people about
that the whole street was full : and the news was spread through
all the town that the fair Childe who came yester eve should be a
knight to-morrow, and was now coming to Court in knightly
garb. Then sprang to the windows they of the town, both men
and women. And when they saw him pass they said that never
had they seen so fair a Childe-knight. So he came to the Court
and alighted from his horse : and the news of him spread through
hall and chamber ; and knights and dames and damsels hurried
forth. And even the King and the Queen went to the windows.
So when the Childe had dismounted, Messire Ywain took him
by the hand, and led him by it up to the Hall.

The King and the Queen came to meet him : and both took
him by his two hands and went to seat themselves on a couch :
while the Childe seated himself before them on the fresh green
grass with which the Hall was spread. And the King gazed on
him right willingly : for if he had seemed fair at his first coming,
it was nothing to the beauty that he now had. And the King
thought he had mightily grown in stature and thews.[1] So the
Queen prayed that God might make him a man of worth, "for
right plenty of beauty has He given him," and she looked at the
Childe very sweetly : and so did he at her as often as he could
covertly direct his eyes towards her. Also marvelled he much how
such great beauty as he saw appear in her could come : for neither
that of his lady, the Lady of the Lake, nor of any woman that he
had ever seen, did he prize aught as compared with hers. And no
wrong had he if he valued no other lady against the Queen : for
she was the Lady of Ladies and the Fountain of Beauty. But if
he had known the great worthiness that was in her he would have
been still more fain to gaze on her. For none, neither poor nor
rich, was her equal.

eldest sons of recognised kings. "Prince" is not used in this sense by the older
Romancers, but only for distinguished knights like Galahault, who is really a king.

[1] There is one admirable word here, *enbarnis*, which has so long been lost to French
that it is not even in Littré. But Dryden's "*burnish* into man" probably preserves it
in English ; for this is certainly not the other "burnish" from *brunir*.

So she asked Monseigneur Ywain what was the Childe's name,
and he answered that he knew not. "And know you," said she,
"whose son he is and of what birth?" "Lady," said he, "nay,
except I know so much as that he is of the land of Gaul. For
his speech bewrayeth him."[1] Then the Queen took him by the
hand and asked him of whom he came. And when he felt it [the
touch] he shuddered as though roused from sleep, and thought
of her so hard that he knew not what she said to him. And she
perceived that he was much abashed, and so asked him a second
time, "Tell me whence you come." So he looked at her very
sheepishly and said, with a sigh, that he knew not. And she
asked him what was his name; and he answered that he knew not
that. So now the Queen saw well that he was abashed and
overthought.[2] But she dared not think that it was for her: and
nevertheless she had some suspicion of it, and so dropped the
talk. But that she might not make the disorder of his mind worse,
she rose from her seat and, in order that no one might think any
evil or perceive what she suspected, said that the Childe seemed
to her not very wise, and whether wise or not had been ill brought
up. "Lady," said Messire Ywain, "between you and me, we
know nothing about him: and perchance he is forbidden[3] to tell
his name or who he is." And she said, "It may well be so," but
she said it so low that the Childe heard her not.

[*Here follows (with a very little surplusage removed perhaps)
the scene which Dante has made world-famous, but which Malory
(I think for reasons) has "cut." I trust it is neither Philistinism
nor perversity which makes me think of it a little, though only a little,
less highly than some have done. There is (and after all this makes
it all the more interesting for us historians) the least little bit of anticipation of Marivaudage about it, and less of the adorable simplicity
such as that (a little subsequent to the last extract given) where
Lancelot, having forgotten to take leave of the Queen on going to his
first adventure, and having returned to do so, kneels to her, receives
her hand to raise him from the ground, " and much was his joy to feel
it bare in his." But the beauty of what follows is incontestable, and
that Guinevere was " exceeding wise in love " is certain.*]

"Ha!" said she then, "I know who you are—Lancelot of
the Lake is your name." And he was silent. "They
know it at court," said she, "this sometime. Messire
Gawain was the first to bring your name there. . . ."
Then she asked him why he had allowed the worst man in

The scene
of the kiss.

---

[1] "Car moult en parole diroit la parole."
[2] Puzzled by the number of new thoughts and emotions.
[3] Ywain suggests one of the commonest things in Romance.

the world to lead him by the bridle.   "Lady," said he, "as one
who had command neither of his heart nor of his body."   "Now
tell me," said she, "were you at last year's assembly ? "   "Yes,
Lady," said he.   "And what arms did you bear ? "   "Lady, they
were all of vermilion."   "By my head," said she, "you say true.
And why did you do such deeds at the meeting the day before
yesterday ? "   Then he began to sigh very very deeply.   And
the Queen cut him short as well, knowing how it was with him.
    "Tell me," she said, "plainly, how it is.   I will never betray
you.   But I know that you did it for some lady.   Now, tell me,
by the faith you owe me, who she is."   "Ah, Lady," said he,
"I see well that it behoves me to speak.   Lady, it is you."   "I!"
said she.   "It was not for me you took the spears that my maiden
brought you.   For I took care to put myself out of the commission."   "Lady," said he, "I did for others what I ought, and
for you what I could."   "Tell me, then, for whom have you
done all the things that you *have* done ? "   "Lady," said he,
"for you."   "How," said she, "do you love me so much ? "
"So much, Lady, as I love neither myself nor any other."   "And
since when have you loved me thus ? "   "Since the hour when
I was called knight and yet was not one." [1]   "Then, by the faith
you owe me, whence came this love that you have set upon me ? "
Now as the Queen said these words it happened that the Lady
of the Puy of Malahault [2] coughed on purpose, and lifted her
head, which she had held down.   And he understood her now,
having oft heard her before : and looked at her and knew her, and
felt in his heart such fear and anguish that he could not answer
the Queen.   Then began he to sigh right deeply, and the tears
fell from his eyes so thick, that the garment he wore was wet to
the knees.   And the more he looked at the Lady of Malahault the
more ill at ease was his heart.   Now the Queen noticed this and
saw that he looked sadly towards the place where her ladies were,
and she reasoned with him.   "Tell me," she said, "whence
comes this love that I am asking you about ? " and he tried as hard
as he could to speak, and said, "Lady, from the time I have said."
"How ? "   "Lady, you did it, when you made me your friend,
if your mouth lied not."   "My friend ? " she said ; "and how ? "
"I came before you when I had taken leave of my Lord the King
all armed except my head and my hands.   And then I commended
you to God, and said that, wherever I was, I was your knight :
and you said that you would have me to be your knight and your
friend.   And then I said, 'Adieu, Lady,' and you said, 'Adieu,

[1] Arthur had, by a set of chances, not actually girded on Lancelot's sword.
[2] Whose prisoner Lancelot had been, who had been ready to fall in love with him,
and to whom he had expressly refused to tell his own love.   Hence his confusion.

fair sweet friend.'   And never has that word left my heart, and
it is that word that has made me a good knight and valiant—if I
be so : nor ever have I been so ill-bested as not to remember that
word.   That word comforts me in all my annoys.   That word
has kept me from all harm, and freed me from all peril, and fills me
whenever I hunger.   Never have I been so poor but that word
has made me rich."   " By my faith," said the Queen, " that word
was spoken in a good hour, and God be praised when He made
me speak it.   Still, I did not set it as high as you did : and to many
a knight have I said it, when I gave no more thought to the saying.
But *your* thought was no base one, but gentle and debonair ;
wherefore joy has come to you of it, and it has made you a good
knight.   Yet, nevertheless, this way is not that of knights who
make great matter to many a lady of many a thing which they have
little at heart.   And your seeming shows me that you love one or
other of these ladies better than you love me.   For you wept for
fear and dared not look straight at them : so that I well see that
your thought is not so much of me as you pretend.   So, by the
faith you owe the thing you love best in the world, tell me which
one of the three you love so much ? "   " Ah ! Lady," said he,
" for the mercy of God, as God shall keep me, never had one of
them my heart in her keeping."   " This will not do," said the
Queen, " you cannot dissemble.   For many another such thing
have I seen, and I know that your heart is there as surely as your
body is here."   And this she said that she might well see how
she might put him ill at ease.   For she thought surely enough
that he meant no love save to her, or ill would it have gone on the
day of the Black Arms.[1]   And she took a keen delight in seeing
and considering his discomfort.   But he was in such anguish that
he wanted little of swooning, save that fear of the ladies before
him kept him back.   And the Queen herself perceived it at the
sight of his changes of colour, and caught him by the shoulder
that he might not fall, and called to Galahault.   Then the prince
sprang forward and ran to his friend, and saw that he was disturbed
thus, and had great pain in his own heart for it, and said, " Ah,
Lady ! tell me, for God's sake, what has happened."   And the
Queen told him the conversation.   " Ah, Lady ! " said Galahault, " mercy, for God's sake, or you may lose me him by such
wrath, and it would be too great pity."   " Certes," said she, " that
is true.   But know you why he has done such feats of arms ? "
" Nay, surely, Lady," said he.   " Sir," said she, " if what he tells
me is true, it was for me."   " Lady," said he, " as God shall keep
me, I can believe it.   For just as he is more valiant than other

---

[1] The day when Lancelot, at her request, had turned against the side of his friend
Galahault and brought victory to Arthur's.

men, so is his heart truer than all theirs." "Verily," said she,
"you would say well that he is valiant if you knew what deeds he
has done since he was made knight," and then she told him all
the chivalry of Lancelot . . . and how he had done it all for a
single word of hers [*Galahault tells her more, and begs mercy for
L.*]. "He could ask me nothing," sighed she, "that I could
fairly refuse him, but he will ask me nothing at all." . .
"Lady," said Galahault, "certainly he has no power to do so.
For one loves nothing that one does not fear." [*And then comes
the immortal kiss, asked by the Prince, delayed a moment by the
Queen's demur as to time and place, brought on by the "Galeotto"-
speech.* "Let us three corner close together as if we were talking
secrets," *vouchsafed by Guinevere in the words,* "Why should I
make me longer prayer for what I wish more than you or he?"
Lancelot still hangs back, but the Queen "takes him by the chin and
kisses him before Galahault with a kiss long enough" *so that the
Lady of Malahault knows it.*] And then said the Queen, who
was a right wise and gracious lady, "Fair sweet friend, so much
have you done that I am yours, and right great joy have I thereof.
Now see to it that the thing be kept secret, as it should be. For
I am one of the ladies of the world who have the fairest fame, and
if my praise grew worse through you, then it would be a foul and
shameful thing."

A little more comment on this cento, and especially
on the central passage of it, can hardly be, and ought
certainly not to be, avoided in such a work as
this, even if, like most summaries, it be something of a repetition. It must surely be
obvious to any careful reader that here is
something much more than — unless his
reading has been as wide elsewhere as it is careful
here—he expected from Romance in the commoner and
half-contemptuous acceptation of that word. Lancelot
he may, though he should not, still class as a mere
amoureux transi—a nobler and pluckier Silvius in an
earlier *As You Like It*, and with a greater than Phoebe
for idol. Malory ought to be enough to set him right
there : he need even not go much beyond Tennyson,
who has comprehended Lancelot pretty correctly, if
not indeed pretty adequately. But Malory has left out
a great deal of the information which would have enabled

Some further remarks on the novel character of the story.

his readers to comprehend Guinevere; and Tennyson, only presenting her in parts, has allowed those parts, especially the final and only full presentation, great as it is, to be too much influenced by his certainly unfortunate other presentation of Arthur as a blameless king.

I do not say that the actual creator of the Vulgate Guinevere, whoever he was, has wrought her into a novel-character of the first class. It would have been not merely a miracle (for miracles often happen), but something more, if he had. If you could take Beatrix Esmond at a better time, Argemone Lavington raised to a higher power, and the spirit of all that is best and strongest and least purely paradoxical in Meredith's heroines, and work these three graces into one woman, adding the passion of Tennyson's own Fatima and the queenliness of Helen herself, it might be something like the achieved Guinevere who is still left to the reader's imagination to achieve. But the Unknown has given the hints of all this; and curiously enough it is only of *English* novel-heroines that I can think in comparison and continuation of her. This book, if it is ever finished, will show, I hope, some knowledge of French ones: I can remember none possessing any touch of Guineveresque quality. Dante, if his poetic nature had taken a different bent, and Shakespeare, if he had only chosen, could have been her portrayers singly; no others that I can think of, and certainly no Frenchman.

But here Guinevere's creator or expounder has done more for her than merely indicate her charm. Her
And the personages. "fear for name and fame" is not exactly "crescent"—it is there from the first, and seems to have nothing either cowardly or merely selfish in it, but only that really "last infirmity of noble minds," the shame of shame even in doing things shameful or shameless. I have seldom seen justice done to her magnificent fearlessness in all her dangers. Her graciousness as a Queen has been more generally admitted, but, once again, the composition and complexity of her fits of jealousy have never, I think, been fully

E

rationalised. Here, once more, we must take into account that difference of age which is so important. *He* thinks nothing of it ; *she* never forgets it. And in almost all the circumstances where this rankling kindles into wrath—whether with no cause at all, as in most cases, or with cause more apparent than real, as in the Elaine business—study of particulars will show how easily they might be wrought out into the great character scenes of which they already contain the suggestion. *This* Guinevere would never have " taken up " (to use purposely a vulgar phrase for what would have been a vulgar thing) with Mordred,[1] either for himself or for the kingdom that he was trying to steal. And I am bound to say again that much as I have read of purely French romance—that is to say, French not merely in language but in certain origin—I know nothing and nobody like her in it.

That Guinevere, like Charlotte, was " a married lady," that, unlike Charlotte, she forgot the fact, and that Lancelot, though somewhat Wertheresque in some of his features, was not quite so " moral " as that very dull young man, are facts which I wish neither to suppress nor to dwell upon. We may cry " Agreed " here to the indictment, and all its consequences. They are not the question.

The question is the suggesting of novel-romance elements which forms the aesthetic solace of this ethical sin. It should be seen at once that the Guinevere of the Vulgate, and her fault or fate, provide a character and career of no small complexity. It has been already said that to represent her as after a fashion intercepted by love for Lancelot on her way to Arthur, like Iseult of Ireland or Margaret of Anjou, is, so to speak, as unhistorical as it is insufficiently artistic. We cannot, indeed, borrow Diderot's speech to Rousseau and say,

---

[1] By the way, the Vulgate Mordred is a more subtle conception than the early stories gave, or than Malory transfers. He is no mere traitor or felon knight, much less a coward, from the first ; but at that first shows a mixture of good and bad qualities in which the "dram of eale" does its usual office. Here once more is a subject made to the hand of a novelist of the first class.

" C'est le pont aux ânes," but it certainly would not have been the way of the Walter whom I favour, though I think it might have been the way of the Chrestien that I know.   Guinevere, when she meets her lover, rescuer, and doomsman, is no longer a girl, and Lancelot is almost a boy.   It is not, in the common and cheap misuse of the term, the most " romantic " arrangement, but some not imperfect in lovelore have held that a woman's love is never so strong as when she is past girlhood and well approaching age, and that man's is never stronger than when he is just not a boy.   Lancelot himself has loved no woman (except his quasi-mother, the Lady of the Lake), and will love none after he has fulfilled the Dead Shepherd's " saw of might."   She *has* loved ;   dispute this and you not only cancel gracious scenes of the text, but spoil the story ;   but she has, though probably she does not yet know it, ceased to love,[1] and not without some reason.   To say no more about Arthur's technical " blamelessness," he has, by the coming of Lancelot, ceased to be altogether heroic.   Though never a mere petulant and ferocious dotard as the *Chansons* too often represent Charlemagne, he is very far from being a wise ruler or even baron.   He makes rash promises and vows, accepts charges on very slight evidence, and seems to have his knights by no means " in hand."   So, too, though never a coward or weakling, he seems pretty nearly to have lost the pluck and prowess which had won Guinevere's love under the walls of Carmelide, and of which the last display is in the great fight with his sister's lover, Sir Accolon.   All this may not excuse Guinevere's conduct to the moralist ;   it certainly makes that conduct artistically probable and legitimate to the critic, as a foundation for novel-character.

Her lover may look less promising, at least at the moment of presentation ;   and indeed it is true that while

---

[1] Some poet or pundit, whether of East or West, or of what place, from Santiago to Samarcand, I know not, has laid it down, that men can love many, but without ceasing to love any; that women love only one at once, but can (to borrow, at fifty years' memory, a phrase of George Lawrence's in *Sans Merci*) "drop their lovers down *oubliettes*" with comparative ease.

" la donna è *im*mobile," in essentials and possibilities
alike, forms of man, though never losing reality and
possibility, pass at times out of possible or at least easy
recognition.   Anybody who sees in the Lancelot of the
foregoing scene only a hobbledehoy and milksop who
happens to have a big chest, strong arms, and plenty of
mere fighting spirit, will never grasp him.   Hardly
better off will be he who takes him—as the story *does*
give some handles for taking him—to be merely one of
the too common examples of humanity who sin and
repent, repent and sin, with a sort of Americanesque
notion of spending dollars in this world and laying them
up in another.   Malory has on the whole done more
justice to the possibilities of the Vulgate Lancelot than
he has to Guinevere, and Tennyson has here improved
on Malory.   He has, indeed, very nearly " got " Lancelot, but not quite.   To get him wholly would have required Tennyson for form and Browning for analysis of
character ;   while even this *mistura mirabilis* would have
been improved for the purpose by touches not merely of
Morris and Swinburne, but of lesser men like Kingsley
and even George Macdonald.   To understand Lancelot
you must previously understand, or by some kind of
intuition divine, the mystical element which his descent
from the Graal-Wardens confers ;   the essential or quint-
essential chivalric quality which his successive creators
agreed in imparting to him ;   the all-conquering gift
so strangely tempered by an entire freedom from the
boasting and the rudeness of the *chanson* hero ;   the
actual checks and disasters which his cross stars bring
on him ;   his utter loyalty in all things save one to the
king ;   and last and mightiest of all, his unquenchable
and unchangeable passion for the Queen.

Hence what they said to him in one of his early
adventures, with no great ill following, " Fair Knight,
thou art unhappy," was always true in a higher sense.
He may have been Lord of Joyous Gard, in title and fact ;
but his own heart was always a Garde Douloureuse—a
cor luctificabile— pillowed on idle triumphs and fearful

hopes and poisoned satisfactions, and bafflements where
he would most fain have succeeded. He has almost
had to have the first kiss forced on him ; he is refused
the last on grounds of which he himself cannot deny the
validity. Guinevere is a tragic figure in the truest and
deepest sense of the term, and, as we have tried to show,
she is amply complex in character and temperament.
But it is questionable whether Lancelot is not more
tragic and more complex still.

It may perhaps without impropriety be repeated that
these are not mere fancies of the writer, but things reasonably suggested by and solidly based upon "the
French books," when these later are collated
and, so to speak, " checked " by Malory and the romances
of adventure branching off from them. But Arthur and
Guinevere and Lancelot by no means exhaust the material
for advanced and complicated novel-work—in character
as well as incident—provided by the older forms of the
Legend. There is Gawain, who has to be put together
from the sort of first draft of Lancelot which he shows
in the earlier versions, and the light-o'-love opposite
which he becomes in the later, a contrast continued in
the Amadis and Galaor figures of the Spanish romances
and their descendants. There is the already glanced at
group of Arthur's sisters or half-sisters, left mere sketches
and hints, but most interesting. Not to be tedious, we
need not dwell on Palomides, a very promising Lancelot
unloved ; on Lamoracke, left provokingly obscure, but
shadowing a most important possibility in the unwritten
romance of one of those very sisters ; Bors, of whom
Tennyson has made something, but not enough, in the
later *Idylls* ; and others. But it is probably unnecessary
to carry the discussion of this matter further. It has
been discussed and illustrated at some length, because
it shows how early the elements, not merely of romance
but of the novel in the fullest sense, existed in French
literature.

[*Here follows the noble passage above referred to between Lancelot
and King Bagdemagus after the death of Meleagraunce, whose cousin*

Lancelot has just slain in single combat for charging him with treason.
He has kept his helm on, but doffs it at the King's request.]

And when the King saw him he ran to kiss him, and began to
make such joy of him as none could overgo. But Lancelot said,
" Ah, Sir ! for God's sake, make no joy or feast for me.   Certainly
you should make none, for if you knew the evil I have done you,
you would hate me above all men in the world."   " Oh ! Lancelot," said he, " tell it me not, for I understand [1] too well what
you would say ; but I will know [1] nothing of it, because it might
be such a thing " as would part them for ever.

---

[1] It is excusable to use two words for the single verb *savoir* to bring out the
meaning.   King Bagdemagus does not " know " as a fact that Lancelot has slain his
son, though he fears it and feels almost sure of it.

CHAPTER III

ROMANS D'AVENTURES

On the whole, however, the most important influence in the development of the novel originally—that of the *nouvelle* or *novella* in French, and Italian taking the second place in order of time—must be assigned to the very numerous and very delightful body of compositions (not very long as a rule,[1] but also never exactly short) to which the name *Romans d'aventures* has been given with a limited connotation. They exist in all languages ; our own English Romances, though sometimes derived from the *chansons* and the Arthurian Legend, are practically all of this class, and in every case but one it is true that they have actual French originals. These *Romans d'aventures* have a habit, not universal but prevailing, of " keying themselves on " to the Arthurian story itself ; but they rarely, if ever, have much to do with the principal parts of it. It is as if their public wanted the connection as a sort of guarantee ; but a considerable proportion keep independence. They are so numerous, so various, and with rare exceptions so interesting, that it is difficult to know which to select for elaborate analysis and translated selection ; but almost the entire *corpus* gives us the important fact of the increased *freedom* of fiction. Even the connection with the Arthurian matter is, as has been

Variety of the present groups. (marginal note)

---

[1] That is, of nothing like the length of the latest forms of the *Chansons de Geste* or the Arthurian Romances proper. Some of the late fourteenth- and fifteenth-century Adventure stories, before they dropped into prose, are indeed long enough, and a great deal too long ; but they show degeneracy.

said, generally of the loosest kind ; that with the Charlemagne cycle hardly exists.   The Graal (or things connected with its legends) may appear : Gawain is a
frequent hero ; other, as one might call them, sociable
features as regards the older stories. present themselves.
But as a rule the man has got his own story which he
wants to tell ; his own special hero and heroine whom
he wants to present.   Furthermore, the old community
of handling, which is so noticeable in the *chansons* more
particularly, disappears almost entirely.   Nothing has
yet been discovered in French, though it may be any day,
to serve as the origin of our *Gawain and the Green Knight*,
and some special features of this are almost certainly the
work of an Englishman.   Our English *Ywain and
Gawain* is, as has been said, rather better than Chrestien's
original.   But, as a rule, the form, which is French form
in language (by no means always certainly or probably
French in nationality of author), is not only the original,
but better ; and besides, it is with it that we are busied
here, though in not a few cases English readers can obtain
an idea, fairly sufficient, of these originals from the
English versions.   As these, however, with the exception of one or two remarkable individuals or even groups,
were seldom written by men of genius, it is best to go
to the sources to see the power and the variety of fictitious
handling which have been mentioned.

The richness, indeed, of these *Romans d'aventures* is
surprising, and they very seldom display the flatness and
triviality which mar by no means all but too
Different views held of it. many of their English imitations.   Some of
the faults which are part cause of these others
they indeed have—the apparently irrational catalogues
of birds and beasts, stuffs and vegetables ; the long
moralisings ; the religious passages sometimes (as it
may seem to mere moderns) interposed in very odd
contexts ; the endless descriptions of battles and single
combats ; the absence of striking characterisation and
varied incident.   Their interest is a peculiar interest,
yet one can hardly call the taste for it " an acquired

taste," because the very large majority of healthy and intelligent children delight in these stories under whatever form they are presented to them, and at least a considerable number of grown-up persons never lose the enjoyment. The disapproval which rested on " romances of chivalry " for a long time was admittedly ignorant and absurd ; and the reasons why this disapproval, at least in its somewhat milder form of neglect, has never been wholly removed, are not very difficult to discover. It is to be feared that *Don Quixote*, great as it is, has done not a little mischief, and by virtue of its greatness is likely to do not a little more, though the *Amadis* group, which it specially satirises, has faults not found in the older tales. The texts, though in most cases easily enough accessible now, are not what may be called obviously and yet unobtrusively so. They are to a very large extent issued by learned societies : and the public, not too unreasonably, is rather suspicious, and not at all avid, of the products of learned societies. They are accompanied by introductions and notes and glossaries— things the public (again not wholly to be blamed) regards without cordiality. Latterly they have been used for educational purposes, and anything used for educational purposes acquires an evil—or at least an unappetising— reputation. In some cases they have been messed and meddled in *usum vulgi*. But their worst enemy recently has been, it may be feared, the irreconcilable opposition of their spirit to what is called the modern spirit—though this latter sometimes takes them up and plays with them in a fashion of maudlin mysticism.

To treat them at large here as Ellis treated some of the English imitations would be impossible in point of *Partenopeus of Blois selected for analysis and translation.* scale and dangerous as a competition ; for Ellis, though a little too prone to Voltairianise or at least Hamiltonise things sometimes too good for that kind of treatment, was a very clever man indeed. For somewhat full abstract and translation we may take one of the most famous, but perhaps not one of the most generally and thoroughly known,

Partenopeus (or *-pex* [1]) *of Blois*, which, though it exists in English, and though the French was very probably written by an Englishman, is not now one of the most widely read and is in parts very charming.   That it is one of the romances on which, from the fact of the resemblance of its central incident to the story of Cupid and Psyche, the good defenders of the bad theory of the classical origin of romance generally have based one of their few plausible arguments, need not occupy us.   For the question is not whether Denis Pyramus or any one else (modernity would not be modernity if his claims were not challenged) told it, but *how* he told it.   Still less need we treat the other question before indicated.   Here is one of the central stories of the world—one of those which Eve told to her children in virtue of the knowledge communicated by the apple, one with which the sons of God courted the daughters of men, or, at latest, one of those which were yarned in the Ark.   It is the story of the unwise lover—in this case the man, not as in Psyche's the woman—who will not be content to enjoy an unseen, but by every other sense enjoyable and adorable love, even though (in this case) the single deprivation is expressly to be terminated.   We have it, of course, in all sorts of forms, languages, and differing conditions.   But we are only concerned with it here as with a gracious example of that kind of romance which, though not exactly a " fairy tale " in the Western sense, is pretty obviously influenced by the Eastern fairy tale itself, and still more obviously influences the modern kind in which " the supernatural " is definitely prominent.

It was perhaps excusable in the good M. Robert, who wrote the Introduction to Crapelet's edition of this poem eighty years ago, to " protest too much " in favour of the author whom he was now presenting practically for the first time—to a changed audience ; but it was unnecessary and a little unfortunate.   Except in one point or group of points, it is vain to try to put *Par-*

---

[1] The *h* (Part*h*-) does occur in both forms, and there are other variations, as " Partenopeus," etc.   But these are trifles.

tenopeus above *Cupid and Psyche* : but it can perfectly
well stand by itself in its own place, and that no low one.
Except in *Floire et Blanchefleur* and of course in *Aucassin
et Nicolette*, the peculiar grace and delicacy of romance
are nowhere so well shown ; and *Partenopeus*, besides
the advantage of length, has that of personages interesting,
besides the absolute hero and heroine.   The Count of
Blois himself is, no doubt, despite his beauty, and his
bravery, and his good nature, rather of a feeble folk.
Psyche has the excuse of her sex, besides the evil counsel
of her sisters, for her curiosity.   But Partenopeus has
not the former ; nor has he even that weaker but still
not quite invalid one which lost Agib, the son of Cassib,
his many-Houried Paradise on Earth.   He is supposed
to be a Frenchman—the somewhat excessive fashion in
which Frenchmen make obedience to the second clause [1]
of the Fifth Commandment atone for some neglect of
other parts of the decalogue is well known, or at least
traditionally believed.   But most certainly a man is not
justified in obeying his mother to the extent of disobeying
—and that in the shabbiest of ways—his lady and
mistress, who is, in fact, according to mediaeval ideas,
virtually, if not virtuously, his wife.   But Melior herself,
the heroine, is an absolutely delightful person from her
first appearance (or rather *non*-appearance) as a sweet
dream come true, to her last in the more orthodox and
public spousals.   The grace of her Dian-like surrender
of herself to her love ; the constancy with which she
holds to the betrothal theory of the time ; the unselfishness with which she not only permits but actually advises
the lover, whom she would so fain, but cannot yet, make
her acknowledged husband, to leave her ;   her frank
forgiveness of his only-just-in-time repented and prevented, but intended, infidelity ; her sorrow at and after
the separation enforced by his breach of pact ; her interviews with her sister, naturally chequered by conflicting
feelings of love and pride and the rest—are all charming.
But she is not the only charming figure.

---

[1] Taking honour to the mother as separate from that to the father.

The " second heroine," a sister or cousin who plays a sort of superior confidante's part, is by no means uncommon in Romance. Alexandrine, for instance, who plays this in *William of Palerne*, is a very nice girl. But Urraque or Urraca,[1] the sister of Melior—whether full and legitimate, or " half " illegitimate, versions differ—is much more elaborately dealt with, and is, in fact, the chief *character* of the piece, and a character rather unusually strong for Romance. She plays the part of reconciler after Partenopeus' fatal folly has estranged him from her sister, and plays it at great length, but with much less tedium than might be expected. But the author is an " incurable feminist," as some one else was once described with a mixture of pity and admiration : and he is not contented with two heroines. There is a third, Persewis, maid of honour to Urraque, and also a fervent admirer of the incomparable Partenopeus, on whose actual beauty great stress is laid, and who in romance, other than his own, is quoted as a modern paragon thereof, worthy to rank with ancient patterns, sacred and profane. Persewis, however, is very young—a " flapper " or a " [bread-and-]buttercup," as successive generations have irreverently called the immature but agreeable creature. The poet lays much emphasis on this youth. She did not " kiss and embrace," he says, just because she was too young, and not because of any foolish prudery or propriety, things which he does not hesitate to pronounce appropriate only to ugly girls. His own attitude to " the fair " is unflinchingly put in one of the most notable and best known passages of the poem (l. 7095 *sq.*) :

When God made all creation, and devised their forms for his creatures, He distributed beauties and good qualities to each in proportion as He loved it. He loved ladies above all things, and therefore made for them the best qualities and beauties. Of mere earth made He everything [else] under Heaven : but the hearts

---

[1] The Spanish-English form is perhaps the prettier. I am sorry to say that the poet, to get a rhyme, sometimes spells it " Urrac*le*," which is *not* pretty. Southey's " Queen Orraca " seems to me to have changed her vowel to disadvantage.

of ladies He made of honey, and gave to them more courtesy than
to any other living creature. And as God loves them, therefore I
love them : hunger and thirst are nothing to me as regards them :
and I cry "Quits" to Him for His Paradise if the bright faces
of ladies enter not therein.

It will be observed, of course, how like this is to the
most famous passage of *Aucassin et Nicolette*. It is less
dreamily beautiful, but there is a certain spirit and
downrightness about it which is agreeable ; nor do I
know anywhere a more forcible statement of the doctrine,
often held by no bad people, that beauty is a personal
testimonial of the Divinity—a scarcely parabolic command
to love and admire its possessors.[1]

If, however, our poet has something of that Romantic
morality to which Ascham—in a conjoined fit[2] of pedantry,
prudery, and Protestantism—gave such an ugly name,
he may excuse it to less strait-laced judges by other
traits. Even the "retainer" of an editor ought not to
have induced M. Robert to say that Melior's original
surrender was "against her will," though she certainly
did make a protest of a kind.[3] But the enchanted and
enchanting Empress's constancy is inviolable. Even
after she has been obliged to banish her foolish lover, or
rather after he has banished himself, she avows herself
his only. She will die, she says, before she takes another
lord ; and for this reason objects for some time to the
proposed tourney for her hand, in which the already
proven invincibility of the Count of Blois makes him
almost a certain victor, because it involves a conditional
consent to admit another mate. To her scrupulousness,
a kind of blunt common-sense, tempering the amiability
of Urraca, is a pleasant set-off, and the freshness of
Persewis completes the effect.

Moreover, there are little bits of almost Chaucerian
vividness and terseness here and there, contrasting oddly
with the *chevilles*—the stock phrases and epithets—else-

[1] The original author of the *Court of Love*, whether Chaucer or another, pretty
certainly knew it ; and Spenser spiritualised the doctrine itself in the *Four Hymns*.
[2] I think the medical people (borrowing, as Science so often does, the language which
she would fain banish from human knowledge) call this sort of thing *a syndrome*.
[3] See below on Urraca's plain speaking.

where. When the tourney actually comes off and Partenopeus is supposed to be prisoner of a felon knight afar off, the two sisters and Persewis take their places at the entrance of the tower crossing the bridge at Melior's capital, " Chef d'Oire." [1]   Melior is labelled only " whom all the world loves and prizes," but Urraca and her damsel " have their faces pale and discoloured—for they have lost much of their beauty—so sorely have they wept Partenopeus."   On the contrary, when, at the close of the first day's tourney, the usual " unknown knights " (in this case the Count of Blois himself and his friend Gaudins) ride off triumphant, they " go joyfully to their hostel with lifted lances, helmets on head, hauberks on back, and shields held proudly as if to begin jousting."

Bel i vinrent et bel s'en vont,

says King Corsols, one of the judges of the tourney, but not in the least aware of their identity.   This may occur elsewhere, but it is by no means one of the commonplaces of Romance, and a well hit-off picture is motived by a sharply cut phrase.[2]

It is this sudden enlivening of the commonplaces of Romance with vivid picture and phrase which puts *Partenopeus* high among its fellows.   The story is very simple, and the variation and multiplication of episodic adventure unusually scanty ;   while the too common genealogical preface is rather exceptionally superfluous. That the Count of Blois is the nephew of Clovis can interest—outside of a peculiar class of antiquarian commentator—no mortal ;   and the identification of " Chef-d'Oire," Melior's enchanted capital, with Constantinople, though likely enough, is not much more important. Clovis and Byzantium (of which the enchantress is Empress) were well-known names and suited the *abonné* of those times. The actual "argument" is of the slightest. One of Spenser's curious doggerel common measures—say :

---

[1] Not too commentatorially identified with Constantinople.

[2] It may be worth noting that in this context appears the original form of an English word quite common recently, but almost unknown a very short time ago—" grouse " in the sense of " complain," " grumble " : " Ce dist Corsols et nul n'en *grouce*."

> A fairy queen grants bliss and troth
>   On terms, unto the knight :
> His mother makes him break his oath,
>   Her sister puts it right—

would almost do ; the following prose abstract is practically exhaustive.

Partenopeus, Count of Blois, nephew of King Clovis
of France, and descendant of famous heroes of antiquity,
including Hector, the most beautiful and one of the most
valiant of men, after displaying his prowess in a war with
the Saracen Sornagur, loses his way while hunting in the
Ardennes.   He at last comes to the seashore, and finds
a ship which in fifteen days takes him to a strange country,
where all is beautiful but entirely solitary.   He finds a
magnificent palace, where he is splendidly guested by
unseen hands, and at last conducted to a gorgeous bedchamber.   In the dark he, not unnaturally, lies awake
speculating on the marvel ; and after a time light foot-
steps approach the bed, and a form, invisible but tangible,
lies down beside him.   He touches it, and finds it warm
and soft and smooth, and though it protests a little, the
natural consequences follow.   Then the lady confesses
that she had heard of him, had (incognita) seen him at
the Court of France, and had, being a white witch as well
as an Empress, brought him to "Chef d'Oire," her capital,
though she denies having intentionally or knowingly
arranged the shepherd's hour itself.[1]   She is, however,
as frank as Juliet and Miranda combined.   She will be
his wife (she makes a most interesting and accurate
profession of Christian orthodoxy) if he will marry her ;
but it is impossible for the remainder of a period of
which two and a half years have still to run, and at the
end of which, and not till then, she has promised her
vassals to choose a husband.   Meanwhile, Partenopeus
must submit to an ordeal not quite so painful as hot
ploughshares.   He must never see her or attempt to

---

[1] No one will be rude enough to disbelieve her, and, as will be seen, her supernatural
powers had limits ; but it was odd, though fortunate, that they should have broken
down exactly at this important juncture.   Who made those rebellious candles take him
to that chamber and couch, unknown to her ?

see her, and he must not, during his stay at Chef d'Oire, see or speak to any other human being. At the same time, hunting, exploring the palace and the city and the country, and all other pastimes independent of visible human companionship, are freely at his disposal by day.

Et moi aurès cascune nuit

says Melior, with the exquisite simplicity which is the charm of the whole piece.

One must be very inquisitive, exceedingly virtuous (the mediaeval value of consummated betrothal being reckoned), superfluously fond of the company of one's miscellaneous fellow-creatures, and a person of very bad taste[1] to boot, in order to decline the bargain. Parthenopeus does not dream of doing so, and for a whole year thinks of nothing but his fairy love and her bounties to him. Then he remembers his uncle-king and his country, and asks leave to visit them, but not with the faintest intention of running away. Melior gives it with the same frankness and kindness with which she has given herself—informing him, in fact, that he *ought* to go, for his uncle is dead and his country in danger. Only, she reminds him of his pledges, and warns him of the misfortunes which await his breach of them. He is then magically wafted back on shipboard as he came.

He has, once more, no intention of playing the truant or traitor, and does his duty bravely and successfully. But the new King has a niece and the Count himself has a mother, who, motherlike, is convinced that her son's mysterious love is a very bad person, if not an actual *maufès* or devil, and is very anxious that he shall marry the niece. She has clerical and chemical resources to help her, and Partenopeus has actually consented, in a fit of aberration, when, with one of the odd Wemmick-like flashes of reflection,[2] not uncommon with knights, he

[1] For Melior, though of invisible beauty, is represented as delightful in every other way, as wise and witty and gracious in speech as becomes a white witch. And when her lover on one occasion thanks her for her *sermon*, there is no satire; he only means *sermo*.

[2] Like Guy of Warwick; still more like Mr. Jaggers's clerk, though the circumstances are reversed. *He* almost says in so many words, "Hullo! here's an engagement ring on my finger. We *can't* have a marriage."

remembers Melior, and unceremoniously makes off to her. He confesses (for he is a good creature though foolish) and is forgiven, Melior being, though not in the least insipid or of a put-up-with-anything disposition, full of " loving *mercy* " in every sense. But the situation is bound to recur, and now, though the time of probation (probation very much tempered !) is nearly over, the mother wins her way. Partenopeus is deluded into accepting an enchanted lantern, which he tries on his unsuspecting mistress at the first possible moment. What he sees, of course, is only a very lovely woman—a woman in the condition best fitted to show her loveliness —whom he has offended irreparably, and lost.

Melior is no scold, but she is also no milksop. She will have nothing more to do with him, for he has shamed her with her people (who now appear), broken her magic power, and, above all, been false to her wish and his word. The entreaties of her sister Urraca (whose gracious figure is now elaborately introduced) are for the time useless, and Partenopeus is only saved from the vengeance of the courtiers and the household by Urraca's protection.[1]

To halt for a moment, the scene of the treason and discovery is another of those singular vividnesses which distinguish this poem and story. The long darkness suddenly flashing into light, and the startled Melior's beauty framed in the splendour of the couch and the bedchamber—the offender at once realising his folly and his crime, and dashing the instrument of his treachery (useless, for all is daylight now, the charm being counter-charmed) against the wall — the half-frightened, half-curious Court ladies and Court servants thronging in—the apparition of Urraca,—all this gives a picture of extra-ordinarily dramatic power. It reminds one a little of Spenser's famous portrayal of Britomart disturbed at night, and the comparison of the two brings out all sorts of " excellent differences."

---

[1] The author, *more suo*, intimates that the Court *ladies* by no means shared these hostile feelings, and would have willingly been in Melior's place.

But to return to the story itself.   Although the invariable cut-and-driedness of romance incidents has been grossly exaggerated, there is one situation which is almost always treated in the same way.   The knight who has, with or without his own fault, incurred the displeasure of his mistress, " doth [*always*] to the green wood go," and there, whether in complete sanity or not, lives for a time a half or wholly savage life, discarding knightly and sometimes any other dress, eating very little, and in considerable danger of being eaten himself. Everybody, from Lancelot to Amadis, does it ; and Partenopeus does it too, but in his own way.   Reaching Blois and utterly rejecting his mother's attempts to excuse herself and console him, he drags out a miserable time in continual penance and self-neglect, till at last, availing himself of (and rather shabbily if piously tricking) a Saracen page,[1] he succeeds in getting off incognito to the vague " Ardennes," where his sadly ended adventure had begun.   These particular Ardennes appear to be reachable by sea (on which they have a coast), and to contain not only ordinary beasts of chase, not only wolves and bears, but lions, tigers, wyverns, dragons, etc. A single unarmed man has practically no chance there, and the Count determines to condemn himself to the fate of the Roman arena.   As a preliminary, he dismounts and turns loose his horse, who is presently attacked by a lion and wounded, but luckily gets a fair blow with his hoof between his enemy's eyes, and kills him.   Then comes another of the flashes (and something more) of the piece. Stung by the pain of his wound and dripping with blood, the animal dashes at full speed, and whinnying at the top of his powers, to the seashore and along it.   The passage is worth translating :

He [*the horse after he has killed the lion*] lifts his tail, and takes to flight down a valley towards nightfall.   Much he looks about him and much he whinnies.   By night-time he has got out of the

---

[1] He induces him to turn Christian on the supposition of being his companion ; and then gives him the slip.   The neophyte's expressions on the occasion are not wholly edifying.

wood and has fled to the sea : but he will not stop there. He
makes the pebbles fly as he gallops and never stops whinnying.
Now the moon has mounted high in the heavens, all clear and
bright and shining : there is not a dark cloud in all the sky, nor
any movement on the sea : sweet and serene is the weather, and
fair and clear and lightened up. And the palfrey whinnies so
loudly that he can be heard far off at sea.

He *is* heard at sea, for a ship is waiting there in the
calm, and on board that ship is Urraca, with a wise captain
named Maruc and a stout crew. The singularity of the
event induces them to land (Maruc knows the dangers
of the region, but Urraca has no fears ; the captain also
knows how to enchant the beasts), and the horse's blood-
marks guide them up the valley. At last they come upon
a miserable creature, in rags, dishevelled, half-starved,
and altogether unrecognisable. After a little time,
however, Urraca does recognise him, and, despite his
forlorn and repulsive condition, takes him in her arms.

Si le descouvre un poi le vis.

Yet another of the uncommon " flashlight " sketches,
where in two short lines one sees the damsel as she has
been described not so long before, " tall and graceful,
her fair hair (which, untressed, reached her feet [now, no
doubt, more suitably arranged]), with forehead broad
and high, and smooth ; grey eyes, large and *seignorous* "
(an admirable word for eyes), " all her face one kiss " ; one
sees her with one arm round the tottering wretch, and
with the " long fingers " of her other white hand clearing
the matted hair from his visage till she can recognise
him.

They take him on board, of course, though to induce
him to go this delightful creature has to give an account
of her sister's feelings (which, to put it mildly, anticipates
the truth very considerably), and also to cry over him a
little.[1]   She takes him to Saleuces,[2] an island principality

[1] The good palfrey is found and in a state to carry his master, who is quite unable to
walk.   One hopes they did not leave the beast to the lions, tigers, wyverns, etc., for
he could hardly hope for such a literal " stroke of luck " again.
[2] The name will suggest, to those who have some wine-lore, no less a vintage than
Château Yquem.   Nothing could be better for a person in the Count's condition as a
restorative.

of her own, and there she and her maid-of-honour, Perse-wis (see above), proceed to cocker and cosset him up exactly as one imagines two such girls would do to " a dear, silly, nice, handsome thing," as a favourite modern actress used to bring down the house by saying, with a sort of shake, half of tears and half of laughter, in her voice.   Indeed the phrase fits Partenopeus precisely. We are told that Urraca would have been formally in love with him if it had not been unsportsgirl-like towards her sister ; and as for Persewis, there is once more a windfall in the description of the " butter-cup's " delight when Urraca, going to see Melior, has to leave her alone with the Count.   The Princess is of course very sorry to go.   " But Persewis would not have minded if she had stayed forty days, or till August," and she " glories greatly " when her rival departs.   No mischief, how-ever, comes of it ; for the child is " too young," as we are earnestly assured, and Partenopeus, to do him iustice, is both too much of a gentleman, and too dolefully in earnest about recovering Melior, to dream of any.

Meanwhile, Urraca is most unselfishly doing her very best to reconcile the lovers, not neglecting the employment of white fibs as before, and occasionally indulging, not merely in satiric observation on poor Melior's irresolution and conflict of feeling, but in decidedly sisterly plainness of speech, reminding the Empress that after all she had entrapped Partenopeus into loving her, and that he had, for two whole years, devoted himself entirely to her love and its conditions. At last a rather complicated and not always quite con-sistently told provisional settlement is arrived at, carrying out, in a manner, the undertakings referred to by Melior in her first interview with her lover.   An immense tourney for the hand of Melior is to be held, with a jury of kings to judge it : and everybody, Christian or pagan, from emperor to vavasour is invited to compete.   But in case of no single victor, a kind of " election " by what may be called the States of Byzantium—kings, dukes, counts, and simple fief-holders—is to decide, and it seems sometimes as if Melior retained something of a personal veto at last. Of the incidents and episodes before this actually comes off, the most noteworthy are a curious instance of the punctilio of chivalry (the Count having once promised Melior that no one but herself shall gird on his sword, makes a difficulty when Urraca and Persewis arm him), and a misfortune by which he, rowing carelessly by himself, falls into the power of a felon knight, Armans of Thenodon. This last incident, however, though it alarms his two benefactresses, is not really unlucky. For, in the first place, Armans is not at home, and his wife, falling a victim, like every woman, to Partenopeus' extraordinary beauty, allows him his parole; while the accident enables him to appear at the tournament incognito—a practice always affected, if possible, by the knights of romance, and in this case possessing some obvious and special advantages.

On his way he meets another knight, Gaudin le Blond, with whom he gladly strikes up brotherhood-in-arms. The three days of the mellay are not *very* different from the innumerable similar scenes elsewhere, nor can the author be said to be specially happy at this kind of business. But any possible tedium is fairly relieved by the shrewd and sometimes jovial remarks made by one of the judging kings, the before-quoted Corsols—met by grumbles from another, Clarin, and by the fears and interest of the three ladies, of whom the ever-faithful and shrewd Urraca is the first to discover Partenopeus. He and Gaudin perform the usual exploits and suffer the usual inconveniences, but at the end it is still undecided whether the Count of Blois or the Soldan of Persia—a good knight, though a pagan, and something of a brag- gart—deserves the priceless prize of Melior's hand with the empire of Byzantium to boot. The " election " follows, and after some doubt goes right, while Melior now offers no objection. But the Soldan, in his *outre- cuidance*, demands single combat. He has, of course, no right to do this, and the Council and the Empress object strongly. But Partenopeus will have no stain on his honour; consents to the fight; deliberately refuses to take advantage of the Soldan when he is unhorsed and pinned down by the animal; assists him to get free; and only after an outrageous menace from the Persian justifies his own claim to belong to the class of champions

> Who *always* cleave their foe
> To the waist

—indeed excels them, by entirely bisecting the Soldan.

An episodic restoration of parole to the widow of Armans (who has actually taken part in the tourney and been killed) should be noticed, and the piece ends, or rather comes close to an end, with the marriages which appropriately follow these well-deserved murders. Marriages—not a marriage only—for King "Lohier" of France most sensibly insists on espousing the delightful Urraca: and Persewis is consoled for the loss of Partenopeus by the suit—refused at first and then granted, with the obviously intense enjoyment of both processes likely in a novice—of his brother-in-arms, to whom the "Emperor of Byzantium" abandons his own two counties in France, adding a third in his new empire, and winning by this generosity almost more popularity than by his prowess.

But, as was hinted, the story does not actually end. There is a great deal about the festivities, and though the author says encouragingly that he "will not devise much of breeches," he *does*—and of many other garments. Indeed the last of his liveliest patches is a mischievous picture of the Court ladies at their toilette: "Let me see that mirror; make my head-dress higher; let me show my mouth more; drop the pleat over the eyes;[1] alter my eyebrows," etc. etc. But beyond the washing of hands before the feast, this French book that Crapelet printed fourscore years ago goeth not. Perhaps it was a mere accident; perhaps the writer had a shrewd notion that whatever he wrote would seem but stale in its reminder of the night when Partenopeus lay awake, and

[1] These two directions obviously refer to the common mediaeval "wimple" arrangement.

seemingly alone, in the enchanted palace—now merely
an ordinary place of splendour and festivity—and when
something came to the bed, "step by step, little by
little," and laid itself beside him.

Such are the contents and such some of the special
traits and features of one of the most famous of those
romances of chivalry, the reading of which with anything
like the same interest as that taken in Homer, seemed to
the Reverend Professor Hugh Blair to be the most
suitable instance he could hit upon of a total lack of
taste.   This is a point, of course, on which each age, and
each reader in each age, must judge for itself and himself.
I think the author of the *Odyssey* (the *Iliad* comes rather
in competition with the *chansons* than with these
romances) was a better poet than the author of *Parthenopeus*; and I also think that he was a better story-teller;
but I do not think that the latter was a bad story-teller,
and I can read him with plenty of interest.   So I can
most of his fellows, no one of whom, I think, ever quite
approaches the insipidity of their worst English imitators.
The knights do not weary me with their exploits, and I
confess that I am hyperbolical enough to like reading
and thinking as well as talking of the ladies very much.
They are of various sorts; but they are generally lovable.
There is no better for affection and faithfulness and
pluck than the Josiane of *Bevis*, whose husband and her
at one time faithful guardian, but at another would-be
ravisher, Ascapart, guard a certain gate not more than
a furlong or two from where I am writing.   It is good
to think of the (to some extent justified) indignation of
l'Orgueilleuse d'Amours when Sir Blancandin rides up
and audaciously kisses her in the midst of her train; and
the companion picture of the tomb where Idoine apparently sleeps in death (while her true knight Amadas
fights with a ghostly foe above) makes a fitting pendant.
If her near namesake with an L prefixed, the Lidoine of
Méraugis de Portlesguez, interests me less, it is because
its author, Raoul de Houdenc, was one of the first to mix
love and moral allegory—a "wanity" which is not my

favourite " wanity." To the Alexandrine of *Guillaume de Palerne* reference has already been made. Blanche-fleur—known all over Europe with her lover Floire (Floris, etc.)—the Saracen slave who charms a Christian prince, and is rescued by him from the Emir of Babylon, to whom she has been sold in hopes of weaning Floris from his attachment, more than deserved her vogue. But, as in the case of the *chansons*, mere cataloguing would be dull and unprofitable, and analysis on the scale accorded to *Partenopeus* impossible. One must only take up once more the note of this whole early part of our history, and impress again on the reader the evident *desire* for the accomplished novel which these numerous romances show ; the inevitable *practice*, in tale-telling of a kind, which the production of them might have given ; and, above all, the openings, germs, suggestions of new devices in fiction which are observable in them, and which remained for others to develop if the first finders left them unimproved.

CHAPTER IV

THE BEGINNINGS OF PROSE FICTION

THE title of this chapter may seem an oversight or an impertinence, considering that large parts of an earlier

Prose novelettes of the thirteenth century. Aucassin et Nicolette not quite typical.

one have been occupied with discussions and translations of the prose Arthurian Romances. It was, however, expressly pointed out that the priority of these is a matter of opinion, not of judgment; and it may be here quite frankly admitted that one of the most serious arguments against that priority is the extreme lateness of Old French Prose in any finished literary form. The excuse, however, if excuse be needed, does not turn on any such hinge as this. It was desired to treat, in the last two chapters, romance matter proper of the larger kind, whether that matter took the form of prose or of verse. Here, on the other hand, the object is to deal with the smaller but more miscellaneous body of fictitious matter (part, no doubt, of a larger) which presents it tolerably early, and in character foretells the immense development of the kind which French was to see later.[1] A portion of this body, sufficient for us, is contained in two little volumes of the *Bibliothèque Elzévirienne*, published rather less than sixty years

---

[1] The position of "origin" assigned already to the sacred matter of the Saint's Life may perhaps be continued here as regards the Sermon. It was, as ought to be pretty generally known, the not ungenial habit of the mediaeval preacher to tell stories freely. We have them in Ælfric's and other English homilies long before there was any regular French prose; and we have, later, large and numerous collections of them—compiled more or less expressly for the use of the clergy—in Latin, English, and French. The Latin story is, in fact, very wide-ranging and sometimes quite of the novel (at least *nouvelle*) kind, as any one may see in Wright's *Latin Stories*, Percy Society, 1842.

ago (1856 and 1858) by MM. L. Moland and Ch. d'Héricault, the first devoted to thirteenth-, the second to fourteenth-century work.   One of these, the now world-famous *Aucassin et Nicolette*, has been so much written about and so often translated already that it cannot be necessary to say a great deal about it here.   It is, more-over, of a mixed kind, a *cante-fable* or blend of prose and verse, with a considerable touch of the dramatic in it.   Its extraordinary charm is a thing long ago settled ; but it is, on the whole, more of a dramatic and lyrical romance—to recouple or releash kinds which Mr. Browning had perhaps best never have put asunder—than of a pure prose tale.

Its companions in the thirteenth-century volume are four in number, and if none of them has the peculiar *L'Empereur* charm, so none has the technical disqualifica-*Constant* tion (if that be not too strong a word) of more so. *Aucassin et Nicolette*.   The first, shortest, and, save for one or two points, least remarkable, *L'Empereur Constant*, is a very much abbreviated and in more than one sense prosaic version of the story out of which Mr. William Morris made his delightful *The Man Born to be King*.   Probably of Greek or Greek-Eastern origin, it begins with an astrological passage in which the Emperor, childless except for a girl, becomes informed of the imminent birth of a man-child, who shall marry his daughter and succeed him.   He discovers the, as it seems, luckless baby ; has it brought to him, and with his own hand attempts to disembowel it, but allows himself, most improbably,[1] to be dissuaded from finishing the operation.   The benevolent knight who has prevented the completion of the crime takes the infant to a monas-tery, where (after a quaint scene of haggling about fees with the surgeon) the victim is patched up, grows to be a fine youth, and comes across the Emperor, to whom the abbot guilelessly, but in this case naturally enough,[2]

[1] This is one, and one of the most glaring, of the *bêtises* which at some times have been urged against Romance at large.   They are not, as a matter of fact, very frequent ; but their occurrence certainly does show the essentially uncritical character of the time.

[2] For of course the knight did not tell the *whole* story.

betrays the secret. The Emperor's murderous thoughts as naturally revive, and the frustration of them by means of the Princess's falling in love with the youth, the changing of " the letters of Bellerophon," and the Emperor's resignation to the inevitable, follow the same course as in the English poem. The latter part is better than the earlier ; and the writer is evidently (as how should he not be ?) a novice ; but his work is the kind of experiment from which better things will come.

These marks of the novice are even more noticeable in a much longer story, *Le Roi Flore et la Belle Jehane*, *Le Roi Flore* which is found not only in the same printed *et la Belle* volume, but in the same original MS. The *Jehane.* fault of this is curious, and—if not to a mere reader for pastime, to a student of fiction—extremely interesting. It is one not at all unknown at the present day, and capable of being used as an argument in favour of the doctrine of the Unities : that is to say, the mixture, by arbitrary and violent process, of two stories which have nothing whatever to do with each other, except that they are, wilfully and with no reason, buckled together at the end. The first, thin and uninteresting enough, is of a certain King Florus, who has a wife, dearly beloved, but barren. After some years and some very unmanly shilly-shallyings, he puts her away, and marries another, with whom (one is feebly glad to find) he is no more lucky, but who has herself the luck to die after some years. Meanwhile, King Florus being left " in a cool barge for future use," the second item, a really interesting story, is, with some intervals, carried on. A Count of high rank and great possessions has an only daughter, whom, after experience of the valour and general worthiness of one of his vassals of no great " having," he bestows on this knight, Robert, the pair being really in love with each other. But another vassal knight of greater wealth, Raoul, plots with one of the wicked old women who abound in these stories, and engages Robert in a rash wager of all his possessions, that during one of those pilgrimages to " St. James,"

which come in so handy, and are generally so unreasonable, he will dishonour the lady. He fails, but, in a
manner not distantly related to the Imogen - Iachimo
scene, acquires what seems to be damning acquaintance
with the young Countess's person-marks. Robert and
Jehane are actually married ; but the felon knight
immediately afterwards brings his charge, and Robert
pays his debt, and flies, a ruined man, from, as he thinks,
his faithless wife, though he takes no vengeance on her.
Jehane disguises herself as a man, joins him on his journey,
supports him with her own means for a time, and enters
into partnership with him in merchandise at Marseilles,
he remaining ignorant of her sex and relation to him.
At last things come right : the felon knight is forced
in single combat (a long and good one) to acknowledge
his lie and give up his plunder, and the excellent but
somewhat obtuse Robert recovers his wife as well. A
good end if ever there was one, and not a badly told
tale in parts. But, from some utterly mistaken idea of
craftsmanship, the teller must needs kill Robert for no
earthly reason, except in order that Jehane may become
the third wife of Florus and bear him children. A more
disastrous " sixth act " has seldom been imagined ; for
most readers will have forgotten all about Florus, who has
had neither art nor part in the main story ; few can care
whether the King has children or not ; and still fewer
can be other than disgusted at the notion of Jehane,
brave, loving, and clever, being, as a widow, made a
mere child-bearing machine to an oldish and rather
contemptible second husband. But, once more, the
mistake is interesting, and is probably the first example
of that fatal error of not knowing when to leave off, which
is even worse than the commoner one (to be found in
some great artists) of " huddling up the story." The
only thing to be said in excuse is that you could cut his
majesty Florus out of the title and tale at once without
even the slightest difficulty, and with no need to mend
or meddle in any other way.

The remaining stories of the thirteenth-century volume

are curiously contrasted. One is a short prose version
of that exquisite *chanson de geste*, *Amis et Amiles*, of
which it has been said above that any one who cannot
" taste " it need never hope to understand mediaeval
literature. The full beauty of the verse story does not
appear in the prose ; but some does.

Of the other, the so-called " Comtesse de Ponthieu "
(though she is not really this, being only the Count's
La Comtesse daughter and the wife of a vassal), I thought
de Ponthieu. rather badly when I first read it thirty or
forty years ago, and till the present occasion I have
never read it since. Now I think better of it, especially
as a story suggestive in story-telling art. The original
stumbling-block, which I still see, though I can get over
or round it better now, was, I think, the character of the
heroine, who inherits not merely the tendency to play fast
and loose with successive husbands, which is observable
in both *chanson* and *roman* heroines, but something of
the very unlovely savagery which is also sometimes
characteristic of them ; while the hero also is put in
" unpleasant " circumstances. He is a gentleman and
a good knight, and though only a vassal of the Count
of Ponthieu, he, as has been said, marries the Count's
daughter, entirely to her and her father's satisfaction.
But they are childless, and the inevitable " monseigneur
Saint *Jakeme* " (St. James of Compostella) suggests
himself for pilgrimage. Thiebault, the knight, obtains
leave from his lady to go, and she, by a device not un-
prettily told, gets from him leave to go too. Unfortunately and unwisely they send their suite on one
morning, and ride alone through a forest, where they are
set upon by eight banditti. Thiebault fights these odds
without flinching, and actually kills three, but is overpowered by sheer numbers. They do not kill him, but
bind and toss him into a thicket, after which they take
vengeance of outrage on the lady and depart, fearing the
return of the meyney. Thiebault feels that his unhappy
wife is guiltless, but unluckily does not assure her of
this, merely asking her to deliver him. So she, seeing a

sword of one of the slain robbers, picks it up, and, " full
of great ire and evil will," cries, " I will deliver you,
sir," and, instead of cutting his bonds, tries to run him
through.   But she only grazes him, and actually cuts
the thongs, so that he shakes himself free, starts up, and
wrests the sword from her with the simple words, " Lady,
it is not to-day that you will kill me."   To which she
replies, " And right sorry I am therefor." [1]   Their
followers come up ; the pair are clothed and set out
again on their journey.   But Thiebault, though treating
his wife with the greatest attention, leaves her at a
monastery, accomplishes his pilgrimage alone, and on his
return escorts her to Ponthieu as if nothing had happened.
Still—though no one knows this or indeed anything
about her actual misfortune and intended crime—he
does not live with her as his wife.   After a time the
Count, who is, as another story has it, a " *h*arbitrary "
Count, insists that Thiebault shall tell him some incident
of his voyage, and the husband (here is the weak point of
the whole) recounts the actual adventure, though not
as of himself and his lady.   The Count will not stand
ambiguity, and at last extorts the truth, which the lady
confirms, repeating her sorrow that she had *not* slain her
husband.   Now the Count is, as has been said, an arbitrary Count, and one day, his county having, as our
Harold knew to his cost, a sea-coast to it, somewhat
less disputable than those of Bohemia and the Ardennes,
embarks, with only his daughter, son-in-law, son, and a
few retainers, taking with him a nice new cask.   Into this,
despite the prayers of her husband and brother, he puts
the lady, and flings it overboard.   She is picked up half-
suffocated by mariners, who carry her to " Aymarie "
and sell her to the Sultan.   She is very beautiful, and
the Sultan promptly proposes conversion and marriage.
She makes no difficulty, bears him two children, and is
apparently quite happy.   But meanwhile the Count of
Ponthieu begins—his son and son-in-law have never
ceased—to feel that he has exercised the paternal rights

---

[1] *I.e.* not sorry for having tried to kill him, but sorry that she had not done so.

rather harshly ; the Archbishop of Rheims very properly
confirms his ideas on this point, and all three go *outremer*
on pilgrimage to the Holy Land. They are captured
by the Saracens of Aymarie, imprisoned, starved, and
finally in immediate danger of being shot to death as an
amusement for the Sultan's bodyguard. But the Sultaness has found out who they are, visits them in prison, and
" reconciliations and forgivenesses of injuries " follow.

After this, things go in an easily guessable manner.
The Countess-Sultana beguiles her easy-going lord into
granting her the lives of the prisoners one after another,
for which she rewards him by carrying them off, with
her son by the second marriage, to Italy, where the boy
is baptized. " The Apostle " (as the Pope is usually
called in Romance), by a rather extensive exercise of his
Apostleship, gives everybody absolution, confirms the
original marriage of Thiebault and the lady who had
been so obstinately sorry that she had not killed him,
and who had suffered the paynim spousals so easily ;
and all goes merrily. There is a postscript which tells
how the daughter of the Sultan and the Countess, who
is termed *La Bele Caitive*, captivates and marries a Turk
of great rank, and becomes the mother of no less a person
than the great Saladin himself—a consummation no
doubt very satisfactory to the Miss Martha Buskbodies
of the mediaeval world.

Now this story might seem to one who read it hastily,
carelessly, or as " not in the vein," to be partly extravagant, partly disagreeable, and, despite its generous
allowance of incident, rather dull, especially if contrasted
with its next neighbour in the printed volume, *Aucassin
et Nicolette* itself. I am afraid there may have been some
of these uncritical conditions about my own first reading.
But a little study shows some remarkable points in it,
though the original writer has not known how to manage
them. The central and most startling one—the attempt
of the Countess to murder her husband—is, when you
think of it, not at all unnatural. The lady is half mad
with her shame ; the witness, victim, and, as she thinks,

probable avenger of that shame is helpless before her, and in his first words at any rate seems to think merely of himself and not of her. Whether this violent outburst of feeling was not likely to result in as violent a revulsion of tenderness is rather a psychological probability than artistically certain. And Thiebault, though an excellent fellow, is a clumsy one. His actual behaviour is somewhat of that " killing-with-kindness " order which exasperates when it does not itself kill or actually reconcile ; and, whether out of delicacy or not, he does not give his wife the only proof that he acknowledges the involuntariness of her actual misfortune, and forgives the voluntariness of her intended crime. His telling the story is inexcusable : and neither his preference of his allegiance as a vassal to his duty as knight, lover, and husband in the case of the Count's cruelty, nor his final acceptance of so many and such peculiar bygones can be called very pretty. But there are possibilities in the story, if they are not exactly made into good gifts.

The contents of the fourteenth-century volume are, with one exception, much less interesting in themselves ; Those of the but from the point of view of the present fourteenth. enquiry they hardly yield to their predecessors. Asseneth. They are three in number : *Asseneth*, *Foulques Fitzwarin*, and *Troilus*. The first, which is very short, is an account of Joseph's courtship of his future wife, in which entirely guiltless proceeding he behaves at first very much as if the daughter of Potipherah were fruit as much forbidden as the wife of Potiphar. For on her being proposed to him (he has come to her father, splendidly dressed and brilliantly handsome, on a mission from Pharaoh) he at first replies that he will love her as his sister. This, considering the Jewish habit of exchanging the names, might not be ominous. But when the damsel, at her father's bidding, offers to kiss him, Joseph puts his hand on her chest and pushes her back, accompanying the action with words (even more insulting in detail than in substance) to the effect that it is not for God-fearing man to kiss an idolatress.

(At this point one would rather like to kick Joseph.) However, when, naturally enough, she cries with vexation, the irreproachable but most unlikable patriarch condescends to pat her on the head and bless her. This she takes humbly and thankfully; deplores his absence, for he is compelled to return to his master; renounces her gods; is consoled by an angel, who feeds her with a miraculous honeycomb possessing a sort of sacramental force, and announces her marriage to Joseph, which takes place almost immediately.

It will be at once seen, by those who know something of the matter, that this is entirely in the style of large portions of the Graal romances ; and so it gives us a fresh and interesting division of the new short prose tale, allying itself to some extent with the allegory which was to be so fruitful both in verse and in prose. It is not particularly attractive in substance ; but is not badly told, and would have made (what it was very likely used as) a good sermon-story.

As *Asseneth*, the first of the three, is by far the shortest, so *Troilus*, the last, is by far the longest. It is, in fact,

Troilus. nearly twenty times the length of the history of Joseph's pious impoliteness, and makes up something like two-thirds of the whole collection. But, except as a variant of one of the famous stories of the world (*v. sup.* Chap. IV.), it has little interest, and is not even directly taken from Benoît de Sainte-Maure, but from Guido delle Colonne and Boccaccio, of whose *Filostrato* it is, in fact, a mere translation, made apparently by a known person of high station, Pierre de Beauvau, one of the chief nobles of Anjou, at the close of the fourteenth and the beginning of the fifteenth century. It thus brings itself into direct connection with Chaucer's poem, and has some small importance for literary history generally. But it has not much for us. It was not Boccaccio's verse but his prose that was really to influence the French Novel.

With the middle piece of the volume, *Foulques Fitz-warin*, it is very different. It is true that the present

G

writer was once "smitten friendly" by a disciple of
the modern severe historical school, who declared that
Foulques the adventures of Fitzwarin, though of course
Fitzwarin. adulterated, were an important historical
document, and nothing so frivolous as a novel.   One
has, however, a reed-like faculty of getting up again
from such smitings : and for my part I do not hesitate
once more to call *Foulques Fitzwarin* the first historical
prose novel in modern literature.   French in language, as
we have it, it is thoroughly English in subject, and, beyond
all doubt, in the original place of composition, while
there is no reason to doubt the assertion that there were
older verse-renderings of the story both in English and
French.   In fact, they may turn up yet.   But the thing
as it stands is a very desirable and even delectable thing,
and well deserved its actual publication, not merely in
the French collection, of which we are speaking, but in
the papers of the too short-lived English Warton Club.

For it is not only our first historical novel, but also
the first, as far as England is concerned, of those outlaw
stories which have always delighted worthy English
youth from *Robin Hood* to *The Black Arrow*.   The
Fitzwarins, as concerns their personalities and genealogies,
may be surrendered without a pang to the historian,
though he shall not have the marrow of the story.   They
never seem to have been quite happy except when they
were in a state of " utlagation," and it was not only John
against whom they rebelled, for one of them died on the
Barons' side at Lewes.

The compiler, whoever he was—it has been said
already and cannot be said too often, that every re-
compiler in the Middle Ages felt it (like the man in
that " foolish " writer, as some call him, Plato) a sacred
duty to add something to the common stock,—was not
exactly a master of his craft, but certainly showed admirable zeal.   There never was a more curious *macédoine*
than this story.   Part of it is, beyond all doubt,
traditional history, with place-names all right, though
distorted by that curious inability to transpronounce or

trans-spell which made the French of the thirteenth
century call Lincoln " Nicole," and their descendants of
the seventeenth call Kensington " Stintinton."   Part is
mere stock or common-form Romance, as when Foulques
goes to sea and has adventures with the usual dragons
and their usual captive princesses. Part, though not
quite dependent on the general stock, is indebted to that
of a particular kind, as in the repeated catching of the
King by the outlaws.   But it is all more or less good
reading ; and there are two episodes in the earlier part
which (one of them especially) merit more detailed
account.

The first still has something of a general character
about it.   It is the story of a certain Payn Peveril (for
we meet many familiar names), who seems to have been
a real person though wrongly dated here, and has one of
those nocturnal combats with demon knights, the best
known examples of which are those recounted in *Marmion*
and its notes.   Peveril's antagonist, however—or rather
the mask which the antagonist takes,—connects with the
oldest legendary history of the island, for he reanimates
the body of Gogmagog, the famous Cornish giant, whom
Corineus slew.   The diabolic Gogmagog, however, seems
neither to have stayed in Cornwall nor gone to Cambridge-
shire, though (oddly enough the French editors do not
seem to have noticed this) Payn Peveril actually held
fiefs in the neighbourhood of those exalted mountains
called now by the name of his foe.   He had a hard fight ;
but luckily his arms were *or* with a cross *édentée azure*,
and this cross constantly turned the giant-devil's mace-
strokes, while it also weakened him, and he had besides
to bear the strokes of Peveril's sword.   So he gave in,
remarking with as much truth as King Padella in similar
circumstances, that it was no good fighting under these
conditions.   Then he tells a story of some length
about the original Gogmagog and his treasure.   The
secret of this he will not reveal, but tells Peveril that he
will be lord of Blanche-lande in Shropshire, and vanishes
with the usual unpleasant accompaniment—*tiel pueur*

dont Payn quida devier. He left his mace, which the knight kept as a testimony to anybody who did not believe the story.

This is not bad ; but the other, which is either true or extraordinarily well invented, is far finer, and, with some omissions, must be analysed and partly translated. Those who know the singular beauty of Ludlow Town and Castle will be able to " stage " it to advantage, but this is not absolutely necessary to its appreciation as a story.

The Peverils have died out by this time, and the honour and lands have gone by marriage to Guarin of Metz, whose son, Foulques Fitzguarin or Warin, starts the subjects of the general story. When the first Foulkes is eighteen, there is war between Sir Joce of Dinan (the name then given to Ludlow) and the Lacies. In one of their skirmishes Sir Walter de Lacy is wounded and captured, with a young knight of his party, Sir Ernault de Lyls. They have courteous treatment in Ludlow Castle, and Ernault makes love to Marion de la Brière, a most gentle damsel, who is the chief maid of the lady of the castle, and as such, of course, herself a lady. He promises her marriage, and she provides him and his chief with means of escape. Whether Lisle (as his name probably was) had at this time any treacherous intentions is not said or hinted. But Lacy, naturally enough, resents his defeat, and watches for an opportunity of *revanche* ; while Sir Joce[lyn], on the other hand, takes his prisoners' escape philosophically, and does not seem to make any enquiry into its cause. At first Lacy thinks of bringing over his Irish vassals to aid him ; but his English neighbours not unnaturally regard this step with dislike, and a sort of peace is made between the enemies. A match is arranged between Sir Joce's daughter Hawyse and Foulques Fitzwarin. Joce then quits Ludlow for a time, leaving, however, a strong garrison there. Marion, who feigns illness, is also left. And now begins the tragic and striking part of the story.

The next day after Joce had gone, Marion sent a message to Sir Ernault de Lyls, begging him, for the great love that there was between them, not to forget the pledges they had exchanged, but to come quickly to speak with her at the castle of Dinan, because the lord and the lady and the bulk of the servants had gone to Hertilande—also to come to the same place by which he had left the castle. [*He replies asking her to send him the exact height of the wall (which she unsuspiciously does by the usual means of a silk thread) and also the number of the household left. Then he seeks his chief, and tells him, with a mixture of some truth, that the object of the Hertilande journey is to gather strength against Lacy, capture his castle of Ewyas, and kill himself—intelligence which he falsely attributes to Marion. He has, of course, little difficulty in persuading Lacy to take the initiative. Sir Ernault is entrusted with a considerable mixed force, and comes by night to the castle.*] The night was very dark, so that no sentinel saw them. Sir Ernault took a squire to carry the ladder of hide, and they went to the window where Marion was waiting for them. And when she saw them, never was any so joyful: so she dropped a cord right down and drew up the hide ladder and fastened it to a battlement. Then Ernault lightly scaled the tower, and took his love in his arms and kissed her: and they made great joy of each other and went into another room and supped, and then went to their couch, and left the ladder hanging.

But the squire who had carried it went to the forces hidden in the garden and elsewhere, and took them to the ladder. And one hundred men, well armed, mounted by it and descended by the Pendover tower and went by the wall behind the chapel, and found the sentinel too heavy with sleep to defend himself: and the knights and the sergeants were cut to pieces crying for mercy in their beds. But Sir Ernault's companions were pitiless, and many a white sheet was dyed red with blood. And at last they tossed the watchman into the deep fosse and broke his neck.

Now Marion de la Brière lay by her lover Sir Ernault and knew nothing of the treason he had done. But she heard a great noise in the castle and rose from her bed, and looked out and heard more clearly the cry of the massacred, and saw knights in white armour. Wherefore she understood that Sir Ernault had deceived and betrayed her, and began to weep bitterly and said, "Ah! that I was ever of mother born: for that by my crime I have lost my lord Sir Joce, who bred me so gently, his castle, and his good folk. Had I not been, nothing had been lost. Alas! that I ever believed this knight! for by his lies he has ruined me, and what is worse, my lord too." Then, all weeping, she drew Sir Ernault's sword and said, "Sir knight! awake, for you have brought strange company into my lord's castle without his leave. I brought in only you and your squire. And since you have deceived me you cannot rightly blame me if I give you your deserts—at least you shall never boast to any other mistress that by deceiving me you conquered the castle and the land of Dinan !" The knight started up, but Marion, with the sword she held drawn, ran him straight through the body, and he died at once. She herself, knowing that if she were taken, ill were the death she should die, and knowing not what to do, let herself fall from a window and broke her neck.

Now this, I venture to think, is not an ordinary story. Tales of treachery, onslaught, massacre, are not rare in the Middle Ages, nor need we go as far as the Middle Ages for them. But the almost heroic insouciance with which the traitor knight forgets everything except his immediate enjoyment, and, provided he has his mistress at his will, concerns himself not in the slightest degree as to what becomes of his companions, is not an every-day touch. Nor is the strong contrast of the chambers of feast and dalliance—undisturbed, voluptuous, terrestrial-paradisaic—with " the horror and the hell " in the courts below. Nor, last of all, the picture of the more than half innocent Marion, night-garbed or ungarbed, but with sword drawn, first hanging over her slumbering betrayer, then dealing the stroke of vengeance, and then falling—white against the dark towers and the darker ravines at their base—to her self-doomed judgment.

Even more, however, than in individual points of interest or excitement, the general survey of these two Something volumes gives matter for thought on our on these, subject. Here are some half-dozen stories or a little more. It is not much, some one may say, for the produce of two hundred years. But what it lacks in volume (and that will be soon made up in French, while it is to be remembered that we have practically nothing to match it in English) it makes up in variety. The peculiarity, some would say the defect, of mediaeval literature—its sheep-like tendency to go in flocks—is quite absent. Not more than two of the eight, *Le Roi Flore* and *La Comtesse de Ponthieu*, can be said to be of the same class, even giving the word class a fairly elastic sense. They are short prose *Romans d'aventures*. But *Asseneth* is a mystical allegory; *Aucassin et Nicolette* is a sort of idyll, almost a lyric, in which the adventure is entirely subordinated to the emotional and poetical interest; *L'Empereur Constant*, though with something of the *Roman d'aventures* in it, has a tendency towards a *moralitas* (" there is no armour against fate ") which never appears in the pure adventurous kind; *Troilus* is an abridgment of a classical romance; and *Foulques Fitzwarin* is, as has been said, an embryonic historical novel. Most, if not all, moreover, give openings for, and one or two even proceed into, character- and even " problem "-writing of the most advanced novel kind. In one or two also, no doubt, that aggression and encroachment of allegory (which is one of the chief notes of these two centuries) makes itself felt, though not to the extent which we shall notice in the next chapter. But almost everywhere a strong *nisus* towards actual tale-telling and the rapid acquisition of proper " plant " for such telling, become evident. In particular, conversation—a thing difficult to bring anyhow into verse-narrative, and impossible there to keep up satisfactorily in various moods —begins to find its way. We may turn, in the next chapter, to matter mostly or wholly in verse forms. But prose fiction is started all the same.

Before we do so, however, it may not be improper to point out that the short story undoubtedly holds—of itself —a peculiar and almost prerogative place in the history and morphology of the novel. After a long and rather unintelligible unpopularity in English—it never suffered in this way in French—it has been, according to the way of the world, a little over-exalted of late perhaps. It is undoubtedly a very difficult thing to do well, and it would be absurd to pretend that any of the foregoing examples is done thoroughly well. The Italian *novella* had to come and show the way.[1] But the short story, even of the rudi-

And on the short story generally.

---

[1] In *prose*. For the very important part played by the home verse *fabliaux* see next chapter.

mentary sort which we have been considering, cannot help being a powerful schoolmaster to bring folk to good practice in the larger kind.   The faults and the merits of that kind, as such, appear in it after a fashion which can hardly fail to be instructive and suggestive.   The faults so frequently charged against that " dear defunct " in our own tongue, the three-volume novel—the faults of long-windedness, of otiose padding, of unnecessary episodes, etc., are almost mechanically or mathematically impossible in the *nouvelle*.   The long book provides pastime in its literal sense, and if it is not obvious in the other the accustomed reader, unless outraged by some extraordinary dulness or silences, goes on, partly like the Pickwickian horse because he can't well help it, and partly because he hopes that something *may* turn up. In the case of the short he sees almost at once whether it is going to have any interest, and if there is none such apparent he throws it aside.

Moreover, as in almost every other case, the shortness is appropriate to *exercise* ; while the prose form does not encourage those terrible *chevilles*—repetitions of stock adjective and substantive and verb and phrase generally— which are so common in verse, and especially in octo-syllabic verse.   It is therefore in many ways healthy, and the space allotted to these early examples of it will not, it is hoped, seem to any impartial reader excessive.

CHAPTER V

IT was shown in the last chapter that fiction, and even prose fiction, of very varied character began to develop
The con- itself in French during the thirteenth and
nection fourteenth centuries. By the fifteenth the
with prose
fiction development was very much greater, and the
of allegory. " disrhyming " of romances, the beginnings of which were very early, came to be a regular, not an occasional, process; while, by its latter part, verse had become not the usual, but the exceptional vehicle of romance, and prose romances of enormous length were popular. But earlier there had still been some obstacles in the way of the prose novel proper. It was the period of the rise and reign of Allegory, and France, preceptress of almost all Europe in most literary kinds, proved herself such in this with the unparalleled example of the *Roman de la Rose*. But the *Roman de la Rose* was itself in verse—the earlier part of it at least in real poetry—and most of its innumerable imitations were in verse likewise. Moreover, though France again had been the first to receive and to turn to use the riches of Eastern apologue, the most famous example of which is *The Seven Wise Masters*, these rather serious matters do not seem to have especially commended themselves to the French people. The place of composition of the most famous of all, the *Gesta Romanorum*, has been fairly settled to be England, though the original language of composition is not likely to have been other than Latin. At any rate, the style of serious allegory, in prose which

should also be literature, never really caught hold of the French taste.

Comic tale-telling, on the other hand, was germane to the very soul of the race, and had shown itself in *chanson* and *roman* episodes at a very early date. But it had been so abundantly, and in so popular a manner, associated with verse as a vehicle in those pieces, in the great beast-epic of *Renart*, and above all in the *fabliaux* and in the earliest farces, that the connection was hard to separate. None of the stories discussed in the last chapter has, it may be noticed, the least comic touch or turn.

As we go on we must disengage ourselves more and more (though with occasional returns to it) from attention

And of the   to verse; and the two great compositions in
fabliaux.   that form, the *Romance of the Rose* and the *Story of the Fox*, especially the former, hardly require much writing about to any educated person. They are indeed most strongly contrasted examples of two modes of tale-telling, both in a manner allegoric, but in other respects utterly different. The mere story of the *Rose*, apart from the dreamy or satiric digressions and developments of its two parts and the elaborate descriptions of the first, can be told in a page or two. An abstract of the various *Renart* books, to give any idea of their real character, would, on the other hand, have to be nearly as long as the less spun-out versions themselves. But the verse *fabliaux* can hardly be passed over so lightly. Many of them formed the actual bases of the prose *nouvelles* that succeeded them; not a few have found repeated presentation in literature; and, above all, they deserve the immense praise of having deliberately introduced ordinary life, and not conventionalised manners, into literary treatment. We have taken some pains to point out touches of that life which are observable in Saint's Life and Romance, in *chanson* and early prose tale. But here the case is altered. Almost everything is real; a good deal is what is called, in one of the senses of a rather misused word, downright " realism."

Few people who have ever heard of the *fabliaux* can
need to be told that this realism in their case implies
extreme freedom of treatment, extending very commonly to the undoubtedly coarse and not seldom to the
merely dirty. There are some—most of them well
known by modern imitations such as Leigh Hunt's
"Palfrey"—which are quite guiltless in this respect ; but
the great majority deal with the usual comic farrago of
satire on women, husbands, monks, and other stock
subjects of raillery, all of which at the time invited
" sculduddery." To translate some of the more amusing,
one would require not merely Chaucerian licence of
treatment but Chaucerian peculiarities of dialect in order
to avoid mere vulgarity. Even Prior, who is our only
modern English *fabliau*-writer of real literary merit—
the work of people like Hanbury Williams and Hall
Stevenson being mostly mere pornography—could hardly
have managed such a piece as " Le Sot Chevalier "—a
riotously "improper " but excessively funny example—
without running the risk of losing that recommendation
of being " a lady's book " with which Johnson rather
capriciously tempered his more general undervaluation.
Sometimes, on the other hand, the joke is trivial enough,
as in the English-French word-play of *anel* for *agnel* (or
-*neau*), which substitutes " donkey" for "lamb "; or, in
the other, on the comparison of a proper name, " Estula,"
with its component syllables " es tu là ? " But the
important point on the whole is that, proper or improper,
romantic or trivial, they all exhibit a constant improvement in the mere art of telling; in discarding of the
stock phrases, the long-winded speeches, and the general
paraphernalia of verse ; in sticking and leading up
smartly to the point ; in coining sharp, lively phrase ; in
the co-ordination of incident and the excision of superfluities. Often they passed without difficulty into direct
dramatic presentation in short farces. But on the whole
their obvious destiny was to be " unrhymed " and to
make their appearance in the famous form of the *nouvelle*
or *novella*, in regard to which it is hard to say whether

Italy was most indebted to France for substance, or France to Italy for form.

It was not, however, merely the intense conservatism of the Middle Ages as to literary form which kept back *The rise of* the prose *nouvelle* to such an extent that, as *the nouvelle* we have seen, only a few examples survive *itself.* from the two whole centuries between 1200 and 1400, while not one of these is of the kind most characteristic ever since, or at least until quite recent days, of French tale-telling. The French octosyllabic couplet, in which the *fabliaux* were without exception or with hardly an exception composed, can, in a long story, become very tiresome because of its want of weight and grasp, and the temptations it offers to a weak rhymester to stuff it with endless tags. But for a short tale in deft hands it can apply its lightness in the best fashion, and put its points with no lack of sting. The *fabliau*-writer or reciter was not required—one imagines that he would have found scant audiences if he had tried it—to spin a long yarn ; he had got to come to his jokes and his business pretty rapidly ; and, as La Fontaine has shown to thousands who have never known—perhaps have never heard of—his early masters, he had an instrument which would answer to his desires perfectly if only he knew how to finger it.

At the same time, both the lover of poetry and the lover of tale must acknowledge that, though alliance between them is not in the least an unholy one, and has produced great and charming children, the best of the poetry is always a sort of extra bonus or solace to the tale, and the tale not unfrequently seems as if it could get on better without the poetry. The one can only aspire somewhat irrelevantly ; the other can never attain quite its full development. So it was no ill day when the prose *nouvelle* came to its own in France.

Les Cent The first remarkable collection was the *Nouvelles* famous *Cent Nouvelles Nouvelles*, traditionally *Nouvelles.* attributed to Louis XI. when Dauphin and an exile in Brabant, with the assistance of friends and

courtiers, but more recently selected by critics that way
minded as part of the baggage they have "commandeered"
for Antoine de la Salle.   The question of authorship is
of scarcely the slightest importance to us; though the
point last mentioned is worth mentioning, because we
shall have to notice the favoured candidate in this
history again.   There are certainly some of the hundred
that he might have written.

In the careless way in which literary history used to
be dealt with, the *Cent Nouvelles Nouvelles* were held to
be mere imitation of the *Decameron* and other Italian
things.   It is, of course, much more than probable that the
Italian *novella* had not a little to do with the precipitation
of the French *nouvelle* from its state of solution in the
fabliau.   But the person or persons who, in imitating
the *Decameron*, produced the *Cent Nouvelles Nouvelles* had
a great deal more to do—and did a great deal less—than
this mere imitation of their original.   As for a group
of included tales, the already-mentioned *Seven Wise
Masters* [1] was known in France much before Boccaccio's
time.   The title was indeed admittedly Italian, but
such an obvious one as to require no positive borrowing, and there is in the French book no story-framework
like that of the plague and the country-house visit; no
cheerful personalities like Fiammetta or Dioneo make
not merely the intervals but the stories themselves alive
with a special interest.   Above all, there is nothing like
the extraordinary mixture of unity and variety—a pure
gift of genius—which succeeds in making the *Decameron*
a real book as well as a bundle of narratives.   Nor is
there anything like the literary brilliancy of the actual
style and handling.

Nevertheless, *Les Cent Nouvelles Nouvelles* is a book
of great interest and value, despite serious defects due
to its time generally and to its place in the history of
fiction in particular.   Its obscenity, on which even Sir
Walter Scott, the least censorious or prudish-prurient
of men, and with Southey, the great witness against

---

[1] Prose as well as verse.

false squeamishness, has been severe,[1] is unfortunately
undeniable. But it is to be doubted whether Sir Walter
knew much of the *fabliaux*; if he had he would have
seen first, that this sort of thing had become an almost
indispensable fashion in the short story, and secondly,
that there is here considerable improvement on the
fabliaux themselves, there being much less mere schoolboy crudity of dirty detail and phrase, though the situations may remain the same. It suffers occasionally
from the heavy and rhetorical style which beset all
European literature (except Italian, which itself did not
wholly escape) in the fifteenth century. But still one
can see in it that improvement of narrative method and
diction which has been referred to : and occasionally, amid
the crowd of tricky wives, tricked husbands, too obliging
and too hardly treated chambermaids, ribald priests and
monks, and the like, one comes across quite different
things and persons, which are, as the phrase goes, almost
startlingly modern, with a mixture of the *un*modern
heightening the appeal. One of the most striking of
these—not very likely to be detected or suspected by a
careless reader under its sub-title of " La Demoiselle
Cavalière," and by no means fully summarised in the
quaint short argument which is in all cases subjoined—
may be briefly analysed.

In one of the great baronial households of Brabant
there lived, after the usual condition of gentle servitude,
a youth named Gerard, who fell in love, after
quite honourable and seemly fashion, with
Katherine, the daughter of the house—a fact
which, naturally, they thought known only
to themselves, when, as naturally, everybody in the
Court had become aware of it. " For the better pre-
vention of scandal," an immediate marriage being
apparently out of the question because of Gerard's
inferiority in rank to his mistress, it is decided by the
intervention of friends that Gerard shall take his leave
of the Brabantine " family." There is a parting of the

*Analysis
of " La
Demoiselle
Cavalière."*

---

[1] In the very delightful imaginative introduction to *Quentin Durward*.

most laudable kind, in which Katherine bestows on her
lover a ring, and a pledge that she will never marry any
one else, and he responds suitably.   Then he sets out,
and on arriving at Bar has no difficulty in establishing
himself in another great household.   Katherine meanwhile is beset with suitors of the best rank and fortune ;
but will have nothing to say to any of them, till one day
comes the formidable moment when a mediaeval father
determines that his daughter shall marry a certain person,
will she nill she.   But if mediaeval fatherhood was
arbitrary, mediaeval religion was supreme, and a demand
to go on pilgrimage before an important change of life
could hardly be refused.   In fact, the parents, taking
the proposal as a mere preliminary of obedience, consent
joyfully, and offer a splendid suite of knights and damsels,
" Nous lui baillerons ung tel gentilhomme et une telle
demoiselle, Ysabeau et Marguerite et Jehanneton."   But
" no," says Mistress Katherine sagely.   The road to
St. Nicolas of Warengeville is not too safe for people
travelling with a costly outfit and a train of women.   Let
her, dressed as a man, and a bastard uncle of hers (who
is evidently the " Will Wimble " of the house) go
quietly on little horses, and it will save time, trouble,
money, and danger.   This the innocent parents consider
to show " great sense and good will," and the pair start
in German dress—Katherine as master, the uncle as
man,—comfortably, too, as one may imagine (for uncles
and nieces generally get on well together, and the bend
sinister need do no harm).   They accomplish their
pilgrimage (a touch worth noticing in Katherine's
character), and then only does she reveal her plan to her
companion.   She tells him, not without a little bribery,
that she wants to go and see Gerard *en Barrois,* and to
stay there for a short time ; but he is to have no doubt
of her keeping her honour safe.   He consents, partly with
an eye to the future main chance (for she is her father's
sole heir), and partly because *elle est si bonne qu'il n'y
fault guère guet sur elle.*   Katherine, taking the name of
Conrad, finds the place, presents herself to the *maître*

d'ostel, an ancient squire, as desirous of entertainment or *ret*ainment, and is very handsomely received. After dinner and due service done to the master, the old squire having heard that Katherine—Conrad—is of Brabant, naturally introduces her countryman Gerard to her. He does not in the least recognise her, and what strikes her as stranger, neither during their own dinner nor after says a word about Brabant itself. Conrad is regularly admitted to Monseigneur's service, and, as a countryman, is to share Gerard's room. They are perfectly good friends, go to see their horses together, etc., but still the formerly passionate lover says not a word of Brabant or his Brabançonian love, and poor Katherine concludes that she has been " put with forgotten sins "—not a bad phrase, though it might be misconstrued. Being, however, as has been already seen, both a plucky girl and a clever one, she determines to carry her part through. At last, when they go to their respective couches in the same chamber, she herself faces the subject, and asks him if he knows any persons in Brabant. " Oh yes." " Does he know " her own father, his former master ? " Yes." " They say," said she, " that there are pretty girls there : did you not know any ? " " Precious few," quoth he, " and I cared nothing about them. Do let me go to sleep ! I am dead tired." " What ! " said she, " can you sleep when there is talk of pretty girls ? *You* are not much of a lover." But he slept "like a pig."

Nevertheless, Katherine does not give up hope, though the next day things are much the same, Gerard talking of nothing but hounds and hawks, Conrad of pretty girls. At last the visitor declares that he [she] does not care for the Barrois, and will go back to Brabant. " Why ? " says Gerard, " what better hunting, etc., can you get there than here ? " " It has nothing," says Conrad, " like the women of Brabant," adding, in reply to a jest of his, an ambiguous declaration that she is actually in love. " Then why did you leave her ? " says Gerard—about the first sensible word he has uttered.

She makes a fiery answer as to Love sometimes banishing
from his servants all sense and reason. But for the time
the subject again drops. It is, however, reopened at
night, and some small pity comes on one for the recreant
Gerard, inasmuch as she keeps him awake by wailing
about her love. At last she " draws " the sluggard to
some extent. " Has not *he* been in love, and does not
he know all about it ? But he was never such a fool as
Conrad, and he is sure that Conrad's lady is not such
either." Another try, and she gets the acknowledgment
of treason out of him. He tells her (what she knows
too well) how he loved a noble damsel in Brabant and had
to leave her, and it really annoyed him for a few days
(it is good to imagine Katherine's face, even in the dark,
at this), though of course he never lost his appetite
or committed any folly of that sort. But he knew his
Ovid (he tells her), and as soon as he came to Bar he made
love to a pretty girl there who was quite amiable to him,
and now he never thinks of the other. There is more
talk, and Katherine insists that he shall introduce her to
his new lady, that she may try this remedy of counter-
love. He consents with perfect nonchalance, and is at
last allowed to go to sleep. No details are given of the
conversation with the rival,[1] except the bitterness of
Katherine's heart at the fact, and at seeing the ring she
had given to Gerard on his hand. This she actually
has the pluck to play with, and, securing it, to slip on her
own. But the man being obviously past praying or
caring for, she arranges with her uncle to depart early in
the morning, writes a letter telling Gerard of the whole
thing and renouncing him, passes the night silently,
leaves the letter, rises quietly and early, and departs, yet
" weeping tenderly," not for the man, but for her own
lost love. The pair reach home safely, and says the
tale-teller, with an agreeable dryness often found here,[2]
" There were some who asked them the adventures of

---

[1] This is one of the points which a modern novelist would certainly have seized ;
but whether to advantage or not is another question.
[2] And of course recognised by the " Antonians " as peculiar to La Salle.

their journey, but whatever they answered they did not boast of the chief one." The conclusion is so spirited and at the very end so scenic and even modern (or, much better, universal), that it must be given in direct translation, with a few *chevilles* (or pieces of padding) left out.

As for Gerard, when he woke and found his companion gone, he thought it must be late, jumped up in haste, and seized his jerkin: but, as he thrust his hand in one of the sleeves, there dropped out a letter which surprised him, for he certainly did not remember having put any there. He picked it up and saw it subscribed "To the disloyal Gerard." If he was startled before he was more so now: but he opened it at last, and saw the signature "Katherine, surnamed Conrad." Even yet he knew not what to think of it: but as he read the blood rose to his face and his heart fluttered, and his whole manner was changed. Still, he read it through, and learnt how his disloyalty had come to the knowledge of her who had wished him so well; and that not at second hand, but from himself to herself; what trouble she had taken to find him; and how (which stung him most) he had slept three nights in her company after all. [*After thinking some time he decides to follow her, and arrives in Brabant on the very day of her marriage : for she has, in the circumstances, kept her word to her parents.*] Then he tried to go up to her and salute her, and make some wretched excuse for his fault. But he was not allowed, for she turned her shoulder on him, and he could never manage to speak to her all through the day. He even stepped forward once to lead her out to dance, but she refused him flatly before all the company, many of whom heard her. And immediately afterwards another gentleman came, who bade the minstrels strike up, and she stepped down from her dais in full view of Gerard and went to dance with him. And so did the disloyal lover lose his lady.

Now whether this, as the book asserts and as is not at all improbable, is a true story or not, cannot matter to any sensible person one farthing. What does matter is that it is a by no means badly told story, that it resorts to no illegitimate sources or seasonings of interest, and that it offers opportunities for amplification and "diversity of administration" to almost any extent. One can fancy it told, at much greater length and with more or less adjustment to different times, by great novelists of the most widely varying classes—by Scott and by Dumas, by Charles Reade and by George Meredith, to mention no living writer, as might easily be done. Both hero and heroine have more character between them than you could extract out of fifty of the usual *nouvelles*, and each lends him or herself to endless further development. Not a few of the separate scenes—the good parents fussing over their daughter's intended cavalcade and her thrifty and ingenious objections; the journey of the uncle and niece (any of the first three of the great novelists mentioned above would have made chapters of this); the dramatic and risky passages at the castle *en Barrois*; the contrast of Katherine's passion and Gerard's sluggishness; and the fashion in which this latter at once brings on the lout's defeat and saves the lady from danger at his hands—all this is novel-matter of almost the first class as regards incident, with no lack of character-openings to boot. Nor could anybody want a better " curtain " than the falling back of the scorned and baffled false lover, the concert of the minstrels, and Katherine's stately stepping down the dais to complete the insult by dancing with another.

One more general point may be noticed in connection with the superiority of this story, and that is the accession The interest of interest, at first sight trivial but really imof *named* portant, which comes from the *naming* of the personages. personages. Both in the earlier *fabliaux* and in these *Nouvelles* themselves, by far the larger number of the actors are simply called by class-names—a " knight," a " damsel," a " merchant and his wife," a " priest," a " varlet." It may seem childish to allow the mere addition of a couple of names like Gerard and Katherine to make this difference of interest, but the fact is that there is a good deal of childishness in human nature, and especially in the enjoyment of story.[1] Only

[1] Only contrast " *Tom, Tom,* the piper's son," with " *There was once* a piper's son," or think how comparatively uninteresting the enormities of another hero or not-hero would have been if he had been anonymous instead of being called "Georgy-Porgy Pudding-and-Pie!" ["Puddenum" is, or used to be, the preferred if corrupt nursery form.] In more elaborate and adorned narrative the influence, not merely of the name but of the beautiful name, comes in, and that of the name itself remains. In that tragic story of Ludlow Castle which was given above (Chap. iv. pp. 84-6), something, for the present writer at least, would have been lost if the traitor had been merely " a

by very slow degrees were writers of fiction to learn the great difference that small matters of this kind make, and how the mere "anecdote," the dry argument or abstract of incident, can be amplified, varied, transformed from a remainder biscuit to an abundant and almost inexhaustible feast, by touches of individual character, setting of interiors, details of conversation, description, nomenclature, and what not. Quite early, as we saw in the case of the *St. Alexis*, persons of narrative gift stumbled upon things of the kind; but it was only after long delays, and hints of many half-conscious kinds, that they became part of recognised craft. Even with such a master of that craft as Boccaccio before them, not all the Italian novelists could catch the pattern; and the French, perhaps naturally enough, were slower still.

It must be remembered, in judging the fifteenth-century French tale, that just as it was to some extent hampered by the long continuing popularity of the verse *fabliau* on the one hand; so it was, as we may say, "bled" on the other by the growing popularity of the farce, which consists of exactly the same material as the *fabliaux* and the *nouvelles* themselves, with the additional liveliness of voice and action. These later additions imposed not the smallest restraint on the license which had characterised and was to characterise the plain verse and prose forms,[1] and no doubt the result was all the more welcome to the taste of the time. But for that very reason the appetites and tastes, which could glut themselves with the full dramatic representation, might care less for the mere narrative, on the famous principle of *segnius irritant*. Nor was the political state of France during the time very favourable to letters. There are, however, two separate fifteenth-century stories which deserve notice. One of them is the rather famous, though probably not widely read, *Petit Jehan de Saintré*

---

knight" instead of Sir Ernault Lisle and the victim merely "a damsel" instead of Marion de la Brière. And would the *bocca bacciata* of Alaciel itself be as gracious if it was merely anybody's?

[1] The amazing farce-insets of Lyndsay's *Satire of the Three Estates* could be paralleled, and were no doubt suggested, by French farces of older date.

of the already mentioned Antoine de la Salle, a certain
work of his this time.   The other is the pleasant, though
to Englishmen intentionally uncomplimentary, *Jehan de
Paris* of an unknown writer.   La Salle's book must
belong to the later middle of the century, though, if he
died in or about 1461, not to a very late middle.   *Jehan
de Paris* has been put by M. de Montaiglon nearer the
close.

   The history of " little John of Saintré and the Lady
of the Beautiful Cousins " [1] has not struck all judges,
Petit Jehan even all English judges,[2] in the same way.
de Saintré. Some have thought it mawkish, rhetorical,
clumsily imitative of the manners of dead chivalry,
and the like.   Others, admitting it to be a late
and " literary " presentation of the stately society it
describes, rank it much higher as such.   Its author was
a bitter enough satirist if he wrote, as he most probably
did, the famous *Quinze Joyes de Mariage*, one of the most
unmitigated pieces of unsweetened irony—next to *A
Tale of a Tub* and *Jonathan Wild*—to be found in literature ; but not couched in narrative form.   The same
quality appears of course in the still more famous farce
of *Pathelin*, which few good judges deny very stoutly
to him, though there is little positive evidence.   In the
Cent Nouvelles Nouvelles again, as has been said, he
certainly had a hand, and possibly a great hand, as well
as perhaps elsewhere.   The satiric touch appears even
in *Petit Jehan* itself ; for, after all the gracious courtship
of the earlier part, the *dame des belles Cousines*, during
an absence of her lover on service, falls a by no means, as
it would seem, very reluctant victim to the vulgar vicious-
ness of a rich churchman, just like the innominatas of the
nouvelles themselves.   But the earlier part *is* gracious—
a word specifically and intensively applicable to it.   It
may be a little unreal ; does not the secondary form and

---

[1] Nobody seems to be entirely certain what this odd title means : though there have
been some obvious and some far-fetched guesses.   But it has, like other *rhétoriqueur*
names of 1450–1550, such as "Traverser of Perilous Ways" and the like, a kind of
fantastic attraction for some people.
[2] If I remember rightly, my friend the late R. L. Stevenson was wont to abuse it.

sense which has been fastened upon reality—" realism "—show that, in the opinion of many people at least, reality is *not* gracious ? The Foozles of this world who " despise all your kickshaws," the Dry-as-dusts who point out— not in the least seeing the real drift of their argument— that the fifteenth century was, in the greater part of Europe if not the whole, at a new point of morals and manners, may urge these things. But the best part of *Petit Jehan* remains a gracious sort of dream for gracious dreamers—a picture of a kind of Utopia of Feminism, when Feminism did not mean votes or anything foolish, but only adoration of the adorable.

It would be impossible to find or even to imagine anything more different than the not much later *Jehan de Paris*, an evident folk-tale[1] of uncertain origin, which very quickly became a popular chapbook and lasted long in that condition. Although we Englishmen provide the fun, he is certainly no Englishman who resents the fact or fails to enjoy the result, not to mention that we " could tell them tales with other endings." It is, for instance, not quite historically demonstrable that in crossing a river many English horsemen would be likely to be drowned, while all the French cavaliers got safe through ; nor that, in scouring a country, the Frenchmen would score all the game and all the best beasts and poultry, while the English bag would consist of starvelings and offal. But no matter for that. The actual tale tells (with the agreeable introductory " How," which has not yet lost its zest for the right palates in chapter-headings) the story of a King and Queen of Spain who have, in recompense for help given them against turbulent barons, contracted their daughter to the King of France for his son ; how they forgot this later, and betrothed her to the King of England, and how that King set out with his train, through France itself, to fetch his bride. As soon

Jehan de Paris.

---

[1] As such, the substance is found in other languages. But the French itself has been traced by some to an earlier *roman d'aventure, Blonde d'Oxford*, in which an English heiress is carried off by a French squire.

as the Dauphin (now king, for his father is dead) hears
of their coming, he disguises himself under the name of
John of Paris, with a splendid train of followers, much
more gorgeous than the English (the "foggy islander"
of course cannot make this out), and sets of *quiproquos*
follow, in each of which the Englishman is outdone
and baffled generally, till at last "John of Paris" enters
Burgos in state, reveals himself, and carries off the
Englishman's bride, with the natural effect of making
him *bien marry et courroucé*, though no fight comes off.

The tale is smartly and succinctly told (there are not
many more than a hundred of the small-sized and large-
printed pages of the *Collection Jannet-Picard*), and there
is a zest and *verve* about it which ought to please any
mood that is for the time in harmony with the much
talked of Comic Spirit. But it certainly does not lose
attraction, and it as certainly does not fail to lend some,
when it is considered side by side with the other "John,"
especially if both are again compared with the certainly
not earlier and probably later "Prose Romances" in
English, to which that rather ambitious title was given
by Mr. Thoms. There is nothing in these in the very
remotest degree resembling *Jehan de Saintré* : you must
get on to the *Arcadia* or at least to *Euphues* before you
come anywhere near that. There is, on the other hand,
in our stuff, a sort of distant community of spirit with
Jehan de Paris ; but it works in an altogether lower and
less imaginative sphere and fashion ; no sense of art
being present, and very little of craft. It is astonishing
that a language which had had, if only in verse, such an
unsurpassable tale-teller as Chaucer, should have been
so backward. But then the whole conditions of the
fifteenth century, especially in England, become only
the more puzzling the longer one studies them. Even
in France, it will be observed, the output of Tale is by
no means large.[1] Nor shall we find it very greatly

[1] Perhaps one should guard against a possible repetition of a not uncommon critical
mistake—that of inferring ignorance from absence of mention. I am quite aware that
no exhaustive catalogue of known French stories in prose has been given ; and the
failure to supplement a former glance at the late prose versions of romance is intentional.

increased even in the next age, though there is one masterpiece in quantity as well as quality. But, for our purpose, the *Cent Nouvelles* and the two separate pieces just discussed continue, and in more and more striking manner, to show the vast possibilities when the way shall have been clearly found and the feet of the way-farers firmly set in it.

They have nothing new in romance-, still less in novel-*character* for us. The *Bibliothèque Elzévirienne* volumes have been dwelt upon, not as a *corpus*, but because they appear to represent, without any unfair manipulation or " window-dressing," the kind at the time with a remarkable combination of interest both individual and contrasted.

CHAPTER VI

RABELAIS

ALTHOUGH—as it is hoped the foregoing chapters may have shown—the amount of energy and of talent, thrown

The anonymity, or at least impersonality, of author-ship up to this point. into the department of French fiction, had from almost the earliest times been remarkably great; although French, if not France, had been the mother of almost all literatures in things fictitious, it can hardly be said that any writer of undeniable genius, entitling him to the first class in the Art of Letters, had shown himself therein. A hundred *chansons de geste* and as many romances *d'aventures* had displayed dispersed talent of a very high kind, and in the best of them, as the present writer has tried to point out, a very "extensive assortment" of the various attractions of the novel had from time to time made its appearance. But this again had been done "dispersedly," as the Shakespearean stage-direction has it. The story is sometimes well told, but the telling is constantly interrupted; the great art of novel-conversation is, as yet, almost unborn; the descriptions, though sometimes very striking, as in the case of those given from *Parthenopeus*—the fatal revelation of Melior's charms and the galloping of the maddened palfrey along the seashore, with the dark monster-haunted wood behind and the bright moonlit sea and galley in front—are more often stock and lifeless; while, above all, the characters are rarely more than sketched, if even that. The one exception — the great Arthurian history, as liberated from its Graal-legend swaddling clothes, and its kite-and-crow battles with Saxons and rival knights, but retaining the mystical motive of the Graal-search itself and the adventures of Lancelot and other knights ; combining all this into a single story, and storing it with incident for a time, and bringing it to a full and final tragic close by the loves of Lancelot himself and Guinevere— this great achievement, it has been frankly confessed, is so much muddled and distracted with episode which becomes positive digression, that some have even dismissed its pretensions to be a whole. Even those who reject this dismissal are not at one as to any single author of the conception, still less of the execution. The present writer has stated his humble, but ever more and more firm conviction that Chrestien did not do it and could not have done it ; others of more note, perhaps of closer acquaintance with MS. sources, but also perhaps not uniting knowledge of the subject with more experience in general literary criticism and in special study of the Novel, will not allow Mapes to have done it.

The *Roman de la Rose*, beautiful as is its earlier part and ingenious as is (sometimes) its later, is, as a *story*, of the thinnest kind. The *Roman de Renart* is a vast collection of small stories of a special class, and the *Fabliaux* are almost a vaster collection (if you do not exclude the "waterings out" of *Renart*) of kinds more general. There is abundance of amusement and some charm ; but nowhere are we much beyond very simple forms of fiction itself. None of the writers of *nouvelles*, except Antoine de la Salle, can be said to be a known personality.

There has always been a good deal of controversy about Rabelais, not all of which perhaps can we escape, Rabelais un- though it certainly will not be invited, and questionably we have no very extensive knowledge of his the first very great known life. But we have some : and that, as a man of writer. genius, he is superior to any single person named and known in earlier French literature, can hardly be contested by any one who is neither a silly paradoxer nor a mere dullard, nor affected by some extra-literary prejudice—religious, moral, or whatever it may be. But perhaps not every one who would admit the greatness of Master Francis as a man of letters, his possession not merely of consummate wit, but of that precious thing, so much rarer in French, actual humour ; his wonderful influence on the future word-book and phrase-book of his own language, nay, not every one who would go almost the whole length of the most uncompromising Pantagruelist, and would allow him profound wisdom, high aspirations for humanity, something of a complete world-philosophy—would at once admit him as a very great novelist. For my own part I have no hesitation in doing so, and to make the admission good must be the object of this chapter.

It may almost be said that his very excellence in this way has " stood in its own light." The readableness of

But the first great novelist? Rabelais is extraordinary. The present writer, after for years making of him almost an Addison according to Johnson's prescription, fell, by mere accident and occupation with other matters, into a way of *not* reading him, except for purposes of mere literary reference, during a long time. On three different occasions more recently, one ten or a dozen years ago, one six or seven, and the third for the purposes of this very book, he put himself again under the Master, and read him right through. It is difficult to imagine a severer test, and I am bound to confess (though I am not bound to specify) that in some, though not many, instances I have found famous and once favourite classics fail to stand it. Not so Master Francis. I do not think that I ever read him with greater interest than at this last time. Indeed I doubt whether I have ever felt the *catholicon*—the pervading virtue of his book—quite so strongly as I have in the days preceding that on which I write these words.

Some objections considered. Of course Momus may find handles—he generally can. " You are suffering from morbid senile relapse into puerile enjoyment of indecency," he or Mrs. Momus (whom later ages have called Grundy) may be kind enough to say. " You were a member of the Rabelais Club of pleasant memory, and think it necessary to live up to your earlier profession." " You have said this in print before [I have not exactly done so] and are bound to stick to it," etc. etc. etc., down to that final, " You are a bad critic, and it doesn't matter what you say," which certainly, in a sense, does leave nothing to be replied. But whether this is because the accused is guilty, or because the Court does not call upon him, is a question which one may leave to others.

Laying it down, then, as a point of fact that Rabelais *has* this curious " holding " quality, whence does he get it ? As everybody ought to know, many good people, admitting the fact, have, as he would himself have said, gone about with lanterns to seek for out-of-the-way reasons and qualities ; while some people, not so good, but also accepting the fact in a way, have grasped at the above-mentioned indecency itself for an explanation. This trick requires little effort to kick it into its native gutter. The greater proportion of the " *Indexable* " part of Rabelais is mere nastiness, which is only attractive to a very small minority of persons at any age, while to expert readers it is but a time-deodorised dunghill by the roadside, not beautiful, but negligible. Of the other part of this kind—the " naughty " part which is not nasty and may be somewhat nice—there is, when you come to consider it dispassionately, not really so very much, and it is seldom used in a seductive fashion. It may tickle, but it does not excite ; may create laughter, but never passion or even desire. Therefore it cannot be this which " holds " any reader but a mere novice or a glutton for garbage.

Less easily dismissible, but, it will seem, not less inadequate is the alleged " key "-interest of the book. Of course there are some people, and more than a person who wishes to think nobly of humanity might desire to find, who seem never to be tired of identifying Grandgousier, Gargantua, and Pantagruel himself with French kings to whom they bear not the slightest resemblance ;

of obliging us English by supposing us to be the Macréons
(who seem to have been very respectable people, but who
inhabit an island singularly unlike England in or anywhere near the time of Rabelais), and so on.   But to a
much larger number of persons—and one dares say to
all true Pantagruelists—these interpretations are either
things that the Master himself would have delighted to
satirise, and would have satirised unsurpassably, or, at
best, mere superfluities and supererogations.   At any rate
there is no possibility of finding in them the magic spell—
the " Fastrada's ring," which binds youth and age alike
to the unique " Alcofribas Nasier."

One must, it is supposed, increase the dose of respect
(though some people, in some cases, find it hard) when
considering a further quality or property—the Riddle-
attraction of Rabelais.   This riddle-attraction—or attractions, for it might be better spoken of in a very large
plural—is of course quite undeniable in itself.   There
are as many second intentions in the ordinary sense,
apparently obvious in *Gargantua* and *Pantagruel*, as there
can have been in the scholastic among the dietary of
La Quinte, or of any possible Chimaera buzzing at
greatest intensity in the extremest vacuum.   On the
other hand, some of us are haunted by the consideration,
" Was there ever any human being more likely than
François Rabelais to echo (with the slightest change)
the words ascribed to Divinity in that famous piece which
is taken, on good external and ultra-internal evidence, to
be Swift's ?

> *I* to such block-heads set my wit !
> *I* [*pose*] such fools !   Go, go—you're bit."

And there is not wanting, amongst us sceptics, a further
section who are quite certain that a not inconsiderable
proportion of the book is not allegory at all, but sheer
" bamming," while others again would transfer the
hackneyed death-bed saying from author to book, and
say that the whole Chronicle is " a great perhaps."

These things—or at least elaborate discussions of
them—lie somewhat, though not so far as may at

first seem, outside our proper business. It must, however, once more be evident, from the facts
and very nature of the case, that the puzzles,
the riddles, the allegories cannot constitute
the main and, so to speak, "universal"
part of the attraction of the book. They

And dismissed as affecting the general attraction of the book.

may be a seasoning to some, a solid cut-and-come-
again to others, but certainly not to the majority.
Even in *Gulliver*—the Great Book's almost, perhaps
quite, as great descendant—these attractions, though
more universal in appeal and less evasively presented,
certainly do not hold any such position. The fact is
that both Rabelais and Swift were consummate tellers
of a story, and (especially if you take the *Polite Conversation* into Swift's claim) consummate originators of the
Novel or larger story, with more than "incidental"
attraction itself. But we are not now busied with Swift.

Not much serious objection will probably be taken
to the place allotted to Master Francis as a tale-teller
pure and simple, although it cannot be said
that all his innumerable critics and commentators have laid sufficient stress on this. From
the uncomfortable birth of Gargantua to the

Which lies, largely if not wholly, in its story-interest.

triumphant recessional scene from the Oracle of the
Bottle, proofs are to be found in every book, every
chapter almost, and indeed almost every page; and a
little more detail may be given on this head later. But
the presentation of Rabelais as a novelist-before-novels
may cause more demur, and even suggest the presence
of the now hopelessly discredited thing—paradox itself.
Of course, if anybody requires regular plot as a necessary
constituent, only paradox could contend for that. It
has been contended—and rightly enough—that in the
general scheme and the two (or if you take in Grandgousier, three) generations of histories of the good
giants, Rabelais is doing nothing more than parody—
is, indeed, doing little more than simply follow the
traditions of Romance—Amiles and Jourdains, Guy and
Rembrun, and many others. But some of us regard

plot as at best a full-dress garment, at the absence of
which the good-natured God or Muse of fiction is quite
willing to wink.   Character, if seldom elaborately presented, except in the case of Panurge, is showered, in
scraps and sketches, all over the book, and description
and dialogue abound.

But it is not on such beggarly special pleading as this
that the claim shall be founded.   It must rest on the
Contrast of unceasing, or practically unceasing, impetus of
the *Moyen* story-interest which carries the reader through.
de Parvenir. A remarkably useful contrast-parallel in this
respect, may be found in that strange book, the
Moyen de Parvenir.   I am of those who think that it
had something to do with Rabelais, that there is some
of his stuff in it, even that he may have actually planned
something like it.   But the " make-up " is not more
inferior in merit to that of *Gargantua* and *Pantagruel*
than it is different in kind.   The *Moyen de Parvenir* is
full of separate stories of the *fabliau* kind, often amusing
and well told, though exceedingly gross as a rule.   These
stories are " set " in a framework of promiscuous conversation, in which a large number of great real persons,
ancient and modern, and a smaller one of invented
characters, or rather names, take part.   Most of this,
though not quite all, is mere *fatrasie*, if not even mere
jargon : and though there are glimmerings of something
more than sense, they are, with evident deliberation,
enveloped in clouds of nonsense.   The thing is not a
whole at all, and the stories have as little to do with each
other or with any general drift as if they were professedly—
what they are practically—a bundle of *fabliaux* or *nouvelles*.
As always happens in such cases—and as the author,
whether he was Béroalde or another, whether or not
he worked on a canvas greater than he could fill, or tried
to patch together things too good for him, no doubt
intended—attempts have been made to interpret the
puzzle here also ; but they are quite obviously vain.

Such a sentence, however, cannot be pronounced in
any such degree or measure on the similar attempts in

the case of *Gargantua* and *Pantagruel*; for a reason

A general which some readers may find unexpected.
theme The unbroken vigour—unbroken even by the
possible. obstacles which it throws in its own way,
like the Catalogue of the Library of Saint-Victor and
the burlesque lists of adjectives, etc., which fill up whole
chapters—with which the story or string of stories is
carried on, may naturally suggest that there *is* a story or
at least a theme. It is a sort of quaint alteration or
catachresis of *Possunt quia posse videntur*. There must
be a general theme, because the writer is so obviously
able to handle any theme he chooses. It may be wiser—
it certainly seems so to the present writer—to disbelieve
in anything but occasional sallies—episodes, as it were,
or even digressions—of political, religious, moral, social
and other satire. It is, on the other hand, a most important thing to admit the undoubted presence—now
and then, and not unfrequently—of a deliberate dropping of the satiric and burlesque mask. This supplies
the presentation of the serious, kindly, and human
personality of the three princes (Grandgousier, Gargantua,
and Pantagruel); this the schemes of education (giving

A reference so large a proportion of the small bulk of *not-*
—to be nonsense written on that matter). Above all,
taken up
later—to the this permits, to one taste at least, the exquisite
last Book. presentation of La Quinte and the fresh roses
in her hand, the originality of which, not only in the
whole book in one sense, but in the particular Book in
the other, is, to that taste, and such argumentative
powers as accompany it, an almost absolute proof of
that Book's genuineness. For if it had been by another
who, *un*like Rabelais, had a special tendency towards
such graceful imagination, he could hardly have refrained
from showing this elsewhere in this long book.[1]

---

[1] A complete argument on this much vexed subject can hardly be wished for here :
but it may be permitted to say that nearly fifty years' consideration of the matter has
left less and less doubt in my mind as to the genuineness of the "*Quart*" or "*Quint*"
Livre as it is variously called—according as *Gargantua* is numbered separately or not.
One of the apparently strongest arguments against its genuineness—the constant presence
of "*Je*" in the narrative—really falls, with the others—the fiercer and more outspoken
character of the satire, the somewhat lessened prominence of Pantagruel, etc. etc.—

But however this may be, it is certain that a critical
reader, especially when he has reason to be startled by
Running the external, if not actually extrinsic, oddities
survey of and excesses of the book, will be justified in
the whole. allowing—it may almost be said that he is
likely to allow—the extraordinary volume of concaten-
ated fictitious interest in the whole book or books. The
usual and obvious " catenations " are indeed almost
ostentatiously wanting. The absence of any real plot
has been sufficiently commented on, with the temptations
conferred by it to substitute a fancied unity of purpose.
The birth, and what we may call the two educations, of
Gargantua ; the repetition, with sufficient differences,
of the same plan in the opening of *Pantagruel*; the
appearance of Panurge and the campaign against the
Dipsodes ; the great marriage debate ; and the voyage
to the Oracle of the Bottle, are connected merely in
" chronicle " fashion. The character-links are hardly
stronger, for though Friar John does play a more or less
important part from almost the beginning to quite the
end, Panurge, the most important and remarkable single
figure, does not appear for a considerable time, and the
rest are shadows. The scene is only in one or two
chapters nominally placed in Nowhere ; but as a whole
it is Nowhere Else, or rather a bewildering mixture of
topical assignments in a very small part of France, and

before one simple consideration. We know from the dates of publication of the other
books that Rabelais was by no means a rapid writer, or at any rate that, if he wrote
rapidly, he " held up " what he did write long, and pretty certainly rewrote a good deal.
Now the previous Book had appeared only a short time before what must have been
the date of his death ; and this could not, according to analogy and precedent, have been
ready, or anything like ready, when he died. On the other hand, time enough passed
between his death and the publication (even of the *Ile Sonnante* fragment) for the MS. to
have passed through other hands and to have been adulterated, even if it was not, when the
Master's hands left it, in various, as well as not finally finished form. I can see nothing
in it really inconsistent with the earlier Books ; nothing unworthy of them (especially
if on the one hand possible meddling, and on the other imperfect revision be allowed
for) ; and much, especially the *Chats Fourrés*, the Quintessence part, and the Conclusion,
without which the whole book would be not only incomplete but terribly impoverished.
I may add that, having a tolerably full knowledge of sixteenth-century French literature,
and a great admiration of it, I know no single other writer or group of other writers
who could, in my critical judgment, by any reasonable possibility have written this
Book. François Rabelais could have done it, and I have no doubt that he did it ;
though whether we have it as he left it no man can say.

I

allegorical or fantastic descriptions of a multitude of Utopias. And yet, once more, it *is* a whole story. As you read it you almost forget what lies behind, you quite forget the breaches of continuity, and press on to what is before, almost as eagerly, if not quite in the same fashion, as if the incidents and the figures were not less exciting than those of *Vingt Ans Après*. Let us hope it may not be excessive to expend a few pages on a sketch of this strange story that is no story, with, it may be, some fragments of translation or paraphrase (for, as even his greatest translator, Urquhart, found, a certain amount of his own *Fay ce que voudras* is necessary with Rabelais) here and there.

Master Francis does not exactly plunge into the middle of things ; but he spends comparatively little time on the preliminaries of the ironical Prologue to the " very illustrious drinkers," on the traditionally necessary but equally ironical genealogy of the hero, on the elaborate verse *amphigouri* of the *Fanfreluches Antidotées*, and on the mock scientific discussion of extraordinarily prolonged periods of pregnancy. Without these, however, he will not come to the stupendous banquet of tripe (properly washed down, and followed by pleasant revel on the "echoing green ") which determined the advent of Gargantua into the world, which enabled Grandgousier, more fortunate than his son on a future occasion, to display his amiability as a husband and a father unchecked by any great sorrow, and which was, as it were, crowned and sealed by that son's first utterance—no miserable and ordinary infant's wail, but the stentorian barytone "*A boire !* " which rings through the book till it passes in the sharper, but not less delectable treble of " *Trinq !* " And then comes a brief piece, not narrative, but as characteristic perhaps of what we may call the ironical *moral* of the narrative as any—a grave remonstrance with those who will not believe in *ceste estrange nativité*.

Gargantua.

I doubt me ye believe not this strange birth assuredly. If ye disbelieve, I care not ; but a respectable man—a man of good sense

—*always* believes what people tell him and what he finds written.
Does not Solomon say (Prov. xiv.), " The innocent
[simple] believeth every word " etc. ? And St. Paul
(1 Cor. xiii.), "Charity believeth all things"? Why
should you *not* believe it ? "Because," says you, "there
is no probability[1] in it." I tell you that for this very and only reason
you ought to believe with a perfect faith. For the Sorbonists say
that faith is the evidence of things of no probability.[2] Is it
against our law or our faith ? against reason ? against the Sacred
Scriptures ?[3] For my part I can find nothing written in the
Holy Bible which is contrary thereto. But if the Will of God
had been so, would you say that He could not have done it ?
Oh for grace' sake do not make a mess of your wits in such
vain thoughts. For I tell you that nothing is impossible with God.

(The birth and education.)

And Divinity being done with, the Classics and pure
fantasy are drawn upon ; the incredulous being finally
knocked down by a citation from Pliny, and a polite
request not to bother any more.

This is, of course, the kind of passage which has been
brought against Rabelais, as similar ones have been
brought against Swift, to justify charges of impiety. But,
again, it is not necessary to bother (*tabuster*) about that.
Any one who cannot see that it is the foolish use of
reverend things and not the things themselves that the
satire hits, is hardly worth argument. But there is no
doubt that this sort of mortar, framework, menstruum,
canvas, or whatever way it may be best metaphored,
helps the apparent continuity of the work marvellously,
leaving, as it were, no rough edges or ill-mended joints.
It is, to use an admirable phrase of Mr. Balfour's about
a greater matter, " the logical glue which holds together
and makes intelligible the multiplicity " of the narrative
units, or perhaps instead of " intelligible " one should
here say " appreciable."

---

[1] It is perhaps hardly necessary, but may not be quite idle, to observe that our
Abstractor of Quintessence takes good care not to quote the other half of the parallelism,
"but the prudent looketh well to his going."

[2] It is possible, but not certain, that he is playing on the two senses of the word
apparence, the ambiguity of which is not so great in English. The A.V., "evidence of
things *not seen*," would not have suited his turn.

[3] In which, it will be remembered, the "liquor called punch," which one notes
with sorrow that Rabelais knew not, but which he certainly would have approved, is
also " nowhere spoken against."

Sometimes the " glue " of ironic comment rather saturates these units of narrative than surrounds or interjoins them, and this is the case with what follows. The infantine peculiarities of Gargantua; his dress and the mystery of its blue and white colours (the blue of heaven and the white of the joy of earth); how his governesses and he played together; what smart answers he made; how he became early both a poet and an experimental philosopher—all this is recounted with a marvellous mixture of wisdom and burlesque, though sometimes, no doubt, with rather too much of *haut goût* seasoning. Then comes the, in Renaissance books, inevitable " Education " section, and it has been already noted briefly how different this is from most of its group (the corresponding part of *Euphues* may be suggested for comparison). Even Rabelais does not escape the main danger—he neglects a little to listen to the wisest voice, " Can't you let him alone ? " But the contrasts in the case of Gargantua, the general tenor (that good prince profiting by his own experience for his son's benefit) in that of Pantagruel, are not too " improving," and are made by their historian's " own sauce " exceedingly piquant. Much as has been written on the subject, it is not easy to be quite certain how far the " Old " Learning was fairly treated by the " New." Rabelais and Erasmus and the authors of the *Epistolae Obscurorum Virorum* are such a tremendous overmatch for any one on the other side, that the most judicial as well as judicious of critics must be rather puzzled as to the real merits of the case. But luckily there is no need to decide. Enjoyment, not decision, is the point, and there is no difficulty in *that*. How Gargantua was transferred from the learned but somewhat, as the vulgar would say, " stick-in-the-mud " tutorship of Master Thubal Holofernes, who spent eighteen years in reading *De Modis Significandi* with his pupil, and Master Jobelin Bridé, who has " become a name "—not exactly of honour; how he was transferred to the less antiquated guidance of Ponocrates, and set out for Paris on the famous dappled

mare, whose exploits in field and town were so alarming,
and who had the bells of Notre Dame hung round her
neck, till they were replaced rather after than because
of the remonstrance of Master Janotus de Bragmardo ;
how for a time, and under Sorbonic direction, he wasted
that time in short and useless study, with long intervals
of card - playing, sleeping, etc. etc., and of course a
great deal of eating and drinking, " not as he ought and
as he ought not "—all this leads up to the moment when
the sage Ponocrates takes him again in hand, and institutes
a strenuous drill in manners, studies, manly exercises,
and the like, ending with one of those extraordinary
flashes of perfect style and noble meaning which it pleases
Rabelais to emit from what some call his " dunghill "
and others his " marine-store."

Also they prayed to God the Creator, adoring Him, and solemnly
repledging to Him their faith, and glorifying Him for His boundless
goodness ; while, giving Him thanks for all time past, they commended themselves to His divine mercy for all the future.   This
done, they turned to their rest.

It is only after this serious training that the first
important division of what may be called the action
begins—the " War of the Cakes," in which
certain outrageous bakers, subjects of King
Picrochole of Lerné, first refuse the custom of the good
Grandgousier's shepherds, and then violently assault
them, the incident being turned by the choleric monarch
into a *casus belli* against the peaceful one.   Invasion, the
early triumph of the aggressor, the triumphant appearance of the invincible Friar John, and the complete
turning of the tables by the advent of Gargantua and his
terrible mare, follow each other in rapid and brilliant
telling, and perhaps no parts of the book are better
known.   The extraordinary felicity with which Rabelaisian irony—here kept in quieter but intenser activity
than almost anywhere else—seizes and renders the
common causes, excuses, manners, etc., of war can
never have escaped competent readers ; but it must

The war.

have struck more persons of late than perhaps at any former time. It would be impertinent to particularise largely; but if the famous adaptation and amplification of the old Pyrrhus story in the counsel of Spadassin and Merdaille to Picrochole were printed in small type as the centre of a fathom-square sheet, the whole margin could be more than filled with extracts, from German books and newspapers, of advice to Kaiser Wilhelm II. Nor is there anything, in literature touching history, where irony has bitten more deeply and lastingly into Life and Time than the brief record of Picrochole's latter days after his downfall.

He was informed by an old hag that his kingdom would be restored to him at the coming of the Cocqsigrues: since then it is not certainly known what has become of him. However, I have been told that he now works for his poor living at Lyons, and is as choleric as ever. And always he bemoans himself to strangers about the Cocqsigrues—yet with a certain hope, according to the old woman's prophecy, that at their coming he will be reinstated in his kingdom.

Edward FitzGerald would have called this "terrible"; and perhaps it is.

But there is much more humour than terror in the rest, and sometimes there are qualities different from either. The rescue of the sacred precincts of the Abbey of Seuillé from the invaders by that glorious monk (a personage at no great remove from our own Friar Tuck, to the later portraits of whom he has lent some of his own traits) pleases the soul well, as do the feats of Gymnast against Tripet, and the fate of the unlucky Touquedillon, and the escalade of La Roche Clermande, and (a little less perhaps) the pure burlesque of the eating of the pilgrims, and the combing out of the cannon balls, and the contrasted sweet reasonableness of the amiable though not at all cowardly Grandgousier. But the advice of the Evil Counsellors to Picrochole is still perhaps the pearl:

Then there appeared before Picrochole the Duke of Mennail, Count Spadassin, and Captain Merdaille, and said to him, "Sire,

this day we make you the most happy and chivalrous prince that
ever has been since the death of Alexander of Macedon."

The Counsel to Picrochole. "Be covered, be covered," said Picrochole. "Gramercy, sire," said they, "but we know our duty.
The means are as follows. You will leave here in
garrison some captain with a small band of men to hold the place,
which seems to us pretty strong, both by nature and by the fortifica-
tions you have contrived. You will, as you know well, divide your
army in half. One half will fall upon this fellow Grandgousier and
his people, and easily discomfit him at the first assault. There we
shall gain money in heaps, for the rascal has plenty. (Rascal we
call him, because a really noble prince never has a penny. To
hoard is the mark of a rascal.)

"The other part will meanwhile draw towards Aunis, Saintonge,
Angoumois, and Gascony, as well as Perigord, Medoc, and Elanes.
Without any resistance they will take towns, castles, and fortresses.
At Bayonne, at St. Jean de Luz, and at Fontarabia you will seize
all the ships, and coasting towards Galicia and Portugal, will
plunder all the seaside places as far as Lisbon, where you will be
reinforced with all the supplies necessary to a conqueror: *Corbleu !*
Spain will surrender, for they are all poltroons. You will pass
the Straits of Seville,[1] and will there erect two columns more
magnificent than those of Hercules for the perpetual memory of
your name. And that Strait shall thenceforward be named the
Sea of Picrochole.

"When that sea has been passed, lo ! comes Barbarossa[2] to
surrender as your slave." "I," said Picrochole, "will extend
mercy to him." "Very well," said they, "on condition that he
is baptized. And then you will assault the kingdoms of Tunis, of
Hippo,[3] of Argier, of Bona, of Corona—to cut it short, all Barbary.
Going further,[4] you will keep in your hands Majorca, Minorca,
Sardinia, Corsica, and the other islands of the Ligurian and Balearic
sea. Coasting to the left[5] you will dominate all Narbonese
Gaul, Provence, the Allobroges, Genoa, Florence, Lucca, and,
begad ! Rome. Poor master Pope is already dying for fear of
you." "I will never kiss his slipper," said Picrochole.

"Italy being taken, behold Naples, Calabria, Apulia, and Sicily

---

[1] Original "Sibyle." I owe to Prof. Ker an important reminder (which I ought not
to have needed) of Dante's "Sibilia" in the famous "Ulysses" passage, *Inf.* xxvi. 110.

[2] The Turkish corsair, not the German Emperor.

[3] Probably erected into a kingdom in honour of St. Augustine.

[4] *Passant oultre*—one of Rabelais' favourite and most *polymorphic* expressions. It
has nearly always an ironical touch in it ; and it enjoys a chapter all to itself in that
mood—V. xvii.

[5] Perhaps this *à gauche* might make as good a short test as any of a reader's sense
of humour. But here also a possible Dantean reminiscence (not suggested to me this
time) comes in ; for in the lines already quoted "dalla man *destra*" occurs.

all at your mercy, and Malta into the bargain. I should like to see those funny knights, formerly of Rhodes, resist you ! if it were only to examine their water." "I should like," said Picrochole, "to go to Loretto." "No, no," said they, "that will be on the way back. Thence we shall take Candia, Cyprus, Rhodes, and the Cyclades, and make a set at Morea. We shall get it at once. By St. Treignan, God keep Jerusalem ! for the soldan is nothing in power to you." "Shall I," said he, "then rebuild the Temple of Solomon ?" "Not yet," said they, "wait a little. Be not so hasty in your enterprises."

And so with the most meticulous exactness (Rabelais' geography is irreproachable, and he carefully avoids the cheap expedient of making Spadassin and Merdaille blunder) and the sagest citations of *Festina lente*, they take him through Asia Minor to the Euphrates and Arabia, while the other army (that which has annihilated Grandgousier) comes round by the northern route, sweeping all Europe from Brittany and the British Isles to Constantinople, where the great rendezvous is made and the universal empire established, Picrochole graciously giving his advisers Syria and Palestine as their fiefs.

"Pretty much like our own days," said Mr. Rigmarole. Have we not heard something very like this lately, as "Berlin to Baghdad," if not "Calais to Calcutta"? And even if we had not, would not the sense and the satire of it be delectable ? A great deal has been left out : the chapter is, for Rabelais, rather a long one. The momentary doubt of the usually undoubting Picrochole as to what they shall drink in the desert, allayed at once by a beautiful scheme of commissariat camels and elephants,[1] which would have done credit to the most modern A.S.C., is very capital. There is, indeed, an unpleasant Echephron [2] who points the old moral of Cineas to Pyrrhus himself. But Picrochole rebuffs him with the invaluable *Passons oultre*, and closes the discussion by anticipating Henri Quatre (who, no doubt, learnt the

---

[1] The King is, however, more difficult to satisfy on this point than on others ; and objects with a delightful *preterite*, "Yes : but we *did not get* our wine fresh and cool " ; whereat they rebuke him with a respectful reminder that great conquerors cannot be always entirely comfortable.
[2] "Suspender of judgment."

phrase from him), crying, " *Qui m'aime, si me suive !* " and ordering all haste in the war.

It is possible that, here or earlier, the not-quite-so-gentle-as-he-is-traditionally-called reader may ejaculate, " This is all true enough ; but it is all very well known, and does not need recapitulation." Is this quite so certain ? No doubt at one time Englishmen did know their Rabelais well. Southey did, for instance, and so, according to the historian of Barsetshire, did, in the next generation, Archdeacon Grantly. More recently my late friend Sir Walter Besant spent a great deal of pains on Master Francis, and mainly owing to his efforts there existed for some years a Rabelais Club (already referred to), which left some pleasant memories. But *is* it quite so certain that the average educated Englishman can at once distinguish Eudemon from Epistemon, give a correct list of the various answers to Panurge's enquiries as to the probable results of his marriage, relate what happened when (as glanced at above and returned to later) *nous passasmes oultre,* and say what the adorable Quintessence admitted to her dainty lips besides second intentions ? I doubt it very much. Even special students of the Great Book, as in other cases, have too often allowed themselves to be distracted from the pure enjoyment of it by idle questions of the kinds above mentioned and others—questions of dates and names and places, of origins and borrowings and imitations—questions the sole justification of which, from the genuine Pantagruelian point of view, is that their utter dryness inevitably suggests the cries—the Morning Hymn and the Evening Voluntary of the book itself—*A boire !* and *Trinq.*

But, even were this not so, a person who has undertaken, wisely or unwisely, to write the history of the French Novel is surely entitled to lay some stress on what seems to him the importance of this its first eminent example. At any rate he proposes *not* to *passer oultre,* but to stick to the line struck out, and exhibit, in reasonable detail, the varieties of novel-matter and manner contained in the book.

The conclusion of *Gargantua*—after the victor has addressed a *concio* to the vanquished, has mildly punished the originators of the trouble or those he could catch (Spadassin and Merdaille having run away " six hours before the battle ") by setting them to work at his newly established printing-press, and has distributed gifts and estates to his followers —may be one of the best known parts of the whole book, but is not of the most strictly novel character, though it has suggested at least one whole novel and parts or pass-ages of others. The " Abbey of Thelema "—the home of the order of *Fay ce que vouldras*—is, if not a devout, a grandiose imagination, and it gives occasion for some admirable writing. But it is one of the purest exercises of " purpose," and one of the least furnished with incident or character, to be found in Rabelais. In order to introduce it, he may even be thought guilty of what is extremely rare with him, a fault of " keeping." He avoids this fault surprisingly in the contrasted burlesque and serious chronicles of Grandgousier and Gargantua himself, as well as in the expanded contrast of Pantagruel and Panurge. Yet the heartiest admirer of " Friar John of the Funnels " (or " Collops," for there is a schism on this point) may fail to see in him a suitable or even a possible Head for an assemblage of gallant gentlemen and stately ladies (both groups being also accomplished scholars) like the Thelemites. But Rabelais, like Shake-speare, had small care for small objections. He wanted to sketch a Paradise of Anti-Monkery, and for this he wanted an Anti-Abbot. Friar John was the handiest person, and he took him. But it is worth noting that the Abbot of Thelema never afterwards appears as such, or in the slightest relation to this miniature but most curious and interesting example of the Renaissance fancy for imaginary countries, cities, institutions, with its splendours of architecture and decoration, its luxurious but not loose living, its gallantry and its learning, its gorgeous dress, its polished manners (the Abbot must have had some trouble to learn them), and its " inscrip-

The peace and the Abbey of Thelema.

tions and enigmas " in verse which is not quite so happy
as the prose. One would not cut it out of the book for
anything, and parallels to it (not merely of the kind above
referred to) have found and may find place in other books
of fiction. But it is only a sort of chantry, in the Court
of the Gentiles too, of the mighty Temple of the Novel.

What it was exactly that made Rabelais " double,"
as it were, on *Gargantua* in the early books of *Pantagruel* [1]
Pantagruel I. it would probably be idle to enquire. His
The deliberate mention in the Prologue of some of
contrasted the most famous romances (with certain others
youth. vainly to be sought now or at any time) might
of course most easily be a mere red herring. It may be,
that as *Gargantua* was not entirely of his own creation,
he determined to " begin at the beginning " in his
original composition. But it matters little or nothing.
We have, once more, a burlesque genealogy with known
persons—Nimrod, Goliath, Polyphemus, etc. etc.—en-
tangled in a chain of imaginaries, one of the latter,
Hurtaly, forming the subject of a solemn discussion of
the question why he is not received among the crew
of the Ark. The unfortunate concomitants of the birth
of Pantagruel—which is fatal to his mother Badebec—
contrast with the less chequered history of Gargantua
and Gargamelle, while the mixed sorrow and joy of
Gargantua at his wife's death and his son's birth
completes this contrast. Pantagruel, though quite as
amiable as his father, if not more so, has in infancy the
natural awkwardnesses of a giant, and a hairy giant too
—devouring cows whole instead of merely milking them,
and tearing to pieces an unfortunate bear who only licked
his infant chops. As was said above, he has no wild-
oats period of education like his father's, but his company
is less carefully chosen than that of Gargantua in the days
of his reformation, and gives his biographer opportunities
for his sharpest satire.

First we have (taken, as everybody is supposed now

---

[1] Of course the first book of the son *preceded* the reconstructed history of the
father ; but this is immaterial.

to know, from Geoffroy Tory, but improved) the
episode of the Limousin scholar with his ." pedantesque " [1]
deformation of French and Latin at once, till the giant
takes him by the throat and he cries for mercy in the
strongest meridional brogue.[2] Then comes the famous
catalogue of the Library of Saint Victor, a fresh attack
on scholastic and monastic degeneracy, and a kind of
joining hands (Ortuinus figures) with the German
guerrilla against the *Obscuri*, and then a long and admirable letter from Gargantua, whence we learn that Grandgousier is dead, and that his son is now the sagest of
monarchs, who has taken to read Greek, and shows no
memory of his governesses or his earlier student days.
And then again comes Panurge.

Many doubtful things have been said about this most
remarkable personage. He has been fathered upon the
Cingar of Folengo, which is too much of a
compliment to that creation of the great

Panurge.

Macaronic, and Falstaff has been fathered upon him,
which is distinctly unfair to Falstaff. Sir John has
absolutely nothing of the ill-nature which characterises
both Cingar and Panurge ; and Panurge is an actual
and contemptible coward, while many good wits have
doubted whether Falstaff is, in the true sense, a coward
at all. But Panurge is certainly one thing—the first
distinct and striking *character* in prose fiction. Morally,
of course, there is little to be said for him, except that,
when he has no temptations to the contrary, he is a " good
fellow " enough. As a human example of *mimesis* in
the true Greek sense, not of " imitation " but of " fictitious
creation," he is, once more, the first real character in
prose fiction—the ancestor, in the literary sense, of
the mighty company in which he has been followed by
the similar creations of the masters from Cervantes to

[1] The correct opposition of this term (Latin or Greek words vernacularised) to
" Macaronic " (vernacular words turned into Latin or Greek form) is not always
observed.

[2] It is very seldom, after his infantine and innocent excesses, that Pantagruel behaves
thus. He is for the most part a quiet and somewhat reserved prince, very generous,
very wise, very devout, and, though tolerating the eccentricities of Panurge and Friar
John, never taking part in them.

Thackeray. The fantastic colouring, and more than
colouring, of the whole book affects him, of course, more
than superficially. One could probably give some not
quite absurd guesses why Rabelais shaped him as he did
—presented him as a very naughty but intensely clever
child, with the monkey element in humanity thrown
into utmost prominence. But it is better not to do so.
Panurge has some Yahooish characteristics, but he is not
a Yahoo—in fact, there is no misanthropy in Rabelais.[1]
He is not merely impish (as in his vengeance on the lady
of Paris), but something worse than impish (as in that
on Dindenault); and yet one cannot call him diabolic,
because he is so intensely human. It is customary, and
fairly correct, to describe his ethos as that of understanding and wit wholly divorced from morality, chivalry, or
religion ; yet he is never Mephistophelian. If one of
the hundred touches which make him a masterpiece is to
be singled out, it might perhaps be the series of rapturous
invitations to his wedding which he gives to his advisers
while he thinks their advice favourable, and the limitations
of enforced politeness which he appends when the unpleasant side of their opinions turns up. And it may
perhaps be added that one of the chief reasons for believing
heartily in the last Book is the delectable and unimprovable
contrast which La Quinte and her court of intellectual
fantastry present to this picture of intellectual materialism.

It was impossible that such a figure should not to a
certain extent dwarf others ; but Rabelais, unlike some
Short view modern character-mongers, never lets his
of the psychology interfere with his story. After
sequels in a few episodes, the chief of which is the great
Book II. sign-duel of Thaumast and Panurge himself,
the campaign against the Dipsodes at once enables
Pantagruel to display himself as a warlike hero of romance,
permits him fantastic exploits parallel to his father's,
and, by installing Panurge in a lordship of the conquered
country and determining him, after " eating his corn in

[1] If Swift had drunk more wine and had not put water in what he did drink, possibly this quality might have been lessened in *him*.

the blade," to "marry and settle," introduces the larger and most original part of the whole work—the debates and counsellings on the marriage in the Third Book, and, after the failure of this, the voyage to settle the matter at the Oracle of the Bottle in the Fourth and Fifth. This "plot," if it may be called so, is fairly central and continuous throughout, but it gives occasion for the most surprising "alarums and excursions," variations and divagations, of the author's inexhaustible humour, learning, inventive fertility, and never-failing faculty of telling a tale. If the book does sometimes in a fashion "hop forty paces in the public street," and at others gambade in a less decorous fashion even than hopping, it is also Cleopatresque in its absolute freedom from staleness and from tedium.

The Third Book has less of apparent variety in it, and less of what might be called striking incident, than any of the others, being all but wholly occupied by the enquiries respecting the marriage of Panurge. But this gives it a "unity" which is of itself attractive to some tastes, while the delightful sonnet to the spirit of Marguerite,

Pantagruel II. (Book III.) The marriage of Panurge and the consultations on it.

Esprit abstraict, ravy et ecstatique,

(perhaps the best example of *rhétoriqueur* poetry), at the beginning, and the last sight (except in letters) of Gargantua at the end, with the curious *coda* on the "herb Pantagruelion" (the ancestor of Joseph de Maistre's famous eulogy of the Executioner), give, as it were, handle and top to it in unique fashion. But the body of it is the thing. The preliminary outrunning of the constable—had there been constables in Salmigondin, but they probably knew the story of the Seigneur of Basché too well—and the remarkable difference between the feudatory and his superior on the subject of debt, serve but as a whet to the project of matrimony which the debtor conceives. Of course, Panurge is the very last man whom a superficial observer of humanity—the very

first whom a somewhat profounder student thereof—
would take as a marrying one. He is " a little failed " ;
he thinks to rest himself while not foregoing his former
delights, and he shuts eyes and ears to the proverb, as
old as Greek in words and as old as the world in fact,
that ." the doer shall suffer." That he should consult
Pantagruel is in the circumstances almost a necessity,
and Pantagruel's conduct is exactly what one would
expect from that good-natured, learned, admirable, but
rather enigmatic personage. Merely " aleatory " decision—by actual use of dice—he rejects as illicit, though
towards the close of the book one of its most delectable
episodes ends in his excusing Mr. Justice Bridoye for
settling law cases in that way. But he recommends the
sortes Virgilianae, and he, others, and Panurge himself
add the experiment of dreams, and the successive con-
sultation of the Sibyl of Panzoust, the dumb Nazdecabre,
the poet Raminagrobis, Epistemon, " Her Trippa,"
Friar John himself, the theologian Hippothadée, the
doctor Rondibilis, the philosopher Trouillogan, and the
professional fool Triboulet. No reader of the most
moderate intelligence can need to be told that the counsellors opine all in the same sense (unfavourable), though
with more or less ambiguity, and that Panurge, with
equal obstinacy and ingenuity, invariably twists the
oracles according to his own wishes. But what no
reader, who came fresh to Rabelais and fasting from
criticism on him, could anticipate, is the astonishing
spontaneity of the various dealings with the same problem,
the zest and vividness of the whole thing, and the unceasing shower of satire on everything human—general,
professional, and individual—which is kept up throughout. There is less pure extravagance, less mere farce,
and (despite the subject) even less " sculduddery " than
in any other Book ; but also in no other does Rabelais
" keep up with humanity " (somewhat, indeed, in the
fashion in which a carter keeps up with his animal,
running and lashing at the same time) so triumphantly.

In no book, moreover, are the curious intervals—or,

as it were, prose choric odes—of interruption more remarkable. Pantagruel's own serious wisdom supplies
not a few of them, and the long and very characteristic
episode of Judge Bridoye and his decision by throw of
dice is very loosely connected with the main subject.
But the most noteworthy of these excursions comes, as has
been said, at the end—the last personal appearance of the
good Gargantua, and the famous discourse, several chapters
long, on the Herb Pantagruelion, otherwise Hemp.

The Fourth Book (Third of *Pantagruel*) starts the
voyage, and begins to lead the commentator who insists
Pantagruel on fixing and interpreting the innumerable real
III. (IV.) or apparent double, treble, and almost cen-
The first
part of the tuple meanings, into a series of dances almost
voyage. illimitable. As has been suggested more than
once, the most reasonable way is probably to regard the
whole as an intentional mixture of covert satire, pure
fooling, not a little deliberate leading astray, and (serving
as vehicle and impelling force at once) the irresistible
narrative impulse animating the writer and carrying the
reader on to the end—any end, if it be only the Other
End of Nowhere. The " curios," living and other, of
Medamothi (Nowhere to begin with !), and the mysterious
appearance of a shipful of travellers coming back from
the Land of Lanterns, whither the Pantagruelian party
is itself bound ; the rather too severely punished ill-
manners of the sheep-dealer Dindenault ; the strange
isles of various nature—such, especially, as the abode of
the bailiffs and process-servers, which gives occasion to
the admirably told story of François Villon and the
Seigneur of Basché ; the great storm—another of the
most famous passages of the book—with the cowardice
of Panurge and the safe landing in the curious country
of the Macréons (long-livers) ; the evil island where
reigns Quaresmeprenant, and the elaborate analysis of
that personage by the learned Xenomanes ; the alarming
Physeter (blowing whale) and his defeat by Pantagruel ;
the land of the Chitterlings, the battle with them, and the
interview and peace-making with their Queen Niphleseth

(a passage at which the sculduddery - hunters have
worked their hardest), and then the islands of the Pape-
figues and the Papimanes, where Rabelais begins his
most obvious and boldest meddling with the great
ecclesiastical-political questions of the day—all these
things and others flit past the reader as if in an actual
voyage. Even here, however, he rather skirts than
actually invades the most dangerous ground. It is the
Decretals, not the doctrines, that are satirised, and
Homenas, bishop of Papimania, despite his adoration
of these forgeries, and the slightly suspicious number
and prettiness of the damsels who wait upon him, is a very
good fellow and an excellent host. There is something
very soothing in his metaphorical way of demanding
wine from his Hebes, " *Clerice*, esclaire icy," the
necessary illumination being provided by a charming
girl with a hanap of " extravagant " wine. These
agreeable if satiric experiences—for the Decretals do no
harm beyond exciting the bile of Master Epistemon (who,
it is to be feared, was a little of a pedant)—are followed
by the once more almost universally known passage of
the " Frozen Words " and the visit to " Messer Gaster,
the world's first Master of Arts " ; by the islands (once
more mysterious) of Chaneph (hypocrisy) and Ganabin
(thieves) ; the book concluding abruptly with an ultra-
farcical *cochonnerie* of the lower kind, relieved partially by
a libellous but impossible story about our Edward the
Fifth and the poet Villon again, as well as by the appearance of an interesting but not previously mentioned
member of the crew of the *Thalamége* (Pantagruel's flag-
ship), the great cat Rodilardus.

One of the peculiarities of the Fifth Book, and perhaps
one of those which have aroused that suspicion about it
which, after what has been said above, it is not necessary further to discuss, is that it is more " in blocks "
than the others.[1] The eight chapters of the *Isle Sonnante*
take up the satire of the Fourth Book on Papimania

---

[1] The first of these, the *Isle Sonnante*, as is well enough known to all students,
appeared separately and before the rest.

and on the "Papegaut," who is here introduced in a much fiercer tone—a tone which, if one cared for hypothetical criticism, might be attributed with about equal probability to a genuine deepening of hostile feeling, to absence of revision, and to possible sophistication by some one into whose hands it fell between the author's death and its publication. But a perfectly impartial critic, who, on the one hand, does not, in Carlyle's admirable phrase, "regard the Universe as a hunting-field from which it were good and pleasant to drive the Pope," and, on the other, is content to regard the extremer Protestants as singularly unpleasant persons without pronouncing Ernulphus-curses on them, may perhaps fail to find in it either the cleverest or the most amusing part of the voyage. The episode of the next Isle—that *des Ferrements*—is obscure, whether it is or is not (as the commentators were sure to suggest) something else beginning with "obsc-," and the succeeding one, with its rocks fashioned like gigantic dice, is not very amusing. But the terrible country of the *Chats Fourrés* and their chief Grippeminaud— an attack on the Law as unsparing as, and much more vivid than that on the Church in the overture—may rank with the best things in Rabelais. The tyrant's ferocious and double-meaning catchword of *Or çà !* and the power at his back, which even Pantagruel thinks it better rather to run away from than to fight openly, which Panurge frankly bribes, and over which even the reckless and invincible Friar John obtains not much triumph, except that of cutting up, after buying it, an old woman's bed — these and the rest have a grim humour not quite like anything else.

The next section—that of the Apedeftes or Uneducated Ones [1]—has been a special object of suspicion ; it is certainly a little difficult, and perhaps a little dull. One is not sorry when the explorers, in the ambiguous way already noted, "*passent*

Marginal notes:
Pantagruel IV. (Book V.) The second part of the voyage. The "Isle Sonnante."

The "Chats Fourrés."

"La Quinte."

---

[1] A sort of dependency or province of the *Chats Fourrés*.

Oultre," and, after difficulties with the wind, come to
" the kingdom of Quintessence, named Entelechy."
Something has been said more than once of this already,
and, it is perhaps unnecessary to say more, or indeed
anything, except to those who themselves " hold of La
Quinte," and who for that very reason require no talking
about her.   " We " (if one may enrol oneself in their
company) would almost rather give up Rabelais altogether
than sacrifice this delightful episode, and abandon the
idea of having the ladies of the Queen for our partners in
Emmelie, and Calabrisme, and the thousand other dances,
of watching the wonderful cures by music, and the interesting process of throwing, not the house out of the window,
but the window out of the house, and the miraculous and
satisfactory transformation of old ladies into young girls,
with very slight alteration of their former youthful selves,
and all the charming topsyturvifications of Entelechy.
Not to mention the gracious if slightly unintelligible
speeches of the exquisite princess, when clear Hesperus
shone once more, and her supper of pure nectar and
ambrosia (not grudging more solid viands to her visitors),
and the great after-supper chess-tournament with living
pieces, and the " invisible disparition " of the lady, and the
departure of the fortunate visitors themselves, duly inscribed and registered as Abstractors of Quintessence.
The whole is like a good dream, and is told so as almost
to be one.

Between this and the final goal of the Country of
Lanterns the interest falls a little.   The island of " Odes "
(not " poems " but " ways "), where the " walks walk "
(*les chemins cheminent*) ; that of " Esclots " (" clogs "),
where dwell the Frères Fredonnants, and where the attack
on monkery is renewed in a rather unsavoury and rather
puerile fashion ; and that of Satin, which is a sort of
Medamothi rehandled, are not first-rate—they would
have been done better, or cut out, had the book ever been
issued by Master Francis.   But the arrival at and the
sojourn in Lanternia itself recovers the full powers of
Rabelais at his best, though one may once more think

that some of the treatment might have been altered in the case just mentioned.

Apart from the usual mixture of serious and purely jocular satire, of learning and licence, of jargonic cata- *The con-* logues, of local references to Western France *clusion and* and the general topography of Utopia, *The Bottle.* this conclusion consists of two main parts— first, a most elaborate description of the Temple, containing underground the Oracle of the Bottle, to which the pilgrims are conducted by a select " Lantern,", and of its priestess Bacbuc, its *adytum* with a fountain, and, in the depth and centre of all, the sacred Bottle itself; and secondly, the ceremonies of the delivery of the Oracle; the divine utterance, *Trinq !* its interpretation by Bacbuc; the very much *ad libitum* reinterpretations of the interpretation by Panurge and Friar John, and the dismissal of the pilgrims by the priestess, *Or allez de par Dieu, qui vous conduise !* [1]

What, it may be asked, is the object of this cumbrous analysis of certainly one of the most famous and (as it at least should be) one of the best known books of the world ? That object has been partly indicated already; but it may be permissible to set it forth more particularly before ending this chapter. Of the importance, on the one hand, of the acquisition by the novel of the greatest known and individual writer of French up to his date, and of the enormous popularity of this example of it, enough may have been said. But the abstract has been given, and the further comment is now added, with the purpose of showing, in a little detail, how immensely the resources and inspirations of future practitioners were enriched and strengthened, varied and multiplied, by *Gargantua* and *Pantagruel.* The book as a whole is to be classed, no doubt, as " Eccentric " fiction. But if you compare with Rabelais that one of his followers [2] who possessed

[1] A MS. " addition " unknown to the old printed forms, appears in some modern ones. It is a mere disfigurement : and is hardly likely even to have been a rejected draft.
[2] Not Swift here, but Sterne. There is far higher genius in *Gulliver* than in *Shandy* ; but the former is not a *fatrasie*, the latter is.

most genius and who worked at his following with most
deliberation, you will find an immense falling off in
richness and variety as well as in strength.   The inferiority of Sterne to Master Francis in his serious pieces,
whether he is whimpering over dead donkeys and dying
lieutenants, or simulating honest indignation against
critics, is too obvious to need insistence.   Nor can one
imagine any one—unless, like Mackenzie and other
misguided contemporaries or juniors, he himself wanted
to whimper, or unless he also aimed at the *fatrasie*—
going to Sterne for pattern or inspiration.   Now Rabelais
is a perpetual fount of inspiration, an inexhaustible
magazine of patterns to the most " serious " novelist
whose seriousness is not of the kind designated by that
term in dissenting slang.   That abounding narrative
faculty which has been so much dwelt on touches so
many subjects, and manages to carry along with it so
many moods, thoughts, and even feelings, that it could
not but suggest to any subsequent writer who had in
him the germ of the novelist's art, how to develop and
work out such schemes as might occur to him.   While,
for his own countrymen at least, the vast improvement
which he made in French prose, and which, with the
accomplishment of his younger contemporaries Amyot
and Montaigne, established the greatness of that prose
itself, was a gain, the extent of which cannot be exaggerated.   Therefore it has seemed not improper to give
him a chapter to himself, and to treat his book with a
minuteness not often to be paralleled in this *History*.[1]

---

[1] That the not quite unknown device of setting up a man of straw in order to knock
him down has not been followed in this chapter, a single piece of evidence out of many
may be cited.   H. Körting in his justly well reputed *Geschichte des Franz. Romans im
XVII. Jahrh.* (Oppeln u. Leipzig, 1891, i. 133 *note*) would rule Rabelais out of the
history of the novel altogether.   This book, which will be quoted again with gratitude
later, displays a painstaking erudition not necessitating any make-weight of sympathy
for its author's early death after great suffering.   It is extremely useful ; but it does
not escape, in this and other places, the censure which, ten years before the war of 1914,
the present writer felt it his duty to express on modern German critics and literary
historians generally (*History of Criticism*, London, 1904, vol. iii. Bks. viii. and ix.),
that on points of literary appreciation, as distinguished from mere philology, " enumera-
tion," bibliographical research, and the like, they are " sadly to seek."   It may not be
impertinent to add that Herr Körting's history happened never to have been read by me
till after the above chapter of the present book was written.

CHAPTER VII

THE SUCCESSORS OF RABELAIS AND THE INFLUENCE OF THE "AMADIS" ROMANCES

In the present chapter we shall endeavour to treat two divisions of actual novel- or at least fiction-writing—strikingly opposed to each other in character; and a third subject, to include which in the title would have made that title too long, and which is not strictly a branch of novel-*writing*, but which had perhaps as important an influence on the progress of the novel itself as anything mentioned or to be mentioned in all this *History*. The first division is composed of the followers—sometimes in the full, always in the chronological sense—of Rabelais, a not very strong folk as a rule, but including one brilliant example of co-operative work, and two interesting, if in some degree problematical, persons. The second, strikingly contrasting with the general if not the universal tendency of the first, is the great translated group of *Amadis* romances, which at once revived romance of the older kind itself, and exercised a most powerful, if not an actually generative, influence on newer forms which were themselves to pass into the novel proper. The third is the increasing body of memoir- and anecdote-writers who, with Brantôme at their head, make actual personages and actual events the subjects of a kind of story-telling, not perhaps invariably of unexceptionable historic accuracy, but furnishing remarkable situations of plot and suggestions of character, together with abundant new examples of the " telling " faculty itself.

The last point, as an apparent digression but really a most important contribution to the History, may Subsidiary perhaps be discussed and dismissed first.   All importance persons who have even a slight knowledge of of Brantôme French literature must be aware how early and other character- and how remarkable are its possessions in mongers. what is vaguely called the " Memoir " department.   There is nothing at the time, in any modern literature known to the present writer, similar to Ville-hardouin, or a little later to Joinville,—one might almost say that there is nothing in any literature at any time superior, if there be anything equal, in its kind to Frois-sart.   In the first two cases there is pure personal ex-perience ; in the third there is, of course, a certain amount of precedent writing on the subject for guidance, and a large gathering of information by word of mouth.   But in all these, and to a less extent in others up to the close of the fifteenth century, there is the indefinable gift of treatment—of "telling a story."   In Villehardouin this gift may be almost wholly, and in principle very mainly, limited to the two great subjects which made the mediaeval end as far as profane matters were concerned—fighting and counselling ; but this is by no means the case in Froissart, whom one is sometimes tempted to regard as a Sir Walter Scott thrown away upon base reality.

With the sixteenth century this gift once more burgeoned and spread itself out—dealing, indeed, very mainly with the somewhat ungrateful subject of the religious disputes and wars, but flowering or fruiting into the unsurpassable gossip—though gossip is too undignified a word—of Pierre de Bourdeilles, Abbé de Brantôme, that Froissart and Pepys in one, with the noble delight in noble things of the first, inex-tricably united to the almost innocent shamelessness of the second, and a narrative gift equal to that of either in idiosyncrasy, and ranging beyond the subjects of both. Himself a soldier and a courtier (his abbacy, like many others, was purely titular and profitable—not professional in the least), his favourite subjects in literature, and obviously his idols in life, were great soldiers and fair ladies, "Bayard and the two Marguerites," as some one has put it. And his vivid irregular fashion of writing adapts itself with equal ease to a gallant feat of arms and a ferocious, half-cut-throat duel, to an exquisite piece of sentimental passion like that which tells us the story how the elder Queen of Navarre rebuked the lover carelessly stepping over the grave of his dead mistress, and to an unquotable anecdote to parallel the details of which, in literature of high rank, one must go to Rabelais himself, to Martial, or to Aristophanes. But, whatever the subject, the faculty of lively communication remains unaltered, and the suggestion of its transference from fact (possibly a little coloured) to pure fiction becomes more and more possible and powerful.[1]

No book has been more subject to the "insupportable advances" of the "key"-monger than the *Heptameron*, The *Heptameron*. and the rage for identifying has gone so far that the pretty old name of "Emarsuite" for one of the characters has been discarded for an alleged and much uglier "Ennasuite," which is indeed said to have MS. authority, but which is avowedly preferred because it can be twisted into "*Anne* à Suite" ("Anne in Waiting"), and so can be fastened to an actual Maid of Honour of Marguerite's. It is only fair, however, to admit that something of the kind is at least suggested by the book itself. Even by those who do not trouble themselves in the least about the personages who may

---

[1] This suggestive influence may be found almost as strongly, though shown with less literary craftsmanship, in Brantôme's successor and to some extent overlapper, Note on Montaigne. Tallemant des Réaux. And it is almost needless to say that in both *subjects* for novel treatment "foison," as both French and English would have said in their time. Nor may it be improper to add that Montaigne himself, though more indirectly, assisted in speeding the novel. The actual telling of a story is indeed not his strongest point : the dulness of the *Travels*, if they were really his (on which point the present writer cannot help entertaining a possibly unorthodox doubt), would sufficiently show this. But the great effect which he produced on French prose could not, as in the somewhat similar case of Dryden in English a century later, but prove of immense aid to the novelist. Except in the deliberately eccentric style, as in Rabelais' own case, or in periods such as the Elizabethan and our own, where there is a coterie ready to admire jargon, you cannot write novels, to interest and satisfy readers, without a style, or a group of styles, providing easy and clear narrative media. We shall see how, in the next century, writers in forms apparently still more alien from the novel helped it in the same way.

or may not have been disguised under the names of Nomerfide (the Neifile of this group) and Longarine, Saffredent and Dagoucin and Gebron (Geb*u*ron they call him now), admit the extreme probability of the Queen having invited identification of herself with Parlamente, the younger matron of the party, and of Hircan her husband with the King of Navarre.[1]   But some (among whom is the present writer) think that this delightful and not too well-fated type of Renaissance amorousness, letteredness, and piety combined made a sort of dichotomy of herself here, and intended the personage of Oisille, the elder duenna (though by no means a very stern one) of the party, to stand for her as well as Parlamente—to whom one really must give the Italian pronunciation to get her out of the abominable suggestion of our " talking-machine."

A much more genuinely literary question has been raised and discussed as to the exact authorship of the book.   That it is entirely Marguerite's, not the most jealous admirers of the Queen need for a moment contend.   She is known to have had a sort of literary court from Marot and Rabelais downwards, some of the members of which were actually resident with her, and not a few of whom—such as Boaistuau and Le Maçon, the translators of Bandello and Boccaccio, and Bonaventure Despériers (*v. inf.*)— were positive experts in the short story.   Moreover, the custom of distributing these collections among different

Character and "problems."

---

[1] The character of this Bourbon prince seems to have been very faithfully though not maliciously drawn by Margaret (for the name, *Gallicé pulchrum*, is *Anglicé pulchrius*, and our form may be permitted in a note) as not ungenial, not exactly ungentlemanly, and by no means hating his wife or being at all unkind to her, but constantly " hard " on her in speech, openly regarding infidelity to her as a matter of course, and not a little tinged by the savagery which (one is afraid) the English wars had helped to introduce among the French nobility ; which the religious wars were deepening, and which, in the times of the Fronde, came almost to its very worst, and, though somewhat tamed later, lasted, and was no mean cause, if not so great a one as some think, of the French Revolution. Margaret's love for her brother was ill rewarded in many ways—among others by brutal scandal—and her later days were embittered by failure to protect the new learning and the new faith she had patronised earlier.   But one never forgets Rabelais' address to her, or the different but still delightful piece in which Marot is supposed to have commemorated her Platonic graciousness ; while her portrait, though drawn in the hard, dry manner of the time, and with the tendency of that time to " make a girl's nose a proboscis," is by no means unsuggestive of actual physical charm.

speakers positively invited collaboration in writing. The present critic and his friend, Mr. Arthur Tilley of King's College, Cambridge, who has long been our chief special- ist in the literature of the French Renaissance, are in an amicable difference as to the part which Despériers in particular may have played in the *Heptameron*; but this is of no great importance here, and though Marguerite's other literary work is distinctly inferior in style, it is not impossible that the peculiar tone of the best parts of it, especially as regards the religious-amorous flavour, was infused by her or under her direct influence. The enthusiasm of Rabelais and Marot; the striking anecdote already mentioned which Brantôme, whose mother had been one of Marguerite's maids of honour, tells us, and one or two other things, suggest this; for Despériers was more of a satirist than of an amorist, and though the charges of atheism brought against him are (*v. inf.* again) scarcely supported by his work, he was certainly no pietist. I should imagine that he revised a good deal and sometimes imparted his nervous and manly, but, in his own *Contes*, sometimes too much summarised style. But some striking phrases, such as "*l'impossibilité* de nostre chair,"[1] may be hers, and the following remarkable speech of Parlamente probably expresses her own senti- ments pretty exactly. It is very noteworthy that Hircan, who is generally represented as "taking up" his wife's utterances with a certain sarcasm, is quite silent here.

"Also," said Parlamente, "I have an opinion that never will
Parlamente a man love God perfectly if he has not perfectly loved
on human some of God's creatures in this world." "But what
and divine do you call 'perfect loving'?" said Saffredent.
love. "Do you reckon as perfect lovers those who are
transis,[2] and who adore ladies at a distance, without daring to make

---

[1] This phrase, though Biblical, of course, in spirit, is not, so far as I remember, any- where found textually in Holy Writ. It may be patristic; in which case I shall be glad of learned information. It sounds rather like St. Augustine. But I do not think it occurs earlier in French, and the word *impossibilité* is not banal in the connection.

[2] The famous phrase "*amoureux transi*" is simply untranslatable by any single word in English for the adjective, or rather participle. Its unmetaphorical use is, of course, commonest in the combination *transi de froid*, "frozen," and so suggests in the other a lover shivering actually under his mistress's shut window, or, metaphorically, under her disdain.

their wishes known?" "I call perfect lovers," answered Parlamente, "those who seek in what they love some perfection—be it beauty, kindness, or good grace,—always striving towards virtue ; and such as have so high and honourable a heart, that they would not, were they to die for it, take for their object the base things which honour and conscience disapprove: for the soul, which is only created that it may return to its Sovereign Good, does naught while it is in the body but long for the attainment of this. But because the senses by which alone it can acquire information are darkened and made carnal by the sin of our first father, they can only show her the visible things which approach closest to perfection—and after these the soul runs, thinking to find in outward beauty, in visible grace, and in moral virtue, grace, beauty, and virtue in sovereign degree. But when she has sought them and tried them, and finds not in them Him whom she loves, she leaves them alone,[1] just as a child, according to his age, likes dolls and other trivialities, the prettiest he sees, and thinks a collection of pebbles actual riches, but as he grows up prefers his dolls alive, and gets together the goods necessary for human life. Yet when he knows, by still wider experience, that in earthly things there is neither perfection nor felicity, he desires to seek the Creator and the Source of these. Nevertheless, if God open not the eye of faith in him he would be in danger of becoming, instead of a merely ignorant man, an infidel philosopher.[2] For Faith alone can demonstrate and make receivable the good that the carnal and animal man cannot understand.

This gives the better Renaissance temper perhaps as well as anything to be found, and may, or should in fairness, be set against the worser tone of mere libertinage in which some even of the ladies indulge here, and still more against that savagery which has been noticed above. This undoubtedly was in Milton's mind when he talked of " Lust hard by Hate," and it makes Hircan coolly observe, after a story has been told in which an old

---

[1] The expression (*passe oultre*) commented on in speaking of Rabelais, and again one which has no English equivalent.

[2] A very early example of the special sense given to this word in French increasingly during the sixteenth, seventeenth, and eighteenth centuries, of "freethinker" deepening to "atheist." Johnson's friend, it will be remembered, regarded Philosophy as something to which the irruption of Cheerfulness was fatal ; Butler, as something acquirable by reading Alexander Ross ; a famous ancient saying, as the remembrancer of death ; and a modern usage, as something which has brass and glass "instruments." But it was Hegel, was it not? or Carlyle? who summarised the French view and its time of prevalence in the phrase, "When every one was a philosopher who did not believe in the Devil."

woman successfully interferes to save a girl's chastity, that in the place of the hero he should certainly have killed the hag and enjoyed the girl. This is obviously said in no bravado, and not in the least humorously : and the spirit of it is exemplified in divers not in the least incredible anecdotes of Brantôme's in the generation immediately following, and of Tallemant des Réaux in the next. The religiosity displayed is of a high temper of Christian Platonism, and we cannot, as we can elsewhere, say what the song says of something else, that " it certainly looks very queer." The knights and ladies do go to mass and vespers ; but to say that they go punctually would be altogether erroneous, for Hircan makes wicked jokes on his and Parlamente's being late for the morning office, and, on one occasion at least, they keep the unhappy monks of the convent where they are staying (who do not seem to dare to begin vespers without them) waiting a whole hour while they are finishing not particularly edifying stories. The less complaisant casuists, even of the Roman Church, would certainly look askance at the piety of the distinguished person (said by tradition to have been King Francis himself) who always paid his respects to Our Lady on his way to illegitimate assignations, and found himself the better therefor on one occasion of danger. But the tone of our extract is invariably that of Oisille and Parlamente. The purer love part of the matter is a little, as the French themselves say, " alembicated." But still the whole is graceful and fascinating, except for a few pieces of mere passionless coarseness, which Oisille generally reproves. And it is scarcely necessary to say what large opportunities these tones and colours of fashion and " quality," of passion and manners, give to the future novelist, whose treatment shall stand to them very much as they stand to the shorter and sometimes almost shorthand written tales of Despériers himself.

With the *Cymbalum Mundi* of this rather mysterious person we need have little to do. It is, down to the dialogue-form, an obvious imitation of Lucian—a story

about the ancient divinities (especially Mercury) and a
Despériers. certain " Book of Destiny " and talking animals,
and a good deal of often rather too transparent
allegory.   It has had, both in its own day and since, a
very bad reputation as being atheistical or at least anti-
Christian, and seems really to have had something to do
with the author's death, by suicide or otherwise.   There
need, however, be very little harm in it; and there is not
very much good as a story, nor, therefore, much for us.
It does not carry the art of its particular kind of fiction
any further than Lucian himself, who is, being much
more of a genius, on the whole a much better model,
even taking him at that rather inferior rate.   The
Contes et Joyeux Devis, on the other hand, though the
extreme brevity of some has perhaps sometimes prejudiced readers against them, have always seemed to the
present writer to form the most remarkable book, as
literature, of all the department at the time except *Gargantua* and *Pantagruel* and the *Heptameron*, and to supply
a strong presumption that their author had more than a
minor hand in the *Heptameron* itself.   It must, of course,
be admitted that the fashion in which they are delivered
may not only offend in one direction, but may possibly
mislead in another.   One may read too much into the
brevity, and so fall into the error of that other Englishman
who was beguiled by the mysterious signs of Despériers'
greatest contemporary's most original creation.   But a
very large and long experience of literary weighing and
measuring ought to be some safeguard against the
mistake of Thaumast.

One remarkable difference which may seem, at first
sight, to be against the theory of Despériers having had
Contes et a large share in the *Heptameron* is the con-
Joyeux Devis. trasted and, as it may seem again at first
sight, antagonistic tone of the two.   There are purely
comic and even farcical passages in Marguerite's book,
but the general colour, as has been said, is religious-
sentimental or courtly-amatory, with by no means
infrequent excursions into the purely tragical.   The

Contes et Joyeux Devis, on the other hand, in the main
continue the wholly jocular tone of the old *fabliaux*. But
Despériers must have been, not only *not* the great man
of letters which the somewhat exaggerated zeal of his
editor, M. Louis Lacour, ranked him as being, but a
very weak and feeble writer, if he could not in this way
write comedy in one book and tragedy in another. In fact
Rabelais gives us (as the greatest writers so often do)
what is in more senses than one a master-key to the
contrast. Despériers has in the *Contes* constant ironic
qualifications and asides which may even have been
directly imitated from his elder and greater contemporary;
Marguerite has others which pair off in the same way
with the most serious Rabelaisian " intervals," to which
attention has been drawn in the last chapter. One
point, however, does seem, at least to me, to emerge from
the critical consideration of these two books with the
other works of the Queen on the one hand and the other
works of Despériers [1] on the other. It is that the latter
had a much crisper and stronger style than Marguerite's
own, and that he had a faculty of grave ironic satire,
going deeper and ranging wider than her " sensibility "
would allow. There is one on the fatal and irremediable
effects of disappointing ladies in their expectations,
wherein there is something more than the mere *grivoiserie*,
which in other hands it might easily have remained.
The very curious Novel XIII.—on King Solomon and
the philosopher's stone and the reason of the failure of
alchemy—is of quite a different type from most things
in these story-collections, and makes one regret that there
is not more of it, and others of the same kind. For
sheer amusement, which need not be shocking to any
but the straitest-laced of persons, the story (XXXIV.) of
a curate completely " scoring off " his bishop (who did
not observe the caution given by Ophelia to Laertes) has
not many superiors in its particular kind.

[1] His translations of the *Andria* and of Plato's *Lysis*; and his verses, the chief charm
of which is to be found in his adoption of the "cut and broken" stanzas which the
French Renaissance loved.

The fancy for these collections of tales spread widely in the sixteenth century, and a respectable number of Other tale- them have found a home in histories of litera-
collections. ture.   Sometimes they present themselves honestly as what they are, and sometimes under a variety of disguises, the most extravagant of which is the title of the rather famous work of Henri Estienne, *Apologie pour Hérodote*.   Others, more or less fantastic, are the *Propos Rustiques* and *Baliverneries* of Noel Du Fail, a Breton squire (as we should say), and his later *Contes d'Eutrapel*; the *Escraignes Dijonnaises* and other books of Tabourot des Accords; the *Matinées* and *Apres Dinées* of Cholières, and, the largest collection of all, the *Sérees* [Soirées] of the Angevin Guillaume Bouchet,[1] while after the close of the actual century, but probably repre-senting earlier work, appeared the above-mentioned *Moyen de Parvenir*, by turns attributed and denied to Béroalde de Verville.   In all these, without exception, the imitation of Rabelais, in different but unmistakable ways, is to be found; and in not a few, that of the *Hep-tameron* and of Despériers; while not unfrequently the same tales are found in more than one collection.   The *fatrasie* character—that is to say, the stuffing together of all sorts of incongruous matter in more or less burlesque style—is common to all of them; the licence of subject and language to most; and there are hardly any, except a few mere modernisings of old *fabliaux*, in which you will not find the famous farrago of the Renaissance—learning, religious partisanship, war, law, love, almost everything. All the writers are far below their great master,[2] and none of them has the appeal of the *Heptameron*.   But the spirit of tale-telling pervades the whole shelf-ful, and there is one more special point of importance " for us."
    It will be observed that some of them actually display

---

[1] Not to be confused with *Jehan* Bouchet the poet, a much older man, indeed some twenty years older than Rabelais, and as dull as Raminagrobis Crétin himself, but the inventor or discoverer of that agreeable *agnomen* " Traverseur des Voies Périlleuses" which has been noted above.
[2] Cholières, I think, deserves the prize for sinking lowest.

in their titles (such as that of Tabourot's book as quoted) the fact that they have a definite provinciality in no bad sense: while Bouchet is as clearly Angevin and Du Fail as distinctly Breton as Des Accords is Burgundian and as the greatest of all had been Tourangeau. It can scarcely be necessary to point out at great length what a reinforcement of vigour and variety must have been brought by this plantation in the different soils of those provinces which have counted for so much—and nearly always for so much good[1]—in French literature and French things generally. The great danger and defect of mediaeval writing had been its tendency to fall into schools and ruts, and the " printed book " (especially such a printed book as Rabelais) was, at least in one way, by no means unlikely to exercise this bad influence afresh. To this the provincial differences opposed a salutary variety of manners, speech, local colour, almost everything. Moreover, manners themselves generally—one of the fairest and most fertile fields of the novel-kingdom—became thus more fully and freely the object and subject of the tale-teller. Character, in the best and most extensive and intensive sense of the word, still lagged behind ; and as the drama necessarily took that up, it was for more reasons than one encouraged, as we may say, in its lagging. But meanwhile Amyot and Calvin[2] and Montaigne were getting the language more fully ready for the prose-writer's use, and the constant " sophistication " of literature with religion, politics, knowledge of the physical world in all ways, commerce, familiarity with foreign nations—everything almost that touched on life—helped to bring on the slow but inevitable appearance of the novel itself. But it had more influences to assimilate and more steps to go through before it could take full form.

The "provincial" character of these.

[1] From all the endless welter of abuse of God's great gift of speech [and writing] about the French Revolution, perhaps nothing has emerged more clearly than that its evils were mainly due to the sterilisation of the regular Provincial assemblies under the later monarchy.

[2] A person not bad of blood will always be glad to mention one of the few good sides of a generally detestable character; and a person of humour must always chuckle at some of the ways in which Calvin's services to French prose were utilised.

No more curious contrast (except, perhaps, the not very dissimilar one which will meet us in the next chapter) The *Amadis* is to be found in the present *History*, or perhaps romances. in any other, than that of the matter just discussed with the great body of *Amadis* romance which, at this same time, was introduced into French literature by the translation or adaptation of Nicolas Herberay des Essarts and his continuators.   That Herberay [1] deserves, according to the best and most catholic students of French, a place with the just-mentioned writers among the formers or reformers of the French tongue, is a point of some importance, but, for us, minor.   Of the controversial part of the *Amadis* subject it must, as in other cases, be once more unnecessary for us to say much. It may be laid down as certain, on every principle of critical logic and research, that the old idea of the Peninsular cycle being borrowed direct from any French original is hopelessly absurd.   There is, notoriously, no external evidence of any such original ever having existed, and there is an immense improbability against any such original ever having existed.   Further, the internal characteristics of the Spanish romances, though, undoubtedly, they might never have come into existence at all but for the French, and though there is a very slight " catch-on " of *Amadis* itself to the universally popular Arthurian legend, are not in the least like those of French or English.   How the actual texts came into that existence ; whether, as used to be thought at first, after some expert criticism was turned on them, the actual original was Portuguese, and the refashioned and prolific form Spanish, is again a question utterly beyond bounds for us.   The quality of the romances themselves—their huge vogue being a matter of fact—and the influence which they exercised on the future development of the

---

[1] He did not confine his good offices to romances of *caballeria*.   In 1539 he turned into French the *Arnalte and Lucenda* of Diego de San Pedro (author of the more widely known *Carcel de Amor*), a very curious if also rather tedious-brief love-story which had great influence in France (see Reynier, *op. cit. inf.* pp. 66-73).   This (though M. Reynier did not know it) was afterwards versified in English by one of our minor Carolines, and will appear in the third volume of the collected edition of them now in course of publication by the Clarendon Press.

L

novel,—these are the things that concern us, and they are quite interesting and important enough to deserve a little attention.

What is certain is that these Spanish romances them-selves — which, as some readers at any rate may be Their char- presumed to know, branch out into endless acteristics. genealogies in the *Amadis* and *Palmerin* lines, besides the more or less outside developments which fared so hardly with the censors of Don Quixote's library —as well as the later French examples of a not dissimilar type, the capital instance of which, for literature, is Lord Berners's translation of *Arthur of Little Britain*—do show the most striking differences, not merely from the original twelfth- and thirteenth-century Charlemagne and Arthur productions, but also from intermediate variants and expansions of these. The most obvious of these discrepancies is the singular amplification of the super-natural elements. Of course these were not absent in the older romance literature, especially in the Arthurian cycle. But there they had certain characteristics which might almost deserve the adjective " critical "—little criticism proper as there was in the Middle Ages. They were very generally religious, and they almost always had what may be called a poetic restraint about them. The whole Graal-story is deliberately modelled on Scriptural suggestions ; the miracle of reconciliation and restoration which concludes *Amis and Amiles* is the work of a duly commissioned angel. There are giants, but they are introduced moderately and equipped in consonance. The Saint's Life, which, as it has been contended, exercised so large an influence on the earlier romance, carried the nature, the poetry, the charm of its supernatural elements into the romance itself.

In the *Amadis* cycle and in romances like *Arthur of* Little Britain all this undergoes a change— Extravagance in incident, not by any means for the better. What has nomencla- been unkindly, but not perhaps unjustly, ture, etc. called the " conjuror's supernatural " takes the place of the poet's variety. One of the personages of the *Knight of the Sun* is a "Bedevilled Faun," and it is really too much not to say that most of such personages are bedevilled. In *Arthur of* (so much the Lesser) *Britain* there is, if I remember rightly, a giant whose formidability partly consists in his spinning round on a sort of bedevilled music-stool: and his class can seldom be met with without three or seven heads, a similarly large number of legs and hands, and the like. This sort of thing has been put down, not without probability, to the Oriental suggestion which would come so readily into Spain. It may be so or it may not. But it certainly imports an element of puerility into romance, which is regrettable, and it diminishes the dignity and the poetry of the things rather lamentably. Whether it diminishes, and still more whether it originally diminished the *readability* of these same things, is quite another question.

Closely connected with it is the fancy for barbaric names of great length and formidable sound, such as Famongomadan, Pintiquinestra, and the like—a trait which, if anybody pleases, may be put down to the distorted echo of more musical [1] appellations in Arabic and other Eastern tongues, or to a certain childishness, for there is no doubt that the youthful mind delights, and always has delighted, in such things. The immense length of these romances even in themselves, and still more with continuations from father to son and grandson, and trains of descendants sometimes alternately named, can be less charged as an innovation, though there is no doubt that it established a rule which had only been an exception before. But, as will have been seen earlier, the continuation of romance genealogically had been not uncommon, and there had been a constant tendency to lengthen from the positively terse *Roland* to the prolix fifteenth-century forms. In fact this went on till the extravagant length of the Scudéry group made itself impossible, and even afterwards, as all readers of Richardson know, there was reluctance to shorten.

---

[1] Not always. Nouzhatoul-aouadat is certainly not as musical as Pintiquinestra, though Nouronnihar as certainly is.

We have, however, still to notice another peculiarity, and the most important by far as concerns the history The "cruel" of the novel: this is the ever-increasing heroine. tendency to exaggerate the "cruelty" of the heroine and the sufferings of the lovers. This peculiarity is not specially noticeable in the earliest and best of the group itself. Amadis suffers plentifully; yet Oriana can hardly be called "cruel." But of the two heroines of *Palmerin*, Polisarda does play the part to some extent, and Miraguarda (whose name it is not perhaps fantastic to interpret as "Admire her but beware of her") is positively ill-natured. Of course the thing was no more a novelty in literature than it was in life. The lines—

> And cruel in the New
> As in the Old one,

may certainly be transferred from the geographical world to the historical. But in classical literature "cruelty" is attributed rather indiscriminately to both sexes. The cliff of Leucas knew no distinction of sex, and Sappho can be set against Anaxarete. Indeed, it was safer for men to be cruel than for women, inasmuch as Aphrodite, among her innumerable good qualities, was very severe upon unkind girls, while one regrets to have to admit that no particular male deity was regularly "affected" to the business of punishing light o' love men, though Eros-Cupid may sometimes have done so. The Eastern mistress, for obvious reasons, had not much chance of playing the Miraguarda part as a rule, though there seems to me more chance of the convention coming from Arab and Hebrew poetry than from any other source. But in the *Arabian Nights* at least, though there are lustful murderesses—eastern Margarets of Burgundy, like Queen Labé of the Magicians,—there is seldom any "cruelty," or even any tantalising, on the part of the heroines.

A hasty rememberer of the sufferings of Lancelot and one or two other heroes of the early and genuine romance might say, "Why go further than this?"

But on a little examination the cases will be found very different. Neither Iseult nor Guinevere is cruel to her lover ; Orgueilleuse has a fair excuse in difference of rank and slight acquaintance ; persons like Tennyson's Ettarre, still more his Vivien, are " sophisticated "— as we have pointed out already. Besides, Vivien and Ettarre are frankly bad women, which is by no means the case with the Polisardas and Miraguardas. They, if they did not introduce the thing—which is, after all, as the old waterman in *Jacob Faithful* says, " Human natur'," —established and conventionalised the Silvius and Phoebe relation of lover and mistress. If Lancelot is banished more than once or twice, it is because of Guinevere's real though unfounded jealousy, not of any coquettish " cruelty " on her part ; if Parthenopeus nearly perishes in his one similar banishment, it is because of his own fault—his fault great and inexcusable. But the Amadisian heroes, as a rule—unless they belong to the light o' love Galaor type, which would not mind cruelty if it were exercised, but would simply laugh and ride away—are almost painfully faithful and deserving ; and their sojourns in Tenebrous Isles, their encounters with Bedevilled Fauns, and the like, are either pure misfortunes or the deliberate results of capricious tyranny on the part of their mistresses.

Now of course this is the sort of thing which may be (and as a matter of fact it no doubt was) tediously abused ; but it is equally evident that in the hands of a novelist of genius, or even of fair talent and craftsmanship, it gives opportunity for extensive and ingenious character-drawing, and for not a little " polite conversation." If *la donna è mobile* generally, she has very special opportunities of exhibiting her mobility in the exercise of her caprice : and if it is the business of the lover (as it is of minorities, according to a Right Honourable politician) to suffer, the *amoureux transi* who has some wits and some power of expression can suffer to the genteelest of tunes with the most ingenious fugues and variations. A great deal of the actual charm of sixteenth- and seventeenth-century poetry in all languages comes from the rendering in verse of this very relation of woman and man. We owe to the " dear Lady Disdain " idea not merely Beatrice, but Beatrix long after her, and many another good thing both in verse and in prose between Shakespeare and Thackeray.

In the *Amadis* group (as in its slightly modernised successor, that of the *Grand Cyrus*), the handling is so preposterously long and the reliefs, of dialogue and other things frequently managed with so little skill, that, except for sheer passing of time, the books have been found difficult to read. The present writer's knowledge of Spanish is too sketchy to enable him to read them in the original with full comfort. *Amadis* and *Palmerin* are legible enough in Southey's translations, made, as one would expect from him, with all due effort to preserve the language of the old English versions where possible. But Herberay's sixteenth - century French is a very attractive and perfectly easy language, thoroughly well suited to the matter. And if anything that has been said is read as despite to these romances, the reading is wrong. They have grave faults, but also real delights, and they have no small " place i' the story." [1]

---

[1] There should be added here a very curious, and now, if not in its own time, very rare book, my first knowledge of which I owed to a work already mentioned,

Note on Hélisenne de Crenne.

M. Gustave Reynier's *Le Roman Sentimental avant l'Astrée* (Paris, 1908), though I was able, after this chapter was composed, to find and read the original in the British Museum. It was first printed in 1538, and bears, like other books of its time, a disproportionately long title, which may, however, be easily shortened, "*Les Angoisses douloureuses qui procèdent d'Amour . . . :* composées par dame Hélisenne de Crenne." This Hélisenne or Hélisaine seems to have been a real person : and not the least of the remarkable group of women authors who illustrate her time in France, though M. Reynier himself admits that "it is difficult to know exactly *who* she was." She appears to have been of Picardy, and other extant and non-extant works are attributed to her. Like almost everybody of her time she wrote in the extreme *rhétoriqueur* style— so much so indeed as to lead even Pasquier into the blunder of supposing that Rabelais hit at her in the dialect of the " Limousin scholar." The *Angoisses*, which M. Reynier's acute examination shows to have been written by some one who must have known Boccaccio's *Fiammetta* (more than once Frenched about this time), is, or gives itself out to be, the autobiography of a girl of noble birth who, married at eleven years old and at first very fond of her husband, becomes at thirteen the object of much courtship from many gallants. Of these she selects, entirely on the love-at-first-sight principle, a very handsome young man who passes in the street. She is well read and tries to keep herself in order by stock examples, classical and romantic, of ill-placed and ill-fated affection. Her husband (who seems to have been a very good fellow for his time) gives her unconsciously what should have been the best help of all, by praising her self-selected lover's good looks and laughing at the young man's habit of staring at her. But she has already spoken frankly of her own *appétit sensuel*, and she proceeds to show this in the fashion which makes the fifteenth century and the early sixteenth a sort of trough of animalism between the altitudes of Mediaeval and Renaissance passion. Her lover turns out to be an utter cad, boastful, blabbing, and almost cowardly (he tells her in the usual stolen church interview, *Je crains merveilleusement monsieur votre mari*). But it makes not the slightest difference ; nor does the at last awakened wrath of an at last not merely threatened but wide-awake husband. Apparently she never has the chance of being actually guilty, for her husband finally, and very properly, shuts her up in a country house under strong duennaship. This finishes the first part, but there are two more, which return to more ancient ways. The lover Guenélic goes off to seek adventures, which he himself recounts, and acquires considerable improvement in them. He comes back, endeavours to free his mistress from her captivity, and does actually fly with her ; but they are pursued ; and though the lover and a friend of his with the rather Amadisian name of "Quezinstra" do their best, the heroine dies of weariness and shock, to be followed by her lover.

This latter part is comparatively commonplace. M. Reynier thinks very highly of the first. It is possible to go with him a certain part of the way, but not, I think, the whole, except from a purely "naturalist" and not at all "sentimental" point of view. Some bold bad men have, of course, maintained that when the other sex is possessed by an *appétit sensuel* this overcomes everything else, and seems, if not actually to exclude, at any rate by no means always or often to excite, that accompanying transcendentalism which is not uncommon with men, and which, comprised with the appetite, makes the love of the great lovers, whether they are represented by Dante or by Donne, by Shakespeare or by Shelley. Whether this be truth or libel *non nostrum est*. But it is certain that Hélisenne, as she represents herself, does not make the smallest attempt to spiritualise (even in the lowest sense) or inspirit the animality of her affection. She wants her lover as she might want a pork chop instead of a mutton one ; and if she is sometimes satisfied with seeing him, it is as if she were looking at that pork chop through a restaurateur's window and finding it better than not seeing it at all and contenting herself with the mutton. Still this result is probably the result at least as much of want of art as of original *mis*feeling ; and the book certainly does deserve notice here.

The original *Œuvres* of Hélisenne form a rather appetising little volume, fat, and close and small printed, as indeed is the case with most, but not quite all, of the books now under notice. The complementary pieces are mainly moralities, as indeed are, in intention, the *Angoisses* themselves. These latter seem to me better worth reprinting than most other things as yet not reprinted, from the *Heptameron* (Hélisenne, be it remembered, preceded Marguerite) for nearly a hundred years. The later parts, though (or perhaps even because) they contrast curiously with the first, are by no means destitute of interest ; and M. Reynier, I think, is a little hard on them if he has perhaps been a little kind to their predecessor. The lingo is indeed almost always stupendous and occasionally terrible. The printer aids sometimes ; for it was not at once that I could emend the description of the B. V. M. as "Mère et Fille de *l'aliltonât* [ant] plasmateur" into "*altitonant*" ("loud-thundering"), while *plasmateur* itself, though perfectly intelligible and legitimate, a favourite with the *rhétoriqueurs*, and borrowed from them even in Middle Scots, is not exactly everybody's word. But from her very exordium she may be fairly judged. "Au temps que la Déesse Cibélé despouilla son glacial et gélide habit, et vestit sa verdoyante robe, tapissée de diverses couleurs, je fus procréé de noblesse." And, after all, there *is* a certain nobility in this fashion of speech and of literary presentation.

CHAPTER VIII

THE SEVENTEENTH-CENTURY NOVEL—I

The Pastoral and Heroic Romance, and the Fairy Story

THE seventeenth century, almost if not quite from its beginning, ranks in French literature as the eighteenth Immense does with us, that is to say, as the time of importance origin of novels or romances which can be of the seventeenth called, in any sense, modern. In its first century in decade appeared the epoch-making pastoral-our subject. heroic Astrée of Honoré d'Urfé;[1] its middle period, from 1620 to 1670, was the principal birth-time of the famous " Heroic " variety, pure and simple; while, from that division into the last third, the curiously contrasted kind of the fairy tale came to add its quota of influence. At various periods, too, individuals of more or less note (and sometimes of much more than almost any of the " school-writers " just mentioned) helped mightily in strengthening and diversifying the subjects and manners of tales. To this period also belongs the continuance and prominence of that element of actual " lived " anecdote and personal history which has been mentioned more than once before. The *Historiettes* of Tallemant contain short suggestions for a hundred novels and romances ; the memoirs, genuine

---

[1] Herr Körting (*v. sup.* p. 133) gave considerable space to Barclay's famous *Argenis*, which also appeared fairly early in the century. To treat, however, a Latin book, written by a Scotsman, with admittedly large if not main reference to European politics, as a " French novel," seems a literary solecism. I do not know whether it is rash to add that the *Argenis* itself seems to me to have been wildly overpraised. It is at any rate one of the few books—one of the still fewer romances—which have defied my own powers of reading at more than one attempt.

or forged, of public and private persons have not seldom, in more modern times, formed the actual basis of some of the greatest fiction. Everybody ought long to have known Thackeray's perhaps rather whimsical declaration that he positively preferred the forged D'Artagnan memoirs of Courtils de Sandras (as far at least as the Gascon himself was concerned) to the work of that Alexander, the truly Great, of which he was nevertheless such a generous admirer: and recently mere English readers have had the opportunity of seeing whether they agree with him. In fact, as the century went on, almost all kinds of literature began to be more or less pervaded with the novel appeal and quality.

The letters of "Notre Dame des Rochers" constantly read like parts or scenes of a novel, and so do various The divisions compositions of her ill-conditioned but not of its unintelligent cousin Bussy-Rabutin. Camus contribution. de Pontcarré in the earlier and Fénelon in the later century determined that the Devil should not have this good prose to himself, and our own Anthony Hamilton showed the way to Voltaire in a kind, of which, though the Devil had nothing immediately to do with it, he might perhaps make use later. In fact, the whole century teems with the spirit of tale-telling, *plus* character-analysis ; and in the eighteenth itself, with a few notable exceptions, there was rather a falling-off from, than a further advance towards, the full blossoming of the aloe in the nineteenth.

It will probably, therefore, not be excessive to give two chapters (and two not short ones) to this period. In the first of them we may take the two apparently opposite, but by no means irreconcilable schools of Pastoral and Heroic Romance [1] and of Fairy Tale, including perhaps

[1] The repetition, in the seventeenth century, of something very like a phenomenon which we noticed in the twelfth, is certainly striking, and may seem at Note on first sight rather uncanny. But those who have made some attempt to marked in- "find the whole" in literature, and in that attempt have at least found fluence of out something about the curious laws of revolution and recurrence Greek which take the place of any progress in a straight line, will deem the Romance. thing natural enough. We declined, in the earlier case, to admit much, if any, direct influence of the accomplished Greek Romance on the Romance of the

only four persons, if so many, of first-rate literary rank—
Urfé,[1] Madeleine de Scudéry, Madame d'Aulnoy, and
Perrault ; in the second, the more isolated but in some
cases not unimportant names and works of Sorel, Scarron,
Furetière, and the capital ones of Madame de la Fayette
and Hamilton. According to the plan previously pursued, less attempt will be made to give exhaustive or
even full lists of practitioners than to illustrate their
practice thoroughly by example, translated or abstracted,
and by criticism ; and it is necessary that this latter
course should be used without mercy to readers or to
the historian himself in this first chapter. For there is
hardly any department of literature which has been more
left to the rather treacherous care of traditional and
second- or seventh-hand judgment than the Heroic
romance.[2]

The Pastoral, as being of the most ancient and in a
literary sense of the highest formal rank, may occupy us
first, but by no means longest. A great deal
of attention (perhaps a great deal more than
was at all necessary) has been paid to the
pastoral element in various kinds of literature. The
thing is certainly curious, and inevitably invited com-

West ; but we showed how classical subjects, whether pure or tinctured with Oriental
influence, induced an immensely important development of this same Western Romance
in two directions—that of manners, character, and passion, and that of marvel. In the
later period classical influences of all sorts are again at work ; but infinitely the larger
part of that work is done by the Greek Romances themselves—pastoral, adventurous,
and sentimental,—the dates of the translations of which will be given presently. And
the newer Oriental kind—coming considerably later still and sharing its nature certainly,
and perhaps its origin, not now with classical mythology, but again, in the most curious
way, with Western folk stories—supplements and diversifies the reinforcement.

[1] Scudéry writes "Urfé," and this confirms the *obiter dictum* of Sainte-Beuve, that
with the Christian name, the "Monsieur," or some other title you use the "*de*," otherwise not. But in this particular instance I think most French writers give the particle.

[2] I myself, in writing a *Short History of French Literature* many years ago, had to
apologise for incomplete knowledge ; and I will not undertake even now to have read
every romance cursorily mentioned in this chapter—indeed, some are not very easy
to get at. But I have done my best to extend my knowledge, assisted by a rather minute
study of the contemporary English heroic romance in prose and verse ; and I believe
I may say that I do now really know the *Grand Cyrus*, though even now I will again
not say that I have read every one of its perhaps two million words, or even the whole
of every one of its more than 12,000 pages. In regard to the *Astrée* I have been less
fortunately situated ; but "I have been there and still would go."

ment; but unfortunately it has peculiar temptations to a kind of comment which, though very fashionable for some time past, is rarely profitable. Pastorals of the most interesting kind actually exist in literature : " pastoral-ism " in the abstract, unless treated in the pure historical manner, is apt, like all similar criticism and discussion of " kinds " in general, to tend to φλυαρία.[1] For a history in a nutshell there is perhaps room even here, because the relations of the thing to fiction cannot be well under-stood without it. That the association of shepherds,[2] with songs, and with the telling of " tales " in both senses, is immensely old, is a fact which the Hebrew Scriptures establish, and almost the earliest Greek mythology and poetry confirm; but the wiser mind, here as elsewhere, will probably be content with the fact, and not enquire too busybodily into the reason. The connection between Sicily—apparently a land of actual pastoral life—and Alexandria—the home of the first professional man-of-letters school, as it may be called—perhaps supplies some-thing more; the actual beauty of the Sicilian-Alexandrian poems, more still; the adoption of the form by Virgil, who was revered at Rome, renowned somewhat hetero-doxically in the Middle Ages, and simply adored by the Renaissance, most of all. So, in English, Spenser and Milton, in French, Marot and others niched it solidly in the nation's poetry; and the certainly charming *Daphnis and Chloe*, when vernacularised, transferred its influence from verse to prose in almost all the countries of Europe.

To what may be called " common-sense " criticism, there is, of course, no form of literature, in either prose or verse, which is more utterly abhorrent and more helplessly exposed. Unsympathetic, and in some points unfair and even unintelligent, as Johnson's criticism of

---

[1] The above remarks are most emphatically *not* intended to refer to the work of Mr. Greg.

[2] The sheep, whether as a beast of most multitude or for more recondite reasons, has, of course, the preference; but it may be permissible to say that no guardian of animals is excluded. Goat-herds in the Greek ran the shepherd hard; neat-herds and swine-herds abound everywhere except, as concerns the last, in Jewry; even the goose-girl figures, and has in Provençal at least a very pretty name—*auquiera*.

Lycidas may seem, to the censure of its actual " pastor-
ality " there is no answer, except that " these things are
an allegory " as well as a convention. To go further
out of mere common-sense objections, and yet stick to
the Devil's-Advocate line, there is no form which lends
itself to—which, indeed, insists upon—conventions of the
most glaring unreality more than the pastoral, and none in
which the decorations, unless managed with extraordinary
genius, have such a tendency to be tawdry at best,
draggled and withered at worst. Nevertheless, the fact
remains that at almost all times, both in ancient literature
and since the revival of letters, as well as in some probably
more spontaneous forms during the Middle Ages themselves,[1] pastorals have been popular with the vulgar, and
practised by the elect ; while within the very last hundred
years such a towering genius as Shelley's, and such a
manifold and effectual talent as Mr. Arnold's, have
selected it for some of their very best work.

Such adoption, moreover, had, for the writer of prose
fiction, some peculiar and pretty obvious inducements.
It has been noticed by all careful students of fiction that
one of the initial difficulties in its way, and one of those
which do not seem to get out of that way very quickly,
is diffidence on the writer's part " how to begin." It
may be said that this is not peculiar to fiction ; but
extends from the poet who never can get beyond the
first lines of his epic to the journalist who sits for an
hour gazing at the blank paper for his article, and returns
home at midnight, if not like Miss Bolo " in a flood of
tears and a sedan chair," at any rate in a tornado of
swearing at himself and (while there were such things)
a hansom cab. Pastoral gives both easy beginning and
supporting framework.

The transformation of the older pastoral form into
the newer began, doubtless, with the rendering into

[1] The mediaeval *pastourelle* is no doubt to some extent conventional and "made in
moulds." But it is by no means so unreal as (whether Greek was so or not) Roman
pastoral pretty certainly was, and as modern has been beyond possibility of doubt. How
good it could be, without any convention at all, Henryson showed once for all in
our own language by *Robene and Makyne*.

French of *Daphnis and Chloe*,[1] which appeared in the same
year with the complete *Heptameron* (1559).
Twelve years later, in 1571, Belleforest's *La
Pyrénée et Pastorale Amoureuse* rather took

Its beginnings in France.

the title than exemplified the kind; but in 1578 the
translation of Montemayor's *Diana* definitely turned
the current into the new-old channel. It was not,
however, till seven years later still that "*Les Bergeries
de Juliette*, de l'invention d'Ollenix du Mont Sacré"
(a rather exceptionally foolish anagram of Nicolas de
Montreux) essayed something original in the style.
Montreux issued his work, of which more presently,
again and again in five instalments, the last of which
appeared thirteen years later than the first. And it has
been proved with immense bibliographical labour by
M. Reynier,[2] that though the last decade of the sixteenth century in France was almost as fertile in short
love-romances[3] as ours was in sonnet-cycles, the pastoral
form was, whether deliberately or not, for the most part
eschewed, though there were one or two exceptions of
little if any consequence. It is indeed noteworthy that
(only four years before the first part of the
Astrée) a second translation of the *Diana* came
out. But it was not till 1607 that this first
part actually appeared, and in the opinion of

Minor romances preceding the Astrée.

its own time generally, and our own time for the most

[1] *Theagenes and Chariclea* had preceded it by thirteen years, though a fresh translation
appeared in the same year, as did the first of *Hysminias and Hysmine*. Achilles Tatius
(*Cleitophon and Leucippe*) had been partly done in 1545, but waited till 1568 for completion.
[2] *Op. cit. sup.*
[3] They are almost always *Amours* after their Greek prototypes, sometimes simple,
often qualified, and these most frequently by such adjectives as "Infortunées et chastes,"
"Constantes et infortunées," "Chastes et heureuses," "Pudiques," etc. etc. Not a few are
taken direct from episodes of Ariosto or other elders; otherwise they are "loves" of
Laoniphile, Lozie, Poliphile and Mellonimphe, Pégase (who has somehow or other
become a nymph) and Léandre, Dachmion and Deflore (a rather unlucky heroine-
name), etc. etc. Their authors are nearly as numerous as their titles; but the chief were
a certain Sieur de Nervèze, whose numerous individual efforts were collected more than
once to the number at least of a good baker's dozen, and a Sieur des Escuteaux, who had
the same fôrtune. Sometimes the Hellenism went rather to seed in such titles as
Erocaligenèse, which supposed itself to be Greek for "Naissance d'un bel amour." It
is only (at least in England) in the very largest libraries, perhaps in the British Museum
alone, that there is any chance of examining these things directly; some of them
escaped even the mighty hunt of M. Reynier himself. What the present writer has
found is treated shortly in the text.

part, though not in that of the interval, made a new
epoch in the history of French fiction.

The general characteristics of this curious and numerous, but almost forgotten, body of work—which must, be
Their it remembered, have exercised influence, more
general or less, on the progress of the novel by the ways
character. of supply, demand, and reaction alike—have
been carefully analysed by M. Reynier, with whom, in
regard to one or two points of opinion, one may differ,
but whose statements of fact are certainly trustworthy.
Short as they usually are, and small as is the literary
power displayed in most of them, it is clear that they,
long before Rambouillet and the *précieuses*, indicate a
distinct reaction against merely brutal and ferocious
manners, with a standard of " courtiership " in both
senses. Our dear Reine Margot herself in one case
prescribes, what one hopes she found not merely in La
Mole, but in others of those transitorily happy ones
whose desiccated hearts did or did not distend the pockets
of her farthingale as live Persian kittens do those of their
merchants. To be a lover you must have " a stocking
void of holes, a ruff, a sword, a plume, *and a knowledge
how to talk*." This last point is illustrated in these
miniature romances after a fashion on which one of the
differences of opinion above hinted at may arise. It is
not, as in the later " Heroics," shown merely in lengthy
harangues, but in short and almost dramatised dialogue.
No doubt this is often clumsy, but it may seem to have
been not a whole mistake in itself—only an abortive
attempt at something which, much later again, had to
come before real novel-writing could be achieved, and
which the harangues of the Scudéry type could never have
provided. There is a little actual history in them—not
the key-cryptograms of the " Heroics " or their adoption
of ancient and distant historic frames. In a very large
proportion, forced marriages, proposed and escaped from,
supply the plot ; in not a few, forced " vocations " to the
conventual life. Elopements are as common as abductions
in the next stage, and are generally conducted with as

much propriety.   Courtships of married women, and lapses by them, are very rare.

No one will be surprised to hear that the " Phébus " or systematised conceit, for which the period is famous, Examples of and which the beloved Marguerite herself did their style. not a little favour, is abundant in them.   From a large selection of M. Reynier's, I cull, as perhaps the most delightful of all these, if not also of all known to me in any language, the following :

During this task, Love, who had ambushed himself, plunged his wings in the tears of the lover, and dried them in the burning breast of the maiden.

"A squadron of sighs" is unambitious, but neat, terse, and very tempting to the imagination.   More complicated is a lady "floating on the sea of the persecution of her Prince, who would fain give her up to the shipwreck of his own concupiscence."

And I like this :

The grafts of our desires being inarched long since in the tree of our loves, the branches thereof bore the lovely bouquets of our hopes.

And this is fine :

Paper ! that the rest of your white surface may not blush at my shame, suffer me to blacken it with my sorrow !

It has always been a sad mystery to me why rude and dull intelligences should sneer at, or denounce, these delightful fantastries, the very stuff of which dreams and love and poetry—the three best things of life—are made.[1]

Montreux   The British Museum possesses not very and the   many of the, I believe, numerous works of Bergeries de Nicolas de Montreux, *alias*, as has been said, Juliette.   Ollenix du Mont Sacré, a " gentleman of Maine," as he scrupulously designates himself.   But it does

---

[1] M. Reynier (most justly, but of course after many predecessors) points out that the common filiation of these things on Marini and Gongora is chronologically impossible. We could, equally of course, supply older examples still in English ; and persons of any reading can carry the thing back through sixteenth- and fifteenth-century examples to the Dark Ages and the late Greek classics—if no further.

possess two parts (the first two) of the *Bergeries de Juliette,*
and I am not in the least surprised that no reader of them
should have worried any librarian into completing the
set. Each of these parts is a stout volume of some five
hundred pages,[1] not very small, of close small print,
filled with stuff of the most deadly dulness. For instance,
Ollenix is desirous to illustrate the magnificence and the
danger of those professional persons of the other sex at
Venice who have filled no small place in literature from
Coryat to Rousseau. So he tells us, without a gleam or
suspicion of humour, that one customer was so astonied
at the decorations of the bedroom, the bed, etc., that he
remained for two whole hours considering them, and
forgetting to pay any attention to the lady. It is satisfactory to know that she revenged herself by raising the
fee to an inordinate amount, and insisting on her absurd
client's lackey being sent to fetch it before the actual
conference took place. But the silliness of the story
itself is a fair sample of Montreux' wits, and these wits
manage to make anything they deal with duller by their
way of telling it.

It is still more unfortunate that our national collection
has none of the numerous fictions [2] of A(ntoine ?) de
Nervèze. His *Amours Diverses* (1606), in
which he collected no less than seven love-
stories, published separately earlier, would be
useful. But it luckily does provide the similarly titled book of Des Escuteaux, who is perhaps the
most representative and prolific writer, next to Montreux
and Nervèze, of the whole, and who seems to me, from
what I have read of the first and what others say of
the second, to be their superior. The collections
consist of (*Amours de* in every case) *Filiris et Isolia,*
dedicated to Isabel (not " -bel*le* ") de Rochechouart;
Clarimond et Antoinette (to Lucresse [*sic*] de Bouillé);
Clidamant et Marilinde (to *Jane* de la Brunetière), and

Marginal note: Des Escuteaux and his *Amours Diverses.*

---

[1] It is fair to say that the first is "make-weighted" with a pastoral play entitled
Athlette, from the heroine's rather curious name.
[2] It *has* two poems and some miscellanea. Something like this is the case with
another bookmaker of the class, Du Souhait.

Ipsilis et Alixée (to Renée de Cossé, Amirale de France !).[1]

Some readers may be a little " put off " by a habit which Des Escuteaux has, especially in the first story of the volume, of prefixing, as in drama, the names of the speakers—*Le Prince, La Princesse,* etc.—to the first paragraphs of the harangues and *histoires* of which these books so largely consist.[2] But it is not universal. The most interesting of the four is, I think, *Clidamant et Marilinde,* for it introduces the religious wars, a sojourn of the lovers on a desert island, which M. Reynier[3] not unjustly calls Crusoe-like, and other "varieties."

I have not seen the other—quite other, and François —Molière's *Semaine Amoureuse,* which belongs to this class, though later than most; but his still later *Polyxène,* a sort of half-way house between these shorter novels and the ever-enlarged "Heroics," is a very fat duodecimo of 1100 pages. The heroine has two lovers—one with the singular name of Cloryman,—but love does not run smooth with either, and she ends by taking the (pagan) veil. The bathos of the thought and style may be judged from the heroine's affecting mention of an entertainment as " the last *ballet* my unhappy father ever saw."

François de Molière— Polyxène.

Not one of the worst of these four or five score minors, though scarcely in itself a positively good thing, is the Sieur du Périer's *La Haine et l'Amour d'Arnoult et de Clarimonde.* It begins with a singularly banal exordium, gravely announcing that Hate and Love *are* among the most important passions, with other statements of a similar kind couched in commonplace language. But it does something to bring the novel from an uninteresting cloudland to earth by dealing

Du Périer— Arnoult et Clarimonde.

---

[1] It may be childish, but the association in this group of ladies—three of them bearing some of the greatest historic names of France, and the fourth that of the admirable critic with no other namesake of whom I ever met—seemed to me interesting. It is perhaps worth adding that Isabel de Rochechouart seems to have been not merely dedicatee but part author of the first tale.

[2] The habit is common with these authors.

[3] He gives more analysis than usual, but complains of the author's "affectation and bad taste." I venture to think this relatively rather harsh, though it is positively too true of the whole group.

M

with the recent and still vividly felt League wars: and there is some ingenuity shown in plotting the conversion of the pair from more than "a little aversion" at the beginning to nuptial union—*not* at the end. For it is one of the points about the book which are not commonplace, though it may be a survival or atavism from mediaeval practice—that the latter part of it is occupied mainly, not with Arnoult and Clarimonde, but with the loves, fortunes, and misfortunes of their daughter Claride.

The *Philocalie* of Du Croset (1593) derives its principal interest from its being not merely a *Bergerie* before the *Astrée*, but, like it, the work of a Forézian gentleman who proudly asserts his territoriality, and dedicates his book to the "Chevalier D'Urfé." And its part name-fellow, the *Philocaste* of Jean Corbin—a very tiny book, the heroine of which is (one would hardly have thought it from her name) a Princess of England—is almost entirely composed of letters, discourse on them, and a few interspersed verses. It belongs to the division of backward-looking novels, semi-chivalrous in type, and its hero is as often called "The Black Knight" as by his name.

Du Croset— Philocalie. Corbin— Philocaste.

The *Roman Satirique* (1624) of Jean de Lannoi is another example of the curious inability to "hit it off" which has been mentioned so often as characterising the period. Its 1100 pages are far too many, though it is fair to say that the print is exceptionally large and loose. Much of it is not in any sense "satiric," and it seems to have derived what popularity it had almost wholly from the "key" interest.

Jean de Lannoi and his Roman Satirique.

The minor works—if the term may be used when the attribution of the major is by no means certain—of Béroalde de Verville have, as is usual, been used both ways as arguments for and against his authorship of the *Moyen de Parvenir*. Les *Aventures de Floride* is simply an attempt, and a big one in size, to *amadigauliser*, as the literary slang of the time went. The *Histoire Véritable*, owing nothing

Béroalde de Verville outside the Moyen de Parvenir.

but its title and part of its idea to Lucian, and sub-titled *Les Princes Fortunés*, is less conventional. It has a large fancy map for a frontispiece; there are fairies in it, and a sort of *pot-pourri* of queernesses which might not impossibly have come from the author or editor of the *Moyen* in his less inconveniently ultra - Pantagruelist moments. *Le Cabinet de Minerve* is actually a glorification of " honest " love. In fact, Béroalde is one of the oddest of " polygraphers," and there is nobody quite like him in English, though some of his fellows may be matched, after a fashion, with our Elizabethan pamphleteers. I have long wished to read the whole of him, but I suppose I never shall.

And it is time to leave these very minor stars and come to the full and gracious moon of the *Astrée* itself.

Honoré d'Urfé, who was three years younger than Shakespeare, and died in the year in which Charles I. The *Astrée*— came to the throne, was a cadet of a very its author. ancient family in the district or minor province of Forez, where his own famous Lignon runs into the Loire. He was a pupil of the Jesuits and early *fort en thème*, was a strenuous *ligueur*, and, though (or perhaps also because) he was very good friends with Henri's estranged wife, Margot, for some time decidedly suspect to Henri IV. For this reason, and others of property, etc., he became almost a naturalised Savoyard, but died in the service of his own country at the beginning of Richelieu's Valtelline war. The most noteworthy thing in his rather eventful life was, however, his marriage. This also has a direct literary interest, at least in tradition, which will have his wife, Diane de Châteaumorand, to be Astrée herself, and so the heroine of " the first [great] sentimental romance." The circumstances of the union, however, were scarcely sentimental, much less romantic. They were even, as people used to say yesterday, " not quite nice," and the Abbé Reure, a devotee of both parties to it, admits that they " *heurte[nt] violemment nos idées.*" In fact Diane was not only eight years older than Honoré and thirty-eight years of age, but she had been for a quarter of a century the wife of his elder brother, Anne, while he himself was a knight of Malta, and vowed to celibacy. Of course (as the Canon points out with irrefragably literal accuracy in logic and law) the marriage being declared null *ab initio* (for the cause most likely to suggest itself, though alleged after extraordinary delay), Diane and Honoré were not sister- and brother-in-law at all, and no " divorce " or even " dispensation " was needed. In the same way, Honoré, having been introduced into the Order of St. John irregularly in various ways, never was a knight of it at all, and could not be bound by its rules. Q.E.D. Wicked people, of course, on the other hand, said that it was a device to retain Diane's great wealth (for Honoré was quite poor in comparison) in the family ; sentimental ones that it was a fortunate and blameless crowning of a long and pure attachment. As a matter of fact, no " permanent children " (to adopt an excellent phrase of the late Mr. Traill's) resulted ; Diane outlived her husband, though but for a short time, and left all her property to her relations of the Lévis family. The pair are also said not to have been the most united of couples. In connection with the *Astrée* their portraits are interesting. Honoré d'Urfé, though he had the benefit of Van Dyck's marvellous art of cavalier creation, must have been a very handsome man. Diane's portrait, by a much harder and dryer hand, purports to have been taken at the age of sixty-four. At first sight there is no beauty in it ; but on reinspection one admits possibilities—a high forehead, rather " enigmatic " eyes, not at all " extinguished," a nose prominent and rather large, but straight and with well, but not too much, developed " wings," and, above all, a full and rather voluptuous mouth. Such may have been the first identified novel-heroine. It is a popular error to think that sixty-four and beauty are incompatibles, but one certainly would have liked to see her at sixteen, or better still and perhaps best of all, at six and twenty.

The *Astrée* itself is not the easiest of subjects to deal with. It is indeed not so huge as the *Grand Cyrus*, but

it is much more difficult to get at—a very rare flower
The book. except in the "grey old gardens" of secular
libraries. It and its author have indeed for a
few years past had the benefit (as a result partly of
another doubtful thing, an *x*-centenary) of one[1] of the
rather-to-seek good specimens among the endless number
of modern literary monographs. But it has never been
reprinted—even extracts of it, with the exception of a
few stock passages, are not common or extensive ; and
though a not small library has been written about it in
successive waves of eulogy, reaction, mostly ignorant
contempt, rehabilitation, and mere book-making; though
there have been (as noted) recent anniversaries and
celebrations, and so forth; though it is one of the not
numerous books which have given a name-type—
Celadon,—and a place—"les bords du Lignon,"—to their
own, if not to universal literature, it seems to be "as a
book " very little known. The faithful monographer above
cited admits merit in Dunlop ; but Dunlop does not say
very much about it.   Herr Körting (*v. sup.*) analyses it.
Possibly there may be, also in German, a comparison,
tempting to those who like such things, between it and
its twenty years' predecessor, Sidney's *Arcadia*, the first
French translation of which, in 1625, just after Urfé's
death, was actually dedicated to his widow. But I
suspect that few English writers about Sidney have
known much of the *Astrée*, and I feel sure that still fewer
French writers[2] on this have known anything of Sidney
save perhaps his name. Of course the indebtedness of
both books to Montemayor's *Diana* is a commonplace.

One of the numerous resemblances between the two,
and one which, considering their respective positions in
Its likeness the history of the French and English novel,
to the   is most interesting, is the strong philosophical
Arcadia. and specially Platonic influence which the
Renaissance exercised on both.[3] Sidney, however full

[1] *La Vie et les Œuvres de Honoré d'Urfé.* Par le Chanoine O. C. Reure, Paris, 1910.
[2] The Abbé Reure, to whom I owe my own knowledge of the translation and
dedication, says nothing more.
[3] M. Reynier, in the useful book so often quoted, has shown that, as one would

of it elsewhere, put less of it in his actual novel ; while, on the other hand, nothing did so much to create and spread the rather rococo notion of pseudo-platonic love in France, and from France throughout Europe, as the *Astrée* itself.   The further union of the philosophic mind with an eminently cavalier temperament—the united *ethos* of scholar, soldier, lover, and courtier—fills out the comparison : and dwarfs such merely mechanical things as the mixed use of prose and verse (which both may have taken, nay pretty certainly did take, from Montemayor) and the pastoralities, for which they in the same way owed royalty to the Spaniard, to Tasso, to Sannazar, and to the Greek romances, let alone Theocritus and

Its philo- Virgil.   And, to confine ourselves henceforward
sophy and to our own special subject, it is this double
its general infusion of idealism — of spiritual and in-
temper. tellectual enthusiasm on the one hand and practical fire of life and act on the other—which makes the great difference, not merely between the *Astrée* and its predecessors of the *Amadis* class, but between it and its successors the strictly " Heroic " romances, though these owe it so much.   The first—except in some points of passion—hardly touch reality at all ; the last are perpetually endeavouring to simulate and insinuate a sort of reality under cover of adventures and conventions which, though fictitious, are hardly at all fantastic.   But the *Astrée* might almost be called a French prose *Faerie Queene*, allowing for the difference of the two nations, languages, vehicles, and *milieux* generally, in its repre-sentation of the above-mentioned cavalier-philosophic *ethos*—a thing never so well realised in France as in Eng-land or in Spain, but of which Honoré d'Urfé, from many traits in life and book, seems to have been a real example, and which certainly vindicates its place in history and literature.

expect, this influence is not absent from the smaller French love-novels which preceded the *Astrée* ; indeed, as we saw, it is obvious, though in a form of more religiosity, as early as the *Heptaméron*.   But it was not till the seventeenth century in France, or till a little before it in some cases with us, that "Love in fantastic triumph sat" between the shadowing wings of sensual and intellectual passion.

The *Astrée* appeared in five instalments, 1607-10-12-19 and posthumously, the several parts being frequently printed: and it is said to be almost impossible to find a copy, all the parts of which are of the first issue in each case.   The two later parts probably, the last certainly, were collaborated in, if not wholly written by, the author's secretary Baro.   But it was by no means Honoré's only work ; indeed the Urfés up to his time were an unusually literary family ; and, while his grandfather Claude collected a remarkable library (whence, at its dispersion in the evil days of the house[1] during the eighteenth century, came some of not the least precious possessions of French public and private collections), his unfortunate brother Anne was a poet.   Honoré himself, besides school exercises, wrote *Epistres Morales* which were rather popular, and display qualities useful in appreciating the novel itself ; a poem in octosyllables, usually and perhaps naturally called " *La* Sireine," but really entitled in the masculine, and having nothing to do with a mermaid ; a curious thing, semi-dramatic in form and in irregular blank verse, entitled *Silvanire ou La Morte Vive*, which was rehandled soon after his death by Corneille's most dangerous rival Mairet ; and an epic called *La Savoisiade*, which seems to have no merit, and all but a very small portion of which is still unprinted.

Its appear-ance and its author's other work.

He remains, therefore, the author of the *Astrée*, and, taking things on the whole (a mighty whole, beyond contest, as far as bulk goes), there are not so many authors of the second rank (for one of the first he can hardly be called) who would lose very much by an exchange with him.   One's estimates of the book are apt to vary in different places, even as, though not in the same degree as, the estimates of others have varied at different times ; but I myself have found that the more I read of it the more I liked and

Its character and appeals.

---

[1] They had, indeed, neither luck nor distinction after Honoré's death: and the last of the family died, like others of the renegade nobles of France, by his own hand, to escape the guillotine which he himself had helped to establish.

esteemed it ; and I believe that, if I had a copy of my own and could turn it over in the proper diurnal and nocturnal fashion, not as duty- but as pleasure-reading, I should like it better still. Certain points that have appealed to me have been noticed already—its combination of sensuous and ideal passion is perhaps the most important of them ; but there are not a few others, themselves by no means void of importance. One is the union, not common in French books between the sixteenth and the nineteenth century, of sentiment and seriousness with something very like humour. Hylas, the not exactly "comic man," but light-o'-love and inconstant shepherd, was rather a bone of contention among critics of the book's own century. But he certainly seasons it well ; and there is one almost Shakespearean scene in which he is concerned—a scene which Benedick and Beatrice, who may have read it not so very many years after their own marriage, must have enjoyed considerably. Hylas and the shepherdess Stella (who is something of a girl-counterpart of his, as in the case just cited) draw up a convention of love [1] between them. The tables, though they are not actually numbered in the original, are twelve, and, shortened a little, run as follows :

1. Neither is to be sovereign over the other.

2. Both are to be at once Lover and Beloved. [They knew *Hylas and* something about the matter, these two, for all their *Stella and* jesting.]
their Con-
vention.   3. There is to be no constraint of any kind.

4. They are to love for as long or as short a time as they please.

5. No charge of infidelity is ever to be brought on either side.

6. It is quite permitted to either or both to love somebody else, and yet to continue loving each other.

7. There is to be no jealousy, no complaints, no sulks.

8. They are to do and say exactly what they please.

9. Words like "faithfulness," etc., are taboo.

10. They may leave off playing whenever they like.

11. And begin again ditto.

---

[1] The more orthodox "laws of love" which Celadon puts up in his "Temple of Astraea" are less amusing.

12. They are to forget both the favours they receive from each other and the offences they may commit against each other.

Now, of course, any one may say of the Land where such a code might be realised, in the very words of one of the most charming of songs, set to one of the happiest of tunes :

> Cette rive, ma chère,
> On ne la connaît guère
> Au pays des amours !

But that is not the question, and if it *were* possible it undoubtedly would be a very agreeable Utopia, combining the transcendental charms of the country of Quintessence with the material ones of the Pays de Cocagne. From its own point of view there seems to be no fault to find with it, except, perhaps, with the first part of the Twelfth Commandment ; for the remembrance of former favours heightens the enjoyment of later ones, and the danger of *nessun maggior dolore* is excluded by the hypothesis of indifference after breach. But a sort of umpire, or at any rate thirdsman, the shepherd Silvandre,[1] when asked his opinion, makes an ingenious objection. To carry out Article Three, he says, there ought to be a Thirteenth :

13. That they may break any of these rules just as they please.

For what comes of this further the reader may go to the book, but enough of it should have been given to show that there is no want of salt, though there is no (or very little) *gros sel*[2] in the *Astrée*.

Yet again there is very considerable narrative power. Abstracts may be found, not merely in older books

Narrative skill frequent. mentioned or to be mentioned, but in the recent publications of Körting and the Abbé Reure, and there is neither room nor need for a fresh one here. As some one (or more than one) has said,

---

[1] He constantly plays this part of referee and moraliser. But he is by no means exempt from the pleasing fever of the place, and some have been profane enough to think his mistress, Diane, more attractive than the divine Astrée herself.

[2] Very delicate persons have been shocked by the advantages afforded to Celadon in his disguise as the Druid's daughter, and the consequent familiarity with the innocent unrecognising heroine. But *honi soit* will cover them.

the book is really a sort of half-allegorical tableau of honourable Love worked out in a crowd of couples (some I believe, have counted as many as sixty), from Celadon and Astrée themselves downwards. The course of these loves is necessarily "accidented," and the accidents are well enough managed from the first, and naturally enough best known, where Celadon flings himself into the river and is rescued, insensible but alive, by nymphs, who all admire him very much, though none of them can affect his passion for Astrée. But one cares—at least I have found myself caring—less for the story than for the way in which it is told—a state of things exactly contrary, as will be seen, to that produced with or in me by the *Grand Cyrus*. There we have a really well, if too intricately, engineered plot, in the telling of which it is difficult to take much interest. Here it is just the reverse. And one of the consequences is that you can dip in the *Astrée* much more refreshingly than in its famous follower, where, if you do so, you constantly "don't know where you are."

One of the most famous things in the book, and one of the most important to its conduct, is the "Fountain The Fountain of the Truth of Love," a few words on which of the Truth will illustrate the general handling very fairly. of Love. This Fountain (presided over by a Druid, a very important personage otherwise, who is a sort of high priest thereof) has nothing in common with the more usual waters which are philtres or anti-philtres, etc. Its function is to be gazed in rather than to be drunk, and if you look into it, loving somebody, you see your mistress. If she loves you, you see yourself as well, beside her, and (which is not so nice) if she loves some one else you see *him*; while if she is fancy-free you see her only. Clidaman, one of the numerous lovers above mentioned, tries the water; and his love, Silvie, presents herself again and again as he looks, "almost setting on fire with her lovely eyes the wave which seemed to laugh around her." But she is quite alone.

The presiding Druid interprets, not merely in the sense already given, but with one of the philosophic commentaries, which, as has been said, are distinctive of the book. The nature of the fountain is to reflect not body but spirit. Spirit includes Will, Memory, and Judgment, and when a man loves, his spirit transforms itself through all these ways into the thing loved. Therefore when he looks into the fountain he sees Her. In the same way She is changed into Him or some one else whom she loves, and He sees that image also ; but if she loves no one He sees her image alone.

" This is very satisfactory " (as Lady Kew would say) to the inquiring mind, but not so much so to the lover. He wants to have the fountain shut up, I suppose (for my notes and memory do not cover this point exactly), that no rival may have the chance denied to himself. He would even destroy it, but that—the Druid tells and shows him—is quite impossible. What can be done shall be. And here comes in another of the agreeable things (to me) in the book—its curious fairy-tale character, which is shown by numerous supernaturalities, much more *humanised* than those of the *Amadis* group, and probably by no means without effect on the fairy-tale proper which was to follow. Clidaman himself happens, in the most natural way in the world, to " keep "—as an ordinary man keeps cats and dogs—a couple of extraordinary big and savage lions and another couple of unicorns to fight, not with each other, but with miscellaneous animals. The lions and the unicorns are forthwith extra-enchanted, so as to guard the fountain—an excellent arrangement, but subject to some awkwardnesses in the sequel. For the lions take turns to seek their meat in the ordinary way, and though they can hurt nobody who does not meddle with the fountain, and have no wish to be man-eaters, complications naturally supervene. And sometimes, besides fighting,[1] and love-making, and love casuistry, and fairy-tales, and oracles, and the finer comedy above mentioned, " Messire d'Urfé " (for he did not live

---

[1] There is plenty of this, including a regular siege of the capital, Marcilly.

too late to have that most gracious of all designations of a gentleman used in regard to him) did not disdain, and could not ill manage, sheer farce. The scene with Cryseide and Arimant and Clorine and the nurse and the ointment in Part III. Book VII., though it contains little or nothing to *effaroucher la pudeur*, is like one of the broader but not broadest tales of the Fabliaux and their descendants.

The book, therefore, has not merely a variety, but a certain liveliness, neither of which is commonplace ; but it would of course be uncritical to suppress its drawbacks. It is far too long: and while bowing to those to the manner born who say that Baro carried out his master's plan well in point of style, and acknowledging that I have paid less attention to Parts IV. and V. than to the others, it seems to me that we could spare a good deal of them. One error, common to almost the whole century in fiction, is sometimes flagrant. Nobody except a pedant need object to the establishment, in the time of the early fifth century and the place of Gaul, of a non-historical kinglet- or queenletdom of Forez or " Séguse " under Amasis (here a feminine name [1]), etc. ; nor, though (as may perhaps be remarked again later) things Merovingian bring little luck in literature, need we absolutely bar Chilperics and Alarics, or a reference to " all the beauties of Neustria." But why, in the midst of the generally gracious *macédoine* of serious and comic loves, and jokes, and adventures, should we have thrust in the entirely unnecessary, however historical, crime whereby Valentinian the Third lost his worthless life and his decaying Empire ? It has, however, been remarked, perhaps often enough, by those who have busied themselves with the history of the novel, how curious it is that the historical variety, though it never succeeded in being born for two thousand

Some drawbacks— awkward history.

---

[1] The constant confusion, in these quasi-classical romances, of masculine and feminine names is a rather curious feature. But the late Sir W. Gilbert played some tricks of the kind in *Pygmalion and Galatea*, and I remember an English novelist, with more pretensions to scholarship than Gilbert, making the particularly unfortunate blunder of attributing to Longus a book called " *Doris* and Chloe."

years after the *Cyropaedia* and more, constantly strove to
be so.   At no time were the throes more frequent than
during the seventeenth century in France ; at no time,
there or anywhere else, were they more abortive.[1]

But it remains on the whole an attractive book, and
the secret of at least part of this attractiveness is no doubt
    But   to be found stated in a sentence of Madame
attractive on de Sévigné's, which has startled some people,
  the whole. that " everything in it is natural and true."
To the startled persons this may seem either a deliberate
paradox, or a mere extravagance of affection, or even
downright bad taste and folly.   But the Lady of all
Beautiful Letter-writers was almost of the family of
Neverout in literary criticism.   If she had been a professional critic (which is perhaps impossible), she might
have safeguarded her dictum by the addition, " according
to its own scheme and division."   It is the neglect of this
implication which has caused the demurs.   " ' Natural ! ' "
and " ' true ! ' " they say, " why, the Pastoral is the most
frankly and in fact outrageously unnatural and false of
all literary kinds.   Does not Urfé himself warn us that
we are not to expect ordinary shepherds and shepherdesses
at all ? "   Or perhaps they go more to detail.   " The
whole book is unabashedly occupied with love-making;
and love is not the whole, it is even a very small part, of
life, that is to say, of truth and nature."   Or, to come
still closer to particulars, " Where, for instance, did
Celadon, who is represented as having been reduced to
utter destitution when, *more heroum*, he started a quasi-
hermit life in the wood, get the decorations, etc., of the
Temple he erected to Love and Astrée ? "   One almost
blushes at having to explain, in a popular style, the
mistakenness, to use the mildest word, of these objections.
The present writer, in a book less ambitious than the
present on the sister subject of the English novel, once
ventured to point out that if you ask " where Sir Guyon
got that particularly convenient padlock with which he

---

[1] It is fair to say that Urfé has been praised for these historical excursions or
incursions of his.

fastened Occasion's tongue, and still more the hundred iron chains with which he bound Furor ? " that is to say, if you ask such a question seriously, you have no business to read romance at all. As to the Love matter, of that it is still less use to talk. There are some who would go so far as to deny the major ; even short of that hardiness it may be safely urged that in poetry and romance Love *is* the chief and principal thing, and that the poet and the romancer are only acting up to their commission in representing it as such. But the source of all these errors is best reached, and if it may be, stopped, by dealing with the first article of the indictment in the same way. What if Pastoral *is* artificial ? That may be an argument against the kind as a whole, but it cannot lie against a particular example of it, because that example is bound to act up to its kind's law. And I think it not extravagant to contend that the *Astrée* acts up to its law in the most inoffensive fashion possible—in such a fashion, in fact, as is hardly ever elsewhere found in the larger specimens, and by no means very often in the smaller. Hardly even in *As You Like It*, certainly not in the *Arcadia*, do the crook and the pipe get less in the way than they do here. A minor cavil has been urged—that the " shepherds " and the " knights," the " shepherdesses " and the " nymphs " are very little distinguishable from each other ; but why should they be ? Urfé had sufficient art to throw over all these things an air of glamour which, to those who can themselves take the benefit of the spell, banishes all inconsistencies, all improbabilities, all specks and knots and the like. It has been said that the *Astrée* has in it something of the genuine fairy-tale element. And the objections taken to it are really not much more reasonable than would be the poser whether even the cleverest of wolves, with or without a whole human grandmother inside it, would find it easy to wrap itself up in bedclothes, or whether, seeing that even walnut shells subject cats to such extreme discomfort, top-boots would not be even more intolerable to the most faithful of feline retainers.

The literary influence and importance of the book have never been denied by any competent criticism which The general had taken the trouble to inform itself of the importance facts. It can be pointed out that while the and influence. " Heroics," great as was their popularity for a time, did not keep it very long, and lost it by sharp and long continued—indeed never reversed—reaction, the influence of the *Astrée* on this later school itself was great, was not effaced by that of its pupils, and worked in directions different, as well as conjoint. It begat or helped to beget the *Précieuses* ; it did a great deal, if not exactly to set, to continue that historical character which, though we have not been able to speak very favourably of its immediate exercise, was at last to be so important. Above all, it reformed and reinforced the " sentimental " novel, as it is called. We have tried to show that there was much more of this in the mediaeval romance proper than it has been the fashion in recent times to allow. There was a great deal in the *Amadis* class, but extravaganzaed out of reason as well as out of rhyme. To us, or some of us, the *Astrée* type may still seem extravagant, but in comparison it brings things back to that truth and nature which were granted it by Madame de Sévigné. Its charms actually soothed the savage breast of Boileau, and it is not surprising that La Fontaine loved it. Few things of the kind are more creditable to the better side of Jean Jacques a full century later, than that he was not indifferent to its beauty ; and there were few greater omissions on the part of *mil-huit-cent-trente* (which, however, had so much to do !) than its comparative neglect to stray on to the gracious banks of the Lignon. All honour to Saint-Marc Girardin (not exactly the man from whom one would have expected it) for having been, as it seems, though in a kind of *palinodic* fashion, the first to render serious attention, and to do fair justice, to this vast and curious wilderness of delights.[1]

[1] Its difficulty of access in the French has been noted. The English translation may be less rare, but it is not a good one even of its kind. And, in face of the most false and misleading statements, never more frequent than at the present moment, about the efficacy of translations, it may be well to insist on the truth. For science, history,

To turn from the Pastoral to the Heroic, the actual readers, English or other, of *Artamène ou le Grand Cyrus*[1]

The *Grand* in late years, have probably been reckonable
Cyrus. rather as single spies (a phrase in this connection of some rather special appropriateness) than in battalions. And it is to be feared that many or most, if not nearly all of them, have opened it with little expectation of pleasure. The traditional estimates are dead against it as a rule; it has constantly served as an example—produced by wiseacres for wiseacres—of the *un*wisdom of our ancestors : and, generous as were Sir Walter's estimates of all literature, and especially of his fellow-craftsmen's and craftswomen's work, the lively passage in *Old Mortality* where Edith Bellenden's reference to the book excites the (in the circumstances justifiable) wrath of the Major—perhaps the only *locus* of ordinary reading that touches *Artamène* with anything but vagueness—is not entirely calculated to make readers read eagerly. But on turning honestly to the book itself, it is possible that considerable relief and even a little astonishment may result. Whether this satisfaction will arise at the very dedication by that vainglorious and yet redoubtable cavalier, Georges de Scudéry, in which he characteristically takes to himself the credit due mainly, if not wholly, to his plain little sister Madeleine, will depend upon taste. It is addressed to Anne Geneviève de Bourbon, Duchess of Longueville, sister of Condé, and adored mistress of many noteworthy persons—the most noteworthy perhaps being the Prince de Marcillac, better

---

philosophy (though in a descending ratio through these three) translations may serve. The man who knows Greek or Latin or any other *literature* only through them knows next to nothing of that literature as such, and in its literary quality. The version may be, as in the leading case of FitzGerald's Omar Khayyam, literature itself of the highest class; but it is quite *other* literature than the original, and is, in fact, a new original itself. It may, while keeping closer, be as good as Catullus on Sappho or as bad as Mr. Gladstone on Toplady in form; but the form, even if copied, is always again *other*.

[1] Some reasons will be given later for taking this first—not the least being the juxtaposition with the *Astrée*. The actual order of the chief "Heroic" authors and books is as follows : Gomberville, *La Caritée*, 1622; *Polexandre*, 1632; *Citherée*, 1640–42. La Calprénède, *Cassandre*, 1642; *Cléopâtre*, 1648; *Faramond*, 1662. Mlle. de Scudéry, *Ibrahim*, 1641; *Artamène*, 1649; *Clélie*, 1656; *Almahide*, 1660.

known, as from his later title, as Duc de la Rochefoucauld,
and a certain Aramis—not so good a man as three friends
of his, but a very accomplished, valiant, and ingenious
Its preface gentleman.   The blue eyes of Madame de
to Madame Longueville (M. de Scudéry takes the liberty
de Longue- to mention specially their charm, if not their
ville. colour) were among the most victorious in
that time of the "raining" and reigning influence of
such things : and somehow one succumbs a little even now
to her as the Queen of that bevy of fair, frail, and occasionally rather ferocious ladies of the Fronde feminine.
(The femininity was perhaps most evident in Madame
de Chevreuse, and the ferocity in Madame de Montbazon.)   Did not Madame de Longueville—did not
they all—figuratively speaking, draw that great philosopher Victor Cousin [1] up in a basket two centuries
after her death, even as had been done, literally if mythic-
ally, to that greater philosopher, Aristotle, ages before ?
But the governor of Our Lady of the Guard [2] says to her
many of these things which that very Aramis delighted to
hear (though not perhaps from the lips of rivals) and
described, rebuking the callousness of Porthos to them,
as fine and worthy of being said by gentlemen.   The
Great Cyrus himself "comes to lay at her Highness's
feet his palms and his trophies."   His historian, achieving
at once advertisement and epigram, is sure that as she
listened kindly to the *Death of Caesar* (his own play),
she will do the same to the Life of Cyrus.   Anne Geneviève herself will become the example of all Princesses
(the Reverend Abraham Adams might have groaned a
little here), just as Cyrus was the pattern of all Princes.
She is not the moon, but the sun [3] of the Court.   The
mingled blood of Bourbon and Montmorency gives her

[1] Cousin relieved his work on "The True, the Good, and the Beautiful" not only
with elaborate disquisitions on the ladies of the Fronde who, though certainly beautiful
were not very very good, but with a long exposition of French society as revealed in the
Grand Cyrus itself.

[2] Scudéry bore, and evidently rejoiced in, this sounding title, which can never have
had a titular to whom it was more appropriate.   The place seems to have been an actual
fortress, though a small one, near Marseilles.

[3] I blushed for my namesake when I found, some time afterwards, that he had copied
this unusual (save in German) feminisation of the sun from Gomberville (*v. inf.* p. 240).

such an *éclat* that it is almost unapproachable. He then digresses a little to glorify her brother, her husband, and Chapelain, the famous author of *La Pucelle*, who had the good fortune to be a friend of the Scudérys, as well as, like them, a strong "Heroic" theorist. After which he comes to that personal inventory which has been referred to, decides that her beauty is of a celestial splendour, and, in fact, a ray of Divinity itself; goes into raptures, not merely over her eyes, but over her hair (which simply effaces sunbeams); the brightness and whiteness of her complexion ; the just proportion of her features; and, above all, her singularly blended air of modesty and gallantry; her intellectual and spiritual match; her bodily graces; and he is finally sure that though somebody's misplaced acuteness may discover faults which nobody else will perceive (Georges would like to see them, no doubt), her extreme kindness will pardon them. A commonplace example of flattery this ? Well, perhaps not. One somehow sees, across the rhetoric, the blue eyes of Anne Geneviève and the bristling mustachios and "swashing outside" and mighty rapier of Georges ; and the thing becomes alive with the life of a not ungracious past, the ills of which were, after all, more or less common to all times, and its charms (like the charms of all things and persons charming) its own.

But the Address to the Reader, though it discards those "temptations of young ladies" (Madame de

The "Address to the Reader."

Longueville can never have been old) which Dr. Johnson recognised, and also the companion attractions of Cape and Sword, is of perhaps directly greater importance for our special and legitimate purpose. Here the brother and sister (probably the sister chiefly) develop some of the principles of their bold adventure, and they are of no small interest. It is allowed that the varying accounts of Cyrus (in which, as almost every one with the slightest tincture of education [1] must be aware, doctors differ remarkably), at least those of Herodotus and Xenophon (they do not, or she does

---

[1] That is classical education : in comparison with which "all others is cagmaggers."

not, seem to have known Ctesias), are confounded, and selected *ad libitum* and *secundum artem* only.   Further " lights " are given by the selection of the " Immortal Heliodorus " and " the great Urfé " as patterns and patrons of the work.   In fact, to any expert in the reading and criticism of novels it is clear that a great principle has been—imperfectly but somehow—laid hold of.

Perhaps, however, " laid hold of " is too strong ; we should do better by borrowing from Dante and saying The opening that the author or authors have " glimpsed of the the Panther,"—have seen that a novel ought "business." not to be a mere chronicle, unselected and miscellaneous, but a work which, whether it has actual unity of plot or not, has unity of interest, and will deal with its facts so as to secure that interest.   At first, indeed, they plunge us into the middle of matters quite excitingly, though perhaps not without more definite suggestion, both to them and to us, of the " immortal " Heliodorus.   The hero, who still bears his false name of Artamène,[1] appears at the head of a small army, the troops of Cyaxares of Media ; and, at the mouth of a twisting valley, suddenly sees before him the town of Sinope in flames, the shipping in the harbour blazing likewise, all but one bark, which seems to be flying from more than the conflagration.   A fine comic-opera situation follows ; for while Artamène is trying to subdue the fire he is attacked by the traitor Aribée, general under the King of Assyria, who is himself shut up in a tower and seems to be hopelessly cut off from rescue by the fire. The invincible hero, however, subdues at once the rebel and the destroying element; captures the Assyrian, who is not only his enemy and that of his master Cyaxares, but his Rival (the word has immense importance in these romances, and is always honoured with a capital there), and learns that the escaping galley carried with it his beloved Mandane, daughter of Cyaxares, of whom he is

[1] I have wavered a little between adopting French or Greek forms of names.   But as the authors are not consistent, and as some of their more fanciful compounds classicalise badly, I have finally decided to stick to the text in every case, except in those of historical persons where French forms such as " Pisistrate " would jar.

in quest, and who has been abducted from her abductor and lover by another, Prince Mazare of Sacia.

All this is lively and business-like enough, and one feels rather a brute in making the observation (necessary, however) that Artamène talks too much and not in the right way. When things in general are " on the edge of a razor " and one is a tried and skilful soldier, one does not, except on the stage, pause to address the unjust Gods, and inquire whether they have consented to the destruction of the most beautiful princess in the world; discuss with one's friends the reduction into cinders [1] of the adorable Mandane, and further enquire, without the slightest chance of answer, " Alas ! unjust Rival ! hast thou not thought rather of thine own preservation than of hers ? " However, for a time, the incidents do carry off the verbiage, and for nearly a hundred small pages there is no great cause for complaint. It is the style of the book; and if you do not like it you must " seek another inn." But what succeeds, for the major part of the first of the twenty volumes, [2] is open to severer criticisms. We fall into interminable discussions, récits, and the like, on the subject of the identity of Artamène and Cyrus, and we see at once the imperfect fashion in which the nature of the novel is conceived. That elaborate explanation— necessary in history, philosophy, and other " serious " works—cannot be cut down too much in fiction, is one truth that has not been learnt. [3] That the stuffing of the story with large patches of solid history or pseudo-history is wrong and disenchanting has not been learnt either; and this is the less surprising and the more pardonable in that very few, if indeed any, of the masters and mistresses of the novel, later and greater than Georges and

The ups and downs of the general conduct of the story.

---

[1] Like Robina in *Mrs. Lirriper's Legacy.*

[2] There are ten parts, each divisible into two *volumes* and three books. There is also a division at the end of the fifth " part " and tenth volume, the first five (ten) having apparently been issued together. The " parts " are continuously paged—running never, I think, to less than 1000 pages and more than once to a little over 1400.

[3] Drama may have done harm here, if those dramatic critics who say that you must never " puzzle the audience " are right. The happy novel-reader is of less captious mood and mould : he trusts his author and hopes his author will pull him through.

Madeleine de Scudéry, have not refused to learn it or have not carelessly forgotten the learning. Even Scott committed the fault sometimes, though never in his very best work. Dumas—when he went out and left the "young men" to fill in, and stayed too long, and made them fill in too much—did it constantly. Yet again, that mixture of excess and defect in talking, which has been noted already, becomes more and more trying in connection with the previously mentioned faults and others. Of *mere* talk there is enough and immensely to spare ; but it is practically never real dialogue, still less real conversation. It is harangue, narrative, soliloquy, what you will, in the less lively theatrical forms of speech watered out in prose, with "passing of compliments" in the most gentlefolkly manner, and a spice of "Phébus" or Euphuism now and then. But it is never real personal talk,[1] while as for conveying the action *by* the talk as the two great masters above mentioned and nearly all others of their kind do, there is no vestige of even an attempt at the feat, or a glimpse of its desirableness.

Again, one sees before long that of one priceless quality—a sense of humour—we shall find, though there is a little mild wit, especially in the words of the ladies named in the note, no trace in the book, but a "terrible *minus* quantity." I do not know that the late Sir William Gilbert was a great student of literature—of classical literature, to judge from the nomenclature of *Pygmalion and Galatea* mentioned above, he certainly was not. But his eyes would surely have glistened at the unconscious and serious anticipation of his own methods at their most Gilbertian, had he ever read pp. 308 *sqq.* of this first volume. Here not only do Cyrus and a famous pirate, by boarding with irresistible valour on each side, "exchange ships," and so find themselves at once to have gained the enemy's and lost their own, but this remarkable manœuvre is repeated more than twenty times without advantage on either side—or

---

[1] Some exception in the way of occasional flashes may be made for two lively maids of honour to be mentioned later, Martésie and Doralise.

without apparently any sensible losses on either side.
From which it would appear that both contented themselves with displays of agility in climbing from vessel
to vessel, and did nothing so impolite as to use their
" javelins, arrows, and cutlasses " (of which, nevertheless,
we hear) against the persons of their competitors in such
agility on the other side.   It did come to an end somehow
after some time ; but one is quite certain that if Mr.
Crummles had had the means of presenting such an
admirable spectacle on any boards, he never would have
contented himself without several encores of the whole
twenty operations.

An experienced reader, therefore, will not need to
spend many hours before he appreciates pretty thoroughly
what he has to expect—of good, of bad, and of indifferent
—from this famous book.   It is, though in a different
sense from Montaigne's, a *livre de bonne foi*.   And we
must remember that the readers whom it directly addressed expected from books of this kind " pastime "
in the most literal and generous, if also humdrum, sense
of the word ; noble sentiments, perhaps a little learning,
possibly a few hidden glances at great people not of
antiquity only.   All these they got here, most faithfully
supplied according to their demand.

Probably nothing will give the reader, who does not
thus read for himself, a better idea of the book than some
Extracts— extract translations, beginning with Artamène's
the introduc- first interview with Mandane,[1] going on to
tion of Cyrus his reflections thereon, and adding a perhaps
to Mandane. slightly shortened version of the great fight
recounted later, in which again some evidence of the
damaging absence of humour, and some suggestions as
to the originals of divers well-known parodies, will be
found.   (It must be remembered that these are all parts
of an enormous *récit* by Chrisante, one of Artamène's

[1] There is an immense "throw-back" after the Sinope affair, in which the previous
history of Artamène and the circumstances of Mandane's abduction are recounted up to
date—I hope that some readers at least will not have forgotten the introduction of
Lancelot to Guinevere. We have here the Middle Age and the *Grand Siècle* like
philippines in a nut-shell.

confidants and captains, to the King of Hircania, a monarch doubtless inured to hardships in the chase of his
native tigers, or requiring some sedative as a change
from it.)

No sooner had the Princess seen my Master than she rose, and
prepared to receive him with much kindness and much joy, having
already heard, by Arbaces, the service he had done to the King,
her father. Artamène then made her two deep bows, and coming
closer to her, but with all the respect due to a person of her condition, he kissed [*no doubt the hem of*] her robe, and presented to her
the King's letter, which she read that very instant. When she had
done, he was going to begin the conversation with a compliment,
after telling her what had brought him ; but the Princess anticipated him in the most obliging manner. "What Divinity,
generous stranger," said she, "has brought you among us to save
all Cappadocia by saving its King ? and to render him a service
which the whole of his servants could not have rendered ?"
"Madam," answered Artamène, "you are right in thinking that
some Divinity has led me hither; and it must have been some
one of those beneficent Divinities who do only good to men, since
it has procured me the honour of being known to you, and the
happiness of being chosen by Fortune to render to the King a
slight service, which might, no doubt, have been better done him
by any other man." "Modesty," said the Princess (smiling and
turning towards the ladies who were nearest her), "is a virtue
which belongs so essentially to our own sex, that I do not know
whether I ought to allow this generous stranger so unjustly to rob
us of it, or—not content with possessing eminently that valour to
which we must make no pretension—to try to be as modest when
he is spoken to of the fineness of his actions as reasonable women
ought to be when they are praised for their beauty. For my part,"
she added, looking at Artamène, "I confess I find your proceeding
a little unfair. And I do not think that I ought to allow it, or to
deprive myself of the power of praising you infinitely, although
you cannot endure it." "Persons like you," retorted Artamène,
but with profound respect, "ought to receive praise from all the
earth, and not to give it lightly. 'Tis a thing, Madam, of which
it is not pleasant to have to repeat ; for which reason I beg you not
to expose yourself to such a danger. Wait, Madam, till I have
the honour of being a little better known to you."

There are several pages more of this *carte* and *tierce*
of compliment ; but perhaps a degenerate and impatient
age may desire that we should pass to the next subject.

Whether it is right or not in so desiring may perhaps be discussed when the three samples have been given.

Artamène has been dismissed with every mark of favour, and lodged in a pavilion overlooking the garden. When he is alone—

After having passed and re-passed all these things over again in his imagination, "Ye gods!" said he, "if, when she is so lovable, it should chance that I cannot make her love me, what would become of the wretched Artamène? But," and he caught himself up suddenly, "since she seems capable of appreciating glory and services, let us continue to act as we have begun! and let us do such great deeds that, even if her inclination resisted, esteem may introduce us, against her will, into her heart! For, after all, whatever men may say, and whatever I may myself have said, one may give a little esteem to what one will never in the least love; but I do not think one can give much esteem to what will never earn a little love. Let us hope, then; let us hope! let us make ourselves worthy to be pitied if we are not worthy to be loved."

His soliloquy in the pavilion. [marginal note]

After which somewhat philosophical meditation it is not surprising that he should be informed by one of his aides-de-camp that the Princess was in the garden. For what were Princesses made? and for what gardens?

The third is a longer passage, but it shall be subjected to that kind of *centoing* which has been found convenient earlier in this volume.

[*The dispute between the kings of Cappadocia on the one hand and of Pontus on the other has been referred to a select combat of two hundred men a side. Artamène, of course, obtains the command of the Cappadocians, to the despair of his explosive but not ungenerous rival, "Philip Dastus." After a very beautiful interview with Mandane (where, once more, the most elegant compliments pass between these gentlefolkliest of all heroes and heroines) and divers preliminaries, the fight comes off.*] [1] They began to advance with heads lowered, without cries or noise of any kind, but in a silence which struck terror. As soon as they were near enough to use their javelins, they launched them with such violence that [*a slight bathos*] these flying weapons had

The Fight of the Four Hundred. [marginal note]

---

[1] To understand the account, it must be remembered that the combat takes place in a position secluded from the two armies and strictly forbidden to lookers-on; also that it is to be absolutely *à outrance*.

a pretty great effect on both sides, but much greater on that of the Cappadocians than on the other. Then, sword in hand and covered by their shields, they came to blows, and Artamène, as we were informed, immolated the first victim [*but how about the javelin " effect " ?*] in this bloody sacrifice. For, having got in front of all his companions by some paces, he killed, with a mighty sword-stroke, the first who offered resistance. [*Despite this, the general struggle continues to go against the Cappadocians, though Artamène's exploits alarm one of the enemy, named Artane, so much that he skulks away to a neighbouring knoll. At last*] things came to such a point that Artamène found himself with fourteen others against forty ; so I leave you to judge, Sir [*Chrisante parle toujours*], whether the party of the King of Pontus did not believe they had conquered, and whether the Cappadocians had not reason to think themselves beaten. But as, in this fight, it was not allowed either to ask or to give quarter, and was necessary either to win or to die, the most despairing became the most valiant. [*The next stage is, that in consequence of enormous efforts on his part, the hero finds himself and his party ten to ten, which " equality " naturally cheers them up. But the wounds of the Cappadocians are the severer ; the ten on their side become seven, with no further loss to the enemy, and at last Artamène finds himself, after three hours' fighting, alone against three, though only slightly wounded. He wisely uses his great agility in retiring and dodging ; separates one enemy from the other two, and kills him ; attacks the two survivors, and, one luckily stumbling over a buckler, kills a second, so that at last the combat is single. During this time the coward Artane abstains from intervening, all the more because the one surviving champion of Pontus is a personal rival of his, and because, by a very ingenious piece of casuistry, he persuades himself that the two combatants are sure to kill each other, and he, Artane, surviving, will obtain the victory for self and country !*]

He is nearly right; but not quite. For after Artamène has wounded the Pontic Pharnaces in six places, and Pharnaces Artamène in four (for we wound "by the card" here), the hero runs Pharnaces through the heart, receiving only a thigh-wound in return. He flourishes both swords, cries " I have conquered ! " and falls in a faint from loss of blood. Artane thinks him dead, and without caring to come close and " mak sicker," goes off to claim the victory. But Artamène revives, finds himself alone, and, with what strength he has left, piles the arms of the dead together, writes with his own blood on a silver shield—

TO
JUPITER
GUARDIAN OF TROPHIES,

and lies beside it as well as he can. The false news
deceives for a short time, but when the stipulated advance
to the field takes place on both sides, the discovery of
the surviving victor introduces a new complication, from
which we may for the moment abstain.

The singlestick rattle of compliment in the interview
first given, and the rather obvious and superfluous
meditations of the second, may seem, if not exactly
disgusting, tedious and jejune. But the " Fight of the
Four Hundred " is not frigid ; and it is only fair to say
that, after the rather absurd passage of *chassé croisé* on
ship-board quoted or at least summarised earlier, the
capture of Artamène by numbers and his surrender to
the generous corsair Thrasybulus are not ill told, while
there are several other good fights before you come to
the end of this very first volume. There is, moreover,
an elaborate portrait of the Princess, evidently intended
to " pick up " that vaguer one of Madame de Longueville
in the Preface, but with the blue of the eyes here fear-
lessly specified. Here also does the celebrated Philidaspes
(most improperly, if it had not been for the justification
to be given later, transmogrified in the above-mentioned
passage by Major Bellenden into " Philip Dastus ?
Philip Devil ") make his appearance. The worst of it is
that most, if not the whole, is done by the *récit* delivered,
as noted above, by Chrisante, one of those representatives
of the no less faithful than strong Gyas and Cloanthus,
whom imitation of the ancients has imposed on Scudéry
and his sister, and inflicted on their readers.

The story of the Cappadocian-Pontic fight [1] is continued in the second volume of the First Part by the
expected delivery of harangues from the two claimants,

[1] It is not perhaps extravagant to suggest that Sir Walter had something of this
fight, as well as of the *Combat des Trente*, in his mind when he composed the famous
record of the Clan Chattan and Clan Quhele battle.

and the obligatory, but to Artane very unwelcome,
The abstract single combat.   He is, of course, vanquished
resumed. and pardoned by his foe,[1] making, if not
full, sufficient confession; and it is not surprising to
hear that the King of Pontus requests to see no more of
him.   The rest—for it must never be forgotten that all
this is " throwing back "—then turns to the rivalry of
Artamène and Philidaspes for the love of Mandane,
while she (again, of course) has not the faintest idea that
either is in love with her.   Philidaspes, who (still, of
course) is not Philidaspes at all, is a rough customer—
(in fact the Major hardly did him injustice in calling him
" Philip Devil "—betraying also perhaps some knowledge
of the text), and it comes to a tussle.   This rather resembles what the contemptuous French early Romantics
called *une boxade* than a formal duel, and Artamène stuns
his man with a blow of the flat.   Cyaxares [2] is very
angry, and imprisons them both, not yet realising their
actual fault.   It does not matter much to Artamène,
who in prison can think, aloud and in the most beautiful
" Phébus," of Mandane.   It matters perhaps a little
more to the reader; for a courteous jailer, Aglatidas,
takes the occasion to relate his own woes in a " History
of Aglatidas and Amestris," which completes the second
volume of the First Part in three hundred and fifty mortal
pages to itself.

The first volume of the Second Part returns to the
main story, or rather the main series of *récits*; for, Chrisante being not unnaturally exhausted after talking for
a thousand pages or so, Feraulas, another of Artamène's
men, takes up the running.   The prisoners are let out,
and Mandane reconciles them, after which—as another
but later contemporary remarks (again of other things,
but probably with some reminiscence of this)—they
become much more mortal enemies than before.   The

---

[1] Praed's delightful Medora might have found the practice of the *Grand Cyrus* rather
oppressive ; but she would have thoroughly approved its principles.
[2] He is King of Cappadocia now, Astyages being alive ; and only succeeds to Media
later.   It must never be forgotten that the *Cyropaedia*, not Herodotus, is the chief
authority relied upon by the authors, though they sometimes mix the two.

reflections and soliloquies of Artamène recur; but a not unimportant, although subordinate, new character appears—not as the first example, but as the foremost representative, in the novel, of the great figure of the " confidante "—in Martésie, Mandane's chief maid of honour. Nobody, it is to be hoped, wants an elaborate account of, the part she plays, but it should be said that she plays it with much more spirit and individuality than her mistress is allowed to show. Then, according to the general plan of all these books, in which fierce wars and faithful loves alternate, there is more fighting, and though Artamène is victorious (as how should he not be, save now and then to prevent monotony ?) he disappears and is thought dead. Of course Mandane cries, and confesses to the confidante, being entirely " finished " by a very exquisite letter which Artamène has written before going into the doubtful battle. However, he is (yet once more, of course) not dead at all. What (as that most sagacious of men, the elder Mr. Weller, would have said) 'd have become of the other seventeen volumes if he had been ? There is one of the *quiproquos* or mis- understandings which are as necessary to this kind of novel as the flirtations and the fisticuffs, brought about by the persistence of an enemy princess in taking Arta- mène for her son Spithridates ;[1] but all comes right for the time, and the hero returns to his friends. The plot, however, thickens. An accident informs Artamène that Philidaspes is really Prince of Assyria, sure to become King when his mother, Nitocris, dies or abdicates, and that, being as he is, and as Artamène knows already, desperately in love with Mandane, he has formed a plot for carrying her off. The difficulties in the way of pre- venting this are great, because, though the hero is already aware that he is Cyrus, it is for many reasons undesirable to inform Cyaxares of the fact ; and at last Philidaspes, helped by the traitor Aribée (*v. sup.*), succeeds in the abduction, after an interlude in which a fresh Rival,

---

[1] There is a very great physical resemblance between the two, and this plays an important and repeated part in the book.

with a still larger R, the King of Pontus himself, turns
up ; and an immense episode, in which Thomyris, Queen
of Scythia, appears, not yet in her more or less historical
part of victress of Cyrus. She is here only a young
sovereign, widowed in her earliest youth, extremely
beautiful (see a portrait of her *inf.*), who has never yet
loved, but who falls instantly in love with Cyrus himself
(when he is sent to her court), and is rather a formidable
person to deal with, inasmuch as, besides having great
wealth and power, she has established a diplomatic
system of intrigue in other countries, which the newest
German or other empire might envy. By the end of
this volume, however, the Artamène-Cyrus confusion is
partly cleared up (though Cyaxares is not yet made aware
of the facts), and the hero is sent after Mandane, to be
disappointed at Sinope, in the fashion recounted some
thousand or two pages before.

With the beginning of vol. iv. (that is to say, part ii.
vol. ii.) we return, though still in retrospect, to the direct
fate of Mandane. Nitocris is dead, Philidaspes has
succeeded to the crown of Assyria, and has carried Mandane off to his own dominions. The situation with so
robustious a person as this prince may seem awkward,
and indeed, as is observed in a later part of the book,
the heroine's repeated sojourns (there are three if not
four of them in all [1]) in the complete power of one of the
Rivals, with a large R, are very trying to Cyrus. However, such a shocking thing as violence is hardly hinted
at, and the Princess always succeeds, as the Creole lady
in *Newton Forster* said she did with the pirates, in
" temporising," while her abductors confine themselves
for the most part to the finest " Phébus." Even the fiery
Philidaspes, though he breaks out sometimes, conveys
his wish that Mandane should accompany him to Babylon
by pointing out that " the Euphrates is jealous of the
Tigris for having first had the honour of her presence,"

[1] The King of Assyria, the King of Pontus, and the later Aryante (*v. inf.*). The
fourth is the " good Rival " Mazare, who, though he also is at one time in possession
of the prize, and though he never is weary of " loving unloved," is too honourable a
gentleman to force his attentions on an unwilling mistress.

and that " the First City of the World ought clearly to possess the most illustrious princess of the Earth." Of course, if there is any base person who cannot derive an Aramisian satisfaction (*v. sup.*) from such things as this, he had better abstain from the *Cyrus*. But happier souls they please—not exquisitely, perhaps, or tumultuously, but still well—with a mild tickle which is not unvoluptuous. One is even a very little sorry for Philip Dastus when he begs his cruel idol to write to him the single word Esperez, and meanwhile kindly puts it in capitals and a line to itself. Almost immediately afterwards an The oracle to oracle juggles with him in fashion delightful to Philidaspes. himself, and puzzling to everybody except the intelligent reader, who, it is hoped, will see the double meaning at once.

> Il t'est permis d'espérer
> De la faire soupirer,
> Malgré sa haine :
> Car un jour entre ses bras,
> Tu rencontreras
> La fin de ta peine.

Alas ! without going further (upon honour and according to fact), one sees the *other* explanation—that Mandane will have to perform the uncomfortable duty— often assigned to heroines—of having Philidaspes die in her lap.

For the present, however, only discomfiture, not death, awaits him. The Medes blockade Babylon to recover their princess ; it suffers from hunger, and Philidaspes, with Mandane and the chivalrous Sacian Prince Mazare, whom we have heard of before, escapes to Sinope. Then the events recorded in the very beginning happen, and Mandane, after escaping the flames of Sinope through Mazare's abduction of her by sea, and suffering shipwreck, falls into the power of the King of Pontus. This calls a halt in the main story ; and, as before, a " Troisième Livre " consists of another huge inset—the hugest yet—of seven hundred pages this time, describing an unusually, if not entirely, independent subject—the loves and fates of a certain Philosipe and a certain Polisante. This volume contains a rather forcible boating-scene, which supplies the theme for the old frontispiece.

Refreshed as usual by this excursion,[1] the author returns (in vol. v., bk. i., chap. iii.) to Cyrus, who is once more in peril, and in a worse one than ever. Cyaxares, arriving at Sinope, does not find his daughter, but does discover that Artamène, whom he does not yet know to be Cyrus and heir to Persia, is in love with her. Owing chiefly to the wiles of a villain, Métrobate, he arrests the Prince, and is on the point of having him executed, despite the protests of the allied kings. But the whole army, with the Persian contingent at its head, assaults the castle, and rescues Cyrus, after the traitor Métrobate has tried to double his treachery and get Cyaxares assassinated. Nobody who remembers the *Letter of Advice* already quoted will doubt what the conduct of Cyrus is. He only accepts the rescue in order that he may post himself at the castle gate, and threaten to kill anybody who attacks Cyaxares.

After this burst, which is really exciting in a way, we must expect something more soporific. Martésie takes the place of her absent mistress to some extent, and a good deal of what might be mistaken for " Passe-relle "[2] flirtation takes place, or would do so, if it were not that Cyrus would, of course, die rather than pay attention to anybody but Mandane herself, and that Feraulas, already mentioned as one of the Faithful Companions, is detailed as Martésie's lover. She is, however, installed as a sort of Vice-Queen of a wordy tourney between four unhappy lovers, who fill up the rest of the volume with their stories of " Amants

---

[1] It is probably, however, not quite fair to leave the reader, even for a time, under the impression that it is *merely* an excursion. Of all the huge and numerous loop-lines, backwaters, ramifications, reticulations, episodes, or whatever they may be called, there is hardly one which has not a real connection with the general plot ; and the appearance of Thomyris here has such connection (as will be duly seen) in a capital and vital degree.

[2] Some readers no doubt will not need to be reminded that this is the original title of *The Marriage of Kitty*,—literally " gangway," but in the sense of " makeshift " or " *locum tenens.*"

Infortunés " (cf. the original title of the *Heptameron*), dealing respectively with and told by—

(1) A lover who is loved, but separated from his mistress.

(2) One who is unloved.

(3) A jealous one.

(4) One whose love is dead.[1]

They do it moderately, in rather less than five hundred pages, and Martésie sums up in a manner worthy of any Mistress of the Rolls, contrasting their fates, and deciding very cleverly against the jealous man.

The first twenty pages or so of the sixth volume (nominally iii. 2) afford a good example of the fashion in which, as may be observed more fully below, even an analysis of the *Grand Cyrus*, though a great advance on mere general description of it, must be still (unless it be itself intolerably voluminous) insufficient. Not very much actually " happens "; but if you simply skip, you miss a fresh illustration of magnanimity not only in Cyrus, but in a formerly mentioned character, Aglatidas, with reference to the heroine Amestris earlier inset in the tale (*v. sup.*). And this is an example of the new and sometimes very ingenious fashion in which these apparent excursions are turned into something like real episodes, or at any rate supply connecting threads of the whole, in a manner not entirely unlike that which some critics have so hastily and unjustly overlooked in Spenser. Then we have an imbroglio about forged letters, and a clearing-up of a former charge against the hero, and (still within the twenty pages) a very curious scene—the last for the time—of that flirtation-without-flirtation between Cyrus and Martésie. She wants to have back a picture of Mandane, which she has lent him to worship ; and he replies, looking at her " attentively " (one wonders whether Mandane, if present, would have been entirely satisfied with his " attention "), addresses her as " Cruel Person," and asks her (he is just setting out for the

---

[1] Cf. John Heywood's Interlude of *Love*. These stories also remind one of the short romances noticed above.

Armenian war) how she thinks he can conquer when she
takes away what should make him invincible. To which
replies Miss Martésie, "You have gained so many
victories [*ahem !*] without this help, that it would seem
you have no need of it." This is very nice, and Martésie,
who is herself, as previously observed, quite nice throughout, lets him have the picture after all. But Cyrus, for
once rather ungraciously, will not allow her lover, and his
henchman, Feraulas to escort her home ; first, because
he wants Feraulas's services himself, and secondly,
because it is unjust that Feraulas should be happy with
Martésie when Cyrus is miserable without Mandane—
an argument which, whether slightly selfish or not, is at
any rate in complete keeping with the whole atmosphere
of the book.

Now, as this is by no means a very exceptional,
certainly not a unique, score of pages, and as it has taken
The advent almost a whole one of ours to give a rather
of Araminta. imperfect notion of its contents, it follows that
it would take about six hundred, if not more, to do
justice to the ten or twelve thousand of the original.
Which (in one of the most immortal of formulas) " is
impossible." We must fall back, therefore, on the
system already pursued for the rest of this volume, and
perhaps even contract its application in some cases. A
rash promise of the now entirely, if not also rather in-
sanely,[1] generous Prince not to marry Mandane without
fighting Philidaspes, or rather the King of Assyria,
beforehand, is important; and an at last minute description of Cyrus's person and equipment as he sets out (on
one of the proudest and finest horses that ever was, with
a war-dress the superbest that can be imagined, and with
Mandane's magnificent scarf put on for the first time) is
not quite omissible. But then things become intricate.
Our old friend Spithridates comes back, and has first
love affairs and afterwards an enormous *récit*-episode

---

[1] No gentleman, of course, could refuse a challenge pure and simple, unless in very
peculiar circumstances ; but hardly Sir Lucius O'Trigger or Captain M'Turk would
oblige a friend to enter into this curious kind of bargain.

with a certain Princess of Pontus, whom Cyrus, reminding one slightly of Bentley on Mr. Pope's *Homer* and Tommy Merton on Cider, pronounces to be *belle, blonde, blanche et bien faite*, but not Mandane; and who has the further charm of possessing, for the first time in literature if one mistakes not, the renowned name of Araminta. A pair of letters between these two will be useful as specimens, and to some, it may be hoped, agreeable in themselves.

SPITHRIDATES TO THE PRINCESS ARAMINTA

I depart, Madam, because you wish it : but, in departing, I am the most unhappy of all men. I know not whither I go ; nor when I shall return ; nor even if you wish that I *should* return ; and yet they tell me I must live and hope. But I should not know how to do either the one or the other, unless you order me to do both by two lines in your own hand. Therefore I beg them of you, divine Princess— in the name of an illustrious person, now no more, [*her brother Sinnesis, who had been a great friend of his*], but who will live for ever in the memory of SPITHRIDATES.

Her correspondence with Spithridates.

[*He can hardly have hoped for anything better than the following answer, which is much more " downright Dunstable " than is usual here.*]

ARAMINTA TO SPITHRIDATES

Live as long as it shall please the Gods to allow you. Hope as long as Araminta lives—she begs you : and even if you yourself wish to live, she orders you to do so.

[*In other words he says, " My own Araminta, say ' Yes ' ! " and she does. This attitude necessarily involves the despair of a Rival, who writes thus :*]

PHARNACES TO THE PRINCESS ARAMINTA

If Fortune seconds my designs, I go to a place where I shall conquer *and* die—where I shall make known, by my generous despair, that if I could not deserve your affection by my services, I shall have at least not made myself unworthy of your compassion by my death.

[*And, to do him justice, he " goes and does it."*]

This episode, however, did not induce Mademoiselle

Madeleine to break her queer custom of having something of the same kind in the Third Book of every Part.
For though there is some " business," it slips into another
regular " History," this time of Prince Thrasybulus, a
naval hero, of whom we have often heard, and his Alcio-
nide, not a bad name for a sailor's mistress.[1]   Finally,
we come back to more events of a rather troublesome
kind : for the *ci-devant* Philidaspes most inconveniently
insists in taking part in the rescuing expedition, which—
saving scandal of great ones—is very much as if Mr.
William Sikes should insist in helping to extract booty
from Mr. Tobias Crackit.   And we finally leave Cyrus
in a decidedly awkward situation morally, and the middle
of a dark wood physically.

Here, according to that paulo-post-future precedent
which she did so much to create, the authoress was quite
Some
interposed
comments. justified in leaving him at the end of a volume ;
and perhaps the present historian is, to compare
small things with great, equally justified in
heaving-to (to borrow from Mr. Kipling) and addressing
a small critical sermon to such crew as he may have
attracted.   We have surveyed not quite a third of the
book ; but this ought in any case—*teste* the loved and
lost " three-decker " which the allusion just made concerns—to give us a notion of the author's quality and of
his or her *faire*.   It should not be very difficult for anybody, unless the foregoing analysis has been very clumsily
done, to discern considerable method in Madeleine's
mild madness, and, what is more, not a little originality.
The method has, no doubt, as it was certain to have in
the circumstances, a regular irregularity, which is, or
would be in anybody but a novice, a little clumsy : and
the originality may want some precedent study to discover it.   But both are there.   The skeleton of this vast
work may perhaps be fairly constructed from what has
already been dissected of the body ; and the method of

---

[1] Another instance of the astonishing interweaving of the book occurs here ; for
here is the first mention of Sappho and other persons and things to be caught up sooner
or later.

clothing the skeleton reveals itself without much difficulty. You have the central idea in the loves of Cyrus
and Mandane, which are to be made as true as possible,
but also running as roughly as may be. Moreover,
whether they run rough or smooth, you are to keep them
in suspense as long as you possibly can. The means of
doing this are laboriously varied and multiplied. The
clumsiest of them—the perpetual intercalation or inter-
polation of " side-shows " in the way of *Histoires*—annoys
modern readers particularly, and has, as a rule, since
been itself beautifully and beneficently lessened, in some
cases altogether discarded, or changed—in emancipation
from the influence of the " Unities "—to the form of
second plots, not ostentatiously severed from the main
one. But, as has been pointed out, a great deal of
trouble is at any rate taken to knit them to the main plot
itself, if not actually and invariably to incorporate them
therewith ; and the means of this are again not altogether
uncraftsmanlike. Sometimes, as in the case of Spithridates, the person, or one of the persons, is introduced first
in the main history ; his own particular concerns are
dealt with later, and, for good or for evil, he returns to the
central scheme. Sometimes, as in that of Amestris, you
have the *Histoire* before the personage enters the main
story. Then there is the other device of varying direct
narrative, as to this main story itself, with *Récit* ; and
always you have a careful peppering in of new characters,
by *histoire*, by *récit*, or by the main story, to create fresh
interests. Again, there is the contrast of " business," as
we have called it—fighting and politics—with love-
making and miscellaneous fine talk. And, lastly, there
are—what, if they were not whelmed in such an ocean
of other things, would attract more notice—the not
unfrequent individual phrases and situations which have
interest in themselves. It must surely be obvious that
in these things are great possibilities for future use,
even if the actual inventor has not made the most of
them.

Their originality may perhaps deserve a little more

comment.[1] The mixture of secondary plots might, by
a person more given to theorise than the present historian
—who pays his readers the compliment of supposing that
that excessively easy and therefore somewhat negligible
business can be done by themselves if they wish—be
traced to an accidental feature of the later mediaeval
romances.   In these the congeries of earlier texts, which
the compiler had not the wits, or at least the desire, to
systematise, provided something like it ; but required
the genius of a Spenser, or the considerable craft of a
Scudéry, to throw it into shape and add the connecting
links.   Many of the other things are to be found in the
Scudéry romance practically for the first time.   And the
suffusion of the whole with a new tone and colour of at
least courtly manners is something more to be counted, as
well as the constant exclusion of the clumsy " conjuror's
supernatural " of the *Amadis* group.   That the fairy
story sprung up, to supply the always graceful supernatural
element in a better form, is a matter which will be dealt
with ,later in this chapter.   The oracles, etc., of the
Cyrus belong, of course, to the historical, not the imaginative side of the presentation ; but may be partly due to
the *Astrée*, the influence of which was, we saw, admitted.
    It may seem unjust that the more this complication
of interests increases, the less complete should be the
Analysis   survey of them ; and yet a moment's thought
resumed.   will show that this is almost a necessity.
Moreover, the methods do not vary much ; it is only
that they are applied to a larger and larger mass of ac-
cumulating material.   The first volume of the Fourth
Part, the seventh of the twenty, follows—though with
that absence of slavish repetition which has been allowed
as one of the graces of the book—the general scheme.
Cyrus gets out of the wood literally, but not figuratively ;
for when he and the King of Assyria have joined forces,
to pursue that rather paradoxical alliance which is to

[1] Such knowledge as I have of the other romances of the " heroic" group shows
them to be, with the possible exception of those of La Calprenède, inferior in this
respect, even allowing for the influence of the *Cyropaedia*.

run in couple with rivalry for love and to end in a personal combat, they see on the other side of a river a chariot, in which Mandane probably or certainly is. But the river is unbridged and unfordable, and no boats can be had ; so that, after trying to swim it and nearly getting drowned, they have to relinquish the game that had been actually in sight. Next, two things happen. First, Martésie appears (as usually to our satisfaction), and in consequence of a series of accidents, shares and solaces Mandane's captivity. Then, on the other side, Panthea, Queen of Susiana, and wife of one of the enemy princes, falls into Cyrus's hands, and with Araminta (who is, it should have, if it has not been, said earlier, sister of the King of Pontus) furnishes valuable hostage for good treatment of Mandane and other Medo-Persian-Phrygian-Hircanian prisoners.

Things having thus been fairly bustled up for a time, a *Histoire* is, of course, imminent, and we have it, of about usual length, concerning the Lydian Princess Palmis and a certain Cléandre ; while, even when this is done, we fall back, not on the main story, but once more on that of Aglatidas and Amestris, which is in a sad plight, for Amestris (who has been married against her will and is *maumariée* too) thinks she is a widow, and finds she is not.

It has just been mentioned that Palmis is a Lydian Princess ; and before the end of this Part Croesus comes personally into the story, being the head of a formidable combination to supplant the King of Pontus, detain Mandane, and, if possible (as the well-known oracle, in the usual ambiguity (*v. inf.*), encourages him to hope), conquer the Medo-Persian empire and make it his own. But the *Histoire* mania—now further excited by consistence in working the personages so obtained in generally— is in great evidence, and "Lygdamis and Cléonice" supply a large proportion of the early and all the middle of the eighth volume, the second of the Fourth Part. There is, however, much more business than usual at the end to make up for any slackness at the beginning.

In a side-action with the Lydians both Cyrus and the King of Assyria are captured by force of numbers, though the former is at once released by the Princess Palmis, as well as Artames, son of Cyrus's Phrygian ally, whom Croesus chooses to consider as a rebel, and intends to put to death. Here, however, the captive Queen and Princess, Panthea and Araminta, come into good play, and exercise strong and successful influence through the husband of the one and the brother of the other. But at the end of book, volume, and part we leave Cyrus once more in the dismals. For though he has actually seen Mandane he cannot get at her, and he has heard three apparently most unfavourable oracles ; the Babylonian one, which was quoted above, and which he, like everybody else, takes as a promise of success to Philidaspes ; the ambiguous Delphic forecast of " the fall of *an* Empire " to Croesus ; and that of his own death at the hands of a hostile queen, the only one which, historically, was to be fulfilled in its apparent sense, while the others were not. He cares, indeed, not much about the two last, but infinitely about the first.

At the opening of the Fifth Part (ninth volume) there is a short but curious " Address to the Reader," announcing the fulfilment of the first half of the promised production, and bidding him not be downhearted, for the first of the second half (the Sixth Part or eleventh volume of the whole) is actually at Press. It may be noticed that there is a swagger about these *avis* and such like things, which probably *is* attributable to Georges, and not to Madeleine.[1]

The inevitable *Histoire* comes earlier than usual in this division, and is of unusual importance ; for it deals with two persons of great distinction, and already intro-

[1] An extract may be worth giving in a note : " For the rest, if there is anybody who is not acquainted enough with all my authors [*this is a very delightful sweep over literature*] to know what was the Ring of Gyges which is spoken of in this volume, let him not imagine that it is Angelica's, with which I chose to adorn Artamène ; and let him, on the contrary, know that it was Ariosto who stole this famous ring which gave his Paladins so much trouble ; that *he* took it from those great men whom I am obliged to follow " [*a sweep of George's plumed hat in the best Molièresque marquis style to Herodotus, Xenophon, and Cicero (who comes in shortly) and the others*].

duced in the story, Queen Panthea and her husband Abradates. It is also one of the longer batch, running to some four hundred pages ; and a notable part in it and in the future main story is played by one Doralise— a pretty name, which Dryden, making it prettier still by substituting a *c* for the *s*, borrowed for his most original and (with that earlier Florimel of *The Maiden Queen*, who is said to have been studied directly off Nell Gwyn) perhaps his most attractive heroine, the Doralice of *Marriage à la Mode*. Another important character, the villain of the sub-plot, is one Mexaris.[1] At the end of the first instalment we leave Cyrus preparing elaborate machines of war to crush the Lydians.

Early in Book II. we hear of a mysterious warrior on the enemy side whom nobody knows, who calls himself Telephanes, and whom Cyrus is very anxious to meet in battle, but for the time cannot. He is also frustrated in his challenge of the King of Pontus to fight for Mandane—a challenge of which Croesus will not hear. At last Telephanes turns out to be no less a person than Mazare, Prince of Sacia, whom we know already as one of the ever-multiplying lovers and abductors of the heroine ; while, after a good deal of confused fighting, another inset *Histoire* of him closes the tenth volume (V. ii.). It is, however, only two hundred pages long— a mere parenthesis compared to others, and it leads up to his giving Cyrus a letter from Mandane—an act of generosity which Philidaspes, otherwise King of Assyria, frankly confesses that he, as another Rival, could never have done. After yet another *Histoire* (now a " foursome ") of Belesis, Hermogenes, Cléodare, and Léonice, Abradates changes sides, carrying us on to an " intricate

---

[1] The opening sentences of this *Histoire* give a curious picture of the etiquette of these spoken narrative episodes, which, from the letters and memoirs of the time, we can see to have been actually practised in the days of *Précieuse* society. [*The story is not of course delivered in the presence of Panthea herself ; but she sends a confidante, Pherenice, to tell it.*] "They were no sooner in Araminta's apartment than, after having made Cyrus sit down, and placed Pherenice on a seat opposite to them, she begged her to begin her narrative and not to hide from them, if it were possible, the smallest thought of Abradates and Panthea. Accordingly this agreeable person, having made them a compliment so as to ask their pardon for the scanty art she brought to the story she was going to tell, actually began as follows : "

impeach " of old and new characters, especially Araminta
and Spithridates, and to the death in battle of the generous
King of Susiana himself, and the grief of Panthea.   There
is, at the close of this volume, a rather interesting *Privilège
du Roi*, signed by Conrart (" *le silencieux Conrart* "), sealed
with " the great seal of yellow wax in a simple tail " (one
ribbon or piece of ferret only ?), and bestowing its rights
" nonobstant Clameur de Haro, Charte Normande, et
autres lettres contraires."

The first volume of the Sixth Part (the eleventh of
the whole and the first of what, as so many words of the
kind are required, we may call the Second Division) has
plenty of business—showing that the author or her adviser
was also a business-like person—to commence the new
venture.   Cyrus, after being victorious in the field and
just about to besiege Sardis in form, receives a " bolt
from the blue " in the shape of a letter " From the
unhappy Mandane to the faithless "—himself !   She
has learnt, she tells him, that his feelings towards her are
changed, requests that she may no longer serve as a
pretext for his ambition, and — rather straining the
prerogatives assumed even by her nearest ancestresses
in literature, the Polisardas and Miraguardas of the
Amadis group, but scarcely dreamt of by the heroines of
ancient Greek Romance—desires that he will send back
to her father Cyaxares all the troops that he is, as she
implies, commanding on false pretences.

Now one half expects that Cyrus, in a transport of
Amadisian-Euphuist-heroism, will comply with this very
modest request.   In fact it is open to any one to contend
that, according to the strictest rules of the game, he ought
to have done so and gone mad, or at least marooned
himself in some desert island, in consequence.   The
sophistication, however, of the stage appears here.   After
a very natural sort of " Well, I never ! " translated into
proper heroic language, he sets to work to identify the
person whom Mandane suspects to be her rival—for she
has carefully abstained from naming anybody.   And he
asks—with an ingenious touch of self-confession which

does the author great credit, if it was consciously laid on—whether it can be Panthea or Araminta, with both of whom he has, in fact, been, if not exactly flirting, carrying on (as the time itself would have said) a " commerce of respectful and obliging admiration." He has a long talk with his confidant Feraulas (whose beloved and really lovable Martésie is, unluckily, not at hand to illuminate the mystery), and then he writes as " The Unfortunate Cyrus to the Unjust Mandane," tells her pretty roundly, though, of course, still respectfully, that if she knew how things really were " she would think herself the cruellest and most unjust person in the world." [I should have added, " just as she is, in fact, the most beautiful."] She is, he says, his first and last passion, and he has never been more than polite to any one else. But she will kindly excuse his not complying with her request to send back his army until he has vanquished all his Rivals—where, no doubt, in the original, the capital was bigger and more menacing than ever, and was written with an appropriate gnashing of teeth.

The traditional balance of luck and love, however, holds; and the armies of Croesus and the King of Pontus begin to melt away; so that, after a short but curious pastoral episode, they have to shut themselves up in the capital. The dead body of Abradates is now found, and his widow Panthea stabs herself upon it. This removes one of Mandane's possible causes of jealousy, but Araminta remains; and, as a matter of fact, it *is* this Princess on whom her suspicion has been cast, arising partly, though helped by makebates, from the often utilised personal resemblance between her actual lover, Prince Spithridates, and Cyrus. The treacherous King of Pontus has, in fact, shown her a letter from Araminta (his sister, be it remembered) which seems to encourage the idea.

All this, however, and more fills but a hundred pages or so, and then we are as usual whelmed in a *Histoire de Timarète et de Parthénie*, which takes up four times the space, and finishes the First Book. The Second opens

smartly enough with the actual siege of Sardis ; but we
cannot get rid of Araminta (it is sad to have to wish that
she was not " our own Araminta " quite so often) and
Spithridates.   Conversations between the still prejudiced
Mandane and the Lydian Princess Palmis—a sensible
and agreeable girl—are better ; but from them we are
hurled into a *Histoire de Sésostre* (the Egyptian prince,
son of Amasis, who is now an ally of Cyrus) *et de Timarète*,
which not only fills the whole of the rest of the volume,
but swells over into the next, being much occupied with
the villainies of a certain Heracleon, who is at the time a
wounded prisoner in Cyrus's Camp.   The siege is kept
up briskly, but Cyrus's courteous release of certain
captives adds fuel to Mandane's wrath as having been
procured by Araminta.   He will do anything for Araminta !   The releases themselves give rise to fresh
" alarums and excursions," among which we again meet
a pretty name (Candiope), borrowed by Dryden.   Doralise is also much to the fore; and we have a regular *Histoire*, though a shorter one than usual, of *Arpalice and
Thrasimède*, which will, as some say, " bulk largely "
later.   The length of this part is, indeed, enormous, the
double volume running to over fourteen hundred pages,
instead of the usual ten or twelve.   But its close is spirited
and sufficiently interim - catastrophic.   Cyrus discovers
in the *enceinte* of Sardis the usual weak point—an apparently impregnable scarped rock, which has been weakly
fortified and garrisoned—takes it by escalade in person
with his best paladins, and after it the city.

But of course he cannot expect to have it all his own
way when not quite twelve-twentieths of the book are
gone, and he finds that Mandane is gone likewise ; the
King of Pontus, who has practically usurped the authority
of Croesus, having once more carried her off—perhaps
not so entirely unwilling as before.   Cyrus pursues, and
while he is absent the King of Assyria (Philidaspes)
shows himself even more of a " Philip Devil " than usual
by putting the captive Lydian prince on a pyre, threatening to burn him if he will not reveal the place of the

Princess's flight, and actually having the torch applied. Of course Cyrus turns up at the nick of time, has the fire put out, rates the King of Assyria soundly for his violence, and apologises handsomely to Croesus. The notion of an apology for nearly roasting a man may appear to have its ludicrous side, but the way in which the historic pyre and the mention of Solon are brought in without discrediting the hero is certainly ingenious. The Mandane-hunt is renewed, but fruitlessly.

At the beginning of Part VII. there are—according to the habit noticed, and in rather extra measure as regards " us " if not " them "—some interesting things. The first is an example—perhaps the best in the book—of the elaborate description (called in Greek rhetorical technique *ecphrasis*) which is so common in the Greek Romances. The subject is an extraordinarily beautiful statue of a woman which Cyrus sees in Croesus's gallery, and which will have sequels later. It, or part of it, may be given :

> But, among all these figures of gold, there was to be seen one of marble, so wonderful, that it obliged Cyrus to stay longer in The statue admiring it than in contemplating any of the others, in the though it was not of such precious material. It is true gallery at that it was executed with such art, and represented Sardis. such a beautiful person, as to prevent any strangeness in its charming a Prince whose eyes were so delicate and so capable of judging all beautiful objects. This statue was of life-size, placed upon a pedestal of gold, on the four sides of which were bas-reliefs of an admirable beauty. On each were seen captives, chained in all sorts of fashions, but chained only by little Loves, unsurpassably executed. As for the figure itself, it represented a girl about eighteen years old, but one of surprising and perfect beauty. Every feature of the face was marvellously fine ;[1] her figure was at once so noble and so graceful that nothing more elegant[2] could be seen ; and her dress was at once so handsome and so unusual, that it had something of each of the usual garbs of Tyrian ladies, of nymphs, and of goddesses ; but more particularly that of the Wingless Victory, as represented by the Athenians,

---

[1] Observe how *vague* what follows is. A scholar and a *modiste*, working in happiest conjunction, might possibly " create " the dress ; but as for the face it might be any one out of those on one hundred chocolate-boxes.

[2] This passage gives a key to the degradation of the word "elegant." It has kept the connotation of " grace," but lost that of " nobility."

with a simple laurel crown on her head.   This statue was so well
set on its base, and had such lively action, that it seemed actually
animated ; the face, the throat, the arms, and the hands were of
white marble, as were the legs and feet, which were partly visible
between the laces of the buskins she wore, and which were to be
seen because, with her left hand, she lifted her gown a little, as if
to walk more easily.   With her right she held back a veil, fastened
behind her head under the crown of laurel, as though to prevent
its being carried away by the breeze, which seemed to agitate it.
The whole of the drapery of the figure was made of divers-
coloured marbles and jaspers ; and, in particular, the gown of
this fair Phoenician, falling in a thousand graceful folds, which
still did not hide the exact proportion of her body, was of jasper,
of a colour so deep that it almost rivalled Tyrian purple itself.   A
scarf, which passed negligently round her neck, and was fastened
on the shoulder, was of a kind of marble, streaked with blue and
white, which was very agreeable to the eye.   The veil was of
the same substance ; but sculptured so artfully that it seemed as
soft as mere gauze.   The laurel crown was of green jasper, and
the buskins, as well as the sash she wore, were again of different
hues.   This sash brought together all the folds of the gown over
the hips ; below, they fell again more carelessly, and still showed
the beauty of her figure.   But what was most worthy of admiration
in the whole piece was the spirit which animated it, and almost
persuaded the spectators that she was just about to walk and talk.
There was even a touch of art in her face, and a certain haughtiness
in her attitude which made her seem to scorn the captives chained
beneath her feet: while the sculptor had so perfectly realised the
indefinable freshness, tenderness, and *embonpoint* of beautiful girls,
that one almost knew her age.

Then come two more startling events.   A wicked
Prince Phraortes bolts with the unwilling Araminta,
and the King of Assyria (*alias* Philidaspes) slips away
in search of Mandane on his own account—two things
inconvenient to Cyrus in some ways, but balancing themselves in others.   For if it is unpleasant to have a very
violent and rather unscrupulous Rival hunting the
beloved on the one hand, that beloved's jealousy, if
not cured, is at least not likely to be increased by the
disappearance of its object.   This last, however, hits
Spithridates, who is, as it has been and will be seen, the
souffre-douleur of the book, much harder.   And the

double situation illustrates once more the extraordinary care taken in systematising—and as one might almost say *syllabising*—the book. It is almost impossible that there should not somewhere exist an actual syllabus of the whole, though, my habit being rather to read books themselves than books about them, I am not aware of one as a fact.[1]

Another characteristic is also well illustrated·in this context, and a further translated extract will show the curious, if not very recondite, love-casuistry which plays so large a part. But these French writers of the seventeenth century[2] did not know one-tenth of the matter that was known by their or others' mediaeval ancestors, by their English and perhaps Spanish contemporaries, or by writers in the nineteenth century. They were not " perfect in love-lore " ; their *Liber Amoris* was, after all, little more than a fashion-book in divers senses of " fashion." But let them speak for themselves :

[*Ménécrate and Thrasimède are going to fight, and have, according to the unqualified legal theory*[3] *and very occasional actual practice of seventeenth-century France, if not of the Medes and Persians, been arrested, though in honourable fashion. The* " *dependence* " *is a certain Arpalice, who loves Thrasimède and is loved by him. But she is ordered by her father's will to marry Ménécrate, who is now quite willing to marry* her, *though* she *hates* him, *and though he has previously been in love with Androclée, to whom he has promised that he will* not *marry the other. A sort of informal* Cour d'Amour *is held on the subject, the President being Cyrus himself, and the judges Princesses Timarète and Palmis, Princes Sesostris and Myrsilus, with* " *Toute la compagnie* " *as assessors and assessoresses. After much discussion, it is decided to disregard the dead father's injunction and the living inconstant's wishes, and to unite Thrasimède and Arpalice. But the chief points of interest lie in the following remarks :*]

The judgment of Cyrus in a court of love.

---

[1] *Abstracts* of all the principal members of this group and others occurred in the *Bibliothèque Universelle des Romans*, which appeared as a periodical at Paris in 1778. But what I do not know is whether any one ever arranged an elaborate tabular syllabus of the book like that of Burton's *Anatomy*. It would lend itself admirably to the process if any one had time and inclination to do the thing.

[2] With the exception, already noted, of Urfé ; and even he is far below Donne.

[3] There were, though not many, actual instances of capital punishment for disregard of the edicts against duelling, and imprisonment was common. But the deterrent effect was very small. Montmorency-Bouteville was the best-known victim.

"As it seems to me," said Cyrus, "what we ought most to consider in this matter is the endeavour to make the fewest possible persons unhappy, and to prevent a combat between two gentlemen of such gallantry, that to whichever side victory inclines, we should have cause to regret the vanquished. For although Ménécrate is inconstant and a little capricious, he has, for all that, both wits and a heart. We must, then, if you please," added he, turning to the two princesses, "consider that if Arpalice were forced to carry out her father's testament and marry Ménécrate, everybody would be unhappy, and he would have to fight two duels,[1] one against Thrasimède and one against Philistion (*Androclée's brother*), the one fighting for his mistress, the other for his sister." "No doubt," said Lycaste, "several people will be unhappy, but, me-thinks, not all; for at any rate Ménécrate will possess *his* mistress." "'Tis true," said Cyrus, "that he will possess Arpalice's beauty; but I am sure that as he would not possess her heart, he could not call himself satisfied; and his greatest happiness in this situation would be having prevented the happiness of his Rival. As for the rest of it, after the first days of his marriage, he would be in despair at having wedded a person who hated him, and whom he, perhaps, would have ceased to love; for, considering Ménécrate's humour, I am the most deceived of all men if the possession of what he loves is not the very thing to kill all love in his heart. As for Arpalice, it is easy to see that, marrying Méné-crate, whom she hates, and *not* marrying Thrasimède, whom she loves, she would be very unhappy indeed; nor could Androclée, on her side, be particularly satisfied to see a man like Ménécrate, whom she loves passionately, the husband of another. Philistion could hardly be any more pleased to see Ménécrate, after promising to marry his sister, actually marrying another. As for Thrasi-mède, it is again easy to perceive that, being as much in love with Arpalice as he is, and knowing that she loves him, he would have good reason for thinking himself one of the unhappiest lovers in the world if his Rival possessed his mistress. Therefore, from what I have said, you will see that by giving Arpalice to Ménécrate, everybody concerned is made miserable; for even Parmenides [*not the philosopher, but a friend of Ménécrate, whose sister, however, has rejected him*], though he may make a show of being still at-tached to the interests of Ménécrate, will be, unless I mistake, well enough pleased that his sister should not marry the brother of a person whom he never wishes to see again, and by whom he has been ill-treated. Then, if we look at the matter from the other side and propose to give Arpalice to Thrasimède, it remains

---

[1] It is amusing, as one reads this, to remember Hume's essay in which he lays stress on the *contrast* between Greek and French ideas in this very matter of the duel.

an unalterable fact that these two people will be happy; that
Philistion will be satisfied; that justice will be done to Androclée;
that nothing disobliging will be done to Parmenides, and that
Ménécrate will be made by force more happy than he wishes to
be; for we shall give him a wife by whom he is loved, and take
from him one by whom he is hated. Moreover, things being so,
even if he refuses to subject his whim to his reason, he can wish
to come to blows with Thrasimède alone, and would have nothing
to ask of Philistion; besides which, his sentiments will change
as soon as Thrasimède is Arpalice's husband. One often fights
with a Rival, thinking to profit by his defeat, when he has not
married the beloved object; but one does not so readily fight the
husband of one's mistress, as being her lover.[1]

Much about the "Good Rival" (as we may call him)
Mazare follows, and there is an illuminative sentence
about our favourite Doralise's *humeur enjouée et critique*,
which, as the rest of her part does, gives us a "light"
as to the origin of those sadly vulgarised lively heroines
of Richardson's whom Lady Mary very justly wanted
to "slipper." Doralise and Martésie are ladies, which
the others, unfortunately, are not. And then we pay for
our *ecphrasis* by an immense *Histoire* of the Tyrian Élise,
its original.

At the beginning of VII. ii. Cyrus is in the doldrums.
Many of his heroes have got their heroines—the personages of bygone *histoires*—and are honeymooning
and (to borrow again from Mr. Kipling) "dancing on the
deck." He is not. Moreover, the army, like all seventeenth-century armies after victory and in comfortable
quarters, is getting rather out of hand; and he learns
that the King of Pontus has carried Mandane off to
Cumae—not the famous Italian Cumae, home of the
Sibyl whom Sir Edward Burne-Jones has fixed for us,
and of many classical memories, but a place somewhere
near Miletus, defended by unpleasant marshes on land,
and open to the sea itself, the element on which Cyrus is
weakest, and by which the endlessly carried off Mandane
may readily be carried off again. He sends about for

---

[1] A curious and rather doubtful position; well worth the consideration of anybody
who wishes to write the much-wanted *History and Philosophy of Duelling*.

help to Phoenicia and elsewhere ; but when, after a smart action by land against the town, a squadron does appear off the port, he is for a time quite uncertain whether it is friend or foe.   Fortunately Cléobuline, Queen of Corinth, a young widow of surpassing beauty and the noblest sentiments, who has sworn never to marry again, has conceived a Platonic-romantic admiration for him, and has sent her fleet to his aid.   She deserves, of course, and still more of course has, a *Histoire de Cléobuline*.   Also the inestimable Martésie writes to say that Mandane has been dispossessed of her suspicions, and that the King of Pontus is, in the race for her favour, nowhere. The city falls, and the lovers meet.   But if anybody thinks for a moment that they are to be happy ever afterwards, Arithmetic, Logic, and Literary History will combine to prove to him that he is very much mistaken.   In order to make these two lovers happy at all, not only time and space, but six extremely solid volumes would have to be annihilated.

The close of VII. ii. and the whole of VIII. i. are occupied with imbroglios of the most characteristic kind. There is a certain Anaxaris, who has been instrumental in preventing Mandane from being, according to her almost invariable custom, carried off from Cumae also. To whom, though he is one of the numerous " unknowns " of the book, Cyrus rashly confides not only the captainship of the Princess's guards, but various and too many other things, especially when " Philip Devil " turns up once more, and, seeing the lovers in apparent harmony, claims the fulfilment of Cyrus's rash promise to fight him before marrying.   This gets wind in a way, and watch is kept on Cyrus by his friends ; but he, thinking of the parlous state of his mistress if both her principal lovers were killed—for Prince Mazare is, so to speak, out of the running, while the King of Pontus is still lying *perdu* somewhere—entrusts the secret to Anaxaris, and begs him to take care of her.   Now Anaxaris—as is so usual— is not Anaxaris at all, but Aryante, Prince of the Massagetae and actually brother of the redoubtable Queen

P

Thomyris ; and he also has fallen a victim to Mandane's fascinations, which appear to be irresistible, though they are, mercifully perhaps, rather taken for granted than made evident to the reader. One would certainly rather have one Doralise or Martésie than twenty Mandanes. However, again in the now expected manner, the fight does not immediately come off. For "Philip Devil," in his usual headlong violence, has provoked another duel with the Assyrian Prince Intaphernes,[1] and has been badly worsted and wounded by his foe, who is unhurt. This puts everything off, and for a long time the main story drops again (except as far as the struggles of Anaxaris between honour and love are depicted), first to a great deal of miscellaneous talk about the quarrel of King and Prince, and then to a regular *Histoire* of the King, Intaphernes, Atergatis, Princess Istrine, and the Princess of Bithynia, Spithridates's sister and daughter of a very robustious and rather usurping King Arsamones, who is a deadly enemy of Cyrus. The dead Queen Nitocris, and the passion for her of a certain Gadates, Intaphernes's father, and also sometimes, if not always, called a "Prince," come in here. The story again introduces the luckless Spithridates himself, who is first, owing to his likeness to Cyrus, persecuted by Thomyris, and then imprisoned by his father Arsamones because he will not give up Araminta and marry Istrine, whom Nitocris had wanted to marry her own son Philidaspes— a good instance of the extraordinary complications and contrarieties in which the book indulges, and of which, if Dickens had been a more "literary" person, he might have thought when he made the unfortunate Augustus Moddle observe that "everybody appears to be somebody else's." Finally, the volume ends with an account of the leisurely progress of Mandane and Cyrus to Ecba-

[1] The author uses "Prince," as indeed one might expect, rather in the Continental than in the English way, and the persons who bear it are not always sons of kings or members of reigning families. The two most agreeable *quiproquos* arising from this difference are probably the fictitious unwillingness of the excellent Miss Higgs to descend from "Princesse de Montcontour" to "Duchesse d'Ivry," and the, it is said, historical contempt of a comparatively recent Papal dignitary for an English Roman Catholic document which had no Princes among the signatories.

tana and Cyaxares, while the King of Assyria recovers
as best he can.   But at certain " tombs " on the route
evidence is found that the King of Pontus has been
recently in the land of the living, and is by no means
disposed to give up Mandane.

The second volume of this part is one of the most
eventless of all, and is mainly occupied by a huge *Histoire*
of Puranius, Prince of Phocaea, his love Cléonisbe, and
others, oddly topped by a passage of the main story,
describing Cyrus's emancipation of the captive Jews.
He is for a time separated from the Princess.

The first pages of IX. i. are lively, though they are
partly a *récit*.   Prince Intaphernes tells Cyrus all about
Anaxaris (Aryante), and how by representing Cyrus as
dead and the King of Assyria in full pursuit of her, he
has succeeded in carrying off Mandane ;   how also he
has had the cunning, by availing himself of the passion
of another high officer, Andramite, for Doralise, to induce him to join, in order that the maid of honour may
accompany her mistress.   Accordingly Cyrus, the King
of Assyria himself, and others start off in fresh pursuit ;
but the King has at first the apparent luck.   He over-
takes the fugitives, and a sharp fight follows.   But the
guards whom Cyrus has placed over the Princess, and
who, in the belief of his death, have followed the ravishers,
are too much for Philidaspes, and he is fatally wounded ;
fulfilling the oracle, as we anticipated long ago, by
dying in Mandane's arms, and honoured with a sigh
from her as for her intended rescuer.

She herself, therefore, is in no better plight, for Aryante
and Andramite continue the flight, with her and her
ladies, to a port on the Euxine, destroying, that they
may not be followed, all the shipping save one craft they
select, and making for the northern shore.   Here after
a time Aryante surrenders Mandane to his sister Thomyris, as he cannot well help doing, though he knows her
violent temper and her tigress-like passion for Cyrus,
and though, also, he is on rather less than brotherly
terms with her, and has a party among the Massagetae

who would gladly see him king. Meanwhile the King of Pontus and Phraortes, Araminta's carrier-off, fight and kill each other, and Araminta is given up—a loss for Mandane, for they have been companions in quasi-captivity, and there is no longer any subject of jealousy between them.

Having thus created a sort of " deadlock " situation such as she loves, and in the interval, while Cyrus is gathering forces to attack Thomyris, the author, as is her fashion likewise, surrenders herself to the joys of digression. We have a great deal of retrospective history of Aryante, and at last the famous Scythian philosopher, Anacharsis, is introduced, bringing with him the rest of the Seven Ancient Sages—with whom we could dispense, but are not allowed to do so. There is a Banquet of them all at the end of the first volume of the Part; and they overflow into the second, telling stories about Pisistratus and others, and discussing " love in the *aib*-stract," as frigidly as might be expected, on such points as, " Can you love the same person *twice* ? "[1] But the last half of this IX. ii. is fortunately business again. There is much hard fighting with Thomyris, who on one occasion wishes to come to actual sword-play with Cyrus, and of whom we have the liveliest *ecphrasis*, or set description, in the whole romance.

As for Thomyris, she was so beautiful that day that there was no one in the world save Mandane, who could have disputed a heart

Thomyris on the war- path.

with her[2] without the risk of losing. This Princess was mounted on a fine black horse, trapped with gold; her dress was of cloth of gold, with green panels shot with a little carnation, and was of the shape of that of Pallas when she is represented as armed. The skirt was caught up on the hip with diamond clasps, and showed buskins of lions' muzzles made to correspond with the rest. Her head-dress was adorned with jewels, and a great number of feathers—carnation, white and green—hung over her beautiful fair tresses, while these, fluttering

---

[1] Nobody, unless I forget, has the wisdom to put the counter-question, "Can you ever cease loving if you have once really loved?" which is to be carefully distinguished from a third, "Can you love more than once?" But there are more approaches to these *arcana* in the *Astrée* than in Mlle. de Scudéry.

[2] A very nice phrase.

at the wind's will, mixed themselves with the plumes as she turned her head, and with their careless curls gave a marvellous lustre to her beauty.   Besides, as her sleeves were turned up, and caught on the shoulder, while she held the bridle of her horse with one hand and her sword with the other, she showed the loveliest arms in the world.   Anger had flushed her complexion, so that she was more beautiful than usual; and the joy of once more seeing Cyrus, and seeing him also in an action respectful towards her,[1] effaced the marks of her immediately preceding fury so completely that he could see nothing but what was amiable and charming.

Thomyris, however, is as treacherous and cruel as she is beautiful; and part of her reason for seeming milder is that more of her troops may turn up and seize him.

On another occasion, owing to false generalship and disorderly advance on the part of the King of Hyrcania, Cyrus is in no small danger, but he "makes good," though at a disastrous expense, and with still greater dangers to meet.   Thomyris's youthful son (for young and beautiful widow as she is, she has been an early married wife and a mother), Spargapises, just of military age, is captured in battle, suffers from his captors' ignorance what has been called "the indelible insult of bonds," and though almost instantly released as soon as he is known, stabs himself as disgraced.   His body is sent to his mother with all sorts of honours, apologies, and regrets, but she, partly out of natural feeling, partly from her excited state, and partly because her mind is poisoned by false insinuations, sends, after transports of maternal and other rage, a message to Cyrus to the effect that if he does not put himself unreservedly in her hands, she will send him back Mandane dead, in the coffin of Spargapises.   And so the last double-volume but one ends with a suitable "fourth act" curtain, as we may perhaps call it.

The last of all, X. i. and ii., exhibits, in a remarkable degree, the general defects and the particular merits and promise of this curious and (it cannot be too often

---

[1] He had refused to cross swords with her, and had lowered his own in salute.

repeated) epoch-making book. In the latter respect more especially it shows the " laborious orient ivory sphere in sphere " fashion in which the endless and, it may sometimes seem, aimless episodes, and digressions, and insets are worked into the general theme. The defects will hardly startle, though they may still annoy, any one who has worked through the whole. But if another wickedly contented himself with a sketch of the story up to this point, and thought to make up by reading this Part of two volumes carefully, he would probably feel these defects very strongly indeed. We—we corrupt moderns —do expect a quickening up for the run-in. The usual beginning may seem to the non-experts to promise this, or at least to give hopes of it ; for though there is a vast deal of talking—with Anacharsis as a go-between and Gélonide (a good confidante), endeavouring to soften Thomyris, one can but expect it—the situation itself is at once difficult and exciting. The position of Aryante in particular is really novel-dramatic. As he is in love with Mandane, he of course does not want his sister to murder her. But inasmuch as he fears Cyrus's rivalry, he does not want him to be near Mandane for two obvious reasons : first, the actual proximity, and, secondly, the danger of Thomyris's temper getting the better (or worse) of her when both the lovers are in her power. So he sends private messengers to the Persian Prince, begging him *not* to surrender. Cyrus, however, still thinks of exchanging himself for Mandane. At this point the neophyte's rage may be excited by being asked to plunge into the regular four-hundred page *Histoire* of a certain Arpasie, who has two lovers—a Persian nobleman Hidaspe, and a supposed Assyrian champion Méliante, who has come with reinforcements for Thomyris. And no doubt the proportion *is* outrageous. But " wait and see," a phrase, it may be observed, which was not, as some seem to think, invented by Mr. Asquith.

At last the business does begin again, and a tremendous battle takes place for the possession of certain forests which lie between the two armies, and are at first held by

the Scythians. Cyrus, however, avails himself of the
services of an engineer who has a secret of combustibles,
sets the forests ablaze, and forces his way through one or
two open defiles, with little loss to himself and very heavy
loss to the enemy, whose main body, however, is still
unbroken.   This affords a fine subject for one of the
curious frontispieces known to all readers of seventeenth
century books.   A further wait for reinforcements takes
place, and the author basely avails herself of it for a no
doubt to herself very congenial (they actually called her
in " precious " circles by the name of the great poetess)
and enormous *Histoire* of no less a person than Sappho,
which fills the last 250 pages of the first (nineteenth)
volume and about as much of the second (twentieth)
or last.   It has very little connection with the text, save
that Sappho and Phaon (for the self-precipitation at Leucas
is treated as a fable) retire to the country of the Sauromatae, to live there a happy, united, but unwed and purely
Platonic (in the silly sense) existence.   The foolish side
of the *précieuse* system comes out here, and the treatment
confirms one's suspicion that the author's classical
knowledge was not very deep.

It does come to an end at last, however, and at last
also we do get our " run-in," such as it is.   The chief
excuse for its existence is that it brings in a certain
Méréonte, who, like his quasi-assonant Méliante, is to
be useful later, and that the tame conclusion is excused
by a Sapphic theory—certainly not to be found in her
too fragmentary works—that " possession ruins love,"
a doctrine remembered and better put by Dryden in a
speech of that very agreeable Doralice, whose name,
though not originally connected with this part of it, he
also, as has been noted, borrowed from the *Grand Cyrus*.

The actual finale begins (so to speak) antithetically
with the last misfortune of the unlucky Spithridates.
His ill-starred likeness to Cyrus, assisted by a suit of
armour which Cyrus has given to him, make the enemy
certain that he is Cyrus himself, and he is furiously
assaulted in an off-action, surrounded, and killed.   His

head is taken to Thomyris, who, herself deceived, exe-
cutes upon it the famous " blood-bath " of history or
legend.[1] Unfortunately it is not only in the Scythian
army that the error spreads. Cyrus's troops are terrified
and give way, so that he is overpowered by numbers and
captured. Fortunately he falls into the hands, not of
Thomyris's own people or of her savage allies, the Geloni
(it is a Gelonian captain who has acted as executioner
in Spithridates's case), but of the supposed Assyrian
leader Méliante, who is an independent person, admires
Cyrus, and, further persuaded by his friend Méréonte
(v. sup.), resolves to let him escape. The difficulties,
however, are great, and the really safest, though apparently the most dangerous way, seems to lie through the
" Royal Tents " (the nomad capital of Thomyris)
themselves. Meanwhile, Aryante is making interest
against his sister ; some of Cyrus's special friends,
disguised as Massagetae, are trying to discover and
rescue him, and the Sauromatae are ready to desert the
Scythian Queen. One of her transports of rage brings on
the catastrophe. She orders the Gelonian bravo to poniard
Mandane, and he actually stabs by mistake her maid-
of-honour Hésionide—the least interesting one, luckily.
Cyrus himself, after escaping notice for a time, is identified, attacked, and nearly slain, when the whole finishes
in a general chaos of rebellion, arrival of friends, flight of
Thomyris, and a hairbreadth escape of Cyrus himself,
which unluckily partakes more of the possible-improbable
than of the impossible-probable. The murders being
done, the marriages would appear to have nothing to
delay them ; but an evil habit, the origin of which is
hard to trace, and which is not quite extinct, still puts
them off. Méliante has got to be rewarded with the
hand of Arpasie, which is accomplished after he has
been discovered, in a manner not entirely romantic, to be
the son of the King of Hyrcania, and both his marriage
and that of Cyrus are interfered with by a supposed
Law of the Medes and of certain minor Asiatic peoples,

[1] Compare the not quite so ingenious adjustment of the intended burning of Croesus.

that a Prince or Princess may not marry a foreigner. Fresh discoveries get rid of this in Méliante's case, while in that of Cyrus a convenient Oracle declares that he who has conquered every kingdom in Asia cannot be considered a foreigner in any. So at last the long chart is finished, Doralise retaining her character as lightener of this rather solid entertainment by declaring that she cannot say she loves her suitor, Prince Myrsilus, because, every phrase that occurs to her is either too strong or too weak. So we bless her, and stop the water channels— or, as the Limousin student might have more excellently said, " claud the rives."

If the reader, having tolerated this long analysis (it is perhaps most probable that he will *not* have done so), General asks what game one pretends to have shown remarks on for so much expenditure of candle, it is, no the book and doubt, not easy to answer him without a fresh, its class. though a lesser, trial of his patience. You cannot " ticket " the *Grand Cyrus*, or any of its fellows, or the whole class, with any complimentary short descrip- tion, such as a certain school of ancient criticism loved, and corresponding to our modern advertisement labels— " grateful and comforting," " necessary in every travel- ling bag," and the like. They are, indeed, as I have endeavoured to indicate indirectly as well as directly, by no means so destitute of interest of the ordinary kind as it has generally been the fashion to think them. From the charge of inordinate length it is, of course, impossible to clear the whole class, and *Artamène* more particularly.[1] Length " no more than reason " is in some judgments a positive advantage in a novel ; but this *is* more than reason. I believe (the *moi*, I trust, is not utterly *haïssable* when it is necessary) that I myself am a rather unusually rapid, without being a careless or unfaithful, reader ; and that I have by nature a very little of that faculty with which some much greater persons have been credited, of being able to see at a glance whether anything on a

---

[1] *Clélie* is about as bad in this respect, *v. inf.* : the others less so.

page needs more than that glance or not, a faculty not likely to have been rendered abortive (though also not, I hope, rendered morbid) by infinite practice in reviewing. I do not say that, even now, I have read every word of this *Artamène* as I should read every word of a sonnet of Shakespeare or a lyric of Shelley, even as I should read every word of a page of Thackeray. I have even skimmed many pages. But I have never found, even in a time of "retired leisure," that I could get through more than three, or at the very utmost four, of the twenty volumes or half-volumes without a day or two of rest or other work between. On the other hand, the book is not significantly piquant in detail to enable me to read attentively fifty or a hundred pages and then lay it down.[1] You do, in a lazy sort of way, want to know what happened—a tribute, no doubt, to Mlle. Madeleine—and so you have to go on ploughing the furrow. But several weeks' collar-work[2] is a great deal to spend on a single book of what is supposed to be pastime; and the pastime becomes occasionally one of doubtful pleasure now and then. In fact, it is, as has been said, best to read in shifts. Secondly, there may, no doubt, be charged a certain unreality about the whole: and a good many other criticisms may be, as some indeed have been already, made without injustice.

The fact is that not only was the time not yet, but something which was very specially of the time stood in the way of the other thing coming, despite the strong *nisus* in its favour excited by various influences spoken of at the beginning of this chapter. This was the devotion—French at almost all times, and specially

[1] I have said that you *can* do this with the *Astrée*, and that this makes for superiority in it : but there also I think absolutely continuous reading of the whole would become "collar-work."

[2] That is to say, several weeks occupied in the manner above indicated. You may sometimes read two of the volumes in a day, but much oftener you will find one enough ; in the actual process for the present history some intervals must be allowed for digestion and *précis* ; and, as above remarked, if other forms of "cheerfulness," in Dr. Johnson's friend Mr. Edwards's phrase, do not "break in " of themselves, you must make them, to keep any freshness in the task. I fancy the twenty volumes were, if not " my *sole* occupation " (like that more cheerful and charitable one of the head-waiter at Limmer's), my main one for nearly twice twenty days.

French at this—to the type. There are some " desperate willins " (as Sam Weller called the greengrocer at the swarry) who fail to see much more than types in Racine, though there is something more in Corneille, and a very great deal more in Molière. In the romances which charmed at home the audiences and spectators of these three great men's work abroad, there is nothing, or next to nothing, else at all. The spirit of the *Epistle to the Pisos*, which acted on the Tragedians in verse, which acted on Boileau in criticism and poetry, was heavier on the novelist than on any of them. Take sufficient generosity, magnanimity, adoration, bravery, courtesy, and so forth, associate the mixture with handsome flesh and royal blood, clothe the body thus formed with brilliant scarfs and shining armour, put it on the best horse that was ever foaled, or kneel it at the feet of the most beautiful princess that ever existed, and you have Cyrus. For the princess herself take beauty, dignity, modesty, graciousness, etc., *quant. suff.*, clothe *them* in garments again magnificent, and submit the total to extreme inconveniences, some dangers, and an immense amount of involuntary travelling, but nothing " irreparable," and you have Mandane. For the rest, with the rare and slight exceptions mentioned, they flit like shadows ticketed with more or less beautiful names. Even Philidaspes, the most prominent male character after the hero by far, is, whether he be " in cog " as that personage or " out of cog " as Prince and King of Assyria, merely a petulant hero—a sort of cheap Achilles, with no idiosyncrasy at all. It is the fault, and in a way the very great fault, of all the kind: and there is nothing more to do with it but to admit it and look for something to set against it.

How great a thing the inception (to use a favourite word of the present day, though it be no favourite of the writer's) of the " psychological " treatment of Love[1] was

---

[1] In this respect the remarks above extend backwards to the *Astrée*, and even to some of the smaller and earlier novels mentioned in connection with it. But the " Heroics," especially Mlle. de Scudéry, *modernise* the treatment not inconsiderably.

may, of course, be variously estimated. The good conceit of itself in which that day so innocently and amusingly indulges will have it, indeed, that the twentieth century has invented this among other varieties of the great and venerable art of extracting nourishment from eggs. "We have," somebody wrote not long ago—the exact words may not be given, but the sense is guaranteed—"perceived that Love is not merely a sentiment, an appetite, or a passion, but a great means of intellectual development." Of course Solomon did not know this, nor Sappho, nor Catullus, nor the fashioners of those "sentiments" of the Middle Ages which brought about the half-fabulous Courts of Love itself, nor Chaucer, nor Spenser, nor Shakespeare, nor Donne. It was reserved for—but one never names contemporaries except *honoris causâ*.

It is—an "of course" of another kind—undeniable that the fashion of love-philosophy which supplies so large a part of the "yarn" of Madeleine de Scudéry's endless rope or web is not *our* fashion. But it is, in a way, a new variety of yarn as compared with anything used before in prose, even in the Greek romances [1] and the *Amadis* group (nay, even in the *Astrée* itself). Among other things, it connects itself more with the actual society, manners, fashions of its day than had ever been the case before, and this is the only interesting side of the "key" part of it. This was the way that they did to some extent talk and act then, though, to be sure, they also talked and acted very differently. It is all very well to say that the Hôtel de Rambouillet is a sort of literary-historical fiction, and the *Précieuses Ridicules* a delightful farce. The fiction was not wholly a fiction, and the farce was very much more than a farce—would have been, indeed, not a farce at all if it had not satirised a fact.

It is, however, in relation to the general history and development of the novel, and therefore in equally important relation to the present *History*, that the import-

---

[1] Achilles Tatius and the author of *Hysminias and Hysmine* come nearest. But the first is too ancient and the last too modern.

ance of the *Grand Cyrus*, or rather of the class of which it was by far the most popular and noteworthy member, is most remarkable.   Indeed this importance can hardly be exaggerated, and is much more likely to be—indeed has nearly always been—undervalued.   Even the jejune and partial analysis which has been given must have shown how many of the elements of the modern novel are here—sometimes, as it were, " in solution," sometimes actually crystallised.   For any one who demands plot there is one—of such gigantic dimensions, indeed, that it is not easy to grasp it, but seen to be singularly well articulated and put together when it is once grasped. Huge as it is, it is not in the least formless, and, as has been several times pointed out, hardly the most (as it may at first appear) wanton and unpardonable episode, digression, or inset lacks its due connection with and " orientation " towards the end.   The contrast of this with the more or less formless chronicle-fashion, the " overthwart and endlong " conduct, of almost all the romances from the Carlovingian and Arthurian [1] to the *Amadis* type, is of the most unmistakable kind.

Again, though character, as has been admitted, in any real live sense, is terribly wanting still; though description is a little general and wants more " streaks in the tulip "; and though conversation is formal and stilted, there is evident, perhaps even in the first, certainly in the second and third cases, an effort to treat them at any rate systematically, in accordance with some principles of art, and perhaps even not without some eye to the actual habits, manners, demands of the time— things which again were quite new in prose fiction, and, in fact, could hardly be said to be anywhere present in literature outside of drama.

To set against these not so very small merits in the present, and very considerable seeds of promise for the future, there are, of course, serious faults or defects—

---

[1] We have indeed endeavoured to discover a "form" of the greatest and best kind in the Arthurian, but it has been acknowledged that it may not have been deliberately reached—or approached—by even a single artist, and that, if it was, the identity of that artist is not quite certain.

defaults which need, however, less insistence, because they are much more generally known, much more obvious, and have been already admitted. The charge of excessive length need hardly be dealt with at all. It has already been said that the most interesting point about it is the opportunity of discovering how it was, in part, a regular, and, in fact, almost the furthest possible, development of a characteristic which had been more or less observable throughout the progress of romance. But it may be added that the law of supply and demand helped ; for people evidently were not in the least bored by bulk, and that the fancy for having a book " on hand " has only lately, if it has actually, died out.[1] Now such a " book on hand " as the *Grand Cyrus* exists, as far as my knowledge goes, in no Western literature, unless you count collections of letters, which is not fair, or such memoirs as Saint-Simon's, which do not appeal to quite the same class of readers.

A far more serious default or defect—not exactly blameworthy, *because* the time was not yet, but certainly to be taken account of—is the almost utter want of character just referred to. From Cyrus and Mandane downwards the people have qualities ; but qualities, though they are necessary to character, do not constitute it. Very faint approaches may be discerned, by very benevolent criticism, in such a personage as Martésie with her shrewdness, her maid-of-honour familiarity with the ways and manners of courtly human beings, and that very pardonable, indeed agreeable, tendency, which has been noticed or imagined, to flirt in respectful fashion with Cyrus, while carrying on more regular business with Feraulas. But it is little more than a suggestion, and it has been frankly admitted that it is perhaps not even that, but an imagination merely. And the same observation may apply to her " second string," Doralise. No others of the women have any character at all, and we have already spoken of the men.

---

[1] The intolerance of anything but scraps is one of the numerous arms and legs of the twentieth century Baal. There are some who have not bowed down to it.

Now these things, in a book very widely read and immensely admired, could not, and did not, fail to have their effect. Nobody—we shall see this more in detail in the next chapter—can fail to perceive that the *Princesse de Clèves* itself is, from one point of view, only a *histoire* of the *Grand Cyrus*, taken out of its preposterous *matrix* of other matter, polished, charged with a great addition of internal fire of character and passion, and left to take its chance alone and unencumbered. Nobody, on the other hand, who knows Richardson and Mademoiselle de Scudéry can doubt the influence of the French book—a century old as it was—on the " father of the English novel." Now any influence exerted on these two was, beyond controversy, an influence exerted on the whole future course of the kind, and it is as exercising such an influence that we have given to the *Great Cyrus* so great a space.

After the exhaustive account given of *Artamène*, it is probably not necessary to apologise for dealing with the rest of Mlle. de Scudéry's novel work, and with that of her comrades in the Heroic romance, at no very great length. *Ibrahim ou L'Illustre Bassa* has sometimes been complimented as showing more endeavour, if not exactly at " local colour," at technical accuracy, than the rest. It is true that the French were, at this time, rather amusingly proud of being the only Western nation treated on something like equal terms by the Sublime Porte, and that the Scudérys (possibly Georges, whose work the Dedication to Mlle. de Rohan, daughter of the famous soldier, pretty certainly is) may have taken some pains to acquire knowledge. " Sandjak " (or " Sanjiac "), not for a district but for its governor, is a little unlucky perhaps ; but " Aderbion " is much nearer " Azerbaijan " than one generally expects in such cases from French writers of the seventeenth or even of other centuries. The Oriental character of the story, however, is but partial. The Illustrious Pasha himself, though First

The other Scudéry romances— Ibrahim.

Vizir and "victorious" general of Soliman the Second, is not a Turk at all, but a " Justinian" or Giustiniani of Genoa, whose beloved Isabelle is a Princess of Monaco, and who at the end, after necessary dangers,[1] retires with her to that Principality, with a punctilious explanation from the author about the Grimaldis. The scene is partly there and at Genoa—the best Genoese families, including the Dorias, appearing—partly at Constantinople : and the business at the latter place is largely concerned with the intrigues, jealousies, and cruelties of Roxelane, who is drawn much more (one regrets to say) as history paints her than as the agreeable creature of Marmontel's subsequent fancy. The book is a mere cockboat beside the mighty argosy of the *Cyrus*, running only to four volumes and some two thousand pages. But though smaller, it is much " stodgier." The *Histoires* break out at once with the story of a certain Alibech—much more proper for the young person than that connected with the same name by Boccaccio,—and those who have acquired some knowledge of Mlle. Madeleine's ways will know what it means when, adopting the improper but defensible practice of " looking at the end," they find that not merely " Justinian " and Isabelle, but a Horace and a Hypolite, a Doria and a Sophronie, an Alphonse and a Léonide are all married on the same day, while a " French Marquis " and an Emilie vow inviolable but celibate constancy to each other ; they will know, that is to say, that in the course of the book all these will have been duly " historiated." To encourage them, a single hint that Léonide sometimes plays a little of the parts of Martésie and Doralise in the *Cyrus* may be thrown in.

There is, however, one sentence in the second volume of *Ibrahim* which is worth quotation and brief comment, because it is a text for the whole management and system of these novels, and accounts for much in their successors almost to the present day. Emilie is telling the *Histoire* of Isabelle, and excuses herself for not beginning at the beginning : " Puisque je sais que vous n'ignorez pas

---

[1] For Soliman is not indisposed to fall in love with his illustrious Bassa's beloved.

l'amour du Prince de Masseran, les violences et les artifices de Julie, la trahison de Féliciane, le généreux ressentiment de Doria [this is another Doria], la mort de cet amant infortuné, et ensuite celle de Julie." In other words, all these things have been the subject of previous histories or of the main text. And so it is always. Diderot admired, or at least excused, that procedure of Richardson's which involved the telling of the conversation of an average dinner-party in something like a small volume. But the "Heroic" method would have made it necessary to tell the previous experiences of the lady you took down to dinner, and the man that you talked to afterwards, while, if extended from aristocratic to democratic ideas, it would have justified a few remarks on the cabmen who brought both, and the butcher and fishmonger who supplied the feast. The inconvenience of this earlier practice made itself felt, and by degrees it dropped off; but it was succeeded by a somewhat similar habit of giving the subsequent history of personages introduced—a thing which, though Scott satirised it in Mrs. Martha Buskbody's insistence on information about the later history of Guse Gibbie,[1] by no means ceased with his time. Both were, in fact, part of the general refusal to accept the conditions of ordinary life. If "tout *passe*" is an exaggeration, it is an exaggeration of the truth: and in fiction, as in fact, the minor shapes must dissolve as well as arise without too much fuss being made about them.[2]

Almahide is, I think, more readable than *Ibrahim*; but the *English* reader must disabuse himself of the idea
Almahide. (if he entertains it) that he will find much of the original of *The Conquest of Granada*. The book does, indeed, open like the play, with the faction-fights of Abencerrages and Zegrys, and it ends with

---

[1] At the close of *Old Mortality*.

[2] One is lost if one begins quoting from these books. But there is another passage at the end of the same volume worth glancing at for its oddity. It is an elaborate chronological "checking" of the age of the different characters ; and, odd as it is, one cannot help remembering that not a few authors from Walter Map (or whoever it was to Thackeray might have been none the worse for similar calculations.

Boabdelin's jealousy of his wife Almahide, while a few of the other names in both are identical. But *Almahide* contains nothing, or hardly anything, of the character of Almanzor, and Dryden has not attempted to touch a hundredth part of the copious matter of the French novel, the early history of Almahide, the usual immense digressions and side-*histoires*, the descriptions (which, as in *Ibrahim*, play, I think, a larger relative part than in the *Cyrus*), and what not.

Copious as these are, however, in both books, they do not fill them out to anything like the length of the *Cyrus* itself, or of its rival in size, and perhaps *Clélie.* superior in attraction, the *Clélie.* I do not plead guilty to inconsistency or change of opinion in this " perhaps " when it is compared with the very much larger space given to the earlier novel. *Le Grand Cyrus* has been estated too firmly, as the type and representative of the whole class, to be dislodged, and there is, as we shall see presently, a good deal of repetition from it in *Clélie* Perhaps the itself. But this latter is the more amusing liveliest of book of the two ; it is, though equally or the set. nearly as big, less labyrinthine ; there is somewhat livelier movement in it, and at the same time this is contrasted with a set or series of interludes of love-casuistry, which are better, I think, than anything of the kind in the *Cyrus*.[1] The most famous feature of these is, of course, the well-known but constantly mis-named " Carte de Tendre " (" Map of the Country of Tenderness "—not of " Tenderness in the *ab*stract," as *du* Tendre would be). The discussion of what constitutes Tenderness comes quite early ; there is later a notable discourse on the respective attractions of Love and of Glory or Ambition ; a sort of Code and Anti-code of lovers [2] occurs as " The Love-Morality of Tiramus," with a set of (not always) contrary criticism thereof ; and a debate of an almost mediaeval kind as to

---

[1] It is not, I hope, frivolous or pusillanimous, but merely honest, to add that, as I have spent much less time on *Clélie* than on the other book, it has had less opportunity of boring me.

[2] Cf. the *Astrée* as noted above.

the respective merits of merry and melancholy mistresses. Moreover, there is a rather remarkable " Vision of Poets " —past, present, and to come—which should be taken in connection with the appearance, as an actual personage, of Anacreon. All this, taken in conjunction with the " business " of the story, helps to give it the superior liveliness with which it has, rightly or wrongly, been credited here.

Of that business itself a complete account cannot, for reasons given more than once, be attempted ; though Rough out- anybody who wants such a thing, without going line of it. to the book itself, may find it in the places also above mentioned. There is no such trick played upon the educated but not wideawake person as (*v. inf.*) in La Calprenède's chief books. Clélie is the real Clelia, if the modern historical student will pass " real " without sniffing, or even if he will not. Her lover, " Aronce," although he probably may be a little disguised from the English reader by his spelling, is so palpably the again real " Aruns," son of Porsena, that one rather wonders how his identity can have been so long concealed in French (where the pronunciations would be practically the same) from the readers of the story. The book begins with a proceeding not quite so like that of the *Cyrus* as some to be mentioned later, but still pretty close to the elder overture. " The illustrious Aronce and the adorable Clelia " are actually going to be married, when there is a fearful storm, an earthquake, and a disappearance of the heroine. She has, of course, been carried off ; one might say, without flippancy, of any heroine of Madeleine de Scudéry's not only that she was, as in a famous and already quoted saying, " very liable to be carried off," but that it was not in nature that she should not be carried off as early and as often as possible. And her abductor is no less a person than Horatius—our own Horatius Cocles—the one who kept the bridge in some of the best known of English verses, not he who provoked, from the sister whom he murdered, the greatest speech in all French tragedy before, and perhaps not merely before, Victor Hugo. Horatius is the Philidaspes of *Clélie*, but, as he was bound to be, an infinitely better fellow and of a better fate. Of course the end knits straight on to the beginning. Clélie and Aronce are united without an earthquake, and Porsena, with obliging gallantry, resigns the crown of Clusium (from which he has himself long been kept out by a " Mezentius," who will hardly work in with Virgil's), not to Aronce, but to Clélie herself. The enormous interval between (the book is practically as long as the *Cyrus*) is occupied by the same, or (*v. sup.*) nearly the same tissue of delays, digressions, and other maze-like devices for setting you off on a new quest when you seem to be quite close to the goal. A large part of the scene is in Carthage, where, reversing the process in regard to Mezentius, Asdrubals and Amilcars make their appearance in a very " mixedly " historical fashion. A Prince of Numidia (who had heard of Numidia in Tarquin's days ?) fights a lively water-combat with Horatius actually as he is carrying Clélie off, over the Lake of Thrasymene. All the stock legends of the Porsena siege and others are duly brought in : and the atrocious Sextus, not contented with his sin against Lucrece, tries to carry off Clélie likewise, but is fortunately or wisely prevented. Otherwise the invariable propriety which from the time of the small love-novels (*v. sup.* pp. 157-162) had distinguished these abductions might possibly have been broken through. These outlines might be expanded (and the process would not be very painful to me) into an abstract quite as long as that of Cyrus; but " It Cannot Be."

One objection, foreshadowed, and perhaps a little more, already, must be allowed against *Clélie*. That tendency to resort to repetition of situations and movements —which has shown itself so often, and which practically distinguishes the very great novelists from those not so great by its absence or presence—is obvious here, though the huge size of the book may conceal it from mere dippers, unless they be experts. The similarity of the openings is, comparatively speaking, a usual thing. It should not happen, and does not in really great writers ; but it is tempting, and is to some extent excused by the brocard about *le premier pas*. It is so nice to put yourself in front of your beginning—to have made sure of it ! But this charity will hardly extend to such a thing as the repetition of Cyrus's foolish promise to fight Philidaspes before he marries Mandane in the case of Aronce, Horatius, and Clélie. The way in which Aronce is kept an " unknown " for some time, and that in which his actual relationship to Porsena is treated, have also too much of the *replica* ; and though a lively skirmish with a pirate which occurs is not quite so absurd as that ready-made series of encores which was described above (pp. 181-2), there is something a little like it in the way in which the hero and his men alternately reduce the enemy to extremity, and run over the deck to rescue friends who are in the pirates' power from being butchered or flung overboard. " Sapho's " invention, though by no means sterile, was evidently somewhat indiscriminate, and she would seem to have thought it rather a pity that a good thing should be used only once.

Nevertheless the compliment given above may be repeated. If I were sent to twelve months' imprisonment of a mild description, and allowed to choose a library, I should include in it, from the heroic or semi-heroic division, *Clélie*, La Calprenède's two chief books, Gomberville's *Polexandre*, and Gombauld's *Endimion* (this partly for the pictures), with, as a matter of course, the *Astrée*, and a choice of one other. By reading slowly and " savouring " the process, I should imagine that, with one's memories of other things, they might be able to last for a year. And it would be one of the best kind of fallows for the brain. In anticipation, let us see something of these others now.

It has seemed, as was said, desirable to follow the common opinion of literary history in giving Madeleine de Scudéry the place of honour, and the largest as well as the foremost share in our account of this curious

stage in the history of the novel. But if, to alter slightly
La Cal- a famous quotation, I might "give a short
prenède : his hint to an impartial *reader*," I should very
comparative strongly advise him to begin his studies (or
cheerfulness. at least his enjoyment) thereof, not with
" Sapho," but with Gauthier de Costes, Seigneur de la
Calprenède, himself according to Tallemant almost the
proverbial " Gascon *et demi* "; a tragic dramatist, as well
as a romantic writer ; a favourite of Mme. de Sévigné,
who seldom went wrong in her preferences, except when
she preferred her very disagreeable daughter to her very
agreeable son ; and more than any one else the inventor,
or at least perfecter, of the hectoring heroic style which
we associate with Dryden's plays. Indeed the Artaban
of *Cléopatre* is much more the original of Almanzor
and Drawcansir than anything in Madeleine, though
Almahide was actually the source of Dryden's story, or
heroine. Besides this, though La Calprenède has rather
less of the intricate-impeach character than his she-
rival, there is much more bustle and "go" in him ; he
has, though his books are proper enough, much less
fear of dealing with " the kissing and that sort of thing,"
as it was once discreetly put; and he is sometimes positively exciting in his imbroglios, as when the beautiful
Amazon princess Menalippe fights a real duel on horse-
back with Prince, afterwards King, Alcamenes of Scythia,
under the impression that he has killed a certain Alcimedon, who was her lover; discovers, after no small time
and considerable damage, that he is Alcimedon himself;
and, like a sensible and agreeable girl, embraces him
heartily in the sight of men and angels.

This is among the numerous *divertissements* of *Cléopatre* (not the earliest, but perhaps the chief of its author's
novels [1]), the heroine of which is not

The laughing queen that caught the world's great hands

herself, but her daughter by Antony, who historically married Juba of Mauretania, and is here courted

---

[1] He also wrote several plays.

by him under the name of Coriolanus, while he is in *Cléopatre*— disgrace with Augustus. La Calprenède (all these romancers are merciful men and women to the historically unlucky, and cruel only, or for the most part, to fictitious char-acters) saves her half-brother Caesarion from his actual death, and, after the due thousands of pages, unites him happily to Queen Candace of Æthiopia. There is the same odd muddle (which made a not un-intelligent Jesuit label this class of books " historia *mixta* ") with many other persons. Perhaps the most curious of all episodes of this kind is the use made of Ovid's " fusca Cypassis." If Mrs. Grundy could be supposed ever to have read the *Amores,* the mere sight of the name of that dusky handmaid—to whom Ovid behaved, by his own confession, in such an exceedingly shabby as well as improper fashion—would make her shudder, if not shriek. But La Calprenède's Cypassis, though actually a maid of honour to Julia, as her original was a handmaid to Corinna, is of unblemished morality, flirted with certainly by Ovid, but really a German princess, Ismenia, in disguise, and beloved by, betrothed to, and in the end united with no less a compatriot than Arminius. This union gives also an illustration of the ingenious fashion in which these writers reconcile and yet omit. La Calprenède, as we have seen, does not give Arminius's wife her usual name of Thusnelda, but, to obviate a complaint from readers who have heard of Varus, he invents a protest on " Herman sla lerman " part against that general, who has trepanned him into captivity and gladiatorship, and makes him warn Augustus that he will be true to the Romans *unless* Varus is sent into his country.[1]

This episode is, in many ways, so curious and charac-teristic, that it seemed worth while to dwell on it for a little ; but the account itself must have shown how impossible it is to repeat the process of

Cléopatre—the Cypassis and Arminius episode.

The book generally.

---

[1] This would supply the ghost of Varus with a crushing answer to " Give me back my legions !" in such form as " Why did you send me with them ? "

general abstract. There are, I think, in the book
(which took twelve years to publish and fills as many
volumes in French, while the English translation is an
immense folio of nearly a thousand pages in double
column, also entitled *Hymen's Praeludia* [1]) fewer separate
Histoires, though there are a good many, than in the
Cyrus, but the intertwined love-plots are almost more
complicated. For instance, the Herod-and-Mariamne
tragedy is brought in with a strictly " proper " lover,
Tiridates, whom Salome uses to provoke Herod's patience,
and who has, at the very opening of the book, proved
himself both a natural philosopher of no mean order by
seeing a fire at sea, and " judging with much likelihood
that it comes from a ship," and a brave fellow by rescuing
from the billows no less a person than the above-mentioned
Queen Candace. From her, however, he exacts immediate, and, as some moderns might think, excessive,
payment by making her listen to his own *Histoire*.

Not the least attractive part of *Cléopatre* to some people
will be that very " Phébus," or amatory conceit, which
made the next ages scorn it. When one of the numerous
" unknowns " of both sexes (in this case a girl) is discovered (rather prettily) lying on a river bank and playing
with the surface of the water, " the earth which sustained
this fair body seemed to produce new grass to receive
her more agreeably "—a phrase which would have
shocked good Bishop Vida many years before, as much
as it would have provoked the greater scorn of Mr.
Addison about as many after. There are many "ecphrases"
or set descriptions of this kind, and they show a good
deal of stock convention. For instance, the wind is
always " most discreetly, most discreetly " ready, as
indeed it was in Mlle. de Scudéry's own chaste stories,
to blow up sleeves or skirts a little, and achieve the dis-
traction of the beholders by what it reveals. But on the
whole, as was hinted above, Gauthier de Costes de La
Calprenède is the most natural creature of the heroic
band.

[1] At another time there might have been a little gentle satire in this, but hardly then.

His earlier *Cassandre* is not much inferior to *Cléopatre*, and has a little more eccentricity about it.   The author
Cassandre.   begins his Second Part by making the ghost of Cassandra herself (who is not the Trojan Cassandra at all) address a certain Calista, whom she mildly accuses of " dragging her from her grave two thousand years after date," adding, as a boast of his own in a Preface, that the very name " Cassandre " has never occurred in the *First* Part—a huge cantle of the work. The fact is that it is an *alias* for Statira, the daughter of Darius and wife of Alexander, and is kept by her during the whole of her later married life with her lover Oroondates, King of Scythia, who has vainly wooed her in early days before her union with the great Emathian conqueror. Here, again, the mere student of " unmixed " history may start up and say, " Why ! this Statira, who was also called Barsine [an independent personage here] was murdered by Roxana after Alexander's death ! " But, as was also said, these romancers exercise the privilege of mercy freely; and though La Calprenède's Roxana is naughty enough for anything (she makes, of course, the most shameless love to Oroondates), she is not allowed to kill her rival, who is made happy, after another series of endless adventures of her own, her lover's, and other people's. The book opens with a lively interest to students of the English novel ; for the famous two cavaliers of G. P. R. James appear, though they are not actually riding at the moment, but have been, and, after resting, see two others in mortal combat. Throughout there is any amount of good fighting, as, for the matter of that, there is in *Cléopatre* also ; and there is less duplication of detail here than in some other respects, for La Calprenède is rather apt to repeat his characters and situations. For instance, the fight between Lysimachus and Thalestris (La Calprenède is fond of Amazons), though *not* in the details, is of course in the idea a replica of that between Alcamenes and Menalippe in *Cléopatre* ; and names recur freely. Moreover, in the less famous story, the whole situation of hero and heroine is exactly

duplicated in respect of the above-mentioned Lysimachus and Parisatis, Cassandra's younger sister, who is made to marry Hephaestion at first, and only awarded, in the same fashion as her elder sister, at last to her true lover.

By the way, the already-mentioned " harmonising " is in few places more oddly shown than by the remark that Plutarch's error in representing Statira as killed was due to the fact that he did not recognise her under her later name of Cassandra—a piece of Gascon half-naïveté, half-jest which Mlle. de Scudéry's Norman shrewdness[1] would hardly have allowed. There is also much more of the supernatural in these books than in hers, and the characters are much less prim. Roxana, who, of course, is meant to be naughty, actually sends a bracelet of her hair to Oroondates ! which, however, that faithful lover of another instantly returns.

La Calprenède's third novel, *Faramond*, is unfinished as his work, and the continuation seems to have more than one claimant to its authorship. If the *Faramond.* " eminent hand " was one Vaumorière, who independently accomplished a minor " heroic " in *Le Grand Scipion*, he was not likely to infuse much fire into the ashes of his predecessor. As it stands in La Calprenède's own part, *Faramond* is a much duller book than *Cassandre* or *Cléopatre*. It must, of course, be remembered that, though patriotism has again and again prompted the French to attack these misty Merovingian times (the *Astrée* itself deals with them in the liberal fashion in which it deals with everything), the result has rarely, if ever, been a success. Indeed I can hardly think of any one—except our own " Twin Brethren " in *Thierry and Theodoret*—who has made anything good out of French history before Charlemagne.[2] The reader, therefore, unless he be a very thorough and conscientious student, had better let *Faramond* alone ; but its elder sisters are much pleasanter company. Indeed the impolite thought will occur that it is much more like the

---

[1] It would seem, however, that the Scudérys were not originally Norman.
[2] Chateaubriand hardly counts in strictness.

Scudéry novels, part of which it succeeded, and may possibly have been the result—not by any means the only one in literature—of an unlucky attempt to beat a rival by copying him or her.

If any one, seeking acquaintance with the works of Marin le Roy, Seigneur de Gomberville, begins at the Gomberville beginning with his earliest work, and one of —La Caritée the earliest of the whole class, *La Caritée* (not " Carit*ie*," as in some reference books), he may not be greatly appetised by the addition to the title, " contenant, sous des temps, des personnes, et des noms supposés, plusieurs rares et véritables histoires de notre temps." For this is a proclamation, as Urfé had *not* proclaimed it,[1] of the wearisome " key " system, which, though undoubtedly it has had its partisans at all times, is loathsome as well as wearisome to true lovers of true literature. To such persons every lovable heroine of romance is, more or less, suggestive of more or fewer women of history, other romance, or experience ; every hero, more or less, though to a smaller extent, recognisable or realisable in the same way ; and every event, one in which such readers have been, might have been, or would have liked to be engaged themselves ; but they do not care the scrape of a match whether the author originally intended her for the Princess of Kennaquhair or for Polly Jones, him and it for corresponding realities. Nor is the sequel particularly ravishing, though it is dedicated to " all fair and virtuous shepherdesses, all generous and perfect shepherds." Perhaps it is because one is not a generous and perfect shepherd that one finds the " Great Pan is Dead " story less impressive in Gomberville's prose than in Milton's verse at no distant period ; is not much refreshed by getting to Rome about the death of Germanicus, and hearing a great deal about his life ; or later still by Egyptian *bergeries*—things in which somehow one does not see a concatenation accordingly ; and is not consoled by having the Phoenix business done—

---

[1] Although some say that almost every one of the numerous *personae* of the *Astrée* had a live original.

oh ! so differently from the fashion of Shakespeare or even of Darley. And when it finishes with a solemn function for the rise of the Nile, the least exclusively modern of readers may prefer Moore or Gautier.

But if any one, deeming not unjustly that he had drunk enough of *Caritée*, were to conclude that he would
Polexandre. drink no more of any of the waters of Gomber-
ville, he would make a mistake. *Cythérée* [1] I cannot yet myself judge of, except at second-hand ; but the first part of *Polexandre*, if not also the continuation, *Le Jeune Alcidiane*,[1] may be very well spoken of. It, that is to say the first part of it, was translated into English by no less a person than William Browne, just at the close of his life ; and, perhaps for this reason, the British Museum does not contain the French original ; but those who cannot attain to this lose the less, because the substance of the book is the principal thing. This makes it one of the liveliest of the whole group, and one does not feel it an idle vaunt when at the end the author observes cheerfully of his at last united hero and heroine, " Since we have so long enjoyed *them*, let us have so much justice as to think it fitting now that *they* should likewise enjoy each other." Yet the unresting and unerring spirit of criticism may observe that even here the verbosity which is the fault of the whole division makes its appearance. For why not suppress most of the words after " them," and merely add, " let them now enjoy each other " ?

The book is, in fact, rather like a modernised " number " of the *Amadis* series,[2] and the author has had the will and the audacity to exchange the stale old Greeks and Romans—not the real Greeks, who can never be stale, or the real Romans, who can stand a good deal of staling, but the conventional classics—as well as the impossible shadows of the Dark Ages, for Lepanto and

---

[1] These books, having been constantly referred to in this fashion, offer a good many traps, into some of which I have fallen in the past, and may have done so even now. For instance, Körting rightly points out that almost every one calls this " *La* Jeune Alcidiane," whereas A. is the hero, who bears his mother's name.

[2] I had made this remark before I knew that Körting had anticipated it.

the Western Main, Turks and Spaniards and Mexicans, and a Prince of Scotland. Here also we find in the hero something more like Almanzor than Artamène, if not than Artaban : and of the whole one may say vulgarly that " the pot boils." Now, with the usual Heroic it too often fails to attain even a gentle simmer.

Jean Camus [de Pontcarre ?],[1] Bishop of Belley and of Arras—friend of St. Francis of Sales and of Honoré

Camus— d'Urfé; author of many " Christian " romances
Palombe, etc. to counteract the bad effects of the others, of a famous *Esprit de Saint François de S.*, and of a very great number of miscellaneous works,—seems to have been a rather remarkable person, and, with less power and more eccentricity, a sort of Fénelon of the first half of the century. His best known novel, *Palombe*, stands practically alone in its group as having had the honour of a modern reprint in the middle of the nineteenth century.[2] The title-giver is a female, not a male, human dove, and of course a married one. Camus was a divine of views which one does not call " liberal," because the word has been almost more sullied by ignoble use in this connection than in any other—but unconventional and independent; and he provoked great wrath among his brethren by reflecting on the abuses of the conventual system. *Palombe* appears to be not uninteresting, but after all it is but one of those parasitic exercises which have rarely been great except in the hands of very great genius. Historically, perhaps, the much less famous *Evènemens Singuliers* (2 vols., 1628) are more important, though they cannot be said to be very amusing. For (to the surprise, perhaps, of a reader who comes to the book without knowing anything about it) it is composed of pure Marmontel-and-Miss-Edgeworth Moral Tales

---

[1] The more recent books which refer to him, and (I think) the British Museum Catalogue, drop this addition. But he was admittedly of the Pontcarré family.

[2] Neither the original, however, nor this revision seems to have enjoyed the further honour of a place in the British Museum. Other books of his which at least sound novelish were *Darie, Aristandre, Diotrèphe, Cléoreste* (of which as well as of *Palombe* analyses may be found in Körting). The last would seem to be the most interesting. But in the bibliography of the Bishop's writings there are at least a dozen more titles of the same kind.

about *L'Ami Desloyal, La Prudente Mère, L'Amour et la Mort, L'Imprécation Maternelle,* and the like. Of course, as one would expect from the time, and the profession of the author, the meal of the morality is a little above the malt of the tale ; but the very titles are " germinal."

François Hédelin, Abbé d'Aubignac, is one of those unfortunate but rarely quite guiltless persons who live Hédelin d'Aubignac —*Macarise.* in literary history much more by the fact of their having attacked or lectured greater men than themselves, and by witticisms directed against them, than by their own actual work, which is sometimes not wholly contemptible. He concerns us here only as the author of a philosophical-heroic romance, rather agreeably entitled *Macarise ou La Reine des Iles Fortunées,* where the bland naïveté of the pedantry would almost disarm the present members of that Critical Regiment, of which the Abbé, in his turn, was not so much a chaplain as a most combatant officer. The very title goes on to neutralise its attractiveness by explaining —with that benignant condescension which is natural to at least some of its author's class—that it " contains the Moral Philosophy of the Stoics under the veil of several agreeable adventures in the form of a Romance " ; and that we may not forget this, various side-notes refer to passages in an *Abrégé* of that philosophy. The net is thus quite frankly set in the sight of the bird, and if he chooses to walk into it, he has only himself to blame. The opening is a fine example of that plunge into the middle of things which Hédelin had learnt from his classical masters to think proper : "Les cruels persécuteurs d'Arianax l'ayant réduit à la nécessité de se précipiter [1] dans les eaux de la Sennatèle avec son frère Dinazel. . . ." The fact that the presupposed gentle reader knows nothing of the persons or the places mentioned is supposed to arouse in him an inextinguishable desire to find out. That he should be at once gratified is, of course, un-

---

[1] Cf. the "self-precipitation" of Céladon. Perhaps no class of writers has ever practised " imitation," in the wrong sense, more than these "heroic" romancers.

thinkable. In fact his attention will soon be diverted from Arianax and Dinazel and the banks of the Sennatèle altogether by the very tragical adventures of a certain Cléarte. He, with a company of friends, visits the country of a tyrant, who is accustomed to welcome strangers and heap them with benefits, till a time comes (the allegory is something obvious) when he demands it all back, with their lives, through a cruel minister (again something "speakingly" named) "Thanate." The head of this company, Cléarte, on receiving the sentence, talks Stoicism for many pages, and when he is exhausted, somebody else takes up the running in such a fascinating manner that it "seemed as if he had only to go on talking to make the victims immortal !" But the atrocious Thanate cuts, at the same moment, the thread of the discourse and the throat of Cléarte—who is, however, transported to the dominions of Macarise,—and *histoires* and " ecphrases " and interspersions of verse follow as usual. But the Abbé is nowise infirm of purpose ; and the book ends with the strangest mixture of love-letters and not very short discourses on the various schools of philosophy, together with a Glossary or Onomasticon interpreting the proper names which have been used after the following fashion : " Alcarinte. *La Crainte*, du mot français par anagramme sans aucun changement," though how you can have an anagram without a change is not explained.

Perhaps one may class, if, indeed, classification is necessary, with the religious romances of Camus and the Gombauld— philosophical romance of Hédelin d'Aubignac, *Endimion*. the earlier allegorical ones of the poet Gombauld, *Endimion* and *Amaranthe*. The latter I have not yet seen. *Endimion* is rather interesting ; there was an early English translation of it; and I have always been of those who believe that Keats, somehow or other, was more directly acquainted with seventeenth-century literature than has generally been allowed.[1] The wanderings

---

[1] I am glad to find the high authority of my friend Sir Sidney Colvin on my side here as to the wider position—though he tells me that he was not, when he read *Endimion*, conscious of any positive indebtedness on Keats' part.

of the hero are as different as possible in detail ; but the fact that there *are* wanderings at all is remarkable, and there are other coincidences with Keats and differences from any classical form, which it might be out of place to dwell on here. Endymion is waked from his Latmian sleep by the infernal clatter of the dwellers at the base of the mountain, who use all the loudest instruments they possess to dispel an eclipse of the moon : and is discovered by his friend Pyzandre, to whom he tells the vicissitudes of his love and sleep. The early revealings of herself by Diana are told with considerable grace, and the whole, which is not too long, is readable. But there are many of the *naïvetés* and awkwardnesses of expression which attracted to the writers of this time the scorn of Boileau and others down to La Harpe. The Dedication to the Queen may perhaps be excused for asserting, in its first words, that as Endymion was put to sleep by the Moon, so he has been reawakened by the Sun,[1] *i.e.* her Majesty. But a Nemesis of this Phébus follows. For, later, it is laid down that " La Lune doit *toujours* sa lumière au Soleil." From which it will follow that Diana owed her splendour to Anne of Austria, or was it Marie de Medicis ?[2] It was fortunate for Gombauld that he did not live under the older dispensation. Artemis was not a forgiving goddess like Aphrodite.

Again, when Diana has disappeared after one of her graciousnesses, her lover makes the following reflection— that the gods apparently can depart *sans être en peine de porter nécessairement les pieds l'un devant l'autre*—an observation proper enough in burlesque, for the idea of a divine goose-step or marking time, instead of the *incessus*, is ludicrous enough. But there is not the slightest sign of humour anywhere in the book. Yet, again, this is a thing one would rather not have said, " Diane cessant de m'être favorable, Ismène [3] *me pouvait tenir lieu de Déesse.*"

---

[1] *V. sup.* p. 177, note 3.

[2] Gombauld seems to have been a devotee of both Queens : and commentators will have it that this whole book is courtship as well as courtiership in disguise.

[3] A kind of intermediary nymph—an enchantress indeed—who has assisted and advised him in his quests for the goddess.

Now it is sadly true that the human race does occasionally entertain, and act upon, reflections of this kind: and persons like Mr. Thomas Moore and Gombauld's own younger contemporary, Sir John Suckling, have put the idea into light and lively verse.   But you do not expect it in a serious romance.

Nevertheless it may be repeated that *Endimion* is one of the most readable of the two classes of books—the smaller sentimental and the longer heroic—between which it stands in scope and character.   The author's practice in the "other harmony" makes the obligatory verse-insertions rather less clumsy than usual ; and it may be permitted to add that the illustrations of the original edition, which are unusually numerous and elaborate, are also rather unusually effective.   "Peggy's face" is too often as "wretched" as Thackeray confessed his own attempts were ; but the compositions are not, as such, despicable—even in the case of the immortal and immortalising kiss-scene itself.   The "delicious event," to quote the same author in another passage, is not actually coming off—but it is very near.   But it was perhaps a pity that either Gombauld or Keats ever *waked* Endymion.

The most recent book[1] but one about Mme. de Villedieu contains (and, oddly enough, confesses itself to contain) very little about her novels, which the plain man might have thought the only reason for writing about her at all. It tells (partly after Tallemant) the little that is known about her (adding a great deal more about other people, things, and places, and a vast amount of conjecture), and not only takes the very dubious "letters" published by herself for gospel, but attributes to her, on the slightest evidence, if any, the anonymous *Mémoires sur la Vie de Henriette Sylvie de Molière*, and, what is more, accepts them as autobiographic ; quotes a good deal of her very valueless verse and that of others, and relates the whole in a most marvellous style, the smallest and most modest effervescences

> Mme. de Villedieu.

---

[1] Emile Magne, *Mme. de V.*, Paris, 1907.

of which are things like this : " La religion arrose
son âme d'une eau parfumée, et les fleurs noirs du répentir
éclosent " or " Soixante ans pesaient sur son crâne
ennuagé d'une perruque."[1] A good bibliography of the
actual work, and not a little useful information about
books and MS. relating to the period, may reconcile one
class of readers to it, and a great deal of scandal another ; but as far as the subject of this history goes no
one will be much wiser when he closes the volume than
he was when he opened it.

The novelist-heroine's actual name was Marie
Catherine Hortense des Jardins, and she never was really
Mme. de Villedieu at all, though there was a real M. de
Villedieu whom she loved, went through a marriage
ceremony and lived with, left, according to some, or
was left by, according to others. But he was already
married, and this marriage was never dissolved. Very
late in life she seems actually to have married a Marquis
de Chaste, who died soon. But most of the time was
spent in rather scandalous adventures, wherein Fouquet's
friend Gourville, the minister Lyonne, and others
figure. In fact she seems to have been a counterpart
as well as a contemporary of our own Afra, though she
never came near Mrs. Behn in poetry or perhaps in fiction.
Her first novel, *Alcidamie*, not to be confounded with
the earlier *Alcidiane*, was a scarcely concealed utilising
of the famous scandal about Tancrède de Rohan (Mlle.
des Jardins' mother had been a dependant on the
Rohan family, and she herself was much befriended by
that formidable and sombre-fated enchantress, Mme.
de Montbazon). In fact, common as is the real or
imputed " key "-interest in these romances from the
Astrée onwards, none seems to have borrowed more from
at least gossip than this. Her later performances, *Les
Annales Galantes de la Grèce* (said to be very rare), *Carmente, Les Amours des Grands Hommes, Les Désordres de*

---

[1] This sometimes causes positive obscurity as to fact. Thus it is impossible to make
out from M. Magne whether Hortense, in her last days, actually married the cousin with
whom she had been intimate in youth, or merely lived with him.

l'Amour, and some smaller pieces, all rely more or less on this or that kind of scandal. Collections appeared three or four times in the earlier eighteenth century.

Since M. Magne wrote (and it is fair to say that the main purpose of his book was frankly avowed by its

Le Grand Alcandre Frustré. appearance as a member of a series entitled *Femmes Galantes*), a somewhat more sober account, definitely devoted in part to the novels, has appeared.[1]   But even this is not exhaustive from our point of view.   The collected editions (of which that of 1702, in 10 vols., said to be the best, is the one I have used) must be consulted if one really wishes to attain a fair knowledge of what " this questionable Hortense " (as Mr. Carlyle would probably have called her) really did in literature ; and no one, even of these, appears to contain the whole of her ascribed compositions.   What used sometimes to be quoted as her principal work, *Le Grand Alcandre Frustré* (the last word being often omitted), is, in fact, a very small book, containing a bit of scandal about the Grand Monarque, of the same kind as those which myriad anonyms of the time printed in Holland, and of which any one who wants them may find specimens enough in the *Bibliothèque Elzévirienne* edition of Bussy-Rabutin.   Its chief—if not its only—attraction is an exceedingly quaint frontispiece—a cavalier and lady standing with joined hands under a chandelier, the torches of which are held by a ring of seven Cupids, so that the lower one hangs downwards, and the disengaged hand of the cavalier, which is raised, seems to be grabbing at him.

Most of the rest, putting aside the doubtful *Henriette de Molière* already referred to, are collections of love-

The collected love-stories. stories, which their titles, rather than their contents, would seem to have represented to the ordinary commentator as loose.   There is really very little impropriety, except of the mildest kind, in any of them,[2] and they chiefly consist of the kind of

---

[1] By M. H. E. Chatenet, Paris, 1911.
[2] There is a little in the verse, most of which belongs to the " flying " kind so common in the century.

quasi-historic anecdote (only better told) which is not uncommon in English, as, for instance, in Croxall's *Novelist*. They are rather well written, but for the most part consist of very " public " material, scarcely made " private " by any striking merit, and distinguished by curious liberties with history, if not with morals.

For instance, in one of her *Amours Galantes* the Elfrida-Ethelwold-Edgar story is told, not only with "*Edward I.* of England" for the deceived and revengeful king, but with a further and more startling intrusion of Eleanor of Guyenne! That of Inez de Castro is treated in a still more audacious manner. Also (with what previous example I know not, but Hortense was exceedingly apt to have previous examples) the names of the heretic to whom Dante was not merciful and of his beloved Margaret—names to which Charles Kingsley made the atonement of two of the most charming of his neglected poems—appear as " Dulcin " and " Marguerite," King and Queen of Lombardy, but guilty of more offensive lubricity than the sternest inquisitor ever charged on the historical Dolcino and his sect. For this King and Queen set up, in cold blood, two courts of divorce, in one of which each is judge, with the direct purpose of providing themselves with a supply of temporary wives and husbands. Some have maintained that no less a thing than the *Princesse de Clèves* itself was suggested by something of Mme. de Villedieu's ; but this seems to me merely the usual plagiarism-hunter's blunder of forgetting that the treatment, not the subject, is the *crux* of originality. Of her longer books, *Alcidamie*, the first, has been spoken of. The *Amours des Grandes Hommes* and *Cléonice ou le Roman Galant* belong to the " keyed " Heroics ; while the *Journal Amoureux*, which runs to nearly five hundred pages, has Diane de Poitiers for its chief heroine. Lastly, *Carmente* (or, as it was reprinted, *Carmante*) is a sort of mixed pastoral, with Theocritus himself introduced, after a fashion noted more than once before.

Their historic liberties.

Carmente, etc.

Her most praised things, recently, have been the story of the loves of Henri IV. and Mme. de Sauve Her value on the whole. (lightly touched on, perhaps "after" her in both senses, by Dumas) in the *Amours Galantes*, and a doubtful story (also attributed to the obscure M. de Preschac of the *Cabinet des Fées* [1]) entitled *L'Illustre Parisienne*, over which folk have quarrelled as to whether it is to be labelled "realist" or not. One regrets, however, to have to say that—except for fresh, if not very strong, evidence of that "questing" character which we find all over the subjects of these two chapters— the interest of Mme. de Villedieu's work can hardly be called great. By a long chapter of accidents, the present writer, who had meant to read her some five-and-thirty years ago, never read her actually till the other day— with all good will, with no extravagant expectation beforehand, but with some disappointment at the result. She is not a bookmaker of the worst kind ; she evidently had wits and literary velleities ; and she does illustrate the blind *nisus* of the time as already indicated. But beyond the bookmaking class she never, I think, gets. Her mere writing is by no means contemptible, and we may end by pointing out two little points of interest in *Carmente*. One is the appearance of the name "Ardélie," which our own Lady Winchelsea took and anglicised as her coterie title. It may occur elsewhere, but I do not recollect it. The other is yet a fresh anticipation of that bold figure of speech which has been cited before from Dickens—one of the characters appearing "in a very clean shepherd's dress *and a profound melancholy.*" Mme. de Villedieu (it is about the only place she has held hitherto, if she has held any, in ordinary Histories of French Literature) has usually been regarded as closing the Heroic school. We may therefore most properly turn from her directly to the last and most cheerful division of the subjects of this chapter—the Fairy Tale.

One of the greatest solaces of the writer of this book,

[1] *V. inf.* upon it.

and, he would fain hope, something of a consolation to
The fairy its readers, has been the possibility, and indeed
tale. advisability, of abstention from certain stock
literary controversies, or at worst of dismissing them
with very brief mention. This solace recurs in reference
to the large, vague, and hotly debated subject of folk-
lore and fairy stories, their connection, and the origin of
the latter. It is true that " the pleasure gives way To a
savour of sorrow," to adopt a charming phrase of Mr.
Dobson's, when I think of the amiable indignation
which the absence of what I shall not say, and perhaps
still more the presence of some things that I shall say,
would have caused in my friend, and his friend, the late
Mr. Andrew Lang.[1] But the irreparable is always
with us. Despite the undoubted omnipresence of the
folk-story, with its " fairy " character in the general
sense, I have always wanted more proof than I have
ever received, that the thing is of Western rather than
of Eastern origin, and that our Western stories of the
kind, in so far as they affected literature before a
very recent period, are independent. But I attach no
particular value to this opinion, and it will influence
nothing that I say here. So with a few more half-words
to the wise, as that Mme. d'Aulnoy had been in
Spain, that the Crusades took place in the eleventh
century, that, independently thereof, Scandinavians had
been " Varangians " very early at Constantinople, etc.
etc., let us come to the two great literary facts—the
chorus of fairy tale-telling proper at the end of the
century (of which the coryphaei are the lady already
mentioned and Perrault), and the epoch-making translation of *The Arabian Nights* by Galland.

In a certain sense, no doubt, the fairy tale may be
said to be merely a variety of the age-old *fabliau* and
nouvelle. But it is, for literary purposes, a distinctly
and importantly new variety—new not merely in subject,

[1] His own admirable introduction to Perrault in the Clarendon Press series will, as
far as our subject is directly concerned, supply whatever a reader, within reason further
curious, can want : and his well-known rainbow series of Fairy Books will give infinite
illustration.

even in the widest possible sense of that rather disputable
Its general (or at least disputed) word, but in that *nescio*
characteristics *quid* between subject and treatment for which
—the happy I know no better term than the somewhat
ending. vague one " atmosphere." It has the priceless
quality of what may be called good childishness ; it gives
not merely Fancy but Imagination the freest play, and,
till it has itself created one, it is free from any convention.
It continued, indeed, always free from those " previous "
conventions which are so intolerable. For it is constantly
forgotten that a convention in its youth is often positively
healthy, and a convention in the prime of its life a very
tolerable thing. It is the *old* conventions which, as
Mahomet rashly acknowledged about something else
(saving himself, however, most dexterously afterwards),
cannot be tolerated in Paradise. Moreover, besides
creating of necessity a sort of fresh dialect in which it
had to be told, and producing a set of personages entirely
unhackreyed, it did an immense service by introducing
a sort of etiquette, quite different from the conventions
above noticed,—a set of manners, as it may almost be
called, which had the strongest and most beneficial
influence—though, like all strong and good things, it
might be perverted—on fiction generally. In this all
sorts of nice things, as in the original prescription for
what girls are made of, were included—variety, gaiety,
colour, surprise, a complete contempt of the contemptible,
or of that large part of it which contains priggishness,
propriety, " prunes, and prism " generally. Moreover (and
here I fear that the above promised abstinence from the
contentious must be for a little time waived) it confirmed
a great principle of novel and romance alike, that if
you can you should " make a good end," as, *teste* Romance
herself, Guinevere did, though the circumstances were
melancholy.

The termination of a fairy tale rarely is, and never
should be, anything but happy. For this reason I have
always disliked—and though some of the mighty have
left their calm seats and endeavoured to annihilate me

for it, I still continue to dislike—that old favourite of some part of the public, *The Yellow Dwarf*. That detestable creature (who does not even amuse me) had no business to triumph ; and, what is more, I don't believe he did. Not being an original writer, I cannot tell the true history as it might be told ; but I can criticise the false. I do not object to this version because of its violation of poetical justice—in which, again, I don't believe. But this is neither poetical, nor just, nor amusing. It is a sort of police report, and I have never much cared for police reports. I should like to have set Maimoune at the Yellow Dwarf: and then there would have been some fun.

It is probably unnecessary to offer any translations here, because the matter is so generally known, and because the books edited by that regretted friend of mine above mentioned have spread it (with much other matter of the same kind) more widely than ever. But the points mentioned above, and perhaps some others, can never be put too firmly to the credit of the fairy tale as regards its influence on fiction, and on French fiction particularly. It remains to be seen, in the next chapter, how what a few purists may call its contamination by, but what we may surely be permitted to call its alliance with, " polite literature " was started, or practically started, through the direct agency of no Frenchman, but of a man who can be claimed by England in the larger and national sense, by Scotland and Ireland and England again in the narrower and more parochial—by Anthony Hamilton. His work, however, must be left till that next chapter, though in this we may, after the " blessed originals " just mentioned, take in their sometimes degenerate successors for nearly a hundred years after Perrault's time.

Well, however, as the simpler and purer fairy-tales may Perrault and Mme. d'Aulnoy. be known to all but twentieth-century children (who are said not to like them), it is doubtful whether many people have considered them in the light in which we have to regard them here, so as

to see in them both a link in the somewhat complicated
chain of novel development, and also one which is not
dead metal, but serves as a medium for introducing
powerful currents of influence on the chain itself.   We
have dwelt on one point—the desirableness, if not
necessity, of shortness in them—as specially valuable at
the time.   No doubt they need not all be as short as
Perrault's, though even among his there are instances
(not to mention *L'Adroite Princesse* for the moment),
such as *Peau d'Âne*, of more than twenty pages, as against
the five of the *Chaperon Rouge* and the ten of *Barbe Bleue*,
Le Chat Botté, and *Cendrillon*.   Mme. d'Aulnoy's run
longer ; but of course the longest [1] of all are mites
to the mammoths of the Scudéry romance.   A fairy
story must never " drag," and in its better, and indeed all
its genuine, forms it never does.   Further (it must be
remembered that " Little Red Riding Hood," in its
unadulterated and " *un*happy ending " form, is not a
fairy story at all, for talking animals are not peculiar
to that), " fairiness," the actual presence of these gracious
or ungracious but always between-human-and-divine-
creatures, is necessary,[2] and their agency must be necessary
too.   In this and other ways it is interesting to contrast
two stories (which are neighbours to each other, with
Peau d'Âne between them, in the convenient one-volume
collection of French Fairy Tale classics published by
Garnier), Mme. d'Aulnoy's *Gracieuse et Percinet* and
L'Adroite Princesse ou Les Aventures de Finette, which
appeared with Perrault's, but which I can hardly believe
to be his.   They are about the same length, but the one
is one of the best and the other one of the worst examples
of its author and of the general style.   It may be worth
while to analyse both very briefly.   As for Perrault's
better work, such analysis should be as unnecessary as it
would be irreverent.

[1] The longest of all, in the useful collection referred to in the text, are the *Oiseau Bleu*
and the charming *Biche au Bois*, each of which runs to nearly sixty pages.   But both,
though very agreeable, are distinctly " sophisticated," and for that very reason useful as
gangways, as it were, from the simpler fairy tale to the complete novel.
[2] Enchanters, ogres, etc. " count " as fairies.

That *Gracieuse et Percinet* is of an essentially " stock " character is not in the least against it, for so it ought to be: and the " stock " company that plays its parts plays them well. The father is perhaps rather excessively foolish and unnatural, but then he almost had to be. The wicked and ugly stepmother tops, but does not overtop, *her* part, and her punishment is not commonplace. Gracieuse herself deserves her name, not only " by her comely face and by her fair bodie," but by her good but not oppressive wits, and her amiable but not faultless disposition. She ought not to have looked into the box ; but then we should not have liked her nearly as much if she had not done so. She was foolishly good in refusing to stay with Percinet ; but we are by no means certain that we should like her better if she had thrown herself into his arms at the first or second time of asking. Besides, where would have been the story ? As for Percinet, he escapes in a wonderful fashion, though partly by help of his lady's little wilfulnesses, the dangers of the handsome, amiable, in a small way always successful, and almost omnipotent hero. There is a sort of ironic tenderness, in his letting Gracieuse again and again go her wilful way and show her foolish filiality, which saves him. He is always ready, and does his spiriting in the politest and best manner, particularly when he shepherds all those amusing but rebellious little people into their box again— a feat which some great novelists have achieved but awkwardly in their own cases. There is even pathos in the apparently melancholy statement that the fairy palace is dead, and that Gracieuse will never see it till she is buried. I should like to have been Percinet, and I should particularly like to have married Gracieuse.

Moreover, the thing is full of small additional seasonings of incident and phrase to the solid feast of fairy working which it provides. Gracieuse's " collation," with its more than twenty pots of different jams, has a delightful realty (which is slightly different from reality) even for those to whom jam has never been the very

*Commented examples—
Gracieuse et Percinet.*

VIII SEVENTEENTH-CENTURY NOVEL 251

highest of human delights, because they prefer savouries
to sweets. Even the abominable duchess seems to have
had a splendid cellar, before she took to filling the casks
with mere gold and jewels to catch the foolish king. It
is impossible to imagine a scene more agreeably com-
pounded of politeness and affection than Percinet's first
introduction of himself to the Princess: and it is extraordinarily nice to find that they knew all about each
other before, though we have had not the slightest
previous information as to the acquaintance. I am very
much afraid that he made his famous horse kick and
plunge when Grognon was on him; but it must be
remembered that he had been made to lead that animal
against his will. The description of the hag's flogging
Gracieuse with feathers instead of scourges is a quite
admirable adaptation of some martyrological stories;
and when, in her dilapidated condition, she remarks that
she wishes he would go away, because she has always
been told that she must not be alone with young gentlemen, one feels that the martyrdom must have been
transferred, in no mock sense, to Percinet himself. If
she borrows Psyche's trials, what good story is not another
good story refreshed ? [1]

But if almost everything is good and well managed in
Gracieuse, it may also be said that almost everything
L'Adroite is badly managed in *Finette*.[2] To begin with,
Princesse. there is that capital error which has been
noticed above, that it is not really a fairy tale at all.
Except the magic *quenouilles*, which themselves are of
the smallest importance in the story, there is nothing in
it beyond the ways of an ordinary adventurous *nouvelle*.
The touch of *grivoiserie* by which the Princesses Nonchalante and Babillarde allow the weaknesses ticketed
in their names to hand them over as a prey to the cunning
and blackguard Prince Riche-Cautèle, under pretence

[1] Apuleius, who has a good deal of the "fairy" element in him, was naturally drawn
upon in this group. The *Psyche* indebtedness reappears, with frank acknowledgment,
in *Serpentin Vert.*
[2] If Perrault really wrote this, the Muses, rewarding him elsewhere for the good
things he said in "The Quarrel," must have punished him here for the silly ones. It
has, in fact, most of the faults which *neo*-classicism attributed to its opposite.

of entirely unceremonised and unwitnessed " marriage,"
is in no way amusing. Finette's escapes from the same
fate are a little better, but the whole is told (as its author
seems to have felt) at much too great length ; and the
dragging in of an actual fairy at the end, to communicate
to the heroine the exceedingly novel and recondite maxim
that " Prudence is the mother of safety," is almost
idiotic. If the thing has any value, it is as an example,
not of a real fairy tale nor of a satire on fairy tales (for
which it is much too much " out of the rules " and much
too stupid), but of something which may save an ordinary
reader, or even student, from attacking, as I fear we shall
have to do, the *Cabinet des Fées* at large, and discovering, by
painful experience, how excessively silly and tedious the
corruption of this wise and delightful kind may be.

One might, of course, draw lessons from others of the
original batches, but this may suffice for the specimen
batch under immediate review. *Peau d'Âne*, one of the
most interesting to " folklorists " and origin-hunters, is,
of course, also in itself interesting to students of literature.
Its combination of the old theme of the incestuous
passion of a father for his daughter, with the special but
not invariable shadow of excuse in the selfish vanity of
the mother's dying request, is quite out of the usual way
of these things. So is the curious series of fairy failures—
things apparently against the whole set of the game—beginning with the unimaginative conception of dresses,
weather-, or sky-, moon-, and sun-colour, rendered futile
by the success of the artists, and ending in the somewhat
banal device of making yourself ugly and running away,
with the odd conclusion-contrast of Peau d'Âne's squalid
appearance in public and her private splendour in the fairy
garments.

Still, the lessons of correction, warning, and instruction to be drawn from these gracious little things, for
The danger the benefit of their younger and more elaborate
of the successors, are not easily exhausted. They
"moral." are, on the whole, very moral, and it is well
that morality, rightly understood, should animate fiction.

But they are occasionally much *too* moral, and then they warn off instead of cheering on. Take, for instance, two other neighbours in the collection just quoted, *Le Prince Chéri* and the ever-delightful *La Belle et La Bête*. Both of these are moral; but the latter is just moral enough, while *Chéri*, with one or two alleviations (of which, perhaps, more presently), is hardly anything if *not* moral, and therefore disgusts, or at any rate bores. On the other hand, " Beauty " is as *bonne* as she is *belle* ; her only fault, that of overstaying her time, is the result of family affection, and her reward and the punishment of the wicked sisters are quite copy-book. But it is not for this part that we love what is perhaps the most engaging of all the tales. It is for Beauty's own charm, which is subtly conveyed ; for the brisk and artistic " revolutions and discoveries "; above all, for the far from merely sentimental pathos of the Beast's all but death *for* love, and the not in the least mawkish bringing of him to life again *by* love.[1]

One may perhaps also make amends to Prince Chéri for the abuse just bestowed on him. His story has at Yet often least one touch which is sovereign for a fiction-redeemed. fault common in the past, and only too probable in the future, at whatever time one takes the " present " of the story. When he is not unjustly turned into a monster of the most allegorical-composite order of monster archi-tecture—a monster to whom dragons and wyverns and chimaeras dire are as ordinary as kittens—what do they do with him ? They put him " with the other monsters." *Ce n'est pas plus raide que ça.* The present writer need hardly fear to be thought an anti-mediaevalist, but he is very much afraid that an average mediaeval romancer might have thought it necessary to catalogue these other monsters with the aid of a Bestiary. On the other hand, there have been times—no matter which—when this abrupt introduction and dismissal of monsters as common objects (for which any respectable community will have proper stables or cages) would have been disallowed,

[1] For a spoiling of this delightful story *v. inf.* on the *Cabinet.*

or explained away, or apologised for, or, worst of all,
charged with a sort of wink or sneer to let the reader
know that the author knew what he was about. Here
there is nothing of this superfluous or offensive sort.
The appropriate and undoubting logic of the style
prevails over all too reasonable difficulties. There are
monsters, or how could Chéri be made into one ? If
there are monsters there must, or in the highest probability may, be other monsters. Put him with them, and
make no fuss about it. If all novelists had had this
aplomb, we should have been spared a great deal of
tediousness, some positive failures, and the spoiling, or
at least the blotting and marring, of many excellent
situations. But to praise the good points of fairy stories,
from the brief consummateness of *Le Chat Botté* to the
longer drawn but still perfectly golden matter of *La Biche
au Bois*, would really be superfluous. One loathes leaving
them ; but one has to do it, so far as the more unsophisticated part of them is concerned. Yet the duty of the
historian will not let him be content with these, and, to
vary "The Brave Lord Willoughby" a little, "turning
to the [*others*] a thousand more," he must "slay," or at
least criticise.

He who ventures on the complete *Cabinet des Fées* [1]
in its more than forty volumes, will provide himself
The main with "cabin furniture" of nearly as good
Cabinet des pastime-quality, at least to my fancy (and
Fées—more yet I may claim to be something of a
on Mme. Balzacian), as the slightly larger shelf-ful
d'Aulnoy.
which suggested itself to the fancy of Mr. Browning
and provoked (*as* "cabin furniture") the indignation
of Mr. Swinburne. But he had better look over the
contents before he takes it on board, or he will find
himself, if his travelling library is anything like as
large as that of the patriarch Photius, in danger of
duplication. For the *Cabinet* holds, not merely the

[1] Its full title, "ou Collection Choisie des C. des F. *et autres Contes Merveilleux*,"
should in justice be remembered, when one feels inclined to grumble at some of the
contents.

Arabian Nights in the original translation of Galland,
but also Hamilton : as well, of course, as much of what
we may call the classical fairy matter proper on which
we have already dwelt, and which is known to all decent
people.   Still, he will find more of Mme. d'Aulnoy
than, unless he is already something of an expert, he
already knows, and perhaps he will not be entirely
rejoiced at the amplification.   She wrote more or less
regular heroic romances,[1] which are very inferior to her
fairy tales ; and though these are not in the *Cabinet*,
she sometimes " mixes the kinds " rather disastrously in
shorter pieces.   The framework of *Don Gabriel Ponce de
Leon*, which enshrines the sad but charming " Golden
Sheep," and a variant of *Cendrillon*, is poor stuff ; and
Les Chevaliers Errans only shows what we knew before,
that the junction of the seventeenth and eighteenth
centuries is not the time or the place in which to find the
loved one, if that loved one is mediaeval.   Still, this
invaluable lady does generally reck and exemplify her
own immortal rede.   " Il me semble," says Prince Mar-
cassin to the fairies, " à vous entendre, qu'il ne faut pas
même croire ce qu'on voit."   And they reply, " La
règle n'est pas toujours générale ; *mais il est indubitable
que l'on doit suspendre son jugement sur bien des choses, et
penser qu'il peut entrer quelque chose de Féerie dans ce que
nous paroît de plus certain.*"

Alas ! it was precisely this *quelque chose de Féerie*
which is wanting in the majority of the minor fairy-tale
Warning writers.   That they should attain the wonder-
against dis- ful simplicity, freshness, and charm of Perrault
appointment. at his best was not to be expected ; hardly
that they should reach the more sophisticated grace of
Hamilton ; but it might have been hoped that some would
come more or less near the lower, and much more unequal, but occasionally very successful art or luck of
Mme. d'Aulnoy herself.   Unfortunately very few of

---

[1] This indeed was the case, in one or other kind of longer fiction writing, with most
of the authors to be mentioned. The total of this in the French eighteenth century was
enormous.

them do. It was easy enough to begin *Il était autrefois un roi et une reine*, to put in a Prince Charming and a Princess Graciosa, and good fairies and bad fairies, and magicians and ogres and talking beasts, and the like. It was not so easy to make all these things work together to produce the peculiar spell which belongs to the true land of Faery, and to that land alone. Still more unfortunately, wrong ways of attempting the object (or some other object) were as easy as the right ways were difficult. They cannot avoid muddling the fairy tale with the heroic romance: and with the half-historical sub-variety of this latter which Mme. de La Fayette introduced. The worst enchanter that ever fairies had to fight with is not such an enemy of theirs as History and Geography—two most respectable persons in their proper places, but fatal here. They will make King Richard of England tell fairy tales to Blondel out of the Austrian tower, and muddle up things about his wicked brother the Count of Mortagne. They will talk of Lemnos and Memphis and other *patatis* and *patatas* of the classical dictionary and the *Grand Cyrus*. In a fashion not perhaps so instantly suicidal, but in a sufficiently annoying fashion, they will invent clumsy " speaking " names, or dog-Latin and cat-Greek ones. And, perhaps worst of all, they prostitute the delicate charms of the fairy tale to clumsy adulation of the reigning monarch, and tedious half-veiled flattery or satire of less exalted persons, or, if " prostitute " be too harsh a word here, attempt to force a marriage between these charms and the dullest moralising. In fact, it is scarcely extravagant to say that, in regard to too many of them—to some of them at least—everything that ought not to be, such as the things just mentioned and others, is there, and everything that ought to be—lightness, brightness, the sense of the impossible in which it is delightful to believe, the dream-feeling, the magic of gratified wish and realised ideal—is not.

Of course, in these other and minor writers that the *Cabinet* has to give, all these disappointments do not

always occur, and the crop is mixed. Mlle. de la
Mlle. de la Force and others. Force [1] was one of those *dames* or *demoiselles de compagnie* who figure so largely in the literary history of the French eighteenth century, and whose group is illustrated by such names as those of Mlle. Delaunay and Mlle. de Lespinasse. Her full name was Charlotte Rose de Caumont de la Force, and she was, if not an adventuress, a person of adventures, who also wrote many quasi-historical romances in the *Princesse de Clèves* manner. Her fairy tales are thin, and marred by weak allegory of the " Carte de Tendre " kind. A " Pays des Délices," very difficult to reach, and constantly personated by a " Pays des Avances," promises little and performs less.

The eleven (it is an exact eleven) called *Les Illustres Fées* is scarcely so illustrious as the All England and the United were, in the memory of some of us, in another and better played kind of cricket. The stories are not very long ; they run to a bare eighteen small pages apiece ; but few readers are likely to wish them longer. *Blanche-Belle* introduces the *sylphes*—an adulteration [2] which generally produces the effect that Thackeray deplored when his misguided friend would have *purée* mixed with *julienne*. *Le Roi Magicien* is painfully destitute of personality ; we want names, and pretty names, for a fairy tale. *Le Prince Roger* is a descendant of Mélusine, and one does not think she would be proud of him. *Fortunio* is better, and *Quiribirini*, one of the numerous stories which turn on remembering or failing to remember an odd name,[3] perhaps better still ; but the rest deserve little praise, and the last, *L'Ile Inaccessible*, appears to be, if it is anything but pure

[1] She is even preceded by a Mme. de Murat, a friend of Mme. de Parabère, but a respectable fairy-tale writer. It does not seem necessary, according to the plan of this book, to give many particulars about these writers ; for it is their writings, not themselves, that our subject regards. The curious may be referred to Walckenaer on the Fairy Tale in general, and Honoré Bonhomme on the *Cabinet* in particular, as well as (*v. inf.*) to the thirty-seventh volume of the collection itself.

[2] There is sometimes alliance and sometimes jealousy on this subject. In one tale the " Comte de Gabalis " is solemnly "had up," tried, and condemned as an impostor.

[3] *Ricdin-Ricdon*, one of those which pass between Cœur de Lion and Blondel, is of the same kind, is also good, and is longer.

dulness, a flat political allegory about England and France.

The style picks up a little in the miscellany called (not without a touch of piquancy) *La Tyrannie des Fées Détruite*, by a Mme. d'*Auneuil*, whom persons of a sceptical turn might imagine to be a sort of factitious rival to Mme. d'Aulnoy.[1] It returns to the Greek or pseudo-Greek names of the heroic romance, and to its questionable device of *histoires* stuck like plums in a pudding. Nor are the *Sans Parangon* and the *Fée des Fées* of the Sieur de Preschac utterly bad. But *Les Aventures d'Abdalla*, besides rashly incurring the danger (to be exemplified and commented on more fully a little later) of vying with the *Arabian Nights*, substitutes for the genuine local colour and speech the *fade* jargon of French eighteenth-century "sensibility"—*autels* and *flammes* and all the rest of the trumpery. But it does worse still—it tries to be instructive, and informs us of the difference between male and female *dives* and *peris*, of the custom of suttee, and of the fact that there are many professional singers and dancers among Indian girls. This is simply intolerable.[2]

The great prominence of the Eastern Tale, indeed, in this collection is likely to be one of the most striking things in it to a new-comer. He would know, of course, that such tales are not uncommon in contemporary English; he would certainly be acquainted with Addison's, Johnson's, Goldsmith's experiments in them, perhaps with those of Hawkesworth and others.[3] He could see for himself that the "accaparation" by France of the peerless *Arabian Nights* themselves must have led to a still greater fancy for them there; and he might possibly have heard

The large proportion of Eastern Tales.

---

[1] She seems, however (see vol. 37 as above), to have been a real person.

[2] The would-be anonymous compiler (he was really Gueulette, on whom *v. inf.*) of this and the other collections now to be noticed, when acknowledging his sufficiently evident *supercherie* and some of his indebtednesses (*e.g.* to Straparola), defends this on Edgeworthian principles. But though it is quite true that a healthy curiosity as to such things may be aroused by tales, it should be left to satisfy itself, not forestalled and spoilt and stunted by immediate information.

[3] The once very popular *Tales of the Genii* (*v. inf.*) which are often referred to by

the tradition (which the present writer [1] never traced to
its source, or connected with any real evidence either
way) that no less a person than Lesage assisted Galland
in his task.   But though the *Nights* themselves form the
most considerable single group in the *Cabinet*, the united
bulk of their congeners or imitations occupies a still
larger space.   There are the rather pale and " moon-
like " but sometimes not uninteresting *Thousand and One
Days*, and the obviously and rather foolishly pastiched
Thousand and One Quarters of an Hour.   There are
Persian Tales—origin of a famous and characteristic
jibe at " Namby Pamby " Philips—and Turkish Tales
which are a fragment of one of the numerous versions of
the *Seven Sages* scheme.   The just mentioned *Adventures
of Abdallah* betray their source and their nature at once ;
the hoary fables of Bidpai and Lokman are modernised
to keep company with these " fakings," and there are
more definitely literary attempts to follow.   *Les Voyages
de Zulma*, again an incomplete thing which actually tails
off towards its failure of an end, shows some ingenuity
in its conception, but suffers, even in the beginning, from
that mixing of kinds which has been pointed out and
reprobated.   An attempt is made to systematise the
fairy idea by representing these gracious creatures as offspring of Destiny and the Earth, with a cruel brother
Time, and an offset of mischievous sisters who exactly
correspond to the good ones—Disgracieuse to Gracieuse,
and so on—and have a queen Laide-des-Laides, who
answers to the good fairy princess, Belle-des-Belles.   A
mortal — Zulma — is, for paternal rather than personal
merits, chosen by Destiny to enjoy the privilege of entering
Les Voyages   and understanding the fairy world, and Gracieuse
de Zulma.   is the fairy assigned as his guide.   The idea is,
as has been said, rather ingenious ; but it is too systematic,

---

Scott and other men of his generation, seem to have dropped out of notice comparatively.
We shall meet them here in French.

[1] The late Mr. Henley was at one time much interested in this point, and consulted
me about it.   But I could tell him nothing ; and I do not know whether he ever
satisfied himself on the subject.   Lesage *is* said (though I am not sure that the evidence
goes beyond *on dit*) to have revised the work of Pétis de La Croix in the *Days* ; and
some of his own certainly corresponds to it.

and like other things in other parts of the collection, " loses
the grace and liberty of the composition" in system. Moreover, the morality, as is rather the wont of these imitators
when they are not (as a few of the partly non-cabinetted
ones are) deliberately naughty, is much too scrupulous.[1]
It is clear that Zulma is in love with Gracieuse, that she
responds to some extent, and that Her Majesty Queen
Belle-des-Belles is a little jealous and inclined to cut
Gracieuse out. But nothing in the finished part of the
story gives us any of the nice love-making that we want.

Madame le Marchand's *Boca* is a story which begins
in Peru but finishes in an " Isle of Ebony," where the
names of Zobeide and Abdelazis seem rather
Fénelon. more at home ; it is not without merit. As for
the fables and stories which Fénelon composed for that
imperfect Marcellus, the Duke of Burgundy, they have
all the merits of style, sense, and good feeling which they
might be expected to have, and it would be absurd to ask
of them qualities which, in the circumstances, they could
not display.

The *Chinese Tales* are about as little Chinese as may
be, consisting of accounts of his punitive metempsychoses
by the Mandarin Fum Hoam (a name afterwards
borrowed in better known work), who seems to have
been excluded from the knowledge of anything particularly Celestial.[2] But they are rather smartly told. On
the other hand, *Florine ou la Belle Italienne*, which is
included in the same volume with the sham *Chinoiseries*,
is one of the worst instances of the confusion of kinds
noted above. It honestly prepares one for what is coming
by a reference in the Preface to Fénelon ; but a list of
dramatis (or *fabulae*) *personae*, which follows, would have
tried the saintliness even of him of Cambrai almost as
much as a German occupation of his archiepiscopal see.
" Agatonphisie," for a personage who represents, we are

[1] Or, as it was once put, with easy epigram, when the artificial fairy tale is not
dreadfully improper it is apt to be dreadfully proper.
[2] Nothing suits the entire group better than the reply of the ferocious and sleepless
but not unintelligent Sultan Hudgiadge, in the *Nouveaux Contes Orientaux*, when his
little benefactress Moradbak says that she will have the honour to-morrow of telling
him a *histoire Mongole*. " Le pays n'y fait rien," says he. And it doesn't.

told, " Le Bon Sens," might break the heart of Clenardus, if not the head of Priscian.

The Thousand and One Quarter Hours, or *Contes Tartares*, have as little of the Tartar as those above mentioned of the Chinese, but if somewhat verbose, they are not wholly devoid of literary quality. The substance is, as in nearly all these cases, *Arabian Nights* rehashed ; but the hashing is not seldom done *secundum artem*, and they have, with the *Les Sultanes de Gujerate* and *Nouveaux Contes Orientaux*, which follow them, the faculty of letting themselves be read.

The best of these [1] (except the French translation of the so-called Sir Charles Morell's (really James Ridley's) *Tales of the Genii* (see above)) is perhaps, on the whole, *Les Sultanes de Gujerate*, where not only are some of the separate tales good, but the frame-story is far more artistically worked in and round and out than is usually the case. But taking them all together, there is one general and obvious, as well as another local and particular objection to them. Although the subtitle (*v. sup.* again) lets them in, the main one regards them with, at best, an oblique countenance. The differences between the Western fairy and the Eastern *peri, dive, djin*, or whatever one choses to call her, him, or it, though not at all easy to define, are exceedingly easy to feel. The magicians and enchanters of the two kinds are nearer to each other, but still not the same. On the other hand, it is impossible for any one who has once felt the strange charm of the *Arabian Nights* not to feel the immense inferiority of these rehashes and *croquettes* and *rissoles*, and so forth, of the noble old haunch or sirloin. Yet again, from the special point of view of this book, though they cannot be simply passed over, they supply practically nothing which marks, or causes, or even promises an advance in the general development of fiction. They may be said to be simply a continuation of, or a relapse upon, the pure romance of adventure, with different dress, manners, and nomenclature. There is hardly a single touch of

[1] All of them, be it remembered, the work of Gueulette (*v. inf.*).

character in any one ; their very morals (and no shame
to them) are arch-known ; and they do not possess style
enough to confer distinction of the kind open to such
things. If you take *Les Quatre Facardins*, before most
of them, and *Vathek* [1] (itself, remember, originally French
in language), after them all, the want of any kind of
genius in their composers becomes almost disgustingly
apparent. Yet even these masterpieces are masterpieces
outside the main run of the novel.

Although, therefore, it would be very ungrateful not
to acknowledge that they do sometimes comply with
Caylus. the demands of that sensible tyrant already
mentioned, Sultan Hudgiadge, and "either
amuse us or send us to sleep," it must be admitted to be
with some relief that one turns once more, at about the
five and twentieth volume, to something like the fairy
tale proper, if to a somewhat artificial and sophisticated
form of it. The Comte de Caylus was a scholar and a
man of unusual brains ; Moncrif showed his mixture of
Scotch and French blood in a corresponding blend of
quaintness and *esprit* ; others, such as Voisenon in one
sex and Voltaire's pet Mlle. de Lubert in the other,
whatever they were, were at any rate not stupid.

To Anne Claude Philippe de Tubières de Grimoard
de Pestels de Lévi, Comte de Caylus, one owes particular
Prince thanks, at least when one comes to the history
Courtebotte et of *Le Prince Courtebotte*, after wrestling with
Princesse the *macédoine* of orientalities just discussed.
Zibeline. It is not, of course, Perrault, and it is not the
best Madame D'Aulnoy. But you are never " put out "
by it ; the hero, if rather a hero of Scott in the uniform
propriety of his conduct, or of Virgil in his success, is not
like Waverley, partly a simpleton, nor like Aeneas, wholly
a cad. One likes the Princess Zibeline both before she
had a heart and afterwards ; it can be very agreeable to
know a nice girl in both states. Perhaps it was not quite

---

[1] The recently recovered "episodes" of this are rather more like the *Cabinet* stories
than *Vathek* itself ; and perhaps a sense of this may have been part of the reason why
Beckford never published them.

cricket of the good fairy to play that trick [1] on the ambassador of King Brandatimor, but it was washed out in fair fight ; and King Biby and his people of poodles are delightful. One wonders whether Dickens, who was better read in this kind of literature than in most, consciously or unconsciously borrowed from Caylus one of his not least known touches.[2]

In the next of the Caylus stories there is an Idea—the capital seems due because the Count was a man of
Rosanie. Science, as science (perhaps better) went then, and because one of his other tales (not the best) is actually called *Le Palais des Idées*. The idea of *Rosanie* is questionable, though the carrying of it out is all right. Two fairies are fighting for the (fairy) crown, and the test is who shall produce the most perfect specimen of the special fairy art of education of mortals. (I may, as a *ci-devant* member of this craft, be permitted to regret that the business has been so largely taken over by persons who are neither fairies in one sex, though there may be some exceptions here, nor enchanters in the other, where exceptions are very rare indeed.) The tutoress of the Princess Rosanie pursues her task, and pursues it triumphantly, by dividing the child into twelve *interim* personalities, each of whom has a special characteristic—beauty, gentleness, vivacity, discretion, and what not. At the close of the prescribed period they are reunited, and their fortunate lover, who has hitherto been distracted between the twelve *eidola*, is blessed with the compound Rosanie. Although it is well known to be the rashest of things for a man to say anything about women—although certainly sillier things have been said by men about women than about any other subject, except, of course, education itself—I venture to demur to the fairy method. Both *a priori* and from experience, I should say that unmixed Beauty would become intolerably

[1] He came to ask, or rather demand, Zibeline's hand for his master : and the fairy made his magnificence appear rags and rubbish.
[2] Mr. Toots's "I'm a-a-fraid you must have got very wet." When Courtebotte returns from his expedition, across six months of snow, to the Ice Mountain on the top of which rests Zibeline's heart, "many thousand persons" ask him, "*Vous avez donc eu bien froid ?*"

vain ; that Discretion would grow into a hypocritical and unpleasant prude ; that Vivacity would develop into Vulgarity; and that the reincarnation of the twelve would be one of the most intolerable creatures ever known, if it were not that the impossibility of the concentrated essences being united in one person, after separation in several, would save the situation by annihilating her.

Caylus, however, makes up in the third tale, *Le Prince Muguet et la Princesse Zaza*, where, though the *Prince Muguet et Princesse Zaza.* principal fairy, she of the *Hêtre*, is rather silly for one of the kind, Muguet is a not quite intolerable coxcomb, and Zaza is positively charming. Her sufferings with a wicked old woman are common ; but her distress when the fairy makes her seem ugly to the Prince, who has actually fallen in love with her true portrait, and the scenes where the two meet under this spell, are among the best in the whole *Cabinet*—which is a bold word. The others, though naturally unequal, never or very seldom lack charm, for the reason that Caylus knew what one has ventured to call the secret of Fairyland—that it is the land of the attained Wish—and that he has the art of scattering rememberable and generative phrases and fancies. *Tourlou et Rirette*, one of the lightest of all, may not impossibly—indeed probably—have suggested Jean Ingelow's great single-speech poem of *Divided*; the Princesses Pimprenelle and Lumineuse are the right sort of Princesses ; *Nonchalante et Papillon, Bleuette et Coquelicot* come and take their places unpretentiously but certainly; Mignonette and Minutieuse are not "out." Caylus is not Hamilton by a long way ; but he has something that Hamilton has not. He is still less Perrault or Madame d'Aulnoy, but he has a sufficient difference from either. With these predecessors he makes the select quartette of the fairy-tale tellers of France.

After him one expects—and meets—a drop. No reasonable person would look for a really great fairy tale from Jean Jacques, because you must forget yourself to write one; and *La Reine Fantasque*, though not bad, is not good. Madame de Villeneuve may, for ought I know, have been an excellent person in other ways, but she deserves one of the worst bolgias in the Inferno of literature for lengthening, muddling, and altogether spoiling the ever-beloved "Beauty and the Beast." Mlle. de Lussan, they say,[1] was too fond of eating, and died of indigestion. A more indigestible thing than her own *Les Veillées de Thessalie*, which figure here (she wrote a great deal more), the present writer has never come across. And as for *Prince Titi*, which fills a volume and a half, it might have been passed without any remark at all if it had not become famous in connection with the Battle of Croker and Macaulay over the body of Boswell's *Johnson*.[2]

A break takes place at the thirtieth volume of the *Cabinet*, and a fresh instalment, later than the first batch, follows, with more particulars about authors. Here we find the attributions of the very large series of imitative Eastern tales already noticed, and to be followed in this new parcel by *Soirées Bretonnes*, to Thomas Simon Gueulette. The thirty-first opens with the *Funestine* of Beauchamps[3]—an ingenious title and heroine-name, for

[1] She is also said to have been a "love-child" of no less a father than Prince Eugene.

[2] Anybody who is curious as to this should look up the matter, as may be done most conveniently in an *excursus* of Napier's edition, where my "friend of" [more than] "forty years," the late Mr. Mowbray Morris, in a note to his own admirable one-volume "Globe" issue, thought that Macaulay was "proved to be absolutely right." Morris, though his published and signed writings were few, and though he pushed to its very furthest the hatred of personal advertisement natural to most English "*gentlemen* of the press," was a man of the world and of letters in most unusual combination; of a true Augustan taste both in criticism and in composition; of wit and of *savoir vivre* such as few possess. But, like all men who are good for anything, he had some crazes: and one of them was Macaulay. I own that I do not think all the honours were on T. B. M.'s side in this mellay: but this is not the place to reason out the matter. What is quite certain is that in this long-winded and mostly trivial performance there is a great deal of intended, or at least suggested, political satire. But Johnson, though he might well think little of *Titi*, need not have despised the whole *Cabinet* (or as he calls it, perhaps using the real title of another issue, *Bibliothèque*), and would not on another occasion. Indeed the diary-notes in which the thing occurs are too much in shorthand to be trustworthy texts.

[3] Pierre François Godard de Beauchamps seems to have been another fair example of the half-scholarly bookmakers of the eighteenth century. He wrote a few light plays and some serious *Recherches sur les Théâtres de France* which are said to have merit. He translated the late and coxcombical but not uninteresting Greek prose romance of *Hysminias and Hysmine*, as well as that painful verse-novel, the *Rhodanthe and Dosicles* of

266 HISTORY OF THE FRENCH NOVEL   сн.

it avoids the unnatural sounds so common, is a quite possible feminine appellation, and though a "speaking" one, is only so to those who understand the learned languages, and so deserve to be spoken to. Moreover, the idea, though not startlingly original or a mark of genius, is good—that of an unlucky child who attracts the malignity of *all* fairies, and is ugly, stupid, ill-natured, and everything that is detestable. Her reformation by the genie Clair-Obscur would not be bad if it were cut a great deal shorter.

It is followed by a series of short tales, beginning with *The Little Green Frog*, and not of the first class, which in turn are succeeded by two (or, as the latter is in two parts, three) longer stories, sometimes attributed to Caylus— *Le Loup Galeux* and *Bellinette et Belline*. The *Soirées Bretonnes* themselves, though apparently the earliest, are not the happiest of Gueulette's *pastiches* ; the speaking names [1] especially are irritating. A certain Madame de Lintot, who does not seem to have had anything to do with the hero of Pope's famous "Ride with a Bookseller," is what may be called "neutral," with *Timandre et Bleuette* and others; nor does a fresh instalment of Moncrif's efforts show the historian of cats at his best. But in vol. xxxiii. Mlle. de Lubert, glanced at before, raises the standard. She should have cut her tales down ; it is the mischief of these later things

---

Theodorus Prodromus : and he composed, under a pseudonym, of course, a naughty *Histoire du Prince Apprius* to match his good *Funestine*. The contrasted ways and works of such bookmakers at various times would make a not uninteresting essay of the Hayward type.

[1] "Engageant," "Adresse," "Parlepeu," etc. The *Avertissement de l'Auteur* is possibly a joke, but more probably an awkward and miss-fire *supercherie* revealing the usual ignorance of the time as to matters mediaeval. "Alienore" (though it would be better without the final *e*) is a pretty as well as historic form of one of the most beautiful and protean of girl's names : but how did her father, a "seigneur *anglais*," come to be called "Rivalon Murmasson"? And did they know much about Arabia Felix in Brittany when "Daniel Dremruz" reigned there between A.D. 680 and 720? Gueulette himself was a barrister and Procureur-Substitut at the Châtelet. He seems to have imitated Hamilton, to whom the editors of the Cabinet rather idly think him "equal," though, inconsistently, they admit that Hamilton "stands alone" and Gueulette does not. On the other hand, they charge Voltaire with actually "tracing" over Gueulette. ("*Zadig* est calqué sur les *Soirées Bretonnes*.") This is again an exaggeration ; but Gueulette had, undoubtedly, a pleasant and exceedingly fertile fancy, and a good knack of narrative.

that they extend too much. But *Lionnette et Coquérico*
is good; *Le Prince Glacé et la Princesse Etincelante* is not
bad; and *La Princesse Camion* attracts, by dint of extravagance in the literal sense. Fairy trials had gone far;
but the necessity of either marrying a beautiful sort of
mermaid or else of *flaying* her, and the subsequent trial,
not of flaying, but braying her in a mortar as a shrimp,
show at least a lively fancy. Nor is the anonymous
Nourjahad—an extremely moral but not dull tale, which
follows—at all contemptible.

The French Bar, inexhaustible in such things, gave
another tale-teller in one Pajon, who, besides the obligatory *polissonneries*, not included in the *Cabinet*, composed
not a few harmless things of some merit. The first,
Eritzine et Paretin, is perhaps the best. Nor is the com-
plement of vol. xxxiv., the *Bibliothèque des Fées et des
Génies* (the title of which was that of a larger collection,
containing much the same matter as the *Cabinet*, and
probably in Johnson's mind when he jotted down *Prince
Titi*), quite barren. *La Princesse Minon-Minette et le
Prince Souci, Apranor et Bellanire, Grisdelin et Charmante*,
are none of them unreadable. The next volume, too, is
better as a whole than any we have had for a long time.
Mme. Fagnan's *Minet Bleu et Louvette* contains, in its
fifteen pages, a good situation by no means ill-treated.
The pair are under the same spell—that of being ugly
and witty for part of the week, handsome, stupid, and
disagreeable for the other part, and of having the times
so arranged that each sees the other at his or her most
repulsive to her or his actual state. The way in which
" Love unconquered in battle " proves, though not
without fairy assistance, victorious here also, is very
ingeniously managed.

One of the cleverest of all the later fairy tales is the
Acajou et Zirphile of Duclos, who, indeed, had sufficient
wits to do anything well, and was a novelist, though not
a very distinguished one, on a larger scale. The tale
itself (which is said to have been written " up to " illustrations of Boucher designed for something else) has,

indeed, a smatch of vulgarity, but a purely superfluous and easily removable one. It is almost as cleverly written as any thing of Voltaire's : and the final situation, where the hero, who has gone through all the mischiefs and triumphs of one of Crébillon's, recovers his only real love, Zirphile, in a torment and tornado of heads separated from bodies and hands separated from arms, is rather capital.

Not much less so, in the different way of a pretty sentimentality, is the *Aglaé ou Naboline* of the painter Coypel ; while the batch of short stories from Mme. Le Prince de Beaumont's *Magasin des Enfants* have had a curious fate. They are rather pooh-poohed by French editors and critics, and they are certainly *very* moral, too much so, in fact, as has been already objected to one of them, *Le Prince Chéri*. But allowances have been allowed even there, and, somehow or other, *Fatal et Fortuné*, *Le Prince Charmant*, *Joliette*, and the rest have recovered more of the root of the matter than most others, and have established a just popularity in translation.

And then comes the shortest, I think, of all the stories in the one and forty volumes ; the silliest as a composition ; the most contemptibly *thought*—but by the accidents of fate endowed later with a tragic-satiric *moralitas* almost if not quite unrivalled in literature. Its author was a certain M. Selis, apparently a very respectable schoolmaster, professor, and bookmaker of not the lowest class—employments and occupations in respect of all of which not a few of us have earned our bread and paid our income-tax. Unluckily for him, there was born in his time a Dauphin, and he wrote a little adulatory tale of the birth, and the editors of the *Cabinet* Appendix thanked him much for giving it them. It is not four pages long ; it tells how an ancestral genie—a great king named Louis —blessed the child, and said that he would be called " the father of his people," and another followed suit with " the father of letters," and a third swore *Ventre Saint Gris!* and named the baby's uncle as "Joseph," and a still greater Louis said other things, and a fairy named

Maria Theresa crowned the blessings. Then came an ogre mounted on a leopard and eating raw meat, who was of Albion, and said he was king of the country, and observed " God ham " [sic], and was told that he would be beaten and made to lay down his arms by the child.

And the Dauphin, unless this *signalement* is strangely delusive, lived to know the worst ogres in the world (their chief was named Simon), who were of his own people, and to die the most unhappy prince or king in that world. And he of the Leopard who said *God ham*, would have saved that Dauphin if he could, and did slay many of his less guiltless relations and subjects, and beat the rest " thorough and thorough," and restored (could they have had the will and wit to profit by it) the race of Louis and Francis, and of the genie who said " Ventre Saint Gris ! " to their throne.   And this was the end of the vaticinations of M. Selis, and such are the tears of things.

The rest of this volume is occupied by a baker's dozen of *Contes Choisis*, the first of which, *Les Trois Epreuves*, seems to imitate Voltaire, and is smartly written, while some of the others are not bad.

Volume xxxvi. is occupied (not too appositely, though inoffensively in itself) by a translation of Wieland's *Don Silvio de Rosalva*, which is a German *Sir Launcelot Greaves* or *Spiritual Quixote*, with fairy tales substituted for romances of chivalry. The author of *Oberon* was seldom, if ever, unreadable, and he is not so here ; but the thing is neither a tale proper (seeing that it fills a whole volume), nor a real fairy tale, nor French, so we may let it alone.

Then this curious collection once more comes to an end, which is not an end, with a very useful though not too absolutely trustworthy volume of *Notices des Auteurs*, containing not only " bio-bibliographical " articles on the actual writers collected, but references to others, great and small, from Marivaux, Lesage, Prévost, and Voltaire downwards, and glances, sometimes with actual *comptes rendus*, at pieces of the class not included. That it is conducted on the somewhat irresponsible and indolent principles of its time might be anticipated from previous things, such as the clause in the Preface to Wieland's just noticed book, that the author had " gone to Weimar, where perhaps he is still," an observation which, from the context, seems not to be so much an attempt at *persiflage* as a pure piece of lazy *naïveté*.   The volume, however, contains a great deal of information such as it is ; some sketches, ingeniously draped or Bowdlerised, of the " naughty " tales excluded from the collection itself, and a few amusing stories.[1]

As, however, has been said, there was to be still another joint to this crocodile, and the four last volumes, xxxviii. to xli. (*not*, as is wrongly said by some, xxxvii. to xl.), contain a somewhat rash continuation of the *Arabian Nights* themselves, with which Cazotte [2] appears to have

---

[1] The best perhaps is of a certain peppery Breton, Saint-Foix, who was successively a mousquetaire, a lieutenant of cavalry, aide-de-camp to " Broglie the War-god," and a long-lived *littérateur* in Paris.   M. de Saint-Foix picked a quarrel in the *foyer* of the opera with an unknown country gentleman, as it seemed, and " gave him a rendezvous." But the other party replied coolly that it " was his custom " to be called on if people had business with him, and gave his address.   Saint-Foix goes next morning, and is received with the utmost politeness and asked to breakfast.   " That's not the question," says the indignant Breton.   " Let us go out."   " I never go out without breakfasting ; *it is my custom*," says the provincial, and does as he says, politely repeating invitations from time to time to his fretting adversary.   At last they do go out, to Saint-Foix's great relief ; but they pass a *café*, and it is once more the stranger's sacred custom to play a game of chess or draughts after breakfast.   The same thing happens with a " turn " in the Tuileries, at which Saint-Foix does not fume quite so much, because it is on the way to the Champs Élysées, where fighting is possible.   The " turn " achieved, he himself proposes to adjourn there.   " What for ? " says the stranger innocently.   " What *for* ? A pretty question *pardieu* !   To fight, of course !   Have you forgotten it ? "   " *Fight !* Why, sir, what are you thinking of ?   What would people say of me ?   A magistrate, a treasurer of France, put sword in hand ?   They would take us for a couple of fools." Which argument being unanswerable, according to the etiquette of the time, Saint-Foix leaves the dignitary—who himself takes good care to tell the story.   It must be remembered—first that no actual *challenge* had passed, merely an ambiguous demand for addresses ; secondly, that the treasurer, as the superior by far in rank, had a right to suppose himself known to his inferiors ; and thirdly, that to challenge a " magistrate " was in France equivalent to being, in the words of a lampoon quoted by Macaulay, " 'Gainst ladies and bishops excessively valiant " in England.

[2] Although there is a good deal of merit in some of these tales, none of them approaches the charming *Diable Amoureux* which Cazotte produced in 1772, twenty years before his famous and tragical death after once escaping the Revolutionary fangs. This little story, which is at least as much of a fairy tale as many things " cabinetted," would be nearly perfect if Cazotte had not unluckily botched it with a double ending, neither of the actual closes being quite satisfactory.   If, in one of them, he had had the pluck to stop at the outcry of the succubus Biondetta when she has at last attained her object,

   " Je suis le diable ! mon cher Alvare, je suis le diable ! "

and let the rest be " wrop in mystery," it would probably have been the best way.   But the bulk of the book is beyond improvement : and there is a fluid grace about the

had a good deal to do, though an actual Arab monk of the name of Chavis is said to have been mainly concerned. They are not bad reading ; but even less of fairy tales than Gueulette's orientalities.

Not much apology is needed, it may be hoped, for the space given to this curious kind ; the bulk of its production, the length of its popularity, and the intrinsic merit of some few of its better examples vindicate its position here. But a confession should take the place of the unnecessary excuse already partly made. The artificial fairy tale of the more regular kind was not, by the law of its being, prevented almost unavoidably from doing service to the novel at large, as the Eastern story was ; but, as a matter of fact, it did little except what will be mentioned in the next paragraph. That it helped to exemplify afresh what had been shown over and over again for centuries, the singular recreative faculty of the nation and the language, was about all. But another national characteristic, the as yet incurable set of the French mind towards types—which, if the second volume of this work ever appears, will, it is hoped, be shown to have spared the later novel—seized on these tales. They are " as like as my fingers to my fingers," and they are not very pretty fingers as a rule. Incidentally they served as frameworks to some of the worst verse in the world, nor, for the most part, did they even encourage

autobiographical *récit* which is very rare indeed, at least in French, except in the unfortunate Gérard de Nerval, who was akin to Cazotte in many ways, and actually edited him. A very carping critic may object to the not obvious nor afterwards explained interposition of a pretty little spaniel between the original diabolic avatar of the hideous camel's head and the subsequent incarnation of the beautiful Biondetto-Biondetta ; especially as the later employment of another dog, to prevent Alvare's succumbing to temptation earlier than he did, is confusing. But this would be "seeking a knot in a reed." Perhaps the greatest merit of the story, next to the pure tale-telling charm above noted, is the singular taste and skill with which Biondetta, except for her repugnance to the marriage ceremony, is prevented from showing the slightest diabolic character during her long cohabitation with Alvare, and her very "comingnesses" are arranged so as to give the idea, not in the least of a temptress, but of an extra-innocent but quite natural *ingénue*. Monk Lewis, of course, knew Cazotte, but he has coarsened his original woefully. It may perhaps be added that the first illustrations, reproduced in Gérard's edition as curiosities, are such in the highest degree. They are ushered with an ironic Preface : and they sometimes make one rub one's eyes and wonder whether Futurism and Cubism are not, like so many other things, merely recooked cabbage.

very good prose. You may get some good out of them ; but unless you like hunting, and are not vexed by frequent failures to " draw," the *Cabinet des Fées* is best left to exploration at second-hand.

To collect the results of this long chapter, we may observe that in these three departments—Pastoral, Heroic, and Fairy—various important elements of *general* novel material and construction are provided in a manner not yet noticed. The Pastoral may seem to be the most obsolete, the most of a mere curiosity. But the singular persistence and, in a way, universality of this apparently fossil convention has been already pointed out ; and it is perhaps only necessary to shift the pointer to the fact that the novels with which one of the most modern, in perhaps the truest sense of that word, of modern novelists, though one of the eldest, Mr. Thomas Hardy, began to make his mark—*Under the Greenwood Tree* and *Far from the Madding Crowd*—may be claimed by the pastoral with some reason. And it has another and a wider claim —that it keeps up, in its own way, the element of the imaginative, of the fanciful—let us say even of the unreal— without which romance cannot live, without which novel is almost repulsive, and which the increasing advances of realism itself were to render more than ever indis- pensable. As for the Heroic, we have already shown how much, with all its faults, it did for the novel generally in construction and in other ways. It has been shown likewise, it is hoped, how the Fairy story, besides that additional provision of imagination, fancy, and dream which has just been said to be so important—mingled with this a kind of realism which was totally lacking in the others, and which showed itself especially in one immensely important department wherein they had been so much to seek. Fairies may be (they are not to my mind) things that "do not happen"; but the best of these fairies are fifty times more natural, not merely than the characters of Scudéry and Gomberville, but than those (I hold to my old blasphemy) of Racine. Animals may

not talk ; but the animals of Perrault and even of Madame
d'Aulnoy talk divinely well, and, what is more, in a way
most humanly probable and interesting.   Never was there
such a triumph of the famous impossible-probable as a
good fairy story.   Except to the mere scientist and to
(of course, quite a different person) the unmitigated fool,
these stories, at least the best of them, fully deserve the
delightful phrase which Southey attributes to a friend of
his.   They are " necessary and voluptuous and right."
They were, to the French eighteenth century and to French
prose, almost what the ballad was to the English eighteenth
century and to English verse; almost what the *Märchen*
was to the prose and verse alike of yet un-Prussianised
Germany.   They were more than twice blessed : for
they were charming in themselves ; they exercised good
influence on other literary productions; and they served
as precious antidotes to bad things that they could not
improve, and almost as precious alternatives to things
good in themselves but of a different kind from theirs.

What, however, none of the kinds discussed in this
chapter gave entirely, while only the fairy story gave
in part, and that in strong contrast to another part of
itself, was a history of ordinary life—high, low, or middle
—dealing with characters more or less representing live
and individual personages; furnished with incidents of
a possible and probable character more or less regularly
constructed; furnished further with effective description
of the usual scenery, manners, and general accessories
of living ; and, finally, giving such conversation as
might be thought necessary in forms suitable to " men
of this world," in the Shakespearian phrase.   In other
words, none of them attained, or even attempted to
fulfil, the full definition of the novel.   The scattered
books to be mentioned in the next chapter did not,
perhaps, in any one case—even Madame de la Fayette's—
quite achieve this ; but in all of them, even in Sorel's,
we see more or less conscious or unconscious attempt
at it.

CHAPTER IX

From " Francion " to " La Princesse de Clèves "—
Anthony Hamilton [1]

JUSTICE has, it is hoped, been done to the great classes of fictitious work which, during the seventeenth century,

<small>The material of the chapter.</small> made fiction, as such, popular with high and low in France. But it is one of the not very numerous safe generalisations or inductions which may be fished out from the wide and treacherous Syrtes of the history of literature, that it is not as a rule from " classes " that the best work comes ; and that, when it does so come, it generally represents a sort of outside and uncovenanted element or constituent of the class. We have, unfortunately, lost the Greek epic, *as* a class ; but we know enough about it, with its few specimens, such as Apollonius Rhodius earlier and Nonnus later, to warn us that, if we had more, we should find Homer not merely better, but different, and this though probably every practitioner was at least trying to imitate or surpass Homer. Dante stands in no class at all, nor does Milton, nor does Shelley ; and though Shakespeare indulgently permits himself to be classed as an " Elizabethan dramatist," what strikes true critics most is again hardly more his " betterness " than his

---

[1] It is perhaps not quite superfluous to point out that the principle of separation in these chapters is quite different from that (between "idealist" and "realist") pursued by Körting and others, and reprobated, partially or wholly, by MM. Le Breton and Brunetière.

difference.   The very astonishment with which we sometimes say of Webster, Dekker, Middleton, that they
come near Shakespeare, is not due, as foolish people
say, to any only less foolish idolatry, but to a true critical
surprise at the approximation of things usually so very
distinct.

The examples in higher forms of literature just
chosen for comparison do not, of course, show any wish
in the chooser to even any French seventeenth-century
novelist with Homer or Shakespeare, with Dante or
Milton or Shelley.   But the work noticed in the last
chapter certainly includes nothing of strong idiosyncrasy.
In other books scattered, in point of time of production,
over great part of the period, such idiosyncrasy is to be
found, though in very various measure.   Now, idiosyncrasy is, if not the only difference or property, the
inseparable accident of all great literature, and it may
exist where literature is not exactly great.   Moreover,
like other abysses, it calls to, and calls into existence, yet
more abysses of its own kind or not-kind ; while school-
and class-work, however good, can never produce anything but more class- and school-work, except by exciting
the always dubious and sometimes very dangerous desire
" to be different."   The instances of this idiosyncrasy
with which we shall now deal are the *Francion* of Charles
Sorel ; the *Roman Comique* of Paul Scarron ; the *Roman
Bourgeois* of Antoine Furetière ; the *Voyages,* as they are
commonly called (though the proper title is different[1]),
à la Lune et au Soleil, of Cyrano de Bergerac, and the
Princesse de Clèves of Mme. de La Fayette; while last
of all will come the remarkable figure of Anthony
Hamilton, less " single-speech "[2] than the others and
than his namesake later, but possessor of greater genius
than any.

The present writer has long ago been found fault with

---

[1] *L'Autre Monde : ou Histoire Comique des États et Empires de la Lune,* etc.

[2] It must be remembered that even Gerard Hamilton made many more speeches, but
only one good one, while the novelists discussed here wrote in most cases many other
books.   But their goodness shows itself in hardly more than a single work in each case.
Anthony Hamilton's is in all his.

for paying too much attention to *Francion*, and he may
Sorel and Francion. possibly (if any one thinks it worth while) be
found fault with again for placing it here.
But he does so from no mere childish desire to persist in
some rebuked naughtiness, but from a sincere belief in
the possession by the book of some historical importance.
Any one who, on Arnoldian principles, declines to take
the historic estimate into account at all, is, on those
principles, justified in neglecting it altogether; whether,
on the other hand, such neglect does not justify a suspicion
of the soundness of the principles themselves, is another
question. Charles Sorel, historiographer of France, was
a very voluminous and usually a very dull writer. His
voluminousness, though beside the enormous compositions of the last chapter it is but a small thing, is not
absent from *Francion*, nor is his dulness. Probably few
people have read the book through, and I am not going
to recommend anybody to do so. But the author does
to some extent deserve the cruel praise of being " dull in
a new way " (or at least of being evidently in quest of a
new way to be dull in), as Johnson wrongfully said of
Gray. His book is not a direct imitation of any one
thing, though an attempt to adapt the Spanish picaresque
style to French realities and fantasies is obvious enough,
as it is likewise in Scarron and others. But this is mixed
with all sorts of other adumbrations, if not wholly original,
yet showing that quest of originality which has been
commended. It is an almost impossible book to analyse,
either in short or long measure. The hero wanders about
France, and has all sorts of adventures, the recounting
of which is not without touches of Rabelais, of the *Moyen
de Parvenir*, perhaps of the rising fancies about the
occult, which generated Rosicrucianism and "astral
spirits" and the rest of it—a whole farrago, in short,
of matters decent and indecent, congruous seldom and
incongruous often. It is not like Sterne, because it is
dull, and at the same time quasi-romantic; while " sensibility " had not come in, though we shall see it do so
within the limits of this chapter. It has a resemblance,

though not very much of one, to the rather later work
of Cyrano. But it is most like two English novels
of far higher merit which were not to appear for a
century or a century and a half—Amory's *John Buncle* and
Graves's *Spiritual Quixote*. As it is well to mention things
together without the danger of misleading those who
run as they read, and mind the running rather than the
reading, let me observe that the liveliest part of *Francion*
is duller than the dullest of *Buncle*, and duller still than the
least lively thing in Graves. The points of resemblance
are in pillar-to-postness, in the endeavour (here almost
entirely a failure, but still an endeavour) to combine
fancy with realism, and above all in freedom from following the rules of any " school." Realism in the good
sense and originality were the two things that the novel
had to achieve. Sorel missed the first and only achieved
a sort of " distanced " position in the second. But he
tried—or groped—for both.

I am bound to say that in Sorel's other chief works of
fiction, the *Berger Extravagant* and *Polyandre*, I find the
The *Berger* same curious mixture of qualities which have
Extravagant made me more lenient than most critics to
and *Francion*. And I do not think it unfair to
Polyandre. add that they also incline me still more to think
that there was perhaps a little of the *Pereant qui ante nos*
feeling in Furetière's attack (*v. inf.* p. 288). Neither
could possibly be called by any sane judge a good book,
and both display the uncritical character,[1] the " pillar-
to-postness," the marine-store and almost rubbish-heap
promiscuity, of the more famous book. Like it, they are
much too big.[2] But the *Berger Extravagant*, in applying
(very early) the *Don Quixote* method, as far as Sorel
could manage it, to the *Astrée*, is sometimes amusing and
by no means always unjust. *Polyandre* is, in part, by no
means unlike an awkward first draft of a *Roman Bourgeois*.

[1] It has been noted, I think, by all who have written about the *Berger*, that Sorel is
a sort of Balak and Balaam in one. He calls on himself to curse the *Astrée*, but he,
sometimes at least, blesses it.

[2] The *Berger* fills two volumes of some nine hundred pages ; *Polyandre*, two of six
hundred each ! But it must be admitted that the print is very large and widely spaced.

The scene in the former, where Lysis—the Extravagant Shepherd and the Don Quixote of the piece,—making an all-night sitting over a poem in honour of his mistress Charité (the Dulcinea), disturbs the unfortunate Clarimond—a sort of " bachelor," the sensible man of the book, and a would-be reformer of Lysis—by constant demands for a rhyme[1] or an epithet, is not bad. The victim revenges himself by giving the most ludicrous words he can think of, which Lysis duly works in, and at last allows Clarimond to go to sleep. But he is quickly waked by the poet running about and shouting, " I've got it ! I've found it. The finest *reprise* [=refrain] ever made ! " And in *Polyandre* there is a sentence (not the only one by many) which not only gives a *point de repère* of an interesting kind in itself, but marks the beginning of the " *farrago libelli* moderni ": " Ils ont des mets qu'ils nomment des *bisques* ; je doute si c'est potage ou fricassée."

Here we have (1) Evidence that Sorel was a man of observation, and took an interest in really interesting things.

(2) A date for the appearance, or the coming into fashion, of an important dish.

(3) An instance of the furnishing of fiction with something more than conventional adventure on the one hand, and conventional harangues or descriptions on the other.

(4) An interesting literary parallel ; for here is the libelled " Charroselles " (*v. inf.* p. 288) two centuries beforehand, feeling a doubt, exactly similar to Thackeray's, as to whether a *bouillabaisse* should be called soup or broth, brew or stew. Those who understand the art and pastime of " book-fishing " will not go away with empty baskets from either of these neglected ponds.

Almost as different a person as can possibly be conceived from Sorel was Paul Scarron, Abbé, " Invalid to

[1] One remembers the story of the greater Corneille calling to the lesser down a trap between their two houses, " Sans-Souci !—une rime ! "

the Queen," husband of the future Mme. de Maintenon,
Scarron and author of burlesques which did him no particular
the *Roman* honour, of plays which, if not bad, were never
Comique. first-rate, of witticisms innumerable, most of
which have perished, and of other things, besides
being a hero of some facts and more legends; but
author also of one book in our own subject of much
intrinsic and more historical interest, and original also
of passages in later books more interesting still to all
good wits. Not a lucky man in life (except for the
possession of a lively wit and an imperturbable temper),
he was never rich, and he suffered long and terribly
from disease—one of the main subjects of his legend, but,
after all discussions and carpings, looking most like
rheumatoid arthritis, one of the most painful and incurable of ailments. But Scarron was, and has been since, by
no means unlucky in literature. He had, though of course
not an unvaried, a great popularity in a troubled and
unscrupulous time: and long after his death two of the
foremost novelists of his country selected him for honourable treatment of curiously different kinds. Somehow
or other the introduction of men of letters of old time
into modern books has not been usually very fortunate,
except in the hands of Thackeray and a very few more.
Among these latter instances may certainly be ranked
the pleasant picture of Scarron's house, and of the
attention paid to him by the as yet unmarried Françoise
d'Aubigné, in Dumas's *Vingt Ans Après*. Nor is it easy
to think of any literary following that, while no doubt
bettering, abstains so completely from robbing, insulting,
or obscuring its model as does Gautier's *Capitaine
Fracasse*.

It is, however, with this pleasant book itself that we
are concerned. Here again, of course, the picaresque
model comes in, and there is a good deal of directly
borrowed matter. But a much greater talent, and
especially a much more acute and critical wit than Sorel's,
brings to that scheme the practical-artistic French gift,
the application of which to the novel is, in fact, the

subject of this whole chapter. Not unkindly judges have, it is true, pronounced it not very amusing ; and an uncritical comparer may find it injured by Gautier's book. The older novel has, indeed, nothing of the magnificent style of the overture of this latter. *Le Château de la Misère* is one of the finest things of the kind in French ; for exciting incident there is no better duel in literature than that of Sigognac and Lampourde ; and the delicate pastel-like costumes and manners and love-making of Gautier's longest and most ambitious romance are not to be expected in the rough " rhyparography "[1] of the seventeenth century. But in itself the *Roman Comique* is no small performance, and historically it is almost great. We have in it, indeed, got entirely out of the pure romance ; but we have also got out of the *fatrasie*—the mingle-mangle of story, jargon, nonsense, and what not,— out of the mere tale of adventure, out of the mere tale of *grivoiserie*. We have borrowed the comic dramatist's mirror—the " Muses' Looking-glass "—and are holding it up to nature without the intervention of the conventionalities of the stage. The company to which we are introduced is, no doubt, pursuing a somewhat artificial vocation ; but it is pursuing it in the way of real life, as many live men and women have pursued it. The mask itself may be of their trade and class ; but it is taken off them, and they are not merely *personae*, they are persons.

To re-read the *Roman Comique* just after reading the *Grand Cyrus* came into the present plan partly by design and partly by accident ; but I had not fully anticipated the advantage of doing so. The contrast of the two, and the general relation between them could, indeed, escape no one ; but an interval of a great many years since the last reading of Scarron's work had not unnaturally caused forgetfulness of the deliberate and minute manner in

---

[1] I have known this word more than once objected to as pedantic. But pedantry in this kind consists in using out-of-the-way terms when common ones are ready to hand. There is no single word in English to express the lower kind of " Dutch-painting " as this Greek word does. And Greek is a recognised and standing source of words for English. If geography, why not rhyparography?—or, if any one prefers it, "rhypography," which, however, is not, I think, so good a form.

which he himself points that contrast, and even now
and then satirises the *Cyrus* by name.   The system of
inset *Histoires*,[1] beginning with the well-told if borrowed
story of Don Carlos of Aragon and his " Invisible Mistress," is, indeed, hardly a contrast except in point of
the respective lengths of the digressions, nor does it seem
to be meant as a parody.   It has been said that this
" inset " system, whether borrowed from the episodes of
the ancients or descended from the constant divagations
of the mediaeval romances, is very old, and proved itself
uncommonly tenacious of life.   But the difference
between the opening of the two books can hardly have
been other than intentional on the part of the later writer ;
and it is a very memorable one, showing nothing less than
the difference between romance and novel, between
academic generalities and " realist " particularism, and
between not a few other pairs of opposites.   It has been
fully allowed that the overture of the *Grand Cyrus* is by
no means devoid of action, even of bustle, and that it is
well done of its kind.   But that kind is strongly marked
in the very fact that there is a sort of faintness in it.   The
burning of Sinope, the distant vessel, the street-fighting
that follows, are what may be called " cartoonish "—
large washes of pale colour.   The talk, such as there is,
is stage-talk of the pseudo-grand style.   It is curious
that Scarron himself speaks of the *Cyrus* as being the most
" furnitured " romance, *le roman le plus meublé*, that he
knows.   To a modern eye the interiors are anything but
distinct, despite the elaborate *ecphrases*, some of which
have been quoted.[2]

Now turn to the opening passage of the *Roman
Comique*, which strikes the new note most sharply.   It is
rather well known, probably even to some who have not
read the original or Tom Brown's congenial translation
of it ; for it has been largely laid under contribution by
the innumerable writers about a much greater person

[1] There is, no doubt, significance in the fact that they are definitely called *nouvelles*.
[2] *V. sup.* p. 204.   The habit of these continues in all the books.   *L'Illustre Bassa*
opens with a most elaborate, but still not very much " alive," procession and sham fight.

than Scarron, Molière. The experiences of the *Illustre Théâtre* were a little later, and apparently not so sordid as those of the company of which Scarron constituted himself historiographer ; but they cannot have been very dissimilar in general kind, and many of the characteristics, such as the assumption now of fantastic names, " Le Destin," " La Rancune," etc., now of rococo-romantic ones, such as " Mademoiselle de l'Étoile," remained long unaltered. But perhaps a fresh translation may be attempted, and the attempt permitted. For though the piece, of course, has recent Spanish and even older Italian examples of a kind, still the change in what may be called " particular universality " is remarkable.

The sun had finished more than half his course, and his chariot, having reached the slope of the world, was running quicker than he wished. If his horses had chosen to avail them- selves of the drop of the road, they would have got through what remained of the day in less than half or quarter of an hour ; but instead of pulling at full strength, they merely amused themselves by curvetting, as they drew in a salt air, which told them the sea, wherein men say their master goes to bed every night, was close at hand. To speak more like a man of this world, and more intelligibly, it was between five and six o'clock, when a cart came into the market-place of Le Mans. This cart was drawn by four very lean oxen, with, for leader, a brood-mare, whose foal scampered about round the cart, like a silly little thing as it was. The cart was full of boxes and trunks, and of great bundles of painted canvas, which made a sort of pyramid, on the top of which appeared a damsel, dressed partly as for town, partly for country. By the side of the cart walked a young man, as ill-dressed as he was good-looking. He had on his face a great patch, which covered one eye and half his cheek, and he carried a large fowling-piece on his shoulder. With this he had slain divers magpies, jays, and crows ; and they made a sort of bandoleer round him, from the bottom whereof hung a pullet and a gosling, looking very like the result of a plundering expedition. Instead of a hat he had only a night-cap, with garters of divers colours twisted round it, which headgear looked like a very un- finished sketch of a turban. His coat was a jacket of grey stuff, girt with a strap, which served also as a sword-belt, the sword being so long that it wanted a fork to draw it neatly for use. He wore breeches trussed, with stockings attached to them, as actors do

The opening scene of this.

when they play an ancient hero ; and he had, instead of shoes, buskins of a classical pattern, muddied up to the ankle. An old man, more ordinarily but still very ill-dressed, walked beside him. He carried on his shoulders a bass-viol, and as he stooped a little in walking, one might, at a distance, have taken him for a large tortoise walking on its hind legs. Some critic may perhaps murmur at this comparison ; but I am speaking of the big tortoises they have in the Indies, and besides I use it at my own risk. Let us return to our caravan.

It passed in front of the tennis-court called the Doe, at the door of which were gathered a number of the topping citizens of the town. The novel appearance of the conveyance and team, and the noise of the mob who had gathered round the cart, induced these honourable burgomasters to cast an eye upon the strangers ; and among others a Deputy-Provost named La Rappinière came up, accosted them, and, with the authority of a magistrate, asked who they were. The young man of whom I have just spoken replied, and without touching his turban (inasmuch as with one of his hands he held his gun and with the other the hilt of his sword, lest it should get between his legs) told the Provost that they were French by birth, actors by profession, that his stage-name was Le Destin, that of his old comrade La Rancune, and that of the lady who was perched like a hen on the top of their baggage, La Caverne. This odd name made some of the company laugh ; whereat the young actor added that it ought not to seem stranger to men with their wits about them than " La Montagne," " La Vallée," " La Rose," or " L'Épine." The talk was interrupted by certain sounds of blows and oaths which were heard from the front of the cart. It was the tennis-court attendant, who had struck the carter without warning, because the oxen and the mare were making too free with a heap of hay which lay before the door. The row was stopped, and the mistress of the court, who was fonder of plays than of sermons or vespers, gave leave, with a generosity unheard of in her kind, to the carter to bait his beasts to their fill. He accepted her offer, and, while the beasts ate, the author rested for a time, and set to work to think what he should say in the next chapter.

The sally in the last sentence, with the other about the tortoise, and the mock solemnity of the opening, illustrate two special characteristics, which will be noticed below, and which may be taken in each case as a sort of revulsion from, or parody of, the solemn ways of the regular romance. There may be even a special reference to the "*Phébus*," the technical name or nickname of the "high language" in these repeated burlesque introductions of the sun. And the almost pert flings and cabrioles of the narrator form a still more obvious and direct Declaration of Independence. But these are mere details, almost trivial compared with the striking contrast of the whole presentation and *faire* of the piece, when taken together with most of the subjects of the last chapter.

It may require a little, but it should not require much, knowledge of literary history to see how modern this is ; it should surely require none to see how vivid it is—how the sharpness of an etching and the colour of a bold picture take the place of the shadowy "academies" of previous French writers.[1] There may be a very little exaggeration even here—in other parts of the book there is certainly some—and Scarron never could forget his tendency to that form of exaggeration which is called burlesque. But the stuff and substance of the piece is reality.

An important item of the same change is to be found in the management of the insets, or some of them. One of the longest and most important is the autobiographical history of Le Destin or Destin (the article is often dropped), the tall young man with the patch on his face. But this is not thrust bodily into the other body of the story, *Cyrus*-fashion ; it is alternated with the passages of that story itself, and that in a comparatively natural manner—night or some startling accident interrupting it; while how even courtiers could find breath to tell, or patience and time to hear, some of the interludes of the *Cyrus* and its fellows is altogether past comprehension. There is some coarseness in Scarron—he would not be a comic writer of the seventeenth century if there were none. Not very long after the beginning the tale is interrupted by a long account of an unseemly practical joke which surely could amuse no mortal after a certain stage of schoolboyhood. But there is little or no positive in-

---

[1] Of course Cervantes is not shadowy.

decency : the book contrasts not more remarkably with
the Aristophanic indulgence of the sixteenth century than
with the sniggering suggestiveness of the eighteenth.
Some remnants of the Heroic convention (which, after
all, did to a great extent reflect the actual manners of the
time) remain, such as the obligatory " compliment."
Le Destin is ready to hang himself because, at his first
meeting with the beautiful Léonore, his shyness prevents
his getting a proper " compliment " out.   On the other
hand, the demand for *esprit*, which was confined in the
Heroics to a few privileged characters, now becomes
almost universal.   There are tricks, but fairly novel
tricks—affectations like " I don't know what they did
next " and the others noted above: while the famous
rhetorical beginnings of chapters appear not only at
the very outset, but at the opening of the second volume,
" Le Soleil donnant aplomb sur les antipodes,"—things
which a century later Fielding, and two centuries later
Dickens, did not disdain to imitate.

Scarron did not live to finish the book, and the third
part or volume, which was tinkered—still more the
Suite, which was added— by somebody else, are very
inferior.   The somewhat unfavourable opinions referred
to above may be partly based on the undoubted fact
that the story is rather formless ; that its most important
machinery is dependent, after all, on the old *rapt* or abduction, the heroines of which are Mademoiselle de l'Étoile
(nominally Le Destin's sister, really his love, and at the
end his wife) and Angélique, daughter of La Caverne, who
is provided with a lover and husband of 12,000 (*livres*) a
year in the person of Léandre, one of the stock theatrical
names, professedly " valet " to Le Destin, but really a
country gentleman's son.   Thus everybody is somebody
else, again in the old way.   Another, and to some tastes
a more serious, blot may be found in the everlasting
practical jokes of the knock-about kind, inflicted on the
unfortunate Ragotin, a sort of amateur member of the
troupe.   But again these " *low* jinks " were an obvious
reaction from (just as the ceremonies were followings of)

the solemnity of the Heroics; and they continued to be popular for nearly two hundred years, as English readers full well do know. Nevertheless these defects merely accompany—they do not mar or still less destroy—the striking characteristics of progress which appear with them, and which, without any elaborate abstract of the book, have been set forth somewhat carefully in the preceding pages. Above all, there is a real and consider-able attempt at character, a trifle *typy* and stagy perhaps, but still aiming at something better; and the older *nouvelle*-fashion is not merely drawn upon, but improved upon, for curious anecdotes, striking situations, effective names. Under the latter heads it is noteworthy that Gautier simply "lifted" the name Sigognac from Scarron, though he attached it to a very different per-sonage; and that Dumas got, from the same source, the startling incident of Aramis suddenly descending on the crupper of D'Artagnan's horse. The jokes may, of course, amuse or not different persons, and even different moods of the same person; the practical ones, as has been hinted, may pall, even when they are not merely vulgar. Practical joking had a long hold of literature, as of life; and it would be sanguine to think that it is dead. Izaak Walton, a curious contemporary-"disparate," as the French say, of Scarron, would not quite have liked the quarrel between the dying inn-keeper, who insists on being buried in his oldest sheet, full of holes and stains, and his wife, who asks him, from a sense rather of decency than of affection, how he can possibly think of appearing thus clad in the Valley of Jehoshaphat? But there is something in the book for many tastes, and a good deal more for the student of the history of the novel.

The couplet-contrast of the Comic Romance of Scarron and the "Bourgeois" Romance of Furetière[1] is one of the most curious among the minor phenomena of literary history; but it repeats itself in that history

---

[1] As far as mere chronology goes, Cyrano, *v. inf.*, should come between; but it would split the parallel.

so often that it becomes, by accumulation, hardly minor.
There is a vast difference between Furetière and Miss
Furetière and Austen, and a still vaster one between Scarron
the *Roman* and Scott; but the two French books stand
Bourgeois. to each other, on however much lower a step
of the stair, very much as *Waverley* stands to *Pride and
Prejudice*, and they carry on a common revulsion against
their forerunners and a common quest for newer and
better developments.   The *Roman Bourgeois*, indeed, is
more definitely, more explicitly, and in further ways of
exodus, a departure from the subjects and treatment of
most of the books noticed in the last chapter.   It is
true that its author attributes to the reading of the regular
romances the conversion of his pretty idiot Javotte from
a mere idiot to something that can, at any rate, hold
her own in conversation, and take an interest in life.[1]
But he also adds the consequence of her elopement,
without apparently any prospect of marriage, but with
an accomplished gentleman who has helped her to
esprit by introducing her to those very same romances;
and he has numerous distinct girds at his predecessors, including one at the multiplied abductions of
Mandane herself.   Moreover his inset tale *L'Amour
Égaré* (itself something of a parody), which contains most
of the " key "-matter, includes a satirical account (not
uncomplimentary to her intellectual, but exceedingly so
to her physical characteristics) of " Sapho " herself.
For after declining to give a full description of poor
Madeleine, for fear of disgusting his readers, he tells us,
in mentioning the extravagant compliments addressed to
her in verse, that she only resembled the Sun in having
a complexion yellowed by jaundice; the Moon in being
freckled; and the Dawn in having a red tip to her nose !
   But this last ill-mannered particularity illustrates the
character, and in its way the value, of the whole book.
A romance, or indeed in the proper sense a story—that is

---

[1] Scarron had, in Le Destin's account of himself, made a distinction between the
pastoral and heroic groups and the "old" romances, meaning thereby not the true
mediaeval specimens but the *Amadis* cycle. Furetière definitely classes all of them
ogether.

to say, *one* story,—it certainly is not: the author admits
the fact frankly, not to say boisterously, and his title seems
to have been definitely suggested by Scarron's.   The two
parts have absolutely no connection with one another,
except that a single personage, who has played a very
subordinate part in the first, plays a prominent but entirely
different one in the second.   This second is wholly occupied by legal matters (Furetière had been " bred to the
law "), and the humours and amours of a certain female
litigant, Collantine, to whom Racine and Wycherley
owe something, with the unlucky author " Charroselles "[1]
and a subordinate judge, Belastre, who has been pitch-
forked by interest into a place which he finally loses
by his utter incapacity and misconduct.   To understand
it requires even more knowledge of old French law terms
generally than parts of Balzac do of specially commercial
and financial lingo.

This " specialising " of the novel is perhaps of more
importance than interest ; but interest itself may be found
in the First Part, where there is, if not much, rather more
of a story, some positive character-drawing, a fair amount
of smart phrase, and a great deal of lively painting of
manners.   There is still a good deal of law, to which
profession most of the male characters belong, but there
are plentiful compensations.

As far as there is any real story or history, it is that of
two girls, both of the legal *bourgeoisie* by rank.   The
prettier, Javotte, has been briefly described above.   She
is the daughter of a rich attorney, and has, before her

---

[1] The time is well known to have been fond of anagrams, and "Charroselles" is
such an obvious one for "Charles Sorel" that for once there is no need to gainsay or
neglect the interpreters. The thing, if really meant for a real person, is a distinct
lampoon, and may perhaps explain the expulsion and persecution of Furetière, by his
colleagues of the Academy, almost as well as the ostensible cause thereof—his compiling,
in competition with the Academy itself, of a French Dictionary, and a very good one,
which was not printed till after his death, and ultimately became the famous
Dictionnaire de Trévoux.   Not that Sorel himself was of much importance, but that the
thing shows the irritable and irritating literary failing in the highest degree.   Furetière
had friends of position, from Boileau, Racine, and Bossuet downwards ; and the
king himself, though he did not interfere, seems to have disapproved the Academy's
action.   But the *Roman* was heavily "slated" for many years, though it had a curious
revival in the earlier part of the next century ; and for the rest of that century and the
first part of the nineteenth it was almost wholly forgotten.

emancipation and elopement, two suitors, both advocates;
the one, Nicodème, young, handsome, well dressed, and
a great flirt, but feather-headed; the other, Bedout, a
middle-aged sloven, collector, and at the same time
miser, but very well off.   The second heroine, Lucrèce,
is also handsome, though rather less so than Javotte: but
she has plenty of wits.   She is, however, in an unfortunate position, being an orphan with no fortune, and living
with an uncle and aunt, the latter of whom has a passion
for gaming, and keeps open house for it, so that Lucrèce
sees rather undesirable society.   Despite her wits, she
falls a victim to a rascally marquis, who first gives her a
written promise of marriage, and afterwards, by one of
the dirtiest tricks ever imagined by a novelist—a trick
which, strange to say, the present writer does not remember to have seen in any other book, obvious though it
is—steals it.[1]   Fortunately for her, Nicodème, who is
of her acquaintance, and a general lover, has also given
her, though not in earnest and for no serious " consideration," a similar promise: and by the help of a busybody
legal friend she gets 2000 crowns out of him to prevent
an action for breach.   And, finally, Bedout, after dis-
placing the unlucky Nicodème (thus left doubly in the
cold), and being himself thrown over by Javotte's elopement, takes to wife, being induced to do so by a cousin,
Lucrèce herself, in blissful ignorance (which is never
removed) of her past.   The cousin, Laurence, has also
been the link of these parts of the tale with an episode of
précieuse society in which the above-mentioned inset
is told; a fourth feminine character, Hyppolyte (*vice*
Philipote), of some individuality, is introduced; Javotte
makes a greater fool of herself than ever; and her future
seducer, Pancrace, makes his appearance.

Thus reduced to " argument" form, the story may
seem even more modern than it really is, and the censures,
apologies, etc., put forward above may appear rather

---

[1] She falls in love with an ebony cabinet at a fair which they visit together, and he
gives it her. But, anticipating that she will use it for her most precious things, he
privately gets a second set of keys from the seller, and in her absence achieves the theft
of the promise.

unjust. But few people will continue to think so after reading the book. The materials, especially with the "trimmings" to be mentioned presently, would have made a very good novel of the completest kind. But, once more, the time had not come, though Furetière was, however unconsciously, doing his best to bring it on. One fault, not quite so easy to define as to feel, is prominent, and continued to be so in all the best novels, or parts of novels, till nearly the middle of the nineteenth century. There is far too much mere *narration*—the things being not smartly brought before the mind's eye as *being* done, and to the mind's ear as *being* said, but recounted, sometimes not even as present things, but as things that *have been* said or done already. This gives a flatness, which is further increased by the habit of not breaking up even the conversation into fresh paragraphs and lines, but running the whole on in solid page-blocks for several pages together. Yet even if this mechanical mistake were as mechanically redressed,[1] the original fault would remain and others would still appear. A scene between Javotte and Lucrèce, to give one instance only, would enliven the book enormously; while, on the other hand, we could very well spare one of the few passages in which Nicodème is allowed to be more than the subject of a *récit*, and which partakes of the knock-about character so long popular, the young man and Javotte bumping each other's foreheads by an awkward slip in saluting, after which he first upsets a piece of porcelain and then drags a mirror down upon himself. There is "action" enough here; while, on the other hand, the important and promising situations of the two promises to Lucrèce, and the stealing by the Marquis of his, are left in the flattest fashion of "recount." But it was very long indeed before novelists understood this matter, and as late as Hope's famous *Anastasius* the fault is present, apparently to the author's knowledge, though he has not removed it.

[1] Any one who has, as the present writer has had, opportunities of actually doing this, will find it a not uninteresting operation, and one which "amply repays the expense" of time and trouble.

To a reader of the book who does not know, or care to pay attention to, the history of the matter, the opening of the *Roman Bourgeois* may seem to promise something quite free, or at any rate much more free than is actually the case, from this fault. But, as we have seen, they generally took some care of their openings, and Furetière availed himself of a custom possibly, to present readers, especially those not of the Roman Church, possessing an air of oddity, and therefore of freshness, which it certainly had not to those of his own day. This was the curious fashion of *quête* or collection at church—not by a commonplace verger, or by respectable churchwardens and sidesmen, but by the prettiest girl whom the *curé* could pitch upon, dressed in her best, and lavishing smiles upon the congregation to induce them to give as lavishly, and to enable her to make a "record" amount.

The original meeting of Nicodème and the fair Javotte takes place in this wise, and enables the author to enlighten us further as to matters quite proper for novel treatment.[1] The device of keeping gold and large silver pieces uppermost in the open "plate"; the counterbalancing mischief of covering them with a handful of copper ; the licensed habit, a rather dangerous one surely, of taking "change" out of that plate, which enables the aspirant for the girl's favour to clear away the obnoxious *sous* as change for a whole pistole—all this has a kind of attraction for which you may search the more than myriad pages of *Artamène* without finding it. The daughter of a citizen's family, in the French seventeenth century, was kept with a strictness which perhaps explains a good deal in the conduct of an Agnes or an Isabelle in comedy. She was almost always tied to her mother's apron-strings, and even an accepted lover had to carry on his courtship under the very superfluous number of *six* eyes at least. But the Church was misericordious.

---

[1] This is a point of importance. Details of a life-like character are most valuable in the novel ; but if they are not " material" in the transferred sense they are simply a bore. Scott undoubtedly learnt this lesson from his prentice work in finishing Strutt's *Queenhoo Hall*, where the story is simply a clumsy vehicle for conveying information about sports and pastimes and costumes and such-like "antiquarities."

The custom of giving and receiving holy water could be improved by the resources of amatory science; but this of the *quête* was, it would seem, still more full of opportunity. Apparently (perhaps because in these city parishes the church was always close by, and the whole proceedings public) the fair *quêteuse* was allowed to walk home alone; and in this instance Nicodème, having ground-baited with his pistole, is permitted to accompany Javotte Vollichon to her father's door—her extreme beauty making up for the equally extreme silliness of her replies to his observations.

The possible objection that these things, fresh and interesting to us, were ordinary and banal to them, would be a rather shallow one. The point is that, in previous fiction, circumstantial verisimilitude of this kind had hardly been tried at all. So it is with the incident of Nicodème sending a rabbit (supposed to be from his own estate, but really from the market—a joke not peculiar to Paris, but specially favoured there), or losing at bowls a capon, to old Vollichon, and on the strength of each inviting himself to dinner; the fresh girds at the extraordinary and still not quite accountable plenty of marquises (Scarron, if I remember rightly, has the verb *se marquiser*); and the contributory (or, as the ancients would have said, symbolic) dinners—as it were, picnics at home — of *bourgeois* society at each other's houses, with not a few other things. A curious plan of a fashion-review, with patterns for the benefit of ladies, is specially noticeable at a period so early in the history of periodicals generally, and is one of the not few points in which there is a certain resemblance between Furetière and Defoe.

It is in this daring to be quotidian and contemporary that his claim to a position in the history of the novel mainly consists. Some might add a third audacity, that of being " middle-class." Scarron had dealt with barn-mummers and innkeepers and some mere riff-raff; but he had included not a few nobles, and had indulged in fighting and other " noble " subjects. There is no fighting in Furetière, and his chief " noble " figure—

the rascal who robbed Lucrèce of her virtue and her keys
—is the sole figure of his class, except Pancrace and the
précieuse Angélique.   This is at once a practical protest
against the common interpretation and extension of
Aristotle's prescription of "distinguished" subjects,
and an unmistakable relinquishment of mere picaresque
squalor.   Above all, it points the way in practice, indirectly
perhaps but inevitably, to the selection of subjects that
the author really *knows*, and that he can treat with the
small vivifying details given by such knowledge, and by
such knowledge alone.   There is an advance in character,
an advance in "interior" description—the Vollichon
family circle, the banter and the gambling at Lucrèce's
home, the humour of a *précieuse* meeting, etc.   In fact,
whatever be the defects [1] in the book, it may almost be
called an advance all round.   A specimen of this, as of
other pioneer novels, may not be superfluous ; it is the
first conversation, after the collection, between Nicodème
and Javotte.

This new kind of gallantry [*his removing the offensive copper
coins as pretended " change " for his pistole*] was noticed by Javotte,
Nicodème who was privately pleased with it, and really thought
takes Javotte herself under an obligation to him. Wherefore, on
home from their leaving the church, she allowed him to accost her
church. with a compliment which he had been meditating all
the time he was waiting for her.   This chance favoured him much,
for Javotte never went out without her mother, who kept her in
such a strait fashion of living that she never allowed her to speak
to a man either abroad or at home.   Had it not been so, he would
have had easy access to her ; for as she was a solicitor's daughter
and he was an advocate, they were in relations of close affinity and
sympathy—such as allow as prompt acquaintance as that of a servant-
maid with a *valet-de-chambre*.[2]
As soon as the service was over and he could join her, he said,
as though with the most delicate attention, " Mademoiselle, as
far as I can judge, you cannot have failed to be lucky in your
collection, being so deserving and so beautiful."   " Alas ! Sir,"

---

[1] To us small, as are not those of its predecessors.
[2] Not a bad instance of the subacid touches which make the book lively, and which
probably supply some explanation of its author's unpopularity. The " furred law-cats "
of all kinds were always a prevailing party in Old France, and required stout gloves to
touch them with.

replied Javotte in the most ingenuous fashion, "you must excuse me. I have just been counting it up with the Father Sacristan, and I have only made 65 livres 5 sous. Now, Mademoiselle Henriette made 90 livres a little time since; 'tis true she collected all through the forty hours'[1] service, and in a place where there was the finest Paradise ever seen." "When I spoke," said Nicodème, " of the luck of your collection, I was not only speaking of the charity you got for the poor and the church; I meant as well what you gained for yourself." " Oh, Sir ! " replied Javotte, " I assure you I gained nothing. There was not a farthing more than I told you ; and besides, can you think I would butter my own bread[2] on such an occasion ? 'Twould be a great sin even to think of it." " I was not speaking," said Nicodème, " of gold or silver. I only meant that nobody can have given you his alms without at the same time giving you his heart." " I don't know," quoth Javotte, " what you mean by hearts; I didn't see one in the plate." " I meant," added Nicodème, " that everybody before whom you stopped must, when he saw such beauty, have vowed to love and serve you, and have given you his heart. For my own part I could not possibly refuse you mine." Javotte answered him naïvely, " Well ! Sir, if you gave it me I must have replied at once, 'God give it back to you.' "[3] "What ! " cried Nicodème rather angrily, " can you jest with me when I am so much in earnest, and treat in such a way the most passionate of all your lovers ? " Whereat Javotte blushed as she answered, " Sir, pray be careful how you speak. I am an honest girl. I have no lovers. Mamma has expressly forbidden me to have any." " I have said nothing to shock you," replied Nicodème. " My passion for you is perfectly honest and pure, and its end is only a lawful suit." " Then, Sir," answered Javotte, " you want to marry me ? You must ask my papa and mamma for that ; for indeed I do not know what they are going to give me when I marry." " We have not got quite so far yet," said Nicodème. " I must be assured beforehand of your esteem, and know that you have admitted me to the honour of being your servant." " Sir," said Javotte, " I am quite satisfied with being my own servant, and I know how to do everything I want."

---

[1] This (often called by its Italian name of Quarant' ore) is a " Devotion " during an exposure of the Sacrament for that time, in memory of the interval between the Crucifixion and the Resurrection of Our Lord. It is a public service, and, I suppose, collections were made *at intervals*. No one, especially no girl, could stand the time straight through. The " Paradise " was, of course, a " decoration."

[2] Javotte says "shoe the mule"—"ferrer la mule"—one of the phrases like " faire danser l'anse du panier " and others, for taking "self-presented testimonials," as Wilkie Collins's Captain Wragge more elegantly and less cryptically calls it.

[3] Of course the regular " thanks " of a collector for pious purposes.

Now this, of course, is not extraordinarily brilliant ; but it is an early—a *very* early—beginning of the right sort of thing—conversation of a natural kind transferred from the boards to the book, sketches of character, touches of manners and of life generally, individual, national, local. The cross-purposes of the almost idiotic *ingénue* and the philandering gallant are already very well done ; and if Javotte had been as clever as she was stupid she could hardly have set forth the inwardness of French marriages more neatly than by the blunt reference to her *dot*, or have at the same moment more thoroughly disconcerted Nicodème's regularly laid-out approaches for a flirtation in form, with only a possible, but in any case distant, termination in anything so prosaic as marriage.[1] The thing as a whole is, in familiar phrase, " all right " in kind and in scheme. It requires some perfecting in detail ; but it is in every reasonable sense perfectible.

It has been possible to speak of one of the pioneer books mentioned in this chapter with more allowance _{Cyrano de} than most of the few critics and historians _{Bergerac and} who have discussed or mentioned it have _{his *Voyages*.} given it, and to recommend the others, not uncritically but quite cheerfully. This satisfactory state of things hardly persists when we reach what seems perhaps, to those who have never read it, not the least considerable of the batch—the *Voyage à la Lune* of Cyrano de Bergerac, as his name is in literary history, though he never called himself so.[2] Cyrano, though he does not seem to have had a very fortunate life, and died young, yet was not all unblest, and has since been rather blessed than banned. Even in his own day Boileau

---

[1] He does later seek this, and only loses her (if she can be called a loss) by his own folly. But his main object is to *conter* (or, as Furetière himself has it, *débiter*) *la fleurette*. It ought, perhaps, to be mentioned, as a possible counterweight or drawback, that the novelist breaks off to discuss the too great matter-of-factness of *bourgeois* girls and women. But he was to have great followers in this also.

[2] He was born and baptized Savinien de Cyrano, and called himself de Cyrano-Bergerac. The sound of the additional designation and some of his legendary peculiarities probably led to his being taken for a Gascon ; but there is no evidence of meridional extraction or seat, and there appears to be some of Breton or other Western connection.

spoke of him with what, in the " Bollevian " fashion, was comparative compliment—that is to say, he said that he did not think Cyrano so bad as somebody else. But long afterwards, in the middle of the nineteenth century, Gautier took him up among his *Grotesques* and embalmed him in the caressing and immortalising amber of his marvellous style and treatment ; while at the end of the same century one of the chief living poets and playwrights of France made him the subject of a popular and really pathetic drama. His *Pedant Joué* is not a stupid comedy, and had the honour of furnishing Molière with some of that " property " which he was, quite rightly, in the habit of commandeering wherever he found it. *La Mort d'Agrippine* is by no means the worst of that curious school of tragedy, so like and so unlike to that of our own " University wits," which was partly exemplified and then transcended by Corneille, and which some of us are abandoned enough to enjoy more as readers, though as critics we may find more faults with it, than we find it possible to do with Racine. But the *Voyage à la Lune*, as well as, though rather less than, its complementary dealing with the Sun, has been praised with none of these allowances. On the contrary, it has had ascribed to it the credit of having furnished, not scraps of dialogue or incident, but a solid suggestion to an even greater than Molière—to Swift ; remarkable intellectual and scientific anticipations have been discovered in it, and in comparatively recent times versions of it have been published to serve as proofs that Cyrano was actually a father [1] of French eighteenth-century *philosophie*—a different thing, once more, from philosophy.

Let us, however, use the utmost possible combination of critical magnanimity with critical justice : and allow these precious additions, which did not form part of the " classical " or " received " text of the author,

[1] There is nothing in the least astonishing in his having been this—if he was. The tendency of the Renaissance towards what is called "free thought" is quite well known ; and the existence, in the seventeenth century, of a sort of school of boisterous and rather vulgar infidelity is familiar—with the names of Bardouville, and Saint-Ibal or Saint-Ibar, as members of it—to all readers of Saint-Evremond, Tallemant, the *Ana*, etc.

not to count against him. *For* him they can only count
with those who still think the puerile and now hopelessly
stale jests about Enoch and Elijah and that sort of thing
clever. But they can be either disregarded or at least
left out of the judgment, and it will yet remain true that
the so-called *Voyage* is a very disappointing book indeed.
As this is one of the cases where the record of personal
experience is not impertinent, I may say that I first read
it some forty years ago, when fresh from reading about
it and its author in " Théo's " prose ; that I therefore
came to it with every prepossession in its favour, and
strove to like it, or to think I did. I read it again, if I
remember rightly, about the time of the excitement
about M. Rostand's *Cyrano*, and liked it less still ; while
when I re-read it carefully for this chapter, I liked it least
of all. There is, of course, a certain fancifulness about
the main idea of a man fastening bottles of dew round him
in the expectation (which is justified) that the sun's heat
will convert the dew into steam and raise him from the
ground. But the reader (it is not necessary to pay him
the bad compliment of explaining the reasons) will soon
see that the scheme is aesthetically awkward, if not positively ludicrous, and scientifically absurd. Throwing off
bottles to lower your level has a superficial resemblance
to the actual principles and practice of ballooning ; but
in the same way it will not here " work " at all.

This, however, would be a matter of no consequence
whatever if the actual results of the experiment were
amusing. Unfortunately they are not. That the aero-
naut's first miss of the Moon drops him into the new
French colony of Canada may have given Cyrano some
means of interesting people then ; but, reversing the
process noticed in the cases of Scarron and Furetière, it
does not in the least do so now. We get nothing out
of it except some very uninteresting gibes at the Jesuits,
and, connected with these, some equally uninteresting discussions whether the flight to the Moon is possible or not.

Still one hopes, like the child or fool of popular saying,
for the Moon itself to atone for Canada, and tolerates

298 HISTORY OF THE FRENCH NOVEL ch.

disappointment till one actually gets there. Alas ! of all Utopias that have ever been Utopiated, Cyrano's is the most uninteresting, even when its negative want of interest does not change into something positively disagreeable. The Lunarians, though probably intended to be, are hardly at all a satire on us Earth-dwellers. They are bigger, and, as far as the male sex is concerned, apparently more awkward and uglier ; and their ideas in religion, morals, taste, etc., are a monotonously direct reversal of our orthodoxies. There is at least one passage which the absence of all " naughty niceness " and the presence of the indescribably nasty make a good " try " for the acme of the disgusting. More of it is less but still nasty ; much of it is silly ; all of it is dull.[1]

Nevertheless it is not quite omissible in such a history as this, or in any history of French literature. For it is a notable instance of the coming and, indeed, actual invasion, by fiction, of regions which had hitherto been the province of more serious kinds ; and it is a link, not unimportant if not particularly meritorious, in the chain of the eccentric novel. Lucian of course had started it long ago, and Rabelais had in a fashion taken it up but a century before. But the fashioners of new commonwealths and societies, More, Campanella, Bacon, had been as a rule very serious. Cyrano, in his way, was serious too ; but the way itself was not one of those for which the ticket has been usually reserved.

But the last of this batch is the most important and the best of the whole. This is *La Princesse de Clèves*, by Marie Madeleine Pioche de Lavergne, Comtesse de la Fayette, friend of Madame de Sévigné and of Huet ; more or less Platonic, and at any rate last, love of La Rochefoucauld ; a woman

Mme. de la Fayette and *La Princesse de Clèves*.

---

[1] Perhaps the dullest part is where (save the mark !) the Demon of Socrates is brought in to talk sometimes mere platitudes, sometimes tame paradoxes which might as well be put in the mouth of any pupil-teacher, or any popular journalist or dramatist, of the present day.—Of the attempt to make Swift Cyrano's debtor one need say little : but among predecessors, if not creditors, Ben Jonson, for his *News from the New World discovered in the Moon*, may at least be mentioned.

evidently of great charm as well as of great ability, and apparently of what was then irreproachable character. She wrote, besides other matter of no small literary value and historical interest, four novels, the minor ones, which require no special notice here, being *Zaïde*, *La Comtesse de Tende*, and (her opening piece) *Madame de Montpensier*. Their motives and methods are much the same as those of the *Princesse de Clèves*, but this is much more effectively treated. In fact, it is one of the very few highly praised books, at the beginnings of departments of literature, which ought not to disappoint candid and not merely studious readers.

It begins with a sketch, very cleverly done, of the Court of Henri II., with the various prominent personages there—the King and the Queen, Diane de Poitiers, Queen Mary of Scotland ("La Reine Dauphine"), "Madame, sœur du Roi" (the second Margaret of Valois—not so clever as her aunt and niece namesakes, and not so beautiful as the latter, but, like both of them, a patroness of men of letters, especially Ronsard, and apparently a very amiable person, though rude things were said of her marriage, rather late in life, to the Duke of Savoy), with many others of, or just below, royal blood. Of these latter there are Mademoiselle de Chartres, the Prince de Clèves, whom she marries, and the Duc de Nemours, who completes the usual "triangle." [1] As is also usual—in a way not unconnected in its usuality with that of triangular sequences—the Princess has more *amitié* and *estime* than *amour* for her husband, though he, less usually, is desperately in love with her. So, very shortly, is Nemours, who is represented as an almost irresistible lady-killer, though no libertine, and of the "respectful" order. His conduct is not quite that of the Elizabethan or Victorian ideal gentleman; for he steals his mistress's portrait while it is being shown to a mixed company; eavesdrops (as will be seen presently) in the most atrocious manner; chatters about his love

[1] The key-mongers, of course, identify the three with the author, her own husband, and La Rochefoucauld.

affairs in a way almost worse; and skulks round the
Princess's country garden at night in a manner exceedingly unlikely to do his passion any good, and nearly
certain to do (as it does) her reputation much harm.
Still, if not an Amadis, he is not in the least a Lovelace,
and that is saying a good deal for a French noble of his
time. The Princess slowly falls in love with him (she
has seen him steal the portrait, though he does not know
this and she dares say nothing for fear of scandal); and
divers Court and other affairs conduct this concealed
amourette (for she prevents all " declaration ") in a
manner very cleverly and not too tediously told, to a
point when, though perfectly virtuous in intention, she
feels that she is in danger of losing self-control.

Probably, though it is the best known part of the
book, it may be well to give the central scene, where
Its central M. de Nemours plays the eavesdropper to
scene. M. and Mme. de Clèves, and overhears the
conversation which, with equal want of manners and of
sense, he afterwards (it is true, without names) retails to
the Vidame de Chartres, a relation of Mme. de Clèves
herself, and a well-known gossip, with a strong
additional effect on the fatal consequences above described. It is pretty long, and some " cutting " will
be necessary.

He [1] heard M. de Clèves say to his wife, " But why do you
wish not to return to Paris ? What can keep you in the country ?
For some time past you have shown a taste for solitude which
surprises me and pains me, because it keeps us apart. In fact,
I find you sadder than usual, and I am afraid that something is
annoying you." " I have no mind-trouble," she answered with
an embarrassed air ; " but the tumult of the Court is so great,
and there is always so much company at home, that both body and
mind must needs grow weary, and one wants only rest." " Rest,"
replied he, " is not the proper thing for a person of your age. Your
position is not, either at home or at Court, a fatiguing one, and I am
rather afraid that you do not like to be with me." " You would

[1] He has ensconced himself in one of the smaller rooms of a garden pavilion outside
of which they are sitting, having left their suite at some distance.

do me a great injustice if you thought so," said she with ever-in-creasing embarrassment, " but I entreat you to leave me here. If you would stay too, I should be delighted—if you would stay here alone and be good enough to do without the endless number of people who never leave you." " Oh! Madam," cried M. de Clèves, " your looks and your words show me that you have reasons for wishing to be alone which I do not know, and which I beg you to tell me." He pressed her a long time to do so without being able to induce her, and after excusing herself in a manner which increased the curiosity of her husband, she remained in deep silence with downcast eyes. Then suddenly recovering her speech, and looking at him, " Do not force me," said she, " to a confession which I am not strong enough to make, though I have several times intended to do so. Think only that prudence forbids a woman of my age, who is her own mistress,[1] to remain exposed to the trials[2] of a Court." " What do you suggest, Madame ? " cried M. de Clèves. " I dare not put it in words for fear of offence." She made no answer, and her silence con-firming her husband in his thought, he went on : " You tell me nothing, and that tells me that I do not deceive myself." " Well then, Sir ! " she answered, throwing herself at his feet, " I will confess to you what never wife has confessed to her husband ; but the innocence of my conduct and my intentions gives me strength to do it. It is the truth that I have reasons for quitting the Court, and that I would fain shun the perils in which people of my age sometimes find themselves. I have never shown any sign of weakness, and I am not afraid of allowing any to appear if you will allow me to retire from the Court, or if I still had Mme. de Chartres to aid in guarding me. However risky may be the step I am taking, I take it joyfully, as a way to keep myself worthy of being yours. I ask your pardon a thousand times if my sentiments are disagreeable to you ; at least my actions shall never displease you. Think how—to do as I am doing—I must have more friendship and more esteem for you than any wife has ever had for any husband. Guide me, pity me, and, if you can, love me still." M. de Clèves had remained, all the time she was speaking, with his head buried in his hands, almost beside himself ; and it had not occurred to him to raise his wife from her position. When she finished, he cast his eyes upon her and saw her at his knees, her face bathed in tears, and so admirably lovely that he was ready

---

[1] *Maîtresse de sa conduite*, a curious but not difficult text as to French ideas of marriage.

[2] I have been obliged to insert "trials" to bring out the meaning of "*exposée au milieu.*" "*Exposée*" has a fuller sense than the simple English verb, and almost equals the legal " exposed for sale."

to die of grief. But he kissed her as he raised her up, and said :

[*The speech which follows is itself admirable as an expression of despairing love, without either anger or mawkishness ; but it is rather long, and the rest of the conversation is longer. The husband naturally, though, as no doubt he expects, vainly, tries to know* who *it is that thus threatens his wife's peace and his own, and for a time the eavesdropper (one wishes for some one behind him with a jack-boot on) is hardly less on thorns than M. de Clèves himself. At last a reference to the portrait-episode (see above) enlightens Nemours, and gives, if not an immediate, a future clue to the unfortunate husband.*]

It will be seen at once that this is far different from anything we have had before—a much further importation of the methods and subjects of poetry and drama into the scheme of prose fiction.

We need only return briefly to the main story, the course of which, as one looks back to it through some 250 years of novels, cannot be very difficult to "*pro*-ticipate." A continuance of Court interviews and gossip, with the garrulity of Nemours himself and the Vidame, as well as the dropping of a letter by the latter, brings a complete *éclaircissement* nearer and nearer. The Countess, though more and more in love, remains virtuous, and indeed hardly exposes herself to direct temptation. But her husband, becoming aware that Nemours is the lover, and also that he is haunting the grounds at Coulommiers by night when the Princess is alone, falls, though his suspicion of actual infidelity is removed too late, into hopeless melancholy and positive illness, till the " broken heart " of fact or fiction releases him. Nemours is only too anxious to marry the widow, but she refuses him, and after a few years of " pious works " in complete retirement, herself dies early.

It is possible that, even in this brief sketch, some faults of the book may appear ; it is certain that actual reading of it will not utterly deprive the fault-finder of his prey. The positive history—of which there is a

good deal, very well told in itself,[1] and the appearance of
which at all is interesting—is introduced in too great
proportions, so as to be largely irrelevant.   Although
we know that this extremely artificial world of love-making
with your neighbours' wives was also real, in a way and
at a time, the reality fails to make up for the artifice, at
least as a novel-subject.   It is like golf, or acting, or
bridge—amusing enough to the participants, no doubt,
but very tedious to hear or read about.[2]   Another point,
again true to the facts of the time, no doubt, but somewhat repulsive in reading, is the almost entire absence of
Christian names.   The characters always speak to each
other as " Monsieur " and " Madame," and are spoken of
accordingly.   I do not think we are ever told either of M.
or of Mme. de Clèves's name.   Now there is one person
at least who cannot " see " a heroine without knowing
her Christian name.   More serious, in different senses
of that word, is the fact that there is still ground for the
complaint made above as to the too *solid* character of the
narrative.   There is, indeed, more positive dialogue, and
this is one of the " advances " of the book.   But even
there the writer has not had the courage to break it up
into actual, not " reported," talk, and the " said he's "
and " said she's," " replied so and so's " and " observed
somebody's " perpetually get in the way of smooth
reading.

So much in the way of alms for Momus.   Fortunately
a much fuller collection of points for admiration offers
itself.   It has been admitted that the historical element[3] is

---

[1] Mme. de la Fayette was a very accomplished woman, and, possibly from her
familiarity with Queen Henrietta Maria, well acquainted with English as well as French
history.   But our proper names, as usual, vanquish her, and she makes Henry VIII.
marry Jane *Seimer* and Catherine *Havart*.

[2] This does not apply to the *main* love story but to the atmosphere generally.   The
Vidame de Chartres, for instance, is represented as in love with (1) Queen Catherine ;
(2) a Mme. de Themines, with whom he is not quite satisfied ; (3) a Mme. de
Martignes, with whom he is ; (4) a lady unnamed, with whom he has *trompé* them
all.   This may be true enough to life ; but it is difficult to make it into good matter of
fiction, especially with a crowd of other people doing much the same.

[3] It ought, perhaps, to be added that though manners, etc., altered not a little
between Henri II. and Louis XIV., the alteration was much less than in most other
histories at most other periods.   It would be easy to find two persons in Tallemant
whose actual experience covered the whole time.

perhaps, in the circumstances and for the story, a trifle irrelevant and even " in the way." But its presence at all is the important point. Some, at any rate, of the details—the relations of that Henri II., with whom, it seems, we may *not* connect the very queer, very rare, but not very beautiful *faïence* once called " Henri Deux " ware,[1] with his wife and his mistress ; his accidental death at the hands of Montgomery ; the history of Henry VIII.'s matrimonial career, and the courtship of his daughter by a French prince (if not *this* French prince)—are historical enough to present a sharp contrast with the cloudy pseudo-classical canvas of the Scudéry romances, or the mere fable-land of others. Any critical Brown ought to have discovered " great capabilities " in it ; and though it was not for more than another century that the true historical novel got itself born, this was almost the nearest experiment to it. But the other side —the purely sentimental—let us not say psychological— side, is of far more consequence ; for here we have not merely aspiration or chance-medley, we have attainment.

There is a not wholly discreditable prejudice against abridgments, especially of novels, and more especially against what are called condensations. But one may think that the simple knife, without any artful or artless aid of interpolated summaries, could carve out of *La Princesse de Clèves*, as it stands, a much shorter but fully intelligible presentation of its passionate, pitiful subject. A slight want of *individual* character may still be desiderated ; it is hardly till *Manon Lescaut* that we get that, but it was not to be expected. Scarcely more to be expected, but present and in no small force, is that truth to life ; that " knowledge of the human heart " which had been hitherto attempted by—we may almost say per- mitted to—the poet, the dramatist, the philosopher, the divine ; but which few, if any, romancers had aimed at. This knowledge is not elaborately but sufficiently " set " with the halls and *ruelles* of the Court, the gardens and

---

[1] You *had* to call it so when I first saw it ; when I last did so it was " Oiron." No doubt it is something else now.

woods of Coulommiers ; it is displayed with the aid of conversation, which, if it seems stilted to us, was not so then ; and the machinery employed for working out the simple plot—as, for instance, in the case of the dropped letter, which, having originally nothing whatever to do with any of the chief characters, becomes an important instrument—is sometimes far from rudimentary in conception, and very effectively used.

It is therefore no wonder that the book did two things—things of unequal value indeed, but very important for us. In the first place, it started the School of " Sensibility "[1] in the novel, and so provided a large and influential portion of eighteenth-century fiction. In the second—small as it is—it almost started the novel proper, the class of prose fiction which, though it may take on a great variety of forms and colours, though it may specialise here and " extravagate " there, yet in the main distinguishes itself from the romance by being first of. all subjective—by putting behaviour, passion, temperament, character, motive before incident and action in the commoner sense—which had had few if any representatives in ancient times, had not been disentangled from the romantic envelope in mediaeval, but was to be the chief new development of modern literature.

There seemed to be several reasons for separating Hamilton from the other fairy-tale writers. The best of all is that he has the same qualification for the present chapter as that which has installed in it the novelists already noticed—that of idiosyncrasy. This leads to, or rather is founded on, the consideration that his tales are fairy-tales only " after a sort," and testify rather to a prevalent fashion than to a natural affection for the kind.[2] Thirdly, he exhibits, in his supernatural matter, a new and powerful influence on fiction generally—that of the first translated *Arabian Nights*. Lastly, he is in turn himself the head of two considerable though widely

[1] For that, see Chapter XII.
[2] See below on the verse Introduction to the *Quatre Facardins*.

different sub-departments of fiction—the decadent and often worthless but largely cultivated department of what we may call the fairy-tale *improper*,[1] and the very important and sometimes consummately excellent " ironic tale," to be often referred to, and sometimes fully discussed, hereafter.

The singularity of Hamilton's position has always been recognised ; but until comparatively recently, his history and family relations were very little understood. Since the present writer discussed him in a paper[2] now a quarter of a century old in print, and older in composition, further light has been thrown on his life and surroundings in the *Dictionary of National Biography*, and more still in a monograph by a lady[3] whose researches will, it is hoped, sooner or later be published. A very little, too, of the unprinted work which was held back at his death has been recovered. But this, it seems, includes nothing of importance ; and his fame will probably always rest, as it has so long and so securely rested, on the *Mémoires de Grammont*, the few but sometimes charming independent verses, some miscellanies not generally enough appreciated, and the admirable group of ironic tales which set a fashion hardly more admirably illustrated since by Voltaire and Beckford[4] and Lord Beaconsfield, to name no others. Of these things the verses,[5] unfortunately, do not concern us at all ; and the *Mémoires* and miscellanies[5] only in so far as they add another, and one of the very best, to the brilliant examples of personal narrative of which the century is so full, and

[1] Including miscellaneous imbecility and unsuitableness as well as moral indecorum.
[2] Written for the *Fortnightly Review* in 1882, but by a chapter of accidents not printed till 1890. Reprinted next year in *Essays on French Novelists* (London, 1891).
[3] Miss Ruth Clark.
[4] The conclusion of *Vathek* is of course undoubtedly more "admirable" than anything of Hamilton's ; but it is in a quite different *genus*.
[5] The piece *Celle que j'adore* is the best of the casual verses, though there are other good songs, etc. Those which alternate with the prose of some of the tales are too often (as in the case of the *Cabinet* insets, *v. sup.*) rather prosaic. Of the prose miscellanies the so-called *Relations* "of different places in Europe," and "of a voyage to Mauritania," contain some of the cream of Hamilton's almost uniquely ironic narrative and commentary. When that great book, "The Nature and History of Irony," which has to be written is written—the last man died with the last century and the next hour seems far off—a contrast of Hamilton and Kinglake will probably form part of it.

which have so close a connection with the novel itself. But the *Tales* are, of course, ours of most obvious right ; and they form one of the most important *points de repère* in our story.

To discuss, on the one hand, how Hamilton's singularly mixed conditions and circumstances of birth[1] and life[2] influenced his literary production would be interesting, but in strictness rather irrelevant. To attempt, on the other, at any great length to consider the influences which produced the kind of tale he wrote would have more relevance, but would, if pursued in similar cases elsewhere, lengthen the book enormously. Two main ancestor or progenitor forces, as they may be called, though both were of very recent date and one actually contemporary, may be specified. The one was the new-born fancy for fairy-tales, and Eastern tales in particular. The other was the now ingrained disposition towards ironic writing which, begun by Rabelais, as a most notable origin, varied and increased by Montaigne and others, had, just before Hamilton, received fresh shaping and tempering from not a few writers, especially Saint-Évremond. There is indeed no doubt that this last remarkable and now far too little read writer,[3] who, let it be remembered, was, like Hamilton, and even more so, an intimate friend of Grammont and also an inmate of Charles's court, was Hamilton's direct and immediate model so far as he had any such—his " master " in the general tone of *persiflage*. But master and pupil chose, as a rule, different subjects, and the idiosyncrasy of each was intense ; it must be remembered, too, that both were of Norman blood, though that of the Hamiltons had long been transfused into the veins of a new nationality, while Saint-Évremond was actually born in Nor-

---

[1] As a member, though a cadet, of a cadet branch of one of the noblest families of Great Britain and Ireland.

[2] As a soldier, a courtier of Charles II., and a Jacobite exile in France.

[3] I may perhaps be allowed to refer to another essay of mine on him in *Miscellaneous Essays* (London, 1892). It contains a full account, and some translation, of the *Conversation du maréchal d'Hocquincourt avec le Père Canaye*, which is at once the author's masterpiece of quiet irony, his greatest pattern for the novelist, and his clearest evidence of influence on Hamilton.

mandy. The Norman (that is to say, the English, with a special intention of difference [1]) in each could be very easily pointed out if such things were our business. But it is the application of this, and of other things in relation to the development of the novel, that we have to deal with.

It is said, and there is good reason for believing it to be true, that all the stories have a more or less pervading vein of " key " application in them. But this, except for persons particularly interested in such things, has now very little attraction. It has been admitted that it probably exists, as indeed it does in almost everything of the day, from the big as well as " great " *Cyrus* to the little, but certainly not much less great, *Princesse de Clèves*. But our subject is what Hamilton writes about these people, not the people about whom he may or may not be writing.

What we have left of Hamilton's tales, as far as they have been printed (and, as was said above, not much more seems to exist), consists of five stories of very unequal length, and in two cases out of the five unfinished. One of the finished pieces, *Fleur d'Épine*, and one of the unfinished—although unfinished it is not only one of the longest, but, unluckily in a way, by far the best of all—*Les Quatre Facardins*, are " frame-work " stories, and avowedly attach themselves, in an irreverent sort of attachment, to the *Arabian Nights*; the others, *Le Bélier*, *Zénéyde* (unfinished), and *L'Enchanteur Faustus*, are independent, and written in the mixed verse-and-prose style which had been made popular by various writers, especially Chapelle, but which cannot be said to be very acceptable in itself. Taken together, they fill a volume of just over 500 average octavo pages in the standard edition of 1812; but their individual length is very unequal. The two longest, the fragmentary *Quatre Facardins* and the finished *Le Bélier*, run each of them to 142 pages; the shortest, *L'Enchanteur Faustus*, has

[1] There are some who hold that *the* "English" differentia, whether shown in letters or in life, whether south or north of Tweed, east or west of St. George's Channel, is always Anglo-Norman.

just five-and-twenty; while *Fleur d'Épine*, in its completeness, has 114, and *Zénéyde*, in its incompleteness,
runs to 78, and might have run, for aught one can tell—
in the mixed tangle of Roman and Merovingian history
in which the author (possibly in ridicule of Madeleine de
Scudéry's classical chronicling) has chosen to plunge it—
to 780 or 78QO, which latter figure would, after all, have
been little more than half the length of the *Grand Cyrus*
itself.

We may take *L'Enchanteur Faustus* first, as it requires
the shortest notice. In fact, if it had not been Hamilton's,
it would hardly require any. Written to a " charmante
Daphné " (evidently one of the English Jacobite exiles,
from a reference to a great-great-grandfather of hers
who was " admiral in Ireland " during Queen Elizabeth's time), it is occupied by a story of the great Queen
herself, who is treated with the mixture of admiration
(for her intelligence and spirit) with " scandal " (about
her person and morals) that might be expected at St.
Germains. The subject is the usual exhibition of dead
beauties (here by, not to, Faustus), with Elizabeth's
affected depreciation of Helen, Cleopatra, and Mariamne,
and her equally affected admiration of Fair Rosamond,[1]
whom she insists on summoning *twice*, despite Faustus's
warning, and with disastrous consequences. Hamilton's
irony is so pervading that one does not know whether
ignorance, carelessness, or intention made him not only
introduce Sidney and Essex as contemporary favourites
of Elizabeth, but actually attribute Rosamond's end to
poor Jane Shore instead of to Queen Eleanor ! This
would matter little if the tale had been stronger ; but
though it is told with Hamilton's usual easy fluency,
the Queen's depreciations, the flattery of the courtiers,
and the rest of it, are rather slightly and obviously handled.
One would give half a dozen like it for that *Second* (but not
necessarily *Last*) *Part* of the *Facardins*, which Crébillon
the younger is said to have actually seen and had the

[1] The " Marian " and Roman comparison of Anne Boleyn's position to Rosamond's is
interesting.

opportunity of saving, a chance which he neglected till too late.

As *L'Enchanteur Faustus* is the shortest of the completed tales, so *Le Bélier* is the longest; indeed, as indicated above, it is the same length as what we have of *Les Quatre Facardins*. It is also—in that unsatisfactory and fragmentary way of knowledge with which literature often has to content itself—much the best known, because of the celebrated address of the giant Moulineau to the hero-beast "Bélier, mon ami, . . . si tu voulais bien commencer par le commencement, tu me ferais plaisir." There are many other agreeable things in it; but it has on the whole a double or more than double portion of the drawback which attends these "key" stories. It was written to please his sister, Madame de Grammont, who had established herself in a country-house, near Versailles. This she transformed from a mere cottage, called Moulineau, into an elegant villa to which she gave the name of Pontalie. There were apparently some difficulties with rustic neighbours, and Anthony wove the whole matter into this story, with the giant and the (of course enchanted) ram just mentioned; and the beautiful Alie who hates all men (or nearly all); and her father, a powerful druid, who is the giant's enemy; and the Prince de Noisy and the Vicomte de Gonesse, and other personages of the environs of Paris, who were no doubt recognisable and interesting once, but who, whether recognisable or not, are not specially interesting now. To repeat that there are good scenes and piquant remarks is merely to say once more that the thing is Hamilton's. But, on the whole, the present writer at any rate has always found it the least interesting (next to *L'Enchanteur Faustus*) of all.

On the other hand, *Zénéyde*—though unfinished, and though containing, in its ostensibly main story, things compared to which the Prince de Noisy and the Vicomte de Gonesse excite to palpitation—has points of remarkable interest about it. One of these—a prefatory sketch of the melancholy court of exiles at St. Germains—is like

nothing else in Hamilton and like very few things anywhere else. This is in no sense fiction—it is, in fact, a
historical document of the most striking kind ; but it
makes background and canvas for fiction itself,[1] and it
gives us, besides, a most vivid picture of the priest-ridden,
caballing little crowd of folk who had made great re-
nunciations but could not make small. It also shows
us in Hamilton a somewhat darker but also a stronger
side of satiric powers, differently nuanced from the quiet
persiflage of the *Contes* themselves. This, however,
though easily " cobbled on " to the special tale, and
possibly not unconnected with it key-fashion, is entirely
separable, and might just as well have formed part of an
actual letter to the " Madame de P.," to whom it is
addressed.

The tale itself, like some if not all the others, but in
a much more strikingly contrasted fashion, again consists
of two strands, interwoven so intimately, however, that
it is almost impossible to separate them, though it is
equally impossible to conceive two things more different
from each other. The ostensible theme is a history of
herself, given by the Nymph of the Seine to the author—
a history of which more presently. But this is introduced
at considerable length, and interrupted more than once,
by scenes and dialogues, between the nymph and her
distinctly unwilling auditor, which are of the most
whimsically humorous character to be found even in
Hamilton himself.

The whole account of the self-introduction of the
nymph to the narrator is extremely quaint, but rather
long to give here as a whole. It is enough to say that
Hamilton represents himself as by no means an ardent
nympholept, or even as flattered by demi-goddess-like
advances, which are of the most obliging description ;
and that the lady has not only to make fuller and fuller

---

[1] It is a sort of brief lift and drop of the curtain which still concealed the true
historical novel ; it has even got a further literary interest as giving the seamy side of
the texture of Macaulay's admirable *Jacobite's Epitaph*. The account would be rather
out of place here, but may be found translated at length (pp. 44-46) in the volume of
Essays on French Novelists more than once referred to.

revelations of her beauty, but at last to exert her supernatural power to some extent in order to carry the recreant
into her "cool grot," not, indeed, under water, but
invisibly situated on land. What there takes place is,
unfortunately, as has been said, mainly the telling of a
very dull story with one not so dull episode. But the
conclusion of the preface exemplifies the whimsicality
even of the writer, and points to the existence of a com-
modity in the fashion of wig-wearing which few who
glory in "their own hair," and despise their periwigged
forefathers, are likely to have thought of :

At these words [*her own*] raising her eyes to heaven, she sighed
several times; and though she tried to keep them back, I saw, coursing
Hamilton the length of her cheeks and falling on her beautiful
and the neck, tears so natural, in the midst of a silence so touch-
Nymph. ing, that I was just about to follow her example.[1] But
she soon recovered herself; and having shown me by a languishing
look that she was not insensible to my sympathetic emotion . . .
[*she enjoins discretion, and then*:—] After having looked at me
attentively for some time she came closer to me, and as she gently
pulled one side of my wig in order to whisper in my ear, I had to
lean over her in a rather familiar manner.[2] Her face touched mine,
and it seemed to me animated by a lively warmth, very different
from the insensibility which I had accused [3] her of shedding upon
me when she came out of the water. Her breath was pure and
fresh, and her goddess-ship, which I had suspected of being something
marshy, had no taint of mud about it. If only I might reveal
all that she said to me in a confidence which I could have wished
longer ! [3] But apparently she got tired of it [3] and let go my wig.
" 'Twould be too tiresome," she said, " to go on talking like this.
Go out there, and leave us alone ! " I turned round, and seeing
no one in the room, I thought this order was addressed to me, so I
was just rising. . . .

This quaint presentation of a craven swain is perhaps
as good an example as could be found of the curious

---

[1] The most unexpected bathos of these last three words is of course intentional,
and is Hamilton all over.

[2] The nymph is lying on a couch, and her companion (who has been recalcitrant
even to this politeness) is sitting beside her.

[3] This is as impudent as the other passages below are imbecile—of course in each
case (as before) with a calculated impudence and imbecility. The miserable creature
had himself obliged her to "come out of the water" by declining to join her there on
the plea that he was never good for an assignation when he was wet !

mixture of French and English in Hamilton. Hardly
any Frenchman could have borne to put even a fictitious
eidolon of himself in such a contemptible light; very
few Englishmen, though they might easily have done
this, would have done it so neatly, and with so quaint
a travesty of romantic situation. But the main story,
as admitted above, is *assommant*, though, just before the
breach, a substitution of three agreeable damsels for the
nymph herself promises something better.

This combination of the dullest with some of the finest
and most characteristic work of the author, would be
rather a puzzle in a more " serious " writer than Hamilton ; but in his case there is no need to distress, or in
any way to cumber, oneself about the matter. The
whole thing was a " compliment," as the age would have
said, to Fantasy ; and the rules of the Court of Quintessence, though not non-existent as dull fools suppose,
are singularly elastic to skilled players.

We are left with what, even as it exists, is by far his
most ambitious attempt, and with one in which, considering
all its actual features, one need not be taking things too
seriously if one decides that he had an aim at something
like a whole—even if the legends [1] about further parts,
actually seen and destroyed by a more than Byzantine
pudibundity, are not taken as wholly gospel.

The completed *Fleur d'Épine* and the uncompleted
Quatre Facardins [2] are in effect continuous parts (and to
all appearance incomplete in more than the finishing of
the second story) of an untitled but intelligibly sketched
continuation of the *Arabian Nights* themselves. Hamilton, like others since, had evidently conceived an affection
for Dinarzade : and a considerable contempt for Schahriar's
notion of the advantages of matrimony. It is less certain,

---

[1] If they are true, and if Maoame de Grammont was the culprit, it is a sad con-
firmation of the old gibe, " Skittish in youth, prudish in age." It can only be pleaded
in extenuation that some youth which was not skittish, such as Sarah Marlborough's,
matured or turned into something worse than " devotion." And Elizabeth Hamilton
was so very pretty !

[2] " Completions " of both *Zénéyde* and *Les Quatre Facardins*, by the Duke de Lévis,
are included in some editions, but they are, after the fashions of such things, very little
good.

but I think possible, that he had anticipated the ideas of those who think that the unmarried sister went at least halves in the composition or remembrance of the stories themselves, or she could not have varied her timing at dawn so adroitly. He had, at any rate, an Irish-Englishman's sense of honest if humorous indignation at the part which she has to play (or rather endure) in these " two years " (much nearer three !), and the sequel in a way revenges her.

I should imagine that Thackeray must have been reminiscent of Hamilton when he devised the part of " Sister Anne " in *Bluebeard's Ghost*. Like her, Hamilton's Dinarzade is slightly flippant ; she would most certainly have observed " Dolly Codlins is the matter " in Anne's place. Like her, she is not unprovided with lovers ; she actually, at the beginning, " takes a night off " that she may entertain the Prince of Trebizond ; and it is the Prince himself who relates the great, but, alas ! torsoed epic of the Facardins,[1] of whom he is himself one. But as there are only two stories, there is no room for much framework, and we see much less of the " resurrected " Dinarzade [2] than we could wish from what we do see and hear.

Fleur d'Épine, which she herself tells, is a capital story, somewhat closer to the usual norm of the *Nights* than is usual with Hamilton. It bases itself on the well-known legends of the Princess with the literally murderous eyes ; but this Princess Luisante is not really the heroine, and is absent from the greater part of the tale, though she is finally provided with the hero's brother, who is a reigning prince, and has everything handsome about him. The actual hero Tarare (French for " Fiddlestick ! " or something of that sort, and of course an assumed name), in order to cure Luisante's eyes of their lethal quality, has to liberate a still more attractive damsel —the title-heroine—putative daughter of a good fairy and

[1] The name is not, like "Tarare," a direct burlesque ; but it suggests a burlesque intention when taken with " facond " and others including, perhaps, even *faquin*.
[2] The Sultaness is almost *persona muta*—and indeed her tongue must have required a rest.

actual victim of a bad one, quite in the orthodox style.
He does this chiefly by the aid of a very amiable mare,
who makes music wherever she goes, and can do wonderful things when her ears are duly manipulated.   It is a
good and pleasant story, with plenty of the direct relish
of the fairy-tale, Eastern and Western, and plenty also of
satirical parody of the serious romance.   But it is not
quite consummate.   The opening, however, as a fair
specimen of Hamilton's style, may be given.

Two thousand four hundred and fifty-three leagues from
here there is an extraordinarily fine country called Cashmere.
The opening In this country reigned a Caliph; that Caliph had a
of *Fleur* daughter, and that daughter had a face; but people
d'Épine. wished more than once that she had never had any.
Her beauty was not insupportable till she was fifteen; but at
that age it became impossible to endure it.   She had the most
beautiful mouth in the world; her nose was a masterpiece;
the lilies of Cashmere—a thousand times whiter than ours—were
discoloured beside her complexion; and it seemed impertinent of
the fresh-blown rose to show itself beside the carnation of her
cheek.   Her forehead was unmatchable for shape and brilliancy;
its whiteness was contrasted with a Vandyke point of hair blacker
and more shining than jet—whence she took her name of
"Luisante"; the shape of her face seemed made to frame so
many wonders.   But her eyes spoilt everything.
   No one had ever been able to look at them long enough to distinguish their exact colour; for as soon as one met her glance it
was like a stroke of lightning.   When she was eight years old
her father, the Caliph, was in the habit of sending for her, to admire
his offspring and give the courtiers the opportunity of paying a
thousand feeble compliments to her youthful beauty; for even
then they used to put out the candles at midnight, no other light
being necessary except that of the little one's eyes.   Yet all this
was nothing but—in the literal sense, and the other—child's play;
it was when her eyes had acquired full strength that they became
no joking matter.

   [*The fatal effects—killing men in twenty-four hours, and
blinding women—are then told, with the complaints of the
nobility whose sons have fallen victims, and the various
suggestions for remedying the evil made at a committee,
which is presided over by the Seneschal of the kingdom . . .*

"*the silliest man who had ever held such an office—so much so that the caliph could not possibly think of choosing any one less silly.*" *Tarare happens to be in this pundit-potentate's service ; and so the story starts.*]

But—and indeed the writer's opinion on this point has already been indicated—Hamilton's masterpiece, *Les Quatre* unfinished as it is, is *Les Quatre Facardins.* *Facardins.* Indeed, though unfinished in one sense, it is, in another, the most finished of all. Beside it the completed *Faustus* is a mere trifle, and not a very interesting trifle. It has no dull parts like *Zénéyde* and even *Le Bélier.* It has much greater complication of interest and variety of treatment than *Fleur d'Épine*, in which, after the opening, Hamilton's peculiar *persiflage*, though not absent, is much less noticeable. It at least suggests, tantalising as the suggestion is, that the author for once really intended to wind up all his threads into a compact ball, or (which is the better image) to weave them into a new and definite pattern. Moreover—this may not be a recommendation to everybody, but it is a very strong one to the present historian,—it has no obvious or insistent " key "-element whatsoever. It is, indeed, not at all unlikely that there *is* one, for the trick was ingrained in the literature and the society of the time. But if so, it is a sleeping dog that neither bites nor barks ; and if you let it alone it will stay in its kennel, and not even obtrude itself upon your view.

To these partly, if not wholly, negative merits it adds positive ones of a very considerable and delectable kind. The connection with the *Arabian Nights* is brought closer still in the fact that it is not only told (as of himself) by the Prince of Trebizond, Dinarzade's servant-cavalier, but is linked—to an important extent, and not at all to Schahriar's unmixed satisfaction—with one of the earliest incidents of the *Nights* themselves, the remarkable story how the Lady from the Sea increases her store of rings at the cost of some exertion and alarm—not to mention the value of the rings themselves—to the Sultan and his brother, the King of Tartary. This lady, with her genie

and her glass box, reappears as " Cristalline la Curieuse "
—one of the two heroines. The other, of whose actual
adventures we hear only the beginning, and that at the
very close of the story, is Mousseline la Sérieuse, who
never laughs, and who, later, escaping literally by the
loss of her last garment, twitched off by the jaws of an
enormous crocodile, afterwards the pest of the country,
finds herself under a mysterious weird. She is never
able to get a similar vestment made for her, either of day-
or night-fashion. Three hundred and seventy-four
dozen of such things, which formed her wardrobe, had
disappeared [1] after the death (actually crocodile-devoured)
of her Mistress of the Robes ; and although she used up
all the linen-drapers' stocks of the capital in trying to get
new ones, they were all somewhat milder varieties of the
shirt of Nessus. For the day-shifts deprived her of all
appetite for food or drink, and the night ones made it
impossible for her to sleep.

This particular incident comes, as has been said, just
at the end of what we have of the book ; indeed there is
nothing more, save a burlesque embassy, amply provided
with painted cloth [2] and monkeys, to the great enchanter
Caramoussal (who has already figured in the book),
and the announcement, by one of the other Facardins,
of its result—a new adventure for champions, who must
either make the Princess laugh or kill the crocodile.
" It is indifferent," we learn from a most Hamiltonian
sentence, " whether you begin with the crocodile or with
the Princess." Indeed there is yet another means of
restoring peace in the Kingdom of Astrachan, according
to the enchanter himself, who modestly disclaims being an
enchanter, observing (again in a thoroughly Hamiltonian
manner) that as he lives on the top of a mountain close
to the stars, they probably tell him more than they tell
other people. It is to collect three spinning-wheels [3]

---

[1] As Hamilton's satiric intention is as sleepless as poor Princess Mousseline herself,
it is not impossible that he remembered the incident recorded by Pepys, or somebody,
how King Charles the Second could not get a sheet of letter paper to write on for all
the Royal Households and Stationery Offices and such-like things in the English world.

[2] I.e. colour-printed cotton from India—a novelty "fashionable" and, therefore,
satirisable in France.   [3] Or " distaffs and spindles " ?

which are scattered over the universe, but of some of
which we have heard earlier in the story.

One takes perhaps a certain pleasure in outraging the
feelings of the giant Moulineau, so hateful to Madame de
Grammont, by beginning not merely in the middle but
at the end—an end, alas! due, if we believe all the legends,
to her own mistaken zeal when she became a *dévote*—a
variety of person for whom her brother [1] certainly had
small affection, though he did not avenge himself on it
in novel-form quite so cruelly as did Marivaux later. It
is, however, quite good to begin at the beginning, though
the verse-preface needs perhaps to be read with eyes of
understanding. Ostensibly, it is a sort of historical
condemnation of all the species of fiction which had been
popular for half a century or so, and is thus very much
to our purpose, though, like almost all the verses included
in these tales, it does not show the poetic power which
the author of *Celle que j'adore* [2] undoubtedly possessed.
Mere tales, he says, have quite banished from court
favour romances, celebrated for their sentiments, from
Cyrus to *Zaïde*, *i.e.* from Mlle. de Scudéry to Mme. de
la Fayette. *Télémaque* had no better fate

> On courut au Palais [3] le rendre,
> Et l'on s'empressa d'y reprendre
> Le Rameau d'Or et l'Oiseau Bleu. [4]

Then came the "Arabian tales," of which he speaks
with a harshness, the sincerity or design of which may be
left to the reader; and then he himself took up the running,
of course obliged by request of irresistible friends of the
other sex. All which may or may not be read with
grains of salt—the salt-merchant of which everybody
is at liberty to choose for himself. Something may be
said on the subject when we, in all modesty, try to sum
up Hamilton and the period.

[1] She is indeed said to have "converted" both him and Grammont, the latter
perhaps the most remarkable achievement of its kind.
[2] Mr. Austin Dobson's charming translation of this was originally intended to appear
in the present writer's essay above mentioned.
[3] The chief region of bookselling. Cf. Corneille's early comedy, *La Galerie du
Palais.*   [4] For note on *Télémaque* see end of chapter.

But we must now give some more account of the
" Four Facardins " themselves. He of Trebizond is
a tributary Prince of Schahriar's, much after the fashion
(it is to be feared here burlesqued) of the innumerable
second- and third-class heroes whom one meets in the
Cyrus. He begins, like Dinarzade,[1] by " cheeking "
the Sultan on his views of matrimony ; and then he tells
how he set out from his dominions in quest of adventures,
and met another bearer of the remarkable name which
his mother had insisted on giving him. This second
adventurer happened to be bearer also of a helmet with a
strange bird, apparently all made of gems, as its crest.
They exchange confidences, which are to the effect that
the Trebizondian Facardin is a lady-killer of the most
extravagant success, while the other (who is afterwards
called Facardin of the Mountain) is always unfortunate
in love ; notwithstanding which he proposes to undertake
the adventure (to be long afterwards defined) of Mousseline la Sérieuse. For the present he contents himself
with two or three more stories (or, rather, one in several
" fyttes "), which reduce the wildest of the *Nights* to
simple village tales—of an island where lions are hunted
with a provision of virgins, chanticleers, and small deer
on an elaborately ruled system ; of a mountain full of
wild beasts, witches, lovely nymphs, savages, and an
enchanter at the top. After an interruption very much
in the style of Chaucer's Host and *Sir Thopas*, from Dinarzade, who is properly rebuked by the Sultan, Facardin
of the Mountain (he has quite early in the story received
the celebrated scratch from a lion's claw, " from his right
shoulder to his left heel ") recounts a shorter adventure
with Princess Sapinelle of Denmark, and at last, after a
fresh outburst from Dinarzade, the Prince of Trebizond
comes to his own affairs.

Then it is that (after some details about the Prince
of Ophir, who has a minim mouth and an enormous
nose, and the Princess of Bactria, whose features were
just the reverse) we recover Cristalline. It is perhaps

---

[1] Who is here herself an improved Doralise.

only here that even Mrs. Grundy, though she may have been uncomfortable elsewhere, can feel really shocked at Hamilton ; others than Mrs. Grundy need not be so even here. The genie has discovered his Lady's little ways, and has resolved to avenge himself on her by strict custody, and by a means of delivery which, if possible, might not have entirely displeased her. The hundred rings are bewitched to their chain, and are only to be recovered by the same process which strung them on it. But this process must be applied by one person in the space of twelve hours, and the conditions are only revealed to him after he has been kidnapped or cajoled within the genie's power. If he refuses to try, he is clad as Omphale clad Hercules, and set to work. If he tries and fails, he is to be flayed alive and burnt. Facardin, to the despair of his secretary, enters—beguiled by a black ambassadress, who merely informs him that a lady wants help—the enchanted boat which takes him to the fatal scene. But when he is to be introduced to the lady he entirely declines to part with his sword ; and when the whole secret is revealed he, with the help of Cristalline, who is really a good-natured creature in more senses than one, slays the three chief minions of the tyrant—a watchmaker who sets the clock, a lock-smith who is to count the detached rings, and a kind of Executioner High-priest who is to do the flaying and burning,—cuts his way with Cristalline herself to the enchanted boat, regaining *terra firma* and (relatively speaking) *terra* not too much enchanted. But at his very landing at the mouth of the crocodile river he again meets Facardin of the Mountain (who has figured in Cristalline's history earlier) with the two others, whose stories we shall never hear ; and is told about Mousseline ; whereat we and the tale "join our ends" as far as is permitted.

It would be easy to pick from this story alone a sort of nosegay of Hamiltonisms like that from Fuller, which Charles Lamb selected so convincingly that some have thought them simply invented. But it would be unjust to Anthony, because, unless each was given in a *matrix* of context, nobody could, in most cases at any rate, do justice to this curious glancing genius of his. It exists in Sydney Smith to some extent—in Thackeray to more—among Englishmen. There is, in French, something of it in Lesage, who possibly learnt it directly from him; and of course a good deal, though of a lower kind, in Voltaire, who certainly did learn it from him. But it is, with that slight indebtedness to Saint-Évremond noticed above, essentially new and original. It is a mixture of English-Irish (that is to say, Anglo-Norman) humour with French wit, almost unattainable at that day except by a man who, in addition to his natural gifts, had the mixed advantages and disadvantages of his exile position.

Frenchmen at the time—there is abundance, not of mere anecdote, but of solid evidence to prove it—knew practically nothing of English literature. Englishmen knew a good deal more of French, and imitated and translated it, sometimes more eagerly than wisely. But they had not as yet assimilated or appreciated it : that was left for the eighteenth century to do. Meanwhile Hamilton brought the double influence to bear, not merely on the French novel, but on the novel in general and on the eccentric novel in particular. To appreciate him properly, he ought to be compared with Rabelais before him and with Voltaire or Sterne—with both, perhaps, as a counsel of perfection—after him. He is a smaller man, both in literature and in humanity, than Master Francis; but the phrase which Voltaire himself rather absurdly used of Swift might be used without any absurdity in reference to him. He *is* a " Rabelais de bonne compagnie," and from the exactly opposite point of view he might be called a Voltaire or a Sterne *de bonne compagnie* likewise. That is to say, he is a gentleman pretty certainly as well as a genius, which Rabelais might have been, at any rate in other circumstances, but did not choose to be, and which neither François Arouet nor Laurence Sterne could have been, however much either had tried, though the metamorphosis is not quite so

Y

utterly inconceivable in Sterne's case as in the other's. Hamilton, it has been confessed, is sometimes "naughty"; but his naughtiness is neither coarse nor sniggering,[1] and he depends upon it so little—a very important point— that he is sometimes most amusing when he is not naughty at all. In other words, he has no need of it, but simply takes it as one of the infinite functions of human comedy. Against which let Mrs. Grundy say what she likes.

It is conceivable that objection may be taken, or at any rate surprise felt, at the fulness with which a group of mostly little books—no one of them produced by an author of the first magnitude as usual estimates run— has been here handled. But the truth is that the actual birth of the French novel took a much longer time than that of the English—a phenomenon explicable, without any national vainglory, by the fact that it came first and gave us patterns and stimulants. The writers surveyed in this chapter, and those who will take their places in the next—at least Scarron, Furetière, Madame de La Fayette and Hamilton, Lesage, Marivaux, and Prévost —whatever objections or limitations may be brought against them, form the central group of the originators of the modern novel. They open the book of life, as distinguished from that of factitious and rather stale literature; they point out the varieties of incident and character; the manners and interiors and fantastic adjustments; the sentiment rising to passion—which are to determine the developments and departments of the fiction of the future. They leave, as far as we have seen them, great opportunities for improvement to those immediate followers to whom we shall now turn. Hamilton is, indeed, not yet much followed, but Lesage far outgoes Scarron in the raising of the picaresque; Marivaux distances Furetière in painting of manners and in what some people call psychology; *Manon Lescaut* throws *La*

---

[1] To put it otherwise in technical French, there is a little *grivoiserie* in him, but absolutely no *polissonnerie*, still less any *cochonnerie*. Or it may be put, best of all, in his own words when, in a short French-Greek dialogue, called *La Volupté*, he makes Aspasia say to Agathon, " Je vous crois fort voluptueux, sans vous croire débauché."

Princesse de Clèves into the shade as regards the greatest
and most novel-breeding of the passions.   But the whole
are really a *bloc*, the continental sense of which is rather
different from our " block."   And perhaps we shall find
that, though none of them was equal in genius to some
who succeeded them in novel-writing, the novel itself
made little progress, and some backsliding, during nearly
a hundred years after they ceased to write.

NOTE ON *TÉLÉMAQUE*

IT may not perhaps be superfluous to give the rest of that criticism
of Hamilton's on *Télémaque*, the conclusion of which has been
quoted above.   " In vain, from the famous coasts of Ithaca, the
wise and renowned Mentor came to enrich us with those treasures
of his which his *Télémaque* contains.   In vain the art of the
teacher delicately displays, in this romance of a rare kind, the
usefulness and the deceitfulness of politics and of love, as well as
that fatal sweetness—frail daughter of luxury—which intoxicates
a conquering hero at the feet of a young mistress or of a skilful
enchantress, such as in each case this Mentor depicts them.   But,
well-versed as he was in human weakness, and elaborately as he
imitated the style and the stories of Greece, the vogue that he
had was of short duration.   Weary of inability to understand the
mysteries which he unfolded, men ran to the Palais to give back
the volume," etc., etc.

Hamilton, no doubt intentionally, has himself made this
criticism rather " mysterious."   It is well known that, if not
quite at first, very soon after its appearance, the fact that the
politics, if not also the morals, of Fénelon's book were directly
at variance with Court standards was recognised.   At a time
when Court favour and fashion were the very breath of the upper
circles, and directly or indirectly ruled the middle, the popularity
of this curious romance-exhortation was, at any rate for a time,
nipped in the bud, to revive only in the permanent but not altogether
satisfactory conditions of a school-book.   Whether Hamilton
dealt discreetly with the matter by purposely confining himself
to the record of a fact, or at least mixing praise to which no exception could be taken, with what might be taken for blame, one
cannot say.   By dotting a few i's, crossing the t's, and perhaps
touching up some hidden letters with the requisite reagent, one
can, however, get a not unfair or unshrewd criticism of the book
out of this envelope.   *Télémaque*, if it is not, as one of Thackeray's

" thorn " correspondents suggested, superior to " *Lovel Parsonage*
and *Framley the Widower*," has, or with some easy suppres-
sions and a very few additions and developments might have,
much more pure romance interest than its centuries of scholastic
use allow it to have for most people. Eucharis is capable of being
much more than she is allowed to show herself; and some Mrs.
Grundys, with more intelligence than the average member of the
clan, have hinted that Calypso might be dangerous if the persons
who read about her were not likely to consider her as too old to
be interesting. The style is, of course, admirable—there has
hardly ever been a better writer of French than Fénelon, who was
also a first-rate narrator and no mean critic. Whether by the
" mysteries " Hamilton himself meant politics, morals, religion,
or all three and other " serious " things, is a point which, once more,
is impossible to settle. But it is quite certain that, whether there
is any difficulty in comprehending them or not, a great many—
probably the huge majority—of novel readers would not care to
take the trouble to comprehend them, and might, even if they
found little difficulty, resent being asked to do so. And so we
have here not the first—for, as has been said, the Heroic romance
itself had much earlier been " conscripted " into the service of
didactics—but the first brilliant, or almost brilliant, example of that
novel of purpose which will meet us so often hereafter. It may
be said to have at once revealed (for the earlier examples were, as
a rule, too dull to be fair tests) the ineradicable defects of the species.
Even when the purpose does not entirely preclude the possibility
of enjoyment, it always gets in the way thereof; and when the
enjoyable matter does not absorb attention to the disregard of the
purpose altogether, it seldom—perhaps never—really helps that
purpose to get itself fulfilled.

CHAPTER X

THE words which closed the last chapter should make it unnecessary to prefix much of the same kind to this, though at the end we may have again to summarise rather more fully.

As was there observed, our figures here are, with the possible exception of Crébillon *Fils*, " larger " persons The subjects than those dealt with before them; and they of the also mark a further transition towards the chapter. condition—the " employment or vocation "— of the novelist proper, though the polygraphic habit which has grown upon all modern literature, and which began in France almost earlier than anywhere else, affects them. Scarron was even more of a dramatist than of a novelist ; and though this was also the case with Lesage and Marivaux—while Prévost was, save for his masterpiece, a polygraph of the polygraphs—their work in fiction was far larger, both positively and comparatively, than his. *Gil Blas* for general popularity, and *Manon Lescaut* for enthusiastic admiration of the elect, rank almost, if not quite, among the greatest novels of the world. Marivaux, for all his irritating habit of leaving things unfinished, and the almost equally irritating affectation of phrase, in which he anticipated some English novelists of the late nineteenth and earliest twentieth century, is almost the first " psychologist " of prose fiction ; that is to say, where Madame de la Fayette had taken the soul-analysis of hardly more than two persons (Nemours scarcely counts) in a single situation, Marivaux gives us an almost complete dissection of the temperament and character of a girl and of a man under many ordinary life-circumstances for a considerable time.

But we must begin, not with him but with Lesage, not merely as the older man by twenty years, but in virtue
Lesage—his of that comparative " greatness " of his greatest
Spanish work which has been glanced at. There is
connections. perhaps a doubt whether *Gil Blas* is as much read now as it used to be ; it is pretty certain that *Le Diable Boiteux* is not. The certainty is a pity ; and if the doubt be true, it is a greater pity still. For more than a century *Gil Blas* was almost as much [1] a classic, either in the original or in translation, in England as it was in France ; and the delight which it gave to thousands of readers was scarcely more important to the history of fiction generally than the influence it exerted upon generation after generation of novelists, not merely in its own country, but on the far greater artists in fiction of the eighteenth and early nineteenth century in England from Fielding to Scott, if not to Dickens. Now, I suppose, that we are told to start with the axiom that even Fielding's structure of humanity is a simple toy-like thing, how much more is Lesage's ? But for those of us who have not bowed the knee to foolish modern Baals, " They reconciled us ; we embraced, and we have since been mortal enemies " ; and the trout ; and the soul of the licentiate ; and Dr. Sangrado ; and the Archbishop of Granada—to mention only the most famous and hackneyed matters—are still things a little larger, a little more complex, a little more eternal and true, than webs of uninteresting analysis told in phrase to which Marivaudage itself is golden and honeyed Atticism.

Yet once more we can banish, with a joyful and quiet mind, a crowd of idle fancies and disputes, apparently but not really affecting our subjects. The myth of a

---

[1] In fact it has been said, and may be said again, that Lesage is one of the prophets who have never had so much justice done them in their own countries as abroad.

direct Spanish origin for *Gil Blas* is almost as easily dispersible by the clear sun of criticism as the exaggeration of the debt of the smaller book to Guevara. On the other hand, the *general* filiation of Lesage on his Spanish predecessors is undeniable, and not worth even shading off and toning down. A man is not ashamed of having good fathers and grandfathers, whose property he now enjoys, before him in life; and why should he be in literature?

Lesage's work, in fiction and out of it, is considerable in bulk, but it is affected (to what extent disadvantage-

Peculiarity ously different judges may judge differently) by of his work some of the peculiarities of the time which have generally. been already mentioned, and by some which have not. It is partly original, partly mere translation, and partly also a mixture of the strangest kind. Further, its composition took place in a way difficult to adjust to later ideas. Lesage was not, like Marivaux, a professed and shameless "*un*finisher," but he took a great deal of time to finish his work.[1] He was not an early-writing author; and when he did begin, he showed something of that same strange need of a suggestion, a "send-off," or whatever anybody likes to call it, which appears even in his greatest work. He began with the *Letters* of Aristaenetus, which, though perhaps they have been abused more than they deserve by people who have never read them, and would never have heard of them if it had not been for Alain René, are certainly not the things that most scholars, with the whole range of Greek literature before them to choose from, would have selected. His second venture was almost worse than his first; for there *are* some prettinesses in Aristaenetus, and except for the one famous passage enshrined by Pope in the *Essay on Criticism*, there is, I believe,[2] nothing good in the continuation of *Don Quixote* by the so-called Avellaneda.

---

[1] The first part of *Gil Blas* appeared in 1715; and nearly twenty years later gossip said that the fourth was not ready, though the author had been paid in advance for it six or seven years earlier.

[2] I have never read it in the original, being, though a great admirer of Spanish, but slightly versed therein.

But at any rate this job, which is attributed to the suggestion of the Abbé de Lyonne, " put " Lesage on Spanish,
and never did fitter seed fall on more fertile soil.

Longinus would, I think, have liked *Gil Blas*, and
indeed Lesage, very much. You might kill ten asses,
And its of the tallest Poitou standard in size and the
variety. purest Zoilus or Momus sub-variety in breed,
under you while going through his " faults." He
translates ; he borrows ; he " plagiarises " about as much
as is possible for anybody who is not a mere dullard to
do. Of set plot there is nothing in his work, whether
you take the two famous pieces, or the major adaptations
like *Estévanille Gonzales* and *Guzman d'Alfarache*, or
the lesser things, more Lucianic than anything else, such
as the *Cheminées de Madrid*[1] and the *Journée des Parques*
and the *Valise Trouvée*. " He worked for his living "
(as M. Anatole France long ago began a paper about him
which is not quite the best of its very admirable author's
work), and though the pot never boiled quite so merrily
as the cook deserved, the fact of the pot-boiling makes
itself constantly felt. *Les chaînes de l'esclavage* must
have cut deep into his soul, and the result of the cutting
is evident enough in his work. But the vital marks on
that work are such as many perfectly free men, who have
wished to take literature as a mistress only, have never
been able to impress on theirs. He died full of years,
but scarcely of the honours due to him, failing in power,
and after a life[2] of very little luck, except as regards
possession of a wife who seems to have been beautiful
in youth and amiable always, with at least one son who
observed the Fifth Commandment to the utmost. But
he lives among the immortals, and there are few names
in our present history which are of more importance to
it than his.

---

[1] This, which is a sort of Appendix to the *Diable Boiteux*, is much the best of these
opera minora.
[2] He had a temper of the most *Breton-Bretonnant* type—not ill-natured but sturdy
and independent, recalcitrant alike to ill-treatment and to patronage. He got on
neither at the Bar, his first profession, nor with the regular actors, and he took
vengeance in his books on both ; while at least one famous anecdote shows his way of
treating a patron—indeed, as it happened, a patroness—who presumed.

Some of his best and least unequal work is indeed denied us. We have nothing to do with his drama, though *Turcaret* is something like a masterpiece in comedy, and *Crispin Rival de son Maître* a capital farce. We cannot even discuss that remarkable *Théâtre de la Foire*, which, though a mere collection of the lightest Harlequinades, has more readable matter of literature in it than the whole English comic drama since Sheridan, with the exception of the productions of the late Sir William Gilbert.

Nor must much be said even of his minor novel work. The later translations and adaptations from the Spanish need hardly any notice for obvious reasons ; whatever is good in them being either not his, or better exemplified in the *Devil* and in *Gil*. The extremely curious and very Defoe-like book—almost if not quite his last —*Vie et Aventures de M. de Beauchesne, Capitaine de Flibustiers*, is rather a subject for a separate essay than for even a paragraph here. But Lesage, from our point of view, is *Le Diable Boiteux* and *Gil Blas*, and to the *Diable Boiteux* and *Gil Blas* let us accordingly turn.

The relations of the earlier and shorter book to the *Diablo Cojuelo* of Luis Velez de Guevara are among the
Le Diable most open secrets of literature. The French-
Boiteux. man, in a sort of prefatory address to his Spanish parent and original, has put the matter fairly enough ; anybody who will take the trouble can " control " or check the statement, by comparing the two books themselves. The idea—the rescuing of an obliging demon from the grasp of an enchanter, and his unroofing the houses of Madrid to amuse his liberator—is entirely Guevara's, and for a not inconsiderable space of time the French follows the Spanish closely. But then it breaks off, and the remainder of the book is, except for the carrying out of the general idea, practically original. The unroofing and revealing of secrets, from being merely casual and confined to a particular neighbourhood, becomes systematised : a lunatic asylum and a prison are subjected to the process ; a set of dreamers are obliged to deliver up

what Queen Mab is doing with them ; and, as an incident, the student Don Cleofas, who has freed Asmodeus,[1] gains through the friendly spirit's means a rich and pretty bride whom the demon—naturally immune from fire—has rescued in Cleofas's likeness from a burning house.

The thing therefore neither has, nor could possibly pretend to have, any merit as a plotted and constructed whole in fiction. It is merely a variety of the old " framed " tale-collection, except that the frame is of the thinnest ; and the individual stories, with a few exceptions, are extremely short, in fact little more than anecdotes. The power and attraction of the book lie simply in the crispness of the style, the ease and flow of the narrative, and the unfailing satiric knowledge of human nature which animates the whole. As it stands, it is double its original length ; for Lesage, finding it popular, and never being under the trammels of a fixed design, very wisely, and for a wonder not unsuccessfully, gave it a continuation. And, except the equally obvious and arbitrary one of the recapture of the spirit by the magician, it has and could have no end. The most famous of the anecdotes about it is that Boileau—in 1707 a very old man—found his page reading it, and declared that such a book and such a critic as he should never pass a night under the same roof. Boileau, though he often said rude, unjust, and uncritical things, did not often say merely silly ones ; and it has been questioned what was his reason for objecting to a book by no means shocking to anybody but Mrs. Grundy Grundified to the very *n*th, excellently written, and quite free from the bombast and the whimsicality which he loathed. Jealousy for Molière,[2] to whom, in virtue of *Turcaret*, Lesage had been set up as a sort of rival ; mere senile ill-

(margin: Lesage and Boileau.)

[1] Asmodeus, according to his usual station in the infernal hierarchy, is *démon de la luxure* : but any fears or hopes which may be aroused by this description, and the circumstances of the action, will be disappointed. Lesage has plenty of risky situations, but his language is strictly " proper."

[2] Against this may be cited his equally anecdotic acceptance of Regnard, who was also "run " against Molière. But Regnard was a "classic" and orthodox in his way ; Lesage was a free-lance, and even a Romantic before Romanticism. Boileau knew that evil, as evil seemed to him, *had* come from Spain ; he saw more coming in this, and if he anticipated more still in the future, 1830 proved him no false prophet.

temper, and other things have been suggested; but the matter is of no real importance even if it is true. Boileau was one of the least catholic and the most arbitrary critics who ever lived; he had long made up and colophoned the catalogue of his approved library; he did not see his son's coat on the new-comer, and so he cursed him. It is not the only occasion on which we may bless what Boileau cursed.

Gil Blas, of course, is in every sense a " bigger " book of literature. That it has, from the point of view of the

Gil Blas—
its peculiar
cosmo-
politanism. straitest sect of the Unitarians—and not of that sect only—much more unity than the *Diable*, would require mere cheap paradox to contend. It has neither the higher unity, say, of *Hamlet*, where every smallest scene and almost personage is connected with the general theme; nor the lower unity of such a thing as *Phèdre*, where everything is pared down, or, as Landor put it in his own case, " boiled off " to a meagre residuum of theme special. It has, at the very most, that species of unity which Aristotle did not like even in epic, that of a succession of events happening to an individual; and while most of these might be omitted, or others substituted for them, without much or any loss, they exist without prejudice to mere additions to themselves. As the excellent Mr. Wall, sometime Professor of Logic at Oxford, and now with God, used to say, " Gentlemen, I can conceive an elephant," so one may conceive a *Gil Blas*, not merely in five instead of four, but in fifty or five hundred volumes. But, on the other hand, it has that still different unity (of which Aristotle does not seem to have thought highly, even if he thought of it at all), that all these miscellaneous experiences do not merely happen to a person with the same name—they happen to the same person.[1] And they have themselves yet another unity, which I hardly remember any critic duly insisting on and discussing, in the fact that they all are possibly human accidents or incidents. Though he was

---

[1] In other words, there is a unity of personality in the attitude which the hero takes to and in them.

a native of one of the most idiosyncratic provinces of not the least idiosyncratic country in Europe, Lesage is a citizen not of Brittany, not of France, not of Europe even, but of the world itself, in far more than the usual sense of cosmopolitanism.   He has indeed coloured background and costume, incident and even personage itself so deeply with essence of " things of Spain," that, as has been said, the Spaniards, the most jealous of all nationalities except the smaller Celtic tribes, have claimed his work for themselves.   Yet though Spain has one of the noblest languages, one of the greatest literatures in quality if not in bulk, one of the most striking histories, and one of the most intensely national characters in the world, it is—perhaps for the very reason last mentioned—as little cosmopolitan as any country, and Lesage, as has been said, is inwardly and utterly cosmopolitan or nothing.

> At Paris, at Rome, at the Hague he's at home ;

and though he seems to have known little of England, and, as most Frenchmen of his time had reason to do, to have disliked us, he has certainly never been anywhere more at home than in London.   In fact—and it bears out what has been said—there is perhaps no capital in Europe where, in the two hundred years he has had to nationalise himself, Lesage has been less at home than at Paris itself.   The French are of course proud of him in a way, but there is hardly one of their great writers about whom they have been less enthusiastic.   The technical, and especially the neo-classically technical, shortcomings which have been pointed out may have had something to do with this ; but the cosmopolitanism has perhaps more.

For us Lesage occupies a position of immense import-
And its adoption of the homme sensuel moyen fashion. ance in the history of the French novel ; but if we were writing a history of the novel at large it would scarcely be lessened, and might even be relatively larger.   He had come to it perhaps by rather strange ways ; but it is no novelty

to find that conjunction of road and goal. The Spanish picaresque romance was not in itself a very great literary kind ; but it had in it a great faculty of *emancipation*. Outside the drama [1] it was about the first division of literature to proclaim boldly the refusal to consider anything human as alien from human literary interest. But, as nearly always happens, it had exaggerated its protests, and become sordid, merely in revolt from the high-flown non-sordidness of previous romance. Lesage took the principle and rejected the application. He dared, practically for the first time, to take the average man of unheroic stamp, the *homme sensuel moyen* of a later French phrase, for his subject. *Gil Blas* is not a virtuous person,[2] but he is not very often an actual scoundrel.[3] (Is there any of us who has never been a scoundrel at all at all ?) He is clever after his fashion, but he is not a genius ; he is a little bit of a coward, but can face it out fairly at a pinch ; he has some luck and ill-luck ; but he does not come in for *montes et maria*, either of gold or of misery. I have no doubt that the comparison of *Gil Blas* and *Don Quixote* has often been made, and it would be rather an *excursus* here. But inferior as Lesage's work is in not a few ways, it has, like other non-quintessential things, much more virtue as model and pattern. Imitations of *Don Quixote* (except Graves's capital book, where the following is of the freest character) have usually been failures. It is hardly an extravagance to say that every novel of miscellaneous adventure since its date owes something, directly or indirectly, to *Gil Blas*.

One of the " faults "—it must be understood that between " faults " with inverted commas and faults without them there is a wide and sometimes an un-

---

[1] And in it too, of course ; as well as in Spain's remarkable but too soon re-enslaved criticism.

[2] As he says of himself (vii. x.) : *Enfin, après un sévère examen je tombais d'accord avec moi-même, que si je n'étais pas un fripon, il ne s'en fallait guère.* And the Duke of Lerma tells him later, " *M. de Santillane, à ce que je vois, vous avez été tant soit peu picaro.*"

[3] The two most undoubted cases—his ugly and, unluckily, repeated acceptance of the part of Pandarus-Leporello—were only too ordinary rascalities in the seventeenth century. The books of the chronicles of England and France show us not merely clerks and valets but gentlemen of every rank, from esquire to duke, eagerly accepting this office.

bridgeable gulf—lies in the fact that the book is after all not much more of a whole, in any sense but that noted above, than *Le Diable Boiteux* itself. The innumerable incidents are to a very large extent episodes merely, and episodes in the loose, not the precise, sense of the term. That is to say, they are not merely detachable ; they might be reattached to almost any number of other stories. But the redeeming feature—which is very much more than a *mere* redeeming feature—is the personality of the hero which has been already referred to. Lesage's scrip and staff, to apply the old images exactly enough, are his inexhaustible fertility in well-told stories and his faculty of delineating a possible and interesting human character.

The characteristics of the successive parts of *Gil Blas* are distinct and interesting, the distinctions themselves being also rather curious. The anecdote cited above as to the Fourth and last volume is certainly confirmed by, and does not seem, as so many anecdotes of the kind do, to have been even possibly drawn from, the volume itself. Although the old power is by no means gone, the marks of its failing are pretty obvious. A glance has been given already to the unnecessary and disgusting repetition of the Pandar business—made, as it is, more disgusting by the distinctly tragic touch infused into it. The actual *finale* is, on the other hand, a good comedy ending of a commonplace kind, except that a comic author, such as Lesage once had been on and off the stage, would certainly have made *Gil Blas* suffer in his second marriage for his misdeeds of various kinds earlier, instead of leaving him in the not too clean cotton or clover of an old rip with a good young wife. If he had wanted a happy ending of a still conventional but satisfactory kind, he should have married Gil to Laure or Estelle (they were, in modern slang, sufficiently " shop-worn goods " not to be ill-mated, and Laure is perhaps the most attractive character in the whole book); have legitimated Lucrèce, as by some odd

Its inequality —in the Second and Fourth Books especially.

crotchet he definitely refuses to do ; [1] have dropped the
later Leporello business, in which his old love and her
daughter are concerned, altogether, and have left us in a
mild sunset of " reconciliation." If anybody scorns this
suggestion as evidence of a futile liking for " rose-pink,"
let him remember that Gil Blas, *ci-devant picaro* and other
ugly things, is actually left lapped in an Elysium not less
improbable and much more undeserved than this. But
it is disagreeable to dwell on the shortcomings of age,
and it has only been done to show that this is a criticism
and not a mere panegyric.

Oddly enough, the Second volume is also open to much
exception of something, though not quite, the same kind ;
it seems as if Lesage, after making strong running, had
a habit of nursing himself and even going to sleep for
a while. The more than questionable habit of *histoire*-
insertions revives ; that of the rascal-hermit *picaro*, " Don
Raphael," is, as the author admits, rather long, and, as
he might have admitted, and as any one else may be
allowed to say, very tiresome. Gil Blas himself goes
through a long period of occultation, and the whole
rather drags.

The First and the Third are the pillars of the house ;
and the Third, though (with the exception of the episode
of the Archbishop, and that eternal sentence governing
the relations of author and critic that " the homily
which has the misfortune not to be approved " by the one
is the very best ever produced by the other) not so well
known, is perhaps even better than anything in the First.
But the later part has, of course, not quite so much
freshness ; and nobody need want anything better than the
successive scenes, slightly glanced at already, in which Gil
Blas is taught, by no means finally,[2] the ways of the world ;
the pure adventure interest of the robbers' cave, so admir-

[1] In a curious passage of Bk. XII. Chap. I. in which Gil disclaims paternity and resigns
it to Marialva. This may have been prompted by a desire to lessen the turpitude of
the go-between business ; but it is a clumsy device, and makes Gil look a fool as well as
a knave.

[2] One of Lesage's triumphs is the way in which, almost to the last, " M. de
Santillane," despite the rogueries practised often on and sometimes by him, retains a
certain gullibility, or at least ingenuousness.

ably managed and so little over-dwelt on ; the experiences of travel and of the capital ; the vivid pictures of *petit maître* and actress life ; the double deception—thoroughly Spanish this, but most freshly and universally handled— by Laure and Gil ; many other well-known things ; all deserve the knowledge and the admiration that they have won. But the Third, in which the hero is hardly ever off the scene from first to last, is my own favourite. He shows himself—not at his best, but humanly enough— in the affair with the ill-fated Lorença, on which the Leyva family might have looked less excusingly if the culprit had been anybody but Gil. The Granada scenes, however, and not by any means merely those with the Archbishop, are of the very first class ; and the re- appearance of Laure, with the admirable coolness by which she hoodwinks her " keeper " Marialva, yields to nothing in the book. For fifty pages it is all novel-gold ; and though Gil Blas, in decamping from the place, and leaving Laure to bear the brunt of a possible discovery, commits one of his least heroic deeds, it is so character- istic that one forgives, not indeed him, but his creator. The whole of the Lerma part is excellent and not in the least improbably impossible ; there is infinitely more " human natur' " in it, as Marryat's waterman would have said, than in the *réchauffé* of the situation with Olivares.

The effect indeed which is produced, in rereading, by *Le Diable Boiteux* and *Gil Blas*, but especially by the latter, is of that especial kind which is a sort of quality—not " *a posteriori* intuition," if such a phrase may be permitted, of " classical " quality.[1] This sensation, which appears, unfortunately, to be unknown to a great many people, is sometimes set down by the more critical or, let us say, the more censorious of them, to a sort of childish prepossession—akin to that which makes a not ill-conditioned child fail to discover any uncomeliness in his mother's or a favourite nurse's face. There is

Lesage's quality—not requiring many words, but indis- putable.

[1] Not of course as opposed to "romantic," but as = "chief and principal."

no retort to such a proposition as this so proper as the argument not *ad hominem*, but *ab* or *ex homine*. The present writer did not read the *Devil* till he had reached quite critical years ; and though he read *Gil Blas* much earlier, he was not (for what reason he cannot say) particularly fond of it until the same period was reached. And yet its attractions cannot possibly be said to be of any recondite or artificial kind, and its defects are likely to be more, not less, recognised as the critical faculty acquires strength and practice. Nevertheless, recent reperusal has made him more conscious than ever of the existence of this quality of a classic in both, but especially in the larger and more famous book. And this is a mere pailful added to an ocean of previous and more important testimony. *Gil Blas* has certainly " classed " itself in the most various instances, of essentially critical, not specially critical but generally acute and appreciative, and more or less unsophisticated and ordinary judgments, as a thing that is past all question, equally enjoyable for its incidents, its character-sketches, and its phrasing— though the first are (for time and country) in no sense out of the way, the second scarcely go beyond the individualised type, and the third is neither gorgeous nor " alambicated," as the French say, nor in any way peculiar, except for its saturation with a sharp, shrewd, salt wit which may be described as the spirit of the popular proverb, somehow bodied and clothed with more purely literary form. It is true that, in the last few clauses, plenty of ground has been indicated for ascription of classicality in the best sense ; and perhaps Lesage himself has summed the whole thing up when, in the " Declaration " of the author at the beginning of *Gil Blas*, he claims " to have set before himself only the representation of human life as it is." He has said it ; and in saying and doing it he has said and done everything for his merits as a novelist and his place in the history of the novel.

The Archbishop of Sens, who had the duty of " answering " Marivaux's " discourse of reception " into the

z

Academy in the usual *aigre-doux* manner, informed
him, with Academic frankness and Archiepis-

Marivaux—
Les Effets copal propriety, that "in the small part of
de la your work which I have run through, I soon
Sympathie (?) recognised that the reading of these agreeable
romances did not suit the austere dignity with which
I am invested, or the purity of the ideas which religion
prescribes me." This was all in the game, both for an
Academician and for an Archbishop, and it probably
did not discompose the novelist much. But if his Grace
had read *Les Effets de la Sympathie*, and had chosen to
criticise it, he might have made its author (always supposing that Marivaux *was* its author, which does not seem
to be at all certain) much more uncomfortable. Although
there is plenty of incident, it is but a dull book, and it
contains not a trace of " Marivaudage " in style. A
hero's father, who dies of poison in the first few pages,
and is shown to have been brought round by an obliging
gaoler in the last few ; a hero himself, who thinks he has
fallen in love with a beautiful and rich widow, playing
good Samaritaness to him after he has fallen in among
thieves, but a page or two later really does fall in love
with a fair unknown looking languishingly out of a
window ; a *corsaire*,[1] with the appropriate name of Tur-
camène, who is robustious almost from the very beginning, and receives at the end a fatal stab with his own
poniard from the superfluous widow, herself also fatally
wounded at the same moment by the same weapon (an
economy of time, incident, and munitions uncommon
off the stage) ; an intermediate personage who, straying
—without any earthly business there—into one of those
park " pavilions " which play so large a part in these
romances, finds a lady asleep on the sofa, with her hand
invitingly dropped, promptly kneels down, and kisses it :
these and many other things fill up a Spanish kind
of story, not uningeniously though rather improbably

[1] The reader must not forget that this formidable word means "privateer" rather
than "pirate" in French, and that this was the golden age of the business in that
country.

engineered, but dependent for its interest almost wholly
on incident ; for though it is not devoid of conversation,
this conversation is without spirit or sparkle. 'It is, in
fact, a " circulating library " novel before—at any rate
at an early period of—circulating libraries : not un-
workmanlike, probably not very unsatisfactory to its
actual readers, and something of a document as to the
kind of satisfaction they demanded ; but not intrinsically
important.

One has not seen much, in English,[1] about Marivaux,
despite the existence, in French, of one of the best [2] of
those monographs which assist the foreign critic so much,
and sometimes perhaps help to beget his own lucubra-
tions. Yet he is one of the most interesting writers of
France, one of the most curious, and, one may almost
say, one of the most puzzling. This latter quality he
owes, in part at least, to a " skiey influence " of the time,
which he shares with Lesage and Prévost, and indeed
to some extent with most French writers of the eighteenth
century—the influence of the polygraphic habit.

He was a dramatist, and a voluminous one, long before
he was a novelist : and some of his thirty or forty plays,
His work in especially *Les Fausses Confidences* and *Le Jeu*
general. *de l'Amour et du Hasard*, still rank among at
least the second-class classics of the French comic stage.
He tried, for a time, one of the worst kinds of merely
fashionable literature, the travesty-burlesque.[3] He was
a journalist, following Addison openly in the title, and to
some extent in the manner, of *Le Spectateur*, which he
afterwards followed by *Le Cabinet d'un Philosophe*, showing, however, here, as he was more specially tempted to
do, his curious, and it would seem unconquerable,
habit of leaving things unfinished, which only does not

---

[1] Those who are curious may find something on him by the present writer, not
identical with the above account, in an essay entitled *A Study of Sensibility*, reprinted in
Essays on French Novelists (London, 1891), and partly, but outside of the Marivaux part,
reproduced in Chap. XII. of the present volume.

[2] By M. Gustave Larroumet. Paris, 1882.

[3] I need hardly say that I am not referring to things like *Rebecca and Rowena* or
A Legend of the Rhine, which "burst the outer shell of sin," and, like Mrs. Martha
Gwynne in the epitaph, " hatch themselves a cherubin " in each case.

appear in his plays, for the simple and obvious reason
that managers will not put an unfinished play on the
stage, and that, if they did, the afterpiece would be prema-
ture and of a very lively character. But the completeness
of his very plays is incomplete ; they " run huddling "
to their conclusion, and are rather bundles of good or
not so good acts and scenes than entire dramas. We are,
however, only concerned with the stories, of which there
are three : the early, complete, but doubtful *Effets de la
Sympathie*, already discussed ; the central in every way,
but endlessly dawdled over, *Marianne*, which never got
finished at all (though Mme. Riccoboni continued it in
Marivaux's own lifetime, and with his placid approval,
and somebody afterwards botched a clumsy *Fin*) ; and *Le
Paysan Parvenu*, the latter part of which is not likely to
be genuine, and, even if so, is not a real conclusion. We
may, however, with some advantage, take it before
Marianne, if only because it is not the book generally
connected with its author's name.

Notwithstanding this comparative oblivion, *Le Paysan
Parvenu* is an almost astonishingly clever and original
Le Paysan book, at least as far as the five of its eight
Parvenu. parts, which are certainly Marivaux's, go. I
have read the three last twice critically, at a long interval
of time, and I feel sure that the positive internal evidence
confirms, against their authenticity, the negative want
of external for it. In any case they add nothing—
they do not, as has been said, even really " conclude "
—and we may, therefore, without any more apology, confine ourselves to the part which is certain. Some readers
may possibly know that when that strangest of strange
persons, Restif de la Bretonne (see the last chapter of this
book), took up the title with the slight change or gloss of
Parvenu to *Perverti*, he was at least partly actuated by
his own very peculiar, but distinctly existing, variety of
moral indignation. And though Pierre Carlet (which was
Marivaux's real name) and " Monsieur Nicolas " (which
was as near a real name as any that Restif had) were, the
one a quite respectable person on ordinary standards, and

the other an infinitely disreputable creature, still the later novelist was perhaps ethically justified. Marivaux's successful rustic does not, so far as we are told, actually do anything that contravenes popular morality, though he is more than once on the point of doing so. He is not a bad-blooded person either ; and he has nothing of the wild-beast element in the French peasantry which history shows us from the Jacquerie to the Revolution, and which some folk try to excuse as the result of aristo-cratic tyranny. But he is an elaborate and exceedingly able portrait of another side of the peasant, and, if we may trust literature, even with some administration of salt, of the French peasant more particularly. He is what we may perhaps be allowed to call unconsciously determined to get on, though he does not go quite to the length of the *quocunque modo*, and has, as far as men are concerned, some scruples. But in relation to the other sex he has few if any, though he is never brutal. He is, as we may say, first " perverted," though not as yet *parvenu*,[1] in the house of a Parisian, himself a *nouveau riche* and *novus homo*, on whose property in Champagne his own father is a wine-farmer. He is early selected for the beginnings of Lady-Booby-like attentions by " Madame," while he, as far as he is capable of the proceeding, falls in love with one of Madame's maids, Geneviève. It does not appear that, if the lady's part of the matter had gone further, Jacob (that is his name) would have been at all like Joseph. But when he finds that the maid is also the object of " Monsieur's " attentions, and when he is asked to take the profits of this affair (the attitude[2] of the girl herself is very skilfully delineated) and marry

---

[1] The reader will perhaps excuse the reminder that the sense in which we (almost exclusively) use this word, and which it had gained in French itself by the time of Talleyrand's famous double-edged sarcasm on person and world (*Il n'est pas parvenu : il est arrivé*), was not quite original. The *parvenu* was simply a person who *had* "got on": the disobliging slur of implication on his former position, and perhaps on his means of freeing himself from it, came later. It is doubtful whether there is much if indeed there is any, of this slur in Marivaux's title.

[2] It is the acme of what may be called innocent corruption. She does not care for her master, nor apparently for vicious pleasure, nor—certainly—for money as such. She does care for Jacob, and wants to marry him ; the money will make this possible ; so she earns it by the means that present themselves, and puts it at his disposal.

her, his own *point d'honneur* is reached.[1] Everything
is, however, cut short by the sudden death, in hopelessly
embarrassed circumstances, of Monsieur, and the consequent cessation of Madame's attraction for a young man
who wishes to better himself. He leaves both her and
Geneviève with perfect nonchalance ; though he has good
reason for believing that the girl really loves him, however
she may have made a peculiar sort of hay when the sun
shone, and that both she and his lady are penniless, or
almost so.

He has, however, the luck which makes the *parvenu*,
if in this instance he can hardly be said to deserve it.
On the Pont Neuf he sees an elderly lady, apparently about
to swoon. He supports her home, and finds that she is
the younger and more attractive of two old-maid and
dévote sisters. The irresistibleness to this class of the
feminine sex (and indeed by no means to this class only)
of a strapping and handsome footman is a commonplace
of satire with eighteenth-century writers, both French
and English. It is exercised possibly on both sisters,
though the elder is a shrew ; certainly on the younger,
and also on their elderly *bonne*, Catherine. But it necessarily leads to trouble. The younger, Mlle. Habert (the
curious hiding of Christian names reappears here),
wants to retain Jacob in the joint service, and Catherine
at least makes no objection, for obvious reasons. But
the elder sister recalcitrates violently, summoning to her
aid her " director," and the younger, who is financially
independent,[2] determines to leave the house. She does
so (*not* taking Catherine with her, though the *bonne*
would willingly have shared Jacob's society), and having
secured lodgings, regularly proposes ·to her (the word

---

[1] He is proof against his master's threats if he refuses ; as well as against the money
if he accepts. Unluckily for Geneviève, when he breaks away she faints. Her door
and the money-box are both left open, and the latter disappears.

[2] Here and elsewhere the curious cheapness of French living (despite what history
tells of crushing taxation, etc.) appears. The *locus classicus* for this is generally taken
to be Mme. de Maintenon's well-known letter about her brother's housekeeping. But
here, well into another century, Mlle. Habert's 4000 *livres* a year are supposed to be
at least relative affluence, while in *Marianne* (*v. inf.*) M. de Climal thinks 500 or 600
enough to tempt her, and his final bequest of double that annuity is represented as
making a far from despicable *dot* even for a good marriage.

may be used almost accurately) " swain." Jacob has no
scruples of delicacy here, though the nymph is thirty years
older than himself, and though he has, if no dislike,
no particular affection for her. But it is an obvious step
upwards, and he makes no difficulties. The elder sister,
however, makes strong efforts to forbid the banns, and
her interest prevails on a " President " (the half-regular
power of the French *noblesse de robe*, though perhaps less
violently exercised, must have been almost as galling as
the irresponsibleness of men of birth and " sword ")
to interpose and actually stop the arranged ceremony.
But Jacob appears in person, and states his case convincingly ; the obstacle is removed, and the pair are made
happy at an extraordinary hour (two or three in the morning),
which seems to have been then fashionable for marriages.
The conventional phrase is fairly justified ; for the bride
is completely satisfied, and Jacob is not displeased.

His marriage, however, interferes not in the very
least with his intention to " get on " by dint of his handsome face and brawny figure. On the very day of his
wedding he goes to visit a lady of position, and also of
devoutness, who is a great friend of the President and
his wife, has been present at the irregular enquiry, and
has done something for him. This quickly results in a
regular assignation, which, however, is comically broken
off. Moreover this lady introduces him to another of
the same temperament — which indeed seems to have
been common with French ladies (the Bellaston type
being not the exception, but the rule). *She* is to introduce
him to her brother-in-law, an influential financier, and
she quickly makes plain the kind of gratitude she expects.
This also is, as far as we are told, rather comically interfered with—Marivaux's dramatic practice made him
good at these disappointments. She does give the
introduction, and her brother-in-law, though a curmud-
geon, is at first disposed to honour her draft. But here
an unexpected change is made by the presentation of
Jacob as a man of noble sentiment. The place he is
to have is one taken from an invalid holder of it, whose

wife comes to beg mercy: whereat Jacob, magnanimously
and to the financier's great wrath, declines to profit by
another's misfortune. Whether the fact that the lady
is very pretty has anything to do with the matter need
not be discussed. His—let us call it at least—good
nature, however, indirectly makes his fortune. Going
to visit the husband and wife whom he has obliged, he
sees a young man attacked by three enemies and ill-
bested. Jacob (who is no coward, and, thanks to his
wife insisting on his being a gentleman and " M. de la
Vallée," has a sword) draws and uses it on the weaker side,
with no skill whatever, but in the downright, swash-and-
stab, short- and tall-sailor fashion, which (in novels at
least) is almost always effective. The assailants decamp,
and the wounded but rescued person, who is of very high
rank, conceives a strong friendship for his rescuer, and,
as was said above, makes his fortune. The last and
doubtful three-eighths of the book kill off poor Mlle.
Habert (who, although Jacob would never have been
unkind to her, was already beginning to be very jealous
and by no means happy), and marry him again to a younger
lady of rank, beauty, fashion, and fortune, in the imparted
possession of all of which we leave him. But, except to
the insatiables of " what happened next," these parts are
as questionably important as they are decidedly doubtful.

The really important points of the book are, in the first
place, the ease and narrative skill with which the story is
told in the difficult form of autobiography, and, secondly,
the vivacity of the characters. Jacob himself is, as will
have been seen already, a piebald sort of personage,
entirely devoid of scruple in some ways, but not ill-
natured, and with his own points of honour. He is
perfectly natural, and so are all the others (not half of
whom have been mentioned) as far as they go. The
cross sister and the " kind " one ; the false prude and false
dévote Mme. de Ferval, and the jolly, reckless, rather
coarse Mme. de Fécour ; the tyrannical, corrupt, and
licentious financier, with others more slightly drawn,
are seldom, if ever, out of drawing. The contemporary

wash of colour passes, as it should, into something "fast"; you are in the Paris of the Regency, but you are at the same time in general human time and place, if not in eternity and infinity.

The general selection, however, of *Marianne* as Marivaux's masterpiece is undoubtedly right, though in more *Marianne—* ways than one it has less engaging power than outline of the *Paysan*, and forebodes to some extent, if the story. it does not actually display, the boring qualities which novels of combined analysis and jargon have developed since. The opening is odd : the author having apparently transplanted to the beginning of a novel the promiscuous slaughter with which we are familiar at the end of a play. Marianne (let us hail the appearance of a Christian-named heroine at last), a small child of the tenderest years, is, with the exception of an ecclesiastic, who takes to his heels and gets off, the sole survivor of a coachful of travellers who are butchered by a gang of footpads,[1] because two of the passengers have rashly endeavoured to defend themselves. Nothing can be found out about the child—an initial improbability, for the party has consisted of father, mother, and servants, as well as Marianne. But the good *curé* of the place and his sister take charge of her, and bring her up carefully (they are themselves "gentle-people," as the good old phrase, now doubtless difficult of application, went) till she is fifteen, is very pretty, and evidently must be disposed of in some way, for her guardians are poor and have no influential relations. The sister, however, takes her to Paris—whither she herself goes to secure, if possible, the succession of a relative—to try to obtain some situation. But the inheritance proves illusory; the sister falls ill at Paris and dies there; while the brother is disabled, and his living has to be, if not transferred to, provided with, a substitute. This second massacre (for the brother dies soon) provides Marivaux with the

---

[1] The much greater blood-thirstiness of the French highwayman, as compared with the English, has been sometimes attributed by humanitarians to the "wheel"—and has often been considered by persons of sense as justifying that implement.

situation he requires—that of a pretty girl, alone in the capital, and absolutely unfriended. Fortunately a bene-volent Director knows a pious gentleman, M. de Climal, who is fond of doing good, and also, as it appears shortly by the story, of pretty girls. Marianne, with the earliest touch of distinct " snobbishness "—let it be proudly pointed out that the example is not English,[1]—declines to go into service, but does not so much mind being a shop-girl, and M. de Climal establishes her with his *lingère*, a certain Mme. Dutour.

This good lady is no procuress, but her morals are of a somewhat accommodating kind, and she sets to work, experiencing very little difficulty in the process, to remove Marianne's scruples about accepting presents from M. de Climal—pointing out, very logically, that there is no obligation to (as Chesterfield put it not long after) *payer de sa personne*; though she is naturally some-what disgusted when the gifts take the form of handsome *lingerie* bought at another shop. When this, and a dress to match, are made up, Marianne as naturally goes to church to show them: and indulges in very shrewd if not particularly amiable remarks on her " even-Christians "—a delightful English archaism, which surely needs no apology for its revival. Coming out, she slips and sprains her ankle, whereupon, still naturally, appears the inevitable young man, a M. de Valville, who, after endless amicable wrangling, procures her a coach, but not without an awkward meeting. For M. de Valville turns out to be the nephew of M. de Climal; and the uncle, with a lady, comes upon the nephew and Marianne; while, a little later, each finds the other in turn at the girl's feet. Result : of course more than suspicion on the younger man's part, and a mixture of wrath and desire to hurry matters on the elder's. He offers Marianne a regular (or irregular) " establishment " at a dependent's of his own, with a small income settled upon her, etc. She refuses indignantly, the indignation being rather sus-

---

[1] The Devil's Advocate may say that Marianne turns out to be of English extrac-tion after all—but it is not Marivaux who tells us so.

piciously divided between her two lovers ; is " planted
there " by the old sinner Climal, and of course requested
to leave by Mme. Dutour ; returns all the presents,
much to her landlady's disgust, and once more seeks,
though in a different mood, the shelter of the Church.
Her old helper the priest for some time absolutely declines
to admit the notion of Climal's rascality ; but fortunately
a charitable lady is more favourable, and Marianne gets
taken in as a *pensionnaire* at a convent. Climal, whose
sister and Valville's mother the lady turns out to be,
falls ill, repents, confesses, and leaves Marianne a
comfortable annuity. Union with Valville is not
opposed by the mother ; but other members of the
family are less obliging, and Valville himself wanders
after an English girl of a Jacobite exiled family, Miss
Warton (Varthon). The story then waters itself out,
before suddenly collapsing, with a huge and uninteresting *Histoire d'une Religieuse.* Whereat some folk may
grumble ; but others, more philosophically, may be
satisfied, in no uncomplimentary sense, without hearing
what finally made Marianne Countess of Three Stars, or
indeed knowing any more of her actual history.

For in fact the entire interest of *Marianne* is concentrated in and on Marianne herself, and the fact that
this is so at once makes continuation superfluous, and
gives the novel its place in the history of fiction. We
have quite enough, as it is, to show us—as the Princess
Augusta said to Fanny Burney of the ill-starred last
of French "Mesdames Royales"—"what sort of a
girl she is." And her biographer has made her a
very interesting sort of girl, and himself in making
her so, a very interesting, and almost entirely novel, sort
of novelist. To say that she is a wholly attractive
character would be entirely false, except from the point
of view of the pure student of art. She is technically
virtuous, which is, of course, greatly to her credit.[1]

[1] To question or qualify Marianne's virtue, even in the slightest degree, may seem
ungracious ; for it certainly withstands what to some girls would have been the hardest
test of all—that is to say, not so much the offer of riches if she consents, as the
apparent certainty of utter destitution if she refuses. At the same time, the Devil's

She is not bad-blooded, but if there were such a word as "good-blooded" it could hardly be applied to her. With all her preserving borax- or formalin-like touch of "good form," she is something of a minx. She is vain, selfish—in fact wrapped up in self—without any sense of other than technical honour. But she is very pretty (which covers a multitude of sins), and she is really clever.

Yet the question at issue is not whether one can approve of Marianne, nor whether one can like her, nor even whether, approving and liking her or not, *Importance of Marianne herself.* one could fall in love with her "for her comely face and for her fair bodie," as King Honour did in the ballad, and as *homo rationalis* usually, though not invariably, does fall in love. The question is whether Marivaux has, in her, created a live girl, and to what extent he has mastered the details of his creation. The only critical answer, I think, must be that he has created such a girl, and that he has not left her a mere outline or type, but has furnished the house as well as built it. She is, in the particular meaning on which Mr. Hardy's defenders insist, as "pure" a "woman" as Tess herself. And if there is a good deal missing from her which fortunately some women have, there is nothing in her

---

Advocate need not be a Kelly or a Cockburn to make out some damaging suggestions. Her vague, and in no way solidly justified, but decided family pride seems to have a good deal to do with her refusal; and though this shows the value of the said family pride, it is not exactly virtue in itself. Still more would appear to be due to the character of the suit and the suitor. M. de Climal is not only old and unattractive; not only a sneak and a libertine; but he is a clumsy person, and he has not, as he might have done, taken Marianne's measure. The mere shock of his sudden transformation from a pious protector into a prospective "keeper," who is making a bid for a new concubine, has evidently an immense effect on her quick nervous temperament. She is not at all the kind of girl to like to be the plaything of an old man; and she is perfectly shrewd enough to see that vengeance, and fear as regards his nephew, have as much as anything else, or more, to do with the way in which he brusques his addresses and hurries his gift. Further, she has already conceived a fancy, at least, for that nephew himself; and one sees the "jury droop," as Dickens has put it, with which the Counsel of the Prince of the Air would hint that, if the offers had come in a more seductive fashion from Valville himself, they might not have been so summarily rejected. But let it be observed that these considerations, while possibly unfair to Marianne, are not in the least derogatory to Marivaux himself. On the contrary, it is greatly to his credit that he should have created a character of sufficient lifelikeness and sufficient complexity to serve as basis for "problem"-discussions of the kind.

which some women have not, and not so very much which
the majority of women have not, in this or that degree.
It is difficult not to smile when one compares her quintessence with the complicated and elusive caricatures of
womanhood which some modern novel-writers—noisily
hailed as *gyno*sophists—have put together, and been
complimented on putting together. What is more, she
is perhaps the first nearly complete character of the kind
that had been presented in novel at her date. This is
a great thing to say for Marivaux, and it can be said without the slightest fear of inability to support the saying.[1]

Although, therefore, we may not care much to enter
into calculations as to the details of the indebtedness of
Marivaux
and
Richardson—
"Mari-
vaudage." Richardson to Marivaux, some approximations
of the two, for critical purposes, may be useful.
One may even see, without too much folly of
the Thaumast kind, an explanation, beyond that
of mere idleness, in the Frenchman's inveterate habit of
not completing. He did not want you to read him "for
the story"; and therefore he cared little for the story itself,
and nothing at all for the technical finishing of it. The
stories of both his characteristic novels are, as has been
fairly shown, of the very thinnest. What he did want to
do was to analyse and "display," in a half-technical
sense of that word, his characters; and he did this as no
man had done before him, and as few have done since,
though many, quite ignorant of their indebtedness, have
taken the method from him indirectly. In the second
place, his combination of method and phrase is for infinite
thoughts. This combination is not *necessary*; there is,
to take up the comparative line, nothing of it in Richardson, nothing in Fielding, nothing in Thackeray. A few
French eighteenth-century writers have it in direct
imitation of Marivaux himself; but it dies out in France,
and in the greatest novel-period there is nothing of it.
It revives in the later nineteenth century, especially with

---

[1] To put the drift of the above in other words, we do not *need* to hear any more
of Marianne in any position, because we have had enough shown us to know generally
what she would do, say, and think, in all positions.

us, and, curiously enough, if we look back to the beginnings of Romance in Greek, there is a good deal there,
the crown and flower being, as has been before remarked,
in Eustathius Macrembolita, but something being noticeable in earlier folk, especially Achilles Tatius, and the
trick having evidently come from those rhetoricians [1] of
whose class the romancers were a kind of offshoot. It
is, however, only fair to say that, if Marivaux thought in
intricate and sometimes startling ways, his actual expression is never obscure. It is a maze, but a maze with an
unbroken clue of speech guiding you through it. [2]

A few examples of method and style may now be
given. Here is Marianne's criticism—rather uncannily
shrewd and very characteristic both of her subject
Examples:—and of herself—of that peculiar placid plump-
Marianne on ness which has been observed by the profane
the *physique* in devout persons, especially in the Roman
and *moral* Church and in certain dissenting sects (Angli-
of Prioresses
and Nuns. canism does not seem to be so favourable to
it), and in " persons of religion " (in the technical sense)
most of all.

This Prioress was a short little person, round and white, with a
double chin, and a complexion at once fresh and placid. You
never see faces like that in worldly persons : it is a kind of *embonpoint* quite different from others—one which has been formed
more quietly and more methodically—that is to say, something
into which there enters more art, more fashioning, nay, more
self-love, than into that of such as we. [3]

As a rule, it is either temperament, or feeding, or laziness and
luxury, which give *us* such of it as we have. But in order to acquire
the kind of which I am speaking, it is necessary to have given oneself
up with a saintlike earnestness to the task. It can only be the result

---

[1] It has been observed that there is actually a Meredithian quality in Aristides of
Smyrna, though he wrote no novel. A tale in Greek, to illustrate the parallel, would
be an admirable subject for a University Prize.

[2] Two descriptions of "Marivaudage" (which, by the way, was partly anticipated
by Fontenelle)—both, if I do not mistake, by Crébillon *fils*—are famous : " Putting down
not only everything you said and thought, but also everything you would like to have
thought and said, but did not," and, " Introducing to each other words which never had
thought of being acquainted." Both of these perhaps hit the modern forms of the
phenomenon even harder than they hit their original butt.

[3] It is only fair to the poor Prioress to say that there is hardly a heroine in fiction
who is more deeply in love with her own pretty little self than Marianne.

of delicate, loving, and devout attention to the comfort and well-being of the body. It shows not only that life—and a healthy life—is an object of desire, but that it is wanted soft, undisturbed, and dainty; and that, while enjoying the pleasures of good health, the person enjoying it bestows on herself all the pettings and the privileges of a perpetual convalescence.

Also this religious plumpness is different in outward form from ours, which is profane of aspect; it does not so much make a face fat, as it makes it grave and decent; and so it gives the countenance an air, not so much joyous, as tranquil and contented.

Further, when you look at these good ladies, you find in them an affable exterior; but perhaps, for all that, an interior indifference. Their faces, and not their souls, give you sympathy and tenderness; they are comely images, which seem to possess sensibility, and which yet have merely a surface of kindness and sentiment.[1]

Acute as this is, it may be said to be somewhat displaced—though it must be remembered that it is the Marianne of fifty, " Mme. la Comtesse de * * *," who is supposed to be writing, not the Marianne of fifteen. No such objection can be taken to what follows.

[*She is, after the breach with Climal, and after Valville has earlier discovered his wicked uncle on his knees before her, packing up the—well! not wages of iniquity, but baits for it—to send back to the giver. A little " cutting " may be made.*]

Thereupon I opened my trunk to take out first the newly bought linen. " Yes, M. de Valville, yes! " said I, pulling it out, " you shall learn to know me and to think of me as you ought." This thought spurred me on, so that, without my exactly thinking of it, it was rather to him than to his uncle that I was returning the whole, all the more so that the return of linen, dress, and money, with a note I should write, could not fail to disabuse Valville, and make him regret the loss of me. He had seemed to me to possess a generous soul; and I applauded myself beforehand on the sorrow which he would feel

She returns the gift-clothes.

---

[1] One does not know whether it was prudence, or that materialism which, though he was no *philosophe*, he shared with most of his contemporaries, which prevented Marivaux from completing this sharp though mildly worded criticism. The above-mentioned profane have hinted that both the placidity and the indifference of the persons concerned, whether Catholic or Calvinist, arise from their certainty of their own safety in another world, and their looking down on less "guaranteed" creatures in this. It may be just permissible to add that a comparison of Chaucer's and Marivaux's prioresses will suggest itself to many persons, and should be found delectable by all fit ones.

at having treated so outrageously a girl so worthy of respectful treatment as I was—for I saw in myself, confessedly, I don't know how many titles to respect.

In the first place I put my bad luck, which was unique ; to add to this bad luck I had virtue, and they went so well together ! Then I was young, and on the top of it all I was pretty, and what more do you want ?   If I had arranged matters designedly to render myself an object of sympathy, to make a generous lover sigh at having maltreated me, I could not have succeeded better ; and, provided I hurt Valville's feelings, I was satisfied.   My little plan was never to see him again in my life-time ; and this seemed to me a very fair and proud one ; for I loved him, and I was even very glad to have loved him, because he had perceived my love, and, seeing me break with him, notwithstanding, would see also what a heart he had had to do with.

The little person goes on very delectably describing the packing, and how she grudged getting rid of the pretty things, and at last sighed and wept—whether for-herself, or Valville, or the beautiful gown, she didn't know.   But, alas ! there is no more room, except to salute her as the agreeable ancestress of all the beloved coquettes and piquant minxes in prose fiction since.   Could anything handsomer be said of her creator ?

It is, though an absolute and stereotyped common-place, an almost equally absolute necessity, to begin any notice of the Abbé Prévost by remarking that nothing of his voluminous work is now, or has been for a long time, read, except *Manon Lescaut.* It may be added, though one is here repeating predecessors to not quite the same extent, that nothing else of his, in fiction at least, is worth reading.   The faithful few who do not dislike old criticism may indeed turn over his *Le Pour et* [*le*] *Contre* not without reward. But his historical and other compilations [1]—his total production in volumes is said to run over the hundred, and the standard edition of his *Œuvres Choisies* extends to thirty-nine not small ones—are admittedly worthless. As to his minor novels—if one may use that term, albeit

Prévost.

---

[1] His books on Margaret of Anjou and William the Conqueror are odd crosses between actual historical essays and the still unborn historical novel.

they are as major in bulk as they are minor in merit

His minor —opinions of importance, and presumably
novels—the founded on actual knowledge, have differed
opinions on
them of somewhat strangely. Sainte-Beuve made some-
Sainte-Beuve. thing of a fight for them, but it was the Sainte-
Beuve of almost the earliest years (1831), when, according
to a weakness of beginners in criticism, he was a little
inclined " to be different," for the sake of difference.
Against *Cléveland* even he lifts up his heel, though in a
rather unfortunate manner, declaring the reading of the
greater part to be " aussi fade que celle d' *Amadis*." Now
to some of us the reading of *Amadis* is not " fade " at all.
But he finds some philosophical and psychological passages of merit. Over the *Mémoires d'un Homme de
Qualité*—that huge and unwieldy galleon to which the
frail shallop of *Manon* was originally attached, and which
has long been stranded on the reefs of oblivion, while its
fly-boat sails for ever more—he is quite enthusiastic,
finds it, though with a certain relativity, " natural,"
" frank," and " well-preserved," gives it a long analysis,
actually discovers in it " an inexpressible savour " surpassing modern " local colour," and thinks the handling
of it comparable in some respects to that of *The Vicar of
Wakefield* ! The *Doyen de Killérine*—the third of Prévost's long books—is " infinitely agreeable," " si l'on y
met un peu de complaisance." (The Sainte-Beuve of
later years would have noticed that an infinity which has
to be made infinite by a little complaisance is curiously
finite). The later and shorter *Histoire d'une Grecque
moderne* is a *joli roman*, and *gracieux*, though it is not so
charming and subtle as Crébillon *fils* would have made it,
and is " knocked off rather haphazardly." Another
critic of 1830, now perhaps too much forgotten, Gustave

And of Planche, does not mention the *Grecque*, and
Planche. brushes aside the three earlier and bigger
books rather hastily, though he allows " interest " to
both *Cléveland* and the *Doyen*. Perhaps, before " coming
to real things " (as Balzac once said of his own work) in
Manon, some remarks, not long, but first-hand, and

2 A

based on actual reading at more than one time of life, as
to her very unreal family, may be permitted here, though
they may differ in opinion from the judgment of these
two redoubtable critics.

I do not think that when I first wrote about Prévost
(I had read *Manon* long before) more than thirty years
ago, in a *Short History of French Literature*,
I paid very much attention to these books.
I evidently had not read the *Grecque Moderne*,
for I said nothing about it. Of the others I
said only that they are " romances of adventure, occupy-
ing a middle place between those of Lesage and Marivaux." It is perfectly true, but of course not very "in-
going," and whatever reading I then gave any of them
had not left very much impression on my mind, when
recently, and for the purpose of the present work, I took
them up again, and the *Histoire* as well. This last is the
story of a young modern Greek slave named Théophé
(a form of which the last syllable seems more modern
than Greek), who is made visible in full harem by her
particularly complaisant master, a Turkish pasha, to a
young Frenchman, admired and bought by this Frenchman (the relater of the story), and freed by him. He
does not at first think of making her his mistress, but later
does propose it, only to meet a refusal of a somewhat
sentimental-romantic character, though she protests not
merely gratitude, but love for him. The latter part of
the book is occupied by what Sainte-Beuve calls " delicate " ambiguities, which leave us in doubt whether her
" cruelty " is shown to others as well, or whether it is
not. In suggesting that Crébillon would have made it
charming, the great critic has perhaps made another of
those slips which show the novitiate. The fact is that
it is an exceedingly dull book : and that to have made it
anything else, while retaining anything like its present
" propriety," either an entire metamorphosis of spirit,
which might have made it as passionate as *Manon* itself,
or the sort of filigree play with thought and phrase which
Marivaux would have given, would be required. As a

The books themselves—Histoire d'une Grecque Moderne.

" Crébillonnade " (*v. inf.*) it might have been both pleasant and subtle, but it could only have been made so by becoming exceedingly indecent.

Still, its comparative (though only comparative) shortness, and a certain possibility rather than actuality
Cléveland. of interest in the situation,[1] may recommend this novel at least to mercy. If the present writer were on a jury trying *Cléveland*, no want of food or fire should induce him to endorse any such recommendation in regard to that intolerable book. It is, to speak frankly, one of the very few books—one of the still fewer novels—which I have found it practically impossible to read even in the " skim and skip and dip " fashion which should, no doubt, be only practised as a work of necessity (*i.e.* duty to others) and of mercy (to oneself) on extraordinary occasions, but which nobody but a prig and a pedant will absolutely disallow. Almost the only good thing I can find to say about it is that Prévost, who lived indeed for some time in England, is now and then, if not always, miraculously correct in his proper names. He can actually spell Hammersmith! Other merit—and this is not constant (in the dips which I have actually made, to rise exhausted from each, and skip rather than even skim to the rest)—I can find none. The beginning is absurd and rather offensive, the hero being a natural son of Cromwell by a woman who has previously been the mistress of Charles I. The continuation is a mish-mash of adventure, sometimes sanguinary, but never exciting, travel (in fancy parts of the West Indies, etc.), and the philosophical disputations which Sainte-Beuve found interesting. As for the end, no two persons seem quite agreed what *is* the end. Sainte-Beuve speaks of it as an attempted suicide of the hero—the most justifiable of all his actions, if he had succeeded. Prévost himself, in the Preface to the *Doyen de Killérine*, repeats

---

[1] Mlle. de Launay, better known as Mme. de Staal-Delaunay, saw, as most would have seen, a resemblance in this to the famous Mlle. Aïssé's. But the latter was bought as a little child by her provident " protector," M. de Ferréol. Mlle. Aïssé herself had earlier read the *Mémoires d'un Homme de Qualité* and did not think much of them. But this was the earlier part. It would be odd if she had not appreciated *Manon* had she read it : but she died in the year of its appearance.

an earlier disavowal (which he says he had previously made in Holland) of a fifth volume, and says that his own work ended with the murder of Cleveland by one of the characters. Again, this is a comprehensible and almost excusable action, and might have followed, though it could not have preceded, the other. But if it was the end, the other was not. A certain kind of critic may say that it is my duty to search and argue this out. But, for my part, I say as a reader to *Cléveland*, " No more *in* thee my steps shall be, For ever and for ever." [1]

Le Doyen de Killérine is not perhaps so .utterly to be excommunicated as *Cléveland*, and, as has been said above,
Le Doyen de some have found real interest in it. It is not,
Killérine. however, free either from the preposterousness or from the dulness of the earlier book, though the first characteristic is less preposterous as such preposterousness goes. The Dean of Killérine (Coleraine) is a Roman Catholic dean, just after the expulsion of James II., when, we learn with some surprise, that neighbourhood was rather specially full of his co-religionists. He is a sort of *lusus naturae*, being bow-legged, humpbacked, pot-bellied, and possessing warts on his brows, which make him a sort of later horned Moses. The eccentricity of his appearance is equalled by that of his conduct. He is the eldest son of an Irish gentleman (nobleman, it would sometimes seem), and his father finds a pretty girl who is somehow willing to marry him. But, feeling no vocation for marriage, he suggests to her (a suggestion perhaps unique in fiction if not in fact) that she should marry his father instead. This singular match comes off, and a second family results, the members of which are, fortunately, not *lusus naturae*, but a brace of very handsome and accomplished boys, George and Patrick, and an extremely pretty girl, Rosa. Of these three, their parents dying when they are something short of full age, the excellent

---

[1] The excellent but rather stupid editor of the [Dutch] *Œuvres Choisies* above noticed has given abstracts of Prévost's novels as well as of Richardson's, which the Abbé translated. These, with Sainte-Beuve's of the *Mémoires*, will help those who want something more than what is in the text, while declining the Sahara of the original. But, curiously enough, the Dutchman does not deal with the end of *Cléveland*.

dean becomes a sort of guardian. He takes them to
the exiled court of Versailles, and his very hen-like
anxieties over the escapades of these most lively ducklings
supply the main subject of the book. It might have
been made amusing by humorous treatment, but Prévost
had no humour in him : and it might have been made
thrilling by passion, but he never, except in the one great
little instance, compressed or distilled his heaps and
floods of sensibility and sensationalism into that. The
scene where a wicked Mme. de S—— plays, and almost
outplays, Potiphar's wife to the good but hideous Dean's
Joseph is one of the most curious in novel-literature,
though one of the least amusing.

We may now go back to the *Mémoires*, partly in compliment to the master of all mid-nineteenth-century
The *Mémoires* critics, but more because of their almost
d'un Homme fortuitous good luck in ushering *Manon* into
de Qualité. the world. There is something in them of
both their successors, *Cléveland* and the *Doyen*, but
it may be admitted that they are less unreadable
than the first, and less trivial than the second. The
plan—if it deserve that name—is odd, one marquis
first telling his own fortunes and voyages and what-
nots, and then serving as Mentor (the application, though
of course not original, is inevitable) to another marquis
in further voyages and adventures. There are Turkish
brides and Spanish murdered damsels ; English politics
and literature, where, unfortunately, the spelling *does*
sometimes break down ; glances backward, in " Histoires " of the *Grand Siècle*, at meetings with Charles de
Sévigné, Racine, etc. ; mysterious remedies, a great deal
of moralising, and a great deal more of weeping. Indeed
the whole of Prévost, like the whole of that " Sensibility
Novel " of which he is a considerable though rather
an outside practitioner, is pervaded with a gentle rain
of tears wherein the personages seem to revel—
indeed admit that they do so—in the midst of their
woes.

On the whole, however, the youthful—or almost

youthful—half-wisdom of Sainte-Beuve is better justified

of its preference for the *Mémoires* than of other things in the same article. I found it, reading it later on purpose and with " preventions " rather the other way, very much more readable than any of its companions (*Manon* is not its companion, but in a way its constituent), without being exactly readable *simpliciter*. All sorts of curious things might be dug out of it: for instance, quite at the beginning, a more definite declaration than I know elsewhere of that curious French title-system which has always been such a puzzle to Englishmen. " Il *se fit appeler* le Comte de . . . et, se voyant un fils, il *lui donna* celui de Marquis de . . ." There is a good deal in it which makes us think that Prévost had read Defoe, and something which makes it not extravagant to fancy that Thackeray had read Prévost. But once more " let us come to the real things—let us speak of " *Manon Lescaut*.

It would be a very interesting question in that study of literature—rather unacademic, or perhaps academic

in the best sense only—which might be so near and is so far—whether the man is most to be envied who reads *Manon Lescaut* for the first time in blissful ignorance of these other things, and even of what has been said of them ; or he who has, by accident or design, toiled through the twenty volumes of the others and comes upon Her. My own case is the former: and I am far from quarrelling with it. But I sometimes like to fancy—now that I have reversed the proceeding— what it would have been like to dare the voices—the endless, dull, half-meaningless, though not threatening voices—of those other books—to refrain even from the appendix to the *Mémoires* as such, and never, till the *Modern Greekess* has been dispatched, return to and possess the entire and perfect jewel of *Manon*. I used to wonder, when, for nearer five and twenty than twenty years, I read for review hundreds of novels, English and French, whether anybody would ever repeat Prévost's extraordinary spurt and " sport " in this wonderful little

book.   I am bound to say that I never knew an instance.
The " first book " which gives a promise—dubious it may
be, but still promising—and is never followed by anything
that fulfils this, is not so very uncommon, though less
common in prose fiction than in poetry.   The not so
very rare " single-speech " poems are also not real
parallels.   It is of the essence of poetry, according
Its to almost every theory, that it should be, occa-
uniqueness. sionally at least, inexplicable and unaccount-
able.   I believe that every human being is capable of
poetry, though I should admit that the exhibition of the
capability would be in most cases—I am sure it would be
in my own—" highly to be deprecated."   But with a
sober prose fiction of some scope and room and verge it
is different.   The face of Helen ; the taste of nectar ;
the vision of the clouds or of the sea ; the passion of a
great action in oneself or others ; the infinite poignancy
of suffering or of pleasure, may draw—once and never
again—immortal verse from an exceedingly mortal
person.   Such things might also draw a phrase or a paragraph of prose.   But they could not extract a systematic
and organised prose tale of some two hundred pages,
each of them much fuller than those of our average six-
shilling stuff ; and yet leave the author, who had never
shown himself capable of producing anything similar
before, unable to produce anything in the least like it
again.   I wonder that the usual literary busybodies have
never busied themselves—perhaps they have, for during
a couple of decades I have not had the opportunity of
knowing everything that goes on in French literature
as I once did—with Prévost, demonstrating that *Manon*
was a posthumous work of the Regent (who was a clever
man), or an expression of a real passion which lay at the
back of Richelieu's debauchery, or written by some
unknown author from whom the Abbé bought it, and
who died early, or something else of the kind.

   There does not, however, appear to be the slightest
chance or hope or fear (whichever expression be preferred)
of the kind.   Although Prévost elsewhere indulges—as

everybody else for a long time in France and England alike did, save creative geniuses like Fielding—in transparently feigned talk about the origins of his stories, he was a very respectable man in his way, and not at all likely to father or to steal any one else's work in a disreputable fashion. There are no other claimants for the book : and though it may be difficult for a foreigner to find the faults of style that Gustave Planche rebukes in Prévost generally, there is nothing in the mere style of *Manon* which sets it above the others.

For once one may concede that the whole attraction of the piece, barring one or two transient but almost Shakespearian flashes of expression—such as the famous " Perfide Manon ! Perfide ! " when she and Des Grieux first meet after her earliest treason—is to be found in its marvellous humanity, its equally marvellous grasp of character, and the intense, the absolutely shattering pathos of the relations of the hero and heroine. There are those, of course, who make much of the *persona tertia,* Tiberge, the virtuous and friendly priest, who has a remarkable command of money for a not highly placed ecclesiastic, lends it with singular want of circumspection, and then meddles with the best of intentions and the most futile or mischievous of results. Very respectable man, Tiberge ; but one with whom *on n'a que faire.* Manon and Des Grieux ; Des Grieux and Manon—these are as all-sufficient to the reader as Manon was more than sufficient to Des Grieux, and as he, alas ! was, if only in some ways, *in*sufficient to Manon.

One of the things which are nuisances in Prévost's other books becomes pardonable, almost admirable, in this. His habit of incessant, straight-on narration by a single person, his avoidance of dialogue properly so called, is, as has been noted, a habit common to all these early novels, and, to our taste if not to that of their early readers, often disastrous. Here it is a positive advantage. Manon speaks very little ; and so much the better. Her " comely face and her fair bodie " (to repeat once more a beloved quotation) speak for her to the ruin of her lover

and herself—to the age-long delectation of readers. On
the other hand, the whole speech is Des Grieux', and
never was a monologue better suited or justified. The
worst of such things is usually that there are in them all
sorts of second thoughts of the author. There is none of
this littleness in the speech of Des Grieux. He is a
gentle youth in the very best sense of the term, and as we
gather—not from anything he says of himself, but from
the general tenor—by no means a " wild gallant ";
affectionate, respectful to his parents, altogether " douce,"
and, indeed, rather (to start with) like Lord Glenvarloch
in *The Fortunes of Nigel.* ·He meets Manon (Prévost
has had the wits to make her a little older than her lover),
and *actum est de* both of them.

But Manon herself ? She talks (it has been said)
very little, and it was not necessary that she should talk
The much. If she had talked as Marianne talks, we
character of should probably hate her, unless, as is equally
its heroine. probable, we ceased to take any interest in
her. She is a girl not of talk but of deeds : and her
deeds are of course quite inexcusable. But still that
great and long unknown verse of Prior, which tells how
a more harmless heroine did various things—

As answered the end of her being created,

fits her, and the deeds create her in their process, according
to the wonderful magic of the novelist's art. Manon
is not in the least a Messalina ; it is not what Messalina
wanted that she wants at all, though she may have no
physical objection to it, and may rejoice in it when it is
shared by her lover. Still less is she a Margaret of
Burgundy, or one of the tigress-enchantresses of the
Fronde, who would kill their lovers after enjoying their
love. It has been said often, and is beyond all doubt
true, that she would have been perfectly happy with Des
Grieux if he had fulfilled the expostulations of George the
Fourth as to Mr. Turveydrop, and had not only been
known to the King, but had had twenty thousand a year.
She wants nobody and nothing but him, as far as the

" Him " is concerned : but she does not want him in a
cottage. And here the subtlety comes in. She does not
in the least mind giving to others what she gives him,
provided that they will give her what he cannot give.
The possibility of this combination is of course not only
shocking to Mrs. Grundy, but deniable by persons who
are not Mrs. Grundy at all. Its existence is not really
doubtful, though hardly anybody, except Prévost and
(I repeat it, little as I am of an Ibsenite) Ibsen in the *Wild
Duck*, has put it into real literature. Manon, like Gina
and probably like others, does not really think what she
gives of immense, or of any great, importance. People
will give her, in exchange for it, what she does think of
great, of immense importance ; the person to whom she
would quite honestly prefer to give it cannot give her these
other things. And she concludes her bargain as com-
posedly as any *bonne* who takes the basket to the shops
and " makes its handle dance "—to use the French idiom
—for her own best advantage. It does annoy her when
she has to part from Des Grieux, and it does annoy her
that Des Grieux should be annoyed at what she does.
But she is made of no nun's flesh, and such soul as she
has is filled with much desire for luxury and pleasure.
The desire of the soul will have its way, and the flesh
lends itself readily enough to the satisfaction thereof.

So, too, there is no such instance known to me of the
presentation of two different characters, in two different
ways, so complete and yet so idiosyncratic
in each. Sainte-Beuve showed what he was
going to become (as well, perhaps, as something
which he was going to lose) in his slight but suggestive remarks on the relation of Des Grieux to the
average *roué* hero of that most *roué* time. It is only a
suggestion ; he does not work it out. But it is worth
working out a little. Des Grieux is *ab initio*, and in some
ways *usque ad finem*, a sort of *ingénu*. He seems to have
no vicious tendencies whatever; and had Manon not
supervened, might have been a very much more exemplary Chevalier de Malte than the usual run of those

dignitaries, who differed chiefly from their uncrossed comrades and brethren in having no wife to be unfaithful to. He is never false to Manon—the incident of one ot Manon's lovers trying vainly to tempt his rival, with a pretty cast-off mistress of his own, is one of the most striking features of the book. He positively reveres, not his mother, who is dead, and reverence for whom would be nothing in a Frenchman, but his father, and even, it would seem, his elder brother—a last stretch of reverence quite unknown to many young English gentlemen who certainly would not do things that Des Grieux did. Except when Manon is concerned, it would seem that he might have been a kind ot saint—as good at least as Tiberge. But his love for her and his desire for her entirely saturate and transform him. That he disobeys his father and disregards his brother is nothing : we all do that in less serious cases than his, and there is almost warrant for it in Scripture. But he cheats at play (let us frankly allow, remembering Grammont and others, that this was not in France the unpardonable sin that it has—for many generations, fortunately—been with us), at the suggestion of his rascally left-hand brother-in-law, in order to supply Manon's wants. He commits an almost deliberate (though he makes some excuses on this point) and almost cowardly murder, on an unarmed lay-brother of Saint-Sulpice, to get to Manon. And, worst of all, he consents to the stealing of moneys given to her by his supplanters in order to feed her extravagance. After this his suborning the King's soldiers to attack the King's constabulary on the King's highway to rescue Manon is nothing. But observe that, though it is certainly not " All for God," it *is* " All for Her." And observe further that all these things—even the murder— were quite common among the rank and file of that French aristocracy which was so busily hurrying on the French Revolution. Only, Des Grieux himself would pretty certainly not have done them if She had never come in his way. And he tells it all with a limpid and convincing clarity (as they would say now) which puts the whole thing before us. No apology is made, and no apology is needed. It is written in the books of the chronicles of Manon and Des Grieux; in the lives of Des Grieux and Manon, suppose them ever to have existed or to exist, it could not but happen.

It is surely not profane (and perhaps it has been done The already) to borrow for these luckless, and, if inevitable- you will, somewhat graceless persons, the ness of both and the words of the mighty colophon of Matthew inestimable- Arnold's most unequal but in parts almost ness of their history. finest poem, at least the first and last lines:

> So rest, for ever rest, immortal pair,

and

> The rustle of the eternal rain of love.

Nor is it perhaps extravagant to claim for their creator— even for their reporter—the position of the first person who definitely vindicated for the novel the possibility of creating a passionate masterpiece, outstripping *La Princesse de Clèves* as *Othello* outstrips *A Woman Killed with Kindness*. As for the enormous remainder of him, if it is very frankly negligible by the mere reader, it is not quite so by the student. He was very popular, and, careless book-maker as he was in a very critical time, his popularity scarcely failed him till his horrible death.[1] It can scarcely be said that, except in the one great cited instance, he heightened or intensified the French novel, but he enlarged its scope, varied its interests, and combined new objectives with its already existing schemes, even in his less good work. In *Manon Lescaut* itself he gave a masterpiece, not only to the novel, not only to France, but to all literature and all the world.

The unfortunate nobleman as to whom Dickens has Crébillon *fils*. left us in doubt whether he was a peer in his own right or the younger son of a Marquis or Duke, pronounced Shakespeare "a clayver man."

---

[1] He had a fit of apoplexy when walking, and instead of being bled was actually cut open by a village super-Sangrado, who thought him dead and only brought him to life—to expire actually in torment.

It was perhaps, in the particular instance, inadequate though true. I hardly know any one in literature of whom it is truer and more adequate than it is of Claude Prosper Jolyot de Crébillon the younger, commonly called Crébillon *fils*.[1] His very name is an abomination to Mrs. Grundy, who probably never read, or even attempted to read, one of his naughty books. Gray's famous tribute[2] to him—also known to a large number who are in much the same case with Mrs. Grundy—is distinctly patronising. But he is a very clever man indeed, and the cleverness of some of his books—especially those in dialogue—is positively amazing.

At the same time it is of the first importance to make the due provisos and allowances, the want of The case which so frequently causes disappointment, against him. if not positive disgust, when readers have been induced by unbalanced laudation to take up works of the literature of other days. There are, undoubtedly, things—many and heavy things—to be said against Crébillon. A may say, " I am not, I think, *Mr.* Grundy : but I cannot stand your Crébillon. I do not like a world where all the men are apparently atheists, and all the women are certainly the other thing mentioned in Donne's famous line. It disgusts and sickens me : and I will have none of it, however clever it may be." B, not quite agreeing with A, may take another tone, and observe, " He *is* clever and he *is* amusing : but he is terribly monotonous. I do not mind a visit to the ' oyster-bearing shores ' now and then, but I do not want to live in Lampsacus. After all, even in a pagan Pantheon, there are other divinities besides a cleverly palliated Priapus and a comparatively ladylike Cotytto. Seven volumes of however delicately veiled ' sculduddery ' are nearly as bad as a whole evening's golf-talk in a St.

---

[1] Crébillon *père*, tragedian and academician, is one of the persons who have never had justice done to them : perhaps because they never quite did justice to themselves. His plays are unequal, rhetorical, and as over-heavy as his son's work is over-light. But, if we want to find the true tragic touch of verse in the French eighteenth century, we must go to him.
[2] " Be it mine to read endless romances of Marivaux and Crébillon."

Andrews hotel, or a long men's dinner, where everybody but yourself is a member of an Amateur Dramatic Society." The present writer is not far from agreeing with B, while he has for A a respect which disguises no shadow of a sneer. Crébillon does harp far too much on one string, and that one of no pure tone : and even the individual handlings of the subject are chargeable throughout his work with *longueurs*, in the greater part of it with sheer tedium. It is very curious, and for us of the greatest importance, to notice how this curse of long-windedness, episodic and hardly episodic " inset," endless talk " about it and about it," besets these pioneers of the modern novel. Whether it was a legacy of the " Heroics " or not it is difficult to say. I think it was—to some extent. But, as we have seen, it exists even in Lesage ; it is found conspicuously in Marivaux ; it " advances insupportably " in Prévost, except when some God intervenes to make him write (and to stop him writing) *Manon*; and it rests heavily even on Crébillon, one of the lightest, if not one of the purest, of literary talents. It is impossible to deny that he suffers from monotony of general theme : and equally impossible to deny that he suffers from spinning out of particular pieces. There is perhaps not a single thing of his which would not have been better if it had been shorter : and two of his liveliest if also most risky pieces, *La Nuit et le Moment* and *Le Hasard au Coin du Feu*, might have been cut down to one half with advantage, and to a quarter with greater advantage still.

There are, however, excuses for Crébillon : and though it may seem a rash thing to say, and even one which gives the case away, there is, at least in these two and parts of *Le Sopha*, hardly a page—even of the parts which, if " cut," would improve the work as a whole— that does not in itself prove the almost elfish cleverness now assigned to him.

The great excuse for him, from the non-literary point of view, is that this world of his—narrow though crowded as it is, corrupt, preposterous, inviting the Judgment that came after it as no period perhaps has ever done,

except that immediately before the Deluge, that of the
earlier Roman empire, and one other—was a real
world in its day, and left, as all real things do,
an abiding mark and influence on what followed.
One of the scores and almost hundreds of
sayings which distinguish him, trivial as he
seems to some and no doubt disgusting as
he seems to others, is made by one of his
most characteristic and most impudent but not most
offensive heroes à la Richelieu, who says, not in soliloquy
nor to a brother roué, but to the mistress of the moment :
" If love-making is not always a pleasure, at any rate it
is always a kind of occupation." That is the keynote
of the Crébillon novel : it is the handbook, with illustrative examples, of the business, employment, or vocation
of flirting, in the most extensive and intensive meanings
of that term comprehensible to the eighteenth century.

Now you should never scamp or hurry over business :
and Crébillon observes this doctrine in the most praiseworthy fashion. With the thorough practic-
ality of his century and of his nation (which
has always been in reality the most practical
of all nations) he sets to work to give us the
ways and manners of his world. It is an odd
world at first sight, but one gets used to its conventions. It is a world of what they used to call,
in the later eighteenth and early nineteenth century,
" high fellers " and of great ladies, all of whom—saving
for glimpses of military and other appointments for the
men, which sometimes take them away and are useful
for change of scene, of theatres, balls, gaming-tables
for men and women both—" have nothing in the world
to do " but carry on that occupation which Clitandre of
" The Night and the Moment," at an extremely suitable
time and in equally appropriate circumstances, refers to
in the words quoted above. There are some other
oddities about this world. In some parts of it nobody
seems to be married. Mrs. Grundy, and even persons
more exercised in actual fact than Mrs. Grundy, would

Side notes:
For the defendant— The veracity of his artificiality and his consummate cleverness.

The Crébillon-esque atmosphere and method.

368 HISTORY OF THE FRENCH NOVEL

expect them all to be, and to neglect the tie. But sometimes Crébillon finds it easier to mask this fact. Often
his ladies are actual widows, which is of course very
convenient, and might be taken as a sign of grace in him
by Mrs. G. : oftener it is difficult to say what they are
legally. They are nearly all duchesses or marchionesses
or countesses, just as the men hold corresponding ranks :
and they all seem to be very well off. But their sole
occupation is that conducted under the three great verbs,
Prendre ; Avoir ; Quitter. These verbs are used rather
more frequently, but by no means exclusively, of and by
the men. Taking the stage nomenclature familiar to
everybody from Molière, which Crébillon also uses in
some of his books, though he exchanges it for proper
names elsewhere, let us suppose a society composed of
Oronte, Clitandre, Eraste, Damis (men), and Cydalise,
Célie, Lucinde, Julie (ladies). Oronte " takes " Lucinde,
" possesses " her for a time, and " quits " her for Julie,
who has been meanwhile " taken," " possessed," and
" quitted " by Eraste. Eraste passes to the conjugation
of the three verbs with Cydalise, who, however, takes
the initiative of " quitting " and conjugates " take " in
joint active and passive with Damis. Meanwhile Célie
and Clitandre are similarly occupied with each other,
and ready to " cut in " with the rest at fresh arrangements. These processes require much serious conversation, and this is related with the same mixture of gravity
and irony which is bestowed on the livelier passages of
action.

The thing, in short, is most like an intensely intricate
dance, with endless figures—with elaborate, innumerable,
and sometimes indescribable stage directions. And the
whole of it is written down carefully by M. Claude
Prosper Jolyot de Crébillon.

He might have occupied his time much better ?
Perhaps, as to the subject of occupation. But with
that we have, if not nothing, very little to do. The
point is, How did he handle these better-let-alone
subjects ? and what contribution, in so handling them,

did he make to the general development of the novel ?

I am bound to say that I think, with the caution given above, he handled them, when he was at his best, singularly well, and gave hints, to be taken or left as they chose, to handlers of less disputable subjects than his.

One at least of the most remarkable things about him is connected with this very disputableness. Voltaire and Sterne were no doubt greater men than Crébillon *fils* : and though both of them dealt with the same class of subject, they also dealt with others, while he did not. But, curiously enough, the reproach of sniggering, which lies so heavily on Laurence Sterne and François Arouet, does not lie on Crébillon. He has an audacity of grave persiflage [1] which is sometimes almost Swiftian in a lower sphere : and it saves him from the unpardonable sin of the snigger. He has also—as, to have this grave persiflage, he almost necessarily must have—a singularly clear and flexible style, which is only made more piquant by the " -assiez's " and " -ussiez's " of the older language. Further, and of still greater importance for the novelist, he has a pretty wit, which sometimes almost approaches humour, and, if not a diabolically, a *diablotin*-ically acute perception of human nature as it affects his subject. This perception rarely fails : and conventional, and very unhealthily conventional, as the Crébillon world is, the people who inhabit it are made real people. He is, in those best things of his at least, never " out." We can see the ever-victorious duke (M. de Clerval of the *Hasard* is perhaps the closest to the Richelieu model of all Crébillon's coxcomb-gallants), who, even after a lady has given him most unequivocal proofs of her affection, refuses for a long time, if not finally, to say that he loves her, because he has himself a graduated scheme of values in that direction, and though she may have touched his heart, etc., she has not quite come up to his " love "

---

[1] Learnt, no doubt, to a great extent from Anthony Hamilton, with whose family, as has been noticed, he had early relations.

standard.[1]   And we know, too, though she is less common, the philosophical Marquise herself, who, " possessing " the most notoriously inconstant lover in all Paris (this same M. de Clerval, it happens), maintains her comparative indifference to the circumstance, alleging that even when he is most inconstant he is always " very affectionate, though a little *extinguished.*"   And in fact he goes off to her from the very fireside, where such curious things have chanced.   Extravagant as are the situations in *La Nuit et le Moment,* the other best thing, they are, but for the *longueurs* already censured, singularly verisimilar on their own postulates.   The trusty coachman, who always drives particularly slowly when a lady accompanies his master in the carriage, but would never think of obeying the check-string if his master's own voice did not authorise it ; the invaluable *soubrette* who will sit up to any hour to play propriety, when her mistress is according a *tête-à-tête,* but who, most naturally, always falls asleep— these complete, at the lower end of the scale, what the dukes and the countesses have begun at the upper.   And Crébillon, despite his verbosity, is never at a loss for pointed sayings to relieve and froth it up.   Nor are these mere *mots* or *pointes* or conceits—there is a singular amount of life-wisdom in them, and a short anthology might be made here, if there were room for it, which would entirely vindicate the assertion.

It is true that the praises just given to Crébillon do not (as was indeed hinted above) apply to the whole Inequality of his work, or even to the larger part of it. of his   An unfavourable critic might indeed say that, general work—a   in strictness, they only apply to parts of *Le* survey of it. *Sopha* and to the two little dialogue-stories just referred to.   The method is, no doubt, one by no means easy to apply on the great scale, and the

---

[1] He goes further, and points out that, as she is his *really* beloved Marquise's most intimate friend, she surely wouldn't wish him to declare himself false to that other lady?—having also previously observed that, after what has occurred, he could never think of deceiving his Célie herself by false declarations. These topsy-turvinesses are among Crébillon's best points, and infinitely superior to the silly " platitudes reversed " which have tried to produce the same effect in more recent times.

restriction of the subject adds to the difficulty. The
longest regular stories of all, *Ah! Quel Conte!* and *Le
Sopha* itself, though they should have been mentioned
in reverse order, are resumptions of the Hamiltonian
idea [1] of chaining things on to the *Arabian Nights*.
Crébillon, however, does not actually resuscitate Shahriar
and the sisters, but substitutes a later Caliph, Shah
Baham, and his Sultana. The Sultan is exceedingly
stupid, but also very talkative, and fond of interrupting
his vizier and the other tale-tellers with wiseacreries ;
the Sultana is an acute enough lady, who governs her
tongue in order to save her neck. The framework is
not bad for a short story, but becomes a little tedious
when it is made to enshrine two volumes, one of them
pretty big. It is better in *Le Sopha* than in *Ah! Quel
Conte!* and some of the tales that it gives us in the former
are almost equal to the two excepted dialogues. Moreover, it is unluckily true that *Ah! Quel Conte!* (an
ejaculation of the Sultana's at the beginning) might be,
as Crébillon himself doubtless foresaw, repeated with a
sinister meaning by a reader at the end. *Tanzaï et
Néadarné* or *L'Écumoire*, another fairy story, though
livelier in its incidents than *Ah! Quel Conte!*—nay,
though it contains some of Crébillon's smartest sayings,
and has perhaps his nicest heroine,—is heavy on the
whole, and in it, the author's *gauffre*-like lightness of
" impropriety " being absent, the tone approaches nearer
to that dismallest form of literature or non-literature—
the deliberate obscene.

Les Égarements du Cœur et de l'Esprit, on the other
hand—one of the author's earliest books—is the furthest
from that most undesirable consummation, and one of
the most curious, if not of the most amusing, of all. It
recounts, from the mouth of the neophyte himself, the
" forming " of a very young man—almost a boy—to
this strange kind of commerce, by an elderly, but not yet

[1] It has been said more than once that Crébillon had early access to Hamilton's MSS.
He refers directly to the Facardins in *Ah! Quel Conte!* and makes one of his characters claim to be grand-daughter of Cristalline la Curieuse herself.

old, and still attractive coquette, Madame de Lursay, whose earlier life has scandalised even the not easily scandalisable society of her time (we are not told quite how), but who has recovered a reputation very slightly tarnished. The hero is flattered, but for a long time too timid and innocent to avail himself of the advantages offered to him ; while, before very long, Madame de Lursay's wiles are interfered with by an " Inconnue-Ingénue," with whom he falls in deep calf-love of a quasi-genuine kind. The book includes sketches of the half-bravo gallants of the time, and is not negligible : but it is not vividly interesting.

Still less so, though they contain some very lively passages, and are the chief *locus* for Crébillon's treatment of the actual trio of husband, wife, and lover, are the *Lettres de la Marquise de M——— au Comte de P———*. The scene in which the husband—unfaithful, peevish, and a *petit maître*—enters his wife's room to find an ancient, gouty Marquis, who cannot get off his knees quick enough, and terminates the situation with all the *aplomb* of the Regency, is rather nice : and the gradual " slide " of the at first quite virtuous writer (the wife herself, of course) is well depicted. But love-letters which are neither half-badinage—which these are not—nor wholly passionate— which these never are till the last,[1] when the writer is describing a state of things which Crébillon could not manage at all—are very difficult things to bring off, and Claude Prosper is not quite equal to the situation.

It will thus be seen that the objectors whom we have called A and B—or at least B—will find that they or he need not read all the pages of all the seven volumes to justify their views : and some other work, still to be mentioned, completes the exhibition. I confess, indeed, once more unblushingly, that I have not read every page of them myself. Had they fallen in my way forty years ago I should, no doubt, have done so ; but forty years of critical

---

[1] Nor perhaps even then, for passion is absolutely unknown to our author. One touch of it would send the curious Rupert's drop of his microcosm to shivers, as *Manon Lescaut* itself in his time, and *Adolphe* long after, show.

experience and exercise give one the power, and grant
one the right, of a more summary procedure in respect of
matter thus postponed, unless it is perceived to be of
very exceptional quality. These larger works of Crébillon's are not good, though they are not by any means so
bad as those of Prévost. There are nuggets, of the shrewd
sense and the neat phrase with which he has been credited,
in nearly all of them : and these the skilled prospector
of reading gold will always detect and profit by. But,
barring the possibility of a collection of such, the *Œuvres
Choisies* of Crébillon need not contain more than the best
parts of *Le Sopha*, the two comparatively short dialogue-
tales, and a longer passage or two from *Tanzaï et Néadarné*.
It would constitute (I was going to say a respectable, but as
that is hardly the right word, I will say rather) a tolerable
volume. Even in a wider representation *Les Heureux
Orphelins* and *Lettres Athéniennes* would yield very little.

The first begins sensationally with the discovery, by a
young English squire in his own park, of a foundling girl
and boy—*not* of his own production—whom he brings up ;
and it ends with a tedious description of how somebody
founded the first *petite maison* in England—a worthy
work indeed. It is also noteworthy for a piece of bad
manners, which, one regrets to say, French writers have
too often committed ; lords and ladies of the best known
names and titles in or near Crébillon's own day—such
as Oxford, Suffolk, Pembroke—being introduced with
the utmost nonchalance.[1] Our novelists have many
faults to charge themselves with, and Anthony Trollope,
in *The Three Clerks*, produced a Frenchman with perhaps
as impossible a name as any English travesty in French
literature. But I do not remember any one introducing,
in a *not* historical novel, a Duc de la Tremoille or a member
of any of the branches of Rohan, at a time when actual
bearers of these titles existed in France. As for the
Lettres Athéniennes, if it were not for completeness, I
should scarcely even mention them. Alcibiades is the

---

[1] Some remarks are made by "Madame *Hépenny*"—a very pleasing phoneticism,
and, though an actual name, not likely to offend any actual person.

374 HISTORY OF THE FRENCH NOVEL CH.

chief male writer; Aspasia the chief female; but all of them, male and female, are equally destitute of Atticism and of interest. The contrast of the contrasts between Crébillon's and Prévost's best and worst work is one of the oddest things in letters. One wonders how Prévost came to write anything so admirable as *Manon Lescaut*; one wonders how Crébillon came to write anything so insufficient as the two books just criticised, and even others.

It may be said, " This being so, why have you given half a chapter to these two writers, even with Lesage and Marivaux to carry it off ? " The reason is that this is (or attempts to be) a history of the French novel, and that, in such a history, the canons of importance are not the same as those of the novel itself. *Gil Blas*, *Marianne*, *Manon Lescaut*, and perhaps even *Le Hasard au Coin du Feu* are interesting in themselves ; but the whole work of their authors is important, and therefore interesting, to the historical student. For these authors carried further —a great deal further—the process of laying the foundations and providing the materials and plant for what was to come. Of actual masterpieces they only achieved the great, but not *equally* great, one of *Gil Blas* and the little one of *Manon Lescaut*. But it is not by masterpieces alone that the world of literature lives in the sense of prolonging its life. One may even say—touching the unclean thing paradox for a moment, and purifying oneself with incense, and salt, and wine—that the masterpieces of literature are more beautiful and memorable and delectable in themselves than fertile in results. They catch up the sum of their own possibilities, and utter it in such a fashion that there is no more to say in that fashion. The dreary imitation *Iliads*, the impossible sham *Divina Commedia*s, the Sheridan-Knowles Shakespearian plays, rise up and terrify or bore us. Whereas these second-rate experimenters, these adventurers in quest of what they themselves hardly know, strike out paths, throw seed, sketch designs which others afterwards pursue, and plant out, and fill up. There are probably

not many persons now who would echo Gray's wish for
eternal romances of either Marivaux or Crébillon ; and
the accompanying remarks in the same letter on *Joseph
Andrews*, though they show some appreciation of the
best characters, are quite inappreciative of the merit of
the novél as a whole. For eternal variations of *Joseph
Andrews*, "*Passe !*" as a French Gray might have said.

Nevertheless, I am myself pretty sure that Marivaux
at least helped Richardson and Fielding, and there can
be no doubt that Crébillon helped Sterne. And what is
more important to our present purpose, they and their
companions in this chapter helped the novel in general,
and the French novel in particular, to an extent far more
considerable. We may not, of course, take the course of
literary history—general or particular—which has been,
as the course which in any case must have been. But
at the same time we cannot neglect the facts. And it is
a quite certain fact that, for the whole of the last half of
the eighteenth century, and nearly the whole of the first
quarter of the nineteenth, the French novel, as a novel,
made singularly little progress. We shall have to deal
in the next chapter, if not in the next two chapters, with
at least two persons of far greater powers than any one
mentioned in the last two. But we shall perhaps be able
to show cause why even Voltaire and Rousseau, why
certainly Diderot, why Marmontel and almost every
one else till we come, not in this volume, to Chateaubriand, whose own position is a little doubtful, somehow
failed to attain the position of a great advancer of the
novel.

These others, whatever their shortcomings, *had*
advanced it by bringing it, in various ways, a great deal
nearer to its actual ideal of a completed picture of real
human life. Lesage had blended with his representation
a good deal of the conventional picaresque ; Marivaux
had abused preciousness of language and petty psychology ; Prévost, save in that marvellous windfall of his
and the Muses which the historian of novels can hardly
mention without taking off his hat if he has one on, or

making his best bow if he has not, had gone wandering after impossible and uninteresting will-o'-the-wisps ; Crébillon had done worse than " abide in his inn," he had abided almost always in his polite [1] bordello. But all of them had meant to be real ; and all of them had, if only now and then, to an extent which even Madame de la Fayette had scarcely achieved before, attained reality.

[1] No sneer is intended in this adjective. Except in one or two of the personages of *Les Égarements*, Crébillon's intended gentlemen are nearly always well-bred, however ill-moralled they may be, and his ladies (with the same caution) are ladies. It is with him, in this last point at any rate, as with our own Congreve, whom he rather closely resembles in some ways : though I was amused the other day to find some twentieth-century critical objections to actresses' rendering of *Love for Love* as " too well-bred." The fact is that the tradition of " breeding " never broke down in France till the *philosophe* period, while with us it lasted till—when shall we say?

CHAPTER XI

THE *PHILOSOPHE* NOVEL

The use of the novel for 'purpose'—Voltaire. It has been for some time a commonplace—though, like most commonplaces, it is probably much more often simply borrowed than an actual and (even in the sense of *communis*) original perception of the borrowers — that nothing shows the comparative inevitableness of the novel in the eighteenth century better than the use of it by persons who would, at other times, have used quite different forms to subserve similar purposes. The chief instance of this with us is, of course, Johnson in *Rasselas*, but it is much more variously and voluminously, if not in any single instance much better, illustrated in France by the three great leaders of the *philosophe* movement ; by considerable, if second-rate figures, more or less connected with that movement, like Marmontel and Bernardin de Saint-Pierre ; and by many lesser writers.

There can be no question that, in more ways than one, Voltaire [1] deserves the first place in this chapter, not only by age, by volume, and by variety of general literary ability, but because he, perhaps more than any of the

---

[1] His *verse* tales, even if stories in verse had not by this time fallen out of our proper range, require little notice. The faculty of "telling" did not remain with him here, perhaps because it was prejudicially affected by the "dryness" and unpoetical quality of his poetry, and of the French poetry of the time generally, perhaps for other reasons. At any rate, as compared with La Fontaine or Prior, he hardly counts. *Le Mondain, Le Pauvre Diable*, etc., are skits or squibs in verse, not tales. The opening one of the usual collection, *Ce qui plaît aux Dames*,—in itself a flat rehandling of Chaucer and Dryden,—is saved by its charming last line—

Ah ! croyez-moi, l'erreur a son mérite,

a rede which he himself might well have recked.

others, is a tale-teller born. That he owes a good deal
to Hamilton, and something directly to Hamilton's
master, Saint-Évremond, has been granted elsewhere;
but that he is dependent on these models to such an
extent as to make his actual production unlikely if the
models had not been ready for him, may be roundly
denied. There are in literature some things which must
have existed, and of which it is not frivolous to say that
if their actual authors had not been there, or had declined
to write them, they would have found somebody else to
do it. Of these, *Candide* is evidently one, and more
than one of *Candide's* smaller companions have at least
something of the same characteristic. Yet one may
also say that if Voltaire himself had not written these,
he must have written other things of the kind. The
mordant wit, the easy, fluent, rippling style, so entirely
free from boisterousness yet with constant " wap " of
wavelet and bursting of foam-bubble; above all, the pure
unadulterated faculty of tale-telling, must have found vent
and play somehow. It had been well if the playfulness
had not been, as playfulness too often is, of what contemporary English called an " unlucky " (that is, a
" mischievous ") kind; and if the author had not been
constantly longing to make somebody or many bodies
uncomfortable,[1] to damage and defile shrines, to exhibit
a misanthropy more really misanthropic, because less
passionate and tragical, than Swift's, and, in fact, as
his patron, persecutor, and counterpart, Frederick the
Jonathan-Wildly Great, most justly observed of him,
to " play monkey - tricks," albeit monkey - tricks of
immense talent, if not actually of genius. If the
recent attempts to interpret monkey-speech were to come
to something, and if, as a consequence, monkeys were
taught to write, one may be sure that prose fiction would
be their favourite department, and that their productions
would be, though almost certainly disreputable, quite cer-

---

[1] In justice to Voltaire it ought to be remembered that no less great, virtuous, and
religious a person than Milton ranked as one of the two objects to which "all mortals
most aspire," " to offend your enemies."

tainly amusing. In fact there would probably be some among these which would be claimed, by critics of a certain type, as hitherto unknown works of Voltaire himself.

Yet if the straightforward tale had not, owing to the influences discussed in the foregoing chapters, acquired a firm hold, it is at least possible that he would not have adopted it (for originality of form was not Voltaire's *forte*), but would have taken the dialogue, or something else capable of serving his purpose. As it was, the particular field or garden had already been marked out and hedged after a fashion ; tools and methods of cultivation had been prepared ; and he set to work to cultivate it with the application and intelligence recommended in the famous moral of his most famous tale—a moral which, it is only fair to say, he did carry out almost invariably. A garden of very questionable plants was his, it may be ; but that is another matter. The fact and the success of the cultivation are both undeniable.

At the same time, Voltaire—if indeed, as was doubted just now, he be a genius at all—is not a genius, or even General a djinn, of the kind that creates and leaves characteristics something Melchisedec-like; alone and isolated of his tales. from what comes before and what comes after. He is an immense talent—perhaps the greatest talent-but-not-genius ever known—who utilises and improves and develops rather than invents. It is from this that his faculty of never boring, except when he has got upon the Scriptures, comes ; it is because of this also that he never conceives anything really, simply, absolutely *great*. His land is never exactly weary, but there is no imposing and sheltering and refreshing rock in it. These *romans* and *contes* and *nouvelles* of his stimulate, but they do not either rest or refresh. They have what is, to some persons at any rate, the theatrical quality, not the poetical or best-prosaic. But as nearly consummate works of art, or at least craft, they stand almost alone.

He had seen [1] the effect of which the fairy tale of the

---

[1] It has been noted above (see p. 266, *note*), how some have directly traced *Zadig* to the work of a person so much inferior to Hamilton as Gueulette.

sophisticated kind was capable, and the attraction which
it had for both vulgars, the great and the small : and he
made the most of it. He kept and heightened its *haut
goût* ; he discarded the limitations to a very partial and
conventional society which Crébillon put on it ; but he
limited it in other ways to commonplace and rather vulgar
fancy, without the touches of imagination which Hamilton
had imparted. Yet he infused an even more accurate
appreciation of certain phases of human nature than those
predecessors or partial contemporaries of his who were
discussed in the last chapter had introduced ; he *practical-
ised* it to the *n*th, and he made it almost invariably subordinate to a direct, though a sometimes more or less
ignoble, purpose. There is no doubt that he had learnt
a great deal from Lucian and from Lucian's French
imitators, perhaps as far back as Bonaventure des Périers ;
there is, I think, little that he had added as much as he
could add from Swift.[1] His stolen or borrowed possessions from these sources, and especially this last, remind
one in essence rather of the pilferings of a " light horse-
man," or river-pirate who has hung round an " old
three-decker," like that celebrated in Mr. Kipling's admirable, poem, and has caught something even of the light
from " her tall poop-lanterns shining so far above him,"
besides picking up overboard trifles, and cutting loose
boats and cables. But when he gets to shore and to his
own workshop, his almost unequalled power of sheer
wit, and his general craftsmanship, bring out of these
lootings something admirable in its own way.

Candide is almost "great," and though the breed of Dr.
Pangloss in its original kind is nearly extinct, the England
which suffered the approach, and has scarcely
Candide. yet allowed itself to comprehend the reality,
of the war of 1914, ought to know that there have been
and are Pangloss*otins* of almost appalling variety. The
book does not really require the smatches of sculduddery,

[1] *Micromégas* and one or two other things are avowed—in fact, Voltaire, if not
" great," was " big " enough to make as a rule little secret of his levies on others ; and
he had, if not an adequate, a considerable, respect for the English Titan.

which he has smeared over it, to be amusing ; for its life-likeness carries it through. As is well known, Johnson admitted the parallel with *Rasselas*, which is among the most extraordinary coincidences of literature. I have often wondered whether anybody ever took the trouble to print the two together. There would be many advantages in doing so ; but they might perhaps be counterbalanced by the fact that some of the most fervent admirers of *Rasselas* would be infinitely shocked by *Candide*, and that perhaps more of the special lovers of *Candide* would find themselves bored to extinction by *Rasselas*. Let those who can not only value but enjoy both be thankful, but not proud.

Many people have written about the Consolations of Old Age, not seldom, it is to be feared, in a " Who's afraid ?" sort of spirit. But there are a few, an apple or two by the banks of Ulai, which we may pluck as the night approaches. One is almost necessarily accidental, for it would be rash and somewhat cold-blooded to plan it. It consists in the reading, after many years, of a book once familiar almost to the point of knowing by heart, and then laid aside, not from weariness or disgust, but merely as things happened. This, as in some other books mentioned in this history, was the case with the present writer in respect of *Candide*. From twenty to forty, or thereabouts, I must have read it over and over again ; the sentences drop into their places almost without exercising any effort of memory to recognise them. From forty to seventy I do not think I read it at all ; because no reason made reading necessary, and chance left it untouched on the shelf. Sometimes, as everybody knows, the result of renewed acquaintance in such cases is more or less severe disappointment ; in a few of the happiest, increased pleasure. But it is perhaps the severest test of a classic (in the exact but limited sense of that word) that its effect shall be practically unchanged, shall have been established in the mind and taste with such a combination of solidity and *netteté*, that no change is possible. I do not think I have ever

found this to be more the case than with the history of
Candide (who was such a good fellow, without being
in the least a prig, as I am afraid Zadig was, that one
wonders how Voltaire came to think of him) and of
Mademoiselle Cunégonde (nobody will ever know
anything about style who does not feel what the continual
repetition in Candide's mouth of the " Mademoiselle "
does) of the indomitable Pangloss, and the detestable
baron, and the forgivable Paquette, and that philosopher
Martin, who did *not* " let cheerfulness break in," and the
admirable Cacambo, who shows that, much as he hated
Rousseau, Voltaire himself was not proof against the
noble savage mania.[1]

As a piece (*v. sup.*) of art or craft, the thing is beyond praise or pay. It could not be improved, on its
own specification, except that perhaps the author might
have told us how Mademoiselle Cunégonde, who had
kept her beauty through some very severe experiences,
suddenly lost it. It is idle as literary, though not as
historical, criticism to say, as has been often said about
the Byng passage, that Voltaire's smartness rather " goes
off through the touch-hole," seeing that the admiral's
execution did very considerably " encourage the others."
It is superfluous to urge the unnecessary " smuts," which
are sometimes not in the least amusing. All these and
other sought-for knots are lost in the admirable smooth-
ness of this reed, which waves in the winds of time with
unwitherable greenness, and slips through the hand, as
you stroke it, with a coaxing tickle. To praise its detail
would again be idle—nobody ought to read such praise
who can read itself; and if anybody, having read its first
page, fails to see that it is, and how it is, praiseworthy,
he never will or would be converted if all the eulogies
of the most golden-mouthed critics of the world were
poured upon him in a steady shower. As a whole it is
undoubtedly the best, and (except part of *Zadig*) it is
nowhere else matched in the book of the romances of
Voltaire, while for those who demand " purposes " and

---

[1] Cacambo was not a savage, but he had savage or, at least, non-European blood in him.

"morals," it stands almost alone. It is the comic "Vanity of Human Wishes" in prose, as *Rasselas* is the tragic or, at least, serious version : and, as has been said, the two make an unsurpassable sandwich, or, at least, *tartine*. Nor could it have been told, in any other way than by prose fiction, with anything like the same effect, either as regards critical judgment or popular acceptance.

Zadig, as has been indicated already, probably ranks in point of merit next to *Candide*. If it had *Zadig* and stopped about half-way, there could be no its satellites. doubt about the matter. The reader is caught at once by one of the most famous and one of the most Voltairian of phrases, " Il savait de la métaphysique ce qu'on a su dans tous les âges, c'est-à-dire fort peu de chose," a little more discussion of which saying, and of others like it, may perhaps be given later. The successive disappointments of the almost too perfect [1] hero are given with the simplicity just edged with irony which is Voltaire's when he is at his best, though he undoubtedly learnt it from the masters already assigned, and— the suggestion would have made him very angry, and would probably have attracted one of his most Yahoo-like descents on this humble and devoted head—from Lesage. But though the said head has no objection—much the reverse—to " happy endings," the romance-finish of *Zadig* has always seemed to it a mistake. Still, how many mistakes would one pardon if they came after such a success ? *Babouc*, the first of those miniature *contes* (they are hardly " tales " in one sense), which Voltaire managed so admirably, has the part-advantage part-disadvantage of being likewise the first of a series of satires on French society, which, piquant as they are, would certainly have been both more piquant and more weighty if there had been fewer of them. It is full of the perfect, if not great, Voltairian phrases,—the involuntary *Mene Tekel*, " Babouc conclut qu'une telle société ne pouvait subsister "; the palinode after a fashion, " Il s'affection-

---

[1] Not in the Grandisonian sense, thank heaven ! But as has been hinted, he is a *little* of a prig.

nait à la ville, dont le peuple était doux [oh ! Nemesis !] poli et bien-faisant, quoique léger, médisant et plein de vanité " ; and the characteristic collection of parallel between Babouc and Jonah, surely not objectionable even to the most orthodox, " Mais quand on a été trois jours dans le corps d'une baleine on n'est pas de si bonne humeur que quand on a été à l'opéra, à la comédie et qu'on a soupé en bonne compagnie."

Memnon, ou La Sagesse Humaine is still less of a tale, only a lively sarcastic apologue ; but he would be a strange person who would quarrel with its half-dozen pages, and much the same may be said of the *Voyages de Scarmentado.* Still, one feels in both of them, and in many of the others, that they are after all not much more than chips of an inferior rehandling of *Gulliver.* *Micromégas,* as has been said, does not disguise its composition as something of the kind ; but the desire to annoy Fontenelle, while complimenting him after a fashion as the " dwarf of Saturn," and perhaps other strokes of personal scratching, have put Voltaire on his mettle. You will not easily find a better

Micromégas. Voltairism of its particular class than, " Il faut bien citer ce qu'on ne comprend point du tout, dans la langue qu'on entend le moins." But, as so often happens, the cracker in the tail is here the principal point. Micromegas, the native of Sirius, who may be Voltaire himself, or anybody else—after his joint tour through the universes (much more amusing than that of the late Mr. Bailey's Festus), with the smaller but still gigantic Saturnian—writes a philosophical treatise to instruct us poor microbes of the earth, and it is taken to Paris, to the secretary of the Academy of Science (Fontenelle himself). " Quand le sécretaire l'eut ouvert il ne vit rien qu'un livre tout blanc. ' Ah ! ' dit-il, ' je m'en étais bien douté.' " Voltaire did a great deal of harm in the world, and perhaps no solid good ; [1] but it is things like this which make one feel

---

[1] He has been allowed a great deal of credit for the Calas and some other similar businesses. It is unlucky that the injustices he combated were somehow always *clerical*, in this or that fashion.

that it would have been a loss had there been no Voltaire.

L'Ingénu, which follows *Candide* in the regular editions, falls perhaps as a whole below all these, and
L'Ingénu.   *L'Homme aux Quarante Ecus*, which follows it, hardly concerns us at all, being mere political economy of a sort in dialogue. *L'Ingénu* is a story, and has many amusing things in it. But it is open to the poser that if Voltaire really accepted the noble savage business he was rather silly, and that if he did not, the piece is a stale and not very biting satire. It is, moreover, somewhat exceptionally full (there is only one to beat it) of the vulgar little·sniggers which suggest the eunuch even more than the schoolboy, and the conclusion is abominable. The seducer and, indirectly, murderer Saint-Pouange may only have done after his kind in regard to Mlle. de Saint-Yves ; but the Ingénu himself neither acted up to his Huron education, nor to his extraction as a French gentleman, in forgiving the man and taking service under him.

La Princesse de Babylone is more like Hamilton than almost any other of the tales, and this, it need hardly
La Princesse be said here, is high praise, even for a work of
de Babylone. Voltaire. For it means that it has what we commonly find in that work, and also something that we do not. But it has that defect which has been noticed already in *Zadig*, and which, by its absence, constitutes the supremacy of *Candide*. There is in it a sort of "break in the middle." The earlier stages of the courtship of Formosante are quite interesting ; but when she and her lover begin ·separately to wander over the world, in order that their chronicler may make satiric observations on the nations thereof, one feels inclined to say, as Mr. Mowbray Morris said to Mr. Matthew Arnold (who thought it was Mr. Traill) :

Can't you give us something new ?

Le Blanc et le Noir rises yet again, and though·it has perhaps not many of Voltaire's *mots de flamme*, it is more

2 c

of a fairy moral tale—neither a merely fantastic mow, nor sicklied over with its morality—than almost any

Some minors.

other. It is noteworthy, too, that the author has hardly any recourse to his usual clove of garlic to give seasoning. *Jeannot et Colin* might have been Marmontel's or Miss Edgeworth's, being merely the usual story of two rustic lads, one of whom becomes rich and corrupt till, later, he is succoured by the other. Now Marmontel and Miss Edgeworth are excellent persons and writers ; but their work is not work for Voltaire.

The *Lettres d'Amabed*[1] are the dirtiest and the dullest of the whole batch, and the *Histoire de Jenni*, though not particularly dirty, is very dull indeed, being the " History of a Good Deist," a thing without which (as Mr. Carlyle used to say) we could do. The same sort of " purpose " mars *Les Oreilles du Comte de Chesterfield*, in which, after the first page, there is practically nothing about Lord Chesterfield or his deafness, but which contains a good deal of Voltaire's crispest writing, especially the definition of that English freedom which he sometimes used to extol. With thirty guineas a year,[2] the materialist doctor Sidrac informs the unfortunate Goudman, who has lost a living by the said deafness, " on peut dire tout ce qu'on pense de la compagnie des Indes, du parlement, de nos colonies, du roi, de l'état en général, de l'homme et de Dieu—ce qui est un grand amusement." But the piece itself would be more amusing if Voltaire could let the Bible alone, though he does not here come under the stroke of Diderot's sledge-hammer as he does in *Amabed*.

One seldom, however, echoes this last wish, and re-members the stroke referred to, more than in reference

---

[1] It was said of them at their appearance "[cet] ouvrage est sans goût, sans finesse, sans invention, un rabâchage de toutes les vieilles polissonneries que l'auteur a débitées sur Moïse et Jésus-Christ, les prophètes et les apôtres, l'Église, les papes, les cardinaux, les prêtres et les moines ; nul intérêt, nulle chaleur, nulle vraisemblance, force ordures, une grosse gaieté. . . . Je n'aime pas la religion : mais je ne la hais pas assez pour trouver cela bon." The authorship, added to the justice of it, makes this one of the most crushing censures ever committed to paper ; for the writer was Diderot (*Œuvres*, Ed. Assézat, vi. 36).

[2] It is a singular coincidence that this was exactly the sum which Johnson mentioned to Boswell as capable of affording decent subsistence in London during the early middle eighteenth century.

to *Le Taureau Blanc*. Here, if there were nobody who reverenced the volume which begins with *Genesis* and ends with *Revelation*, the whole thing would be utterly dead and stupid : except for a few crispnesses of the Egyptian Mambrès, which could, almost without a single exception, have been uttered on any other theme. The identification of Nebuchadnezzar with the bull Apis is not precisely an effort of genius ; but the assembling, and putting through their paces, of Balaam's ass and Jonah's whale, the serpent of Eden, and the raven of the Ark, with the three prophets Jeremiah, Ezekiel, and Daniel, and with an historical King Amasis and an unhistorical Princess Amaside thrown in, is less a *conte à dormir debout*, as Voltaire's countrymen and he himself would say, than a tale to make a man sleep when he is running at full speed—a very dried poppy-head of the garden of tales. On the other hand, the very short and very early *Le Crocheteur Borgne*, which, curiously enough, Voltaire never printed, and the not much longer *Cosi-Sancta*, which he printed in his queer ostrich-like manner, are, though a little naughty, quite nice ; and have a freshness and demure grace about their naughtiness which contrasts remarkably with the ugly and wearisome snigger of later work.

The half-dozen others,[1] filling scarce twenty pages between them, which conclude the usual collection, _{Voltaire—the} need little comment; but a " Kehl " note _{Kehl edition} to the first of them is for considerable _{—and Plato.} thoughts :

> M. de Voltaire s'est égayé quelquefois sur Platon, dont le galimatias, regardé autrefois comme sublime, a fait plus de mal au genre humain qu'on ne le croit communément.

One should not hurry over this, but muse a little. In copying the note, I felt almost inclined to write " *M. de* Platon " in order to put the whole thing in a consistent key ; for somehow " Plato " by itself, even in the

---

[1] *Songe de Platon, Bababec et les Fakirs, Aventure de la Mémoire, Les Aveugles Juges des Conteurs, Aventure Indienne,* and *Voyage de la Raison.*

French form, transports one into such a very different world that adjustment of clocks and compasses becomes at once necessary and difficult. " Galimatias " is good, " autrefois " is possibly better, the " evils inflicted on the human race " better still, but *égayé* perhaps best of all. The monkey, we know, makes itself gay with the elephant, and probably would do so with the lion and the tiger if these animals had not an unpleasant way of dealing with jokers. And the tomtit and canary have, no doubt, at least private agreement that the utterances of the nightingale are *galimatias*, while the carrion crow thinks the eagle a fool for dwelling so high and flying so much higher. But as for the other side of the matter, how thin and poor and puerile even those smartest things of Voltaire's, some of which have been quoted and praised, sound, if one attempts to read them after the last sentence of the *Apology*, or after passage on passage of the rest of the " galimatias " of Plato !

Nevertheless, though you may answer a fool according to his folly, you should not, especially when he is not a fool absolute, judge him solely thereby. When Voltaire was making himself gay with Plato, with the Bible, and with some other things, he was talking, not merely of something which he did not completely understand, but of something altogether outside the range of his comprehension. But in the judgment of literature the process of " cancelling " does not exist. A quality is not destroyed or neutralised by a defect, and, properly speaking (though it is hard for the critic to observe this), to strike a balance between the two is impossible. It is right to enter the non-values ; but the values remain and require chief attention.

From what has been already said, it will be clear that there is no disposition here to give Voltaire anything *An attempt* short of the fullest credit, both as an individual *at different* writer of prose fiction and as a link in the chain *evaluation* of its French producers. He worked for the *of himself.* most part in miniature, and even *Candide* runs but to its bare hundred pages. But these are of the first quality in their own way, and give the book the same position for the century, in satiric and comic fiction, which *Manon Lescaut* holds in that of passion. That both should have taken this form, while, earlier, *Manon*, if written at all, would probably have been a poem, and *Candide* would have been a treatise, shows on the one side the importance of the position which the novel had assumed, and on the other the immense advantages which it gave, as a kind, to the artist in literature. I like poetry better than anything, but though the subject could have been, and often has been, treated satirically in verse, a verse *narrative* could hardly have avoided inferiority, while even Berkeley (who himself borrowed a little of novel-form for *Alciphron*) could not have made *Candide* more effective than it is. It is of course true that Voltaire's powers as a " fictionist " were probably limited in fact, to the departments, or the department, which he actually occupied, and out of which he wisely did not go. He must have a satiric purpose, and he must be allowed a very free choice of subject and seasoning. In particular, it may be noted that he has no grasp whatever of individual character. Even Candide is but a " humour," and Pangloss a very decided one; as are Martin, Gordon in *L'Ingénu*, and others. His women are all slightly varied outline-sketches of what he thought women in general were, not persons. Plot he never attempted; and racy as his dialogue often is, it is on the whole merely a setting for these very sparkles of wit some of which have been quoted.

It is in these scintillations, after all, that the chief delight of his tales consists; and though, as has been honestly confessed and shown, he learnt this to some extent from others, he made the thing definitely his own. When the Babylonian public has been slightly " elevated " by the refreshments distributed at the great tournament for the hand of the Princess Formosante, it decides that war, etc., is folly, and that the essence of human nature is to enjoy itself, " Cette excellente morale," says Voltaire gravely, " n'a jamais été démentie " (the

words really should be made to come at the foot of a page
so that you might have to turn over before coming to the
conclusion of the sentence) "que par les faits." Again,
in the description of the Utopia of the Gangarides (same
story), where not only men but beasts and birds are all
perfectly wise, well conducted, and happy, a paragraph
of quite sober description, without any flinging up of
heels or thrusting of tongue in cheek, ends, "Nous
avons surtout des perroquets qui prêchent à mer-
veille," and for once Voltaire exercises on himself the
Swiftian control, which he too often neglected, and
drops his beloved satire of clerics after this gentle touch
at it.[1]

He is of course not constantly at his best; but he is
so often enough to make him, as was said at the beginning, very delectable reading, especially for the second
time and later, which will be admitted to be no common
praise. When you read him for the first time his bad
taste, his obsession with certain subjects, his repetition of
the same gibes, and other things which have been duly
mentioned, strike and may disgust—will certainly more
or less displease anybody but a partisan on the same side.
On a second or later reading you are prepared for them,
and either skip them altogether or pass them by without
special notice, repeating the enjoyment of what is better
in an unalloyed fashion. And so doth the excellent old
chestnut-myth, which probably most of us have heard
told with all innocence as an original witticism, justify
itself, and one should "prefer the second hour" of the
reading to the first. But if there is a first there will
almost certainly be a second, and it will be a very great
pity if there is no reading at all.

According to the estimate of the common or vulgate
(I do not say "vulgar," though in the best English there

---

[1] It is only fair to mention in this place, and in justice to a much abused institution,
that this Babylonian story is said to be the only thing of its kind and its author that
escaped the Roman censorship. If this is true, the unfeathered *perroquets* were not so
spiteful as the feathered ones too often are. Or perhaps each chuckled at the satire on
his brethren.

is little or no difference) literary history, Rousseau[1]
ranks far higher in the scale of novel-writing
than Voltaire, having left long and ambitious
books of the kind against Voltaire's handful of
short, shorter, and shortest stories. It might
be possible to accept this in one sense, but in one which
would utterly disconcert the usual valuers. The *Confessions*, if it were not an autobiography, would be one
of the great novels of the world. A large part of it is
probably or certainly "fictionised"; if the whole were
fictitious, it would lose much of its repulsiveness, retain
(except for a few very matter-of-fact judges) all its interest,
and gain the enormous advantage of art over mere
reportage of fact. Of course Rousseau's art of another
kind, his mere mastery of style and presentation, does
redeem this *reportage* to some extent; but this would
remain if the thing were wholly fiction, and the other
art of invention, divination, *mimesis*—call it what you
will—would come in. Yet it is not worth while to be
idly unlike other people and claim it as an actual novel.
It may be worth while to point out how it displays some
of the great gifts of the novel-writer. The first of these
—the greatest and, in fact, the mother of all the rest—is
the sheer faculty, so often mentioned but not, alas! so
invariably found, of telling the tale and holding the
reader, not with any glittering eye or any enchantment,
white or black, but with the pure grasping—or, as French
admirably has it, "enfisting"—power of the tale itself.
Round this there cluster—or, rather, in this necessarily
abide—the subsidiary arts of managing the various
parts of the story, of constructing characters sufficient
to carry it on, of varnishing it with description, and to
some extent, though naturally to a lesser one than if it
had been fiction pure and simple, "lacing" it, in both

---

[1] As with other controverted points, not strictly relevant, it is permissible for us to
neglect protests about *la légende des philosophes* and the like. Of course Rousseau was not
only, at one time or another, the personal enemy of Voltaire and Diderot—he was, at
one time or another, the personal enemy of everybody, including (not at any one but at
all times) himself—but held principles very different from theirs. Yet their names will
always be found together: and for our object the junction is real.

senses of the word, with dialogue. Commonplace (but not the best commonplace) taste often cries " Oh ! if this were only true ! " The wiser mind is fain some-times—not often, for things are not often good enough —to say, " Oh ! if this were only *false* ! "

But if a severe auditor were to strike the *Confessions* out of Rousseau's novel-account to the good, on the score

The ambiguous position of *Émile*. of technical insufficiency or disqualification, he could hardly refuse to do the same with *Émile* on the other side of the sheet. In fact its second title (*de l'Éducation*), its opening re-marks, and the vastly larger part of the text, not only do not pretend to be a novel but frankly decline to be one. In what way exactly the treatise, from the mere assumption of a supposed " soaring human boy " named Émile, who serves as the victim of a few *Sandford-and-Merton*-like illustrations, burgeoned into the romance of actual novel-kind with Sophie in the Fifth Book, and the purely novel-natured, but unfinished and hardly begun, sequel of *Émile et Sophie ou Les Solitaires*, it is impossible to say. From the sketch of the intended conclusion of this latter given by Prévost [1] it would seem that we have not lost much, though with Rousseau the treatment is so constantly above the substance that one cannot tell. As it is, the novel part is nearly worthless. Neither Émile nor Sophie is made in the least a live person ; the catastrophe of their at first ideal union might be shown, by an advocate of very moderate skill, to be largely if not wholly due to the meddlesome, muddle-headed, and almost inevitably mischievous advice given to them just after their marriage by their foolish Mentor ; and one neither finds nor foresees any real novel interest whatever. Anilities in the very worst style of the eighteenth century —such as the story how Émile instigated mutiny in an Algerian slave-gang, failed, made a noble protest, and instead of being impaled, flayed, burnt alive, or otherwise taught not to do so, was made overseer of his own projects

---

[1] Not the Abbé, who had been dead for some years, but a Genevese professor who saw a good deal of Jean-Jacques in his later days.

of reformed discipline—are sufficiently unrefreshing in fact. And the sort of " double arrangement " fore-shadowed in the professorial programme of the un-written part, where, in something like Davenant and Dryden's degradation of *The Tempest*, Émile and Sophie, she still refusing to be pardoned her fault, are brought together after all, and are married, in an actual though not consummated cross-bigamy, with a mysterious couple, also marooned on a desert island, is the sort of thing that Rousseau never could have managed, though Voltaire, probably to the discontent of Mrs. Grundy, could have done it in one way, and Sir William Gilbert would have done it delightfully in another. But Jean-Jacques's absolute lack of humour would have ensured a rather ghastly failure, relieved, it may be, by a few beautiful passages.

If, therefore, Rousseau had nothing but *Émile*, or even nothing but *Émile* and the *Confessions* to put to his credit, he could but obtain a position in our "utmost, last, provincial band," and that more because of his general literary powers than of special right. But, as everybody knows, there is a third book among his works which, whether universally or only by a majority, whether in whole or in part, whether with heavy deductions and allowances or with light ones, has been reckoned among the greatest and most epoch-making novels of the world. The full title of it is *Julie, ou la Nouvelle Héloïse, ou Lettres de deux Amans, habitans d'une petite ville au pied des Alpes, recueillies et publiées, par J. J. Rousseau.*[1] Despite its immense fame, direct and at second-hand—for Byron's famous outburst, though scarcely less rhetorical, is decidedly more poetical than most things of his, and has inscribed itself in the general memory—one rather doubts whether the book is as much read as it once was. Quotations, references, and those half-unconscious reminiscences of borrowing

La Nouvelle Héloïse.

---

[1] "For short" *La Nouvelle Héloïse* has been usually adopted. I prefer *Julie* as actually the first title, and for other reasons with which it is unnecessary to trouble the reader.

which are more eloquent than anything else, have not recently been very common either in English or in French. It has had the fate—elsewhere, I think, alluded to—of one of the two kinds of great literature, that it has in a manner seeded itself out. An intense love-novel—it is some time since we have seen one till the other day— would be a descendant of Rousseau's book, but would not bear more than a family likeness to it. Yet this, of itself, is a great testimony.

Except in rhetoric or rhapsody, the allowances and deductions above referred to must be heavy ; and, accord-

Its numerous and grave faults.

ing to a custom honoured both by time and good result, it is well to get them off first. That peculiarity of being a novelist only *par interim*, much more than Aramis was a mousque-taire, appears, even in *Julie*, so glaringly as to be dangerous and almost fatal. The book fills, in the ordinary one-volume editions, nearly five hundred pages of very small and very close print. Of these the First Part contains rather more than a hundred, and it would be infinitely better if the whole of the rest, except a few passages (which would be almost equally good as fragments), were in the bosom of the ocean buried. Large parts of them are mere discussions of some of Rousseau's own fads ; clumsy parodies of Voltaire's satiric manners-painting ; waterings out of the least good traits in the hero and heroine ; uninteresting and superfluous appearances of the third and only other real person, Claire ; a dreary account of Julie's married life ; tedious eccentricities of the impossible and not very agreeable Lord Edward Bomston, who shares with Dickens's Lord Frederick Verisopht the peculiarity of being alternately a peer and a person with a courtesy " Lord "-ship ; a rather silly end for the heroine herself ; [1] and finally, a rather repulsive and quite incongruous acknowledgment of affection for the creature Saint-Preux, with a refusal to " implement " it

---

[1] She dies after slipping into the lake in a successful attempt to rescue one of her children ; but neither is drowned, and she does not succumb rapidly enough for "shock" to account for it, or slowly enough for any other intelligible malady to hold its course.

(as they say in Scotland) matrimonially, by Claire, who is by this time a widow.[1] If mutilating books [2] were not a crime deserving terrible retribution in this life or after it, one could be excused for tearing off the Second, Third, Fourth, Fifth, and Sixth Parts, with the *Amours de Lord Edouard* which follow. If one was rich, one would be amply justified in having a copy of Part I., and the fragments above indicated, printed for oneself on vellum.

But this is not all. Even the First Part—even the presentation of the three protagonists—is open to some, The minor and even to severe, criticism. The most characters. guiltless, but necessarily much the least important, is Claire. She is, of course, an obvious " borrow " from Richardson's lively second heroines; but she is infinitely superior to them. It is at first sight, though not perhaps for long, curious—and it is certainly a very great compliment to Madame de Warens or Vuarrens and Madame d'Houdetot, and perhaps other objects of his affections—that Rousseau, cad as he was, and impossible as it was for him to draw a gentleman, could and did draw ladies. It was horribly bad taste in both Julie and Claire to love such a creature as Saint-Preux; but then *cela s'est vu* from the time of the Lady of the Strachy downwards, if not from that of Princess Michal. But Claire is faithful and true as steel, and she is lively without being, as Charlotte Grandison certainly is, vulgar. She is very much more a really " reasonable woman," even putting passion aside, than the somewhat sermonising and syllogising Julie; and it would have been both agreeable and tormenting to be M. d'Orbe. (Tormenting because she only half-loved him, and agreeable because she did love him a little, and, whether it was little or much, allowed herself to be his.) He himself,

---

[1] There is another curious anticipation of Dickens here: for Julie, as Dora does with Agnes, entreats Claire to "fill her vacant place "—though, by the way, not with her husband. And a third parallel, between Saint-Preux and Bradley Headstone, need not be quite farcical.

[2] You *may* tear out Introductions, if you do it neatly ; and this I say, having written many.

slight and rather " put upon " as he is, is also much
the most agreeable of the " second " male characters.
Of Bomston and Wolmar we shall speak presently ; and
there is so little of the Baron d'Étange that one really
does not know whether he was or was not something more
than the tyrannical husband and father, and the ill-
mannered specimen of the lesser nobility, that it pleased
Saint-Preux or Rousseau to represent him as being. He
had provocation enough, even in the case of his otherwise hardly pardonable insolence to Bomston.[1]

But Saint-Preux himself ? How early was the obvious
jest made that he is about as little of a *preux* as he is of
a saint ? I have heard, or dreamt, of a schoolboy who, being accidentally somewhat preco-
cious in French, and having read the book,
ejaculated, "*What* a sweep he is ! " and I remember no time of my life at which I should not have
heartily agreed with that youth. I do not suppose that
either of us—though perhaps we ought to be ashamed
of ourselves for not doing so—founded our condemnation
on Saint-Preux's " forgetfulness of all but love." That
is a " forfeit," in French and English sense alike, which
has itself registered and settled in various tariffs and
codes, none of which concerns the present history. It is
not even that he is a most unreasonable creature now and
then ; that can be pardoned, being understood, though
he really does strain the benefit of *amare et sapere* etc.
It is that, except when he is in the altitudes of passion,
and not always then, he never " knows how to behave,"
as the simple and sufficient old phrase had it. If M.
d'Étange had had the wits, and had deigned to do it, he
might even, without knowing his deepest cause of quarrel

The delinquencies of Saint-Preux.

---

[1] Also Rousseau, without meaning it, has made him by no means a fool. When, on
learning from his wife and daughter that Saint-Preux had been officiating as " coach,"
he asked if this genius was a gentleman, and on hearing that he was not, replied,
" What have you paid him, then ? " it was not, as the novelist and his hero took it,
in their vanity, to be, mere insolence of caste. M. d'Étange knew perfectly well that
though he could not trust a French gentleman with his wife, there was not nearly so
much danger with his daughter—while a *roturier* was not only entitled to be paid, and
might accept pay without derogation, but was not unlikely, as the old North Country
saying goes, to take it in malt if he did not receive it in meal.

with the treacherous tutor, have pointed out that Saint-
Preux's claim to be one of God Almighty's gentlemen
was as groundless as his " proofs," in the French technical
sense of gentility, were non-existent.   It is impossible
to imagine anything in worse taste than his reply to the
Baron's no doubt offensive letter, and Julie's enclosed
renunciation.   Even the adoring Julie herself, and the
hardly less adoring Claire—the latter not in the least a
prude, nor given to giving herself " airs "—are constantly
obliged to pull him up for his want of *délicatesse*.   He is
evidently a coxcomb, still more evidently a prig ; selfish
beyond even that selfishness which is venial in a lover ;
not in the least, though he can exceed in wine, a " good
fellow," and in many ways thoroughly unmanly.   A
good English school and college might have made him
tolerable : but it is rather to be doubted, and it is certain
that his way as a transgressor would have been hard at
both.   As it is, he is very largely the embodiment—and
it is more charitable than uncharitable to regard him as
largely the cause—of the faults of the worst kind of French,
and not quite only French, novel-hero ever since.

One approaches Julie herself, in critical intent, with
mixed feelings.   One would rather say nothing but good
And the of her, and there is plenty of good to say : how
less charm- much will be seen in a moment.   Most of
ing points what is not so good belongs, in fact, to the
of Julie. dreary bulk of sequel tacked on by mis-
Her
redemption. taken judgment to that more than true history
of a hundred pages, which leaves her in despair, and
might well have left her altogether.   Even here she is
not faultless, quite independently of her sins according
to Mrs. Grundy and the Pharisees.   If she had not been,
as Claire herself fondly but truly calls her, such a *pré-
cheresse*, she might not have fallen a victim to such a
prig.   One never can quite forgive her for loving him,
except on the all-excusing ground that she loved him so
much ; and though she is perhaps not far beyond the
licence of " All's fair, in certain conditions," there is no
doubt that, like her part-pattern Clarissa, she is not

passionately attached to the truth. It might be possible
to add some cavils, but for the irresistible plea just
glanced at, which stops one.

Quia multum amavit! Nobody—at least no woman—
had loved like that in a prose novel before ; nobody at
all except Des Grieux, and he is but as a sketch to an
elaborate picture. She will wander after Pallas, and
would like to think that she would like to be of the train
of Dian (one shudders at imagining the scowl and the
shrug and the twist of the skirt of the goddess !). But
the kiss of Aphrodite has been on her, and has mastered
her whole nature. How the thing could be done, out of
poetry, has always been a marvel to me ; but I have
explained it by the supposition that the absolute impossibility of writing poetry at this time in French
necessitated the break-out in prose. Rousseau's wonderful style—so impossible to analyse, but so irresistible—
does much ; the animating sense of his native scenery
something. But, after all, what gives the thing its
irresistibleness is the strange command he had of Passion
and of Sorrow—two words, the first of which is actually,
in the original sense, a synonym of the second, though it
has been expanded to cover the very opposite.

But it would be unfair to Rousseau, especially in such
a place as this, to confine the praise of *Julie* as a novel
to its exhibition of passion, or even to the
charm of Julie herself. Within its proper
limits—which are, let it be repeated, almost
if not quite exactly those of the First Part—
many other gifts of the particular class of artist are shown.
The dangerous letter-scheme, which lends itself so easily,
and in the other parts surrenders itself so helplessly and
hopelessly, to mere " piffle " about this and that, is
kept well in hand. Much as Rousseau owes to Richardson, he has steered entirely clear of that system of word-
for-word and incident-for-incident reporting which makes
the Englishman's work so sickening to some. You
have enough of each and no more, this happy mean
affecting both dialogue and description. The plot (or

rather the action) is constantly present, probably managed, always enlivened by the imminence of disastrous discovery. As has been already pointed out, one may dislike—or feel little interest in—some of the few characters; but it is impossible to say that they are out of drawing or keeping. Saint-Preux, objectionable and almost loathsome as he may be sometimes, is a thoroughly human creature, and is undoubtedly what Rousseau meant him to be, for the very simple reason that he is (like the Byronic hero who followed) what Rousseau wished to be, if not exactly what he was, himself. Bomston is more of a lay figure; but then the *Anglais philosophe de qualité* of the French imagination in the eighteenth century *was* a lay figure, and, as has been excellently said by De Quincey in another matter, nothing can be wrong which conforms to the principles of its own ideal. As for Julie and Claire, they once more

> Answer the ends of their being created.

Even the " talking-book " is here hardly excessive, and comes legitimately under the excuse of showing how the relations between the hero and heroine originally got themselves established.[1]

Are we, then, from the excellence of the " Confessions " *in pari materia* and *in ipsa* of *Julie*, to lament

But little probability of more good work in novel from its author.

that Rousseau did not take to novel-writing as a special and serious occupation ? Probably not. The extreme weakness and almost *fadeur* of the strictly novel part of *Émile*, and the going-off of *Julie* itself, are very open warnings; the mere absence of any other attempts worth mentioning[2] is evidence of a kind; and the character of

---

[1] I observe that I have not yet fulfilled the promise of saying something of Wolmar, but the less said of him the better. He belongs wholly to that latter portion which has been wished away; he is a respectable Deist—than which it is essentially impossible, one would suppose, for orthodoxy and unorthodoxy alike to imagine anything more uninteresting; and his behaviour to Saint-Preux appears to me to be simply nauseous. He cannot, like Rowena, "forgive as a Christian," because he is not one, and any other form of forgiveness or even of tolerance is, in the circumstances, disgusting. But it was Rousseau's way to be disgusting sometimes.

[2] We have spoken of his attempt at the fairy tale; *qui* Gomersal *non odit* in English verse, *amet Le Lévite d'Ephraïm* in French prose, etc. etc.

all the rest of the work, and of all this part of the work but the opening of *Julie*, and even of that opening itself, counsel abstention, here as everywhere, from quarrelling with Providence. Rousseau's superhuman concentration on himself, while it has inspired the relevant parts of the *Confessions* and of *Julie*, has spoilt a good deal else that we have, and would assuredly have spoilt other things that we have not. It has been observed, by all acute students of the novel, that the egotistic variety will not bear heavy crops of fruit by itself; and that it is incapable, or capable with very great difficulty, of letting the observed and so far altruistic kind grow from the same stool. Of what is sometimes called the dramatic faculty (though, in fact, it is only one side of that),—the faculty which in different guise and with different means the general novelist must also possess,—Rousseau had nothing. He could put himself in no other man's skin, being so absolutely wrapped up in his own, which was itself much too sensitive to be disturbed, much less shed. Anything or anybody that was (to use Mill's language) a permanent or even a temporary possibility of sensation to him was within his power ; anything out of immediate or closely impending contact was not. Now some of the great novelists have the external power—or at least the will to use that power—alone, others have had both ; but Rousseau had the internal only, and so was, except by miracle of intensive exercise, incapable of further range.

Neither of the disabilities which weighed on Voltaire and Rousseau—the incapacity of the former to construct any complex character, and of the latter to portray any but his own, or some other brought into intensest communion, actually or as a matter of wish, with his own—weighed upon the third of the great trio of *philosophe* leaders. There is every probability that Diderot might have been a very great novelist if he had lived a hundred years later ; and not a little evidence that he only missed being such, even as it was, because of that mysterious curse which

The different case of Diderot.

was epigrammatically expressed about him long ago
(I really forget who said it first), " Good pages, no good
book." So far from being self-centred or of limited
interests, he could, as hardly any other man ever could,
claim the hackneyed *Homo sum*, etc., as his rightful
motto.   He had, when he allowed himself to give it
fair play, an admirable gift of tale-telling ; he could
create character, and set it to work, almost after the fashion
of the very greatest novelists ; his universal interest and
" curiosity " included such vivid appreciation of literature,
and of art, and of other things useful to the novel-writer,
that he never could have been at a loss for various kinds of
" seasoning."   He had keen observation, an admittedly
marvellous flow of ideas, and a style which (though, like
everything else about him, careless) was of singular
vigour and freshness when, once more, he let it have fair
play.   But his time, his nature, and his circumstances
combined to throw in his way traps and snares and nets
which he could not, or would not, avoid.   His anti-
religiosity, though sometimes greatly exaggerated, was
a bad stumbling-block ; although he was free from the
snigger of Voltaire and of Sterne, you could not prevent
him, as Horace Walpole complains of his distinguished
sire, from blurting out the most improper remarks and
stories at the most inconvenient times and in the most
unsuitable companies ; while his very multiscience, and
his fertility of thought and imagination, kept him in
a whirl which hindered his " settling " to anything.
Although in one sense he had the finest and wisest
critical taste of any man then living—I do not bar even
Gray or even Lessing—his taste in some other ways was
utterly untrustworthy and sometimes horribly bad ; while
even his strictly critical faculty seems never to have been
exercised on his own books—a failure forming part of
the " ostrich-like indifference " with which he produced
and abandoned them.[1]

[1] He did not even, as Rousseau did with his human offspring, habitually take them
to the Foundling Hospital—that is to say, in the case of literature, the anonymous press.
He left them in MS., gave them away, and in some cases behaved to them in such an
incomprehensible fashion that one wonders how they ever came to light.

402 HISTORY OF THE FRENCH NOVEL ch.

It is sometimes contended, and in many cases, no doubt, is the fact, that "Selections" are disgraceful and unscholarly. But what has been said will show that this is an exceptional case. The present writer waded through the whole of the twenty-volume edition of Assézat and Tourneux when it first appeared, and is very glad he did; nor is there perhaps one volume (he does not say one page, chapter, or even work) which he has not revisited more or fewer times during the forty years in which (alas! for the preterite) they remained on his shelves. But it is scarcely to be expected that every one, that many, or that more than a very few readers, have done or will do the same. It so happens, however, that Génin's *Œuvres Choisies*—though it has been abused by some anti-Ydgrunites as too much Bowdlerised— gives a remarkably full and satisfactory idea of this great and seldom [1] quite rightly valued writer. It must have cost much, besides use of paste and scissors, to do; for the extracts are often very short, and the bulk of matter to be thoroughly searched for extraction is, as has just been said, huge. A third volume might perhaps be added;[2] but the actual two are far from unrepresentative, while the Bowdlerising is by no means ultra-Bowdlerish.

The reader, even of this selection, will see how, in quite miscellaneous or heterogeneous writing, Diderot bubbles out into a perfectly told tale or anecdote, no matter what the envelope (as we may call it) of this tale or anecdote may be. All his work is more or less like conversation : and these excursus are like the stories which, if good, are among the best, just as, if bad, they are the worst, sets-off to conversation itself. Next to these come the longer *histoires*—as one would call them in the Heroic novel and its successors—things sometimes found by themselves,

His gifts, and the waste of them.

The various display of them.

---

[1] Carlyle's *Essay* and Lord Morley of Blackburn's book are excepted. But Carlyle had not the whole before him, and Lord Morley was principally dealing with the *Encyclopédie*.

[2] Especially as Génin, like Carlyle, did not know all. There is, I believe, a later selection, but I have not seen it.

sometimes ensconced in larger work [1]—the story of
Desroches and Mme. de la Carlière, *Les Deux Amis de
Bourbonne*, the almost famous *Le Marquis des Arcis et
Mme. de la Pommeraye*, of which more may be said
presently ; and things which are not exactly tales, but
which have the tale-quality in part, like the charming
*Regrets sur ma Vieille Robe de Chambre, Ceci n'est pas un
conte*, etc. Thirdly, and to be spoken of in more detail,
come the things that are nearest actual novels, and in
some cases are called so, *Le Neveu de Rameau*, the
"unspeakable" *Bijoux Indiscrets, Jacques le Fataliste*
(the matrix of *Le Marquis des Arcis*), and *La Religieuse*.

The "unspeakable" one does not need much speaking
from any point of view. If it is not positively what
Carlyle called it, "the beastliest of all dull novels, past,
present, or to come," it really would require a most
unpleasant apprenticeship to scavenging in order to
discover a dirtier and duller. The framework is a flat
imitation of Crébillon, the "insets" are sometimes
mere pornography, and the whole thing is evidently
scribbled at a gallop—it was actually a few days' work,
to get money, from some French Curll or Drybutter, to
give (the appropriateness of the thing at least is humorous)
to the mistress of the moment, a Madame de Puisieux,[2]
who, if she was like Crébillon's heroines in morals,
cannot have been like the best of them in manners. Its
existence shows, of course, Diderot's worst side, that is
to say, the combination of want of breeding with readiness
to get money anyhow. If it is worth reading at all,
which may be doubted, it is to show the real, if equivocal,
value of Crébillon himself. For it is vulgar, which he
never is.

Le Neveu de Rameau has only touches of obscenity,

---

[1] Even the long, odd, and sometimes tedious *Rêve de D'Alembert*, which Carlyle
thought "we could have done without," but which others have extolled, has vivid
narrative touches, though one is not much surprised at Mlle. de Lespinasse having been
by no means grateful for the part assigned to her.
[2] The cleansing effect of war is an old *cliché*. It has been curiously illustrated in
this case : for the first proof of the present passage reached me on the very same day
with the news of the expulsion of the Germans from the village of Puisieux. So the
name got "*red*-washed" from its old reproach.

and it has been enormously praised by great persons.
Le Neveu It is very clever, but it seems to me that, as
de Rameau. a notable critic is said to have observed of
something else, " it has been praised quite enough."
It is a sketch, worked out in a sort of monologue,[1] of something like Diderot's own character
without his genius and without his good fellowship—a
gutter-snipe of art and letters possessed of some talent
and of infinite impudence. It shows Diderot's own
power of observation and easy fluid representation of
character and manners, but not, as I venture to think,
much more.

Jacques le Fataliste is what may be called, without
pedantry or preciousness, eminently a " document."
Jacques le It is a document of Diderot's genius only
Fataliste. indirectly (save in part), and to those who can
read not only in the lines but between them : it is a
document, directly, of the insatiable and restless energy
of the man, and of the damage which this restlessness,
with its accompanying and inevitable want of self-
criticism, imposed upon that genius. Diderot, though
he did not rhapsodise about Sterne as he rhapsodised
about Richardson, was, like most of his countrymen
then, a great admirer of " Tristram," and in an evil hour
he took it into his head to Shandyise. The book starts
with an actual adaptation of Sterne,[2] which is more than
once repeated ; its scheme—of a master (who is as different as possible from my Uncle Toby, except that when
not in a passion he is rather good-natured, and at almost
all times very easily humbugged) and a man (who is
what Trim never is, both insolent and indecent)—is at
least partially the same. But the most constant and the
most unfortunate imitation is of Sterne's literally eccentric, or rather zigzag and pillar-to-post, fashion of narration.
In the Englishman's own hands, by some prestidigitation
of genius, this never becomes boring, though it probably

[1] There really are touches of resemblance in it to Browning, especially in things like *Mr. Sludge the Medium.*
[2] The corporal's wound in the knee.

would have become so if either book had been finished ; for which reason we may be quite certain that it was not only his death which left both in fragments.   In the hands of his imitators the boredom—simple or in the form of irritation—has been almost invariable ; [1] and with all his great intellectual power, his tale-telling faculty, his *bonhomie*, and other good qualities, Diderot has not escaped it—has, in fact, rushed upon it and compelled it to come in.   It is comparatively of little moment that the main ostensible theme—the very unedifying account of the loves, or at least the erotic exercises, of Jacques and his master—is deliberately, tediously, inartistically interrupted and " put off."   The great feature of the book, which has redeemed it with some who would otherwise condemn it entirely, the Arcis and La Pommeraye episode (*v. inf.*), is handled after a fashion which suggests Mr. Ruskin's famous denunciation in another art.   The *ink*pot is " flung in the face of the public " by a purely farcical series of interruptions, occasioned by the affairs of the inn-landlady, who tells the story, by her servants, dog, customers, and Heaven only knows what else ; while the minor incidents and accidents of the book are treated in the same way, in and out of proportion to their own importance ; the author's " simple plan," though by no means " good old rule," being that *everything* shall be interrupted.   Although, in the erotic part, the author never returns quite to his worst *Bijoux Indiscrets* style, he once or twice goes very near it, except that he is not quite so dull ; and when the book comes to an end in a very lame and impotent fashion (the farce being kept up to the last, and even this end being " recounted " and not made part of the mainly dialogic action), one is rather relieved at there being no more. One has seen talent ; one has almost glimpsed genius ; but what one has been most impressed with is the glaring fashion in which both the certainty and the possibility have been thrown away.

[1] Of course, there *are* exceptions, and with one of the chief of them, Xavier de Maistre, we may have, before long, to deal.

The story which has been referred to in passing as muddled, or, to adopt a better French word, for which Its "Arcis- we have no exact equivalent, *affublé* (travestied Pommeraye" and overlaid) with eccentricities and inter-episode. ruptions, the *Histoire* of the Marquis des Arcis and the Marquise de la Pommeraye, has received a great deal of praise, most of which it deserves. The Marquis and the Marquise have entered upon one of the fashionable *liaisons* which Crébillon described in his own way. Diderot describes this one in another. The Marquis gets tired—it is fair to say that he has offered marriage at the very first, but Madame de la Pommeraye, a widow with an unpleasant first experience of the state, has declined it. He shows his tiredness in a gentlemanly manner, but not very mistakably. His mistress, who is not at first *femina furens*, but who possesses some feminine characteristics in a dangerous degree, as he might perhaps have found out earlier if he had been a different person, determines to make sure of it. She intimates *her* tired-ness, and the Marquis makes his first step downwards by jumping at the release. They are—the old, old hopeless folly!—to remain friends, but friends only. But she really loves him, and after almost assuring herself that he has really ceased to love her (which, in the real language of love, means that he has never loved her at all), devises a further, a very clever, but a rather diabolical system of last proof, involving vengeance if it fails. She has known, in exercises of charity (the *femme du monde* has seldom quite abandoned these), a mother and daughter who, having lost their means, have taken to a questionable, or rather a very unquestionable manner of life, keeping a sort of private gaming-house, and extending to those frequenters of it who choose, what the late George Augustus Sala not inelegantly called, in an actual police-court instance, " the thorough hospitality characteristic of their domicile." She prevails on them to leave the house, get rid of all their belongings (down to clothes) which could possibly be identified, change their name, move to another quarter of Paris, and set up as *dévotes*

under the full protection of the local clergy. Then she
manages an introduction, of an apparently accidental
kind, to the Marquis. He falls in love at once with the
daughter, who is very pretty, and with masculine (or at
least *some* masculine) fatuity, makes Madame de la
Pommeraye his confidante. She gives him rope, but
he uses it, of course, only to hang himself. He tries the
usual temptations ; but though the mother at least would
not refuse them, Madame de la Pommeraye's hand on
the pair is too tight. At last he offers marriage, and—
with her at least apparent consent—is married. The
next day she tells him the truth. But her diabolism
fails. At first there is of course a furious outburst. But
the girl is beautiful, affectionate, and humble ; the
mother is pensioned off ; the Marquis and Marquise des
Arcis retire for some years to those invaluable *terres*,
after a sojourn at which everything is forgotten ; and
the story ends. Diderot, by not too skilfully throwing
in casuistical attacks and defences of the two principal
characters, but telling us nothing of Madame de la
Pommeraye's subsequent feelings or history, does what
he can, unluckily after his too frequent fashion, to spoil
or at least to blunt his tale. It is not necessary to imitate
him by discussing the *pros* and *cons* at length. I think
myself that the Marquis, both earlier and later, is made
rather too much of a *benêt*, or, in plain English, a nin-
compoop. But nincompoops exist : in fact how many
of us are not nincompoops in certain circumstances ?
Madame de la Pommeraye is, I fear, rather true, and is
certainly sketched with extraordinary ability. On a
larger scale the thing would probably, at that time and
by so hasty and careless a workman, have been quite
spoilt. But it is obviously the skeleton—and something
more—of a really great novel.

It may seem that a critic who speaks in this fashion,
after an initial promise of laudation, is a sort of Balaam
La Religieuse. topsyturvied, and merely curses where he is
expected to bless. But ample warning was
given of the peculiar position of Diderot, and when we

come to his latest known and by far his best novel, *La Religieuse*, the paradox (he was himself very fond of paradoxes,[1] though not of the wretched things which now disgrace the name) remains. The very subject of the book, or of the greatest part of it, was for a long time, if it is not still, taboo; and even if this had not been the case, it has other drawbacks. It originated in, and to some extent still retains traces of, one of the silly and ill-bred " mystifications " in which the eighteenth and early nineteenth century delighted.[2] It is, at least in appearance, badly tainted with purpose ; and while it is actually left unfinished, the last pages of it, as they stand, are utterly unworthy of the earlier part, and in fact quite uninteresting. Momus or Zoilus must be allowed to say so much : but having heard him, let us cease to listen to the half-god or the whole philologist.

Yet *La Religieuse*, for all its drawbacks, is almost a great, and might conceivably have been a very great book. Madame d'Holbach is credited by Diderot's own generosity with having suggested its crowning *mot*,[3] and her influence may have been in other ways good by governing the force and fire, so often wasted or ill-directed, of Diderot's genius. Sœur Sainte-Suzanne is the youngest daughter of a respectable middle-class family. She perceives, or half-perceives (for, though no fool, she is a guileless and unsuspicious creature), that she is unwelcome there ; the most certain sign of which is that, while her sisters are married and dowered handsomely, she is condemned to be a nun. She has, though quite real piety, no " vocation," and though she allows herself to be coaxed through her novitiate, she at last, in face of almost insuperable difficulties, summons up

Its story.

---

[1] His longest, most avowed, and most famous, the *Paradoxe sur le Comédien*, has been worthily Englished by Mr. Walter H. Pollock.

[2] Its heroine, Suzanne Simonin, was, as far as the attempt to relieve herself of her vows went, a real person ; and a benevolent nobleman, the Marquis de Croixmare, actually interested himself in this attempt—which failed. But Diderot and his evil angel Grimm got up sham letters between themselves and her patron, which are usually printed with the book.

[3] *Mon père, je suis damnée* . . . the opening words, and the only ones given, of the confession of the half-mad abbess.

courage enough to refuse, at the very altar, the final profession. There is, of course, a terrible scandal ; she has more black looks in the family than ever, and at last her mother confesses that she is an illegitimate child, and therefore hated by her putative father, whose love for his wife, however, has induced him to forgive her, and not actually renounce (as indeed, by French law, he could not) the child. Broken in heart and spirit, Suzanne at last accepts her doom. She is fortunate in one abbess, but the next persecutes her, brings all sorts of false accusations against her, strips, starves, imprisons, and actually tortures her by means of the *amende honorable*. She manages to get her complaints known and to secure a counsel, and though she cannot obtain liberation from her vows, the priest who conducts the ecclesiastical part of the enquiry is a just man, and utterly repudiates the methods of persecution, while he and her lay lawyer procure her transference to another convent. Here her last trial (except those of the foolish post-*scrap*, as we may call it) begins, as well as the most equivocal and the greatest part of the book. Her new superior is in every respect different from any she has known—of a luxurious temperament, good-natured, though capricious, and inclined to be very much too affectionate. Her temptation of the innocent Suzanne is defeated by this very innocence, and by timely revelation, though the revealer does not know what she reveals, to a " director " ; and the wayward and corrupted fancy turns by degrees to actual madness, which proves fatal, Suzanne remaining unharmed, though a piece of not inexcusable eavesdropping removes the ignorance of her innocence.

If the subject be not simply ruled out, and the book indexed for silence, it is practically impossible to suggest A hardly missed, if masterpiece. that it could have been treated better. Even the earlier parts, which could easily have been made dull, are not so ; and it is noteworthy that, anti-religionist as Diderot was, and directly as the book is aimed at the conventual system,[1]

[1] Evangelical Protestantism has more than once adopted the principle that the Devil

all the priests who are introduced are men of honour, justice, and humanity. But the wonder is in the treatment of the "scabrous" part of the matter by the author of Diderot's other books. Whether Madame d'Holbach's [1] influence, as has been suggested, was more widely and subtly extended than we know, or whatever else may be the cause, there is not a coarse word, not even a coarsely drawn situation, in the whole. Suzanne's innocence is, in the subtlest manner, prevented from being in the least *bête*. The fluctuations and ficklenesses of the abbess's passion, and in a less degree of that of another young nun, whom Suzanne has partially ousted from her favour, are marvellously and almost inoffensively drawn, and the stages by which erotomania passes into mania general and mortal, are sketched slightly, but with equal power. There is, I suppose, hardly a book which one ought to discommend to the young person more than *La Religieuse*. There are not many in which the powers required by the novelist, in delineating morbid, and not only morbid, character, are more brilliantly shown.

It is not the least remarkable thing about this remarkable book, and not the least characteristic of its most remarkable author, that its very survival has something extraordinary about it. Grimm, who was more likely than any one else to know, apparently thought it was destroyed or lost; it never appeared at all during Diderot's life, nor for a dozen years after his death, nor till seven after the outbreak of the Revolution, and six

---

should not be allowed to have all the best tunes: and I remember in my youth an English religious novel of ultra-anti-Roman purpose, which, though, of course, dropping the "scabrousness," had, as I long afterwards recognised when I came to read *La Religieuse*, almost certainly borrowed a good deal from our most unsaintly Denis of Langres.

[1] She seems to have been, in many ways, far too good for her society, and altogether a lady.—The opinions of the late M. Brunetière and mine on French literature were often very different—though he was good enough not to disapprove of some of my work on it. But with the terms of his expression of mere opinion one had seldom to quarrel. I must, however, take exception to his attribution of *grossièreté* to *La Religieuse*. Diderot, as has been fully admitted, *was* too often *grossier*: sometimes when it was almost irrelevant to the subject. But here, "scabrous" as the subject might be, the treatment is scrupulously *not* coarse. Nor do I think, after intimate and long familiarity with the whole of his work, that he was ever a *faux bonhomme*.

after the suppression of the religious orders in France.
That it might have brought its author into difficulties is
more than probable ; but the undisguised editor of the
Encyclopédie, the author, earlier, of the actually disgraceful
Bijoux Indiscrets, and the much more than suspected
principal begetter of the *Système de la Nature*, could not
have been much influenced by this. The true cause of
its abscondence, as in so much else of his work, was undoubtedly that ultra-Bohemian quality of indifference
which distinguished Diderot—the first in a way, probably
for ever the greatest, and, above all, the most altruistic of
literary Bohemians. Ask him to do something definite,
especially for somebody else's profit, to be done off-
hand, and it was done. Ask him to bear the brunt of a
dangerous, laborious, by no means lucrative, but rather
exciting adventure, and he would, one cannot quite say
consecrate, but devote (which has two senses) his life to
it. But set him to elaborate artistic creation, confine
him to it, and expect him to finish it, and you were certain
to be disappointed. At another time, even at this time,
if his surroundings and his society, his education and his
breeding had been less unfortunate, he might, as it
seems to me, have become a very great novelist indeed.
As it is, he is a great possibility of novel and of much
other writing, with occasional outbursts of actuality.
The *Encyclopédie* itself, for aught I care, might have gone
in all its copies, and with all possibility of recovering or
remembering it on earth, to the place where so many
people at the time would have liked to send it. But
in the rest of him, and even in some of his own Encyclopædia articles,[1] there is much of quite different stuff. And
among the various gifts, critical and creative, which this
stuff shows, not the least, I think, was the half-used and
mostly ill-used gift of novel-writing.

What has been called the second generation of the
philosophes, who were naturally the pupils of the first,

---

[1] They have hardly had a fair opportunity of comparison with Voltaire's *Dictionnaire
Philosophique* ; but they can stand it.

" were not like [that] first," that is to say, they did not
reproduce the special talents of their immediate
masters in this department of ours, save in two
instances. Diderot's genius did not propa-
gate itself in the novel way at all :[1] indeed, as has been
said, his best novel was not known till this second generation itself was waning. The most brilliant of his direct
hearers, Joubert, took to another department ; or rather,
in his famous *Pensées*, isolated and perfected the utterances
scattered through the master's immense and disorderly
work. Naigeon, the most devoted, who might have
taken for his motto a slight alteration of the Mahometan
confession of faith, " There is no God ; but there is
only one Diderot, and I am his prophet," was a dull
fellow, and also, to adopt a Carlylian epithet, a " dull-
snuffling " one, who could not have told a neck-tale if
the Hairibee of the guillotine had caught him and given
him a merciful chance. Voltaire in Marmontel, and
Rousseau in Bernardin de Saint-Pierre, were more fortunate, though both the juniors considerably transformed
their masters' fashions ; and Marmontel was always
more or less, and latterly altogether, an apostate from
the principle that the first and last duty of man is summed
up in *écrasons l'infâme*.

The successors— Marmontel.

This latter writer has had vicissitudes both in English
and French appreciation. We translated him early,
and he had an immense influence on the general Edgeworthian school, and on Miss Edgeworth herself. Much
later Mr. Ruskin " took him up." [2] But neither his
good nor his bad points have, for a long time, been such
as greatly to commend themselves, either to the major
part of the nineteenth century, or to what has yet passed
of the twentieth, on either side of the channel.

He was, no doubt, only a second-class man of letters,

---

[1] Unless Dulaurens' not quite stupid, but formless and discreditable, *Compère Mathieu*
be excepted.

[2] In consequence of which Mr. Ruskin's favourite publisher, the late Mr. George
Allen, asked the present writer, some twenty years ago, to revise and " introduce " the
old translation of his *Contes Moraux*. The volume had, at least, the advantage of very
charming illustrations by Miss Chris. Hammond.

and though he ranks really high in this class, he was
unfortunately much influenced by more or less passing fashions, fads, and fancies of his time—*sensibilité*
(see next chapter) philosophism, politico-philanthropic
economy, and what not. He was also much of a "polygraph," and naturally a good deal of his polygraphy
does not concern us, though parts of his *Memoirs*,
especially the rather well-known accounts of his
sufferings as a new-comer[1] in the atrocious Bastille,
show capital tale-telling faculty. His unequal criticism,
sometimes very acute, hardly concerns us at all ; his
Essai sur les Romans being very disappointing.[2] But he
wrote not a little which must, in different ways and
"strengths," be classed as actual fiction, and this concerns us pretty nearly, both as evidencing that general
set towards the novel which is so important, and also in
detail.

It divides itself quite obviously into two classes, the
almost didactic matter of *Bélisaire* and *Les Incas*, and the
still partly didactic, but much more " fictionised " *Contes Moraux*. The first part (which
is evidently of the family of *Télémaque*) may
be rapidly dismissed. Except for its good
French and good intentions, it has long had, and is likely
always to have, very little to say for itself. We have seen
that Prévost attempted a sort of quasi-historical novel.
Of actual history there is little in *Bélisaire*, rather more
in *Les Incas*. But historical fact and story-telling art
are entirely subordinated in both to moral purpose,

His "Tele-machic" imitations worth little. (marginal note)

---

[1] They were even worse than Leigh Hunt's in the strictly English counterpart
torture-house for the victims of tyranny—consisting, for instance, in the supply of so
good a dinner, at His Most Christian Majesty's expense, for the prisoner's servant,
that the prisoner ate it himself, and had afterwards, on the principles of rigid virtue and
distributive justice, to resign, to the minion who accompanied him, his own still better
one which came later, also supplied by the tyrant.

[2] One expects something of value from the part-contemporary, part-successor of the
novelists from Lesage to Rousseau. But where it is not mere blether about virtue and
vice, and *le cœur humain* and so on, it has some of the worst faults of eighteenth-century
criticism. He thinks it would have been more "moral" if Mme. de Clèves had
actually succumbed as a punishment for her self-reliance (certainly one of the most
remarkable topsyturvifications of morality ever crotcheted) ; is, of course, infinitely
shocked at being asked and induced to "interest himself in a prostitute and a card-
sharper " by *Manon Lescaut* ; and, equally of course, extols Richardson, though it is fair
to say that he speaks well of *Tom Jones*.

endless talk about virtue and the affections and justice
and all the rest of it—the sort of thing, in short, which
provoked the immortal outburst, "In the name of
the Devil and his grandmother, *be* virtuous and have
done with it !" There is, as has just been said, a great
deal of this in the *Contes* also ; but fortunately there is
something else.

The something else is not to be found in the "Sensibility" parts,[1] and could not be expected to be. They
do, indeed, contain perhaps the most absolutely
ludicrous instance of the absurdest side of that
remarkable thing, except Mackenzie's great
trouvaille of the press-gang who unanimously
melted into tears [2] at the plea of an affectionate father.
Marmontel's masterpiece is not so very far removed in
subject from this. It represents a good young man,
who stirs up the timorous captain and crew of a ship
against an Algerine pirate, and in the ensuing engagement, sabre in hand, makes a terrible carnage : "As soon
as he sees an African coming on board, he runs to him
and cuts him in half, crying, ' My poor mother !' "
The filial hero varies this a little, when " disembowelling "
the Algerine commander, by requesting the Deity to
" have pity on " his parent — a proceeding faintly
suggestive of a survival in his mind of the human-sacrifice
period.

*The best
of his Contes
Moraux
worth a
good deal.*

Fortunately, as has been said, it is not always thus : and
some of the tales are amusing in almost the highest
degree, being nearly as witty as Voltaire's, and entirely
free from ill-nature and sculduddery. Not that Marmontel—though a great advocate for marriage, and even
(for a Frenchman of his time) wonderfully favourable
to falling in love *before* marriage—pretends to be altogether superior to the customs of his own day. We still

---

[1] See next chapter.
[2] I wonder whether any one else has noticed that Thackeray, in the very agreeable
illustration to one of not quite his greatest "letterpress " things, *A New Naval Drama*
(Oxford Ed. vol. viii. p. 421), makes the pressgang weep ostentatiously in the picture,
though not in the text, where they only wave their cutlasses. It may be merely a
coincidence : but it may not.

sometimes have the " Prendre-Avoir-Quitter " series
of Crébillon,[1] though with fewer details ; and Mrs.
Newcome would have been almost more horrified than
she was at *Joseph Andrews* by the perusal of one of
Marmontel's most well-intentioned things, *Annette et
Lubin*. But he never lays himself out for attractions of
a doubtful kind, and none of his best stories, even when
they may sometimes involve bowing in the house of
Ashtoreth as well as that of Rimmon, derive their bait
from this kind. Indeed they rather " assume and pass
it by " as a fashion of the time.

.We may take three or four of them as examples. One
is the very first of the collection, *Alcibiade ou le Moi*.
Alcibiade Hardly anybody need be told that the Alci-
ou le Moi. biades of the tale, though nominally, is not in
the least really the Alcibiades of history, or that his
Athens is altogether Paris ; while his Socrates is a
kind of *philosophe*, the good points of Voltaire, Rousseau, and Diderot being combined with the faults of none
of them, and his ladies are persons who—with one
exception—simply could not have existed in Greece.
This Alcibiades wishes to be loved " for himself," and is
(not without reason) very doubtful whether he ever has
been, though he is the most popular and " successful "
man in Athens. His *avoir*, for the moment, is concerned
with a " Prude." (Were there prudes in Greece ? I
think Diogenes would have gladly lent his lantern for
the search.) He is desperately afraid that she only
loves him for *her*self. He determines to try her ; takes
her, not at her deeds, but at her words, which are, of
course, such as would have made the Greeks laugh as
inextinguishably as their gods once did. She expresses
gratitude for his unselfishness, but is anything but
pleased. Divers experiments are tried by her, and
when at last he hopes she will not tempt him any more,
exclaiming that he is really " l'amant le plus fidèle, le
plus tendre et le plus respectueux " . . . " et le plus sot,"

---

[1] There are reasons for thinking that Marmontel was deliberately "antidoting
the *fanfreluches*" of the older tale-teller.

adds she, sharply, concluding the conversation and shutting her, let us say, doors [1] on him.

He is furious, and tries " Glicerie " (the form might be more Greek), an *ingénue* of fifteen, who was " like a rose," who had attracted already the vows of the most gallant youths, etc. The most brilliant of these youths instantly retire before the invincible Alcibiades. But in the first place she wishes that before " explanations " [2] take place, a marriage shall be arranged ; while he, oddly enough, wishes that the explanations should precede the hymen. Also she is particular about the consent of her parents : and, finally, when he asks her whether she will swear constancy against every trial, to be his, and his only, whatever happens, she replies, with equal firmness and point, " Never ! " So he is furious again. But there is a widow, and, as we have seen in former cases, there was not, in the French eighteenth century, the illiberal prejudice against widows expressed by Mr. Weller. She is, of course, inconsolable for her dear first, but admits, after a time, the possibility of a dear second. Only it must be kept secret as yet. For a time Alcibiades behaves nobly, but somehow or other he finds that everybody knows the fact ; he is treated by his lady-love with obvious superiority ; and breaks with her. An interlude with a " magistrate's " wife, on less proper and more Crébillonish lines, is not more successful. So one day meeting by the seashore a beautiful courtesan, Erigone, he determines, in the not contemptible language of that single-speech poetess, Maria del Occidente, to " descend and sip a lower draught." He is happy after a fashion with her for two whole months : but at the end of that time he is beaten in a chariot race, and, going to Erigone for consolation, finds the winner's vehicle at her door. Socrates, on being consulted, recommends Glicerie as, after all, the best of them, in a rather sensible discourse. But the concluding

[1] In the original, suiting the rest of the setting, it is *rideaux*.
[2] " Explanations " is quite admirable, and, I think, neither borrowed from, nor, which is more surprising, by others.

words of the sage and the story are, as indeed might be
expected from Xanthippe's husband, not entirely opti-
mist: " If your wife is well conducted and amiable,
you will be a happy man ; if she is ill-tempered and a
coquette, you will become a philosopher—so you must
gain in any case." An " obvious," perhaps, but a neat
and uncommonly well-told story.

Soliman the Second is probably the best known of
Marmontel's tales, and it certainly has great merits.

Soliman the Second. It is hardly inferior in wit to Voltaire, and is
entirely free from the smears of uncomeliness
and the sniggers of bad taste which he would have been
sure to put in. The subject is, of course, partly historical,
though the reader of Knollys (and one knows more
unhappy persons) will look in vain there, not, indeed, for
Roxelana, but for the *nez retroussé*, which is the important
point of the story. The great Sultan tires of his Asiatic
harem, complaisant but uninteresting, and orders European damsels to be caught or bought for him. The
most noteworthy of the catch or batch are Elmire, Delia,
and Roxelane. Elmire comes first to Soliman's notice,
charms him by her sentimental ways, and reigns for a
time, but loses her piquancy, and (by no means wholly
to her satisfaction) is able to avail herself of the conditional enfranchisement, and return to her country, which
his magnanimity has granted her. Her immediate
supplanter, Delia, is an admirable singer, and possessed
of many of the qualifications of an accomplished *hetæra*.
But for that very reason the Sultan tires of her likewise ;
and for the same, she is not inconsolable or restive :
indeed she acts as a sort of Lady Pandara, if not to
introduce, at any rate to tame, the third, Roxelane, a
French girl of no very regular beauty, but with infinite
attractions, and in particular possessed of what Mr.
Dobson elegantly calls " a madding ineffable nose " of
the *retroussé* type.

The first thing the Sultan hears of this damsel is
that the Master of the Eunuchs cannot in the least
manage her ; for she merely laughs at all he says. The

2 E

Sultan, out of curiosity, orders her to be brought to him, and she immediately cries : " Thank Heaven ! here is a face like a man's. Of course you are the sublime Sultan whose slave I have the honour to be ? Please cashier this disgusting old rascal." To which extremely irreverent address Soliman makes a dignified reply of the proper kind, including due reference to " obedience " and his " will." This brings down a small pageful of raillery from the young person, who asks " whether this is Turkish gallantry ? " suggests that the restrictions of the seraglio involve a fear that " the skies should rain men," and more than hints that she should be very glad if they did. For the moment Soliman, though much taken with her, finds no way of saving his dignity ex- cept by a retreat. The next time he sends for her, or rather announces his own arrival, she tells the messenger to pack himself off : and when the Commander of the Faithful does visit her and gives a little good advice, she is still incorrigible. She will, once more, have nothing to do with the words *dois* and *devoir*. When asked if she knows what he is and what *she* is, she answers with perfect *aplomb*, " What we are ? You are powerful, and I am pretty ; so we are quite on an equality." In the most painfully confidential and at the same time quite decent manner, she asks him what he can possibly do with five hundred wives ? and, still more intolerably, tells him that she likes his looks, and has already loved people who were not worth him. The horror with which this Turkish soldan, himself so full of sin, ejaculates, " Vous *avez* aimé ? ". may be easily imagined, and again she simply puts him to flight. When he gets over it a little, he sends Delia to negotiate. But Roxelane tells the go-between to stay to supper, declaring that she herself does not feel inclined for a *tête-à-tête* yet, and finally sends him off with this obliging predecessor and sub- stitute, presenting her with the legendary handkerchief, which she has actually borrowed from the guileless Padishah. There is some, but not too much more of it ; there can but be one end ; and as he takes her to the

Mosque to make her legitimate Sultana, quite contrary to proper Mussulman usage, he says to himself, " Is it really possible that a little *retroussé* nose should upset the laws of an empire ? " Probably, though Marmontel does not say so, he looked down at the said nose, as he communed with himself, and decided that cause and effect were not unworthy of each other. There is hardly a righter and better hit-off tale of the kind, even in French.

" The Four Flasks " or " The Adventures of Alcidonis of Megara," a sort of outside fairy tale, is good, *The Four* but not quite so good as either of the former. *Flasks.* Alcidonis has a fairy protectress, if not exactly godmother, who gives him the flasks in question to use in amatory adventures. One, with purple liquor in it, sets the drinker in full tide of passion ; the second (rose-coloured) causes a sort of flirtation ; the third (blue) leads to sentimental and moderate affection ; and the last (pure white) recovers the experimenter from the effects of any of the others. He tries all, and all but the last are unsatisfactory, though, much as in the case of Alcibiades and Glicerie, the blue has a second chance, the results of which are not revealed. This is the least important of the group, but is well told.

There is also much good in *Heureusement,* the nearest to a " Crébillonnade " of all, though the Crébillonesque *Heureuse-* situations are ingeniously broken off short. *ment.* It is told by an old marquise [1] to an almost equally old abbé, her crony, who only at the last discovers that, long ago, he himself was very nearly the shepherd of the proverbial hour. And *Le Mari Sylphe,* which is still more directly connected with one of Crébillon's actual pieces, and with some of the weaker stories (*v. sup.*) of the *Cabinet des Fées,* would be good if it were not much too long. Others might be mentioned, but my own favourite, though it has nothing quite so magnetic in it as the *nez de Roxelane,* is *Le Philosophe Soi-disant,* a sort

---

[1] She declares that she has never actually "stooped to folly" ; but admits that on more than one occasion it was only an accidental interruption which "luckily" (*heureusement*) saved her.

of apology for his own clan, in a satire on its less
worthy members, which may seem to hit rather unfairly
at Rousseau, but which is exceedingly amusing.

Clarice—one of those so useful young widows of whom
the novelists of this time might have pleaded that they
took their ideas of them from the Apostle St.
Le Philosophe Soi-disant. Paul—has for some time been anxious to know
a *philosophe*, though she has been warned that
there are *philosophes* and *philosophes*, and that the right
kind is neither common nor very fond of society. She
expresses surprise, and says that she has always heard
a *philosophe* defined as an odd creature who makes it his
business to be like nobody else. " Oh," she is told,
" there is no difficulty about *that* kind," and one, by name
Ariste, is shortly added to her country-house party.
She politely asks him whether he is not a *philosophe*, and
whether philosophy is not a very beautiful thing? He
replies (his special line being sententiousness) that it is
simply the knowledge of good and evil, or, if she prefers
it, Wisdom. " Only that ? " says wicked Doris ; but
Clarice helps him from replying to the scoffer by going
on to ask whether the fruit of Wisdom is not happiness ?
" And, Madame, the making others happy." " Dear
me," says naïve Lucinde, half under her breath, " I
must be a *philosophe*, for I have been told a hundred
times that it only depended on myself to be happy by
making others happy." There is more wickedness from
Doris ; but Ariste, with a contemptuous smile, explains
that the word " happiness " has more than one meaning,
and that the *philosophe* kind is different from that at the
disposal and dispensation of a pretty woman. Clarice,
admitting this, asks what *his* kind of happiness is ? The
company then proceeds, in the most reprehensible fashion,
to " draw " the sage : and they get from him, among other
things, an admission that he despises everybody, and an
unmistakable touch of disgust when somebody speaks of
" his *semblables*." [1]

Clarice, however, still plays the amiable and polite

---

[1] It is necessary to retain the French here : for our " likes " is ambiguous.

hostess, lets him take her to dinner, and says playfully that she means to reconcile him to humanity. He altogether declines. Man is a vicious beast, who persecutes and devours others, he says, making all the time a particularly good dinner while denouncing the slaughter of animals, and eulogising the "sparkling brook" while getting slightly drunk. He declaims against the folly and crime of the modern world in not making philosophers kings, and announces his intention of seeking complete solitude. But Clarice, still polite, decides that he must stay with them a little while, in order to enlighten and improve the company.

After this, Ariste, in an alley alone, to digest his dinner and walk off his wine, persuades himself that Clarice has fallen in love with him, and that, to secure her face and her fortune, he has only got to go on playing the misanthrope and give her a chance of "taming the bear." The company, perfectly well knowing his thoughts, determine to play up to them—not for his greater glory; and Clarice, not quite willingly, agrees to take the principal part. In a long *tête-à-tête* he makes his clumsy court, airs his cheap philosophy, and lets by no means the mere suggestion of a cloven foot appear, on the subject of virtue and vice. However, she stands it, though rather disgusted, and confesses to him that people are suggesting a certain Cléon, a member of the party, as her second husband; whereon he decries marriage, but proposes himself as a lover. She reports progress, and is applauded; but the Présidente de Ponval, another widow, fat, fifty, fond of good fare, possessed of a fine fortune, but very far from foolish, vows that *she* will make the greatest fool of Ariste. Cléon, however, accepts his part; and appears to be much disturbed at Clarice's attentions to Ariste, who, being shown to his room, declaims against its luxuries, but avails himself of them very cheerfully. In the morning he, though rather doubtfully, accepts a bath; but on his appearance in company Clarice makes remonstrances on his dress, etc., and actually prevails on him to let a valet curl his hair. This is an improvement; but she does not like his brown coat.[1] He must write to Paris and order a suit of *gris-de-lin clair*, and after some wrangling he consents. But now the Présidente takes up the running. After expressing the extremest admiration for his coiffure, she makes a dead set at him, tells him she wants a second husband whom she can love for himself, and goes off with a passionate glance, the company letting him casually know that she has ten thousand crowns a year. He affects to despise this, which is duly reported to her next morning. She vows vengeance; but he dreams of her (and the crowns) meanwhile, and with that morning the new suit arrives. He is admiring himself in it when Cléon comes in, and throws himself on his mercy. He adores Clarice; Ariste is evidently gaining fatally on her affections; will he not be generous and abstain from using his advantages? But if *he* is really in love Cléon will give her up.

The hook is, of course, more than singly baited and barbed. Ariste can at once play the magnanimous man, and be rewarded by the Présidente's ten thousand a year. He will be off with Clarice and on with Mme. de Ponval, whom he visits in his new splendour. She admires it hugely, but is alarmed at seeing him in Clarice's favourite colour. An admirable conversation follows, in which she constantly draws her ill-bred, ill-blooded, and self-besotted suitor into addressing her with insults, under the guise of compliments, and affects to enjoy them. He next visits Clarice, with whom he finds Cléon, in the depths of despair. She begins to admire the coat, and to pride herself on her choice, when he interrupts her, and solemnly resigns her to Cléon. Doris and Lucinde come in, and everybody is astounded at Ariste's generosity as he takes Clarice's hand and places it in that of his rival. Then he goes to the Présidente, and tells her what he has done. She expresses her delight, and he falls at her feet. Thereupon she throws round his neck a

---

[1] Cf. the stories, contradictory of each other, as to *our* brown-coated philosopher's appearance in France. (Boswell, p. 322, Globe ed.)

rose-coloured ribbon (*her* colours), calls him " her Charming man," [1] and insists on showing him to the public as
her conquest and captive. He has no time to refuse, for
the door opens and they all appear. " Le voilà," says
she, " cet homme si fier qui soupire à mes genoux pour les
beaux yeux de ma cassette ! Je vous le livre. Mon rôle
est joué." So Ariste, tearing his curled hair, and the *gris-
de-lin clair* coat, and, doubtless, the Présidente's " red rose
chain," cursing also terribly, goes off to write a book
against the age, and to prove that nobody is wise but
himself.

I can hardly imagine more than one cavil being made
against this by the most carping of critics and the most
wedded to the crotchet of " kinds "—that it is too
dramatic for a *story*, and that we ought to have had it as
a drama. If this were further twisted into an accusation
of plagiarism from the actual theatre, I think it could be
rebutted at once. The situations separately might be
found in many dramas ; the characters in more ; but I
at least am not aware of any one in which they had been
similarly put together. Of course most if not all of us
have seen actresses who would make Clarice charming,
Madame de Ponval amusing, and Doris and Lucinde
very delectable adjuncts ; as well as actors by whom the
parts of Cléon and Ariste would be very effectively worked
out. But why we should be troubled to dress, journey,
waste time and money, and get a headache, by going to
the theatre, when we can enjoy all this " in some close
corner of [our] brain," I cannot see. As I read the
story in some twenty minutes, I can see *my* Clarice,
my Madame de Ponval, *my* Doris and Lucinde and
Cléon and Ariste and Jasmin—the silent but doubtless highly appreciative valet, — and I rather doubt
whether the best company in the world could give me
quite that.

But, even in saying this, full justice has not yet been

---

[1] Cf. again the bestowal of this title by Horace Walpole, in his later days, on
Edward Jerningham, playwright, poetaster, and *petit maître*, who, unluckily for himself,
lived into the more roughly satirical times of the Revolutionary War.

done to Marmontel. He has, from our special point of view, made a real further progress towards the ideal of the ordinary novel—the presentation of ordinary life. He has borrowed no supernatural aid;[1] he has laid under contribution no "fie-fie" seasonings; he has sacrificed nothing, or next to nothing, in these best pieces, whatever he may have done elsewhere, to purpose and crotchet. He has discarded stuffing, digression, episode, and other things which weighed on and hampered his predecessors. In fact there are times when it seems almost unjust, in this part of his work, to "second" him in the way we have done; though it must be admitted that if you take his production as a whole he relapses into the second order.

A real advance in these.

The actual books, in anything that can be called fiction, of Bernardin de Saint-Pierre are of far less merit than Marmontel's; but most people who have even the slightest knowledge of French literature know why he cannot be excluded here. Personally, he seems to have been an ineffectual sort of creature, and in a large part of his rather voluminous work he is (when he ceases to produce a sort of languid amusement) a distinctly boring one.[2] He appears to have been unlucky, but to have helped his own bad luck with the only signs of effectualness that he ever showed. It is annoying, no doubt, to get remonstrances from headquarters as to your not sending any work (plans, reports, etc.) as an engineer, and to find, or think you

Bernardin de Saint-Pierre.

---

[1] "The *sylph*ishness of *Le Mari Sylphe* is only an ingenious and defensible fraud; and the philtre-flasks of *Alcidonis* are little more than "properties."

[2] Here is a specimen of his largest and most ambitious production, the *Études de la Nature*. "La femelle du tigre, exhalant l'odeur du carnage, fait retentir les solitudes de l'Afrique de ses miaulements affreux, et paraît remplie d'attraits à ses cruels amants." By an odd chance, I once saw a real scene contrasting remarkably with Saint-Pierre's sentimental melodrama. It was in the Clifton Zoological Gardens, which, as possibly some readers may know, were at one time regarded as particularly home-like by the larger carnivora. It was a very fine day, and an equally fine young tigress was endeavouring to attract the attention of her cruel lover. She rolled delicately about, like a very large, very pretty, and exceptionally graceful cat; she made fantastic gestures with her paws and tail; and she purred literally "as gently as any sucking dove"—*roucoulement* was the only word for it. But her "lover," though he certainly looked "cruel" and as if he would very much like to eat *me*, appeared totally indifferent to her attractions.

find, that your immediate C.O. has suppressed them.
But when you charge him with his disgraceful proceeding,
and he, as any French officer in his position at his time
was likely to do, puts his hand on his sword, it is un-
diplomatic to rush on another officer who happens
to be present, grab at and draw his weapon (you are
apparently not entitled to one), and attack your chief.
Nor when, after some more unsuccessful experiences at
home and abroad, you are on half or no pay, and want
employment, would it seem to be exactly the wisdom
of Solomon to give a minister the choice of employing
you on (1) the civilisation of Corsica, (2) the exploration of the unknown parts of the Western Continent,
(3) the discovery of the sources of the Nile, and (4) a
pedestrian tour throughout India. But, except in the
first instance (for the " Citizen of Geneva " did not meddle
much with cold steel), it was all very like a pupil, and (in the
Citizen's later years) a friend, of Rousseau, carrying out
his master's ideas with a stronger dose of Christianity, but
with quite as little common sense. I have not seen (or
remembered) any more exact account of Saint-Pierre's
relations with Napoleon than that given by the excellent
Aimé-Martin, an academic euphemiser of the French
kind. But, even reading between his lines, they must
have been very funny.[1]

Paul et Virginie, however, is one of those books which,
having attained and long kept a European reputation,
cannot be neglected, and it may be added that it does
deserve, though for one thing only, never to be entirely
forgotten. It is chock-full of *sensibilité*, the characters
have no real character, and all healthy-minded persons
have long ago agreed that the concomitant facts, if not
causes, of Virginie's fate are more nasty than the nastiest
thing in Diderot or Rabelais.[2] But the descriptions of

---

[1] So, also, when one is told that he called his son Paul and his daughter Virginie, it
is cheerful to remember, with a pleasant sense of contrast, Scott's good-humoured
contempt for the tourists who wanted to know whether Abbotsford was to be called
Tullyveolan or Tillietudlem.

[2] As the story is not now, I believe, the universal school-book it once was, something more than mere allusion may be desirable. The ship in which Virginie is

the scenery of Mauritius, as sets-off to a novel, are some-thing new, and something immensely important. *La Chaumière Indienne*, though less of a story in size and general texture, is much better from the point of view of taste. It has touches of real irony, and almost of humour, though its hero, the good pariah, is a creature nearly as uninteresting as he is impossible. Yet his " black and polished " baby is a vivid property, and the descriptions are again famous. The shorter pieces, *Le Café de Surate*, etc., require little notice.

It will, however, have been seen by anybody who can " seize points," that this *philosophe* novel, as such, is a really important agent in bringing on the novel itself to its state of full age. That men like the three chiefs should take up the form is a great thing ; that men who are not quite chiefs, like Marmontel and Saint-Pierre, should carry it on, is not a small one. They all do something to get it out of the rough ; to discard—if sometimes also they add—irrelevances ; to modernise this one kind which is perhaps the predestined and acceptable literary product of modernity. Voltaire originates little, but puts his immense power and *diable au corps* into the body of fiction. Rousseau enchains passion in its service, as Madame de la Fayette, as even Prévost, had not been able to do before. Diderot indicates, in whatever ques-tionable material, the vast possibilities of psychological analysis. Marmontel—doing, like other second-rate talents, almost more *useful* work than his betters—rescues the *conte* from the " demi-rep " condition into which it had fallen, and, owing to the multifariousness of his examples, does not entirely subjugate it even to honest purpose ; while Bernardin de Saint-Pierre carries the suggestions of Rousseau still further in the invaluable department of

---

returning to the Isle of France gets into shallows during a hurricane, and is being beaten to pieces close to land. One stalwart sailor, stripped to swim for his life, approaches Virginie, imploring her to strip likewise and let him try to pilot her through the surf. But she (like the lady in the coach, at an early part of *Joseph Andrews*) won't so much as look at a naked man, clasps her arms round her own garments, and is very deservedly drowned. The sailor, to one's great relief, is not.

description. No one, except on the small scale, is great in plot ; no one produces a really individual character ;[1] and it can hardly be said that any one provides thoroughly achieved novel dialogue. But they have inspired and enlivened the whole thing as a whole ; and if, against this, is to be set the crime of purpose, that is one not difficult to discard.[2]

[1] Julie herself is an intense type rather than individual.
[2] I have not thought it necessary, except in regard to those of them who have been touched in treating of the *Cabinet des Fées*, to speak at any length of the minor tale-tellers of the century. They are sometimes not bad reading ; but as a whole minor in almost all senses.

CHAPTER XII

"SENSIBILITY." MINOR AND LATER NOVELISTS.

THE FRENCH NOVEL, c. 1800

FREQUENT reference has been made, in the last two chapters, to the curious phenomenon called in French "Sensibility." *sensibilité* (with a derivative of contempt, *sensiblerie*), the exact English form of which supplies part of the title, and the meaning an even greater part of the subject, of one of Miss Austen's novels. The thing itself appears first definitely [1] in Madame de la Fayette, largely, though not unmixedly, in Marivaux, and to some extent in Prévost and Marmontel, while it is, as it were, sublimed in Rousseau, and present very strongly in Saint-Pierre. There are, however, some minor writers and books displaying it in some cases even more extensively and intensively; and in this final chapter of the present volume they may appropriately find a place, not merely because some of them are late, but because Sensibility is not confined to any part of the century, but, beginning before its birth, continued till after its end. We may thus have to encroach on the nineteenth a little, but more in appearance than in reality. In quintessence, and as a reigning fashion, Sensibility was the property of the eighteenth century.[2]

---

[1] We have seen above how things were "shaping for" it, in the Pastoral and Heroic romances. But the shape was not definitely taken in them.

[2] In the following pages, and here only in this volume, the author has utilised, though with very considerable alterations, some previously published work, *A Study of Sensibility*, which appeared originally in the *Fortnightly Review* for September 1882, and was republished in a volume (*Essays on French Novelists*, London, 1891) which has been for some years out of print. Much of the original essay, dealing with Marivaux and

To recur for a moment to Miss Austen and *Sense and Sensibility*, everybody has laughed, let us hope not un-

A glance at Miss Austen. kindly, over Marianne Dashwood's woes. But she herself was only an example, exagger- ated in the genial fashion of her creatress, of the proper and recognised standard of feminine feeling in and long before her time. The " man of feeling " was admitted as something out of the way—on which side of the way opinions might differ. But the woman of feeling was emphatically the accepted type—a type which lasted far into the next century, though it was obsolete at least by the Mid-Victorian period, of which some do so vainly talk. The extraordinary development of emotion which was expected from women need not be illustrated merely from love-stories. The wonderful transports of Miss Ferrier's heroines at sight of their long-lost mothers ; even those of sober Fanny Price in *Mansfield Park*, at the recovery of her estimable but not particularly interesting brother William, give the key-note much better than any more questionable ecstasies. " Sensibility, so charming," was the pet affectation of the period—an affectation carried on till it became quite natural, and was only cured by the half-caricature, half-reaction of Byronism.

The thing, however, was not English in origin, and never was thoroughly English at all. The main current

The thing essentially French. of the Sensibility novelists, who impressed their curious morals or manners on all men and women in civilised Europe, was French in unbroken succession, from the day when Madame de la Fayette first broke ground against the ponderous romances of Madeleine de Scudéry, to the day when Benjamin Constant forged, in *Adolphe*, the link between eighteenth - century and nineteenth - century romance, between the novel of sentiment and the novel of analysis.

Of the relations to it of the greater novelists of the

others already treated here, has been removed, and the whole has been cut down, revised, and adjusted to its new contexts. But it seemed unnecessary to waste time in an endeavour to say the same thing differently about matters which, though as a whole indispensable, are, with perhaps one exception, individually not of the first importance.

main century we have already spoken : and as for the two
greatest of the extreme close, Chateaubriand
Its history. and Madame de Stael, they mix too many
secondary purposes with their philandering, and moreover
do not form part of the plan of the present volume. For
the true Sensibility, the odd quintessence of conventional
feeling, played at steadily till it is half real, if not wholly
so, which ends in the peculiarities of two such wholesome
young Britonesses as Marianne Dashwood and Fanny
Price, we must look elsewhere. After Madame de la
Fayette, and excluding with her other names already
treated, we come to Madame de Fontaines, Madame de
Tencin (most heartless and therefore naturally not
least sentimental of women), Madame Riccoboni, the
group of lady-novelists of whom Mesdames de Souza
and de Duras are the chief, and, finally, the two really
remarkable names of Xavier de Maistre and Benjamin
Constant. These are our " documents." Even the minor
subjects of this inquiry are pleasant pieces of literary
bric-à-brac ; perhaps they are something a little more
than that. For Sensibility was actually once a great
power in the world. Transformed a little, it did wonderful things in the hands of Rousseau and Goethe and
Chateaubriand and Byron. It lingers in odd nooks
and corners even at the present day, when it is usually
and irreverently called " gush," and Heaven only knows
whether it may not be resuscitated in full force before
some of us are dead.[1] For it has exactly the peculiarities
which characterise all recurrent fashions—the appeal to
something which is genuine connected with the suggestion of a great deal that is not.

In the followers of Madame de la Fayette[2] we find
that a good many years have passed by. The jargon
appropriated to the subject has grown still more official ;
and instead of using it to express genuine sentiments,

---

[1] These words were originally written more than thirty years ago. I am not sure
that there was not something prophetic in them.
[2] Madame de Fontaines in *La Comtesse de Savoie* and *Amenophis* "follows her leader"
in more senses than one—including a sort of pseudo-historical setting or insetting which
became almost a habit. But she is hardly important.

which in another language might deserve expression well
Mme. de Tencin and Le Comte de Comminge. enough, the characters are constantly suspected by the callous modern reader of elaborately, though perhaps unconsciously, feigning the sentiments which the jargon seems to imply that they ought to have. This is somewhat less noticeable in the work of Madame de Tencin than elsewhere, because d'Alembert's mother was so very much cleverer a person than the generality of the novel-writers of her day that she could hardly fail to hide defects more cunningly. But it is evident enough in the *Comte de Comminge* and in the *Malheurs de l'Amour*. Having as questionable morals as any lady of the time (the time of the Regency), Madame de Tencin of course always had a moral purpose in her writings, and this again gives her books a certain difference. But, like the former, this difference only exposes, all the more clearly, the defects of the style, and the drawbacks from which it was almost impossible that those who practised it should escape.

Madame de Tencin tried to escape by several gates. Besides her moral purposes and her *esprit*, she indulged in a good deal of rather complicated and sometimes extravagant incident. *M. de Comminge*, which is very short, contains, not to mention other things, the rather startling detail of a son who, out of chivalrous affection for his lady-love, burns certain of his father's title-deeds which he has been charged to recover, and the still more startling incident of the heroine living for some years in disguise as a monk. The following epistle, however, from the heroine to the hero, will show better than anything else the topsy-turvy condition which sensibility had already reached. All that need be said in explanation of it is that the father (who is furious with his son, and not unreasonably so) has shut him up in a dungeon, in order to force him to give up his beloved Adelaide.[1]

---

[1] Readers of Thackeray may remember in *The Paris Sketch Book* ("On the French School of Painting," p. 52, Oxford ed.) some remarks on Jacquand's picture, "The Death of Adelaide de Comminge," which he thought "neither more nor less than beautiful." But from his "it appears," in reference to the circumstances, it would seem that he did not know the book, save perhaps from a catalogue-extract or summary.

Your father's fury has told me all I owe you: I know what your generosity had concealed from me. I know, too, the terrible situation in which you are, and I have no means of extracting you therefrom save one. This will perhaps make you more unhappy still. But I shall be as unhappy as yourself, *and this gives me the courage to do what I am required to do.* They would have me, by engaging myself to another, give a pledge never to be yours: 'tis at this price that M. de Comminge sets your liberty. It will cost me perhaps my life, certainly my peace. But I am resolved. I shall in a few days be married to the Marquis de Bénavidés. What I know of his character forewarns me of what I shall have to suffer; *but I owe you at least so much constancy as to make only misery for myself in the engagement I am contracting.*

The extremity of calculated absurdity indicated by the italicised passages was reached, let it be remembered, by one of the cleverest women of the century: and the chief excuse for it is that the restrictions of the La Fayette novel, confined as it was to the upper classes and to a limited number of elaborately distressing situations, were very embarrassing.

Madame Riccoboni, mentioned earlier as continuing *Marianne*, shows the completed product very fairly. Her *Histoire du Marquis de Cressy* is a capital example of the kind. The Marquis is beloved by a charming girl of sixteen and by a charming widow of six-and-twenty. An envious rival betrays his attentions to Adelaide de Bugei, and her father makes her write an epistle which pretty clearly gives him the option of a declaration in form or a rupture. For a Sensible man, it must be confessed, the Marquis does not get out of the difficulty too well. She has slipped into her father's formal note the highly Sensible postscript, " Vous dire de m'oublier ? Ah ! Jamais. On m'a forcé de l'écrire ; rien ne peut m'obliger à le penser ni le désirer." Apparently it was not leap-year, for the Marquis replied in a letter nearly as bad as Willoughby's celebrated epistle in *Sense and Sensibility*.

> MADEMOISELLE,—Nothing can console me for having been the innocent cause of fault being found with the conduct of a person so worthy of respect as you. I shall approve whatever you may

think proper to do, without considering myself entitled to ask the reason of your behaviour. How happy should I be, mademoiselle, if my fortune, and the arrangements which it forces me to make, did not deprive me of the sweet hope of an honour of which my respect and my sentiments would perhaps make me worthy, but which my present circumstances permit me not to seek.

Sensibility does not seem to have seen anything very unhandsome in this broad refusal to throw the handkerchief; but though not unhandsome, it could not be considered satisfactory to the heart. So M. de Cressy despatches this private note to Adelaide by "Machiavel the waiting-maid"—

Is it permitted to a wretch who has deprived himself of the greatest of blessings, to dare to ask your pardon and your pity? Never did love kindle a flame purer and more ardent than that with which my heart burns for the amiable Adelaide. Why have I not been able to give her those proofs of it which she had the right to expect? Ah! mademoiselle, how could I bind you to the lot of a wretch all whose wishes even you perhaps would not fulfil? who, when he possessed you, though master of so dear, so precious a blessing, might regret others less estimable, but which have been the object of his hope and desire, etc. etc.

This means that M. de Cressy is ambitious, and wants a wife who will assist his views. The compliment is doubtful, and Adelaide receives it in approved fashion. She opens it "with a violent emotion," and her "trouble was so great in reading it through, that she had to begin it again many times before she understood it." The exceedingly dubious nature of the compliment, however, strikes her, and "tears of regret and indignation rise to her eyes"—tears which indeed are excusable even from a different point of view than that of Sensibility. She is far, however, from blaming that sacred emotion. "Ce n'est pas," she says; "de notre sensibilité, mais de l'objet qui l'a fait naître, que nous devons nous plaindre." This point seems arguable if it were proper to argue with a lady.

The next letter to be cited is from Adelaide's unconscious rival, whose conduct is—translated into the

language of Sensibility, and adjusted to the manners of
the time and class—a ludicrous anticipation of the Pickwickian widow. She buys a handsome scarf, and sends
it anonymously to the victorious Marquis just before a
Court ball, with this letter—

A sentiment, tender, timid, and shy of making itself known,
gives me an interest in penetrating the secrets of your heart. You
are thought indifferent; you seem to me insensible. Perhaps
you are happy, and discreet in your happiness. Deign to tell me
the secret of your soul, and be sure that I am not unworthy of your
confidence. If you have no love for any one, wear this scarf
at the ball. Your compliance may lead you to a fate which others
envy. She who feels inclined to prefer you is worthy of your
attentions, and the step she takes to let you know it is the first
weakness which she has to confess.

The modesty of this perhaps leaves something to
desire, but its Sensibility is irreproachable. There is
no need to analyse the story of the *Marquis de Cressy*,
which is a very little book [1] and not extremely edifying.
But it supplies us with another *locus classicus* on sentimental manners. M. de Cressy has behaved very badly
to Adelaide, and has married the widow with the scarf.
He receives a letter from Adelaide on the day on which
she takes the black veil—

'Tis from the depths of an asylum, where I fear no more the
perfidy of your sex, that I bid you an eternal adieu. Birth,
wealth, honours, all vanish from my sight. My youth withered
by grief, my power of enjoyment destroyed, love past, memory
present, and regret still too deeply felt, all combine to bury me
in this retreat.

And so forth, all of which, if a little high-flown,
is not specially unnatural; but the oddity of the passage
is to come. Most men would be a little embarrassed at
receiving such a letter as this in presence of their wives

---

[1] The extreme shortness of all these books may be just worth noticing. Reaction
from the enormous romances of the preceding century may have had something
to do with it; and the popularity of the "tale" something more. But the *causa
verissima* was probably the impossibility of keeping up sentiment at high pressure for
any length of time, incident, or talk.

(it is to be observed that the unhappy Adelaide is profuse of pardons to Madame as well as to Monsieur de Cressy), and most wives would not be pleased when they read it. But Madame de Cressy has the finest Sensibility of the amiable kind. She reads it, and then—

> The Marquise, having finished this letter, cast herself into the arms of her husband, and clasping him with an inexpressible tenderness, "Weep, sir, weep," she cried, bathing him with her own tears; "you cannot show too much sensibility for a heart so noble, so constant in its love. Amiable and dear Adelaide ! 'Tis done, then, and we have lost you for ever. Ah ! why must I reproach myself with having deprived you of the only possession which excited your desires ? Can I not enjoy this sweet boon without telling myself that my happiness has destroyed yours ?"

All Madame Riccoboni's work is, with a little good-will, more or less interesting. Much of it is full of italics, which never were used so freely in France as in England, but which seem to suit the queer, exaggerated, topsy-turvyfied senti-ments and expressions very well. The *His-toire d'Ernestine* in particular is a charming little novelette. But if it were possible to give an abstract of any of her work here, *Milady Catesby*, which does us the honour to take its scene and personages from England, would be the one to choose. *Milady Catesby* is well worth com-paring with *Evelina*, which is some twenty years its junior, and the sentimental parts of which are quite in the same tone with it. Lord Ossery is indeed even more "sensible" than Lord Orville, but then he is described in French. Lady Catesby herself is, however, a model of the style, as when she writes—

[margin note: Her other work— Milady Catesby.]

> Oh ! my dear Henrietta ! What agitation in my senses ! what trouble in my soul ! . . . I have seen him. . . . He has spoken to me. . . . Himself. . . . He was at the ball. . . . Yes ! he. Lord Ossery. . . . Ah ! tell me not again to see him. . . . Bid me not hear him once more.

That will do for Lady Catesby, who really had no particular occasion or excuse for all this excitement

except Sensibility.   But Sensibility was getting more and
more exacting.   The hero of a novel must always be in
the heroics, the heroine in a continual state of palpitation.
We are already a long way from Madame de la Fayette's
stately passions, from Marianne's whimsical *minauderies*.
All the resources of typography—exclamations, points,
dashes—have to be called in to express the generally
disturbed state of things.   Now unfortunately this sort
of perpetual tempest in a teacup (for it generally is in a
teacup) requires unusual genius to make it anything
but ludicrous.   I myself have not the least desire to
laugh when I read such a book as *La Nouvelle Héloïse*,
and I venture to think that any one who does laugh must
have something of the fool and something of the brute
in his composition.   But then Rousseau is Rousseau,
and there are not many like him.   At the Madame
Riccobonis of this world, however clever they may be,
it is difficult not to laugh, when they have to dance on
such extraordinary tight ropes as those which Sensibility
prescribed.

The writers who were contemporary with Madame
Riccoboni's later days, and who followed her, pushed
Mme. de the thing, if it were possible, even farther.   In
Beaumont— Madame de Genlis's tiny novelette of *Made-*
Lettres du
Marquis de *moiselle de Clermont,* the amount of tears shed,
Roselle. the way in which the knees of the characters
knock together, their palenesses, blushes, tears, sighs,
and other performances of the same kind, are surprising.
In the *Lettres du Marquis de Roselle* of Madame Élie de
Beaumont (wife of the young advocate who defended the
Calas family), a long scene between a brother and sister,
in which the sister seeks to deter the brother from what
she regards as a misalliance, ends (or at least almost ends,
for the usual flood of tears is the actual conclusion) in
this remarkable passage.

" And I," cried he suddenly with a kind of fury, " I suppose
that a sister who loves her brother, pities and does not insult him ;
that the Marquis de Roselle knows better what can make him
happy than the Countess of St. Séver ; and that he is free, independ-

ent, able to dispose of himself, in spite of all opposition." With these words he turned to leave the room brusquely. I run to him, I stop him, he resists. " My brother ! " " I have no sister." He makes a movement to free himself : he was about to escape me. " Oh, my father ! " I cried. " Oh, my mother ! come to my help." At these sacred names he started, stopped, and *allowed himself to be conducted to a sofa.*

This unlucky termination might be paralleled from many other places, even from the agreeable writings of Mme. de Madame de Souza. This writer, by the way, Souza. when the father of one of her heroes refuses to consent to his son's marriage, makes the stern parent yield to a representation that by not doing so he will " authorise by anticipation a want of filial attachment and respect " in the grandchildren who do not as yet exist. These excursions into the preposterous in search of something new in the way of noble sentiment or affecting emotion—these whippings and spurrings of the feelings and the fancy—characterise all the later work of the school.

Two names of great literary value and interest close the list of the novelists of Sensibility in France, and show Xavier de at once its Nemesis and its caricature. They Maistre. were almost contemporaries, and by a curious coincidence neither was a Frenchman by birth. It would be impossible to imagine a greater contrast than existed personally between Xavier de Maistre and Henri Benjamin de Constant-Rebecque, commonly called Benjamin Constant. But their personalities, interesting as both are, are not the matter of principal concern here. The *Voyage autour de ma Chambre*, its sequel the *Expédition Nocturne*, and the *Lépreux de la Cité d'Aoste*, exhibit one branch of the river of Sensibility (if one may be permitted to draw up a new Carte de Tendre), losing itself in agreeable trifling with the surface of life, and in generous, but fleeting, and slightly, though not consciously, insincere indulgence of the emotions. In *Adolphe* the river rushes violently down a steep place, and *in nigras lethargi mergitur undas*. It is to be hoped that most people who will read these pages know Xavier de Maistre's charming little books ; it is probable that at least some of them do not know *Adolphe*. Constant is the more strictly original of the two authors, for Xavier de Maistre owes a heavy debt to Sterne, though he employs the borrowed capital so well that he makes it his own, while *Adolphe* can only be said to come after *Werther* and *René* in time, not in the least to follow them in nature.

The *Voyage autour de ma Chambre* (readers may be informed or reminded) is a whimsical description of the author's meditations and experiences when confined to barracks for some military peccadillo. After a fashion which has found endless imitators since, the prisoner contemplates the various objects in his room, spins little romances to himself about them and about his beloved Madame de Hautcastel, moralises on the faithfulness of his servant Joannetti, and so forth. The *Expédition Nocturne*, a less popular sequel, is not very different in plan. The *Lépreux de la Cité d'Aoste* is a very short story, telling how the narrator finds a sufferer from the most terrible of all diseases lodged in a garden-house, and of their dialogue. The chief merit of these works, as of the less mannerised and more direct *Prisonnier du Caucase* and *Jeune Sibérienne*, resides in their dainty style, in their singular narrative power (Sainte-Beuve says justly enough that the *Prisonnier du Caucase* has been equalled by no other writer except Mérimée), and in the remarkable charm of the personality of the author, which escapes at every moment from the work. The pleasant picture of the Chevalier de B—— in the *Soirées de St. Péters-bourg*, which Joseph de Maistre is said to have drawn from his less formidable brother, often suggests itself as one follows the whimsicalities of the *Voyage* and the *Expédition*. The affectation is so natural, the mannerism so simple, that it is some time before one realises how great in degree both are.

Looked at from a certain point of view, Xavier de

Maistre illustrates the effect of the Sensibility theory on a thoroughly good-natured, cultivated, and well-bred man of no particular force of character or strength of emotion. He has not the least intention of taking Sensibility seriously, but it is the proper thing to take it somehow or other. So he sets himself to work to be a man of feeling and a humorist at the same time. His encounter with the leper is so freshly and simply told, there is such an air of genuineness about it, that it seems at first sight not merely harsh, but unappreciative, to compare it to Sterne's account of his proceedings with his monks and donkeys, his imaginary prisoners, and his fictitious ensigns. Yet there is a real contact between them. Both have the chief note of Sensibility, the taking an emotion as a thing to be savoured and degusted deliberately—to be dealt with on scientific principles and strictly according to the rules of the game. One result of this proceeding, when pursued for a considerable time, is unavoidably a certain amount of frivolity, especially in dealing with emotions directly affecting the player. Sympathy such as that displayed with the leper may be strong and genuine, because there is no danger about it ; there is the *suave mari magno* preservative from the risk of a too deep emotion. But in matters which directly affect the interest of the individual it does not do to be too serious. The tear of Sensibility must not be dropped in a manner giving real pain to the dropper. Hence the humoristic attitude. When Xavier de Maistre informs us that " le grand art de l'homme de génie est de savoir bien élever sa bête," he means a great deal more than he supposes himself to mean. The great art of an easy-going person, who believes it to be his duty to be " sensible," is to arrange for a series of emotions which can be taken gently.

The author of the *Voyage* takes his without any extravagance. He takes good care not to burn his fingers metaphorically in this matter, though he tells us that in a fit of absence he did so literally. His affec-

His illustrations of the lighter side of Sensibility.

tion for Madame de Hautcastel is certainly not a very passionate kind of affection, for all his elaborately counted and described heartbeats as he is dusting her portrait. Indeed, with his usual candour, he leaves us in no doubt about the matter. " La froide raison," he says, " reprit bientôt son empire." Of course it did ; the intelligent, and in the other sense sensible, person who wishes to preserve his repose must take care of that. We do not even believe that he really dropped a tear of repentance on his left shoe when he had unreasonably rated his servant ; it is out of keeping with his own part. He borrowed that tear, either ironically or by oversight, from Sterne, just as he did " Ma chère Jenny." He is much more in his element when he proves that a lover is to his mistress, when she is about to go to a ball, only a "decimal of a lover," a kind of amatory tailor or ninth part of man ; or when, in the *Expédition*, he meditates on a lady's slipper in the balcony fathoms below his garret.

All this illustrates what may be called the attempt to get rid of Sensibility by the humorist gate of escape. A sign of decadence. Supposing no such attempt consciously to exist, it is, at any rate, the sign of an approaching downfall of Sensibility, of a feeling, on the part of those who have to do with it, that it is an edged tool, and an awkward one to handle. In comparing Xavier de Maistre with his master Sterne, it is very noticeable that while the one in disposition is thoroughly insincere, and the other thoroughly sincere, yet the insincere man is a true believer in Sensibility, and the sincere one evidently a semi-heretic. How far Sterne consciously simulated his droppings of warm tears, and how far he really meant them, may be a matter of dispute. But he was quite sincere in believing that they were very creditable things, and very admirable ones. Xavier de Maistre does not seem by any means so well convinced of this. He is, at times, not merely evidently pretending and making believe, but laughing at himself for pretending and making believe. He still thinks Sensibility a *gratissimus error*, a very pretty game for persons of refine-

ment to play at, and he plays at it with a great deal of
industry and with a most exquisite skill. But the spirit
of Voltaire, who himself did his *sensibilité* (in real life,
if not in literature) as sincerely as Sterne, has affected
Xavier de Maistre " with a difference." The Savoyard
gentleman is entirely and unexceptionably orthodox in
religion ; it may be doubted whether a severe inquisition
in matters of Sensibility would let him off scatheless. It
is not merely that he jests—as, for instance, that when he
is imagining the scene at the Rape of the Sabines, he
suddenly fancies that he hears a cry of despair from one
of the visitors. " Dieux immortels ! Pourquoi n'ai-
je amené ma femme à la fête ? " That is quite proper
and allowable. It is the general tone of levity in the
most sentimental moments, the undercurrent of mockery
at his own feelings in this man of feeling, which is so
shocking to Sensibility, and yet it was precisely this that
was inevitable.

Sensibility, to carry it out properly, required, like
other elaborate games, a very peculiar and elaborate
arrangement of conditions. The parties must be in
earnest so far as not to have the slightest suspicion that
they were making themselves ridiculous, and yet not in
earnest enough to make themselves really miserable.
They must have plenty of time to spare, and not be distracted by business, serious study, political excitement, or
other disturbing causes. On the other hand, to get too
much absorbed, and arrive at Werther's end, was destruc-
tive not only to the individual player, but to the spirit
of the game. As the century grew older, and this danger
of absorption grew stronger, that game became more and
more difficult to play seriously enough, and yet not too
seriously. When the players did not blow their brains
out, they often fell into the mere libertinism from which
Sensibility, properly so called, is separated by a clear
enough line. Two such examples in real life as Rousseau
and Mademoiselle de Lespinasse, one such demonstration of the same moral in fiction as *Werther*, were
enough to discourage the man of feeling. Therefore,

when he still exists, he takes to motley, the only wear for the human race in troublesome circumstances which beset it with unpleasant recurrence. When you cannot exactly believe anything in religion, in politics, in literature, in art, and yet neither wish nor know how to do without it, the safe way is to make a not too grotesque joke of it. This is a text on which a long sermon might be hung were it worth while. But as it is, it is sufficient to point out that Xavier de Maistre is an extremely remarkable illustration of the fact in the particular region of sentimental fiction.

Benjamin Constant's masterpiece, which (the sequel to it never having appeared, though it was in existence in manuscript less than a century ago) is also his only purely literary work, is a very small book, but it calls here for something more than a very small mention. The books which make an end are almost fewer in literature than those which make a beginning, and this is one of them. Like most such books, it made a beginning also, showing the way to Beyle, and through Beyle to all the analytic school of the nineteenth century. Space would not here suffice to discuss the singular character of its author, to whom Sainte-Beuve certainly did some injustice, as the letters to Madame Recamier show, but whose political and personal experiences as certainly call for a large allowance of charity. The theory of *Adolphe's* best editor, M. de Lescure (which also was the accepted theory long before M. de Lescure's time), that the heroine of the novel was Madame de Staël, will not, I think, hold water. In every characteristic, personal and mental, Ellénore and Madame de Staël are at opposite poles. Ellénore was beautiful, Madame de Staël was very nearly hideous ; Ellénore was careless of her social position, Corinne was as great a slave to society as any one who ever lived ; Ellénore was somewhat uncultivated, had little *esprit*, was indifferent to flattery, took not much upon herself in any way except in exacting affection where no affection existed; the good Corinne was one of the cleverest women of her time, and thought herself one of the cleverest of all times, could not endure that any one in company should be of a different opinion on this point, and insisted on general admiration and homage.

However, this is a very minor matter, and anybody is at liberty to regard the differences as deliberate attempts to disguise the truth. What is important is that Madame de Staël was almost the last genuine devotee of Sensibility, and that *Adolphe* was certainly written by a lover of Madame de Staël, who had, from his youth up, been a Man of Feeling of a singularly unfeeling kind. When Constant wrote the book he had run through the whole gamut of Sensibility. He had been instructed as a youth [1] by ancient women of letters; he had married and got rid of his wife *à la mode Germanorum*; he had frequently taken a hint from *Werther*, and threatened suicide with the best possible results; he had given, perhaps, the most atrocious example of the atrocious want of taste which accompanied the decadence of Sensibility, by marrying Charlotte von Hardenburg out of pique, because Madame de Staël would not marry him, then going to live with his bride near Coppet, and finally deserting her, newly married as she was, for her very uncomely but intellectually interesting rival. In short, according to the theory of a certain ethical school, that the philosopher who discusses virtue should be thoroughly conversant with vice, Benjamin Constant was a past master in Sensibility. It was at a late period in his career, and when he had only one trial to go through (the trial of, as it seems to me, a sincere and hopeless affection for Madame Recamier), that he wrote *Adolphe*. But the book has nothing whatever to do with 1815, the date which it bears. It is, as has been said, the history of the Nemesis of Sensibility, the prose commentary by anticipation on Mr. Swinburne's admirable "Stage Love"—

---

[1] *Vide* on the process Crébillon's *Les Égarements du Cœur et de l'Esprit*, as above, pp. 371, 372.

Time was chorus, gave them cues to laugh and cry,
They would kill, befool, amuse him, let him die ;
Set him webs to weave to-day and break to-morrow,
Till he died for good in play and rose in sorrow.

That is a history, in one stanza, of Sensibility, and no
better account than *Adolphe* exists of the rising in sorrow.

The story of the book opens in full eighteenth century.
A young man, fresh from the University of Göttingen,
goes to finish his education at the *residenz* of D——.
Here he finds much society, courtly and other. His
chief resort is the house of a certain Count de P——, who
lives, unmarried, with a Polish lady named Ellénore.
In the easy-going days of Sensibility the *ménage* holds a
certain place in society, though it is looked upon a little
askance. But Ellénore is, on her own theory, thoroughly
respectable, and the Count de P——, though in danger
of his fortune, is a man of position and rank. As for
Adolphe, he is the result of the struggle between Sensibility, an unquiet and ironic nature, and the teaching of
a father who, though not unquiet, is more ironically
given than himself. His main character is all that a
young man's should be from the point of view of Sensibility. " Je ne demandais alors qu'à me livrer à ces
impressions primitives et fougueuses," etc. But his
father snubs the primitive and fiery impressions, and the
son, feeling that they are a mistake, is only more determined to experience them. Alternately expanding himself as Sensibility demands, and making ironic jests as
his own nature and his father's teaching suggest, he
acquires the character of " un homme immoral, un
homme peu sûr," the last of which expressions may be
paralleled from the British repertory by " an ill-regulated
young man," or " a young man on whom you can never
depend."

All this time Adolphe is not in love, and as the dominant teaching of Sensibility lays it down that he ought to
be, he feels that he is wrong. " ' Je veux être aimé,' me
dis-je, et je regardai autour de moi. Je ne voyais personne qui m'inspirait de l'amour ; personne qui me

parut susceptible d'en prendre." In parallel case the
ordinary man would resign himself as easily as if he were
in face of the two conditions of having no appetite and
no dinner ready. But this will not do for the pupil of
Sensibility. He must make what he does not find, and
so Adolphe pitches on the luckless Ellénore, who " me
parut une conquête digne de moi." To do Sensibility
justice, it would not, at an earlier time, have used language
so crude as this, but it had come to it now. Here is
the portrait of the victim, drawn by her ten years younger
lover.

Ellénore's wits were not above the ordinary, but her thoughts
were just, and her expression, simple as it was, was sometimes
striking by reason of the nobility and elevation of the thought.
She was full of prejudices, but she was always prejudiced against
her own interest. There was nothing she set more value on than
regularity of conduct, precisely because her own conduct was con-
ventionally irregular.[1] She was very religious, because religion
rigidly condemned her mode of life. In conversation she frowned
on pleasantries which would have seemed quite innocent to other
women, because she feared that her circumstances might encourage
the use of such as were not innocent. She would have liked to
admit to her society none but men of the highest rank and most
irreproachable reputation, because those women with whom she
shuddered at the thought of being classed usually tolerate mixed
society, and, giving up the hope of respect, seek only amusement.
In short, Ellénore and her destiny were at daggers drawn ; every
word, every action of hers was a kind of protest against her social
position. And as she felt that facts were too strong for her, and
that the situation could be changed by no efforts of hers, she was
exceedingly miserable. . . . The struggle between her feelings
and her circumstances had affected her temper. She was often
silent and dreamy : sometimes, however, she spoke with impetu-
osity. Beset as she was by a constant preoccupation, she was
never quite calm in the midst of the most miscellaneous conversation, and for this very reason her manner had an unrest and an air
of surprise about it which made her more piquant than she was
by nature. Her strange position, in short, took the place of new
and original ideas in her.

The difference of note from the earlier eighteenth
century will strike everybody here. If we are still some

---

[1] The parallel with " George Eliot " will strike most people.

way from Emma Bovary, it is only in point of language :
we are poles asunder from Marianne. But the hero is
still, in his own belief, acting under the influence of
Sensibility. He is not in the least impassioned, he is not
a mére libertine, but he has a " besoin d'amour." He
wants a "conquête." He is still actuated by the odd
mixture of vanity, convention, sensuality, which goes
by the name of our subject. But his love is a " dessin
de lui plaire " ; he has taken an " engagement envers
son amour propre." In other words, he is playing the
game from the lower point of view—the mere point of
view of winning. It does not take him very long to win.
Ellénore at first behaves unexceptionably, refuses to
receive him after his first declaration, and retires to the
country. But she returns, and the exemplary Adolphe
has recourse to the threat which, if his creator's bio-
graphers may be believed, Constant himself was very
fond of employing in similar cases, and which the great
popularity of *Werther* made terrible to the compassionate
and foolish feminine mind. He will kill himself. She
hesitates, and very soon she does not hesitate any longer.
The reader feels that Adolphe is quite worthless, that
nothing but the fact of his having been brought up in a
time when Sensibility was dominant saves him. But the
following passage, from the point of view alike of nature
and of expression, again pacifies the critic : [1]

I passed several hours at her feet, declaring myself the happiest
of men, lavishing on her assurances of eternal affection, devotion,
and respect. She told me what she had suffered in trying to keep
me at a distance, how often she had hoped that I should detect her
notwithstanding her efforts, how at every sound that fell on her
ears she had hoped for my arrival; what trouble, joy, and fear she
had felt on seeing me again; how she had distrusted herself, and
how, to unite prudence and inclination, she had sought once more
the distractions of society and the crowds which she formerly
avoided. I made her repeat the smallest details, and this history
of a few weeks seemed to us the history of a whole life. Love

---

[1] But for uniformity's sake I should not have translated this, for fear of doing it
injustice. " Not presume to dictate," in Mr. Jingle's constantly useful phrase, but
it seems to me one of the finest in French prose.

makes up, as it were by magic, for the absence of far-reaching memory. All other affections have need of the past : love, as by enchantment, makes its own past and throws it round us. It gives us the feeling of having lived for years with one who yesterday was all but a stranger. Itself a mere point of light, it dominates and illuminates all time. A little while and it was not : a little while and it will be no more : but, as long as it exists, its light is reflected alike on the past and on the future.

This calm, he goes on to say, lasted but a short time ; and, indeed, no one who has read the book so far is likely to suppose that it did. Adolphe has entered into the *liaison* to play the game, Ellénore (unluckily for herself) to be loved. The difference soon brings discord. In the earlier Sensibility days men and women were nearly on equal terms. It was only in the most strictly meta-phorical way that the unhappy lover was bound to expire, and his beloved rarely took the method of wringing his bosom recommended by Goldsmith, when anybody else of proper Sensibility was there to console her. But the game had become unequal between the Charlottes and the Werthers, the Adolphes and the Ellénores. The Count de P—— naturally perceives the state of affairs before long, and as naturally does not like it. Adolphe, having played his game and won it, does not care to go on playing for love merely. " Ellénore était sans doute un vif plaisir dans mon existence, mais elle n'était pas plus un but—elle était devenue un lien." But Ellénore does not see this accurate distinction. After many vicissitudes and a few scenes (" Nous vécûmes ainsi quatre mois dans des rapports forcés, quelque fois doux, jamais complétement libres, y rencontrant encore du plaisir mais n'y trouvant plus de charme ") a crisis comes. The Count forbids Ellénore to receive Adolphe any more : and she thereupon breaks the ten years old union, and leaves her children and home.

Her young lover receives this riveting of his chains with consternation, but he does his best. He defends her in public, he fights with a man who speaks lightly of her, but this is not what she wants.

Of course I ought to have consoled her. I ought to have pressed her to my heart and said, " Let us live for each other ; let us forget the misjudgments of men ; let us be happy in our mutual regard and our mutual love." I tried to do so, but what can a resolution made out of duty do to revive a sentiment that is extinct ? Ellénore and I each concealed something from the other. She dared not tell me her troubles, arising from a sacrifice which she knew I had not asked of her. I had accepted that sacrifice ; I dared not complain of ills which I had foreseen, and which I had not had courage enough to forestall. We were therefore silent on the very subject which occupied us both incessantly. We were prodigal of caresses, we babbled of love, but when we spoke of it we spoke for fear of speaking of something else.

Here is the full Nemesis of the sentiment that, to use Constant's own words, is " neither passion nor duty," and has the strength of neither, when it finds itself in presence of a stronger than itself. There were none of these unpleasant meetings in Sensibility proper. There sentiment met sentiment, and " exchanged itself," in Chamfort's famous phrase. When the rate of exchange became unsatisfactory it sought some other customer— a facile and agreeable process, which was quite consistent in practice with all the sighs and flames. Adolphe is not to be quit so easily of his conquest. He is recalled by his father, and his correspondence with Ellénore is described in one of the astonishingly true passages which make the book so remarkable.

During my absence I wrote regularly to Ellénore. I was divided between the desire of not hurting her feelings and the desire of truthfully representing my own. I should have liked her to guess what I felt, but to guess it without being hurt by it. I felt a certain satisfaction when I had substituted the words " affection," " friendship," " devotion," for the word " love." Then suddenly I saw poor Ellénore sitting sad and solitary, with nothing but my letters for consolation : and at the end of two cold and artificial pages I added in a hurry a few phrases of ardour or of tenderness suited to deceive her afresh. In this way, never saying enough to satisfy her, I always said enough to mislead her, a species of double-dealing the very success of which was against my wishes and prolonged my misery.

This situation, however, does not last. Unable to
bear his absence, and half puzzled, half pained by his
letters, Ellénore follows him, and his father for the first
time expresses displeasure at this compromising step.
Ellénore being threatened with police measures, Adolphe
is once more perforce thrown on her side, and elopes with
her to neutral territory. Then events march quickly.
Her father's Polish property, long confiscated, is restored
to him and left to her. She takes Adolphe (still struggling between his obligations to her and his desire to be
free) to Warsaw, rejects an offer of semi-reconciliation
from the Count de P———, grows fonder and more exacting the more weary of her yoke her lover becomes ; and
at last, discovering his real sentiments from a correspondence of his with an artful old diplomatic friend of
his father's, falls desperately ill and dies in his arms. A
prologue and epilogue, which hint that Adolphe, far from
taking his place in the world (from which he had thought
his *liaison* debarred him), wandered about in aimless
remorse, might perhaps be cut away with advantage,
though they are defensible, not merely on the old theory
of political justice, but on sound critical grounds.

This was the end of sensibility in more senses than
one. It is true that, five years later than *Adolphe*,
_{Mme. de} appeared Madame de Duras's agreeable novel-
_{Duras's} ettes of *Ourika* and *Édouard*, in which some-
"postscript." thing of the old tone revives. But they were
written late in their author's life, and avowedly as a
reminiscence of a past state of sentiment and of society.
" Le ton de cette société," says Madame de Duras
herself, " était l'engouement." As happy a sentence,
perhaps, as can be anywhere found to describe what has
been much written about, and, perhaps it may be said
without presumption, much miswritten about. *Engouement* itself is a nearly untranslatable word.[1] It may be
clumsily but not inaccurately defined as a state of fanciful
interest in persons and things which is rather more serious
than mere caprice, and a good deal less serious than

[1] " Craze " has been suggested ; but is, I think, hardly an exact synonym.

genuine enthusiasm. The word expresses exactly the
attitude of French polite society in the eighteenth century
to a vast number of subjects, and, what is more, it helps
to explain the *sensibilité* which dominated that society.
The two terms mutually involve each other, and *sensibilité* stands to mere flirtation on the one hand, and

Sensibilité genuine passion on the other, exactly as *engoue-*
and *ment* does to caprice and enthusiasm. People
engouement. flirted admirably in the sixteenth and seventeenth centuries, and the art was, I fancy, recovered in
the nineteenth with some success, but I do not think
they flirted, properly speaking, in the eighteenth.[1] Sensibility (and its companion " sensuality ") prevented that.
Yet, on the other hand, they did not, till the society
itself and its sentiments with it were breaking up, indulge
in anything that can be called real passion. Sensibility
prevented that also. The kind of love-making which was
popular may be compared without much fancifulness to
the favourite card-game of the period, quadrille. You
changed partners pretty often, and the stakes were not
very serious ; but the rules of the game were elaborate
and precise, and it did not admit of being treated with
levity.

Only a small part, though the most original and not
the least remarkable part, of the representation of this

Some final curious phenomenon in literature has been
words on attempted in this discussion. The English
the matter. and German developments of it are interesting
and famous, and, merely as literature, contain perhaps
better work than the French, but they are not so original,
and they are out of our province. Marivaux[2] served

---

[1] This may seem to contradict, or at any rate to be inconsistent with, a passage
above (p. 367) on the " flirtations " of Crébillon's personages. It is, however, only a
more strictly accurate use of the word.

[2] Two remarkable and short passages of his, not quoted in the special notice of him,
may be given—one in English, because of its remarkable anticipation of the state of
mind of Catherine Morland in *Northanger Abbey* ; the other in French, as a curious " conclusion of the whole matter." They are both from *Marianne*.

" I had resolved not to sleep another night in the house. I cannot indeed tell you
what was the exact object of my fear, or why it was so lively. All that I know is that
I constantly beheld before me the countenance of my landlord, to which I had hitherto
paid no particular attention, and then I began to find terrible things in this countenance.

directly as model to both English and German novelists,
though the peculiarity of the national temperament
quickly made itself felt in both cases. In England the
great and healthy genius of Fielding applied the humour
cure to Sensibility at a very early period ; in Germany
the literature of Sensibility rapidly became the literature
of suicide—a consummation than which nothing could
be more alien from the original conception. It is true
that there is a good deal of dying in the works of Madame
de la Fayette and her imitators. But it is quite transparent stage-dying, and the virtuous Prince of Clèves
and the penitent Adelaide in the *Comte de Comminge* do
not disturb the mind at all. We know that, as soon as
the curtain has dropped, they will get up again and go
home to supper quite comfortably. It is otherwise with
Werther and Adolphe. With all the first-named young
man's extravagance, four generations have known perfectly
well that there is something besides absurdity in him, while
in Adolphe there is no extravagance at all. The wind of
Sensibility had been sown, in literature and in life, for many
a long year, and the whirlwind had begun to be reaped.[1]

This, however, is the moral side of the matter, with
which we have not much to do. As a division of literature these sentimental novels, artificial as they
are, have a good deal of interest ; and in a *History* such as the present they have very great
importance. They are so entirely different in atmosphere
from the work of later times, that reading them has all
the refreshing effect of a visit to a strange country ; and
yet one feels that they themselves have opened that

Its importance here.

His wife's face, too, seemed to be gloomy and dark ; the servants looked like scoundrels ;
all their faces made me in a state of unbearable alarm. I saw before me swords,
daggers, murders, thefts, insults. My blood grew cold at the perils I imagined."

"Enfin ces agitations, tant agréables que pénibles, s'affaiblirent et se passèrent. L'âme
s'accoutume à tout ; sa sensibilité s'use : et je me familiarisais avec mes espérances et
mes inquiétudes."

[1] Since, long ago, I formed the opinion of *Adolphe* embodied above, I have, I think,
seen French criticisms which took it rather differently—as a personal confession of
the "confusions of a wasted youth," misled by passion. The reader must judge which
is the juster view.

country for comiñg writers as well as readers. They are often extraordinarily ingenious, and the books to which in form they set the example, though the power of the writers made them something very different in matter— *Julie*, *La Religieuse*, *Paul et Virginie*,[1] *Corinne*, *René*— give their progenitors not a little importance, or at least not a little interest of curiosity. Besides, it was in the school of Sensibility that the author of *Manon Lescaut* somehow or other developed that wonderful little book. I do not know that it would be prudent to recommend modern readers to study Sensibility for themselves in the original documents just surveyed. Disappointment and possibly maledictions would probably be the result of any such attempt, except in the case of Xavier de Maistre and Constant. But these others are just the cases in which the office of historical critic justifies itself. It is often said (and· nobody knows the truth of it better than critics themselves) that a diligent perusal of all the studies and *causeries* that have ever been written, on any one of the really great writers, will not give as much knowledge of them as half an hour's reading of their own work. But then in that case the metal is virgin, and to be had on the surface and for the picking up. The case is different where tons of ore have to be crushed and smelted, in order to produce a few pennyweights of metal.

Whatever fault may be found with the " Sensibility " novel, it is, as a rule, " written by gentlemen [and ladies] for [ladies and] gentlemen." Of the work of two curious writers, who may furnish the last detailed notices of this volume, as much cannot, unfortunately, be said.

It may, from different points of view, surprise different classes of readers to find Restif de la Bretonne (or Restif de la as some would call him, Rétif) mentioned Bretonne. here at all—at any rate to find him taken seriously, and not entirely without a certain respect. One of these classes, consisting of those who know

---

[1] By a little allowance for influence, if not for intrinsic value.

nothing about him save at second-hand, may ground
their surprise on the notion that his work is not only
matter for the *Index Expurgatorius*, but also vulgar and
unliterary, such as a French Ned Ward, without even
Ned's gutter-wit, might have written.   And these might
derive some support from the stock ticket-jingle *Rousseau
du ruisseau*, which, though not without some real per-
tinency, is directly misleading.   Another class, consisting
of some at least, if not most, of those who have read him
to some extent, may urge that Decency—taking her
revenge for the axiom of the boatswain in *Mr. Midshipman
Easy* — forbids Duty to let him in.   And yet others,
less under the control of any Mrs. Grundy, literary or
moral, may ask why he is let in, and Choderlos de Laclos [1]
and Louvet de Courray, with some more, kept out, as
they most assuredly will be.

In the first place, there is no vulgarity in Restif.   If
he had had a more regular education and society, literary
or other, and could have kept his mind, which was to a
certainty slightly unhinged, off the continual obsession of
morbid subjects, he might have been a very considerable
man of letters, and he is no mean one, so far as style goes, [2]
as it is.   He avails himself duly of the obscurity of a
learned language when he has to use (which is regrettably
often) words that do not appear in the dictionary of the
Academy : and there is not the slightest evidence of his
having taken to pornography for money, as Louvet and
Laclos—as, one must regretfully add, Diderot, if not
even Crébillon—certainly did.   When a certain subject,
or group of subjects, gets hold of a man—especially one
of those whom a rather celebrated French lady called *les
cérébraux*—he can think of nothing else : and though this
is not absolutely true of Restif (for he had several minor
crazes), it is very nearly true of him, and perhaps more

---

[1] On representations from persons of distinction I have given Laclos a place in an
outhouse (see " Add. and Corr."). But I have made this place as much of a penitentiary
as I could.

[2] I must apologise by anticipation to the *official* French critic. To him, I know,
even if he is no mere minor Malherbe, Restif's style is very faulty ; but I should not
presume to take his point of view, either for praise or blame.

true than of any one else who can be called a man of letters.

Probably no one has read all he wrote;[1] even the late M. Assézat, who knew more about him than anybody else, does not, I think, pretend to have done so. He was himself a printer, and therefore found exceptional means of getting the mischief, which his by no means idle hands found to do, into publicity of a kind, though even their subject does not seem to have made his books popular.[2] His largest work, *Les Contemporaines*, is in forty-two volumes, and contains some three hundred different sections, reminding one vaguely, though the differences in detail are very great, of Amory's plan, at least, for the *Memoirs of Several Ladies*. His most remarkable by far, the quasi-autobiographical *Monsieur Nicolas*,[3] is in fourteen. He could write with positive moral purpose, as in the protest against *Le Paysan Parvenu*, above referred to; in *La Vie de Mon Père* (a book agreeably free from any variety of that sin of Ham which some biographical writings of

[1] There is a separate bibliography by Cubières-Palmézeaux (1875). The useful *Dictionnaire des Littératures* of Vapereau contains a list of between thirty and forty separate works of Restif's, divided into nearer two than one hundred volumes. He followed Prévost in *Nouveaux Mémoires d'un Homme de Qualité* as he had followed Marivaux in the *Paysan Perverti*. He completed this work of his own with *La Paysanne Pervertie*; he wrote, besides the *Pornographe*, numerous books of social, general, and would-be philosophical reform—*Le Mimographe*, dealing with the stage; *Les Gynographes*, with a general plan for rearranging the status of women; *L'Andrographe*, a "whole duty of man" of a very novel kind; *Le Thesmographe*, etc.,—besides, close upon the end and after the autobiography above described, a *Philosophie de M. Nicolas*. His more or less directly narrative pieces, *Le Pied de Fanchette*, *Lucile*, *Adèle*, *La Femme Infidèle*, *Ingénue Saxancour*, are nearly always more or less tinged with biography of himself and of persons closely connected with him, as *La Vie de Mon Père*, his most respectable book, is wholly. It may be added, perhaps, that the notice in Vapereau, while not bearing very hard on Restif on the whole, repeats the words *cynisme* and *cynique* in regard to him. Unless the term is in part limited and in part extended, so as to mean nothing but "exposure of things generally kept secret without apparent shame," it is entirely misplaced. Not merely outside of, but actually in his erotomania, Restif was a sentimental philanthropist of the all but most genuine kind, tainted indeed with the vanity and self-centredness which had reached their acme in Rousseau, but very much more certainly sincere, and of a temperament as different as possible from what is commonly called cynicism.

[2] There are, however, contradictory statements on this point.

[3] Nicolas [Edme] Restif being apparently his baptismal name, and "de la Bretonne" merely one of the self-bestowed agnominal flourishes so common in the French eighteenth century. He chose to consider the surname evidence of descent from the Emperor Pertinax; and as for his Christian name he seems to have varied it freely. Rose Lambelin, one of his harem, and a *soubrette* of some literature, used to address him as "Anne-Augustin," Anne being, as no doubt most readers know, a masculine as well as a feminine *prénom* in French.

sons about their fathers display); and in the unpleasantly
titled *Pornographe*, which is also morally intended, and
dull enough to be as moral as Mrs. Trimmer or Dr.
Forsyth.

Indeed, this moral intention, so often idly and offens-
ively put forward by those who are themselves mere
pornographers, pervades Restif throughout, and, while
it certainly sometimes does carry dulness with it, undoubtedly contributes at others a kind of piquancy,
because of its evident sincerity, and the quaint contrast
with the subjects the author is handling.   These subjects
make explicit dealing with himself difficult, if not impossible : but his *differentia* as regards them may, with
the aid of a little dexterity, be put without offence.   In
the first place, as regards the comparison with Rousseau,
Restif is almost a gentleman : and he could not possibly
have been guilty of Rousseau's blackguard tale-telling
in the cases of Madame de Warens (or, as I believe, we
are now told to spell it " Vuarrens ") or Madame de
Larnage.   The way in which he speaks of his one ideal-
ised mistress, Madame " Parangon," is almost romantic.
He is, indeed, savage in respect to his wife—whom he
seems to have married in a sort of *clairvoyant* mixture of
knowledge of her evil nature and fascination by her
personal charms and allurements, though he had had
no difficulty in enjoying these without marriage.   But
into none other of his scores and hundreds of actual
loves in some cases and at least passing intimacies in
others,[1] does he ever appear to have taken either the
Restoration and Regency tone on the one hand, or
that of " sickly sentimentality " on the other.   Against
commerce for money he lifts up his testimony un-
ceasingly ;   he has, as his one editor has put it, a
manie de paternité, and denounces any vice discon-
nected with it.   With the privileges of Solomon or
Haroun al Raschid, Restif would have been perfectly

---

[1] Some, and perhaps not a few of their objects, may have been imaginary "dream-
mistresses," created by Morpheus in an impurer mood than when he created Lamb's
" dream-children."   But some, I believe, have been identified ; and others of the singular
" Calendar " affixed to *Monsieur Nicolas* have probably escaped identification.

contented: and he never would have availed himself
of that of Schahriar before the two divine sisters put a
stop to it.

All this, however, strictly speaking, is outside our
present subject, and is merely intended as a sort of excuse
for the introduction of a writer who has been unfairly
ostracised, not as a passport for Restif to the young
person. But his actual qualities as tale-teller are very
remarkable. The second title of *Monsieur Nicolas—Le
Cœur Humain Dévoilé*—ambitious as it is, is not fatuous.
It is a human heart in a singularly morbid condition
which is unveiled: but as, if I remember rightly, either
Goethe or Schiller, or both, saw and said near the time,
there is no charlatanery about the unveiling, and no
bungling about the autopsy. Restif has been compared,
and not unfairly, to Defoe, as well as to Rousseau; in a
certain way he may be likened to Pepys; and all four
share an intense and unaffected reality, combined,
however, in the Frenchman's case with a sort of exaggeration of a dreamy kind, and with other dream-character,
which reminds one of Borrow, and even of De Quincey.
His absolute shamelessness is less unconnected with this
dream-quality than may at first appear, and, as in all such
cases, is made much less offensive by it. Could he
ever have taken holiday from his day-long and night-
long devotion to

> Cotytto or Venus
> Astarte or Ashtoreth,

he might have been a most remarkable novelist, and as it
is his *mere* narrative faculty is such as by no means every
novelist possesses. Moreover, he counts, once more, in
the advance towards real things in fiction. " A pretty
kind of reality ! " cries Mrs. Grundy. But the real is
not always the pretty, and the pretty is not always the
real.

There is also a good deal that is curious, as well as
many things that are disgusting, for the student of the

novel in Pigault-Lebrun.[1] In the first place, one is
Pigault-
Lebrun—
the differ-
ence of his
positive and
relative
importance. constantly reminded of that redeeming point
which the benevolent Joe Gargery found in
Mr. Pumblechook—

> And, wotsume'er the failings on his part,
> He were a corn-and-seedsman in his hart.

If Pigault cannot exactly be said to have been a
good novelist, he " were " a novelist " in his hart."

---

[1] It has not been necessary (and this is fortunate, for even if it had been necessary,
it would have been scarcely possible) to give biographies of the various authors mentioned
His life and
the reasons
for giving it. in this book, except in special cases. Something was generally known of
most of them in the days before education received a large E, with laws
and rates to suit : and something is still, in a way, supposed to be known
since. But of the life of Pigault, who called himself Lebrun, it may be
desirable to say something, for more reasons than one. In the first place, this life had
rather more to do with his work than is always the case ; in the second, very little will
be found about him in most histories of French literature ; in the third, there will be
found assigned to him, in the text—not out of crotchet, or contumacy, or desire to innovate,
but as a result of rather painful reading—a considerably higher place in the history of
the novel than he has usually occupied. His correct name—till, by one of the
extremest eccentricities of the French *Chats-Fourrés*, he was formally unbegot by his
Roman father, and the unbegetting (*plus* declaration of death) confirmed by the
Parlement of Paris—was the imposing one of Charles Antoine Guillaume Pigault de
L'Épinoy. The paternal Pigault, as may be guessed from his proceedings, was himself a
lawyer, but of an old Calais family tracing itself to Queen Philippa's *protégé*, Eustache de
Saint-Pierre ; and, besides the mysterious life-in-death or death-in-life, Charles Antoine
Guillaume had to suffer from him, while such things existed, several *lettres de cachet*.
The son certainly did his best to deserve them. Having been settled, on leaving school
as a clerk in an English commercial house, he seduced his master's daughter, ran away
with her, and would no doubt have married her—for Pigault was never a really ba
fellow—if she had not been drowned in the vessel which carried the pair back to
France. He escaped—one hopes not without trying to save her. After another scandal
—not the second only—of the same kind, he did marry the victim, and the marriage
was the occasion of the singular exertion of *patria potestas* referred to above. At least
two *lettres de cachet* had preceded it, and it is said that only the taking of the Bastille
prevented the issue, or at least the effect, of a third. Meanwhile, he had been a
gentleman-trooper in the *gendarmerie d'élite de la petite maison du roi*, which, seeing that
the *roi* was Louis Quinze, probably did not conduct itself after the fashion of the
Thundering Legion, or of Cromwell's Ironsides, or even of Captain Steele's " Christian
Hero." The life of this establishment, though as probably merry, was not long, and
Pigault became an actor—a very bad but rather popular actor, it was said. Like other
bad actors he wrote plays, which, if not good (they are certainly not very cheerful to
read), were far from unsuccessful. But it was not till after the Revolution, and till he
was near forty, that he undertook prose fiction ; his first book being *L'Enfant du
Carnaval* in 1792 (noticed in text). The revolutionary fury, however, of which there
are so many traces in his writings, caught him ; he went back to soldiering and fought at
Valmy. He did not stay long in the army, but went on novel-writing, his success
having the rather unexpected, and certainly very unusual, effect of reconciling his father.
Indeed, this arbitrary parent wished not only to recall him to life, which was perhaps
superfluous, but to " make an eldest son of him." This, Pigault, who was a loose fish
and a vulgar fellow, but, as was said above, not a scoundrel, could not suffer ; and he
shared and shared alike with his brothers and sisters. Under the Empire he obtained a
place in the customs, and held it under succeeding reigns till 1824, dying eleven years later

Beside his *polissonneries*, his frequent dulness, his singular gropings and failures at anything like good novelist *faire*, one constantly finds what might be pedantically and barbarously called a " novelistic velleity." His much too ambitiously titled *Mélanges Littéraires* turn to stories, though stories touched with the *polisson* brush. His *Nouvelles* testify at least to his ambition and his industry in the craft of fiction. " Je ne suis pas Voltaire," he says somewhere, in reference, I think, to his plays, not his tales. He most certainly is not ; neither is he Marmontel, as far as the tale is concerned. But as for the longer novel, in a blind and blundering way, constantly trapped and hindered by his want of genius and his want of taste, by his literary ill-breeding and other faults, he seems to have more of a " glimmering " of the real business than they have, or than any other Frenchman had before him.

Pigault-Lebrun [1] spent nearly half of his long life His general in the nineteenth century, and did not die till character- Scott was dead in England, and the great series istics. of novel-romances had begun, with Hugo and others, in France. But he was a man of nearly fifty

---

at over eighty, and having written novels continuously till a short time before his death, and till the very eve of 1830. This odd career was crowned by an odd accident, for his daughter's son was Emile Augier. I never knew this fact till after the death of my friend, the late Mr. H. D. Traill. If I had, I should certainly have asked him to write an Imaginary Conversation between grandfather and grandson. Some years (1822–1824) before his last novel, a complete edition of novels, plays, and very valueless miscellanies had been issued in twenty octavo volumes. The reader, like the river Iser in Campbell's great poem, will be justified for the most part in "rolling rapidly" through them. But he will find his course rather unexpectedly delayed sometimes, and it is the fact and the reasons of these delays which must form the subject of the text.— There is no doubt that Pigault was very largely read abroad as well as at home. We know that Miss Matilda Crawley read him before Waterloo. She must have inherited from her father, Sir Walpole, a strong stomach : and must have been less affected by the change of times than was the case with her contemporary, Scott's old friend, who having enjoyed " your bonny Mrs. Behn " in her youth, could not read her in age. For our poor maligned Afra (in her prose stories at any rate, and most of her verse, if not in her plays) is an anticipated model of Victorian prudery and nicety compared with Pigault. I cannot help thinking that Marryat knew him too. Chapter and verse may not be forthcoming, and the resemblance may be accounted for by common likeness to Smollett : but not, to my thinking, quite sufficiently.

[1] He had a younger brother, in a small way also a novelist, and, apparently, in the Radcliffian style, who extra-named himself rather in the manner of 1830—Pigault-*Maubaillarck*. I have not yet come across this junior's work.—For remarks of Hugo himself on Pigault and Restif, see note at end of chapter.

in 1800, and the character of his work, except in one
all-important point, or group of points, is thoroughly
of the eighteenth, while even the excepted characteristics
are of a more really transitional kind than anything in
Chateaubriand and Madame de Staël, whom we have
postponed, as well as in Constant and Xavier de Maistre,
whom we have admitted. He has no high reputation
in literature, and, except from our own special point of
view, he does not deserve even a demi-reputation.
Although he is not deliberately pornographic, he is
exceedingly coarse, with a great deal of the nastiness
which is not even naughty, but nastiness pure and
simple. There is, in fact, and in more ways than one,
something in him of an extremely inferior ·Smollett.
Comparing him with his elder contemporary, Restif de
la Bretonne, he is vulgar, which Restif never is. Passing
to more purely literary matters, it would be difficult,
from the side of literature as an art—I do not say as a
craft—to say anything for him whatever. His style [1] is,
I should suppose (for I think no foreigner has any business
to do more than " suppose " in that matter), simply
wretched ; he has sentences as long as Milton's or
Clarendon's or Mr. Ruskin's, not merely without the
grandeur of the first, the beauty of the last, and the weighty
sense of the second, but lacking any flash of graceful,
pithy, or witty phrase ; character of the model-theatre
and cut-out paper kind; a mere accumulation of incidents
instead of a plot ; hardly an attempt at dialogue, and,
where description is attempted at all, utter ineffectiveness
or sheer rhyparography.[2]

It is a fair *riposte* to the last paragraph to ask, " Then
why do you drag him in here at all ? " But the counter-
parry is easy. The excepted points above supply it.
With all his faults—admitting, too, that every generation
since his time has supplied some, and most much
better, examples of his kind—the fact remains that he
was the first considerable representative, in his own

---

[1] At least in his early books ; it improves a little later. But see note on p. 453.
[2] For a defence of this word, *v. sup.* p. 280, *note.*

country, of that variety of professional novelist who can
spin yarns, of the sort that his audience or public [1] wants,
with unwearied industry, in great volume, and of a quality
which, such as it is, does not vary very much. He is,
in short, the first notable French novelist-tradesman—
the first who gives us notice that novel-production is
established as a business. There is even a little more than
this to be said for him. He has really made considerable
progress, if we compare him with his predecessors and
contemporaries, in the direction of the novel of ordinary
life, as that life was in his own day. There are extravagances of course, but they are scarcely flagrant. His
atmosphere is what the cooks, housemaids, footmen,
what the grocers and small- or middle-class persons who,
I suppose, chiefly read him, were, or would have liked to
be, accustomed to. His scene is not a paradise in either
the common or the Greek sense ; it is a sort of cabbage-
garden, with a cabbage-garden's lack of beauty, of ex-
quisiteness in any form, with its presence of untidiness,
and sometimes of evil odour, but with its own usefulness,
and with a cultivator of the most sedulous. Pigault-
Lebrun, for France, may be said to be the first author-
in-chief of the circulating library. It may not be a
position of exceeding honour ; but it is certainly one
which gives him a place in the story of the novel, and
which justifies not merely these general remarks on him,
but some analysis (not too abundant) of his particular
works. As for translating him, a Frenchman might as
well spend his time in translating the English newspaper
feuilletons of " family " papers in the earlier and middle
nineteenth century. Indeed that *Minnigrey*, which I
remember reading as a boy, and which long afterwards
my friend, the late Mr. Henley, used to extol as one of
the masterpieces of literature, is worth all Pigault put
together and a great deal more.

The worst of it is, that to be amused by him—to be,

---

[1] It may be objected, " Did not the Scudérys and others do this?" The answer is
that their public was not, strictly speaking, a " public" at all—it was a larger or smaller
coterie.

except as a student, even interested in a large part of his
L'Enfant du work—you must be almost as ill-bred in litera-
Carnaval ture as he himself is.   He is like a person who
and Les
Barons de has had before him no models for imitation or
Felsheim. avoidance in behaviour : and this is where
his successor, Paul de Kock, by the mere fact of being
his successor, had a great advantage over him. But
to the student he *is* interesting, and the interest has
nothing factitious in it, and nothing to be ashamed of.
There is something almost pathetic in his struggles to
master his art: and his frequent remonstrances with critics
and readers appear to show a genuine consciousness of
his state, which is not always the case with such things.

The book which stands first in his Works, *L'Enfant
du Carnaval*, starts with an ultra-Smollettian [1] passage of
coarseness, and relapses now and then.   The body of
it—occupied with the history of a base-born child, who
tumbles into the good graces of a Milord and his little
daughter, is named by them " Happy," and becomes
first the girl's lover and then her husband—is a heap of
extravagances, which, nevertheless, bring the picaresque
pattern, from which they are in part evidently traced,
to a point, not of course anywhere approaching in genius
Don Quixote or *Gil Blas*, but somehow or other a good
deal nearer general modern life.   *Les Barons de Felsheim*,
which succeeds it, seems to have taken its origin from a
suggestion of the opening of *Candide*, and continues with
a still wilder series of adventures, satirising German
ways, but to some extent perhaps inspired by German
literature.   Very commonly Pigault falls into a sort
of burlesque melodramatic style, with frequent interludes of horse-play, resembling that of the ineffably
dreary persons who knock each others' hats off
on the music-hall stage.   There is even something
dreamlike about him, though of a very low order of
dream ; he has at any rate the dream-habit of constantly

[1] It has been said that Pigault spent some time in England, and he shows more
knowledge of English things and books than was common with Frenchmen before, and
for a long time after, his day.   Nor does he, even during the Great War, exhibit any signs
of acute Anglophobia.

attempting something and finding that he cannot bring
it off.

At the close of one of his most extravagant, most
indecent, and stupidest novels, *La Folie Espagnole*—a
supposed tale of chivalry, which of course shows utter
ignorance of time, place, and circumstance, and is, in
fact, only a sort of travestied *Gil Blas*, with a rank infusion
of further vulgarised Voltairianism[1]—the author has a
rather curious note to the reader, whom he imagines
(with considerable probability) to be throwing the book
away with a suggested cry of " Quelles misères ! quel
fatras ! " He had, he says, previously offered *Angélique
et Jeanneton*, a little work of a very different kind, and
the public would neither buy nor read it. His publisher complained, and he must try to please. As for
La Folie, everybody, including his cook, can understand
this. One remembers similar expostulations from more
respectable authors ; but it is quite certain that Pigault-
Lebrun—a Lebrun so different from his contemporary
" Pindare " of that name—thoroughly meant what he
said. He was drawing a bow, always at a venture, with
no higher aim than to hit his public, and he did hit it
oftener than he missed. So much the worse, perhaps,
both for him and for his public ; but the fact is a fact,
and it is in the observation and correlation of facts that
history consists.

Angélique et Jeanneton itself, as might be expected
from the above reference, is, among its author's works,
Angélique et something like *Le Rêve* among Zola's ; it is
Jeanneton. his endeavour to be strictly proper. But, as
it is also one of his most Sternian exercises, the propriety is chequered. It begins in sufficiently startling
fashion ; a single gentleman of easy fortune and
amiable disposition, putting his latchkey in the door of
his chambers one night, is touched and accosted by an
interesting young person with an " argentine " voice.

[1] Pigault's adoration for Voltaire reaches the ludicrous, though we can seldom laugh *with* him. It led him once to compose one of the very dullest books in literature, *Le Citateur*, a string of anti-Christian gibes and arguments from his idol and others.

This may look *louche*; but the silvery accents appeal only for relief of needs, which, as it shortly appears, are those most properly to be supplied by a maternity hospital. It is to be understood that the suppliant is an entire stranger to the hero. He behaves in the most amiable and, indeed, noble fashion, instals her in his rooms, turns himself and his servant out to the nearest hotel, fetches the proper ministress, and, not content with this Good Samaritanism, effects a legitimate union between Jeanneton and her lover, half gives and half procures them a comfortable maintenance, resists temptation of repayment (*not* in coin) on more than one occasion, and sets out, on foot, to Caudebec, to see about a heritage which has come to Jeanneton's husband. On the way he falls in with Angélique (a lady this time), falls also in love with her, and marries her. The later part of the story, as is rather the way with Pigault, becomes more "accidented." There are violent scenes, jealousies, not surprising, between the two heroines, etc. But the motto-title of Marmontel's *Heureusement* governs all, and the end is peace, though not without some spots in its sun. That the public of 1799 did not like the book and did like *La Folie Espagnole* is not surprising; but the bearing of this double attempt on the growth of novel-writing as a regular craft is important.

Perhaps on the whole *Mon Oncle Thomas*, which seems to have been one of the most popular, is also one of the most representative, if not the best, of Pigault-Lebrun's novels. Its opening, and not its opening only, is indeed full of that mere nastiness which we, with Smollett and others to our discredit, cannot disclaim for our own parallel period, and which was much worse among the French, who have a choice selection of epithets for it. But the fortunes of the youthful Thomas—child of a prostitute of the lowest class, though a very good mother, who afterwards marries a miserly and ruffianly corporal of police—are told with a good deal of spirit—one even thinks of *Colonel Jack*—and the author shows his curious vulgar

Mon Oncle Thomas.

common sense, and his knowledge of human nature of a certain kind, pretty frequently, at least in the earlier part of the book.

Jérôme is another of Pigault's favourite studies of boys—distinctly blackguard boys as a rule—from their mischievous, or, as the early English eighteenth century would have put it, "unlucky" child-hood, to their most undeserved reward with a good and pretty wife (whom one sincerely pities), and more or less of a fortune. There is, however, more vigour in *Jérôme* than in most, and, if one has the knack of "combing out" the silly and stale Voltairianism, and paying little attention to the far from exciting sculduddery, the book may be read. It contains, in particular, one of the most finished of its author's sketches, of a type which he really did something to introduce into his country's literature— that of the Revolutionary and Napoleonic *routier* or professional soldier—brave as you like, and—at least at some times when neither drunk nor under the influence of the garden god—not ungenerous; with a certain simplicity too : but as braggart as he is brave ; a mere brute beast as regards the other sex ; utterly ignorant, save of military matters, and in fact a kind of caricature of the older type, which the innocent Rymer was so wrath with Shakespeare for neglecting in Iago.

Jérôme.

It may seem that too much space is being given to a reprobate and often dull author ; but something has been said already to rebut the complaint, and something more may be added now and again. French literature, from the death of Chénier to the appearance of Lamartine, has generally been held to contain hardly more than two names— those of Chateaubriand and Madame de Staël—which can even "seem to be" those of "pillars" ; and it may appear fantastic and almost insulting to mention one, who in long stretches of his work might almost be called a mere muckheap-raker, in company with them. Yet, in respect to the progress of his own department, it may be doubted whether he is not even more than their equal. *René*

The redeem-ing points of these.

and *Corinne* contain great suggestions, but they are
suggestions rather for literature generally than for the
novel proper. Pigault used the improperest materials ;
he lacked not merely taste, but that humour which sometimes excuses taste's absence ; power of creating real
character, decency almost always, sense very often.[1]
But all the same, he made the novel *march*, as it had not
marched, save in isolated instances of genius, before.

Yet Pigault could hardly have deserved even the very
modified praise which has been given to him, if he had
Others— been constant to the muckheap. He could
Adélaïde de never quite help approaching it now and
Méran and then ; but as time went on and the Empire
Tableaux de
Société. substituted a sort of modified decency for the
Feasts of Republican Reason and ribaldry, he tried
things less uncomely. *Adélaïde de Méran* (his longest
single book), *Tableaux de Société*, *L'Officieux*, and others,
are of this class ; and without presenting a single masterpiece in their own kind, they all, more or less, give evidence
of that advance in the kind generally with which their
author has been credited. *Adélaïde* is very strongly
reminiscent of Richardson, and more than reminiscent
of " Sensibility " ; it is written in letters—though all
by and to the same persons, except a few extracts—and
there is no individuality of character. Pigault, it has
been said, never has any, though he has some of type.
But by exercising the most violent constraint upon
himself, he indulges only in one rape (though there have
been narrow escapes before), in not more than two or three
questionable incidents, and in practically no " improper "
details—conduct almost deserving the description of
magnanimity and self-denial. Moreover, the thing
really is a modern novel, though a bad and rickety one ;
the indefinable *naturaleza* is present in it after a strange
fashion. There is less perhaps in the very inappropriately
named *Tableaux de Société*—the autobiography of a certain

---

[1] Yet sometimes—when, for instance, one thinks of the rottenness-to-the-core of Dean
Farrar's *Eric*, or the *spiritus vulgaritatis fortissimus* of Mark Twain's *A Yankee at the
Court of King Arthur*—one feels a little ashamed of abusing Pigault.

Fanchette de Francheville, who, somewhat originally for a French heroine, starts by being in the most frantic state of mutual passion with her husband, though this is soon to be succeeded by an infatuation (for some time virtuously resisted) on her side for a handsome young naval officer, and by several others (not at all virtuously resisted) for divers ladies on the husband's. With his usual unskilfulness in managing character, Pigault makes very little of the opportunities given by his heroine's almost unconscious transference of her affections to Sainte-Luce ; while he turns the uxorious husband, not out of jealousy merely, into a faithless one, and something like a general ruffian, after a very clumsy and " unconvincing " fashion. As for his throwing in, at the end, another fatal passion on part of their daughter for her mother's lover, it is, though managed with what is for the author, perfect cleanliness, entirely robbed of its always doubtful effect by the actual marriage of Fanchette and her sailor, and that immediately after the poor girl's death. If he had had the pluck to make this break off the whole thing, the book might have been a striking novel, as it is actually an attempt at one ; but Pigault, like his friends of the gallery, was almost inviolably constant to happy endings.[1]

L'Officieux. *L'Officieux*, if he had only had a little humour, might have been as good comically as the *Tableaux* might have been tragically ; for it is the history, sometimes not ill-sketched as far as action goes, of a *parvenu* rich, but brave and extremely well-intentioned marquis, who is perpetually getting into fearful scrapes from his incorrigible habit of meddling with other people's affairs to do them good. The situations—as where the marquis, having, through an extravagance of officiousness, got himself put under arrest by his commanding officer, and at the same time insulted by a comrade, insists on fighting the necessary duel in his own drawing-room, and thereby reconciling duty and honour,

---

[1] There was, of course, a milder and perhaps more effective possibility—to make the young turn to the young, and leave Madame de Francheville no solace for her sin. But for this also Pigault would have lacked audacity.

to the great terror of a lady with whom he has been
having a tender interview in the adjoining apartment—
are sometimes good farce, and almost good comedy;
but Pigault, like Shadwell, has neither the pen nor the
wits to make the most of them.

La Famille Luceval—something of an expanded and
considerably Pigaultified story *à la* Marmontel—is duller
than any of these, and the opening is marred by an
exaggerated study of a classical mania on the part of the
hero; but still the novel quality is not quite absent
from it.

Of the rest, *M. Botte*, which seems to have been a
favourite, is a rather conventional extravaganza with a
Further rich, testy, but occasionally generous uncle; a
examples. nephew who falls in love with the charming
but penniless daughter of an *émigré*; a noble rustic, who
manages to keep some of his exiled landlord's property
together, etc. *M. de Roberval*, though in its original
issue not so long as *Adélaïde de Méran*, becomes longer
by a *suite* of another full volume, and is a rather tedious
chronicle of ups and downs. There may be silence
about the remainder.

The stock and, as it may be called, "semi-official"
ticket for Pigault-Lebrun in such French literary history
Last words as takes notice of him, appears to be *verve*:
on him. and the recognised dictionary-sense of *verve*
is "heat of imagination, which animates the artist in
his composition." In the higher sense in which the
word imagination is used with us, it could never be
applied here; but he certainly has a good deal of "go,"
which is perhaps not wholly improper as a colloquial
Anglicising of the label. These semi-official descriptions,
which have always pleased the Latin races, are of more
authority in France than in England, though as long as
we go on calling Chaucer "the father of English poetry"
and Wyclif "the father of English prose" we need not
boast ourselves too much. But Pigault has this "go"—
never perhaps for a whole book, but sometimes for passages of considerable length, which possess "carrying"

power. It undoubtedly gave him his original popularity, and we need not despise it now, inasmuch as it makes less tedious the task of ascertaining and justifying his true place in the further " domestication "—if only in domesticities too often mean and grimy—of the French novel.

There are more reasons than the convenience of furnishing a separately published first volume with an interim conclusion, for making, at the close of this, a few remarks on the general state of the French novel at the end of the eighteenth century. No thoroughly similar point is reached in the literary history of France, or of any country known to me, in regard to a particular department of literature. In England—the only place which can, in this same department, be even considered in comparison, although at this very time two novelists, vastly superior to any of whom France has to boast, were just writing, or just about to write, and were a little later to revolutionise the novel itself—the general state and history of the kind had, for nearly two generations, reached a stage far beyond anything that France could claim. She had made earlier " running " ; on the whole period of some seven hundred years she had always, till very recently, been in front. But in the novel, as distinguished from the romance, she had absolutely nothing to show like our great quartette of the mid-eighteenth century, and hardly anything to match the later developments of Miss Burney and others in domestic, of Mrs. Radcliffe and others still in revived romantic fiction. Very great Frenchmen or French writers had written novels ; but, with the exceptions of Lesage in *Gil Blas*, Prévost in that everlastingly wonderful " single-speech " of his, and Rousseau in *La Nouvelle Héloïse*, none had written a great novel. No single writer of any greatness had been a novelist pure and simple. No species[1] of fiction,

The French novel in 1800.

---

[1] For the story "species" of *Gil Blas* was not new, was of foreign origin, and was open to some objection ; while the other two books just named derived their attraction, in the one case to a very small extent, in the other to hardly any at all, from the story itself.

except the short tale, in which, through varying forms,
France held an age-long mastery, had been thoroughly
developed in her literature.

The main point, where England went right and
France went wrong—to be only in the most equivocal
way corrected by such a writer as Pigault-Lebrun—was
the recognition of the connection—the intimate and all
but necessary connection—of the completed novel with
ordinary life. Look over the long history of fiction
which we have surveyed in the last three or four or five
chapters. There is much and sometimes great literary
talent ; sometimes, again, even genius ; there are
episodes of reality ; there are most artful adjustments
of type and convention and the like, of fashion in morals
(or immorals) and sentiments. But a real objective novel
of ordinary life, such as *Tom Jones*, or even *Humphry
Clinker*, nay, such inferior approaches to it as exist elsewhere in English, you will not find. Of the Scudéry
romances we need not speak again ; for all their key-
references to persons, and their abstention from the
supernatural, etc., they are, as wholes, hardly more real
than *Amadis* and its family themselves. Scarron has
some and Furetière more objectivity that may be argued
for, but the Spanish picaresque has become a convention,
and they, especially Scarron, are aiming more at the
pattern than at the life-model. Madame de la Fayette
has much, and some of her followers a little, real passion ;
but her manners, descriptions, etc., are all conventional,
though of another kind. The fairy tales are of course
not " real." Marivaux is aiming directly at Sensibility,
preciousness, " psychology," if you like, but not at
holding up the glass to any ordinary nature as such.[1]
And though Crébillon might plead that his convention
was actually the convention of hundreds and almost
thousands of accomplished ladies and gentlemen, no
one can deny that it was almost as much a convention
as the historical or legendary acting of the *Comédie*

---

[1] Not that Jacob and Marianne are unnatural—quite the contrary—but that their
situations are conventionalised.

Humaine by living persons a hundred years later at Venice.

No writer perhaps illustrates what is being said better than Prévost. No one of his books, voluminous as they are, has the very slightest reality, except *Manon Lescaut*; and that, like *La Princesse de Clèves*, though with much more intensity and fortunately with no alloy of convention whatever, is simply a study of passion, not of life at large at all. With the greater men the case alters to some extent in proportion to their greatness, but, again with one exception, not to such an extent as to affect the general rule. Voltaire avowedly never attempts ordinary representation of ordinary life—save as the merest by-work, it is all " purpose," satire, fancy. Rousseau may not, in one sense, go beyond that life in *Julie*, but in touching it he is almost as limited and exclusive as Prévost in his masterpiece. Diderot has to get hold of the abnormal, if not the unreal, before he can give you something like a true novel. Marmontel is half-fanciful, and though he does touch reality, subordinates it constantly to half-allegorical and wholly moral purpose. All the minor " Sensibility " folk follow their leaders, and so do all the minor *conteurs*.

The people (believed to be a numerous folk) who are uncomfortable with a fact unless some explanation of it is given, may be humoured here. The failure of a very literary nation—applying the most disciplined literary language in Europe to a department, in the earlier stages of which they had led Europe itself—to get out of the trammels which we had easily discarded, is almost demonstrably connected with the very nature of their own literary character. Until the most recent years, if not up to the very present day, few Frenchmen have ever been happy without a type, a " kind," a set of type- and kind-rules, a classification and specification, as it were, which has to be filled up and worked over. Of all this the novel had nothing in ancient times, while in modern it had only been wrestling and struggling towards something of the sort, and had only in one country

discovered, and not quite consciously there, that the
beauty of the novel lies in having no type, no kind, no
rules, no limitations, no general precept or motto for
the craftsman except " Here is the whole of human life
before you. Copy it, or, better, recreate it—with
variation and decoration *ad libitum*—as faithfully, but as
freely, as you can." Of this great fact even Fielding,
the creator of the modern novel, was perhaps not wholly
aware as a matter of theory, though he made no error
about it in practice. Indeed the " comic prose epic "
notion *might* reduce to rules like those of the verse. Both
Scott and Miss Austen abstained likewise from formal-
ising it. But every really great novel has illustrated it ;
and attempts, such as have been recently made, to contest
it and draw up a novelists' code, have certainly not yet
justified themselves according to the Covenant of Works,
and have at least not disposed some of us to welcome
them as a Covenant of Faith. It is because Pigault-
Lebrun, though a low kind of creature from every point
of view, except that of mere craftsmanship, did, like
his betters, recognise the fact in practice, that he has been
allowed here a place of greater consideration than perhaps
has ever fallen to his lot before in literary history.

Still, even putting out of sight the new developments
which had shown the irrepressible vitality of the French
conte, the seven hundred years had not been wasted.
The product of the first half of them remained, indeed,
at this time sealed up in the " gazophile " of the older
age, or was popularised only by well-meaning mis-
interpreters like the Comte de Tressan;[1] but the treasure-
house was very soon to be broken open and utilised. It
is open to any one to contend—it is, indeed, pretty much
the opinion of the present writer—that it was this very
neglect which had made the progress of the seventeenth
and eighteenth centuries themselves so slow and so
imperfect in its total results. For those who like to look
for literary causes outside literature, there may be other
explanations. But any intelligent reader can do some-

[1] *Corps d'Extraits de Romans de Chevalerie.* 4 vols. Paris, 1782.

thing for himself if he has the facts before him. It is these facts that it has been and will be our business to give and to summarise here.

They have been given ; let us attempt to summarise them in the briefest possible way. France possibly did not invent Romance ; no man or men could do that ; it was a sort of deferred heritage which Humankind, like the Heir of Lynne, discovered when it was ready to hang itself (speaking in terms of literature) during the Dark Ages. But she certainly grew the seed for all other countries, and dispersed the growth to the ends of the earth. Very much the same was the case with the short tale in the " Middle " period. From the fifteenth century to the eighteenth (both included) she entered upon a curious kind of wilderness, studded with oases of a more curious character still. In one of them Rabelais was born, and found Quintessence, and of that finding—more fortunate than the result of True Thomas finding the Elf Queen—was born Pantagruelism. In another came Lesage, and though his work was scarcely original, it was consummate. None of these happy sojourns produced a *Don Quixote* or a *Tom Jones*, but divers smaller things resulted. And again and again, as had happened in the Middle Ages themselves, but on a smaller scale, what France did found development and improvement in other lands ; while her own miniature masterpieces, from the best of the *Cent Nouvelles Nouvelles* and the *Heptameron*, through all others that we noticed down to *Adolphe*, showed the enormous power which was working half blindly. How the strength got eyes, and the eyes found the right objects to fix upon, must be left, if fortune favour, for the next volume to tell.[1]

[1] The link between the two suggested at p. 458, *note*, is as follows. That Victor Hugo should, as he does in the Preface to *Han d'Islande* and elsewhere, sneer at Pigault, is not very wonderful : for, besides the difference between *canaille* and *caballerta*, the author of *M. Botte* was the most popular novelist of Hugo's youth. But why he has, in Part IV. Book VII. of *Les Misérables* selected Restif as " undermining the masses in the most unwholesome way of all " is not nearly so clear, especially as he opposes this way to the " wholesomeness " of, among others—Diderot !

APPENDICES

CHRONOLOGICAL CONSPECTUS OF THE PRINCIPAL WORKS OF FRENCH FICTION NOTICED IN THIS VOLUME

11TH CENTURY

Vie de Saint Alexis (probably).
Roland and one or two other *Chansons* (possibly).

12TH CENTURY

Most of the older *Chansons*.
Arthurian Legend (in some of its forms).
Roman de Troie, Romans d'Alexandre (older forms).

13TH CENTURY

Rest of the more genuine *Chansons*.
Rest of ditto Arthuriad and " Matter of Rome."
Romans d'Aventures (many).
Early Fabliaux (probably).
Roman de la Rose and *Roman de Renart* (older parts).
Prose Stories (*Aucassin et Nicolette*), etc.

14TH CENTURY

Rehandlings, and younger examples, of all kinds above mentioned.

15TH CENTURY

Ditto, but only latest forms of all but Prose Stories, and many of
    the others rendered into prose.
Cent Nouvelles Nouvelles. First *edition*, 1480, but written much
    earlier.
Petit Jehan de Saintré, about 1459, or earlier.
Jehan de Paris. Uncertain, but before 1500.

16TH CENTURY

Rabelais. First Book of *Pantagruel* (Second of the whole, 1533;
    Gargantua, 1535; rest of *Pantagruel* at intervals, to the
    (posthumous) Fifth Book in 1564.
Marguerite de Navarre. *Heptameron.* Written before (probably
    some time before) Marguerite's death in 1549. Imperfectly
    published as *Les Amants Fortunés*, etc., in 1558; com-
    pletely, under its permanent title, next year.
Bonaventure Despériers. *Cymbalum Mundi*, 1537; *Contes et
    Joyeux Devis*, 1558, but written at least fourteen years earlier,
    as the author died in 1544.
Hélisenne de Crenne. *Les Angoisses*, etc., 1538.
Amadis Romances. Date of Spanish or Portuguese originals
    uncertain. Herberay published the first part of his French
    translation of *Amadis* itself in 1540.
Many of the small pastoral and adventurous stories noticed
at the beginning of Chapter VIII. appeared in the last fifteen
years of the sixteenth century, the remainder in the first quarter
of the seventeenth. But of the Greek and Spanish compositions,
which had so great an influence on them and on the subsequent
" Heroic " School, the work of Heliodorus had been translated
as early as 1546, and the *Diana* of Montemayor in 1578.

17TH CENTURY

Honoré d'Urfé. *L'Astrée*, 1607–19. (First three parts in
    Urfé's lifetime, fourth and fifth after his death in 1625.)
" Heroic " Romance, 1622–60, as regards its principal examples,
    the exact dates of which are given in a note to p. 176.
    Madame de Villedieu wrote almost up to her death in 1683.
Fairy Tales, etc. The common idea that Perrault not only
    produced the masterpieces but set the fashion of the kind is
    inexact. Madame d'Aulnoy's *Contes des Fées* appeared in
    1682, whereas Perrault's *Contes de ma Mère L'Oye* did not
    come till fifteen years later, in 1697. The precise dates of the
    writing of Hamilton's Tales are not, I think, known. They
    must, for the most part, have been between the appearance of
    Galland's *Arabian Nights*, 1704, and the author's death in
    1720. As for the *Cabinet* and its later constituents, see
    below on the eighteenth century.
Sorel, Ch. *Francion*, 1622; *Le Berger Extravagant*, 1627.
Scarron, P. *Le Roman Comique*, 1651.
Cyrano de Bergerac. *Histoire Comique*, etc., 1655.
Furetière, A. *Le Roman Bourgeois*, 1666.

La Fayette, Madame de. *La Princesse de Clèves*, 1678. Her first book, *La Princesse de Montpensier* (much slighter but well written), had appeared eighteen years earlier, and *Zaïde* or *Zayde* in 1670, fathered by Segrais.

Fénelon. *Télémaque*, 1699.

18TH CENTURY

Cabinet des Fées, containing not only the authors or translators mentioned under the head of the preceding century, but a series of later writings down to the eve of the Revolution. Gueulette's adaptations and imitations ranged from the *Soirées Bretonnes*, published in 1712 during Hamilton's lifetime, to the *Thousand and One Hours*, 1733, the other collections mentioned in the text coming between. It may be worth mentioning that, being an industrious editor as well as tale-teller and playwright, he reprinted *Le Petit Jehan de Saintré* in 1724 and Rabelais in 1732. Caylus's tales seem to have been scattered over the middle third of the century from about 1730 to his death in 1765. Cazotte's *Diable Amoureux* (not in the *Cabinet*) is of 1772—he had written very inferior things of the tale kind' full thirty years earlier. Mme. Le Prince de Beaumont (who was long an actual governess in England) wrote her numerous "books for the young" for the most part between 1757 (*Le Magazin des Enfants*) and 1774 (*Contes Moraux*).

Lesage. *Le Diable Boiteux*, 1707; *Gil Blas de Santillane*, 1715–35.

Marivaux. *Les Effets Surprenants*, 1713–14; *Marianne*, 1731–36; *Le Paysan Parvenu*, 1735.

Prévost. *Mémoires d'un Homme de Qualité*, 1728–32, followed by *Manon Lescaut*, 1733; *Cléveland*, 1732–39; *Le Doyen de Killérine*, 1735; *Histoire d'une Grecque Moderne*, 1741.

(It may not be impertinent to draw attention to the fact that Prévost, like Defoe—though not quite to the same extent, and in the middle, not towards the end of his career—concentrated the novel-part of an enormous polygraphic production upon a few years.)

Crébillon *fils*. *Lettres de la Marquise*, 1732; *Tanzaï et Néadarné*, 1734; *Les Égarements*, 1736; *Le Sopha*, 1745; *La Nuit et le Moment*, 1755; *Le Hasard au Coin du Feu*, 1763; *Ah! Quel Conte!* 1764.

Voltaire's *Tales* were distributed over a large part of his long and insatiably busy life; but none of his best are very early. *Zadig* is of 1747; *Micromégas* of 1752; *Candide* of 1759;

L'Ingénu and *La Princesse de Babylone* of 1767 and 1768 respectively.

Rousseau.   *La Nouvelle Héloïse*, 1760 ; *Émile*, 1762.

Diderot.   *Les Bijoux Indiscrets*, 1748.   *Jacques le Fataliste* and *La Religieuse* were posthumously published, but must have been written much earlier than their author's death in 1784.

Marmontel.   *Contes Moraux* appeared in the official or semi-official *Mercure de France*, with which the author was connected from 1753–60, being its manager or editor for the last two of these years.   *Bélisaire* came out in 1767.

Bernardin de Saint-Pierre.   *Paul et Virginie*, 1787 ; *La Chaumière Indienne*, 1790.

" Sensibility " Novels :—

   Madame de Tencin.   *Le Comte de Comminge*, 1735 ; *Les Malheurs de l'Amour*, 1747.

   Madame Riccoboni.   *Le Marquis de Cressy*, 1758 ; *Lettres de Julie Catesby*, 1759 ; *Ernestine*, 1762.

   Madame Élie de Beaumont.   *Le Marquis de Roselle*, 1764.

   Madame de Souza.   *Adèle de Senanges*, 1794.

   Madame de Genlis.   *Mlle. de Clermont*, 1802.

   Madame de Duras.   *Ourika*, 1823 ; *Édouard*, 1825.

   Xavier de Maistre.   *Voyage autour de ma Chambre*, 1794 ; *Le Lépreux de la Cité d'Aoste*, 1812 ; *Les Prisonniers du Caucase*, *La Jeune Sibérienne*, 1825.

   Benjamin Constant.   *Adolphe*, 1815.

Restif de la Bretonne.   *Le Pied de Fanchette*, 1769 ; *Adèle*, 1772 ; *Le Paysan Perverti*, 1775–76 ; *Les Contemporaines*, 1780–85 ; *Ingénue Saxancour*, 1789 ; *Monsieur Nicolas*, 1794–97.

Pigault-Lebrun.   *L'Enfant du Carnaval*, 1792 ; *Les Barons de Felsheim*, 1798 ; *Angélique et Jeanneton*, *Mon Oncle Thomas*, *La Folie Espagnole*, 1799 ; *M. Botte*, 1802 ; *Jérôme*, 1804 ; *Tableaux de Société*, 1813 ; *Adélaïde de Méran*, 1815 ; *M. de Roberval*, *L'Officieux*, 1818.

BIBLIOGRAPHICAL NOTES

(Although it is probably idle to attempt to satisfy or placate the contemporary *helluo* of bibliography, it may be respectful to other readers to observe that this is not intended to deal with the whole subject, but only as a companion, or chrestomathic guide, to this book itself.)

CHAPTER I

Apollonius of Tyre. Ed. Thorpe. London, 1834.

English Novel, The. By the present writer. London (Dent), 1913.

French Literature, A Short History of. By the present writer. Oxford, 1882, and often reprinted.

Greek Romances, The. Most convenient editions of originals— Didot's *Erotici Graeci,* Paris, 1856, or Teubner's, ed. Herscher, Leipzig, 1858. English translations in Bohn's Library. For those who prefer books about things to the things themselves, there is a very good English monograph by Wolff (Columbia University Series, New York).

Hymn of St. Eulalia. Quoted in most histories of French literature, *e.g.* that entered above, pp. 4, 5.

Life of St. Alexis. Ed. G. Paris and L. Pannier. Paris, 1872–87.

CHAPTER II

Alexander Legends ("Matter of Rome"). The most important editions of romances concerning Alexander are Michelant's of the great poem from which, according to the most general theory, the "Alexandrine" or twelve-syllabled verse takes its name (Stuttgart, 1846), and M. Paul Meyer's *Alexandre le Grand dans la Littérature Française au moyen âge* (2 vols., Paris, 1886), a monograph of the very first order, with plentiful reproduction of texts.

Arthurian Legend, The. No complete bibliography of this is possible here—a note of some fulness will be found in the writer's *Short History* (see above on Chapter I.). The most

479

important books for an English reader who wishes to supplement Malory are M. Paulin Paris's abstract of the whole,
Les Romans de la Table Ronde (5 vols., Paris, 1869–77),
a very charming set of handy volumes, beautifully printed and
illustrated; and, now at last, Dr. Sommer's stately edition
of the "Vulgate" texts, completed recently, I believe
(Carnegie Institution, Washington, U.S.A.).

Chansons de Gestes. The first sentence of the last entry applies
here with greater fulness. The editions of *Roland* are very
numerous; and those of other *chansons*, though there are
not often two or more of the same, run to scores of volumes.
The most important books about them are M. Léon Gautier's
Les Épopées Françaises (4 vols., Paris, 1892) and M. Bédier's
Les Légendes Épiques (4 vols., Paris, 1908–13).

Sainte-More, B. de. *Roman de Troie.* Ed. Joly. Rouen, 1870.
Edited a second time in the series of the Société des Anciens
Textes Français.

CHAPTER III

The bibliography of the *Romans d'Aventures* generally is again
too complicated and voluminous to be attempted here. A
fair amount of information will be found, as regards the
two sides, French and English, of the matter, in the writer's
Short Histories of the two literatures—*French* as above,
English (Macmillan, 9th ed., London, 1914), and in his
Romance and Allegory, referred to in the text. Short of the
texts themselves, but for fuller information than general
histories contain, Dunlop's well-known book, reprinted in
Bohn's Library with valuable additions, and Ellis's *Early
English Romances*, especially the latter, will be found of
greatest value.

Partenopeus de Blois. 2 vols. Paris, 1834.

CHAPTER IV

Nouvelles du 13ᵉ et du 14ᵐᵉ Siècle. Ed. L. Moland et Ch.
d'Hericault. Bibliothèque Elzévirienne. 2 vols. Paris,
1856.

CHAPTER V

Cent Nouvelles Nouvelles, Les. Numerous editions in the cheap
collections of French classics.

Fabliaux. Ed. A. de Montaiglon et G. Raynaud. 6 vols.
Paris, 1872–88.

Jehan de Paris. Ed. Montaiglon. Paris, 1874.

Petit Jehan de Saintré. Ed. Guichard. Paris, 1843.
Roman de la Rose. Ed. F. Michel. Paris, 1864.
Roman de Renart. The completest (but not a complete) edition of the different parts is that of Méon and Chabaille (5 vols., Paris, 1826–35). The main or " Ancien " Renart was re-edited by E. Martin (3 vols., Paris and Strasbourg, 1882–87).

CHAPTER VI

Rabelais. Editions of the original very numerous : and of Urquhart's famous English translation more than one or two recently. The cheapest and handiest of the former, *without* commentary, is that in the Collection Garnier. Of commentaries and books *on* Rabelais there is no end.

CHAPTER VII

Amadis Romances. No modern reprints of Herberay and his followers. Southey's English versions of *Amadis* and *Palmerin* are not difficult to obtain.
Despériers, B. *Contes et Joyeuse Devis*, etc. Ed. Lacour. 2 vols. Paris, 1866.
Marguerite de Navarre, The *Heptameron.* Editions again numerous, including cheap ones in the collections.
Moyen de Parvenir, Le. Ed. Jacob. Paris, 1860. (For Hélisenne de Crenne see text, and Reynier—*v. inf.* on next chapter.)

CHAPTER VIII

(The general histories and bibliographies of M. Reynier and Herr Körting, as well as the monographs of MM. Chatenay, Magne, and Reure, will be found registered in the notes to text, and references to them in the index. The original editions are also given in text or note. Modern reprints—except of the fairy stories and one or two others—are almost entirely wanting. For the Greek Romances see above under Chapter I. The *Astrée*, after its first issues, appeared as a whole in 1637 and 1647, the latter being the edition referred to in " Add. and Corr." But the later eighteenth-century (1733) version of the Abbé Souchay is said to be " doctored." I have not thought it worth while to look up either this or the earlier abridgment (*La Nouvelle Astrée* of 1713), though this latter is not ill spoken of. For the *Cabinet des Fées* (41 vols., Geneva, 1785–89) see text.

Chapter IX

Sorel. *Francion* is in the Collection Garnier, *Le Berger Extravagant* and *Polyandre* only in the originals.
Scarron. *Le Roman Comique*. The 1752 edition (3 vols.) is useful, but there are reprints.
Furetière. *Le Roman Bourgeois*. Collection Jannet et Picard, 1854.
Cyrano de Bergerac. *Voyages*, etc. Ed. Jacob. Paris, 1858.
Mme. de la Fayette. *La Princesse de Clèves*. Paris, 1881.

Chapter X

For those who wish to study Lesage and Prévost at large, the combined Dutch *Œuvres Choisies*, in 54 vols. (Amsterdam, 1783), will offer a convenient, if not exactly handy, opportunity. Separate editions of the *Diable Boiteux* and *Gil Blas* are very, and of *Manon Lescaut* fairly, numerous.
Marivaux. *Œuvres*. 12 vols. Paris, 1781.
Crébillon *fils*. *Œuvres Complètes*. 7 vols. Londres, 1772.

Chapter XI

The work, in novel, of Voltaire and Rousseau is in all the cheap collections of Didot, Garnier, etc. Of that of Diderot there have recently been several partial collections, but I think no complete one. It is better to take the *Œuvres*, by Assézat and Tourneux, mentioned in the text (20 vols., Paris, 1875–77).
Marmontel's *Œuvres* appeared in 19 vols. (Paris, 1818), and I have used, and once possessed, a more modern and compacter issue in 7 vols. (Paris, 1820?). The *Contes Moraux* appeared together in 1770 and later.
Bernardin de Saint-Pierre. *Œuvres*. 12 vols. 1834. Very numerous separate editions (or sometimes with *La Chaumière Indienne*) of *Paul et Virginie*.

Chapter XII

Minor "Sensibility" novels. Most of them in a handsome 7-vol. edition (Paris, *n.d.*) in Garnier's *Bibliothèque Amusante*. This also includes Marivaux.
X. de Maistre. Editions numerous.
B. Constant. *Adolphe*. Paris, 1842 ; and with Introduction by M. Anatole France (1889) ; besides M. de Lescure's noticed in text.
Restif de la Bretonne. Selection of *Les Contemporaines*, by Assézat. 3 vols. Paris, 1875–76.
Pigault-Lebrun. Edition mentioned in text.

INDEX

(The dates given in this Index are confined to *persons* directly dealt with in this volume. Those of the more important *books* noticed will be found in the Chronological Conspectus. In other respects I have made it as full as possible, in an *Index nominum*, as regards both authors and titles.)

THE END

Printed by R. & R. CLARK, LIMITED, *Edinburgh.*

A HISTORY OF
ENGLISH PROSODY

FROM THE TWELFTH CENTURY
TO THE PRESENT DAY

By Dr. GEORGE SAINTSBURY

Three Vols. 8vo.

Vol. I. From the Origins to Spenser. 10s. net.
Vol. II. From Shakespeare to Crabbe. 15s. net.
Vol. III. From Blake to Swinburne. 15s. net.

SOME PRESS OPINIONS OF VOLUME I.

THE ATHENÆUM.—"A thing complete and convincing beyond any former work from the same hand. 'Hardly any one who takes a sufficient interest in prosody to induce him to read this book' will fail to find it absorbing, and even entertaining, as only one other book on the subject of versification is: the *Petit Traité de poésie française* of Théodore de Banville. . . . We await the second and third volumes of this admirable undertaking with impatience. To stop reading it at the end of the first volume leaves one in just such a state of suspense as if it had been a novel of adventure, and not the story of the adventures of prosody. 'I am myself quite sure,' says Prof. Saintsbury, 'that English prosody is, and has been, a living thing for seven hundred years at least.' That he sees it living is his supreme praise, and such praise belongs to him only among historians of English verse."

THE TIMES.—"To Professor Saintsbury English prosody is a living thing, and not an abstraction. He has read poetry for pleasure long before he began to read it with a scientific purpose, and so he has learnt what poetry is before making up his mind what it ought to be. It is a common fault of writers upon prosody that they set out to discover the laws of music without ever training their ears to apprehend music. They theorise very plausibly at large, but they betray their incapacity so soon as they proceed to scan a difficult line. Professor Saintsbury never fails in this way. He knows a good line from a bad one, and he knows how a good line ought to be read, even though he may sometimes be doubtful how it ought to be scanned. He has, therefore, the knowledge most essential to a writer upon prosody. . . . His object, as he constantly insists, is to write a history, to tell us what has happened to our prosody from the time when it began to be English and ceased to be Anglo-Saxon; not to tell us whether it has happened rightly or wrongly, nor even to be too ready to tell us why or how it has happened."

Professor W. P. Ker in the *SCOTTISH HISTORICAL REVIEW.*—"The history of verse, as Mr. Saintsbury takes it, is one aspect of the history of poetry; that is to say, the minute examination of structure does not leave out of account the nature of the living thing; we are not kept all the time at the microscope. This is the great beauty of his book; it is a history of English poetry in one particular form or mode. . . . The author perceives that the form of verse is not separable from the soul of poetry; poetry 'has neither kernel nor husk, but is all one,' to adapt the phrase of another critic."

MACMILLAN AND CO., Ltd., LONDON.

A HISTORY OF
ENGLISH PROSODY

By Dr. GEORGE SAINTSBURY

SOME PRESS OPINIONS OF VOLUME II.

THE ATHENÆUM.—"We have read this volume with as eager an impatience as that with which we read the first, for the author is in love with his subject; he sees 'that English prosody is and has been a living thing for seven hundred years at least,' and, knowing that metre, verse pure and simple, is a means of expressing emotion, he here sets out to show us its development and variety during the most splendid years of our national consciousness."

THE STANDARD.—"The second volume of Professor Saintsbury's elaborate work on English prosody is even more interesting than his former volume. Extending as it does from Shakespeare to Crabbe, it covers the great period of English poetry and deals with the final development of the prosodic system. It reveals the encyclopædic knowledge of English literature and the minute scholarship which render the Edinburgh professor so eminently suited to this inquiry, which is, we think, the most important literary adventure he has undertaken. . . . It is certainly the best book on the subject of which it treats, and it will be long indeed before it is likely to be superseded."

THE CAMBRIDGE REVIEW.—"It is the capacity of being able to depart from traditional opinion, the evidence shown on every page of independent thought based upon a first-hand study of documents, which make the present volume one of the most stimulating that even Professor Saintsbury has written. The work, as a whole, is a fine testimony to his lack of pedantry, to his catholicity of taste, to his sturdy common sense, and it exhibits a virtue rare among prosodists (dare we say among scholars generally?)—courtesy to opponents."

THE PALL MALL GAZETTE.—"This volume is even more fascinating than was the first. For here there are even greater names concerned — Shakespeare and Milton. . . . It appears to us that Professor Saintsbury hardly writes a page in which he does not advance by some degree his view of the right laws of verse. We cannot imagine any one seriously defending, after this majestical work, the old syllabic notion of scansion. . . . The book is written with all the liveliness of style, richness of argument, and wealth of material that we expect. Not only is it a history of prosody; but it is full of acute judgments on poetry and poets."

MACMILLAN AND CO., Ltd., LONDON.

OTHER WORKS

BY

DR. GEORGE SAINTSBURY

A HISTORY OF ENGLISH PROSE
RHYTHM. 8vo. 14s. net.

A HISTORY OF ELIZABETHAN LITERA-
TURE. Crown 8vo. 7s. 6d.

A HISTORY OF NINETEENTH CENTURY
LITERATURE (1780–1900). Crown 8vo. 7s. 6d.

A SHORT HISTORY OF ENGLISH
LITERATURE. Crown 8vo. 8s. 6d. Also in five parts.
2s. each.

HISTORICAL MANUAL OF ENGLISH
PROSODY. Crown 8vo. 5s. net.

A FIRST BOOK OF ENGLISH LITERA-
TURE. Globe 8vo. 1s. 6d.

DRYDEN. Library Edition. Crown 8vo. 2s. net.
Popular Edition, Crown 8vo, 1s. 6d. Sewed, 1s. Pocket
Edition, Fcap. 8vo, 1s. net. [*English Men of Letters.*

MACMILLAN AND CO., LTD., LONDON.

3